Why You Need This New Edition

If you're wondering why you should buy this new edition of *Public Relations*, here are 7 good reasons!

We, as authors, share a belief in the value of providing you with the most up-to-date statistics, the latest research, and the most current examples of public relations practice. The fifth edition of *Public Relations: A Values-Driven Approach* reflects our belief that if you are to be prepared for a future in public relations, you need the most current coverage of these exciting and important changes. We remain committed to the book's focus on the role of values in our personal and professional lives. Additionally, every effort has been made to present relevant information in the conversational style of writing that you, our readers, prefer. We value you and your investment in your education.

In our best effort to reflect the public relations profession as it is today, we have made substantial revisions in this new fifth edition. Some changes in this new edition include:

1. A NEW four-color design, which grabs and maintains your attention and enhances your overall learning experience, especially if you're a visual learner.

2. The introduction of new information on the contingency theory of accommodation, the reflective paradigm, agenda building, due diligence, and heuristic versus theoretical approaches in an effort to enhance your understanding of the strong theoretical underpinnings throughout the text.

3. Analyses of new-media tactics, including consumer-generated media, social media news releases, microblogging, social bookmarking, digital newsrooms, and mobile marketing to keep you up-to-date with continually changing media platforms and dynamics.

4. A NEW chapter on multimedia message development focuses on the application of critical thinking and creative thinking and gives you the skills to create stronger, more effective multimedia messages.

5. A vigorously updated feature program that includes 17 NEW Case Studies, 10 NEW QuickBreaks, 6 NEW Memos from the Field, and a new feature in every chapter, Social Media Apps, that allows you to assess the impact of social media on the chapter topic.

6. The latest reports on the status and future of the profession, including new data on salary, diversity, job duties, job satisfaction, use of social media, and ethics challenges provide you with an accurate and current perspective of the industry.

7. Discussions of the public relations implications of recent events, including the BP oil spill, the Great Recession, Wall Street scandals, global warming, health care, campaign financing, product recalls, changes in societal demographics, and the growth of social media so that you can apply what you're learning in the text to real-life current events.

PEARSON

Public Relations

A Values-Driven Approach

Fifth Edition

David W. Guth

The University of Kansas

Charles Marsh

The University of Kansas

Allyn & Bacon

Boston Columbus Indianapolis New York San Francisco Upper Saddle River
Amsterdam Cape Town Dubai London Madrid Milan Munich Paris Montréal
Toronto Delhi Mexico City São Paulo Sydney Hong Kong Seoul Singapore Taipei Tokyo

Editor-in-Chief, Communication: Karon Bowers
Senior Acquisitions Editor: Jeanne Zalesky
Editorial Assistant: Stephanie Chaisson
Associate Development Editor: Angela G. Mallowes
Senior Marketing Manager: Wendy Gordon
Media Producer: Megan Higginbotham
Managing Editor: Linda Mihatov Behrens
Associate Managing Editor: Bayani Mendoza de Leon
Production Manager: Raegan Keida Heerema
Project Coordination, Text Design, and Electronic Page Makeup:
   Elm Street Publishing Services
Composition: Integra Software Services Pvt. Ltd.
Cover Art Director: Pat Smythe
Cover Designer: Nancy Sacks
Cover Illustration/Photo: Cesare Naldi/Veer
Senior Manufacturing Buyer: Mary Ann Gloriande
Printer and Binder: RR Donnelley, Crawfordsville, In
Cover Printer: Coral Graphics Services Inc

For permission to use copyrighted material, grateful acknowledgment is made to the copyright holders
on pp. 434–436, which are hereby made part of this copyright page.

Library of Congress Cataloging-in-Publication Data

Guth, David.
   Public relations : a values-driven approach / David W. Guth, Charles Marsh.—5th ed.
      p. cm.
   Includes bibliographical references and index.
   ISBN-13: 978-0-205-81180-9
   ISBN-10: 0-205-81180-9
   1. Public relations.   2. Public relations—Moral and ethical aspects.
   3. Public relations—Case studies.   I. Marsh, Charles,   II. Title.
   HM1221.G87 2011
   659.2—dc22

                                                                      2010036821

Copyright © 2012, 2009, 2006 by Pearson Education, Inc.

All rights reserved. No part of this publication may be reproduced, stored in a retrieval system, or
transmitted, in any form or by any means, electronic, mechanical, photocopying, recording, or
otherwise, without the prior written permission of the publisher. Printed in the United States. To obtain
permission to use material from this work, please submit a written request to Pearson Education, Inc.,
Permissions Department, 501 Boylston Street, Suite 900, Boston, MA 02116, fax: (617) 671 2290. For
information regarding permissions, call (617) 671 2295 or e-mail: permissionsus@pearson.com.

Allyn & Bacon
is an imprint of

5 6 7 8 9 10—DOC—15 14

ISBN-13: 978-0-205-81180-9
ISBN-10:   0-205-81180-9

www.pearsonhighered.com

CONTENTS

SECTION ONE   FOUNDATIONS OF PUBLIC RELATIONS

This section lays the foundations for the practice of values-driven public relations. Public relations, a discipline that is often misunderstood, is important to the conduct and maintenance of free societies. These six chapters bring the profession, the issues confronting it, and its values into focus.

CHAPTER 6
Ethics and Social Responsibility in Public Relations

SECTION TWO   THE PUBLIC RELATIONS PROCESS

Now that the foundations for the practice of public relations have been established, this section of the book focuses on the discipline's four-step process: research, planning, communication, and evaluation. Although this process is both strategic and tactical, an emphasis on values remains at its core. Successful practitioners rely on critical thinking skills introduced in these five chapters.

CHAPTER 9
Communication: The Tactics of Public Relations   254

SECTION THREE   PUBLIC RELATIONS TODAY AND TOMORROW

Public relations practitioners operate in a dynamic and intense environment. We live in a time of great changes that test our values. The final section of this book examines the profession's critical issues. Emerging professionals will confront many, if not most, of these challenges in the coming years. These five chapters bring those challenges into focus.

PREFACE

In the three years since the publication of the fourth edition of this book, the world has been a tumultuous place. There have been armed conflicts around the globe, including Iraq, Afghanistan, and the Darfur region of Sudan. When human beings haven't been trying to kill one another, many have struggled against the forces of nature. Catastrophic earthquakes rocked more than one developing nation. An Icelandic volcano shut down air travel over Europe. Many countries, including the United States, have struggled with weighty issues such as immigration, nuclear proliferation, health care, sexism, racism, violence, and the delicate balance between national security and personal freedoms. Even the sports and entertainment pages of our newspapers often read like a police blotter.

It is in this environment that young women and men prepare for what the U.S. government says is one of the fastest growing careers: public relations. And it is why the authors of this book remain committed to what we call values-driven public relations.

The late and highly respected public relations historian Scott Cutlip wrote about the practitioner's potential for helping what he called "our segmented, scattered society" to replace "misinformation with information, discord with concord." Although the profession has fallen short of that goal, we join Professor Cutlip in that hope. It all comes down to who you are, what you believe, and how you want to be seen by others. It all comes down to whether your actions will match your words.

It all comes down to values.

It has been more than 100 years since the first public relations agency opened in the United States. During the 20th century, the practice of public relations grew from a vague notion to a powerful force in democratic societies. Today, although the profession has made impressive gains in respect and access to power, public relations has a public relations problem. Although its roots date back to the beginning of recorded history, the fact remains that public relations—both as a profession and as a discipline—remains largely misunderstood.

Public relations is an honorable profession with a glorious past and a brilliant future. Like any other human pursuit, it also has its share of flaws. However, at a time when much of the world is embracing democratic institutions for the first time, public relations is an important catalyst for bringing change and promoting consensus. Through the practice of public relations, organizations and individuals communicate their ideas and advance their goals in the marketplace of ideas.

Public Relations: A Values-Driven Approach introduces this dynamic profession to the practitioners of the 21st century. Through a realistic blend of theory and practical examples, this book seeks to remove the veil of mystery that has shrouded the profession from its very beginnings. Using the conversational style of writing favored by today's college students, this book takes the reader on a journey of discovery, often through the eyes of leading practitioners and scholars.

VALUES-DRIVEN PUBLIC RELATIONS

As the title suggests, however, these pages contain more than just a recitation of facts and concepts. This book champions what we call *values-driven public relations*: an approach that challenges practitioners to align their efforts with the values of their organization, their profession, their targeted publics, and society itself.

Values-driven public relations is a logical response to a dynamic and diverse society in which complex issues and competing values bring different groups of people into conflict. This approach links communication with an organization's values, mission, and goals. Today, public and private organizations are increasingly held accountable for their actions by a variety of stakeholders. No longer is an organization's behavior measured solely by traditional indicators of success, such as profits, stock dividends, and jobs created. Additional measures of social worth now include an organization's relationships with its employees, its communities, its customers, and its physical environment. Stakeholders expect decisions to be made within an ethical framework. *Public Relations: A Values-Driven Approach* prepares future practitioners and the organizations they represent for a world of increased responsibility, scrutiny, and accountability.

PUBLIC RELATIONS IN THE SOCIAL CONTEXT

Another notable feature of this book is its discussion of relevant issues within a broader social context. Public relations did not develop, nor is it practiced, in a vacuum. Throughout history, the practice of public relations has been shaped by great social forces. Its emergence in the United States was linked to the Industrial Revolution and the related Populist Era reforms. The 20th century's military and social conflicts served as catalysts for the profession's growth. Public relations was also transformed by the economic globalization and technological advances of the 1980s and 1990s. *Public Relations: A Values-Driven Approach* provides this broad social context so that future practitioners can have a clearer understanding of the so-called real world they are about to enter. The book includes full chapters on history, ethics, law, cross-cultural communication, and the role of the profession in the Digital Age. Throughout the book, students are directed to online sources of further information.

FEATURES

A major goal of this book is to strengthen students' problem-solving skills. Every chapter opens with a hypothetical but realistic **Real World** scenario. Each scenario places students in the shoes of a practitioner and challenges them to create an ethical, values-driven, effective solution. Each chapter also includes relevant case studies that expose students to successful as well as unsuccessful public relations approaches. Following each scenario and case study are questions designed to engage students in a meaningful analysis of the issues raised. The book further promotes problem-solving skills by introducing a variety of processes that guide students through the stages of research, planning, communication, evaluation, and ethical decision making.

Public Relations: A Values-Driven Approach also contains pedagogical elements that engage students in the subject matter. Each chapter begins with a list of **learning objectives** that set the stage for the topics that lie ahead. **QuickChecks**, a series of questions focusing on the book's content, are interspersed throughout each chapter. **Social Media Apps** document how blogs and other new media are changing the profession. Lively and relevant **QuickBreaks** bring depth and texture to each chapter. In keeping with the values focus of this text, **Values Statements** from a broad range of organizations are scattered throughout the book. A list of **key terms** appears in each chapter opener, and a full **glossary** is provided at the end of the book. Each chapter also includes a **Memo from the Field**, a message to students from one of today's leading public relations professionals. These professionals represent a broad range of public and private interests and reflect the diversity of the society upon which they wield so much influence.

Chapter-by-Chapter Revisions

Substantial changes have been made in every chapter of the fifth edition of *Public Relations: A Values-Driven Approach*. New current events include the election of Barack Obama, Wall Street's Meltdown Monday, the British Petroleum oil spill, the philanthropic work of rock star Bono, the opportunities and challenges of new media, the shootings at Northern Illinois University, and crises ranging from Toyota to Tiger Woods. In addition to a sentence-by-sentence and image-by-image review, the chapters contain the following revisions and additions:

Chapter 1: Heuristic versus theoretical approaches; contingency theory of accommodation; the reflective paradigm; a new Social Media Apps sidebar on social media and public relations; a new Memo from the Field; and two new case studies ("Got 2B Safe!" and "Meltdown Monday").

Chapter 2: A new "Real World" scenario; a new Social Media Apps on social media duties; new data on job duties, salaries, and satisfaction; new data on interview thank-you notes; and an updated case study on public relations blunders.

Chapter 3: Two new QuickBreaks on public relations during the American Revolution and the role of public relations in western expansion; a new Social Media Apps on Edward L. Bernays' influence on bloggers; and a new case study ("The Fog of War").

Chapter 4: New data on employee publics, news media publics, government publics, investor publics, multicultural community publics, constituent publics, and business publics; a new Social Media Apps on social media and employee relations; and a new case study ("Big Brother Is Botching: Amazon's Orwellian Debacle").

Chapter 5: Agenda building; a new Social Media Apps on the role of social media in political protests; and two new case studies ("Broken News" and "Flying Against the Wind").

Chapter 6: An updated list of PRSA Professional Standards Advisories; a new Social Media Apps on ethics challenges in social media; incorporation of new reports, including the Edelman Trust Barometer 2010; revised application of the Potter Box; a new Memo from the Field; and a new case study ("A Dirty Campaign for Clean Coal").

Chapter 7: The concept of due diligence; weighted media cost; an updated Memo from the Field; a new Social Media Apps on monitoring social media; and a new case study ("The Green Police").

Chapter 8: Updated examples of public relations plans; a new Social Media Apps on standing social media plans; a new QuickBreak on the most used and most effective strategies in public relations; and a new case study ("Good Intentions, Bad Planning: The Breast Cancer-Screening Debate").

Chapter 9: A new QuickBreak on consumer generated media; new coverage of microblogging and social bookmarking services; expanded coverage of social media news releases; new coverage of digital newsrooms; updated section on pitching; new material on online trolls; new coverage of *Citizens United v. the Federal Elections Commission*; a new QuickBreak on mobile marketing; and a new case study ("'Lying Is a Whole Different Thing': An April Fools' News Release").

Chapter 10: An entirely new chapter with information on multimedia message development; critical and creative thinking processes; organizational schemes; writing and editing tips; and a new case study ("Capitalizing on Tragedy: The Marketing of a Plane Crash").

Chapter 11: The role of social media in Barack Obama's election; the risks and rewards of social media; the latest statistics on Internet and social media use; a new QuickBreak ("I'm with Coco"); a new Social Media Apps on Web 3.0; and new case study ("It Can Happen to Anybody").

Chapter 12: A new QuickBreak on the unintended consequences of swine flu; Toyota's public relations disaster; a new Social Media Apps on Domino's

YouTube crisis; a new Memo from the Field; and a new case study ("Gunman on Campus").

Chapter 13: New data on international IMC; a new Social Media Apps on social media turf battles between public relations and marketing; new data on most-used social media marketing tactics; a new QuickBreak on mobile marketing; and a new case study ("Ford Has a Social Media Idea").

Chapter 14: New examples of culture clashes; updated information on international entrepreneurialism; new data on diversity among public relations practitioners; a new Social Media Apps on international blogs; and a new case study ("Walmart Works to 'Export Our Culture'").

Chapter 15: A new QuickBreak on election finance law; the Bernard Madoff scandal; a new Values Statement; the Fairness Doctrine; Internet libel law; a new Social Media Apps on new regulations on blogger transparency; and two new case studies ("Ethanol 2.0" and "The Black List").

Chapter 16: Public relations in China, India, and Japan; updated U.S. and world population figures; updated information on the growing economic clout of Hispanics/Latinos; updated information on salaries and gender equity; a new Social Media Apps on Facebook's demographics; a new case study ("Social Media Kat Fight"); and an updated case study ("Gun and Greens").

RESOURCES IN PRINT AND ONLINE

Name of Supplement	Available in Print	Available Online	Instructor or Student Supplement	Description
Instructor's Manual and Test Bank (ISBN: 0205811825)		✓	Instructor Supplement	Prepared by the authors, David W. Guth and Charles Marsh, the Instructor's Manual and Test Bank contains sample syllabi, discussions of chapter-opening scenarios, and answers to chapter discussion and case study questions. In addition, the Test Bank portion of the manual contains numerous multiple choice, true/false, fill-in-the-blank, and essay questions. Available for download at www.pearsonhighered.com/irc; access code required.
MyTest (ISBN: 0205032508)		✓	Instructor Supplement	This flexible, online test generating software includes all questions found in the Test Bank section of the printed Instructor's Manual. This computerized software allows instructors to create their own personalized exams, to edit any or all of the existing test questions, and to add new questions. Other special features of this program include random generation of test questions, creation of alternate versions of the same test, scrambling of question sequence, and test preview before printing. Available at www.pearsonmytest.com; access code required.
PowerPoint™ Presentation Package (ISBN: 0205032516)		✓	Instructor Supplement	Prepared by the authors, David W. Guth and Charles Marsh, this book-specific package provides a basis for your lecture with PowerPoint™ slides for each chapter of the book. New to this edition are additional discussion launching

(continued)

Name of Supplement	Available in Print	Available Online	Instructor or Student Supplement	Description
				questions and suggested class activities imbedded right in the presentations for each chapter! Available for download at www .pearsonhighered.com/irc; access code required.
Public Relations Study Site		✓	Student Supplement	This open access Web site features public relations study materials for students, including flashcards and a complete set of practice tests for all major topics. Students will also find Web links to valuable sites for further exploration of major topics. Available at www.pearsonpublicrel.com.
MyCommunicationLab		✓	Instructor & Student Supplement	MyCommunicationLab is a state-of-the-art, interactive and instructive solution for communication courses. Designed to be used as a supplement to a traditional lecture course, or to completely administer an online course, MyCommunicationLab combines a Pearson eText, MySearchLab™, Pearson's Media-Share, multimedia, video clips, activities, research support, tests, and quizzes to completely engage students. MyCommunicationLab can be packaged with your text and is available for purchase at www.mycommunicationlab.com; access code required. See next page for more details.

SAVE TIME AND IMPROVE RESULTS WITH

mycommunicationlab

Designed to amplify a traditional course in numerous ways or to administer a course online, **MyCommunicationLab** for Public Relations courses combines pedagogy and assessment with an array of multimedia activities – videos, a portfolio builder, assessments, research support, multiple newsfeeds—to make learning more effective for all types of students. Now featuring more resources, including a video upload tool, this new release of **MyCommunicationLab** is visually richer and even more interactive than the previous version—a leap forward in design with more tools and features to enrich learning and aid students in classroom success.

TEACHING AND LEARNING TOOLS

NEW VERSION! Pearson eText: Identical in content and design to the printed text, a Pearson eText provides students access to their text whenever and wherever they need it. In addition to contextually placed multimedia features in every chapter, our new Pearson eText allows students to take notes and highlight, just like a traditional book.

Videos and Video Quizzes: Interactive videos provide students with the opportunity to watch video reports about well-known public relations cases and interviews with public relations professionals and scholars. Many videos are annotated with critical thinking questions or include short, assignable quizzes that report to the instructor's gradebook.

Assessments: Every chapter includes a variety of assessment options. Pre-and Post-tests for every chapter generate a customized study plan for further assessment and focus students on areas in which they need to improve. Quick Reviews after every major section in a chapter enable students to immediately check what they learned while reading the chapter. Chapter exams can be used as practice for in-class exams or can be used to completely administer an exam online.

ABC News RSS feeds: MyCommunicationLab provides online news feeds from ABC News, updated hourly, to help students choose and research public relations assignments and keep up with the news.

MySearchLab: Pearson's MySearchLab™ is the easiest way for students to start a research assignment or paper. Complete with extensive help on the research process and four databases of credible and reliable source material, MySearchLab™ helps students quickly and efficiently make the most of their research time. In addition to an extensive research database, MySearchLab™ also includes AutoCite, which assists in the creation of a "Works Cited" document.

CUTTING EDGE TECHNOLOGY

Portfolio Builder: The easy-to-use Portfolio Builder guides students step-by-step as they develop each part of their portfolio. This tool allows students to practice writing various types of press releases and other public relations documents. With only a few clicks, students can create portfolios of their work that they can e-mail, print and download.

MediaShare: With this new video upload tool, students are able to upload group assignments, video news releases and video reflections, for their instructor and classmates to watch (whether face-to-face or online) and provide online feedback and comments. Structured much like a social networking site, MediaShare can help promote a sense of community among students.

Audio Chapter Summaries: Every chapter includes a streaming audio chapter summary, perfect for students reviewing material before a test or instructors reviewing material before class.

ONLINE ADMINISTRATION

No matter what course management system you use—or if you do not use one at all, but still wish to easily capture your students' grade and track their performance—Pearson has a MyCommunicationLab option to suit your needs. Contact one of Pearson's Technology Specialists for more information and assistance.

A MyCommunicationLab access code is no additional cost when packaged with selected Pearson Communication texts. To get started, contact your local Pearson Publisher's Representative at www.pearsonhighered.com/replocator.

ACKNOWLEDGMENTS

The authors want to thank the dozens of people, many unknown to us before the writing of this book, who contributed greatly to this effort. The authors want to thank Dean Ann Brill and the faculty, staff, students, and alumni of the William Allen White School of Journalism and Mass Communications at the University of Kansas for their advice, support, and patience during this project. The authors also extend their gratitude to the dozens of companies, agencies, and individuals who gave their permission for the use of photographs, publications, and other artwork used in the text.

Sixteen men and women gave their valuable time to write memos to students who will read this book. The authors gratefully acknowledge the contributions of Gary McCormick of HGTV; John Echeveste of Valencia, Pérez & Echeveste Public Relations; Edward M. Block, formerly of AT&T; David A. Narsavage of The Friday Group; Jane Hazel of Health Canada; Mike Swenson of Barkley; David Rockland of Ketchum; Timothy S. Brown of Alstom; Josh Dysart of Draftfob; Regina Lynch-Hudson of The Write Publicist; Craig Settles of Successful.com; Melanie Magara of Northern Illinois University; Vin Cipolla of The Municipal Art Society; Bill Imada of IW Group; James F. Haggerty of The PR Consulting Group, Inc.; and Rebecca Timms, 2009–2010 National President of PRSSA.

A group of dedicated educators provided many suggestions for this fifth edition and, in doing so, helped the authors maintain a focus on the needs of students who read this book: Daniel D. Fultz, Bluffton University; Marjorie Keesah Nadler, Miami University; Brent Northup, Carroll College; Astrid Sheil, Northern Arizona University; Amy Thurlow, Mount Saint Vincent University; Lois Boynton, University of North Carolina at Chapel Hill; Christina Yoshimura, The University of Montana; Bobbi Reid Doggett, University of North Florida; and Dan Walsch George Mason University.

Once the text was written and the necessary artwork and permissions secured, the burden of this project shifted to the talented editors, designers, and technicians of Allyn and Bacon, including Karon Bowers, Jeanne Zalesky, and Angela Mallowes as well as the team at Integra Software Services, Inc.

Public Relations: A Values-Driven Approach would not have become a reality without the unwavering love and support of our families. They are our inspiration and motivation.

David W. Guth, APR
Charles Marsh, Ph.D.

The authors of this book come from very different backgrounds but share a passion for public relations education. Both are associate professors at the William Allen White School of Journalism and Mass Communications at the University of Kansas. In addition to this textbook, they have collaborated on two textbooks: *Adventures in Public Relations: Case Studies and Critical Thinking* and, with colleague Bonnie Poovey Short, *Strategic Writing: Multimedia Writing for Public Relations, Advertising and More.*

Before becoming an educator, David W. Guth served as a broadcast journalist in six states and won numerous local, state, regional, and national reporting honors, including the prestigious George Foster Peabody Award. He has also served as a public relations practitioner in the public and private sectors, including holding several positions in North Carolina state government. As an educator, Guth coauthored *Media Guide for Attorneys*, a publication that received regional and national awards. In addition to his teaching and research responsibilities, Guth has served as crisis communications consultant to several government agencies and public utilities. Guth is an accredited member of the Public Relations Society of America. His international experience includes public relations work in Japan, Italy, Russia, and Turkmenistan.

Charles Marsh has a Ph.D. in English literature and 20 years of business communications experience. He is the former editor of *American Way*, the in-flight magazine of American Airlines, and the former senior editor of corporate publications for J.C. Penney. He is the author of *A Quick and (Not) Dirty Guide to Business Writing* (Prentice Hall, 1997) and has won national and regional awards for writing and editing. In addition to teaching, Marsh has been a communications consultant to J.C. Penney, Ralston Purina, the USA Film Festival, the United States Information Agency, the American Management Association, and other organizations. His international experience includes public relations work in France, Italy, Spain, Kyrgyzstan, and Costa Rica.

1

What Is Public Relations?

OBJECTIVES

After studying this chapter, you will be able to

- explain the definition of public relations
- understand the different theories or models of public relations practice
- describe the four-step public relations process
- appreciate the role of personal, organizational, and societal values in the practice of public relations

KEY TERMS

Accredited Business Communicator (ABC), p. 12

Accredited in Public Relations (APR), p. 12

advertising, p. 11

axioms, p. 8

branding, p. 4

communication, p. 13

contingency theory of accommodation, p. 10

Cutlip, Center, and Broom models, p. 9

REAL WORLD

Questions, Questions

You have heard the question many times: "What is your major?" If your major is English, advertising, business, engineering, history, or any of dozens of other career paths, your answer will usually evoke a response along the lines of, "Oh, that's nice." However, those who respond by saying "public relations" often get a second, more difficult question: "What's that?" How do you answer?

OK, maybe it isn't fair to ask that question just one paragraph into your new textbook. Nor will it be comforting to learn that in the century since this dynamic and vital profession was first given its name, neither those who work in it or study it have come to an agreement on what it is.

Where will public relations fit into your career plans? What role does it play in society? What is its place in the Digital Age? Whose values should public relations practitioners follow? And, perhaps most important, when will the authors of this book stop asking a series of annoying questions and begin helping you answer them?

The answer to that last question is: right now. In the coming pages, we hope to open your eyes to a profession with the capacity to do nothing less than change the world. These pages are filled with examples of how the profession has shaped and continues to shape society. But as you read this book and learn more about values-driven public relations, yet one more question may come to mind: "Where do I fit in?"

PUBLIC RELATIONS: EVERYWHERE YOU LOOK

It appears as if the public relations profession has a public relations problem.

Over the past decade, surveys have consistently shown public attitudes toward the practice of public relations as being lukewarm, at best. According to a 2010 Gallup survey, more respondents said they had a negative view of the "advertising and public relations industry" than those who said their view was positive.[1] A 2005 study concluded that while people value what public relation practitioners do, they also mistrust practitioner motives.[2] However, there's some good news: A 2009 study of graduate students concluded that the more people learn more about the profession, the higher their opinion of it.[3] Read on. Maybe we can change some minds.

The term *public relations* and its abbreviation, *PR*, are often used (and abused) by those who have little or no understanding of its meaning. Some treat *public relations* as a synonym for words such as *publicity, propaganda, spin,* and *hype.* Some use the term as a pejorative, something inherently sinister. Others think of it as fluff, lacking in substance. The news media often contribute to the confusion. According to a study of 100 news stories that used the term *public relations,* fewer than 5 percent of them used it correctly. Researcher Julie K. Henderson wrote that 37 percent of the stories used *public relations* in a negative manner, and only 17 percent contained a positive reference.[4]

There are times when it is easy to see public relations at work. As we move deeper into the 21st century, a variety of critical issues—questions of war and peace, disputes between science and religion, and the balance between public safety and personal freedoms—have dominated the news. Public relations practitioners often play a highly visible role in these debates by articulating their clients' values and orchestrating events that grab the public's attention. Other practitioners contribute by communicating vital information to help people important to the success of their organization cope with what are, by any measure, difficult times.

However, it may be more often that people do not recognize the connection between public relations actions and their outcomes. For example, who would expect anyone to take seriously a guy who carries a urinal through his office? The Florida Department of Health hoped everyone would. The potty-toting character played by actor Ben Spring was known to Floridians as "The Fifth Guy"—the one person in five who, according to research, does not wash hands after visiting the restroom. Spring would also engage in other unsanitary behaviors, such as sneezing and coughing without covering his nose or mouth.[5] The edgy and humorous 2008 public relations campaign was created with a serious purpose in mind: to convince people to take steps to halt the spread of highly contagious germs and avoid a much-feared avian flu pandemic. Using a mix of broadcast announcements, posters, and personal appearances, Tallahassee-based Salter-Mitchell generated nationwide media coverage for The Fifth Guy campaign and, most important, made people more health-conscious.[6]

Many try to define public relations strictly in terms of these kinds of high-profile images. However, *publicity* and *public relations* are not synonymous. As you will learn in Chapter 9, publicity is just one of many tactics used by public relations practitioners. Perhaps it is best to think of public relations as a tapestry, with many parts intricately woven into one whole cloth.

Public relations fosters mutually beneficial relationships. During the 1980s, the Adolph Coors Company was under fire from civil rights and feminist groups over its hiring practices. The brewer also was transitioning from a family-owned private company to a stockholder-owned public company. Through a variety of tactics that included the creation of eight employee diversity councils, Coors reached out to publics it once had viewed as its sharpest critics. These initiatives brought both financial and social rewards. What is now known as the Molson-Coors Brewing Company posted $3 billion in net sales in 2009 and has been recognized for its diversity efforts by both the media and private organizations, including *Fortune*, *Business Ethics*, and the Human Rights Campaign Foundation.[7]

Public relations also builds corporate and product identities, a process known as **branding.** In their 2002 book *The Fall of Advertising and the Rise of PR*, authors Al and Laura Ries shook up Madison Avenue with the argument that it was public relations—not advertising—that successfully launched brands such as Starbucks, Palm, The Body Shop, Walmart, and Red Bull. They said the key to this success was the credibility associated with effective public relations.[8]

Some of the best public relations activity occurs when it appears as if nothing at all has happened. Few think to attribute high employee morale, increased productivity, or good corporate citizenship to public relations. But they should. When an orchestra sells out a concert or when a growing number of people decide against drinking and driving, it is easy to forget that these successes may well be benefits of sound public relations strategies. Even knowing where to vote, go to school, and shop is often the result of good public relations.

Public relations casts a broad net.

The Search for a Definition

So what is public relations? To update a phrase from a popular 1950s television game show, that is the million-dollar question. Unfortunately, there is no definitive answer. The modern practice of public relations first came under serious study in the early 1900s, and educators and practitioners have struggled ever since with its definition. Even in the 21st century, defining public relations remains an issue.

This confusion was illustrated in a survey of accountants, attorneys, and public relations practitioners. The three groups were selected because they had something in common: a counselor relationship with their clients. Each group was asked about its profession and its place within organizational structures. Although the accountants and attorneys clearly understood their roles, the public relations practitioners did not. This caused the study's authors to raise a pertinent question: If public relations

Public relations often takes center stage in world affairs. On this occasion, White House Press Secretary Robert Gibbs held a March 2010 daily press briefing in the Rose Garden of the White House.

(White House photo by Chuck Kennedy)

practitioners are unclear about who they are and what they do, why should they expect anyone else to understand?[9]

There isn't even any consensus on what to call the profession. Because of the supposedly negative connotations carried by the term *public relations*, many organizations opt to use euphemisms such as "public affairs," "public information," "corporate communications," or "community outreach" to describe the function. Nor is there consensus on the most appropriate placement of the public relations function within organizations. Sometimes it stands alone and reports directly to the chief executive officer. However, it also exists under the umbrella of other departments such as legal or marketing. The Chrysler Corporation's decision to move its public relations function to its human resources department following its acquisition by Cerberus Capital Management in 2007 was controversial. Chrysler's human resources chief said the move was part of a "cultural transformation" and a search for "synergies and efficiencies." Former Chrysler corporate communications head Jason Vines countered, "Public relations is a service for the entire organization and has to be its voice. That's why public relations should have unfiltered access to the CEO."[10]

Public Relations Defined

In 1976, in an effort to eliminate some of the confusion, public relations pioneer and scholar Rex Harlow compiled 472 definitions of public relations. From those, Harlow came up with his own 87-word definition, which stressed public relations' role as a management function that "helps establish and maintain mutual lines of communication, understanding, acceptance, and cooperation between an organization and its publics."[11]

In recent years, some have referred to public relations as *reputation management, perception management*, or *image management*. However, others express misgivings. They say these are superficial titles that do not reflect the depth of the profession.[12]

One area of agreement among public relations practitioners is the definition of the term **public:** any group of people who share common interests or values in a particular situation—especially interests or values they might be willing to act upon. When a public has a relationship with your organization, the public is called a **stakeholder,** meaning that it has a stake in your organization or in an issue potentially involving your organization.

The fact is that as long as people are people, they will continue to view the world with differing perspectives. That's why it may be best to avoid the debate over the exact wording of a public relations definition and, instead, to concentrate on the various elements of the profession itself. Here is where one finds consensus. Common to any comprehensive definition of public relations are the following elements:

- *Public relations is a management function.* The relationship between an organization and the publics important to its success must be a top concern of the organization's leadership. The public relations practitioner provides counsel on the timing, manner, and form important relationship-building actions should take. In other words, practitioners aren't just soldiers who follow orders;

QUICKBREAK 1.1

The Definition Debate

The struggle to define the profession of public relations continues well into its second century. Although many may see this as an intellectual exercise, others say the failure to reach a consensus on what, exactly, public relations is may undermine its future.

The **Public Relations Society of America (PRSA)** has tried to lay the matter to rest on several occasions. The PRSA Assembly adopted an Official Statement on Public Relations in 1982: "Public relations helps our complex, pluralistic society to reach decisions and function more effectively by contributing to mutual understanding among groups and institutions. It serves to bring the public and public policies into harmony."

The statement went on to describe public relations as a management function that encompasses monitoring and interpreting public opinion, counseling management on communication and social responsibility issues, and researching and managing organizational communication.[13]

Recognizing that its own attempt at defining the profession ran more than 400 words, PRSA settled on a more concise and somewhat vague alternative in 1982: "Public relations helps an organization and its publics adapt mutually to each other."[14]

PRSA's efforts to define public relations appear only to have invigorated the debate. The argument over what public relations is and how it should be defined raged throughout the1990s and into the new century. Practitioners, scholars, and textbook writers (including the authors of this book) continue to add fuel to this fire.

The challenge is deceptively simple: Find concise terminology that captures the values, purpose, and spirit of a complex and dynamic profession. The solution, however, remains elusive.

"If the field of public relations wishes to master its own destiny, it must settle on a definition," wrote James G. Hutton of Fairleigh Dickinson University. To that end, he proposed a three-word definition: "managing strategic relationships." While acknowledging his definition's potential drawbacks, Hutton believed that it captured the essential elements of the profession.[15]

Predictably, this attempt to settle the debate was met with skepticism. Writing in *Public Relations Review* in 2001, four European public relations professors found Hutton's approach "commendable, yet a bit flawed." Their major complaint was that Hutton's definition—and most U.S.-based definitions—focused only on U.S. theories and practices. "It is only after we are able to take into consideration the full richness of the present state of thinking and practicing public relations around the globe that we will be able to draw conclusions towards what the public relations profession is in the world at the beginning of the 21st century," the European scholars wrote.[16]

Even with dramatic advances in public relations research and technology during the last century, we are no closer to defining the profession than when Edward L. Bernays first coined the phrase "public relations counsel" in 1923. As one author wrote more than 40 years ago, public relations remains a discipline "of some 100,000 whose common bond is the profession and whose common woe is that no two of them can ever agree on what that profession is."[17] ■

they're also generals who help shape policy. And like all managers, they must be able to measure the degree of their success in their various projects.

■ *Public relations involves two-way communication.* Communication is not just telling people about an organization's needs. It also involves listening to those same people speak of their concerns. This willingness to listen is an essential part of the relationship-building process.

■ *Public relations is a planned activity.* Actions taken on behalf of an organization must be carefully planned and consistent with the organization's values and goals. And because the relationship between an organization and the publics important to its success is a top concern, these actions must also be consistent with the publics' values and goals.

■ *Public relations is a research-based social science.* Formal and informal research is conducted to allow an organization to communicate effectively, possessing a full understanding of the environment in which it operates and the issues it confronts. Public relations practitioners and educators also share their knowledge with others in the industry through various professional and academic publications.

■ *Public relations is socially responsible.* A practitioner's responsibilities extend beyond organizational goals. Practitioners and the people they represent are expected to play a constructive role in society.

You may have noticed a common theme running throughout this list: the concept of **relationship management.** Farsighted, well-managed organizations know they must have good relationships with publics important to their success. A landmark study that sought to define excellence in public relations noted that having good relationships with these publics can save an organization money by reducing the likelihood of threats such as litigation, regulation, boycotts, or lost revenue that result from falling out of favor with these groups. At the same time, the study said that an organization makes more money by cultivating good relationships with consumers, donors, shareholders, and legislators.[18] Therefore, nurturing these relationships is one of the most important roles public relations practitioners can play.

However one chooses to frame its definition, there is one other important aspect to public relations: It plays a critical role in the free flow of information in democratic societies. When American colonists declared their independence from Great Britain in 1776, they said, "Governments are instituted among men, deriving their just powers from the consent of the governed."[19] The meaning of this phrase is clear: For democratic societies to function in a healthy manner, the government and the people must reach a consensus on matters of importance. Consent cannot occur without the exchange of information and ideas. That, in turn, requires communication. Those who cannot communicate effectively in democratic societies are left at a distinct and sometimes dangerous disadvantage.

Public relations plays a critical role in effective communications. Through public relations, individuals and organizations enter the great marketplace of ideas. And, through the proper application of public relations, practitioners participate in the search for consensus.

MARRYING THEORY AND PRACTICE

Because the profession is difficult to define, one might reasonably ask why developing a specific definition of public relations really matters. Some might argue that although they lack the right words to describe public relations, they still know it when they see it. They might also contend that the lessons learned by trial and error are far more tangible—and therefore more useful—than abstract theory. In doing so, they are taking a **heuristic** or practical approach to problem solving. In other words, these practitioners use educated guesses based upon trial and error to reach a satisfactory solution. A heuristic approach is not much different from learning how to drive a car: The driver initially learns from the experiences of others and, gradually, through his or her own experience, gains in confidence and competence.

Although heuristic problem solving can be both useful and easy, it also has its drawbacks. Decision making by trial and error can be very costly in many ways. It can take a lot of time, drain human and financial resources, and not always lead to the best results. It can lead to errors that ultimately cause more harm than good. There is also the trap that comes with allowing the prevailing conventional wisdom to go unchallenged. History is filled with examples of great social and technological advancements created because someone chose not to accept the idea of "that's the way it has always been."

On the other hand, some practitioners choose to take a **theoretical** or scientific approach, in which decisions rest on tried and tested models verified through social science research. Theory brings a sense of order and structure to social interactions, just as it does to describing the physical actions of nature. In the case of public relations, theory helps us understand better a constantly evolving profession. However, by definition, theories are educated guesses about the way things are—based on formal research, to be certain, but still conjectural. Because of the complexity of human beings, social science has fewer **axioms,** self-evident or universally recognized truths, than the natural sciences. Returning to the example of driving a car, there is a lot more certainty in explaining the physics behind one car's being faster than another than in using social science theory to explain why racecar driver Helio Castroneves has consistently driven faster than most of his peers.

As discussed in greater detail in Chapter 3, the discipline we call public relations has evolved from the birth of the Industrial Revolution to today's Digital Revolution. In this environment, the 21st-century practitioner requires a healthy balance between practice and theory. We should not discount personal experience, nor should we dismiss theories based on years of research and refinement. Employers value critical-thinking, problem-solving, analytical employees who consider all the options before them, both theoretical and practical.

Public Relations Models and Theories

Since the dramatic growth of the profession following the Second World War, a number of scholars have attempted to describe the practice of public relations through the creation of theories or models. These artifacts are meant to describe the complex roles practitioners play within organizations. As you will see, as the profession continued to evolve and challenges facing practitioners became more complex, so did efforts to describe public relations practice.

CUTLIP, CENTER, AND BROOM MODELS   During the early 1980s, public relations scholars Scott M. Cutlip, Allen H. Center, and Glen M. Broom categorized the actions of practitioners into one of four models: *expert prescriber* (seen as an authority on both public relations problems and solutions), *communication technician* (hired primarily for writing and editing skills), *communication facilitator* (who serves as a liaison, interpreter and mediator between the organization and its publics), and *problem-solving process facilitator* (who collaborates with other managers by helping them define and solve problems).[20] Although every practitioner might play some or all of these roles to varying degrees, the three scholars said that one of these models eventually emerges as a practitioner's dominant role.

HUNT AND GRUNIG MODELS   Also in the early 1980s, scholars Todd T. Hunt and James E. Grunig developed their own four-model approach to describe public

SOCIAL MEDIA APPS

Social Media and Public Relations

These are exciting times to be in public relations. Although some might struggle to adjust in a brave new digital world, the profession of public relations continues to flourish. Because public relations practitioners traditionally have been early adopters of new technologies, they have always been among the first to embrace change. And in the 21st century, the only constant is change.

As you read this book, you will learn that the practice of public relations involves the targeting of strategic, values-driven messages toward specific audiences, using media those publics prefer. In recent years, that has increasingly meant the use of social media.

What are *social media*? It's a term we hear a lot these days. Certainly, we think of YouTube, Twitter, and Facebook when we think of social media. What each has in common is interactivity. Unlike traditional media, such as newspapers and television, Internet-based social media promote multisided conversations. They also are platforms for networking and exchanging user-generated content.

Here's another important question to ponder: Why are social media important to public relations? Simply put, there's a conversation taking place in cyberspace, and practitioners—often the point of contact between an organization and its stakeholders—need to be a part of it. It once took weeks and months for important news to filter around the world; today that occurs in a nanosecond. Fortunes and reputations can be made or lost in the blink of an eye. And, as the reach of traditional media fragments, social media offer highly targeted channels for delivering timely and specialized messages.

In coming chapters, we will use this space to examine the challenges, opportunities, and issues of public relations and social media. Prepare to download! ■

relations functions. Whereas the Cutlip, Center, and Broom models focused on the *individual's* role in the organization, the Hunt and Grunig models focused on the ways the *public relations function* interacts with the organization and its publics. Those four models are *press agentry/publicity* (the focus is on gaining media coverage), *public information* (the practitioner serves as a "journalist in residence" focused on dissemination of information), *two-way asymmetrical* (research is used to influence publics to accept a particular point of view), and *two-way symmetrical* (the focus is on two-way communication as a means of conflict resolution.)[21] Just a few years later, Grunig, in collaboration with his wife, Larissa A. Grunig, defined two-way symmetry as **normative,** the ideal standard or model for achieving excellence in public relations. However, they acknowledged that there is often a gap between the ideal and reality of public relations.[22]

CONTINGENCY THEORY OF ACCOMMODATION   The notion of two-way symmetry as the normative public relations model was challenged as being simplistic and unrealistic by four researchers representing both the profession and scholars in 1997. Led by Professor Glen Cameron, the researchers stated that the four-model approach "fails to capture the complexity and multiplicity of the public relations environment."[23] Instead, they proposed a **contingency theory of accommodation** in public relations. The four researchers suggested that the practice of public relations rests somewhere within a continuum from *pure accommodation* (where one builds trusts and maintains important relationships) to *pure advocacy* (where one argues on behalf of a particular cause or position). They said practitioners find themselves at different places along that continuum at different times. A practitioner's location on that continuum at any given moment depends on one or more of 87 variables, including threats an organization might face, the issues confronting it, the dominant organizational culture, and the personal characteristics of the practitioner.[24]

REFLECTIVE PARADIGM A/K/A REFLECTION   The **reflective paradigm** developed from European social research theory in the first decade of the new millennium has gained acceptance in the United States. As noted in Chapter 3, public relations practitioners have historically struggled to enhance the credibility of themselves and their profession. The reflective paradigm—often referred to in the United States as *reflection*—takes a much broader view. "The most important problem in public relations is the societal legitimization of organizations," European scholars Betteke Van Ruler and Dejan Verçiç wrote in *Communication Yearbook* in 2005. "Because current public relations models are too much oriented at a public's or stakeholder's level, they are insufficient to cope with societal issues."[25] To put it another way, reflection focuses on simultaneous interactions with a broad range of stakeholders and recognizes that organizations can achieve only as much as society permits. Within this broad social context, Van Ruler and Vercic defined the four characteristics of communications managers as being *counseling* (analyzing changing values, norms, and issues in society), *coaching* (educating members of their organization to behave competently within societal norms), *conceptualizing* (developing strategies for building and maintaining public trust), and *executing* (creating and carrying out the tactics that support those trust-building strategies).

Public Relations and Marketing

Another definitional issue is whether public relations should be considered a separate discipline at all. Some very learned people argue that public relations is a component of a different field encompassing many persuasive communications: **integrated marketing communications (IMC)**. (This topic is discussed in significant detail in Chapter 13.) However, other equally learned individuals bristle at the thought of public relations' being covered by an all-encompassing IMC umbrella.

The authors of this book support the latter view. We see IMC as a consumer-focused marriage of three distinct disciplines: advertising, marketing, and some functions of public relations. As you may have noticed, some people think of public relations as "free advertising" and of advertising as marketing. However, each term represents a distinct discipline:

- **Advertising** is the use of controlled media (media in which one pays for the privilege of dictating message content, placement, and frequency) in an attempt to influence the actions of targeted publics.
- **Marketing** is the process of researching, creating, refining, and promoting a product or service and distributing that product or service to targeted consumers.
- **Public relations** is the management of relationships between an organization and its publics.

Not every marketing situation requires the use of all three disciplines. Marketing, the central concept in IMC, focuses on consumers. We respectfully suggest that public relations practitioners engage in relationships that go far beyond consumer communications. Although this is a debate that may best be conducted in an atmosphere that includes beverages and peanuts, the debate is indicative of the broader struggle public relations practitioners have faced since the dawn of the 20th century: to have public relations accepted as a separate and significant profession.

At this point, you might ask which model of public relations is best. The answer depends on what is important to you. In that all the models attempt to describe the best way to practice public relations, we can say that they all value effectiveness. The earliest models of public relations placed a higher value on relationships among practitioners, the clients and organizations they serve, and stakeholders important to their success. Recent models value social legitimacy more highly. Although scholars and practitioners might disagree on which model most accurately describes public relations, the common thread of values plays an important role in each. However, before we focus on the role of values in public relations, it would be useful first to describe how public relations is done.

 QUICK CHECK

1. What are the five essential elements in the definition of public relations?
2. How do heuristic and theoretical problem solving differ?
3. What is the reflective paradigm, and how does it differ from other models of public relations?
4. How do public relations and marketing differ?

QUICKBREAK 1.2

A Profession or a Trade?

Adding to the confusion about what public relations is and where it fits into an organization's structure is an ongoing debate: Is public relations a profession or is it a trade? This is a debate over more than mere semantics and prestige. The salaries practitioners earn, their influence on decision making, and the degree to which they are regulated hang in the balance.

Generally recognized qualities that distinguish professions from other career pursuits are

- the need for a certain level of education as a prerequisite to entering the profession;
- support of the profession by ongoing research published in scholarly journals or in professional association publications;
- the establishment of ethical standards, usually in the form of a code of ethics; and
- some form of licensing or government control.

Doctors and lawyers are professionals who clearly meet these criteria. Both have to receive an advanced academic degree and are expected to remain informed on the latest developments in their fields. Both professions are supported by significant bodies of research and have established codes of ethics. And one cannot be a doctor or lawyer until a state licensing board gives its stamp of approval.

When it comes to public relations, the dividing line between profession and trade is not as well defined. In one nationwide survey, there was little consensus on what constitutes a standard of professional performance. Answers varied significantly, depending on the respondent's age, level of education, race, level of experience, and geographic location.[26]

Licensing proponents, including the late Edward L. Bernays, an acknowledged "father" of modern public relations, see licensing as a way of weeding out unqualified practitioners and raising the stature and salaries of those who are licensed. Others see government-sanctioned licensing as burdensome and as an infringement on First Amendment rights to freedom of expression.

Organizations such as PRSA and the **International Association of Business Communicators (IABC)** have sought to promote public relations as a profession through the establishment of voluntary accreditation programs. Practitioners must gain a certain level of experience and demonstrate a certain degree of knowledge before receiving accreditation: **APR,** for **Accredited in Public Relations,** by PRSA and/or **ABC,** for **Accredited Business Communicator,** by IABC. With the creation of the **Universal Accreditation Program** in 1998, PRSA opened its accreditation process to members of eight additional public relations organizations, including the National School Public Relations Association and the Religion Communicators Council.[27] Both IABC and PRSA also promote professionalism with support of scholarly research and through the enforcement of codes of ethics. ■

THE PUBLIC RELATIONS PROCESS

First the good news: Most public relations experts agree that public relations is conducted within the framework of a four-step process. But would this really be public relations if there were agreement on what to label each of the steps? Remember: This is public relations, the profession of a thousand definitions.

The Traditional Four-Step Model of the Public Relations Process

A variety of names have been used to describe the four steps of the public relations process. Some instructors, in an effort to help students memorize the various steps for the inevitable midterm exam, have favored the use of acronyms such as ROPE (research, objectives, programming, and evaluation) and RACE (research, action, communication, and evaluation). In adding our two cents' worth to the debate over what to call each of the four steps, we opt for a more straightforward, if less glamorous, approach: research, planning, communication, and evaluation.

1. **Research** is the discovery phase of a problem-solving process: practitioners' use of formal and informal methods of information gathering to learn about an organization, the challenges and opportunities it faces, and the publics important to its success.
2. **Planning** is the strategy phase of the problem-solving process, in which practitioners use the information gathered during research. From that information, they develop effective and efficient strategies to meet the needs of their clients or organizations.
3. **Communication** is the execution phase of the public relations process. This is where practitioners direct messages to specific publics in support of specified goals. But good plans are flexible: Because changes can occur suddenly in the social or business environment, sometimes it's necessary to adjust, overhaul, or abandon the planned strategies. It's worth repeating here that effective communication is two-way, involving listening to publics as well as sending them messages.
4. **Evaluation** is the measurement of how efficiently and effectively a public relations effort met the organization's goals.

Although there is a simple elegance in defining the public relations process using this traditional model, it does not reflect the real world. It depicts a linear process: Step two follows step one, step three follows step two, and so forth (see Figure 1.1). How often does your own life move in such an orderly fashion? If you are like most people, life is constantly changing and full of surprises. Public relations is no different.

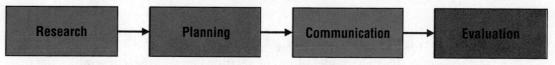

FIGURE 1.1
The Traditional Four-Step Model of the Public Relations Process

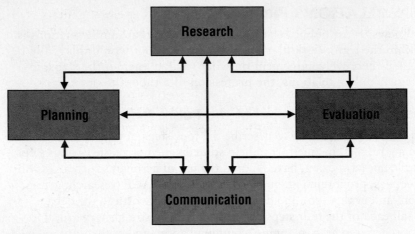

FIGURE 1.2
The Dynamic Model of the Public Relations Process

The Dynamic Model of the Public Relations Process

In the real world, public relations involves a dynamic process (see Figure 1.2). Although practitioners move along a general path of research, planning, communication, and evaluation, it is often necessary to switch directions. They do this because the world is an ever-changing place. To put it another way, what was true yesterday may not be true tomorrow.

For example, the implication of the traditional four-step model is that evaluation is the last thing done. However, in this era of downsizing and increased accountability, evaluation should occur during *every* phase of the public relations process. Research should identify ways to measure the effects of a public relations program. Those measurements should then be built into any plan that is developed. As the plan moves into the communication phase, practitioners should be sensitive to the need to adjust their efforts to any miscalculations or changes in the environment.

That, in turn, may require additional research. Finally, the evaluation phase provides critical information on whether the goals of the plan were met. But it also sets the stage for future actions.

The public relations process is not a step-by-step process followed much like a cook follows a recipe. It is a critical-thinking process involving a constant analysis and reevaluation of information.

THE ROLE OF VALUES IN PUBLIC RELATIONS

Although the dynamic model of public relations more closely resembles the real world, it is still missing a key component: **values.** For the purposes of this discussion, values are defined as the fundamental beliefs and standards that drive behavior and decision making. To put it another way, values are the filters through which we see the world and the world sees us. Everyone has values. Organizations have values. Actions communicate values. Even thoughtless actions taken with little regard for one's beliefs and standards communicate a value.

Think about the process you and your friends follow when planning a spring break trip. As you begin to research where to go, you first identify your values: fun, companionship, safety, price, and so forth. Those core values establish the framework within which you'll gather research, plan your trip, go on your trip, and, finally, evaluate its success.

Let's use a second hypothetical example to illustrate what we mean. If an organization says it values the opinions of its employees, it would not make any sense for that organization to conduct research that doesn't take into account the employees' opinions. And it would make even less sense to launch a plan that, in the pursuit of some other short-term gain, winds up showing that the organization is insensitive to employee concerns. That is why it is necessary to understand an organization's values before engaging in the public relations process. And because good relationships with important publics are critical to any organization's success, it is equally important to understand the values of those publics. Some may argue that this approach limits information gathering and creativity. However, that is exactly what values are supposed to do: establish the boundaries within which we are willing to operate.

This lack of focus on values is perhaps the biggest flaw in the traditional four-step model of public relations. At a time when organizations are being held accountable far beyond the balance sheet, their values-inspired mission and goals must be at the forefront of all their research, planning, communication, and evaluation.

A common complaint against public relations practitioners is that they occasionally act as if the ends justify the means. Some choose to flirt with or even to ignore the boundaries of ethics. Others, failing to pause and consider their organization's core values, sometimes find themselves in the uncomfortable position of trying to place their actions in an ethical framework after the fact. Isn't it much better to snuff out a fire before it causes irreparable damage? Issues of values, ethics, and social responsibility must be addressed throughout the public relations process: The continued growth of public relations as a profession depends on it.

 QUICK CHECK

1. What are the four steps of the traditional public relations process?
2. Why is public relations considered a dynamic process?
3. What are values, and what role should they play in the public relations process?
4. Is public relations a profession? Why or why not?

Actions Speak Louder Than Words—Part I

Too often, unintended actions speak louder than the lofty words found in a mission statement:

■ During the fall 2008 economic crisis, American International Group officials accepted $85 billion in federal government loans in an effort to avoid bankruptcy. Less than a week later, the company spent $440,000 at a California retreat to reward its most successful insurance agents. Another group of AIG executives and their spouses flew to Las Vegas in private jets for a conference. Although AIG initially defended the expenditures, it cancelled more than 160 planned events that would have cost an additional $8 million.[28] In a letter to U.S. Treasury Secretary Henry Paulson, AIG Chair and Chief Executive Officer Edward M. Liddy said, "We owe our employees and the American public new standards and approaches"[29] (see Case Study 1.2).

■ Frantic residents of New York flooded emergency switchboards in April 2009 when a jet aircraft made several low-level passes over lower Manhattan, a scene eerily reminiscent of the September 11, 2001, terrorist attacks on the World Trade Center. But it wasn't a terrorist act—it was a photo op. The director of the White House Military Office authorized the flight of an Air Force One backup jet for the purpose of getting a picture of the president's plane flying above the Statute of Liberty. The publicity effort not only cost taxpayers $329,000; it cost Louis Caldera, the man who authorized the flight, his job.[30] It also prompted the New York *Daily News* to ask the obvious question: "Anyone in the White House ever hear of Photoshop?"[31]

■ It was supposed to be a "Journey of Harmony," a 21-nation torch run designed to promote the 2008 Olympic Games in Beijing. The Chinese government had spent eight years and billions of dollars to showcase its emerging clout on the world stage. However, the torch run organizers got a lot more than they had bargained for as protests against China's human rights record marred the event in London, Paris, and San Francisco. Chinese officials said most people were angry with the protesters. Not everyone agreed. "What is most dramatic is to see how broad and deep the support has become," said one protest organizer. "You almost have to feel sorry for the Chinese because it's turned completely against the public image they wanted to present."[32]

Why did things backfire so badly in each of these examples? Simply put, if you talk the talk, you have to walk the walk. Actions—and the values they reflect—speak louder than words.

VALUES-DRIVEN PUBLIC RELATIONS

How can organizations try to ensure that their actions match their words? We advocate an approach we call **values-driven public relations**. Values-driven public relations incorporates a dynamic version of the four-phase process of research, planning, communication, and evaluation into the framework defined by an organization's core values (see Figure 1.3). We offer an alternate definition of public relations:

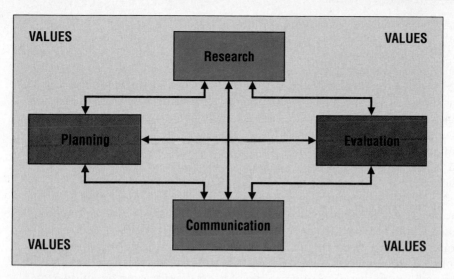

FIGURE 1.3

Values-Driven Public Relations

Public relations is the values-driven management of relationships between an organization and the publics that can affect its success.

Values-driven public relations is the process of uncovering not just where an organization wishes to go but also the principles the organization will observe in getting there. The process begins with the consideration of values during the research phase—those of the organization and the various publics important to its success. Those values, in turn, are incorporated into planning and communications. Values-driven public relations also means being accountable for adherence to those values when we evaluate our actions.

If that sounds easy, it isn't. We live in an increasingly diverse and complex world. New technology and the forces of globalization bring different interests into greater contact—and often into conflict. The Business Roundtable Institute for Corporate Ethics and the Arthur W. Page Society studied the dynamics of public trust in 2009. Their first recommendation focused on values. "Enterprises must focus not only on claiming or codifying a set of beliefs and operating principles, but on being consistently true to them in all their behavior and relationships," the report said. "Otherwise, they will be seen as unreliable and untrustworthy."[33]

Actions Speak Louder Than Words—Part II

Today, a variety of publics are holding public and private organizations more socially accountable. No longer is the bottom line seen as the only thing that matters. Although social responsibility may seem idealistic to some, its applications are very real-world:

■ Honeywell Hometown Solutions, a corporate citizenship initiative of Honeywell International, focuses the company's philanthropic and volunteer efforts in four areas that "align with Honeywell's heritage, products and people: science and math education, family safety and security, housing and shelter, and humanitarian relief." Since its inception, Honeywell's *Got 2B Safe* anti-child abduction program has reached more than 5 million third-grade students (see Case Study 1.1). *FMA Live!*, a traveling stage show designed to encourage math and science education, has been seen by 140,000 middle school students. More than 1,000 homes and community centers have been rehabilitated through the company's community outreach.[34]

- In an effort to curb violence in Puerto Rico's public schools, several community and private organizations collaborated in 2008 to create "Armate de Valor," which means "Arm Yourself with Courage." According to research, most teenagers were reluctant to discuss weapon-related threats at school out of fear that they would be identified. Nearly one in 10 students surveyed said they had missed school because they did not feel safe. Public and in-school educational efforts, combined with the launch of an anonymous hotline, resulted in the safe resolution of 44 weapon-related incidents in the program's first six months.[35]

- Although one in three U.S. women die of heart disease, only one in five believes she is at risk. To counter these sobering statistics, the American Heart Association teamed with Edelman in the "Go Red For Women (GRFW) Untold Stories Campaign" in 2007–08. Recognizing the value of peer-to-peer communication, the campaign featured the personal stories of heart disease survivors through a variety of publicity channels, including online, and in a nationally syndicated television documentary. In addition to generating more than 771 million media impressions for its heart health messages, the campaign resulted in more than 1 million women taking an online heart checkup before June 2008–18 months earlier than originally targeted.[36]

Whose Values Should You Follow?

In the research phase of the public relations process, an organization must, of course, identify and consider its own values—but it must also do more: It must identify the values of involved publics and, perhaps—as in the reflective paradigm— the values of society itself. Sometimes it can be difficult to decide which values to

As the frenetic pace of activity on the floor of the Chicago Board of Trade vividly demonstrates, an increasing number of publics demand instant information. A challenge to 21st century practitioners is to meet that demand in an accurate and values-driven way.

(U.S. Census Bureau)

VALUES STATEMENT 1.1

Hallmark Cards

Hallmark Cards, founded in 1910, is the leader in the personal expression industry. The Kansas City, Missouri, company reported consolidated net revenues of $4.3 billion in 2008. Hallmark products are distributed in more than 30 languages to more than 100 countries.

This Is Hallmark
We Believe:

That our products and services must enrich people's lives.

That creativity and quality—in our products, services and all that we do—are essential to our success.

That innovation in all areas of our business is essential to attaining and sustaining leadership.

That the people of Hallmark are our company's most valuable resource.

That distinguished financial performance is imperative to accomplish our broader purpose.

That our private ownership must be preserved.

We Value and Are Committed To:

Excellence in all we do.

High standards of ethics and integrity.

Caring and responsible corporate citizenship for Kansas City and for each community in which we operate.

These beliefs and values guide our business strategies, our corporate behavior, and our relationships with business partners, suppliers, customers, communities and each other.

—Hallmark Beliefs & Values Statement ■

follow. If there is conflict between organizational and societal values, organizations must make a difficult choice.

This does not imply that one must always adhere to society's values. For example, there was a time in the United States when society condoned slavery, denied women the right to vote, and allowed children to work long hours in unhealthy conditions. An organization may choose to swim against the tide of public opinion. If it chooses to do so, however, it should do so by choice, not chance. Values-driven public relations can be a catalyst for making this crucial decision.

Values-driven public relations is similar to the traditional four-step approach to public relations but it has significant differences. In values-driven public relations,

QUICKBREAK 1.3

How Organizations Establish Their Values

J.C. Penney has *The Penney Idea,* a group of seven governing values written in 1913. One of the values is "To test our every policy, method, and act in this wise: Does it square with what is right and just?"

Hallmark Cards has *This Is Hallmark,* a statement of "Beliefs and Values." One of the statement's five beliefs declares "distinguished financial performance is imperative to accomplish our broader purpose." One of the statement's four values is "ethical and moral conduct at all times and in all our relationships."

Johnson & Johnson is governed by the one-page *Johnson & Johnson Credo,* which begins, "We believe our first responsibility is to the doctors, nurses, and patients, to the mothers and fathers, and all others who use our products and services."

How did these respected, successful organizations—and others like them—develop their written statements of values? Each organization has its own system, but two ingredients seem common to the values identification process. First, it's a job for a dedicated committee, not an individual. Debating with others helps us clarify what we truly believe. Second, a statement of values must be written, must be well known, and must play an active part in an organization's everyday operations. Only in that way can it be tested and improved.

If an organization lacks a written statement of values, its public relations program is a ship without a rudder. An organization can begin to develop a **values statement** by forming a committee or committees to answer these questions:

1. Why are we in business?
2. What does our organization want to be known for—both today and a generation from now?
3. What should our publics expect from us?
4. What are our highest priorities?
5. Where do we want to go, and whom do we want along for the ride?
6. What should our role be in our community and in our industry?
7. Whose organization is this?
8. To whom do we have obligations?
9. Why should someone want to work for this organization?

The answers to these questions should be used to create a short statement of the organization's core values. Stating each value as a principle can help you move from a values statement to a **mission statement**; in other words, stating each value as a principle can help you move from an idea to a proposed action. For example, J.C. Penney values justice in all its actions. In *The Penney Idea,* that value is stated as a principle: "To test our every policy, method, and act in this wise: Does it square with what is right and just?"

Let's look for a moment at the first question: "Why are we in business?" The obvious answer for many organizations might seem to be "to make money." But it's not money that people crave as much as it is what money can provide: a nice home, food, education, the ability to help others. Hallmark's statement of beliefs and values notes that money is not an end; rather, it's a means toward accomplishing Hallmark's broader purpose.

The *Johnson & Johnson Credo* has served that company particularly well. The company won praise from customers, politicians, journalists, and other key publics for its immediate willingness to put the safety of its customers ahead of company profits during two product-tampering incidents in the 1980s. By adhering to its *Credo,* Johnson & Johnson emerged as one of the most respected companies in the world.

Like many strong, values-driven organizations, Johnson & Johnson periodically evaluates its *Credo* in the context of current business situations. In a values-driven organization, a statement of values or a mission statement should be as much a part of the everyday environment as coffee, meetings, and lunch plans. ■

the role of organizational, public, and societal values is explicit rather than implicit. Values-driven public relations also employs a decidedly nonlinear process, in which there are constant checkbacks on values, research, strategies, and execution. Most important, the practice of values-driven public relations answers the most ardent critics of public relations by placing ethical decision making first.

Welcome to values-driven public relations.

 QUICK CHECK

1. How do you define *values-driven public relations,* and how does it differ from the traditional definition of public relations?
2. In values-driven public relations, whose values should we follow?
3. What are some examples of public relations decisions in which values played a key role?

SUMMARY

Public relations is the values-driven management of relationships between an organization and the publics that can affect its success. Although scholars and practitioners may differ on a precise definition for the profession or on a specific model for its practice, there is a consensus that public relations is a management function, involves two-way communication, is a planned activity, is a social science based in research, and is socially responsible. There is also broad agreement that relationship building is at the heart of good public relations. That requires knowledge of values, the beliefs and standards that govern one's actions. And not just our own values but also those of the various publics important to our success.

The manner in which public relations is practiced depends largely on the structure of the organization it serves. Although public relations should be a major concern of management, some organizations relegate its practitioners to the role of technicians. Some view public relations as an element of integrated marketing communications. However, others—including the authors of this book—view it as a separate and distinct profession.

The traditional view of public relations is that it is performed through a four-step process: research, planning, communication, and evaluation. The problem with that view is that public relations is a dynamic process in which any of these four phases can occur at any time. When practitioners conduct this process while closely adhering to values—those of the practitioner, the organization, and the society—the process evolves into what is known as values-driven public relations: the values-driven management of relationships between an organization and the publics that can affect its success.

DISCUSSION QUESTIONS

1. Before you read this chapter, how would you have defined *public relations*?
2. What are the four models or theories of public relations discussed in this chapter? How are they similar and how do they differ?
3. In your opinion, should some form of licensing be mandatory for public relations practitioners?
4. What role does relationship management play in public relations?
5. In the opening scenario in this chapter, you were challenged to ask yourself where you fit into the profession of public relations. Based on what you have learned already, what is your answer now, and is it different from before?

MEMO FROM THE FIELD

GARY MCCORMICK
Director of Partnership Marketing; HGTV
Knoxville, Tennessee

Gary McCormick, APR, Fellow PRSA, is the director of partnership marketing for HGTV, one of the six cable networks owned by Scripps Networks Interactive. He is responsible for identifying opportunities to partner with other companies and brands to provide off-channel exposure for the leading home and lifestyle cable network and its on-air talent that will increase ratings and awareness with viewers. Before moving to HGTV, McCormick served as the director of public relations for DIY Network and Fine Living TV Network, where he directed their media relations and special events, including DIY's national partnership with Habitat for Humanity. Active since 1985 in the Public Relations Society of America (PRSA), he served as its chair and CEO in 2010. In addition, McCormick serves on the board of directors for Plank Center for Public Relations Leadership at the University of Alabama and the University of Florida Department of Public Relations Advisory Council. He served as the president of the PRSA Foundation in 2006 and 2007 and has been a co-chair of the Champions for PRSSA since 2005. McCormick, as the 2006 Recipient of the Educators Academy David Ferguson Award, has been recognized for his contributions to public relations education.

From rather inauspicious beginnings, public relations could clearly have been its own best client for many decades. Today, however, professionals entering this field have an unprecedented opportunity to demonstrate their value to companies and clients. It's time to quit being defensive and become confident about our contributions.

Public relations professionals are now faced with a "new normal." The convergence of multiple factors has positioned public relations as a growing and rapidly evolving profession with new opportunities for graduates as well as for long-time professionals. You are looking at entering the field at a turning point for business and communications.

First, advances in technology have delivered an engaged consumer who demands to be heard through social media, blogs, and comments on news media and company websites. Clearly, public relations is best positioned as the most effective means to manage those relationships. However, our industry must continue to train professionals to integrate these interactions into their overall communications strategies, not as a stand-alone tactic or initiative, stressing outcome over output.

Second, the changing role of traditional media requires public relations to build better and stronger relationships to compete for coverage. In addition, we will have to understand how to identify, prioritize, and develop the relationships with social media to provide balance and enhance our efforts for awareness with growing audiences that increasingly segment their input from media.

Third, but perhaps most important, is the challenge that business faces in relation to its credibility of message. With a marked reduction in trust of business by the public, which is largely a result of the lack of transparency and openness in corporate communications, public relations offers these companies the best skills and approach to repair this damage. By providing strategic counsel to our companies and clients on how to build and manage better relationships with employees, customers, media, and investors, we can start to develop better reputations, deliver value and returns to the bottom line, and help distinguish companies from their competitors.

Last, but not least, today our news cycle is clearly 24/7, worldwide, and immediate. Never before has information reached so many so quickly and, in many cases, without verification or context. The fact that "being first" now often trumps "being true" will challenge public relations professionals to be prepared to help clients and companies understand and handle the immediacy and reach of information that previously would never have become public.

All these factors and many more make public relations a dynamic, diverse, and growing profession that has established its role and value to companies and clients. Beyond the media relations and crisis communications, public relations has integrated itself into the strategic, mission-critical pillars of business, building brand, safeguarding reputation, and maintaining consumer and customer relationships. It has moved beyond publicity and promotion to supporting all facets of what companies must do today to remain viable and successful.

I hope you find your study of the public relations profession engaging and enlightening. If it becomes your career choice, you will find that it's a lifelong study of human behavior, relationships, and managing change that will continue to engage and enlighten as well as reward you personally and professionally. ■

CASE STUDY 1.1 Got 2B Safe!

Following a one-year study, the U.S. Justice Department reported that an average of 2,185 children under the age of 18 were reported missing each day—with one of every three missing children a victim of abduction.[37] The National Center for Missing and Exploited Children (NCMEC) estimates that one child (10–17 years old) out of every seven has received a sexual solicitation or approach over the Internet.[38]

When executives at Honeywell International first looked into the issue of child safety, they found a lot of programs geared toward finding children after they had gone missing but none designed to prevent child abduction. That led to a partnership with NCMEC and the creation of *Got 2B Safe!*, a program to help children make good, quick decisions when faced with the threat of abduction.

"Whereas the whole national dialogue is around finding kids, very little has been done to provide children the skills and behaviors that would prevent them from being abducted or exploited in the first place," said Honeywell's Michael Holland.[39]

According to its 2009 annual report, Honeywell is a "diversified technology company" based in Morris Township, New Jersey, with a net annual income of nearly $2.8 billion. Its business includes aerospace products and services, security and life safety products and services, and the manufacture of specialty chemicals and materials for industrial use.[40]

Honeywell partnered with NCMEC in 2003, the same year it launched Honeywell Hometown Solutions, a new approach to corporate citizenship. According to its website, Honeywell Hometown Solution focuses on "four important societal needs that align with Honeywell's heritage, products and people: science and math education; family safety and security; housing and shelter; and humanitarian relief." Since its inception, Honeywell Hometown Solutions programs have received more than 40 awards for corporate social responsibility and cause marketing.[41]

When Honeywell executives first looked into the issue of missing and exploited children, they conducted a nationwide survey. What they learned surprised them: Whereas abductions ranked behind only drugs as the greatest safety concern among parents and grandparents, more than one third of the respondents did not know that children are more likely to be abducted by someone the children know than by someone they don't. Only 7 percent of the parents and 3 percent of the grandparents knew that teenagers are at the greatest risk.

Honeywell also engaged other partners in its anti-abduction campaign. *Weekly Reader*, which has provided school children with educational reading materials for more than a century, joined in the effort. The company also hired New York–based Peppercom Strategic Communications for its public relations expertise.

Starting with the 2003 school year, *Got 2B Safe!* materials were delivered to 25,000 third grade teachers. They included safety tips, hands-on activities, and strategies for helping children be safer wherever they may be.[42] Since then, *Got 2B Safe!* materials have been distributed annually to nearly all of the 72,319 elementary schools and to 5 million students in the United States. Including its marketing and public relations efforts, the campaign reaches nearly 30 million people each year.[43]

Part of the program's success comes from its focus on teachers. After implementing the campaign, Honeywell and Peppercom conducted follow-up interviews with 25 teachers. The teachers said they care about child abduction education but lacked the necessary time and resources to do it. This, in turn, led to creation of an incentive awards program. To enter, educators nationwide were asked to submit lesson plans or essays on how they teach *Got 2B Safe!* principles. In 2009, the fourth year of the awards, five grand-prize winners each received a $10,000 eco-classroom makeover. Another 100 teachers received $500 worth of school supplies. More than 1,000 teachers entered.

"I've always tried to incorporate a unit of safety in my classroom," said Jessica Beamon, a 2008 winner. "The simple *Got 2B Safe!* rules clearly resonate with my students and help educate them to make safe choices."[44]

"The *Got 2B Safe!* program speaks directly to our mission by putting child safety tools into the hands of educators, parents, and, ultimately, children," said Ernie Allen, NCMEC president and CEO. "We are grateful to Honeywell for its continued support and to these exceptional teachers for the differences they are making in the lives of the children they teach."[45]

Others took note of the campaign as well. *Got 2B Safe!* has received eight corporate responsibility awards and a 2009 Silver Anvil Award from the Public Relations Society of America.

DISCUSSION QUESTIONS

1. Why did Honeywell choose child-abduction prevention as a focus of its corporate outreach?
2. What role did research play in the *Got 2B Safe!* program?
3. What benefits, if any, does Honeywell receive from the *Got 2B Safe!* program?
4. If Honeywell had chosen to donate the money it invests in Honeywell Hometown solutions instead of administering the program, would the company have received the same benefits? ■

CASE STUDY 1.2 Meltdown Monday

Prior to September 15, 2008—known on Wall Street as Meltdown Monday—a very small percentage of U.S. residents could tell you what AIG stood for, let alone what the huge financial company did. However, within a few months, most had a greater understanding of the American International Group—and didn't like it.

"Forget al Qaeda, Weapons of Mass Destruction and the Axis of Evil," wrote CNN correspondent Jonathan Mann in March 2009. "A once obscure acronym is on the lips of President Barack Obama, just about every politician in Washington and a lot of angry taxpayers nationwide.

"It's AIG."[46]

AIG had been one of the most trusted names on Wall Street. Just a year earlier, the insurance conglomerate reported that it had assets of approximately $1 trillion, with $110 billion in annual revenues and 116,000 employees in 130 countries. But that was before Meltdown Monday, when, by AIG's own admission, it was "on the brink of failure and in need of government assistance."[47]

Because this is not a global economics textbook, this case study does not explore the cause and effects of the 2008 recession, the deepest economic slowdown since the Great Depression. However, it is important to know that the U.S. government decided that the collapse of AIG would severely weaken the economy. Over the next few months, the company received $170 billion in bailout money and an $85 billion loan from the Federal Reserve.[48]

It wasn't long before many taxpayers wondered about their investment. Within days of receiving its loan, AIG spent $440,000 wining and dining its most successful independent life insurance agents at a posh California resort. At about the same time, a team of AIG executives, accompanied by their wives, flew on private jets to Las Vegas for a conference. ABC News also reported that the company was paying "hundreds of thousands of dollars" for a luxury suite at New York's Madison Square Garden.[49]

In a letter to the Secretary of the Treasury, AIG Chairman and CEO Edward M. Liddy said that only 10 of the 100 people attending the California event were AIG employees and that "this sort of gathering has been standard practice in our industry for many years and was planned many months before the Federal Reserve's loan to AIG."[50] Soon thereafter, AIG announced plans to cancel more than 160 planned events, including a $750,000 conference in Las Vegas and a $350,000 sales conference on the Georgia coast.[51]

More fuel was poured on the fire when it was learned in March 2009 that AIG paid out $165 million in bonuses to executives in the company's financial products unit—the same business unit many blamed for the company's near collapse. The company said it was legally obligated to pay the bonuses and said they were needed to retain AIG's best employees. A senior Obama administration official told the *New York Times*, "It is unacceptable for Wall Street firms receiving government assistance to handout million-dollar bonuses, while hard-working Americans bear the burden of this economic crisis." Under political pressure and threatened litigation, approximately one half of the bonus money was returned. However, most of the bonuses went to individuals living outside of the United States and beyond U.S. law.[52]

Very little in this world is black and white, especially when it comes to high finance. AIG was just one of many corporations under intense public scrutiny following Meltdown Monday. Some analysts have argued that the apparently lavish practices described here reflect the reality of doing business on Wall Street. Nevertheless, the view from Main Street is far more critical.

"Trust is at the bottom of all financial transactions, and for many investors and trading partners, that trust has been undermined," said Timothy S. Brown, 2008 chair of the PRSA's Financial Communications Professional Interest Section. "As the next phase of this financial crisis unfolds, financial communicators will continue to play a pivotal role in recontextualizing risk and rebuilding the trust of their organizations' stakeholders."[53]

DISCUSSION QUESTIONS

1. According to AIG, almost all the people "wined and dined" at the California resort were not AIG employees and were being rewarded for outstanding financial performance. Should this change the public's perception of the event?

2. Is there any merit to AIG's claim that some of the apparently lavish activities in which it had been engaged were "standard industry practice"?

3. What roles should public relations practitioners have been playing following Meltdown Monday?

4. If, as Timothy S. Brown said, "trust is at the bottom of all financial transactions," what should public relations practitioners do to restore trust when it has been undermined? ■

NOTES

1. Jeffrey M. Jones, "Americans Continue to Rate Real Estate Industry Negatively," Gallup News Service, 27 August 2010, online, www.gallup.com.

2. "Executive, Congressional and Consumer Attitudes Toward Media, Marketing and the Public Relations Profession," Harris Interactive Research, prepared for the Public Relations Society of America, June 2005, online, www.prsa.org.

3. Lisa Fall and Jeremy Hughes, "Reflections of Perceptions: Measuring the Effects Public Relations Education Has on Non-majors' Attitudes Toward the Discipline," *Public Relations Journal*, v. 3, no. 2 (spring 2009), online, www.prsa.org/prjournal.

4. Julie K. Henderson, "Negative Connotations in the Use of the Term 'Public Relations' in the Print Media," *Public Relations Review* (spring 1998): 45–54.

5. Steve Liner, "The Fifth Guy (with the Urinal) Takes PR's Silver Anvil," *Tallahassee Democrat*, 11 June 2008, A7.

6. Silver Anvil Award Campaign Profile 6BW-0805B14: The Fifth Guy—Florida Department of Health Hygiene Campaign, Public Relations Society of America, online, www.prsa.org/awards/silverAnvil/.

7. Molson Coors Brewing Company website, www.molsoncoors.com.

8. Al Ries and Laura Ries, *The Fall of Advertising and the Rise of PR* (New York: HarperCollins, 2002).

9. Eric Denig, ed., *A Geography of Public Relations Trends: Selected Proceedings of the 10th Public Relations World Congress* (Dordrecht, the Netherlands: Martinus Nijhoff, 1985), 244–249.

10. Chris Cobb, "Driving Public Relations: Chrysler Moves PR Under the HR Umbrella, Spurs Debate About Where PR Reports," *The Public Relations Strategist*, Summer 2008, 6–7.

11. Rex F. Harlow, "Building a Public Relations Definition," *Public Relations Review* (winter 1976): 36.

12. J. G. Hutton et al., "Reputation Management: The New Face of Corporate Public Relations?" *Public Relations Review* 27, no. 3 (fall 2001), 247–261.

13. "Official Statement on Public Relations," *Public Relations Tactics: The Blue Book. The Green Book 2003* (New York: PRSA, 2003), B3.

14. "About Public Relations," Public Relations Society of America, online, www.prsa.org.

15. James G. Hutton, "The Definitions, Dimensions, and Domain of Public Relations," *Public Relations Review* 25, no. 1 (summer 1999): 199–214.

16. Dejan Verčiç, Betteke van Ruler, Gerhard Bütschi, and Bertil Flodin, "On the Definition of Public Relations: A European View," *Public Relations Review* 27, no. 4 (winter 2001): 373–387.

17. John E. Marston, *The Nature of Public Relations* (New York: McGraw-Hill, 1963), 4.

18. James E. Grunig, ed., *Excellence in Public Relations and Communication Management* (Hillsdale, N.J.: Lawrence Erlbaum, 1992), 1–30.

19. *Declaration of Independence* (Washington, D.C.: Commission on the Bicentennial of the United States Constitution).

20. Scott M. Cutlip, Allen H. Center, and Glen M. Broom, *Effective Public Relations*, 6th ed. (Englewood Cliffs, N.J.: Prentice-Hall, 1985), 68–70.

21. Todd Hunt and James E. Grunig, *Managing Public Relations* (New York: Holt, Rinehart & Winston, 1984), 22.

22. James E. Grunig and Larissa A. Grunig, "Models of Public Relations and Communication" in J.E. Gruing (ed.) *Excellence in Public Relations and Communication Management*, (Hillsdale, N.J.: Lawrence Erlbaum Associates, 1992), 285–326.

23. Amanda E. Cancel, Glen T. Cameron, Lynne M. Sallot, and Michael A. Mitrook, "It Depends: A Contingency Theory of Accommodation in Public Relations," *Journal of Public Relations Research*, v. 9, no. 1, (1997): 32–33.

24. Cancel et al., 31–63.

25. Betteke Van Ruler and Dejan Verčiç, "Reflective Communication Management, Future Ways for Public Relations Research," *Communication Yearbook 29*, 2009, 239.

26. Glen T. Cameron, Lynne M. Sallot, and Ruth Ann Weaver Lariscy, "Developing Standards of Professional Performance in Public Relations," *Public Relations Review* (spring 1996): 43–61.

27. "Universal Accreditation Board," Public Relations Society of America, online, www.prsa.org.

28. Joseph Rhee and Richard Esposito, "AIG Still Paying for Luxury Suite at Madison Square Garden," ABC News, 16 October 2008, online, www.abcnews.go.com.

29. AIG Chair and CEO Edward M. Liddy in a letter to Treasury Secretary Henry Paulson, 8 October 2008, posted online by ABC News, www.abcnews.go.com.

30. Jeff Zeleny, "After Flyover of Air Force One Backup, Military Office Director Resigns," the *New York Times*, 8 May 2009, online. www.nytimes.com.

31. Owen Moritz, "Create-Your-Own NYC Air Force One Flyover Photo . . . We Did," *Daily News*, 29 April 2009, online, www.nydn.com.

32. Katrin Bennhold and Elisabeth Rosenthal, "Olympic Torch Goes Out, Briefly, in Paris," the *New York Times*, 8 April 2008, online, www.nytimes.com.

33. *The Dynamics of Public Trust in Business— Emerging Opportunities for Leaders*, Business Roundtable for Corporate Ethics and the Arthur W. Page Society, 2009, 28.

34. "About Us: Honeywell Hometown Solutions," online, http://www51.honeywell.com/ hhs/ aboutus.html.

35. Silver Anvil Award Campaign Profile 6BW-0915B04: Arm Yourself with Courage/ Armate

de Valor, Public Relations Society of America, online, www.prsa.org/awards/ silverAnvil/.

36. Silver Anvil Award Campaign Profile 6BW-0916D08: Go Red for Women (GRFW), Public Relations Society of America, online, www.prsa.org/awards/silverAnvil/.

37. Andrea J. Sedlak, David Finkelhor, Heather Hammer and Dana J. Schultz, "National Estimates of Missing Children: An Overview," *National Incidence Studies of Missing, Abducted, Runaway, and Throwaway Children*, Office of Juvenile Justice and Delinquency Prevention, U.S. Justice Department, 2002, 5.

38. David Finkelhor, Kimberly J. Mitchell, and Janis Wolak, *Online Victimization of Youth: Five Years Later*, National Center for Missing and Exploited Children, 2006, 7–8.

39. Mark Hand, "Got 2B Safe! Takes Preventative Tack in Kids Safety Effort," *PRweek* (U.S. ed.), 25 July 2005: 19.

40. Honeywell International 10-K SEC filing, 13 February 2009, online, http://investor.honeywell.com.

41. "About Us: Honeywell Hometown Solutions."

42. "Honeywell and NCMEC Join Forces," *Security*, December 2003, 12.

43. Silver Anvil Award Campaign Profile 6BW-091A06.

44. "Honeywell and National Center for Missing and Exploited Children Announce Fourth Annual Search for America's 'Safest Teachers,'" PR Newswire, 11 February 2009, online, www.prnewswire.com.

45. "Five Teachers Awarded $10,000 Classroom Makeover for Dedication to Child Safety," PR Newswire, 12 May 2009, online, www.prnewswire.com.

46. Jonathan Mann, "America Has a New Enemy," CNN.com, posted 20 March 2009, online www.cnn.com/2009/POLITICS/ 03/20/ pm.aig.obama.

47. "About AIG," American International Group, Inc. website, www.aigcorporate.com/aboutaig/index.html.

48. "House Passes Bill to Limit Executive Compensation," CNN.com, posted 1 April 2009, www.cnn.com/2009/POLITICS/04/01/house.bonus.bill.

49. Rhee and Esposito.

50. Liddy.

51. Rhee and Esposito.

52. Edmund L. Andrews and Peter Baker, "Bonus Money at Troubled AIG Draws Heavy Criticism," the *New York Times*, 16 March 2009, online www.nytimes.com.

53. "Wall Street Woes," *The Public Relations Strategist*, Fall 2008, 7.

2

Jobs in Public Relations

REAL WORLD
The Internship Interview

Tomorrow is the big day: You'll be interviewing for your first public relations internship. You've done your research, learning about your potential employer's products and services, awards, and mission and values statements. You're ready with good answers to standard questions, including "What are your strengths and weaknesses?" and "Where would you like to be in 10 years?"

As you continue to research your potential employer online, you learn that its interviewers have a favorite question: "If we hired you and treated you as a beginning professional, what do you think your duties would be?"

You know that's a good question because you've wondered the same thing: What are the job duties of public relations professionals? How do they spend their days?

Wouldn't it be great, you think, if *you* could ask the questions. Not only could you learn about job duties; you also might find out where the jobs are, how to get them, and what they pay. You could even ask about job satisfaction.

Where, you wonder, could you find such information? (Hint: Keep reading.)

JOBS IN PUBLIC RELATIONS: AN OVERVIEW

What do public relations practitioners do? This chapter will get very specific, but from Chapter 1, you already know the general answer to that question: Public relations practitioners build and maintain relationships with essential publics. This general answer illustrates an important theory in public relations: resource dependency theory, which can help you understand and explain jobs in public relations.

Resource dependency theory consists of three basic beliefs:[1]

1. To fulfill their values-driven business goals, organizations need resources such as raw materials, fair media coverage, and good people to work for the organization.
2. Some of those key resources are *not* controlled by the organization.
3. To acquire those resources, organizations build productive relationships with the publics that control the resources.

So what do public relations practitioners do? They help an organization achieve its most important goals by building productive relationships with resource holders. From the standpoint of resource dependency theory, public relations duties are among the most important functions in any organization: Poor relationships lead to diminished resources—and diminished resources lead to unfulfilled goals and a failed organization. Public relations jobs are vital to an organization's success.

PUBLIC RELATIONS ACTIVITIES AND DUTIES

Let's imagine that you're in the internship interview discussed in the "Real World" scenario that opens this chapter. You've just been asked the big question: *If we hired you and treated you as a beginning professional, what do you think your duties would be?"*

To show that you understand the vital role public relations plays in achieving organizational goals, you could begin your answer with a quick review of resource dependency theory. But after that brief explanation, you know you need to be more specific. Fortunately, public relations researchers devote a great deal of time to answering the big question of job duties. Professor David Dozier, who has extensively studied the daily duties and tasks of public relations practitioners, groups public relations practitioners into two broad categories:

1. **Public relations managers:** They solve problems, advise organizational leaders, make policy decisions, and take responsibility for the success or failure of public relations programs. Public relations managers are most often found in organizations that operate in rapidly changing environments and in organizations that encourage employee input.
2. **Public relations technicians:** They rarely make key strategic decisions, and they rarely advise others within the organization. Instead, their primary role is to prepare communications that help execute the public relations policies created by others. They are more likely to be found in organizations in which the environment is stable and predictable.[2] Many organizations employ both public relations managers and public relations technicians.

As you might expect, oftentimes it's not a matter of being always a manager and never a technician or vice versa. Several studies show that public relations practitioners can have jobs that combine both managerial and technical duties.[3]

Several recent surveys of how public relations practitioners spend their time can help us be even more specific about job duties. For example, a survey of practitioners working for government agencies in California identified these Top 10 duties in order of time spent:[4]

1. Media relations tasks, including writing news releases (p. 266) and pitching story ideas (p. 270)
2. Website and online media tasks
3. Newsletter writing and production
4. Community engagement and outreach
5. Promotion of the organization's specific services
6. Counseling organizational leaders on communication issues
7. Employee communications
8. Special events management
9. Working with elected officials
10. Crisis communications

Survey respondents reported that their top two job-related challenges were a lack of time and strained communications budgets.

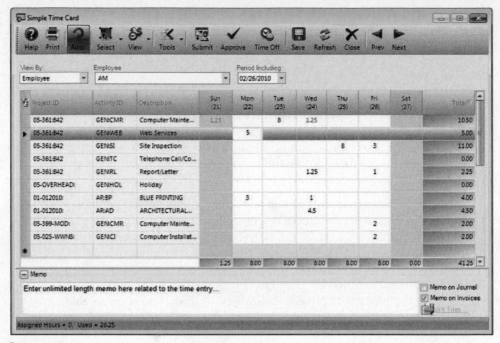

Time Sheet
For billing purposes, public relations practitioners often record how they spend each working day.

(Courtesy of BillQuick and BQE Software, Inc.)

An extensive 2008 survey of the membership of the Public Relations Society of America revealed that members spent the majority of their time engaged in these activities (in order): media relations; writing/editing; marketing communications; corporate communications (image and reputation building); community relations; counseling organizational leaders; employee communications; and special events. Ranking near the bottom of the list were investor relations and fundraising activities.[5]

More recently, a 2010 survey conducted by the Institute for Public Relations predicted that the top duties for public relations managers in the year 2015 would be these:[6]

1. Linking organizational communication strategies to overall organizational goals; decreasing the emphasis on simple publicity
2. Demonstrating "broader analytical and critiquing skills" to an organization's top managers
3. Mastering strategic communication skills that go beyond public relations tactics (see Chapter 13: Public Relations and Marketing)
4. Gaining status as an organization's "chief reputation officer"
5. Increasing public relations' emphasis on engagement with all key stakeholders; decreasing the emphasis on media relations
6. Demonstrating the specific value of public relations programs to an organization's top management

QUICKBREAK 2.1

Student Misperceptions of Public Relations Careers

As a college student, you probably have realized that professors will study just about anything. Professor Shannon Bowen of the University of Maryland studies you: students in introductory courses in public relations.[7] Bowen's research has identified four qualities of the public relations profession that often surprise students in introductory courses.

1. *Diversity of duties.* "You can do more things throughout the field," said one student. "I never realized you can take on so many roles." Bowen's research found that many students had believed that public relations was simply publicity.
2. *Management responsibilities.* "I never realized there was so much management in PR," said another student. Bowen discovered that students in introductory courses had expected simply to learn about news releases and other tactics. The profession's focus on research-based planning surprised many.
3. *Research.* "I didn't know that research and statistics were a part of it or I might not have taken this course," confessed a candid third student. Despite the occasional difficulty of research, Bowen found that research pleased many students by increasing the legitimacy and credibility of public relations.
4. *Relationship maintenance.* "Now I understand that PR has to manage good relationships by using research, research, research, and getting background knowledge," concluded a fourth student. Bowen found that most new students had viewed public relations simply as a one-way communication process.

Bowen reports that although the unforeseen challenges of public relations discourage some students, they inspire others. "It certainly feels like it is a more difficult and challenging field than I thought," said one student, "but it offers advancement and more responsibility." ■

7. Staying current with "changes and trends in communication technologies and practices"
8. Implementing reflective views of public relations (see p. 10) that help an organization maintain social legitimacy and its social license to do business
9. Developing improved cross-cultural communication abilities to respond to the increasing cultural diversity of key publics
10. Gaining an increased voice in "public policy-making, particularly on sustainability and corporate social responsibility issues"

What can we learn from this avalanche of surveys? Within public relations, media relations remains very important, although building relationships with other publics may soon overtake it; writing and editing skills are indispensable; and online/digital/social media skills are rapidly gaining importance.

SOCIAL MEDIA APPS

Social Media Job Duties

To assess the growing importance of social media tactics such as Facebook pages and YouTube videos, a recent survey asked public relations and marketing employers to rank the importance of various skills sought in job applicants. The survey found that although social media skills are very important in hiring decisions, traditional media relations skills still get top priority.[8] In order of importance, the skills sought in job applicants were:

1. Mainstream media relations (such as writing news releases and pitching story ideas)
2. Social networking (such as developing Facebook pages)
3. Blogging and podcasting
4. Microblogging (such as writing brief Twitter messages, or tweets)
5. Search engine optimization (such as ensuring the presence of key words and terms)
6. E-mail marketing
7. Web content management
8. Social bookmarking (such as developing websites, like Delicious, that organize online bookmarks, which are links to other websites)

A second survey of public relations practitioners found that only 4 percent of professionals spent more than 50 percent of their time working with social media; 11 percent spent 26–50 percent of their time in such activities; 30 percent spent 11–25 percent of their time; 48 percent spent 1–10 percent of their time; and 7 percent spent no time working with social media.[9] ■

Let's add a final public relations task that's rarely mentioned in surveys of working professionals: recording how you spend your time. Public relations agencies generally bill clients by the hour, and in an agency your supervisors will want to know how you spend each 15-minute block of time. Many corporations, odd as it may seem, also chart time in this manner. For example, a corporation's public relations department may bill the corporation's college recruiting department for the preparation of brochures and websites. An important part of ensuring the financial success of your organization or your department may well be your scrupulously detailed record of how you've spent your working days.

 QUICK CHECK

1. What specific job duties consume the most time in public relations?
2. How do the job duties of a public relations manager differ from those of a public relations technician?
3. Why do public relations practitioners record how they spend their working hours?

WHERE THE JOBS ARE

Now that you have a clearer concept of job duties in public relations, a logical next question is *where:* Where do such jobs exist? Broadly speaking, jobs in public relations exist in five employment settings:

1. corporations
2. nonprofit organizations and trade associations
3. governments
4. public relations agencies
5. independent public relations consultancies

Each of these five areas contains a variety of sometimes startlingly different public relations jobs. Ideally, however, each job helps an organization fulfill its values-driven mission and goals by building important relationships and securing necessary resources. To help you answer the "Real World" scenario question about jobs and job duties, let's examine the different jobs within these five categories.

Corporations

Not only do corporations offer most of the jobs in public relations, but they also offer the greatest variety of jobs. Corporations are organizations that produce goods or services for a profit. They include manufacturers such as The North Face, for-profit health-care providers such as Humana, retailers such as The Gap, sports organizations such as NASCAR, and a host of other for-profit organizations.

In most corporations, public relations jobs focus on specific publics. Corporate public relations practitioners often specialize in one of the following: employee relations, media relations, government relations, community relations, business-to-business relations, or consumer relations (marketing communications). If the

News Conference
Studies show that media relations activities, such as this news conference sponsored by the National Oceanic and Atmospheric Administration, remain a top public relations job duty.

(Courtesy of the National Oceanic and Atmospheric Administration)

corporation is publicly owned—that is, if it sells stock—some practitioners specialize in investor relations. In each of these areas, ideally, practitioners conduct research; advise the organization's top management; and plan, execute, and evaluate relationship-management programs.

Ideally, public relations practitioners should understand and appreciate all sides of a relationship between their organization and a particular public. Practitioners call this function **boundary spanning** because they span the boundaries that separate their organization from important publics. As boundary spanners, practitioners act for the good of relationships, knowing that healthy relationships are vital to their organization's success. And as boundary spanners, practitioners must sometimes ask their own organizations to change to benefit an important relationship.

One difficulty with the concept of boundary spanning is that it suggests a simple relationship between only two parties. In actuality, public relations practitioners often are intersection managers, operating at points where several publics come together simultaneously. Experienced practitioners know that their relationship-building efforts with one public can affect relationships with other publics. For example, a corporation's cost-cutting measures might please stockholders but discourage employees. In such cases, an organization's public relations team must be keenly aware of the values of the organization and the affected publics.

Although we certainly don't want to downplay the importance of research and counseling, the reality is that most young practitioners begin their careers by creating communications such as newsletter stories and social media news releases. Therefore, let's look at some of the traditional entry-level tasks. These tasks are described more fully in Chapter 9 (Communication: The Tactics of Public Relations).

- **Employee relations:** Communication tasks in employee relations can include production of newsletters and magazines, video programs, websites, wikis, and special events.
- **Media relations:** Communication tasks can include production of news releases and e-mail pitches and assistance with news conferences. More advanced communication tasks can include speechwriting and preparing scripts for video news releases. Media-related counseling duties can include preparing executives for interviews.
- **Government relations** (sometimes known as *public affairs*): Communication tasks can include producing brochures, reports, social bookmarking websites, and videos for lobbies and political action committees. Advanced duties can include testifying before government fact-finding commissions, monitoring the activities of government units at all levels, and preparing reports.
- **Community relations:** Communication tasks can include maintaining contact with local special-interest groups such as environmental organizations. New practitioners also often help coordinate social networking sites, such as Facebook pages, and special events, such as tours of their organization's facilities. Upper-level duties can include overseeing a corporation's charitable contributions, organizing employee volunteer efforts, and lending support to special events such as blood drives and United Way fundraising campaigns.

- **Business-to-business relations,** also known as *B2B:* Communication tasks focus on building strong relationships with related businesses such as suppliers and distributors. Entry-level duties can include writing for newsletters and websites and helping plan special events. Management duties can include orientation meetings to discuss shared values and goals.
- **Consumer relations,** also known as *marketing communications:* Communication tasks usually focus on product publicity. Such duties can include preparing news releases and e-mail pitches, implementing direct-mail campaigns (including texting), organizing special promotional events, enlisting

close window ⊠

NEW STUDY DEMONSTRATES IMPORTANCE AND IMPACT OF DIGITAL MEDIA IN U.S. AND EUROPEAN POLICY MAKING

TRANS-ATLANTIC POLL OF SENIOR CONGRESSIONAL AND PARLIAMENTARIAN STAFF REVEALS REGULAR USAGE OF DIGITAL TOOLS TO RESEARCH AND INFLUENCE POLICY, REACH CONSTITUENTS

November 03, 2009, -- A new five-country study of senior staff in the U.S. Congress and European Parliaments released today revealed the influential role of online resources and social media networks in setting policy and communicating with constituents in political capitals across the Atlantic.

The poll showed staffers regularly access digital outlets and social media to research, influence and set policy. Nearly every staffer (96%) uses online resources for public policy research, more than half (54%) reported learning of policy issues for the first time online and one in five (19%) actually changed policy positions based on information and opinions they found online.

The Capital Staffer Index, conducted by StrategyOne and involving interviews of nearly 400 senior congressional and parliamentarian staff in Washington, D.C., Brussels, London, Paris and Berlin, revealed that social networks like Facebook are becoming an increasingly important resource for staffers.

Sixty percent said they access the social medium for personal reasons, but in addition, nearly one-third use it for communicating with professional colleagues (28%), one in five (21%) to reach out to constituents, and one in ten (9%) to research policy issues. In addition, blogs are an important resource for staffers with two in five (39%) using blogs and social media sites in the past 30 days to monitor news about issues and the same percentage (39%) to monitor constituent opinion about an issue.

"When it comes to policy development and public affairs, we're seeing a digital about-face as staffers and elected officials move from face time to Facebook and other social media to research and communicate on critical issues," said Jere Sullivan, Vice Chairman of Global Public Affairs, Edelman. "Traditional communications and advocacy channels remain important and effective in all countries, but the growing influence of online cannot be overlooked and needs to be included in the mix of tools for communicating about and forming consensus on important policy issues."

News Release

An enduring part of public relations involves delivering stories to news media through news releases. This news release, from the Edelman public relations agency, reports on government use of social media and other online media.

(Courtesy of Edelman)

and training celebrity spokespeople, writing blogs, and coordinating communication efforts with advertising campaigns.

■ **Investor relations:** Communication activities that target investors and investment analysts can include producing newsletters, blogs, and other forms of correspondence directed at stockholders, producing an annual financial report to stockholders, planning and conducting an annual meeting for stockholders, maintaining a flow of information to investment analysts, and other activities designed to inform investors about a corporation's financial health and business goals. Investor relations practitioners often oversee the legally required disclosure of financial information to stockholders and to the government.

Nonprofit Organizations and Trade Associations

Nonprofit organizations can include universities, hospitals, churches, foundations, and other groups that provide a service without the expectation of earning a profit. Some nonprofit organizations, of course, are local. Others, such as the United Way, are nationally known. Still others, such as the Red Cross and Amnesty International, have international duties and reputations. Trade associations are often grouped with nonprofit organizations because, like those organizations, they offer services without the primary motive of earning a profit. Trade associations include such groups as the American Library Association and the International Guild of Professional Butlers.

Public relations duties within a nonprofit organization often are similar to public relations duties within a corporation. Well-run nonprofit organizations have practitioners in employee relations, media relations, government relations, community relations, and, sometimes, marketing communications. However, because nonprofit organizations have no stockholders, they don't engage in investor relations activities. Instead, they have donor relations, fundraising, and, if appropriate, member relations.

Communication tasks in donor relations, fundraising, and member relations can include producing newsletters, videos, podcasts, and websites; writing direct-mail solicitations; and organizing special events.

Trade associations offer their members benefits that can include insurance programs, continuing education, networking, and a unified voice in efforts to influence legislative processes. Public relations jobs in trade associations include member relations, media relations, government relations, and marketing communications. Communication tasks in member relations are often designed to educate and update members through newsletters and other publications, websites, microblogging, videos, and special events such as annual conventions. The American Medical Association, for example, offers its members the prestigious *Journal of the American Medical Association,* both online and on paper. Another task in member relations involves recruiting new members through such actions as direct-mail campaigns.

Governments

Public relations jobs exist at all levels of government: international (as in the United Nations or the European Union), federal, state, and local. Political parties and independent agencies created by a government, such as the U.S. Postal Service, also employ public relations practitioners.

VALUES STATEMENT 2.1

Public Relations Society of America

PRSA is the world's largest organization for public relations professionals. Its 21,000 plus members, organized in more than 100 chapters, represent business and industry, technology, counseling firms, government, associations, hospitals, schools, professional services firms, and nonprofit organizations.

PRSA Member Statement of Professional Values

This statement presents the core values of PRSA members and, more broadly, of the public relations profession. These values provide the foundation for the Member Code of Ethics and set the industry standard for the professional practice of public relations. These values are the fundamental beliefs that guide our behaviors and decision-making process. We believe our professional values are vital to the integrity of the profession as a whole.

Advocacy

- We serve the public interest by acting as responsible advocates for those we represent.
- We provide a voice in the marketplace of ideas, facts, and viewpoints to aid informed public debate.

Honesty

- We adhere to the highest standards of accuracy and truth in advancing the interests of those we represent and in communicating with the public.

Expertise

- We acquire and responsibly use specialized knowledge and experience.
- We advance the profession through continued professional development, research, and education.
- We build mutual understanding, credibility, and relationships among a wide array of institutions and audiences.

Independence

- We provide objective counsel to those we represent.
- We are accountable for our actions.

Loyalty

- We are faithful to those we represent, while honoring our obligation to serve the public interest.

Fairness

- We deal fairly with clients, employers, competitors, peers, vendors, the media, and the general public.
- We respect all opinions and support the right of free expression.

—From "PRSA Member Code of Ethics 2000," PRSA website ∎

Public relations jobs within government units generally focus on four key publics: voters, the news media, employees, and special-interest groups.

Government public relations practitioners operate under a variety of job titles, including **press secretary**, **public information officer**, **public affairs officer**, and **communications specialist**. Entry-level communication duties can include writing news releases, responding to constituent concerns, writing position papers that help politicians articulate their beliefs, and helping build digital newsrooms of documents, images, videos, and links. Upper-level duties can include speaking with reporters, writing speeches for politicians, and briefing officials on public opinion.

At the federal level in the United States, the term *public relations*, with its connotation of persuasive communication, is rarely used. Public relations practitioners within the federal government prefer euphemisms such as *public information*. One reason for their skittishness is the United States Code (a compilation of the permanent governing laws of the United States). Title 5, Section 3107 of the code flatly declares, "Appropriated funds may not be used to pay a publicity expert unless specifically appropriated for that purpose." Similar restrictions can exist at state and local levels.

QUICKBREAK 2.2

The Values of Successful Employers

What do enduring, successful companies have in common? In the book *Built to Last: Successful Habits of Visionary Companies,* authors James Collins and Jerry Porras examine the workings of companies that have thrived despite occasional adversity and changing environments.[10] One foundation of such companies, the authors say, is a set of clear, strongly held, companywide core values:

> Core values [are] the organization's essential and enduring tenets—a small set of general guiding principles; not to be confused with specific cultural or operating practices; not to be compromised for financial gain or short-term expediency. . . .
>
> The crucial variable is not the content of a company's ideology, but how deeply it believes its ideology and how consistently it lives, breathes and expresses it in all that it does. Visionary companies do not ask, "What should we value?" They ask, "What do we actually value deep down to our toes?"

Built to Last examines the long-term success of 20 companies, including IBM, Johnson & Johnson, Motorola, Procter & Gamble, and Walt Disney. "Yes, they seek profits," say the authors, "but they're equally guided by a core ideology—core values and a sense of purpose beyond just making money."

As you consider a career in public relations and as you evaluate the different kinds of employers and job duties, be sure to study the values of those employers. Many organizations now list their values statements on their websites. What, if anything, do those organizations say they value? Do their actions match their beliefs? Are their values so clear that they can guide public relations policies and actions? In the words of James Collins and Jerry Porras, will you select an employer that's built to last? ■

Because many people incorrectly equate public relations with publicity, government units tend to avoid that term. Voters in most countries clearly don't want their tax dollars used for campaigns to persuade them of the wisdom of governmental actions and policies. However, voters also insist that government officials communicate with citizens and respond to their needs and concerns. So public relations *does* exist at all levels of government—but rarely, if ever, is it called by that name.

Public Relations Agencies

Public relations agencies assist with the public relations activities of other organizations. Corporations, nonprofit organizations, trade associations, governments, and even individuals hire public relations agencies to help manage and execute various public relations functions. A corporation, for example, may have its own in-house public relations staff, but for its annual report to stockholders or for a complicated overseas venture, it may hire a public relations agency for research, planning, communication, and evaluation. As we'll discuss in Chapter 13, many public relations agencies have merged with advertising agencies to provide a wide range of integrated, consumer-focused communications.

Practitioners in public relations agencies often are assigned to accounts. An account includes all the public relations activities planned and executed for one particular client. Individual accounts are managed by an **account supervisor** and, often, one

Special Event

U.S. Census Bureau Director Robert Groves greets Nickelodeon's Dora the Explorer at a child-care center in Washington, D.C. Groves and Dora were promoting the need for parents to include children in their 2010 Census forms.

(Courtesy of the U.S. Census Bureau, Public Information Office)

or more **account executives**. Also working on each account are writers, who often are called communications specialists; designers; production supervisors; researchers; and online specialists for website design and maintenance. Workers within an account sometimes wear more than one hat; for example, a writer may also be a researcher. Additionally, practitioners often are assigned to more than one account.

Public relations agencies can range from small shops with only a handful of employees to divisions within advertising agencies to huge international operations such as Hill & Knowlton, Burson-Marsteller, Fleishman-Hillard, and Edelman.

Independent Public Relations Consultancies

An **independent public relations consultant** is, essentially, a one-person public relations agency. Organizations or individuals hire the consultant to assist with particular public relations functions. Generally, however, a public relations consultant offers a smaller range of services than an agency. Many consultants, in fact, specialize in a particular area of public relations, such as crisis communications, speechwriting, website design, or training others in the basics of good public relations.

Some independent consultants, however, thrive as generalists. In the book *Real People Working in Communications*, author Jan Goldberg writes:

> Those who work as generalists in the field must be able to perform a wide array of duties at the same time. On any given week they may write press releases for one client, design a brochure for another, approach an editor for a third, meet with a talk show host for a fourth, implement a promotion for a fifth, set up a press conference for a sixth, put together a press kit for a seventh, work out the beginnings of a client contract for an eighth, and field media questions for a ninth![11]

Note that eighth duty well. Like public relations agencies, independent consultants often must seek new clients even as they conduct business for current clients. The major appeal of independent consulting is also its biggest burden: The consultant alone bears the responsibility for success or failure.

Beyond the Office Walls: Postmodern Public Relations

Postmodernism is a philosophical perspective that almost defies definition—not even postmodernists agree on what it is and isn't. But broadly speaking, postmodernism challenges conventional wisdom and social traditions; it seeks out voices and opinions that the mainstream tends to ignore. Postmodern critics point out that discussions of public relations (like this one, so far) generally focus only on jobs with paychecks.[12] Those critics correctly add that public relations skills can transcend the ordinary workplace. For example, volunteers for activist organizations often work to build relationships with reporters and government officials. Is that a salaried job? Not really—but it remains public relations. The theory and the practice of public relations are not limited to the workplace. In fact, the growth of social media outlets such as Facebook and YouTube has increased the ability of individual activists to build widespread relationships.

QUICKBREAK 2.3

Getting That First Job or Internship

You might be reading this chapter and thinking, "Great. I'm beginning to understand where and what the jobs are. But how do I get one?" Although the *Occupational Outlook Handbook* from the U.S. Bureau of Labor Statistics reports that "employment of public relations specialists is expected to grow 24 percent from 2008 to 2018, much faster than the average for all occupations," it adds this caution: "Keen competition is expected for entry-level jobs."[13]

We'll examine your future in public relations more thoroughly in Chapter 16. But let's preview a few dos and don'ts about communicating with potential employers.

Do This:

- Do thoroughly research a potential employer before applying.
- Do send an error-free application letter and a flawless résumé, whether online or on paper.
- Do realize that, according to one national survey, almost one-third of employers will check you out on websites such as Facebook and Flickr.[14]
- Do prepare for a job interview by reviewing your research on the potential employer and developing knowledgeable questions to ask.
- Do create a portfolio of real work done for real clients, including work done as an intern or volunteer.

Don't Do This:

- Don't send a form letter or generic e-mail asking for a job. Instead, include specific, organization-related information that shows why you want this particular job.
- Don't ask about salary. Let the potential employer introduce that subject.
- Don't forget to send a brief thank-you note after each interview.

A CareerBuilder.com survey reports that 25 percent of employers prefer an e-mail thank-you note; 19 percent prefer an e-mail note followed by a paper note; 23 percent prefer only a handwritten note; and 21 percent prefer only a typed note.[15]

Comprehensive studies over the past decade confirm that good writing is the top quality public relations employers seek in new employees.[16] One study of almost 1,000 public relations professionals identified the top three desired qualities for entry-level employees:

1. Strong written/oral communication skills
2. willingness to learn/enthusiasm
3. personality/culture fit[17]

One more thing, *étudiants*. Experts say "the ability to communicate in a foreign language may open up employment opportunities."[18]

Bonne chance. ■

QUICK CHECK

1. What are the five broad areas of employment within public relations?
2. What criticism do postmodern theorists sometimes level against descriptions of public relations jobs?
3. How does the United States Code affect public relations within the U.S. federal government?

WORKING CONDITIONS AND SALARIES

The U.S. Bureau of Labor Statistics reports that public relations technicians work 35 to 40 hours a week—"but unpaid overtime is common." Approximately two thirds of public relations managers work more than 40 hours a week, according to the BLS, and "long hours, including evenings and weekends are common." The BLS offers this description of working conditions:

> Occasionally, [public relations practitioners] must be at the job or on call around the clock, especially if there is an emergency or crisis. Schedules often have to be rearranged so that workers can meet deadlines, deliver speeches, attend meetings and community activities, and travel.[19]

According to a University of Georgia study, the median starting public relations salary for 2009 graduates of U.S. journalism and mass communication programs was $30,000. Slightly more than 60 percent of those new hires received some form of medical insurance as part of their salary and benefits package.[20]

Each year, *PRWeek* magazine surveys thousands of public relations professionals to determine average annual salaries. Its 2010 report included these findings:[21]

- Median salary for practitioners of 0–2 years' experience was $37,000; 3–4 years, $52,000; 5–6 years, $60,000; 7–10 years, $85,000; 11–15 years, $104,000; 16–20 years, $132,000; 21–plus years, $150,000.
- Evidence of gender inequities remains: Overall median salary for men with more than five years on the job was $130,000; for women, the figure was $90,000. Median salary for men with fewer than five years on the job was $50,000; for women, the figure was $43,000. For more on the important issue of gender inequities in public relations, see pp. 504–511.
- Median salary for corporate jobs was $110,000; for individual consultants, $85,000; for agency jobs, $78,000; for government jobs, $75,000; for trade association jobs, $74,000; and for nonprofit organization jobs, $61,000.

National surveys can provide significant insights into practitioner salaries, but their findings, at best, are only approximations of what you might expect to earn. However, as we'll see in the next section, public relations practitioners enjoy their jobs so much that they have some surprising opinions about salary.

QUICKBREAK 2.4

The People in Public Relations

A recent survey of Public Relations Society of America membership offered this snapshot of PRSA members.[22]

- Seventy percent are female. Older members are more likely to be male; younger members are more likely to be female.
- Eighty-seven percent are white; 5 percent are black; 1 percent are Asian; and 5 percent are of Hispanic, Spanish, or Latino origin.
- Thirty-three percent have a master's degree; 4 percent have a Ph.D.
- Twenty-six percent work for corporations; 20 percent work for agencies; 17 percent work for nonprofit organizations or trade associations; 13 percent work for education institutions; 10 percent work for the government or the military; and 6 percent work as independent consultants.
- Forty percent work in organizations of 100 or fewer employees; 16 percent work in organizations of 101–500 employees; 23 percent work in organizations of 501–5,000 employees; and 21 percent work in organizations of more than 5,000 employees.
- Nineteen percent earn $35,000–$49,999 a year; 46 percent earn $50,000–$99,999 a year; 13 percent earn $100,000–$149,999 a year; 4 percent earn $150,000–$199,999 a year; and 3 percent earn $200,000 or more a year. ■

THE BEST PART OF PUBLIC RELATIONS JOBS

What's the best part of a public relations job? What kind of question is that? Money, cash, paycheck, salary—right?

Wrong, say the people with those jobs.

A decade ago, an extensive survey of the members of the International Association of Business Communicators and the Public Relations Society of America found that salary ranked seventh on the list of important job-satisfaction attributes.[23] Some 95.5 percent of respondents said that salary was important to job satisfaction—but that high percentage was exceeded by the 99.4 percent who said creative opportunity was important, the 99.2 percent who said access to technology was important, the 97.7 percent who said professional development opportunities were important, and the 96.2 percent who said recognition by colleagues was important.[24]

Overall job satisfaction among public relations practitioners remains high, with more than 90 percent of all practitioners saying that they would "recommend PR as a career to a friend or family member."[25] Sixty-six percent agree with the statement "I am committed to a career in PR/communications." Twenty percent say that no amount of money could lure them away from their current jobs; another 43 percent say it would take a raise of at least 20 percent. Eighty-one percent say they are not considering jobs in fields other than public relations.[26] *Fortune* magazine ranked public relations management as one of its Top 50 jobs, giving "job security" and "benefit to society" grades of "B" and "personal satisfaction" a grade of "A."[27]

QUICK CHECK

1. What is the average annual starting salary for entry-level jobs in public relations?
2. Do women practitioners earn as much as men practitioners?
3. How many hours per week do public relations managers work?
4. Is salary the most important aspect of a job in public relations?

SUMMARY

For all their differences, public relations jobs have one thing in common: Ideally, each public relations job has the mission of helping an organization build productive relationships with the publics necessary to its success. Most of the jobs in public relations can be found in five broad settings: corporations, nonprofit organizations and trade associations, government, public relations agencies, and independent public relations consultancies.

Within those five broad areas, jobs and job duties vary widely. Public relations practitioners function as managers who counsel other managers and design public relations programs or as technicians who prepare communications. Oftentimes, a practitioner fulfills both roles, depending on the task at hand. In all public relations jobs, the importance of social media is growing.

Salaries vary within the profession, but studies of practitioners show that salary is not the most important factor in job satisfaction. Such qualities as creative opportunity rank higher than salary in many surveys. Studies of public relations practitioners show that most enjoy their work and are not seeking career changes.

DISCUSSION QUESTIONS

1. Why do corporations have so many different areas of employment for public relations practitioners?
2. What evidence, if any, indicates that discrimination might exist in public relations salaries?
3. What are the attractive elements of a public relations manager's job? What are the attractive elements of a public relations technician's job?
4. What do you consider to be the most important element of job satisfaction? How does your answer compare with the findings of national studies?
5. Now that you've read this chapter, what is your opinion of the public relations profession? Does it seem to be an attractive career? Why or why not?

MEMO FROM THE FIELD

JOHN ECHEVESTE
Partner; Valencia, Pérez & Echeveste Public Relations
Pasadena, California

John Echeveste is a partner with Valencia, Pérez & Echeveste Public
Relations based in Pasadena, California. Established in 1988, VPE is
one of the country's largest Hispanic-owned agencies, handling a
diverse roster of consumer, social-marketing, and public affairs
accounts. Echeveste has helped develop public relations programs
for major national brands such as McDonald's, AT&T, Disneyland,
Target Stores, DirecTV, and General Mills. He is a founding member of the Hispanic Public
Relations Association and recipient of its Premio Award. He also received the Public Relations
Society of America Pioneer Award in 1994. He served as president of the Public Relations
Global Network, an association of 30 worldwide PR agencies, in 2003–2004. He is a graduate
of California State University Fullerton with a bachelor's degree in communications.

I spent two years in high school and four in college studying for a career in journalism,
only to discover after nine months as a reporter that it wasn't the job for me.

What happened? After my short stint as a news and feature reporter at one of the
largest dailies in Los Angeles County, I realized that I was too far removed from the center
of the action. Nothing wrong at all with being a journalist, but what I discovered all too
soon was that reporting was a hands-off job and I was a hands-on person. So I put my
journalistic skills to work and bounced around, working for a big corporation (stifling),
managing a few political campaigns (exciting, but no future), and writing a documentary
film (great fun, little money). In all of these positions, I was developing strategies, testing
ideas, making things happen, and seeing results. That, for me, was a lot more satisfying
and a lot more challenging than reporting on the things other people were doing. When
I combined all these experiences, they pointed in one clear direction: public relations.

I mention this because the road to a PR career isn't always a straight one, and many of
us don't end up in the professions we thought we would. But after 30-some years in the
profession, the one thing I can tell you is this: Public relations puts you right in the center
of the action.

So 20 years after starting an agency, I never regret that early career correction. Every day
has brought new challenges, new discoveries, and new opportunities. And what keeps me
most energized is working with bright new faces eager to make their own mark in the field.

So what does it take to succeed in this ever-changing profession? Here are the top
qualities I look for when interviewing candidates:

- *Learn to write like a reporter.* I can't overemphasize the importance of good writing skills.
  I can't overemphasize the importance of good writing skills. It's essential to everything else
  in the profession and the foundation of a successful career. The best way to learn good
  writing is by taking journalism writing classes—learn to write like a reporter and how to

(*continued*)

write under deadline. Even better, take an internship with a news organization where you can see the inner workings of a news operation and get some solid writing experience.

- *Be inquisitive.* In public relations, you need to know a little about a lot of things. What I mean by that is that you need to be aware of what's happening in the world and how it impacts your clients or your organization. That means reading a daily newspaper thoroughly, monitoring news and trade magazines, and watching news/public affairs programs. The most effective PR practitioner is the one who arrives in the office every morning knowing what the day's top news stories are. Stay up with trends and with what's happening outside of the office.

- *Show common sense.* This is one they don't teach you in college. I'm convinced that the most effective public relations programs are those that are the most straightforward. Too often, we develop convoluted, confusing initiatives that fall flat on their face. Keep it simple.

- *Be committed.* Anyone expecting PR to be a 9-to-5 job should seek employment elsewhere. Deadlines (and clients) don't wait. You need to be willing to put in the long hours that can make the difference. And on top of that, you need to find the time to be involved in a worthwhile community or charitable cause that exposes you to a whole new universe of contacts and issues.

- *Be an expert.* People who come in with a level of expertise in another field—sports, fashion, health care, a foreign language, music, etc.—are a step ahead of the rest. Your passions and hobbies can be an important personal marketing tool that adds extra value to your credentials.

Public relations is an evolving profession. I've seen it grow to become more inclusive and responsive to our multicultural society; to be used as a powerful marketing tool in launching new products and services and building brand equity; and to become a more valued management function. It is also a profession that thrives on those who are the brightest, most creative, and most enthusiastic self-starters. So if you're willing to work long hours, answer to multiple bosses, and make less money than many of your college colleagues in exchange for being where the action is, then welcome to the wild, wonderful, sometimes wacky world of public relations. Enjoy the ride! ■

CASE STUDY 2.1 Stormy Weather: Eight Months in a Professional's Life

College students who monitor weather reports in anticipation of Spring Break know that March often enters like a lion and exits like a lamb. But for Carrie Martin, senior officer of strategic planning and communication for the American Red Cross, March 2006 began like a lamb and roared out like a dragon.

On March 2, Martin won one of the most coveted prizes in U.S. public relations: Public Relations Professional of the Year, as named by *PRWeek* magazine. The profession's elite gathered at New York's Tavern on the Green restaurant to honor Martin and approximately 32 other award-winning public relations campaigns, tactics, teams, and individuals. In naming Martin the best of the best, the editors of *PRWeek* declared:

> Martin showed adaptability and eagerness to expand her role at the Red Cross, and became a valued thinker and contributor to the communication and marketing department's senior management team. Over the past year, she was tapped to serve as the lead of the Red Cross media team made up of individuals representing each line of service in the organization. Hosting biweekly meetings, Martin increased communication and coordination among media team members and was able to provide management with a clearer picture of the organization's proactive media outreach activities.[28]

At almost the same moment Martin was accepting her award, national news media were directing their attention to a federal report titled *A Failure of Initiative: Final Report of the Select Bipartisan Committee to Investigate the Preparation for and Response to Hurricane Katrina.* The report included these devastating conclusions: "Katrina, however, was too much for the Red Cross. . . . The Red Cross was challenged by the sometimes-disorganized manner in which shelters were established. Some shelters were unknown to the Red Cross until after they were already opened by local officials."[29] Other reports accused the Red Cross of waste and fraud in its Katrina efforts.[30]

U.S. Senator Charles Grassley, then chairman of the Senate Finance Committee, declared, "After hurricanes devastated the Gulf Coast in 2005, Americans again responded with tremendous generosity by donating hundreds of millions of dollars. It's a shame the Red Cross leadership did not rise to the occasion. Unlike the heroic efforts put forth by Red Cross volunteers in the aftermath of the disaster, the top dogs at the Red Cross failed their mission."[31]

Only days before the awards ceremony in New York, Martin helped craft an official response to the congressional report: The Red Cross announced that it already had begun its own investigation. In response to Senator Grassley's allegations, Martin served as the media contact person for a Red Cross news release that announced, "We are fully cooperating with the Senate Finance Committee and Chairman Grassley in response to their questions regarding the operations of the American Red Cross. The American Red Cross is committed to learning from our prior challenges and making the necessary changes to improve the delivery of services to the American people."[32]

On March 24, Martin announced through a national news release that the Red Cross was investigating allegations of financial misdeeds involving Hurricane Katrina volunteers.[33] Days later, another Red Cross news release revealed that the organization was turning its findings over to the FBI.[34] Exactly 28 days had passed since Martin had received her Professional of the Year award.

On April 4, the Red Cross announced the formation of the Independent Governance Advisory Panel to recommend any necessary changes to improve the organization's disaster relief efforts. During the next seven months, as the panel met and pondered changes, the Red Cross went about its business, assisting victims of storms in Tennessee, earthquakes in Indonesia and Pakistan, floods in New England, war in Lebanon, measles in Kenya, and much more.

In November, Red Cross leadership met with Grassley to discuss the changes proposed by the advisory group and accepted by the organization. Grassley was impressed. "I'm pleased with the vote by the board of the Red Cross to make real changes to the governance at the American Red Cross," he said. "The board has followed the recommendations of the Independent Governance Advisory Panel to make the changes necessary that will help ensure that the Red Cross has the necessary leadership and governance to succeed."[35]

After that statement—seven months and 28 days after the magical evening at Tavern on the Green—public relations' Professional of the Year Carrie Martin may have had time to breathe a sigh of relief and enjoy her award.

DISCUSSION QUESTIONS

1. Red Cross news releases may have helped publicize the organization's problems. Should the organization have kept silent about its responses to government charges? Why or why not?

2. How might Martin have conducted boundary spanning during the response of the Red Cross to government charges?

3. Organizations that rely on volunteers may have difficulty operating on shared values. How might such organizations avoid values clashes with volunteers?

4. What were your impressions of disaster relief during Hurricane Katrina? In your opinion, how did the Red Cross and other agencies perform? ∎

CASE STUDY 2.2 A List to Avoid

One of the highlights (or lowlights, if it shines on you) of the year for public relations practitioners is the release of an irreverent list of the worst public relations disasters of the past 12 months. Compiled since 1995 by Fineman Public Relations of San Francisco, the list balances an utter lack of mercy with a wicked sense of humor. It offers a wealth of case studies on how *not* to conduct successful public relations.

Among the recent winners of this dubious distinction:[36]

- *Grand Theft Auto:* "As if best selling video game 'Grand Theft Auto, San Andreas' didn't have enough violence and debauchery already, its maker, Rockstar Games, added hidden animated sex scenes. The soft-core porn ignited a political firestorm, forcing a new 'adults-only' rating, reported the *Wall Street Journal.* Other coverage said Best Buy and Circuit City pulled the game from their stores."

- *WPYX-FM, Latham, New York:* "As a promotion, the radio station holds what it calls 'Ugliest Bride' contests. From newspaper wedding announcements, the radio hosts pick the bride they deem the ugliest. Callers win by guessing which photograph was chosen. [Once], in a departure from usual practices, the station aired the bride's full name and place of employment. Hello, $300,000 lawsuit, an AP story, and a mean-spirited image."

- *Kanye West:* "Storming the stage in protest at a nationally televised awards show is practically an annual event for Kanye West, but his 'performance' at this year's [2009] MTV Video Music Awards was particularly ill-advised. When an allegedly inebriated West took the microphone from teenage country artist and Best Female Video winner Taylor Swift, claiming that Beyonce—not Swift—deserved the award, he crossed a critical line."

- *Target Stores:* "Those Salvation Army bell ringers with collection kettles outside department stores have been around for a century and are as meaningful to many consumers as any store-hired Santa Claus. So when Minneapolis-based Target announced it would ban Salvation Army collectors at all its stores, outraged consumers called for a national boycott."

- *Goldman Sachs*: "After taking a severe media drubbing, it makes sense for the big banks to conduct public outreach demonstrating some level of humility. But many have criticized Goldman Sachs CEO and spokesperson Lloyd Blankfein for statements published in the November 8 [2009] edition of the UK's *Sunday Times* in which Blankfein claimed the company was 'doing God's work.'"

- *United Airlines:* "Musician Dave Carroll was frustrated by United Airlines' nine-month refusal to compensate him for $1,200 in repairs after he witnessed United baggage handlers literally tossing guitars, including his own $3,500

Taylor. . . . Carroll vowed that he would write and record songs about the experience—complete with music videos—and publish them online. The first YouTube video amassed *over three million views in a single week.* Within two days, United was in touch with Carroll, offering the long-awaited compensation. . . ."

- *Nike*: "When self-described 'good, solid' marathoner and elementary school teacher Arien O'Connell unexpectedly clocked the fastest time in October's San Francisco Women's Marathon . . . race sponsor Nike had a golden opportunity to support those who 'just do it.' However, Nike only checked times of those in the allegedly 'elite' front-running pack [and] would not recognize her victory. . . ."

There you have it: how not to conduct successful public relations. If you decide to pursue a career in this wonderful, challenging profession, we hope you'll set many lofty goals for yourself. One of them should be never to appear on the annual Fineman list.

DISCUSSION QUESTIONS

1. Which of the above public relations blunders is, in your opinion, the worst? Why?
2. Many of the above gaffes were committed by people not in public relations. How could public relations practitioners within the organizations have prevented those errors?
3. Should the organizations cited respond to their presence on the annual Fineman list? Or should they ignore it?
4. Suppose that you're head of public relations for each of the above organizations or individuals. The terrible event has just happened. Now the reporters are at your door. What do you tell them? ∎

NOTES

1. Larissa Grunig, James Grunig, and William Ehling, "What Is an Effective Organization?" in *Excellence in Public Relations and Communication Management* (Hillsdale, N.J.: Lawrence Erlbaum, 1992), 77, 80.
2. David Dozier, "The Organizational Roles of Communications and Public Relations Practitioners," in *Excellence in Public Relations and Communication Management,* ed. James E. Grunig (Hillsdale, N.J.: Lawrence Erlbaum, 1992), 341–352.
3. Greg Leichty and Jeff Springston, "Elaborating Public Relations Roles," *Journalism and Mass Communications Quarterly* (summer 1996): 467–468; Toth, Serini, Wright, and Emig; *Occupational Outlook Handbook,* 2006–2007.
4. "CAPIO State of the Profession 2009 Survey," California Association of Public Information Officials, May 2009, online, http://www.capio.org/news/2009.
5. "PRSA 2008 Member Value Perception and Satisfaction Study," Public Relations Society of America, 2008, online, www.prsa.org.
6. Tom Watson and Chindu Sreedharan, "The Senior Communicator of the Future—Competencies and Training Needs," Institute for Public Relations, March 2010, online, www.instituteforpr.com.
7. Shannon A. Bowen, "'I Thought It Would Be More Glamorous': Preconceptions and Misconceptions among Students in the Public Relations Principles Course," *Public Relations Review* 29 (2003): 199–214.
8. "Digital Readiness Report: Essential Online Public Relations and Marketing Skills," a report by iPressroom, Trendstream, Korn/Ferry International, and Public Relations Society of America, 2009, online, www.ipressroom.com.
9. Donald K. Wright and Michelle D. Hinson, "An Updated Look at the Impact of Social Media on Public Relations Practice," *Public Relations Journal* 3, no. 2, spring 2009, online, www.prsa.org.
10. James Collins and Jerry Porras, *Built to Last: Successful Habits of Visionary Companies* (New York: HarperBusiness, 1994), 8, 73, 88.
11. Jan Goldberg, *Real People Working in Public Relations* (Lincolnwood, Ill.: VGM Career Horizons, 1997), 88.

12. Patricia A. Curtin and T. Kenn Gaither, "Privileging Identity, Difference, and Power: The Circuit of Culture as a Basis for Public Relations Theory," *Journal of Public Relations Research* 17 (2005): 94.

13. *Occupational Outlook Handbook, 2010–2011,* U.S. Bureau of Labor Statistics, online, www.bls.gov.

14. "More Than One Quarter of Organizations Have Googled Job Candidate Profiles," news release issued by the National Association of Colleges and Employers, 11 July 2006, online, www.naceweb.org.

15. Rosemary Haefner, "No Thank You Could Mean No Job," CareerBuilder.com, 29 July 2009 (survey conducted 17–27 May 2005), online, www.careerbuilder.com/Article/CB-300.

16. Don Stacks, Carl Botan, and Judy Van Slyke Turk, "Perceptions of Public Relations Education," *Public Relations Review* 25 (1999): 9–29; "Workinpr.com State of the Industry Survey 2002," online, www.workinpr.com; "Qualities/ Skills Employers Look for in New Hires," National Association of Colleges and Employers, online, www.jobweb.com/joboutlook/2004outlook; "Council of Public Relations Firms Survey Shows Continued Industry Growth so Far in 2006," news release issued by the Council of Public Relations Firms, 7 June 2006, online, www.prfirms.org.

17. "Workinpr.com State of the Industry Survey 2002."

18. *Occupational Outlook Handbook*, 2010–2011.

19. *Occupational Outlook Handbook*, 2010–2011.

20. Lee B. Becker, Tudor Vlad, Paris Desnoes, and Devora Olin, "2009 Annual Survey of Journalism & Mass Communication Graduates," online, www.uga.edu/AnnualSurveys.

21. "*PRWeek* 2010 Salary Survey," *PRWeek*, March 2010, online, www.prweekus.com.

22. "PRSA 2008 Member Value Perception and Satisfaction Study."

23. "Profile 2000: A Survey of the Profession, Part I," *Communication World,* June/July 2000, A1–A32; "PRSA/IABC Salary Survey 2000," online, www.prsa.org/ppc.

24. "Profile 2000: A Survey of the Profession, Part I"; "PRSA/IABC Salary Survey 2000."

25. "*PRWeek* Diversity Survey 2009," *PRWeek* and Hill & Knowlton, December 2009, online, www.prweekus.com.

26. "*PRWeek* 2010 Salary Survey."

27. "Best Jobs in America," *Fortune*/CNNMoney.com, November 2009, online, http://money.cnn.com.

28. "PR Professional of the Year," *PRWeek Online*, March 2006, online, www.prweek.com/us/events/awards.

29. "A Failure of Initiative: Final Report of the Select Bipartisan Committee to Investigate the Preparation for and Response to Hurricane Katrina," report issued by the U.S. House of Representatives, 15 February 2006, online, www.gpoacess.gov/congress/index.html.

30. Tom Vanden Brook, "Red Cross to Release Results of Fraud Inquiry," *USA Today,* 27 March 2006, 3A.

31. "Raising a Red Flag: Wake Up Call for the Red Cross," news release issued by U.S. Senator Charles Grassley, 15 March 2006, online, www.senate.gov/~grassley.

32. "American Red Cross Response to Senator Grassley Letter of February 27, 2006," news release issued by American Red Cross, 27 February 2006, online, www.redcross.org.

33. "Statement: American Red Cross Currently Investigating Allegations," news release issued by American Red Cross, 24 March 2006, online, www.redcross.org.

34. "Red Cross Refers New Orleans Investigation to Federal Bureau of Investigation," news release issued by American Red Cross, 30 March 2006, online, www.redcross.org.

35. "Grassley Comments on Red Cross Governance Reforms," news release issued by U.S. Senator Charles Grassley, 30 October 2006, online, www.senate.gov/~grassley.

36. Fineman Public Relations' annual list is released through PR Newswire and can be accessed online via LexisNexis.

3

A Brief History of Public Relations

OBJECTIVES

After studying this chapter, you will be able to

- discuss how public relations evolved before it was formally recognized and given a name
- identify the forces that have shaped the modern profession's development

- recognize the major figures and events that influenced the growth of public relations
- explain the issues and trends that are shaping the future of public relations

KEY TERMS

Bernays, Edward L., p. 67
Committee for Public Information (CPI), p. 66

REAL WORLD

Risky Business

Countries, much like corporations and individuals, often engage in public relations practices to attain their goals. That's why you were excited when officials of the Democratic Republic of Tranquility, a small South Seas island nation known for its tropical beauty, asked your agency to submit a bid for a tourism promotional campaign. They promised generous compensation in exchange for your expertise.

This seemed like just the break your struggling firm needed—until you did your research.

You learned that the Democratic Republic of Tranquility is neither democratic nor tranquil. It is run by a brutal military regime that has been widely condemned for its human rights abuses. You also learned that the government wants to boost tourism revenues to support a military expansion that threatens neighboring countries.

On what basis should you decide whether to bid for this contract? Is everyone entitled to public relations counsel? Does history provide any examples from which you can learn?

WHY HISTORY IS IMPORTANT TO YOU

At first glance, public relations appears to be a 20th-century invention. It is logical to link the emergence of the profession to the dramatic growth in mass communication technology during that century.

However, a closer examination reveals a remarkable history—a discipline practiced in many forms long before the nephew of a famous doctor gave it a name. History also tells about a profession that, at its very best, has been a positive force for change and, at its worst, has created challenges we continue to face.

History and the public relations profession are both values-driven. Both are filled with examples of when people acted—or failed to act—on their beliefs and standards. Both are also open to each observer's interpretation—also shaped by values. You faced this challenge in the opening scenario of this chapter: What values will govern your decision on whether to bid for the Tranquility contract? Can public relations help change a client's bad behavior? Does the client's reputation matter?

The "Real World" scenario also posed the question, "Does history provide any examples from which you can learn?" For this particular scenario, history provides a dramatic—some might say tragic—example involving two public relations pioneers. Two men, confronted by similar choices, chose different paths—one to acclaim, the other to ignominy.

History is full of examples in which people have learned—or failed to learn—from the actions of others. William Shakespeare wrote in *The Tempest,* "What is past is prologue." To put it another way: Pay attention to history. You may be watching coming attractions.

PREMODERN PUBLIC RELATIONS

Although the phrase "public relations" did not attain its current meaning until the 20th century, the practice of public relations has been evident since the dawn of recorded history. One example of public relations, in which primitive agricultural extension agents gave advice on how to grow better crops, dates back to 1800 BC in what is now Iraq.

Some historians believe that the development of public relations is a direct result of Western civilization's first true democracy: the city-state of Athens led by Pericles from 461 to 429 BC. The dictatorships of the past had been overthrown, and suddenly the male citizens of Athens were free to debate, create, and implement public policy. In that environment, citizens began to study public opinion and the methods of influencing it. That study, known as **rhetoric,** is often seen as the beginning of public relations as a social science based on research, planning, and two-way communication. The practice of rhetoric fell into disuse with the demise of democratic Athens but flourished again in the freedoms of the final century of the Roman republic (100 BC), when a philosophy of *vox populi,* the voice of the people, was embraced.

The spread of Christianity during the Middle Ages could, in a modern context, be linked to the application of public relations techniques. Before the development of mass communication technologies, the faith was passed along by missionaries using word of mouth. Among the most notable of these missionaries was Francis of Assisi, who spread his teachings of self-imposed poverty and service to the poor across Europe and the Middle East. He died in 1226, but his religious order, the Franciscans, survives to this day. Johannes Gutenberg's Bible, printed in 1456 by means of a revolutionary movable type process, heralded the use of mass communication technologies. The Catholic Church's outreach efforts became more formalized in the 1600s when it established the *Congregatio de Propaganda Fide,* or Congregation for the Propagation of the Faith, to spread church doctrine.

Trends Leading to the Development of Modern Public Relations

The growth of modern public relations was not limited to just one nation. Aspects of what we now know as public relations emerged independently in several societies. For example, organized government public relations efforts in the United Kingdom preceded those in the United States by more than a decade. The National Association of

Local Government Officers began in 1905, in part to educate the public about the role of local government in British society.[1] However, the earliest development of the profession appears to have emerged in the United States, where privately owned business and industry embraced public relations in the 1880s. In comparison, private sector public relations was not prominent in Britain until after the Second World War.[2]

The march toward modern public relations began in earnest in the United States after the Civil War. To a large degree, this development paralleled the country's transition from an agricultural to an industrial society. The **Industrial Revolution** brought with it growing pains, which, in turn, redefined the relationships among government, business, and the people. Historians often refer to this period of reforms as the **Progressive Era,** which ran from the 1890s to the United States' entrance into World War I in 1917. It was a period in which democracy as well as social and governmental institutions matured. Public opinion grew more important; the nation reexamined and, to a certain extent, redefined itself.

Let's look more closely at how the development of modern public relations is linked to five social trends that had their beginnings in the Progressive Era.

THE GROWTH OF INSTITUTIONS   The Industrial Revolution spawned the growth of big companies. The resulting concentration of wealth among early 20th-century industrialists, such as J. P. Morgan, Andrew Carnegie, and John D. Rockefeller, ran against the traditional American inclination toward decentralized power, as evidenced in the checks and balances established in the Constitution. This, in turn, led to increased regulation of these businesses and consequent growth in the size of government. As business, government, and labor organizations grew larger, the need for effective communication increased. All three sectors experienced a second growth spurt in the economic boom that followed the end of World War II.

THE EXPANSION OF DEMOCRACY   Progressive Era reforms such as giving women the right to vote and the direct election of U.S. senators brought more people into the political process and increased the need for public discussion of policy issues. That expansion continued into the mid- to late 20th century. As a result of the civil rights movement, black citizens and other minority groups gained greater access to the political process. During the Vietnam War, 18-year-olds were also given the right to vote. With the fall of communist governments in Europe and Asia near the end of the 20th century came a growing need for effective communication in emerging democratic societies.

IMPROVEMENTS IN COMMUNICATIONS   In the early 1900s, the growth of national news services such as the Associated Press and the birth of national magazines such as the *Ladies' Home Journal* gave muckraking reporters a wider audience. The introduction of commercial radio in 1920 and commercial television in 1947 launched the era of instantaneous electronic communication. Developments in satellite and computer technology in the second half of the 20th century further revolutionized communications. With the dramatic expansion of the Internet in the 1990s, the power to communicate with mass publics began shifting away from media companies and toward individuals.

A great wave of immigrants (shown here receiving health inspections on arrival at Ellis Island) changed U.S. society and helped set the stage for the development of the new profession of public relations.

(Courtesy of The Statue of Liberty–Ellis Island Foundation, Inc.)

THE GROWTH OF ADVOCACY In the late 1800s, a wave of immigrants who brought Old World political ideas to the New World—and, to some extent, the reaction of native-born citizens to this human wave from abroad—gave birth to increased political activism. Newspapers evolved from the organs of partisan "yellow journalism" of the 19th century into instruments of social advocacy in the early 20th century. The period after World War II also witnessed the growth of significant social advocacy, including movements for civil rights, women's rights, environmentalism, consumerism, antiwar ideals, children's rights, multinationalism, rights for persons with disabilities, and gay rights. Both those who advocated change and the institutions forced to deal with it found an increasing need for public relations.

THE SEARCH FOR CONSENSUS U.S. society is built upon consensus. The nation at one time believed itself to be a melting pot in which various cultures and philosophies would combine into something distinctly American. In recent decades, however, that concept has been largely discredited. It is now accepted that people can *both* be American and retain other cultural identities. Beyond the United States, the world population is growing at a rapid rate. The emergence of a global economy has highlighted the increasing competition for Earth's dwindling resources. With the threat of thermonuclear war on one hand and global environmental disaster on the other, the need to span cultural and philosophical differences is greater than ever.

As you will read in the coming pages, the development of public relations closely mirrors the growth of the United States. Although the profession evolved in other societies as well, it was in the United States—the great experiment in democracy—that public relations flourished.

Pre–20th Century America

Although it would be more than a century before the discipline had a name, the use of public relations tactics was evident in pre-Revolutionary America. Perhaps the most famous example is the Boston Tea Party, a publicity event designed to focus attention on British taxation without representation. After the Revolution, public relations tactics were used to change the course of history. In what some have described as history's finest public relations effort, the **Federalist Papers** appeared in newspapers between October 1787 and April 1788. Written by Alexander Hamilton, James Madison, and John Jay under the single nom de plume Publius, these essays helped lead the reluctant former colonies to ratify the Constitution of the United States.

The ratification of the Constitution and the Bill of Rights in 1789 remains the most important event in the development of public relations in the United States. The 45 words of the **First Amendment** define the liberties that allow the free practice of this vital profession:

> Congress shall make no law respecting an establishment of religion, or prohibiting the free exercise thereof; or abridging the freedom of speech, or of the press; or the right of the people peaceably to assemble, and to petition the Government for a redress of grievances.

This guarantee of free expression, however, is not absolute. It is constantly being interpreted and refined by the U.S. Supreme Court. But more than two centuries after ratification, the First Amendment still stands as the singular liberty that distinguishes U.S. democracy and, as a consequence, the practice of public relations in the United States.

In the 1800s, democracy in the United States continued to mature. Public education was introduced, which resulted in a more literate and well-informed society. As the right to vote was extended to men who did not own property, vigorous public debate emerged. The influence of that debate on the government was clear when President Andrew Jackson appointed Amos Kendall to his so-called kitchen cabinet. Kendall was the first presidential press secretary, serving as Jackson's pollster, counselor, speechwriter, and publicist.

Two other figures in the premodern period of public relations are worth noting. During the Civil War, Jay Cooke headed the United States' first fundraising drive: Through an appeal to patriotism, Cooke sold government bonds to finance the Union's war effort. Better known, but less fondly remembered by practitioners, is Phineas T. Barnum, who created his circus in 1871 and later proclaimed it to be "The Greatest Show on Earth." Barnum was the father of press agentry in this

QUICKBREAK 3.1

Revolutionary PR

At the beginning of 1776, the fate of people living in what was then known as British America was very much an open question. Self-proclaimed patriots had been in armed rebellion against the Crown for more than eight months. Both sides were preparing for a long and bloody struggle. American public opinion on the burning issue of the day, independence from Great Britain, was deeply divided.

In this turbulent environment two very different men engaged in a critical public relations battle for the hearts and minds of colonists. Thomas Paine, a corset-maker and schoolteacher who had recently emigrated from England, had a passion for liberty and flair for writing. His counterpart was James Chalmers, a Maryland planter and slaveholder loyal to the King. Their weapon—or tactic—of choice was the pamphlet, the mass medium of the 18th century.

Paine created a stir with the publication of *Common Sense*, the first open demand for a break from England. Using a writing style easily understood by colonists, Paine systematically and persuasively presented the case for American independence.

"I have heard it asserted by some, that as America has flourished under her former connection with Great Britain, the same connection is necessary towards her future happiness," Paine wrote. "We may well assert that because a child has thrived on milk, that it is to never have meat, or that the first twenty years of our lives is to become a precedent for the next twenty."[3]

These words electrified the colonies. However, for Chalmers, Paine's polemic was nothing short of high treason. He decided to counter with his own dissertation, *Plain Truth.* However, as his readers would soon discover, Chalmers' arguments were neither plain nor true. His pamphlet was little more than a collection of cumbersome rhetoric and twisted logic sprinkled with occasional name-calling.

"The judicious reader will therefore perceive that malevolence only is requisite to declaim against and arraign the most perfect governments," Chalmers wrote. "Our *Political Quack* avails himself of this trite expedient to cajole the people into the abject slavery under the delusive name of independence."[4]

Paine was the decisive winner of this public relations battle. He also would be remembered for another series of essays, *The American Crisis*, which bolstered waning public opinion during the darkest days of the conflict. Ironically, his inflammatory writings and revolutionary zeal would eventually force him into exile from the nation he helped create. As for Chalmers, he fought with British Loyalists and fled into exile at war's end. He spent his final days doing what he had done in 1776, unsuccessfully trying to rewrite history. ■

country. A master showman, Barnum generated extensive newspaper coverage of his often bizarre enterprises through exaggeration, distortion, and outright lies. To the shame of the profession, some wanna be publicists still practice Barnum's "publicity for publicity's sake" approach today.

QUICK CHECK

1. What are some of the earliest examples of public relations—even before the profession was known as public relations?
2. What are the major social trends that have influenced the development of public relations?
3. What remains the most important event in the development of public relations in the United States?

THE SEEDBED YEARS

U.S. society underwent profound changes in the period following the Civil War. The Industrial Revolution transformed the nation's economy and helped fuel a flood of immigration. As already noted, reaction to the growth of mammoth corporations spawned a progressive movement and calls for reform. In this environment, publicity was first embraced as a means for shining a public light on government and corporate wrongdoing. New York banker Henry Clews proclaimed in 1906 that publicity was "our great remedy." However, by the 1920s, it was considered a corporate tool. One journalism professor condemned publicity as a weapon used to control public opinion.[5]

This evolution of publicity signaled the birth of a new industry, public relations. Public relations historian Scott Cutlip called this period the **"Seedbed Years,"** a time in which the new profession began to take root.[6] It was during this period of growth in U.S. society that organizations first felt the need for formalizing their communications. For example, in 1888 the Mutual Life Insurance Company created a "literary bureau" to publicize its services. One year later, George Westinghouse hired a newspaper reporter to help him earn public favor in his battle with Thomas Edison over competing electricity distribution systems.

The nation's first public relations agency, the **Publicity Bureau** in Boston, was created in 1900 in recognition of the fact that corporations needed to voice their concerns amid a rising tide of critics. The Publicity Bureau came to epitomize the practice—and the challenges—of modern public relations in its infancy. The Publicity Bureau's clients, which included American Telephone & Telegraph and the nation's railroads, hoped that this new craft known as publicity might stem the increasing threat of government regulation.[7]

Other pioneering practitioners would soon follow. William Wolf Smith opened the national capital's first "publicity business" in 1902. The Parker and Lee agency, the nation's third, opened in New York City in 1904. However, it folded after only four years. That was a common fate of these early agencies.

Credibility was their problem. Publicity agents zealous to put forward a favorable view of their clients often provided inaccurate information. Sources were often hidden, creating a public increasingly suspicious of anything carrying a "publicity" label. There were also ethically challenged reporters—moonlighters— who wrote bylined stories for their newspapers in the morning and anonymous publicity releases in the afternoon.

Early public relations practitioners also faced stiff resistance from newspaper publishers. Some of this hostility stemmed from the tactics of early practitioners,

QUICKBREAK 3.2

Thank You for Smoking

Thank You for Smoking, a 2006 film based on Christopher Buckley's novel, follows the exploits of lobbyist Nick Naylor, who, as one reviewer noted, championed the cause of the tobacco industry "ruthlessly and with a commendable lack of shame."[8] It is a funny movie—one that hits too close for comfort for many public relations practitioners.

Public relations has a long—and controversial—association with the tobacco industry. In the eyes of many, this collaboration has stained the profession's reputation. The most memorable moment in this relationship came on Easter Sunday 1929. Public relations pioneer Edward L. Bernays recruited 10 debutantes to walk down New York's Fifth Avenue carrying lighted cigarettes aloft in protest of restrictions against women's smoking in public places. The so-called Torches of Freedom march generated nationwide publicity and made it more socially acceptable for women to smoke. Bernays wrote decades later that "a beginning had been made, one I regret today."[9]

A 1952 *Reader's Digest* article, "Cancer by the Carton," dramatically brought home the danger of smoking to Americans. The tobacco industry responded by creating the Tobacco Institute Research Committee, which it said would sponsor research into health issues raised by smoking. It evolved into the Tobacco Institute, which at its height employed more than 120 public relations practitioners and spent more than $20 million annually promoting tobacco.[10]

A major shift in public policy came in the 1990s, fueled by the publication of internal industry documents suggesting that tobacco executives had ignored research showing smoking was harmful. Those documents also raised doubts about industry claims that it doesn't encourage smoking among minors.

Under the threat of a mountain of personal injury lawsuits, the tobacco industry finally admitted in 1997 that cigarettes are addictive and harmful to health. It also agreed to submit to nicotine regulation by the Food and Drug Administration, restrict its marketing tactics, and earmark more than $200 billion for health and antismoking education programs.[11]

In an ironic twist, public relations practitioners—once scorned for doing Big Tobacco's bidding—are now being praised for their role in reducing the rate of cigarette smoking. A 2003 report in the *Journal of the National Cancer Institute* credited a federal antismoking campaign with a decline in tobacco use. And it said the reason this effort succeeded where others had failed was because of the effective use of public relations.[12] ■

which included bribes, gifts, and outrageous publicity stunts. Journalists also resented the growing number of people at their doorsteps seeking news coverage. Many journalists were contemptuous of former colleagues who switched to public relations careers. This was ironic because many of the same critics complained bitterly about their own poor wages, negative reputations, and difficult working conditions.[13]

Theodore Roosevelt (1858–1919)

Theodore Roosevelt, the nation's youngest president, is best remembered for using the White House as a "bully pulpit," from which he could rally public opinion in favor of his reform policies.

(Courtesy of the Library of Congress)

Early publicity efforts—especially those targeted at halting the increasing influence of government regulation—achieved only limited success for yet another reason: Theodore Roosevelt. The youngest person to date to serve as president, Roosevelt dramatically transformed the relationships among the White House, big business, and the electorate. Before Roosevelt's succession to the presidency upon the assassination of William McKinley in 1901, the attitude widely held by Washington officials was, in essence, "What is good for big business is good for America." But Roosevelt saw big business' increasing concentration of power—an estimated 10 percent of the population at that time owned 90 percent of the wealth—as a threat to democracy. Roosevelt's administration proceeded to sue 44 major corporations in an attempt to break up monopolies and increase business competition.

Roosevelt also understood—probably better than any other person of his time—the power of harnessing public opinion. He transformed the presidency into what he called his "bully pulpit." Traditional power brokers were opposed to the reforms of Roosevelt's Square Deal, but the president understood the mood of the people and courted their favor through the muckraking press. As researcher Blaire Atherton French has written,

> Theodore Roosevelt was the first to initiate close and continuous ties with reporters, and may be accurately called the founder of presidential press conferences. He brought the press into the White House literally as well as figuratively. The tale goes that he looked out his window one rainy day and saw a group of reporters manning their usual post by the White House gate. Their purpose was to question those coming and going from the White

House and in that way to gather news or leads. When T. R. saw them miserable, wet, and cold, he ordered that there be a room in the White House set aside just for them. In doing so, T. R. granted them a status they had never previously enjoyed and would subsequently never lose.[14]

Although many of his proposed reforms were thwarted by a stubborn Congress, much of Theodore Roosevelt's success and widespread popularity was a result of his skillful application of public relations. As another researcher has written, Roosevelt "figured out how a president can use the news media to guide public opinion. He did not just hand out information and leave matters in the hands of reporters. He created news."[15]

Ivy Ledbetter Lee (1877–1934)

A man who deserves more credit for the growth of public relations than he has received is **Ivy Ledbetter Lee**. His was a career that began in triumph and ended in a controversy that outlived him.

VALUES STATEMENT 3.1

Declaration of Principles

Ivy Ledbetter Lee and George Parker, veterans of Democratic Party politics, joined forces in 1904 to form the public relations firm of Parker and Lee. The agency drew public criticism for its representation of anthracite coal operators during a 1906 miner's strike. In an effort to stem the tide of hostile muckraking reporters who doubted the veracity of the agency's public statements, Lee issued his "Declaration of Principles."

This is not a secret press bureau. All our work is done in the open. We aim to supply news. This is not an advertising agency; if you think any of our matter ought properly to go to your business office, do not use it. Our matter is accurate. Further details on any subject treated will be supplied promptly, and any editor will be assisted most cheerfully in verifying directly any statement of fact. Upon inquiry, full information will be given to any editor concerning those on whose behalf an article is sent out. In brief, our plan is, frankly and openly, on behalf of business concerns and public institutions, to supply to the press and public of the United States prompt and accurate information concerning subjects which it is of value and interest to the public to know about. Corporations and public institutions give out much information in which the news point is lost to view. Nevertheless, it is quite as important to the public to have this news as it is to the establishments themselves to give it currency. I send out only matter every detail of which I am willing to assist any editor in verifying for himself. I am always at your service for the purpose of enabling you to obtain more complete information concerning any of the subjects brought forward in my copy.

—Published in *American Magazine,* September 1906[16] ■

The son of a Methodist minister in Georgia, Lee studied at Princeton and worked as a newspaper reporter and stringer. After a brief foray into politics, Lee joined George E. Parker, once President Grover Cleveland's publicity manager, to form a publicity bureau in 1904. The new agency boasted three values: "Accuracy, Authenticity, and Interest."[17]

This philosophy evolved in 1906 into Lee's **"Declaration of Principles,"** the first articulation of the concept that public relations practitioners (although the term *public relations* had not yet been coined) have a public responsibility that extends beyond obligations to a client. "This is not a secret press bureau," Lee wrote. "All of our work is done in the open." (See Values Statement 3.1.)

Lee's "Declaration of Principles" also declared, "In brief, our plan is, frankly and openly, on behalf of business concerns and public institutions, to supply the press and public of the United States prompt and accurate information concerning subjects which it is of value and interest to the public to know about."[18]

Lee's statement, issued at a time when he was representing management's side in a coal strike, changed the direction of the evolving field of public relations. He established ethical standards by which others could judge his work. In doing so, he also brought credibility and professionalism to the field.

Of course, actions speak louder than words, and Lee did not always live up to his own words. Perhaps a kinder interpretation is that he often defined accuracy in very

Although credited with bringing an ethical foundation to the fledgling profession of public relations, Ivy Lee is most remembered for unfortunate choices that damaged his reputation.

(Courtesy of the Mudd Manuscript Library, Princeton University Library)

narrow terms. For Lee, accuracy meant correctly reflecting the views of the client—but it did not mean checking to see whether the client's statements were truthful. Because of that questionable logic, during his controversial career Lee often supplied misleading or false information to reporters. The resulting mistrust of Lee and his motives would eventually be his undoing.

Lee had an impressive list of clients. It was Lee who, along with pioneer practitioner Harry Bruno, helped promote public acceptance of the new field of aviation. Lee was crucial in gaining the needed financial support for a nation-wide publicity tour by aviator Charles A. Lindbergh. Lee is also credited for his work with what would eventually become General Mills and the creation of three of its most enduring symbols: Betty Crocker; Gold Medal Flour; and Wheaties, the Breakfast of Champions.[19]

You are judged by the company you keep. The appropriateness of representing controversial clients is an age-old problem for public relations practitioners—for example, will you decide to represent the Democratic Republic of Tranquility described in this chapter's opening "Real World" scenario? Many of Lee's clients were controversial at the time they retained his services. They included the Anthracite Coal Operators, the Pennsylvania Railroad, and John D. Rockefeller.

However, it would be Lee's worldview and extensive travels that would cause the most damage to his reputation. In many ways, Lee was a man ahead of his times. He supported recognition of Soviet Russia at a time when most of his compatriots were fearful of the recent communist revolution in that country. Lee was scorned for his desire for cooperation between the two nations. In less than a decade, however, cooperation between the United States and the Soviet Union would lead to an Allied victory in World War II.

The sharpest criticism was leveled at Lee's work in 1934 on behalf of I. G. Farben, the German Dye Trust. This episode occurred at a time shortly after Adolf Hitler assumed power in Germany. Lee's services were retained by industrialists to help counter a growing anti-German sentiment in the United States. Lee accepted a $25,000 fee with the stipulation that he only provide counsel and not disseminate information for the Germans within the United States. Lee, often referred to by his detractors as "Poison Ivy," was accused of being a Nazi sympathizer. Making matters worse, Lee ignored the advice he had often given others and refused to answer reporters' questions about his German business interests. In what now appears to be a very naive notion, Lee thought he could positively influence the behavior of the government of the Third Reich. In fairness, Lee was not the only person to underestimate the evil embodied in Adolf Hitler. However, this association would stain his name long after his death in 1934.

WAR AND PROPAGANDA

America's entrance into World War I in 1917 had a profound effect on both society and the growth of public relations. The war thrust the United States onto the world stage—a place where many U.S. citizens were reluctant to be.

Isolationism grew out of a desire to separate the New World from the problems of Europe. In an earlier time, that had been quite possible. However, with the Industrial Revolution came the growth of U.S. economic power and ties to other nations that were an unavoidable consequence of a growing global economy.

World War I also focused public attention on the use of the mass media as tools of persuasion. People were becoming more familiar with the concept of **propaganda,** which is the attempt to have a viewpoint accepted at the exclusion of all others. The word's etymology stems from the Roman Catholic Church's efforts to propagate the faith during the 17th century. *Propaganda,* as a term, did not carry the negative connotations at the beginning of World War I that it does today. However, its abuse by its most evil practitioner, Nazi Propaganda Minister Joseph Goebbels, discredited propaganda both as a word and as a practice.

To rally the nation behind the war, President Woodrow Wilson established the **Committee for Public Information (CPI).** It became better known as the Creel Committee, after its chairman, former journalist George Creel. Creel was a longtime Wilson friend who had tried to persuade him to run for president as early as 1905, while Wilson was still president of Princeton University. Wilson had been reelected to the White House in 1916 on a promise that he would keep the United States out of the bloody conflict that had been raging across Europe since 1914. With involvement in the war now on the horizon, Wilson leaned toward the advice of his military experts that the press should be strictly censored. Creel, however, as military historian Thomas Flemming has noted, "convinced Wilson that the country needed not suppression but the expression of a coherent pro-war policy."[20]

During the two years that the United States was at war, the CPI churned out more than 75 million pamphlets and books with titles ranging from "Why We Are Fighting" to "What Our Enemy Really Is." Through what may have been the largest speakers' bureau ever created, the **Four-Minute Men,** 75,000 speakers gave 755,190 talks to drum up home front morale.[21] (The name "Four-Minute Men" came from the length of time volunteers spoke between reel changes at cinemas, which were the most important form of mass entertainment at the time.) CPI filmmakers also produced features such as *Pershing's Crusaders* and *Under Four Flags.* These films not only fanned patriotic fires but also raised $852,744.30— not bad for the days when the price of a movie ticket was only a nickel.[22]

QUICK CHECK

1. Why did most of the early publicity agencies fail?
2. What contributions did Ivy Ledbetter Lee make to the development of public relations?
3. In what ways did the outbreak of World War I influence the growth of public relations?

SOCIAL MEDIA APPS

Blogging Bernays

If you had asked Edward L. Bernays about social media, he probably would have thought you were talking about the society pages of the *New York Times*. Although the self-proclaimed father of public relations died before the birth of blogs, it wasn't long before he became a hot topic online.

Bernays acquaintances Shelley and Barry Spector created the Museum of Public Relations (www.prmuseum.com) in 1997. The online museum, which receives more than 90,000 hits a month, features images of the legendary practitioner's personal memorabilia as well as the video recollections of Bernays himself.[23] Another place where Bernays has a huge Web presence is PRhistory.com, the brainchild of Alex Breve and his graduate project at Rowan University.[24]

Bernays might not have heard of social media, but his name often surfaces in them. "Bernays would have loved Ashton Kutcher race to 1 million followers," media relations specialist Jeff Rutherford said in his blog.[25] Another blog, *Search Engine Journal*, speculates that "Eddy would be a great link builder because he knew how to build the perception of authority, make people express themselves by accomplishing his goals, and how to start conversations that end up benefiting his clients."[26]

Of course, Bernays is not always portrayed in a favorable light. Some cast him as a master manipulator. One blogger told readers, "For your own protection, spend time meeting and learning about Edward Bernays, the Father of Public Relations. Dead but alive and controlling and current."[27]

No one knows how he would have reacted to this online chatter. However, with his bent toward self-promotion, Bernays probably would have enjoyed knowing that he remains a topic of many online conversations. ■

Edward L. Bernays (1891–1995)

World War I and the propaganda surrounding it sparked interest in the study and manipulation of public opinion. There was a growing demand for publicity agents to represent the interests of private companies and public agencies. The Creel Committee proved to be a training ground for many of these practitioners. Notable among them was **Edward L. Bernays,** an acknowledged "father" of public relations. Although Bernays had served as a press agent in several capacities before joining the Creel Committee in 1917, it was after the war that he made his indelible mark.

The Austrian-born Bernays was a nephew of Sigmund Freud, and he played a major role in having Freud's theories on psychoanalysis introduced to America. Before joining the CPI, Bernays served as a newspaper reporter and a theatrical press agent. For the most part, Bernays received high marks for his work with the Creel Committee. However, Bernays' lifelong propensity for self-promotion eventually led to

QUICKBREAK 3.3

"Go West, Young Man"

Horace Greeley, the powerful publisher of the *New York Tribune* in the mid-19th century, is best remembered for popularizing the phrase, "Go West, Young Man, Go West." Greeley advocated Manifest Destiny, the belief that the American nation should become a continental power.[28] While Greeley used the power of the press to promote his beliefs, others used the power of public relations to advance western expansion.

Many public relations historians dismiss these early efforts as press agentry. Certainly, some of the earliest attempts to lure European settlers to the New World would not meet today's ethical standards. When Captain Arthur Barlowe returned to England in 1584 after founding a colony on the coast of present-day North Carolina, he described it to his benefactor Sir Walter Raleigh as the most "plentiful, sweet, fruitful and wholesome of all the world." Apparently, it wasn't. The first attempt at a permanent English settlement in North America failed, and its inhabitants disappeared without a trace. Even the legend of frontiersman Daniel Boone was inflated by schoolteacher-turned-landowner John Filson hoping to lure settlers to Kentucky.[29]

However, other historians have noted a degree of sophistication in some of these early efforts. One example of successful public relations—decades before the profession was given that name—came from the Burlington and Missouri Railroad in 1869. To encourage immigrants to settle railroad lands in the American West, the company opened an office in Liverpool, England, a major point of embarkation. From there, the railroad orchestrated a public information campaign that would make modern practitioners envious.

The Burlington and Missouri's campaign was based on research. It targeted people most likely to emigrate: those living in areas of high unemployment or civil unrest or where minority groups faced persecution. It used tactics one might see today: 10,000 two-color handbills; 10,000 large circulars with maps; 50,000 small circulars distributed at hotels and bars; and advertising inserts in English and Scottish newspapers. Campaign literature relied on sources credible to targeted publics, such as scientists, preachers, and newly settled emigrants writing home to their former friends and neighbors.[30]

The Industrial Revolution fueled the migration to the American Frontier. Improvements in printing and transportation, as well as the invention of the telegraph and photography, helped spread the word—real and exaggerated—of a land of unlimited promise. The positive drumbeat of publicity was aided by the "booster press," frontier newspaper editors eager to recruit additional settlers—potential subscribers and advertisers—to their small towns.[31]

Although it would be a bit of a stretch to suggest that pioneering practitioners led the great westward migration, one fact is indisputable: Long before the term *public relations* came into vogue in the 20th century, the profession played a crucial role in the opening of the frontier. ■

Edward L. Bernays, an acknowledged "father" of public relations, was the nephew of famed psychoanalyst Sigmund Freud and the first person to coin the phrase "public relations counsel."

(Courtesy of the Museum of Public Relations, www.prmuseum.com)

the dismantling of the CPI. At the war's end, Bernays traveled with President Wilson to Paris for the Versailles Peace Conference to provide the president with technical assistance in dealing with reporters. Bernays issued a news release upon his departure, announcing that he and 15 other employees of CPI were traveling to France as the "United States Official Press Mission to the Peace Conference." In the release Bernays wrote that "the announced object of the expedition is 'to interpret the work of the Peace Conference by keeping up a worldwide propaganda to disseminate American accomplishments and ideals.' "[32] Creel was angry that Bernays had overstated the CPI's role. Wilson's detractors in Congress began to look upon the CPI as the president's personal publicity machine and pulled its plug.

The inevitable finger-pointing ensued. Creel blamed Bernays for undercutting the mission of the CPI in a search for personal glory. For his part, Bernays cast blame on Creel for helping to lose the peace. "Lack of effective public relations between President Wilson and the people of the United States, historians confirm, was one of the reasons for the rejection of the League of Nations by the United States," Bernays wrote.[33]

It was Bernays who, in his 1923 book, *Crystallizing Public Opinion,* popularized the phrase "public relations counsel." He said he used the phrase because of the negative connotations attached to terms such as *propagandist, publicist,* and *press agent:*

> I wanted something broader than publicity or press-agentry. I called what I did "publicity direction," by which I meant directing the actions of a client to result in the desired publicity. A year later Doris [Bernays' wife] and I coined the phrase "counsel on public relations," which we thought described our activity better—giving professional advice to our clients on their public relationships, regardless of whether such an activity resulted in publicity.[34]

Bernays was not the first to use the term *public relations.* President Thomas Jefferson used it in an address to Congress in 1807. Attorney Dorman Eaton also used the term in an 1882 talk before the Yale Law School graduating class.[35] However, Bernays was the first to use it to describe the discipline that bears its name.

In his book, Bernays was also the first to articulate the two-way communication concept of public relations. In the same year that *Crystallizing Public Opinion* was published, Bernays taught the first public relations course, at New York University.

QUICKBREAK 3.4

The Mother of Public Relations

If Edward L. Bernays is most often credited with being the father of public relations, it is both logical and just that his wife, Doris E. Fleischman, be recognized as the profession's mother. Fleischman was more than Bernays' life partner. She was an equal—yet often invisible—business partner in one of history's most important and successful public relations agencies.

The original power couple of public relations met as children at a beach resort on Long Island, where their families had summer cottages.[36] Fleischman, whose father was a prominent attorney, became a women's page writer for the New York Tribune in 1914 and a freelance writer in 1916. She went to work for Bernays in the summer of 1919 at $50 a week as a staff writer. (He paid his male staff writers $75 a week.) At that time, Bernays was engaged in what he called "publicity direction" for clients such as opera legend Enrico Caruso and the Russian Ballet.[37]

Bernays and Fleischman married on September 16, 1922. In an act that would come to symbolize this partnership, Fleischman—with her new husband's encouragement—registered at the Waldorf-Astoria for their wedding night using her maiden name. "I had an inner fear that marriage (though I wanted it fiercely with Doris) would take away some of my liberties as an individual if there were always a Mrs. added to my name," Bernays wrote in his memoirs. "I wanted both the ties and the freedom."[38] During their 58 years of marriage, Fleischman and Bernays were truly a team. "My relationship with Doris was at two levels," Bernays wrote. "At the office we were fairly businesslike and professional, but after working hours our relationship became highly personal."[39] Bernays gives credit to his wife for helping him coin the phrase "public relations counsel." Bernays told one interviewer that his wife "played an equally important role with mine, except that her insight and judgment are better than mine."[40]

Although they may have been equal partners, they certainly haven't received equal recognition: Fleischman remains a shadow lingering in the background of Bernays' career. That is largely because of the way this unique partnership operated. Although the couple collaborated closely on all projects, Bernays made all the client contacts and speeches—and not just because of his propensity for self-promotion. It was a time when women were a rarity in the business world. Many companies were uncomfortable and unwilling to embrace women's ideas. Though this reality was a bitter pill to swallow, the couple played the game by the rules of the day and, by all measures, won.

Even though Doris Fleischman has not received the acclaim achieved by her husband, Bernays was his wife's greatest champion. "These are difficult times, being alone after 58 years of happy twenty-four-hour-a-day companionship," Bernays wrote after Fleischman's death in 1980. "She was a rare woman."[41] ■

Through the years, Bernays promoted the interests of a wide variety of clients, including the American Tobacco Company, Lithuanians seeking independence from the Soviet Union, and Procter & Gamble. Bernays took credit for pushing CBS Radio to develop news programming to build up its image. He also acknowledged his role in encouraging women to smoke cigarettes—something he said he regretted much later in life.

Public relations historian Scott Cutlip wrote that Bernays believed in self-promotion to the point that he lost the respect of many of his contemporaries. In one instance, Bernays was fired from an account he had with General Motors because he had gotten more credit for GM's Depression-era relief efforts than had the company.[42] Nevertheless, in recognition of his role in the advancement of public relations, *Life* magazine named Bernays to its list of the 100 most influential Americans of the 20th century.

Bernays remained a leading advocate for professional public relations until his death at the age of 103 in 1995. Late in his life, Bernays favored the licensing of public relations professionals. "Any dumbbell, nitwit or crook can call himself a public relations practitioner," Bernays told an interviewer. "The only way to protect yourself from dumbbells and crooks is to install intellectual and social values that are meaningful and keep out people who only hand out circulars in Harvard Square."[43]

Why Bernays and Not Lee?

Why isn't Ivy Ledbetter Lee, whose "Declaration of Principles" preceded Edward L. Bernays' *Crystallizing Public Opinion* by 17 years, considered the real founder of modern public relations? It appears that timing and circumstances favored Bernays.

That both men deserve recognition is without question. At a time when what was to become known as public relations was in its infancy, Lee gave the profession credibility and ethical standards. Later, Bernays gave the emerging profession a name and direction.

However, it is also true that both men were not saints. Lee proclaimed the value of truth and accuracy, but he didn't always apply those standards to his own work. As for Bernays, his penchant for self-promotion cost him numerous contracts, caused him to be despised by many of his competitors, and may even have helped dash hopes for a lasting world peace after World War I.

Both men faced a similar fork in the road during their careers. Their choices helped seal their reputations. With what may have been good intentions, Lee worked for the Nazis. Bernays declined the same opportunity.

Lee's death in 1934 stilled his voice and ended any chance he might have had to salvage his tarnished reputation. Bernays, however, outlived his contemporary critics. In his writings and in his promotional literature, Bernays actively portrayed himself as the "father of public relations," and he was embraced by an industry that had itself sought recognition and acceptance for so long. Now that they are gone, perhaps history will treat both men as the flawed but notable figures they really were.

An Office of War Information artist designs a poster to boost public morale. During the Second World War, OWI served as a training ground for a generation of public relations practitioners.

(Library of Congress)

THE POSTWAR BOOM

Government public relations efforts expanded at the start of U.S. involvement in World War II, when a 1942 presidential order created the **Office of War Information (OWI)**. Headed by veteran newspaper and radio commentator Elmer Davis, OWI had a twofold mission: to coordinate and control the flow of information from the battlefield to the home front and to engage in experiments in psychological warfare against the enemy. The OWI was the forerunner of the United States Information Agency, which had more than 7,300 employees and an annual budget of approximately $1 billion prior to being absorbed by the U.S. State Department in 1999.

Like its predecessor, the Committee for Public Information, OWI became a breeding ground for a new generation of public relations practitioners. During World War II, approximately 100,000 people were trained as public information officers.[44] Once the war was over, many of these "battle-hardened" practitioners turned their wartime activities into careers.

The postwar period witnessed a rapid growth in public relations education. It was during this period, in 1948, that the Public Relations Society of America was formed by the merger of the National Association of Public Relations Counsel and the American Council on Public Relations. The International Association of Business Communicators began in 1970, following the merger of the American Association of Industrial Editors and the International Council of Industrial Editors.

Postwar Social Activism

The period following World War II in many ways resembled the period of the Industrial Revolution: It was a time of significant growth in the size of government, businesses, industries, organizations, and population. The United States was the only economic power to emerge from World War II with its industrial base virtually untouched by the destruction of war. A consumer economy that had been slowed by the Great Depression and put on hold by the war was finally unleashed. Great advances were made in telecommunications, including the introduction of the most important mass communication medium of the 20th century—television.

The postwar decades also saw great social reform and upheaval, including the civil rights movement, consumerism, environmentalism, the antiwar movement, women's rights, gay rights, and multinationalism. Looming over all of this was the Cold War and the constant threat of thermonuclear war. Never had there been a time when the need for effective communication among nations, organizations, and individuals was greater.

In the highly competitive environment of the postwar period, public relations was seen by corporations as well as consumer advocates as a means for achieving strategic goals. This often led to a clash of values. One of the most significant conflicts came in what *Fortune* magazine called "the Railroad-Truckers Brawl." Because of the competitive pressures that came with the growth of the consumer economy, a group of railroad executives hired the public relations firm of Carl Byoir & Associates to orchestrate a campaign to increase government regulation of the trucking industry. This included weight restrictions the railroad executives said were designed to minimize the wear and tear on public highways. It also had the effect of making long-haul trucking less cost effective. When these efforts succeeded, the trucking industry fought back. It filed an antitrust suit in 1956 that, in essence, accused railroad executives of using public relations tactics to create an illegal monopoly in the long distance freight industry. The case was decided five years later by the U.S. Supreme Court, which unanimously ruled for the railroad executives. As researchers Karla K. Gower and Margot Opdycke Lamme noted, "It was the first time that the Supreme Court directly addressed public relations, establishing it as a legitimate activity when used in furtherance of a political agenda."[45]

Consumer advocate Ralph Nader also used public relations tactics to change the way big businesses operate. Nader burst on the scene in 1965 with his landmark book, *Unsafe at Any Speed,* in which he documented safety problems associated with automobiles, especially General Motors' Corvair. Unhappy with the negative publicity, GM sought to discredit Nader, prompting the consumer advocate to sue the company for investigating his private life. General Motors settled out of court and paid Nader $425,000—which he used to create a watchdog group, the Project on Corporate Responsibility (PCR). Nader then became a GM shareholder, which gave him access to the company's annual meetings. Although GM management defeated several PCR resolutions placed before shareholders, Nader was successful in coaxing GM to change its operations in several areas, including concessions on minority representation on the board of directors, environmental awareness, and consumer safety.[46]

Ironically, during the Industrial Revolution, many advocates of social change saw public relations as an attempt by big business to maintain the status quo. During the social upheavals of the second half of the 20th century, that view changed. Grassroots organizations adopted public relations tactics to influence the actions of business and government. In many ways, the flow of public relations had reversed.

In the spirit of "if you can't beat 'em, join 'em," well-managed companies came to realize the importance of cultivating important publics through public relations. As Edward Grefe and Martin Linsky note in their book *The New Corporate Activism*,

> A new breed of public affairs professionals began emerging who recognized that to build grassroots constituent support, it was necessary to present potential coalition allies with a positive program they could support.

QUICKBREAK 3.5

Other Notable Figures from Public Relations' Past

Leone Baxter—with her husband and partner, *Clem Whitaker*, formed the first agency specializing in political campaigns in 1933.

Carl Byoir—a Creel Committee veteran; formed one of the earliest public relations firms, Carl Byoir & Associates.

Harwood Childs—a Princeton University political scientist who expanded upon Bernays' theories and stressed that practitioners should be students of "social effects and corporate conduct."

Pendleton Dudley—an influential figure in early public relations whose firm evolved through the years to DAY, which was acquired by Ogilvy & Mather.

Rex Harlow—a practitioner and educator; founded the American Council on Public Relations, which evolved into the Public Relations Society of America in 1948.

E. H. Heinrichs—a former Pittsburgh newspaper reporter hired by Westinghouse in 1889 to run the nation's first corporate public relations department.

John W. Hill—with partner *Don Knowlton* created Hill & Knowlton, one of the world's largest public relations firms, in Cleveland in 1927.

George V. S. Michaelis—a leading force behind the creation of the Publicity Bureau, the nation's first public relations agency.

Arthur W. Page—a vice president with American Telephone & Telegraph in 1927 who set the standard for corporate public relations, particularly employee relations.

Theodore Vail—organized the first public relations program for AT&T, based on the then revolutionary concept that public utilities had to please their customers through good service and fair rates.

Hamilton Wright—a vigorous promoter of the growing state of Florida and a pioneer in the promotion of land development and in representing foreign nations in the United States. ■

Following the example of grassroots organizers, these professionals fostered strategies that would not be simply against something but equally *for* something.[47]

Late–20th century public relations practitioners became increasingly important in a wide variety of areas, including crisis communications, community relations, employee relations, and investor relations. Practitioners also played a part in strategic planning, although the scope of their role varied widely throughout the industry.

 QUICK CHECK

1. Why is Edward L. Bernays most often credited as being the "father" of modern public relations?
2. How did the end of World War II influence the growth of public relations?
3. In what ways have social movements such as civil rights, women's rights, and consumerism affected the development of public relations?

THE INFORMATION AGE

Changes in the world's economic climate brought dramatic consequences starting in the 1970s. The United States had an aging industrial infrastructure that made it difficult for U.S. businesses to compete with more modern facilities in other nations. Former adversaries Germany and Japan, having risen from the ashes of war, began to compete successfully against U.S. companies both in this country and abroad. Those nations had also adopted many management practices that had been pioneered in the United States but seemingly forgotten here. As a result, business and industry began a sometimes painful process of modernizing and **downsizing**. They trimmed layers of middle management, sold unprofitable divisions, and focused on core enterprises. Jobs that had once seemed certain to last forever suddenly disappeared.

The downsizing trend had a major impact on public relations. Many in-house public relations departments were either reduced or eliminated entirely. This, in turn, created opportunities for agencies and private consultants to fill the gaps. The irony, of course, is that this downsizing occurred at a time when organizations needed public relations practitioners more than ever—especially when it came to explaining why people were being laid off while their employers reported record revenues and rising executive salaries. A positive development has been a greater awareness of the need for corporate responsibility and volunteerism—areas in which public relations play a major role.

At the same time these economic changes were occurring, a technological revolution was taking place. With the invention of silicon microprocessing chips, computers became more powerful, smaller, and more affordable. Desktop publishing came into existence, along with fax machines, e-mail, and teleconferencing. Information became the nation's top commodity. Workers, especially public relations practitioners, became more productive, and a record number of new jobs were created. Unfortunately, these new information-based jobs often paid lower salaries than the old ones they replaced.

Public Relations Takes a Higher Profile

Another important change came in the demographic makeup of the workforce. Women entered the job market in record numbers. Civil rights legislation also created opportunities for African Americans and other minority workers. The face of immigration also changed. A century earlier, the majority of immigrants coming to the United States had been from Europe. The nearly 20 million foreign-born residents counted by the U.S. census in 1990 presented a different picture. Of that number, 44 percent had been added in the 1980s; and of the new arrivals, almost half came from Latin America and nearly one third from Asia.

Public relations practitioners began to take on a much higher and sometimes negative profile during the 1970s and 1980s, especially in the area of government and politics. This trend actually had begun in the 1960s, when a large percentage of citizens felt that the Johnson administration was not telling the truth about its conduct of the Vietnam War, creating what commentators often referred to as a "credibility gap." In the 1970s, public relations also was criticized for its role during the Watergate scandal. In reality, many of that scandal's principal figures had advertising, not public relations, backgrounds.

Following Bill Clinton's use of rapid-response public relations tactics to defeat incumbent George Bush in the 1992 presidential election, public awareness of political counselors—so-called spin doctors—increased dramatically. Some of these counselors, such as James Carville and George Stephanopoulos, later became network political pundits, a role once exclusively held by reporters. Political public relations took center stage in the presidential election stalemate of 2000. Both George W. Bush and Al Gore, trying to appear presidential and above the fray, relied heavily on surrogate spokespersons during the 36-day deadlock.

THE NEW MILLENNIUM

Any thoughts that the new millennium might bring a period of peace and prosperity were dashed by the terrorist attacks of September 11, 2001. Within a few weeks, the United States was at war against Al Qaeda in Afghanistan. In March 2003, the U.S. launched a controversial war against Iraq. As the first decade of the 21st century drew to a close, fighting continued in the longest wars in U.S. history.

Things were no more tranquil on the home front. Corporate scandals involving major corporations such as Enron and WorldCom shook investor confidence in 2001. These problems foreshadowed a financial meltdown in 2008. The economies of the world's industrialized nations fell into the deepest recession since the Great Depression of the 1930s. These economic tremors—as well as an accompanying decline in public trust in institutions, public and private—resulted in tighter regulation and increased demands for corporate social responsibility.

During the first decade of the new millennium, the nation witnessed a number of disasters, some of natural origin, some human created, and, as was the case with Hurricane Katrina, some that were both. Rational, civil discourse was often replaced by angry confrontations, such as the raucous health care reform debate of 2009. It was also the decade that saw a decline in traditional media and the rise of social media.

At the center of this maelstrom was public relations. The new millennium has seen both the best and the worst of the profession. Practitioners earned praise for building consensus among disparate groups. They also played a major role in cause-marketing efforts. Unfortunately, the failure to find weapons of mass destruction in Iraq led many to wonder whether our leaders and their official spokespersons had been truthful. Practitioners also were criticized for misleading investors in the march up to the 2008 meltdown.

At a time when the public relations industry should be celebrating a century of achievement, it finds itself answering the very same questions about integrity and values confronted by Ivy Lee and Edward Bernays. This raises a question all practitioners should ponder: Must history repeat itself?

 QUICK CHECK

1. How has corporate downsizing affected public relations practitioners?
2. In addition to downsizing, what other social forces influenced the development of public relations near the end of the 20th century?
3. After more than a century of evolution, why does the profession of public relations still face questions about its values and integrity?

SUMMARY

Although public relations did not acquire its name until the 20th century, it has been practiced in some form since the beginnings of recorded time. At the time the United States was formed, public relations tactics were used to rally colonists to the cause of independence and later to support the adoption of the new nation's Constitution.

Modern public relations was born during the Industrial Revolution and began to take root during the period known as the Progressive Era. Its development throughout the past century has been nurtured by great social trends—the growth of institutions, the expansion of democracy, technological improvements in communications, the growth of advocacy, and the search for consensus. The profession's development has also been advanced by historical figures such as Theodore Roosevelt, Ivy Ledbetter Lee, Edward L. Bernays, and Doris Fleischman.

At the start of the 21st century, public relations had begun to take a more central role in social discourse in the United States. Practitioners began to acquire more public visibility—even on some occasions when they would have preferred otherwise. With the introduction of the Internet, social media, and other technological advances, public relations practitioners faced both challenges and opportunities. Despite all that has changed, the profession continues to confront the same issues it has faced since its infancy: building its own credibility while helping to achieve global consensus.

DISCUSSION QUESTIONS

1. Whom do you consider the "father of public relations," Ivy Ledbetter Lee or Edward L. Bernays? Why did you choose one man over the other?
2. In addition to Lee and Bernays, who are some of the other major figures who contributed to the development of modern public relations?
3. What major forces shaped the development of public relations in the 20th century?
4. What is propaganda, and why has its use been largely discredited?
5. What do you consider the most significant lesson to be learned from the history of public relations?
6. Would you accept the Democratic Republic of Tranquility as a client? Why or why not?

MEMO FROM THE FIELD

EDWARD M. BLOCK
Former Senior Vice President; AT&T Corporation
Key West, Florida

Edward M. Block was senior vice president for public relations, advertising, and employee information at AT&T Corporation for 12 years. He was also assistant to the chairman of the board and a member of the Office of the Chairman. He has received numerous awards for achievements in public relations, including the Public Relations Society of America's Gold Anvil. Most recently, he was cited by *PRWeek* magazine as among the 100 most influential public relations people of the 20th century.

On page 74, you will find the names of Theodore N. Vail and Arthur W. Page, two executives whose pioneering ideas remain as enduring principles of corporate relationship building.

Vail is the chief executive whose utterly unique business model built the Bell Telephone System, a quasi-monopoly that created a new industry and dominated telephone service in the United States for nearly a century, becoming, at its zenith, the biggest company in the world. He welcomed government regulation, believed that profits need only be sufficient to sustain good service, and established a company-paid pension trust based on identical payout formulas for all employees, management as well as nonmanagement. He invested heavily in research to ensure continuous innovation. He also employed national magazine advertising to explain the policies and plans of the company to the public, no doubt the first demonstration of what would be called "transparency" today. These were remarkable innovations in an era best remembered for its robber barons.

Page elaborated and institutionalized Vail's concepts throughout that giant enterprise. A former magazine editor, he was hired by the parent company, AT&T, in 1926.

He thus became the first individual elected to a senior executive position in charge of what we now call public relations. Subsequently, he was elected to the board of directors. He established modern public relations organizations in the Bell companies, delegating to them a cluster of responsibilities still found in most communications departments in U.S. corporations: employee information. Media relations. Community relations. Financial information. Institutional advertising and communications policy. Philanthropy.

Page was above all a counselor, and he made counseling a top priority in the far-flung PR organizations he created. He persistently argued—and demonstrated throughout his career—that when you get your corporate policies and business practices right your public relations programs will succeed. Conversely, he argued, that when your corporate policies are out of sync with the expectations of your publics you cannot sustain effective constituency relationships—so don't bother. Moreover, he warned, communications efforts intended to support wrongheaded policies will only make matters worse.

As an important extension of this focus, Page conceived of public relations as an institutional mind-set, not a functional department, and therefore a priority consideration in every decision, not only by top management, but also by supervisors in the field or on the shop floor. His conception is perhaps best summed up in the modern understanding of the term *corporate culture.* He ardently believed that public relations is everyone's job, a bias, an attitude that strives to fashion policies, actions, and business practices that project integrity and build trust over time.

People employed in the PR departments that Page established were expected to be experts in the communications arts and were hired and incessantly trained in these skills. But more important, they were widely deployed throughout the Bell companies' operating divisions to provide on-the-spot counsel in matters large or small. Their peers in the functional departments routinely took account of their judgments and acted on them.

The Page emphasis on counseling may seem a quaint idea in an era that seems to prize so many of the currently fashionable communications functions such as marketing support and investor relations. But his disciples abound and continue to insist that counseling will sooner or later reassert its importance. Why? Because counseling is by definition a value-added function, providing, as it does, a unique and critical perspective in managing the affairs of businesses whose constituencies are many and varied. Moreover, timely counseling is not overhead. It comes free as part of a total communications package.

Today, a 300-plus member Arthur W. Page Society exists expressly to promote his concepts in a context of contemporary business issues and to serve the needs of senior corporate executives as well as public relations counseling firms.

The Page concepts are captured, albeit cryptically, in the following "principles" espoused by the society's members: Tell the truth. Prove it with action. Listen to the customer. Conduct public relations as if the whole company depends upon it. Remain calm, patient, and good humored, especially in the face of criticism.

When you think about them, these admonitions are nothing more complicated than plain, old-fashioned horse sense. Makes you wonder why so many businesses today seem not to have any. ■

CASE STUDY 3.1 The March of Dimes

One of the greatest ironies of the 20th century was that a man who successfully hid his physical disabilities from most Americans was also the most visible spokesperson in the fight against the disease that had crippled him.

Franklin Delano Roosevelt was the only person elected president of the United States four times. From his inauguration in March 1933 until his death in April 1945, FDR held a commanding presence in the minds of U.S. citizens. Historians consider him among the greatest of presidents for having led the United States through the Great Depression and to the brink of victory in the Second World War.

He is also remembered for his courage in overcoming polio (poliomyelitis), a viral disease that attacks the central nervous system and can lead to paralysis and death. Children were most often the victims of the disease, which is transmitted through contaminated food and water. When FDR contracted polio at the age of 39 in 1921, he lost the use of his legs. But with careful event planning, the assistance of the Secret Service, and the acquiescence of the news media, the extent of Roosevelt's physical disability was unknown to most people.[48]

Although FDR may have hidden his own physical limitations, he was not shy in showing his

Franklin D. Roosevelt (center), shown here in Warm Springs, Georgia, in 1932, managed to hide from the U.S. public his inability to walk. Note that in this carefully staged photograph, FDR steadies himself by holding the arm of an unidentified man.

(Courtesy of the Franklin D. Roosevelt Presidential Library and Museum)

support for others who had suffered the same fate. Initially, his efforts centered on Warm Springs, Georgia, where he had first gone in 1924 to bathe in the area's therapeutic warm spring waters. Roosevelt purchased the property in 1926. A year later, with the help of former law partner Basil O'Connor, FDR established the nonprofit Warm Springs Foundation as a center for polio therapy and research.[49]

With the onset of the Great Depression, the Warm Springs Foundation faced severe financial difficulties. A nationwide series of Birthday Balls was organized on January 30, 1934, coinciding with President Roosevelt's 52nd birthday. The Birthday Balls ranged from a lavish gala at New York's Waldorf-Astoria to a wheelchair dance for patients at Warm Springs.[50] The event was promoted with the slogan "Dance so that others may walk." It was so successful that it was repeated for several years.[51]

"Birthday Balls exploited the prestige of the presidency to collect monies for the Warm Springs Foundation," according to media historian Douglas Gomery. "It was often difficult to tell the difference between these polio balls and similar fundraisers staged by the Democratic Party."[52]

Though the close connection between charity and politics may have been coincidental, it is undeniable. Although Roosevelt had genuine sympathy for polio victims, being seen as their champion also helped his public image. Gomery notes that several interest groups, especially the entertainment industry, embraced the Birthday Balls as a means to gain favor from the Roosevelt administration.[53]

The relationship between FDR and the entertainment industry spawned the signature fundraising campaign for which Roosevelt is best remembered, the March of Dimes. Roosevelt established the National Foundation for Infantile Paralysis on January 3, 1938. It marked the creation of the first permanent self-sustaining source of medical research funding based on small individual contributions rather than on money given by a few wealthy patrons. Eddie Cantor,

a 1930s film and radio star, called this grassroots fundraising effort the "March of Dimes," a play on the title of a popular newsreel series of the day, *The March of Time.* Cantor asked the public to send dimes to the White House to support polio research.

Two days after Cantor's initial radio appeal, the White House received 30,000 pieces of mail, virtually all of which had coins taped to the letters. The next day, the White House received 150,000 letters.[54] This is especially impressive when you consider that a dime in the 1930s was the equivalent of $1.27 in today's money. "The March of Dimes had become the most beloved (and richest) charity in the USA with coffers brimming over with totals measured in the millions of dollars," Gomery wrote.[55]

The story did not end with FDR's death on April 12, 1945. On the 10th anniversary of Roosevelt's passing, March of Dimes officials announced that a polio vaccine developed by Dr. Jonas Salk with their support was both safe and effective. As a result, the threat of polio has been virtually eradicated in most of the world.

This grassroots fundraising effort, which tapped into the generosity of a nation at the height of its worst economic crisis, has had one other lasting imprint. To commemorate Roosevelt's crusade against polio, the U.S Mint began issuing dimes with FDR's image on January 30, 1946, the 64th anniversary of his birth.

DISCUSSION QUESTIONS

1. In your opinion, why was the March of Dimes so successful, especially in the midst of the Great Depression?
2. In hindsight, does Roosevelt's decision to hide his personal disability undermine his credibility as a champion of polio victims?
3. The case mentions the relationship between the charity and partisan politics. What were the benefits and risks of this relationship?
4. At the time of its creation, what made the March of Dimes unique among medical research charities? ■

CASE STUDY 3.2 The Fog of War

When the United States and its allies invaded Iraq in 2003, they said they did so in the belief that dictator Saddam Hussein's regime either had or was attempting to acquire weapons of mass destruction. No such weapons have been uncovered. Since then, there has been an intense debate on whether the decision for war was based on faulty intelligence or a calculated manipulation of public opinion.

Although consensus on that issue remains elusive, many have noted a striking similarity between the 2003 invasion and the Persian Gulf War a dozen years earlier: One of the key justifications for war was later proven untrue.

Iraq invaded and occupied its oil-rich neighbor Kuwait in August 1990. When the Hussein regime ignored international pressure demanding that it remove its troops, a U.S.-led coalition invaded and liberated the country.

A key figure in this controversy was a 15-year-old girl identified only as Nayirah. Approximately three months before the U.S.-led coalition began to take Kuwait back by force, Nayirah tearfully testified before the Congressional Human Rights Caucus about Iraqi atrocities she said she had seen at a Kuwait City hospital. Caucus Chairman Tom Lantos (D-Calif.) agreed to conceal her family name to protect relatives still in occupied Kuwait.

"While I was there, I saw the Iraqi soldiers come into the hospital with guns, and go into the room where fifteen babies were in incubators," Nayirah said. "They took the babies out of the incubators, took the incubators, and left the babies on the cold floor to die." A Kuwaiti surgeon later repeated the same story in testimony before the United Nations Security Council and claimed to have supervised the burial of 120 newborn babies.[56]

Nayirah's testimony was arranged by public relations firm Hill & Knowlton on behalf of its client, Citizens for a Free Kuwait.[57] The group,

which described itself as a broad-based coalition of Kuwaiti expatriates, paid Hill & Knowlton an estimated $10 million for its services.[58] The agency hired an opinion research firm to gauge the public's mood. Although public opinion was decidedly against going to war to protect oil supplies, surveys suggested that war might be more acceptable if it were aimed at ending atrocities.

Nayirah's testimony had the desired effect. President George H. W. Bush mentioned the incubator incident several times in his public remarks. Seven U.S. senators cited the incubator incident before voting their support of a resolution giving the president authority to use force against Iraq. The resolution passed by only five votes.[59]

It wasn't until after the war that the incubator story unraveled. Independent human rights organizations were unable to verify the incident. An ABC News crew that entered Kuwait as the country was being liberated found the incubators right where they were supposed to be.[60] One report concluded that there had been no mass slaughter of babies, although at least seven babies died when medical equipment was moved.[61]

However, the most disturbing revelation was that Nayirah, the tearful 15-year-old hospital volunteer, was the daughter of Saud al-Sabah, Kuwait's ambassador to the United States. Rep. Lantos, who died in 2008, argued that Nayirah's true identity did not undermine her credibility.

"That doesn't wash," editorialized the New York Times. "Had her identity been known, her accusations surely would have faced greater skepticism and been questioned more closely."

The Times also questioned the relationship between the Congressional Human Rights Caucus and Hill & Knowlton. The caucus, a private foundation and not an official committee of Congress, rented Washington office space from Hill & Knowlton at a reduced rate. The paper also reported that Citizens for a Free Kuwait donated $50,000 to the caucus foundation and financed several trips by its members.[62]

And there's more. The Kuwaiti surgeon who testified before the United Nations was actually a dentist who later admitted that he had no direct knowledge of the incubator incident. Whereas the membership of Citizens for a Free Kuwait included people outside the government, almost all of the $12 million raised for the pro-war campaign came from Kuwait's ruling family.

Over the years, Hill & Knowlton officials have defended their actions. They have said, in essence, that everyone has a right to public relations counsel. The late Susanne A. Roschwalb of American University agreed—but to a point.

"Hill & Knowlton had the right to represent Kuwaiti expatriates and the Government of Kuwait in an attempt to go to war to defend its interests in the Persian Gulf," Roschwalb wrote in *Public Relations Review.* "The firm did not take into account that intense scrutiny by the media and special interests, whistle blowers and competitors ultimately would make all of its actions public knowledge.

"It would have saved itself serious loss of reputation, business and performance had it assessed the Kuwaiti campaign in terms of its merits, and with an emphasis on the consequences."[63]

DISCUSSION QUESTIONS

1. Do you agree with the decision to conceal Nayirah's identity?
2. What obligation did Hill & Knowlton have toward verifying the incubator list?
3. Considering the circumstances—the occupation of their homeland by a hostile power— was Kuwait's deception of U.S. officials, media, and the public in this matter an acceptable tactic?
4. Do you agree with the statement "Everyone has a right to public relations counsel"? ∎

NOTES

1. Jacquie L'Etang, "State Propaganda and Bureaucratic Intelligence: The Creation of Public Relations in 20th Century Britain," *Public Relations Review* (winter 1998): 413.
2. L'Etang.
3. Norman Foerster, Norman S. Grabo, Russel B. Nye, E. Fred Carlisle, and Robert Falk, eds., *American Poetry and Prose*, 5th ed./part 1 (New York: Houghton Mifflin, 1970), 139.
4. James Chalmers, *Plain Truth: Remarks on a Late Pamphlet, Entitled Common Sense*, Philadelphia, 1776, online: www.loyalamericanregiment.org.
5. Kevin Stoker and Brad L. Rawlins, "The 'Light' of Publicity in the Progressive Era—From Searchlight to Flashlight," *Journalism History* 30, no. 4 (winter 2005): 117.
6. Scott M. Cutlip, *The Unseen Power: Public Relations: A History* (Hillsdale, N.J.: Lawrence Erlbaum, 1994), 1.
7. Cutlip, 10–25.
8. Andy Dougan, "Smokey and the Bandit," *Evening Times* (Glasgow), 15 June 2006, 4, via LexisNexis.
9. Edward L. Bernays, *Biography of an Idea: Memoirs of Public Relations Counsel Edward L. Bernays* (New York: Simon & Schuster, 1965), 387.
10. John Stauber and Sheldon Rampton, "How the American Tobacco Industry Employs PR Scum to Continue Its Murderous Assault on Human Lives," *Tucson Weekly,* 22 November 1995.
11. "States' Attorneys Are Weighing Whether to Sign Deal," Associated Press, as reported in the *Kansas City Star,* 18 November 1998, A4.
12. Frances A. Stillman et al., "Evaluation of the American Stop Smoking Intervention Study (ASSIST): A Report of Outcomes," *Journal of the National Cancer Institute* 95, no. 22 (19 November 2003) 1681–1691.

13. Fred Fedler and Denise DeLorme, "Journalists' Hostility Toward Public Relations: A Historical Analysis," paper presented at the Association for Education in Journalism and Mass Communication annual conference, Miami, Fla., August 2002.

14. Blaire Atherton French, *The Presidential Press Conference: Its History and Role in the American Political System* (Lanham, Md.: University Press of America, 1982), 3.

15. Carolyn Smith, *Presidential Press Conferences: A Critical Approach* (New York: Praeger, 1990), 22.

16. Cutlip, 45.

17. Cutlip, 37–45.

18. Cutlip, 45.

19. Cutlip, 139.

20. Thomas Flemming, "When the United States Entered World War I, Propagandist George Creel Set Out to Stifle Anti-War Sentiment," *Military History,* The History Net, online, www.thehistorynet.com.

21. Charles A. Lubbers, "George Creel and the Four-Minute Men: A Milestone in Public Relations History," *Business Research Yearbook: Global Business Perspectives,* vol. III (New York: International Academy of Business Disciplines, 1996), 719.

22. Flemming.

23. "The Museum of Public Relations," Spector & Associates, online: www .spectorandassociates.net.

24. "About the Webmaster," PRhistory.com, online: http://faculty.camdencc.edu/abreve/prhistory/home/about.htm.

25. "What Would Edward Bernays Be Doing Today If He Were Alive and Working in PR?" Jeff Rutherford Media Relations, posted 29 July 2009, online: http://jeffrutherford.com.

26. "What Edward Bernays Has Taught Me about Link Building,"*Search Engine Journal,* posted 29 January 2010, online: http://www.searchenginejournal.com.

27. "Manipulating People. Edward Bernays, Managing the Masses, and Teabagging," *The Joy of Equivocating; and the Fear of Fog. Uses of Uncertainty in Politics, History,"* posted 31 January 2010, online: http://joyofequivocating.blogspot.com.

28. Jean Folkerts, Dwight L. Teeter, Jr., and Edward Caudill, *Voices of a Nation: History of Mass Media in the United States,* 5th ed., (New York: Allyn and Bacon, 2009), 150.

29. Cutlip, xiv–xv.

30. Andy Piasecki, "Blowing the Railroad Trumpet: Public Relations on the American Frontier," *Public Relations Review*, 26, no. 1: 53–65.

31. Folkerts et al., 145.

32. Bernays, 161.

33. Bernays, 177–178.

34. Bernays, 288.

35. Kathleen O'Neill, "U.S. Public Relations Evolves to Meet Society's Needs," *Public Relations Journal,* November 1991, 28.

36. Bernays, 218.

37. Susan Henry, "Anonymous in Her Own Name: Public Relations Pioneer Doris Fleischman," *Journalism History* 23, no. 2 (summer 1997): 52.

38. Bernays, 217.

39. Bernays, 216.

40. Cutlip, 169–170.

41. Cutlip, 170.

42. Cutlip, 159–225.

43. Alvin M. Hattal, "The Father of Public Relations: Edward L. Bernays," *Communication World,* January 1992, 15.

44. Cutlip, 528.

45. Karla K. Gower and Margot Opdycke Lamme, "Public Relations on Trial—'The Railroad–Truckers Brawl,'" *Journalism History* 29, no. 1 (spring 2003): 12–20.

46. Patrick Jackson and Allen H. Center, *Public Relations Practices: Managerial Case Studies and Problems,* 5th ed. (Englewood Cliffs, N.J.: Prentice Hall, 1995), 167–178.

47. Edward A. Grefe and Martin Linsky, *The New Corporate Activism* (New York: McGraw-Hill, 1995), 3 (emphasis in original).

48. "Franklin Roosevelt Founds March of Dimes—January 3: This Date in History," the History Channel, online, www. historychannel.com/tdih.

49. "The March of Dimes Story," March of Dimes, online, www.marchofdimes.com.

50. Douglas Gomery, "Health Politics and Movie Power," *Historical Journal of Film, Radio and Television* 15, no. 1 (1995): 127–128.

51. William H. Helfand, Jan Lazarus, and Paul Theerman, "'. . . So That Others May Walk': The March of Dimes," *American Journal of Public Health,* 1 February 2002: 158.

52. Gomery, 128.

53. Gomery, 131.

54. Gomery, 131.

55. Gomery, 132.

56. Transcript, "Plan to Sell the War," *20/20*, ABC News, 17 January 1992.

57. "Deception on Capitol Hill, *New York Times*, 15 January 1992: A20.

58. Susanne A. Roschwalb, "The Hill & Knowlton Cases: A Brief on the Controversy," *Public Relations Review* 20 (fall 1994): 267–276.

59. Thomas J. Mickey, "A Postmodern View of Public Relations: Sign and Reality," *Public Relations Review* 23 (fall 1997): 271–284.

60. "The Plan to Sell the War."

61. Mickey.

62. "Deception on Capitol Hill."

63. Roschwalb.

The Publics in Public Relations

OBJECTIVES

After studying this chapter, you will be able to

- define the term *public* as it is used in public relations
- name and describe the different kinds of publics
- list the kinds of information that practitioners should gather about each public
- identify and describe the traditional publics in public relations

KEY TERMS

REAL WORLD
Pop Goes Your Wednesday

Wednesday starts peacefully at the Kablooie Microwave Popcorn Company, where you are director of public relations. You are planning to spend the morning getting ready for next week's annual meeting of stockholders. Kablooie is a new company, and you are eager to tell stockholders about its recently completed Statement of Values, which begins with these words: "Kablooie Microwave Popcorn Company exists to provide value at a fair price to its customers; to provide a competitive return on investment to its stockholders; to provide a humane workplace and fair salaries and benefits to its employees; and to be a good citizen in its communities."

Then:

■ Your assistant tells you his 13-year-old daughter just telephoned. A new viral video shows Kablooie Microwave Popcorn blowing the doors off microwave ovens and injuring teens. A Google search finds the video in a dozen online sites. One comment posted with the video says that a popular rock star has been hospitalized in critical condition after being injured by a Kablooie explosion. In other comments, kids are telling one another to boycott your product. Microbloggers are posting links to the video.

■ Your assistant is still talking when a reporter from your local newspaper calls to ask about the rumor that Kablooie Microwave Popcorn is exploding in microwave ovens and injuring people. You emphatically deny the rumor and promise to call back in 15 minutes.

■ A beep from your computer tells you that a new e-mail message has arrived. It's from a nationally known investment analyst, asking whether there are any new issues you're expecting to deal with at next week's annual meeting for stockholders. Evidently, she hasn't yet heard about the online video.

■ Your secretary brings you a letter from a local Boy Scout troop. In two days, the troop will begin selling your product door to door as a fundraising project. The letter is thanking you for the early delivery of 10,000 packages of Kablooie Microwave Popcorn.

You immediately decide to implement your company's crisis communications plan (see Chapter 12). Like all good public relations plans, it asks you to identify the most important publics with whom you must communicate.

In this scenario, who are your publics? Which are the most important? Can the new Statement of Values help?

WHAT IS A PUBLIC?

Public relations. That's what we call this challenging, rewarding business.

Take a good look at that first word: **public.** That's where we start. Publics are literally the first word in our profession.

So what is a public? As you may recall from Chapter 1, a public is any group whose members have a common interest or common values in a particular situation. A political party can be a public. Upper-level managers in a corporation can be a public. Fans of a popular music group can be a public.

The word *stakeholder* (not *stockholder*) often substitutes for the word *public,* but the two words aren't interchangeable. Some publics may have no connection with the organization that a public relations practitioner represents. But as we note in Chapter 1, a **stakeholder,** or stakeholder group, has a stake, or an interest, in an organization or issue that potentially involves the organization. For any given organization, then, all stakeholder groups are publics—but not all publics are stakeholders.

Counting all the publics even in just the United States would be like trying to count the stars—an impossible task. So which publics matter in public relations? With which publics do we build and manage values-driven relationships? Certain publics become important to an organization as its values and values-based goals interact with the environment. Those publics become stakeholders. For example, to fulfill its values-driven goal of healing people, a nonprofit hospital must have a good relationship with the community's physicians. The hospital's values somehow must fit comfortably with the values of the physicians if this vital relationship is to work.

Another example: To fulfill its goal of being a clean, attractive facility, that same hospital must have a good relationship with its custodians. The hospital needs to understand the values of the custodians—such as fair wages—to make that relationship work. As an organization's values interact with the values of different publics, relationships—good or bad—are born. In fact, if we know the specific values-driven goals of an organization and we know the environment in which it operates, we can predict with some accuracy the essential relationships that can help the organization attain its goals.

Sometimes, however, a relationship surprises an organization. A public in the organization's environment can discover a relationship before the organization does. Often, a clash of values triggers that unexpected relationship. For example, a Midwestern county government trying to build a highway around a growing metropolitan area was surprised when Native Americans strongly opposed the proposed route. The highway passed too near, they said, to an area they used for worship. A values-driven goal of the county government—easing traffic congestion within the metropolitan area—had clashed with a religious value of Native Americans in the area. As one values system met another, a relationship was born.

Why Do We Need Relationships with Publics?

Now, what about that second word in public relations: *relations?* Why do organizations build and maintain values-driven relationships with a variety of publics? (We're glad that they do: The relationship-management process provides interesting, rewarding jobs for thousands of public relations practitioners.) But, again, it's worth asking: Why do organizations need relationships with different publics?

In Chapter 2, you encountered **resource dependency theory,** which, again, consists of three simple beliefs:

1. To fulfill their values, organizations need resources such as raw materials and people to work for the organization.
2. Some of those key resources are *not* controlled by the organization.
3. To acquire those key resources, organizations build productive relationships with the publics that control the resources.

First and foremost, therefore, public relations practitioners must build relationships with publics that possess resources organizations need to fulfill their values-driven goals.

Resource dependency theory can even help us determine which publics will receive most of our relationship-management efforts. Clearly, our most important publics are those that possess the resources our organization needs the most. For example, Pitney Bowes, an international message-management company, focuses on resource dependency theory in the first sentence of its values statement: "Pitney Bowes' relationships with our four constituent groups—customers, employees, stockholders, and the communities—are critical to our success and reputation."[1] In public relations, we build relationships with publics to secure the resources our organizations need to survive and fulfill their values.

Resource dependency theory, therefore, helps explain values-driven public relations. As we describe in Chapter 1, values-driven public relations brings the entire public relations process—research, planning, communication, and evaluation—into a framework defined by an organization's core values. In the planning phase, practitioners establish values-driven public relations goals. To reach those goals, practitioners often must acquire resources held by other publics; this is where resource dependency theory meets values-driven public relations. If our goals are values-driven, the resources we acquire from targeted publics bring our organization closer to fulfilling its values.

Resource dependency theory also helps explain the two-way symmetrical model, the most successful of the four models of public relations (see Chapter 1). Two-way symmetrical public relations works best when there is an exchange of resources. If an organization wants to acquire the resources it needs, it must be willing to give the resource holders something they need. For example, news media have resources most organizations need, including fair and accurate coverage. In return, those organizations have resources news media need, including a willingness to respond to journalists' questions promptly and honestly. In a two-way symmetrical relationship, an organization agrees to exchange resources to fulfill its values-driven goals.

THE PUBLICS IN PUBLIC RELATIONS

Publics may be as impossible to count as the stars, but, like the stars, they can be grouped into categories, including:

- traditional and nontraditional publics.
- latent, aware, and active publics.
- intervening publics.
- primary and secondary publics.

■ internal and external publics.

■ domestic and international publics.

Why bother to group publics into categories? Because knowing which category or categories a public belongs to can provide insight into how to build a productive relationship with it. The thoughtful process of deciding which category or categories a public belongs to can help us learn from our own experiences as well as from those of others. So let's examine these categories.

TRADITIONAL AND NONTRADITIONAL PUBLICS

Traditional publics are groups with which organizations have ongoing, long-term relationships. As shown in Figure 4.1, traditional publics include employees, news media, governments, investors, customers, multicultural community groups, and

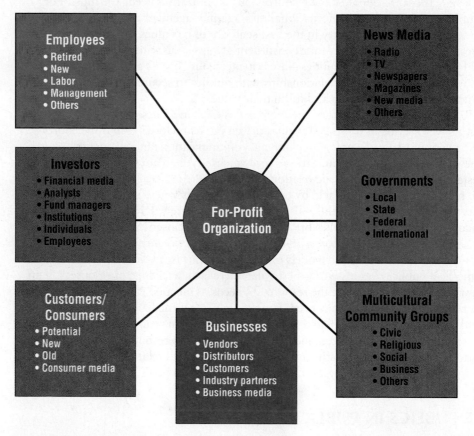

FIGURE 4.1

Traditional Publics in Public Relations

A for-profit organization can have dozens of primary publics. Not pictured in this diagram is the most important public for government public relations practitioners: constituents and voters.

constituents (voters). The fact that these publics are traditional, however, doesn't mean that public relations practitioners can take them for granted. Organizations that ignore the values of employees or of the news media, for example, quickly learn to their sorrow how powerful those publics can be. In Pop Goes Your Wednesday, the "Real World" scenario that opens this chapter, the investment analyst who e-mails you with a request for information represents a traditional public.

Nontraditional publics are groups that usually are unfamiliar to an organization. For example, in Pop Goes Your Wednesday, the high-tech teenagers constitute a nontraditional public—a group with which Kablooie hasn't had an ongoing, long-term relationship. Nontraditional publics can be hard to study and might lead you to try some innovative relationship-building strategies. Nontraditional publics are often sparked by changes in a society—such as the growth of viral videos and related technologies.

Nontraditional publics can be new and challenging, but it's possible that one day they'll become traditional publics. For example, women from an impoverished fishing village in Nigeria shut down a nearby ChevronTexaco oil terminal by entering the facility and refusing to leave. They wanted the corporation to help them improve living conditions in the village. In ensuing negotiations, cultures collided as corporate leaders met with village leaders—but a relationship emerged. "We are friends forever," said a satisfied leader of the protesters.[2]

Closer to home, the gradual evolution of gay and lesbian publics from nontraditional to increasingly traditional publics was illustrated by President Barack Obama's 2010 directive mandating that U.S. hospitals, at a patient's request, remove restrictions on visits from gay and lesbian partners. In the words of the Associated Press, "Obama's move to grant same-sex partners full visitation rights . . . is the latest example of his making concessions to liberals without getting too far ahead of public opinion."[3]

In corporate America, United Airlines, Saturn automobiles, and the San Diego Padres baseball team are among organizations that openly market to gay and lesbian consumers. Other organizations, such as the Walt Disney Company, have extended insurance benefits to the life partners of gay and lesbian employees.[4] But, as the international Gay and Lesbian Alliance Against Defamation has noted, legal restrictions on adoption by gay parents and the prohibition of homosexuality within some religious denominations shows that the terms *traditional* and *nontraditional* are relative.[5]

Latent, Aware, and Active Publics

Public relations scholars often categorize publics as *latent, aware,* or *active.*[6] A **latent public** is a group whose values have come into contact with the values of your organization but whose members haven't yet realized it; the members of that public are not yet aware of the relationship. An **aware public** is a group whose members are aware of the intersection of their values with those of your organization but haven't organized any kind of response to the relationship. An **active public,** however, not only recognizes the relationship between itself and your organization but is also working to manage that relationship on its own terms. In Pop Goes Your Wednesday, the teenagers watching and commenting on the online video are more than just a nontraditional public; they're also an active public.

Intervening Publics

Let's say that in our Kablooie Microwave Popcorn scenario, you wisely keep your promise to the local newspaper reporter who telephoned. You call her back in 15 minutes and report that you've checked with the top five manufacturers of microwave ovens, and none are reporting problems with Kablooie popcorn. In fact, they've said that such a defect in their ovens is impossible. You give the reporter the names of the public relations officials for those manufacturers, and you e-mail her a statement from Kablooie's chief executive officer in which he denies the rumors. You even invite her to come tour your factory's quality-control department.

Why spend so much time with one reporter? You know the answer to that: because she has thousands of local readers to whom you want to send the message that Kablooie popcorn is safe. In public relations, any public that helps you send a message to another public is called an **intervening public.** In the Kablooie scenario, one of your most important publics consists of the people of Kablooie Microwave Popcorn's hometown; they're a high-priority public that you're targeting with a specific message to maintain the good relationship between Kablooie and its hometown. If the local newspaper can help you send that message, it is an intervening public.

Primary and Secondary Publics

Publics can also be divided into primary publics and secondary publics. If a public can directly affect your organization's pursuit of its values-driven goals—if it possesses resources that you must have—that public is definitely a **primary public,** a public of great importance. **Secondary publics** are also important. You want to have a good relationship with them—but their ability to affect your organization's pursuit of its goals is minimal. Because resources such as time and money are scarce, public relations practitioners spend most of their time building and managing relationships with primary publics. If resources permit, they also build and manage relationships with secondary publics.

Rea Carey, executive director of the National Gay and Lesbian Task Force, addresses a session of the Los Angeles Leadership Awards. The task force website declares, "The mission of the National Gay and Lesbian Task Force is to build the political power of the lesbian, gay, bisexual, and transgender (LGBT) community from the ground up."

(Courtesy of the National Gay and Lesbian Task Force)

In Pop Goes Your Wednesday, your company's investors are a primary public; your Statement of Values emphasizes that fact. A bad relationship with investors and the people who advise them could immediately and seriously harm the financial security of Kablooie. In this scenario, a secondary public would be sellers of microwave ovens. Because they might have to field a few questions, you might contact them—if time permits. But you wisely decide first to devote your attention to the primary publics that can influence the success of Kablooie Microwave Popcorn.

Internal and External Publics

Publics are either **internal publics** or **external publics;** that is, either they're inside your organization or outside it. Kablooie's employees are an internal public—as well as a primary public. You'd be smart to inform them of the rumors so that they're not surprised by reports in the news media or by inquisitive friends and neighbors. External publics would include investment analysts, news media, the Boy Scouts, and the online teenagers.

Sometimes, however, the line between internal and external isn't clearly drawn. For example, the alumni of your college or university technically are an external public; they're no longer enrolled, and most have probably moved away. But many of them don't *feel* external—to their dying day, they will be Jayhawks or Tarheels or Longhorns or Terrapins or whatever mascot brings a tear of pride to their eyes. Smart public relations practitioners identify such feelings and, when appropriate, treat such a public as a member of the organization's family. Although the Kablooie Microwave Popcorn Company is a new organization, imagine it 30 years from now. Will its loyal retired employees feel like an internal or an external public?

Domestic and International Publics

Last but not least, publics are either domestic publics or international publics. **Domestic publics** are those within your own country. But proximity doesn't necessarily mean familiarity. As we saw previously, some domestic publics can be nontraditional publics, requiring effective cross-cultural communication efforts.

International publics are those beyond your country's borders. Increasingly, public relations practitioners are dealing with international publics. For example, suppose that the factory that supplies the packages for Kablooie popcorn is in Mexico.

A variety of cross-cultural considerations now confront you. Do you speak Spanish? Does the factory manager there speak English? If your crisis has occurred on May 5 or September 16, will the factory manager answer a telephone call to his or her office? Probably not: Those days are national holidays in Mexico.

The lines between domestic and international publics also can blur. Perhaps Kablooie has plans for international distribution using a company based in the United States but with worldwide operations. Certainly consumers of the popcorn would include both domestic and international publics.

QUICKBREAK 4.1

I'll Scratch Your Back (Social Exchange Theory)

Earlier in this chapter, we noted that resource dependency theory provides an explanation for why organizations form relationships with publics: Those publics have resources the organization needs to achieve its goals.

So far, so good. But resource dependency theory is a one-way street: It focuses on one side of a relationship, describing an organization's reliance on resources held by others. Why should those resource-holding publics agree to relationships with the organization? What's in it for them?

We'll answer this question more fully in Chapter 7 in our discussion of "components of relationships." But, for now, **social exchange theory** helps provide a preliminary answer. If resource dependency theory explains our need for relationships, social exchange theory explains why the publics on the other end of those relationships may agree to work with us.

As its name suggests, social exchange theory holds that an exchange of resources occurs in successful relationships: Each party in the relationship gets something that it wants or needs. And as long as both parties believe that the benefits of the relationship outweigh the costs, the relationship continues. On the positive side, we now can improve relationships by understanding how they work. On the negative side, we now have to wonder if key publics may be on the lookout for a better cost–benefit relationship.

"According to social exchange theory, then, unless our expectations are met or exceeded, we will select other viable alternatives if they are available," say public relations scholars John Ledingham and Stephen Bruning.[7]

The two-way symmetrical model of public relations embraces both resource dependency theory and social exchange theory: It acknowledges that organizations need relationships and that win–win relationships are the most productive and successful.

You've probably heard the crude expression "You scratch my back, and I'll scratch yours." If you understand that, you've begun to understand social exchange theory. ■

WHAT DO WE NEED TO KNOW ABOUT EACH PUBLIC?

No two publics are the same. And yet the kinds of information we need to gather about each public are remarkably similar. To manage a productive, values-driven relationship with a public, we must be able to answer seven questions about it:

1. *How much can the public influence our organization's ability to achieve our goals?* How dependent is our organization on the resources controlled by this public? In other words, is the public a primary public or a secondary public? As much as public relations practitioners would like to have positive, well-maintained relationships with every public, that ideal is simply too impractical;

it would stretch their resources too thin. Public relations practitioners must focus most of their attention and efforts on the relationships that spell the difference between success and failure for their organizations.

2. *What is the public's stake, or value, in its relationship with our organization?* As we noted earlier, a relationship between a public and an organization is born when values intersect. What values does the public hold that have brought it into contact with your organization? For example, investors value steady increases in the price of the stock they own. Customers value getting their money's worth. Employees value, among other things, interesting work and good salaries.

Identifying the value or values a public seeks to realize in its relationship with your organization is one of the most important things you can do in public relations. It allows you to explore the possibility of a relationship in which both sides win: The public's values can be recognized and honored, and your organization can achieve its goal for the relationship. That's the heart of values-driven public relations.

3. *Who are the opinion leaders and decision makers for the public?* Members of a public turn to **opinion leaders** for advice and leadership. Stockholders, for example, often turn to successful investment analysts for advice. Employees may turn to union leaders or trusted supervisors. If we can identify the opinion leaders of a public, perhaps we can build a relationship with them that will strengthen our relationship with the entire public.

Not every public has well-defined, easily identifiable opinion leaders, however. For example, in the scenario that opens this chapter, who are the opinion leaders for the millions of teenagers watching the viral video? That particular public is so large that we might be wise to divide it into smaller publics—based on geography or on the particular websites the teenagers frequent—and look for opinion leaders of those smaller groups.

Decision makers are people who have the authority to dictate actions and establish policies for publics. Some publics have easily identifiable decision makers. For example, decision makers for news media are the editors, publishers, directors, and producers who oversee the content of newspapers, magazines, radio programs, television programs, or websites. The decision maker of a local environmental group probably would be the group's president or board of directors—though any important decision might involve a vote among members. Decision makers can be determined by the goal your organization is trying to achieve. For example, when a company wants to build a new factory, one set of decision makers from which it needs approval may be a local zoning board.

Some publics, however, don't have easily identifiable decision makers. Latent publics or aware publics (as opposed to active publics) can be only loosely organized at best. For example, suppose your organization wants to improve its relationship with local alternative rock musicians. Who are the decision makers for that diverse group? Perhaps the best we can do is to point to opinion leaders for our targeted public.

Even within a single, well-defined public, opinion leaders and decision makers can vary, depending on the issue. For example, a local taxpayers group might have one opinion leader for issues involving sales taxes but a different opinion leader for property tax issues. And on simple matters such as scheduling meetings, the president of the group may be the decision maker. But on more important decisions, such as organizing a protest at City Hall, the board of directors might have to call for a vote among members.

Despite the difficulties, public relations practitioners seek to identify and to build relationships with decision makers and opinion leaders because they often have influence over publics that can be essential to an organization's success.

4. *What is the demographic profile of the public?* **Demographic information** is provable data about who a public is. For example, besides telling us how many members a public has, a demographic profile of a public might include information about age, sex, income, education, and number of children per family. For each of these characteristics, we would probably want medians and ranges. For example, we probably would like to know the median age of an important public (the age that represents a halfway point, with half the public younger and half the public older than the median age). The range of ages would specify the age of the youngest member of the public as well as the age of its oldest member. Demographic information can help us understand who a public is, how important that public might be to our organization, and what its values might be.

In our Kablooie Microwave Popcorn scenario, we might consider grocery-store chains that carry our product as a public. Although demographic characteristics such as age and gender might not influence our communications with that large public, we certainly might rank the members of that public by how much Kablooie Microwave Popcorn each company purchases for resale. That information could help us subdivide our grocery-store chain public into smaller publics and provide direction on which chains we might choose to contact first.

5. *What is the psychographic profile of the public?* **Psychographic information** is data about what members of a public think, believe, feel, and value. For example, are they politically liberal, moderate, or conservative? Are they religious? Agnostic? Atheistic? Do they like sophisticated technology or fear it—or, perhaps, are they indifferent to it? Psychographic information can be harder to collect and measure than demographic information, but it's no less important. Like demographic information, a psychographic profile can help us understand who a public is and what its values might be.

6. *What is the public's opinion of our organization?* Any television sitcom about high school students eventually has a scene in which one student wants to date another and is desperately trying to find out that person's opinion of him or her. It's the same in public relations, though perhaps a little less stressful. A public's opinion of our organization is one of the foundations of our relationship. That opinion tells us whether we approach the relationship as friends, unknowns, or enemies. It would be an embarrassing waste of resources, for example, to create a communications program for a public that we think is hostile, only to discover that that public has a favorable impression of us and is puzzled by our actions.

7. *What is the public's opinion (if any) of the issue in question?* As we've noted before, sometimes a particular issue creates a relationship between an organization and a public. For example, the false stories about Kablooie Microwave Popcorn have suddenly created a relationship between Kablooie and owners of websites that host potentially libelous videos. We need to learn what the public thinks about the issue; in particular, we need to know which of the public's values are supported or threatened by the issue.

Coorientation

Coorientation is a public relations research process that can help us discover where our organization agrees and disagrees with an important public on a particular issue. Coorientation can eliminate damaging misperceptions about what each side believes. Because it seeks to identify accurate points of agreement and disagreement, scholar James Grunig says that coorientation is the "parent" of the two-way symmetrical model of public relations.[8] As you'll see, coorientation can get a little like the comedy routine in which one actor says, "I think that you think that I think . . ." In part, coorientation involves asking these four questions:

1. What is our organization's view of this issue?
2. What is the particular public's view of this issue?
3. What does our organization *think* the public's view is? (Does this agree with reality?)
4. What does the particular public *think* our organization's view is? (Does this agree with reality?)

Let's apply these four basic questions of coorientation to a portion of our Kablooie popcorn scenario:

1. Our view of the situation is that the video and rumors are provably false, but we're concerned that the rumors could influence investment analysts.
2. Quick research on our part shows that investment analysts aren't worried at all. They've encountered such rumors before, and they're laughing. They still like our stock.
3. More research shows that our organization's leaders believe investment analysts are troubled by the rumors. Our CEO has asked us to initiate an emergency webcast for the analysts. (Our management team's opinion clashes with reality.)
4. Our research has shown that investment analysts don't think our organization is worried. (That's wrong, but perhaps we can learn from it.)

To honor our CEO's request, we might want to develop a ready-if-needed plan for a webcast, but in the Kablooie case, coorientation can help keep our organization from overreacting to the crisis. Letting the analysts laugh may be our best option. Using coorientation to discover the perceptions and misperceptions of two different publics can help public relations practitioners manage the relationship effectively.

As we said in Chapter 1, the public relations process begins with research. Answering, to the best of our ability, the seven questions listed above is one of the most important parts of public relations research.

QUICK CHECK

1. In public relations, what is the definition of the word *public*? Of *stakeholder*?
2. What differences separate latent, aware, and active publics?
3. What are the differences between demographic information and psychographic information?
4. What is resource dependency theory?
5. What is coorientation?

THE TRADITIONAL PUBLICS IN PUBLIC RELATIONS

Earlier in this chapter, we introduced the term *traditional publics*—that is, publics with which organizations have long-term, ongoing relationships. As we noted, *traditional* can be a misleading word. A group that is a traditional public for one organization might be a nontraditional public for another. Many organizations, however, do have long-term relationships with well-established traditional publics, including employees, the news media, governments, investors, consumers, multicultural community groups, constituents (voters), and businesses. In the next several pages, we'll offer brief descriptions of those publics—and, because they change every day, we'll also offer sources you can consult to update your knowledge of these important publics in public relations.

EMPLOYEE PUBLICS: FAQS

1. *What resources do employees have that their organizations need?*
   Primarily commitment. Organizations with committed employees have greater innovation, reduced absenteeism, and significantly greater profits.
2. *What are the greatest challenges to building successful relationships with employees?*
   Poor communication breeds distrust and low morale. Employee publics are more diverse than ever. New communications technologies are replacing face-to-face communication.
3. *Where can I find more information on employee publics?*
   • *Communication World* magazine, published by the International Association of Business Communicators
   • U.S. Bureau of Labor Statistics, online at www.bls.gov
   • Society for Human Resource Management, online at www.shrm.org

Employees

As the old joke goes, we have good news and bad news. The good news is that employee job satisfaction is approaching record highs; the numbers, in fact, have trended upward since 2002.[9] In an analysis of several comprehensive surveys, the American Enterprise Institute reports, "Poll questions from leading survey organizations show that the vast majority of workers are highly satisfied with their jobs."[10] So what's the bad news? The economic recession that began in 2008 has caused job-security concerns to skyrocket. In just one year, from 2008 to 2009, the number of employees worried about losing their jobs jumped from 15 percent to 31 percent. The number worried about reduced hours jumped from 14 percent to 27 percent. The number that worried about reduced wages jumped from 16 percent to 32 percent. Finally, the number worried about reduction of benefits such as health care jumped from 27 percent to 46 percent.[11]

"Not only have people seen many co-workers, friends, and family members laid off, but they know they are increasingly on their own for everything from health care, to managing their career, to planning for a secure retirement," concluded a report from Towers Watson, a worldwide employee-relations agency. "This represents a profound shift for employees and employers alike."[12]

Unfortunately, there's more bad news. Even as they try to address employee concerns, 52 percent of organizational communication departments report budget cuts, and 35 percent report staff cuts. Survey research from IABC shows that a lack of internal communication is the second most common reason for employee turnover, following recession-related layoffs.[13]

Yet another sour note in the overall high levels of job satisfaction is widespread employee desire for even better supervisors. Worldwide, 64 percent of workers say that "trustworthiness" is a top trait they want in a supervisor; only 47 percent, however, say they have trustworthy managers. Slightly more than half of workers cite "sincere interest in employee well-being" as a top trait for supervisors; only 38 percent, however, say their supervisors show that interest. And slightly more than half list "commitment to developing critical talent" as a top trait; only 41 percent, however, say their supervisors demonstrate that commitment.[14]

One problem with such data is that it treats employees as a mass, undifferentiated public. New research, however, shows that an employee's age can dramatically affect workplace values and perspectives. Older employees (ages 55 and over), for example, tend to value, in order, job security, workplace safety, opportunities to use particular skills, benefits, the nature of the job, communication with senior management, and salary.

Like their older counterparts, younger employees (ages 36–55) place top priority on job security. After that, their top workplace values, in order, are benefits, salary, opportunities to use particular skills, and recognition for good work.

As the youngest employees (ages 18–35) buy homes, get married, and pay off college loans, they tend to place the highest value on salary. After salary, their top workplace values, in order, are benefits, job security, relationship with the boss, opportunities to use particular skills, and communication with senior management.

Within the group of youngest employees is the so-called Millennial Generation, born between 1981 and 1992, a group that includes many readers of this book. New research shows that even within the younger third of the American work-force, Millennials constitute a distinct group:

- Millennials say that their top values in life are, in order, being a good parent, having a successful marriage, helping others in need, owning a home, and living a "very religious" life.
- The economic recession that began in 2008 meant that Millennials were the last hired and the first fired. However, they remained more optimistic about career prospects than older co-workers.
- Only 31 percent of Millennials say their salaries are sufficient to support the lifestyles they desire. That percentage rises to 46 percent for workers ages 46–64. Again, however, the Millennials are an optimistic public: 88 percent say they anticipate sufficient earnings in the future.
- The Millennials are the least likely age group among employees to have health insurance: 61 percent compared with 82 percent for employees 30 and older.[15]

Age is not the only demographic factor that affects employee values. Sex can play a role: Female employees place more value on workplace security and relationships with supervisors, for example, than do their male counterparts.[16] Likewise, national origin can influence workplace values. Employees in Brazil and China, for example, rank the possibility of promotion as the most attractive quality of a job; German employees favor challenging work. British employees rank competitive salary as the second most attractive quality, following only the possibility of promotion; employees in China and India don't rank competitive salary among the three most attractive qualities. "These differences came through not just in nationality, age, or gender, but also in such aspects as job level, function, and career orientation," concluded a 2010 worldwide survey of employees.[17]

Why should we be so meticulous in subdividing the employee public and collecting data on each group? Employees often are the most important public in public relations. Think about it: If your organization's employees aren't on your side, the quality of your relationships with other publics might not matter.

By 2016, women will constitute 47 percent of the U.S. workforce, according to the U.S. Department of Labor. The department reports that women currently account for "51 percent of all workers in the high-paying management, professional, and related occupations."

(Courtesy of the U.S. Census Bureau, Public Information Office)

SOCIAL MEDIA APPS

Workplace Media: Facebook versus Face-to-Face

With the advent of social media, public relations practitioners have a dazzling array of interactive media they can use to build relationships with employee publics. So which media do employees prefer? Let's keep that question in mind—but, first, some statistics.

Approximately 80 percent of North American employers say they frequently use social media to communicate with their employees. Blogs are most common, followed by interactive discussion boards, podcasts, internal social networks, wikis, and Twitter.[18]

Worldwide, usage figures diminish: Only 10 percent of organizations use social media programs for employee relations, although almost a third believe that such programs could increase productivity.[19]

Measuring the effectiveness of internal social media programs remains a challenge. In North America, almost half of the organizations that have such programs don't measure their effectiveness. Another third measure only usage. Only 1 percent of organizations use surveys to measure the effectiveness of their internal social media programs.[20]

And now let's return that opening question: Which media do employees prefer? For decades, studies have shown that employees prefer to get important information about their organizations through face-to-face meetings with their supervisors.[21] A 2010 world-wide survey of business organizations showed a strong response to that preferred medium: For general business information, 12 percent of organizations included social media in their communications plans; 73 percent included staff meetings. For special business strategies related to economic downturns, 11 percent of organizations included social media; 65 percent included staff meetings.[22]

Of course, every organization and every communications situation are different, but broadly speaking, in employee relations, face-to-face beats Facebook. ∎

The News Media

As a good reporter might say, here are the facts: Old media, such as the *New York Times*, face financial uncertainty, and new media, including online news aggregators such as the *Huffington Post* and the *Drudge Report*, wonder who will report the news if the old media collapse.[23] Traditional journalists in older media acknowledge increasing concerns about staff cuts and tightening budgets.[24] Journalists in new media may be thrilled that "six in ten Americans get some news online in a typical day," but they also face the reality that "of the 4,600 [online news] sites, the top 7 percent collect 80 percent of the traffic."[25]

Additionally, "The State of the News Media: 2010," published by the Pew Project for Excellence in Journalism, identifies these emerging trends:[26]

- News media outlets increasingly are specializing in particular topics such as sports, politics, or finances. The comprehensive "all the news that's fit to print" newspaper model is declining.
- Old media, such as newspapers, excel in reporting. New media, such as blogs, excel in commentary. Successful new models will find ways to blend those strengths.
- The speed of new communications technologies and the desire to beat competitors to a story may be damaging journalism's traditional watchdog role: "What is squeezed is the supplemental reporting that would unearth more facts and context about events."
- Cutbacks in old media hurt the quality of new media, which still rely on reporters within newspapers and television for much of their content.
- As newsrooms get smaller, they rely more on information providers—such as public relations professionals.

The final two trends might hold the key to building successful relationships with journalists in both old and new media: As staff sizes diminish at older media, stress and workloads increase—as does the need for reliable information from public relations professionals. And as journalists in new media begin to do more of their own reporting, they, too, will need reliable information from public relations professionals.

Within all news media publics are important decision makers known as **gatekeepers:** editors or producers who decide which stories to include and which

NEWS MEDIA PUBLICS: FAQS

1. *What resources do news media have that organizations need?*
   Fair coverage and the willingness to consider news stories offered by public relations practitioners. The relative objectivity and credibility of the news media can provide what is called an *independent endorsement* or *third-party endorsement* of an organization's news.

2. *What is the greatest challenge to building successful relationships with news media?*
   A mutual lack of knowledge. Research shows that journalists and public relations practitioners alike value accuracy and fairness—but neither party believes the other holds those values.[27]

3. *Where can I find more information on news media publics?*
   - American Society of Newspaper Editors, online at www.asne.org
   - Poynter Institute for Media Studies, online at www.poynter.org
   - *The State of the News Media: An Annual Report on American Journalism*, the Pew Project for Excellence in Journalism, online at www.stateofthemedia.org

stories to reject. Without the consent of the gatekeepers, public relations practitioners cannot use the news media as intervening publics. Gatekeepers value news that serves the interests of their audiences. If public relations practitioners can supply that kind of audience-focused news, they should have productive relationships with the gatekeepers of the news media.

Because of the First Amendment and its guarantee of freedom of the press, news media in the United States can, with few limitations, report whatever they perceive to be news. But in emerging democracies around the world, freedom of the press is, so to speak, a hotly contested front-page issue. As new freedoms give rise to modern news media, government officials and journalists around the world are debating the limits of freedom.

In the United States, a continuing problem for the news media is the disproportionately small number of minority journalists. In the wake of violent race riots during the struggle for civil rights, the report of the Kerner Commission in 1968 blasted the U.S. news media for their lack of minority journalists. However, in 1998 the American Society of Newspaper Editors conceded that it would not reach its year 2000 goal of having the minority population of newsrooms reflect the actual minority percentages of the U.S. population.[28] ASNE's new target date is 2025.[29] Currently, diversity in the U.S. news media looks something like this:

- Approximately 13 percent of newspaper journalists are members of minority groups: 4.88 percent are black, 4.63 percent are Hispanic, 3.27 percent are Asian American, and 0.48 percent are Native American.[30]
- Approximately 22 percent of television journalists are members of minority groups: 10.1 percent are black, 8.7 percent are Hispanic, 2.3 percent are Asian American, and 0.4 percent are Native American.[31]
- Approximately 6 percent of radio journalists are members of minority groups: 3.3 percent are black, 0.7 percent are Hispanic, 1.1 percent are Native American, and 1.1 percent are Asian American.[32]

Any discussion of modern news media must include the concept of **convergence of media**—that is, a blending of media made possible by digital technology. (For more on convergence and digital technology, please see Chapter 11.) Simply put, digital technology allows journalists to move words, sounds, and images back and forth among radio, TV, newspapers, magazines, and websites.

The news media can be an aggressive public. Even before the scandal that interrupted Tiger Woods' career in 2010, the championship golfer was a center of attention for journalists.

(Courtesy of Samantha L. Quigley and the U.S. Department of Defense)

> ## VALUES STATEMENT 4.1
>
> ### PepsiCo
>
> Tracing its origins to a popular soda pop first developed in 1898, PepsiCo emerged in 1965 as a corporation that specializes in soft drinks and snack foods. Its headquarters are in Purchase, New York.
>
> > PepsiCo's overall mission is to increase the value of our shareholders' investment. We do this through sales growth, cost controls and wise investment of resources. We believe our commercial success depends upon offering quality and value to our consumers and customers; providing products that are safe, wholesome, economically efficient and environmentally sound; and providing a fair return to our investors while adhering to the highest standards of integrity.
> >
> > —"Mission Statement," PepsiCo website ■

As a consequence, members of the news media can offer their news in more than one format. Some experts predict that portable devices such as the Apple iPad will help newspapers and magazines make the final leap from paper to a solely online existence, thus blurring the distinctions among newspapers, magazines, news websites, and television stations.

Whatever their media or personal backgrounds may be, however, almost all journalists value one thing that public relations professionals can supply: information—relevant, accurate, complete, timely information.

Governments

You've probably heard that the nine most feared words in the English language are "I'm from the government, and I'm here to help." Government workers actually *can* help public relations practitioners by providing information and interpreting legislation. But they can also harm a practitioner's organization by adopting unfavorable legislation or regulations. As we note elsewhere in this book, too, a continuing issue in public relations is government licensing of public relations practitioners. That hasn't happened yet in the United States, but the debate isn't over.

Who are the members of this influential public? They range from the local chief of police to the president of the United States. Government officials exist at the city/county level, the state level, and the federal level.

THE FEDERAL GOVERNMENT   At the federal level, there were 2.8 million nonmilitary employees in 2010.[33] The U.S. Bureau of Labor Statistics expects that number to increase by 10 percent by 2018, compared with a growth rate of 11 percent for nongovernmental jobs in the United States.[34] Federal employees range from the 535 members of Congress to the 728,820 who work for the postal service and the 3,871 who work in federal libraries.[35]

The federal Office of Personnel Management reports that 68.5 percent of federal employees say they are satisfied with their jobs. Employees with the highest levels of satisfaction work in the Nuclear Regulatory Commission; those with the lowest levels work in the Department of Transportation. Among the highest areas of job satisfaction are the match of job skills to organizational mission and the promotion of teamwork. Among the lowest areas of job satisfaction are awards/acknowledgment and family friendliness.[36]

By some measures, the federal workforce is more diverse than the private-sector workforce: 17.9 percent of federal employees are black, compared with 10 percent in the private workforce; 7.9 percent are Hispanic, compared with 13.2 percent in the private workforce; 5.4 percent are of Asian/Pacific Islands origins, compared with 4.3 percent in the private workforce; 1.9 percent are Native Americans, compared with 0.7 percent in the private workforce; and 44.2 percent are women, compared with 45.6 percent in the private workforce.[37]

Most visible among these employees, of course, are the members of Congress, each of whom has his or her own values and agendas. An excellent source for studying each member of Congress as well as the top issues among each member's constituency is *The Almanac of American Politics,* which offers state-by-state and district-by-district analyses of senators, representatives, voters, and issues.

Lobbyists who work with federal employees, particularly with elected officials, have at least one bit of advice for public relations practitioners: Be well prepared and work fast.[38] Although 60 percent of federal employees believe their workload is reasonable, only 51.2 percent believe they have the necessary resources to get the job done.[39]

STATE AND LOCAL GOVERNMENTS   At last measurement, there were 5.2 million state government employees and 14.2 million local government employees in the United

GOVERNMENT PUBLICS: FAQS

1. *What resources do governments have that organizations need?*
   Fair, nonrestrictive regulations, protection from unfair competition in the marketplace, and interpretations or explanations of existing laws.
2. *What is the greatest challenge to building successful relationships with government publics?*
   The slow growth of the U.S. federal governments is increasing the workload of federal employees and transferring new and sometimes unfamiliar tasks to state and local government employees.
3. *Where can I find more information on government publics?*
   - *The Almanac of American Politics,* published by the National Journal Group
   - *Governing: The Magazine of States and Localities,* published by Congressional Quarterly, Inc., online at www.governing.com
   - FedStats, online at www.fedstats.gov

States—a total of 19.4 million.[40] The U.S. Bureau of Labor Statistics expects that number to increase to 21.9 million by 2014.[41] In this swirl of numbers, public relations practitioners should appreciate an important trend: State and local governments are growing at a faster rate than the federal government—in many cases taking on functions that formerly existed at the federal level.

Nationwide, 54.6 percent of full-time state and local government employees are men; 45.4 percent are women; 68.1 percent are white; 18.9 percent are black; and 9.1 percent are Hispanic.[42] Diversity figures for individual state governments generally can be found on state government websites, often in annual reports to the governor and state citizens. The majority of state and local government employees are teachers, police officers, or government administrators.[43]

Research conducted by the Pew Center for the States has found that salary and benefits are among "the most important predictors of employee retention." Benefits that state government employees rated most highly included "long-term care insurance, same-sex domestic partner benefits, and family leave." State employees also expressed preferences for programs that showed concern for their families, including "telecommuting, compressed work weeks, and flexible work hours."[44]

Elected officials at all levels of government want to serve their constituents well and be reelected. Public relations practitioners who can help government officials pursue those values will find them to be willing partners in building productive relationships.

QUICK CHECK

1. What do employees value in their jobs?
2. In media relations, what is an independent endorsement?
3. What does the comparatively rapid growth of state and local government workforces mean for public relations practitioners?
4. For public relations practitioners, what essential resources do employee, media, and government publics possess?

Investors

Companies that sell stock have relationships with investors. The investor public encompasses individual stockholders—and much more:

- Financial analysts study the stock markets to advise investors.
- Financial news media include the *Wall Street Journal, Business Week* magazine, the *Mad Money* television show, and websites such as Value Line, at www.valueline.com.
- **Mutual fund managers** supervise what might be called investment clubs. For a fee, mutual fund managers invest a member's contributions (usually monthly payments) into a diverse collection of stocks and bonds. The popularity of mutual funds has soared in the past 30 years.

QUICKBREAK 4.2

Your Tax Dollars at Work

As you're reading this sentence, the federal government of the United States is collecting information about you, your friends, your family—and millions of other Americans.

Sounds scary, right? But that storehouse of information can be incredibly useful to public relations practitioners. Even better, much of the information is online and can be easily accessed at FedStats (www.fedstats.gov).

Need the ethnic makeup of your county? Try the Bureau of the Census. You can reach it through FedStats.

Need employment projections for the coming decades? Try the Bureau of Labor Statistics. You can reach it through FedStats.

Need data on farmers? Try the National Agricultural Statistics Service. On older Americans? Try the Administration on Aging. On prisoners? Try the Federal Bureau of Prisons.

FedStats can connect you to dozens of federal agencies that gather information on the publics that make up public relations. As a taxpayer, you're footing the bill for all those studies, so get your money's worth: Bookmark FedStats for your Web browser. ■

- So-called **institutional investors** are large companies or institutions that generally buy huge amounts of stock. The California Public Employees Retirement System, for example, is the largest public pension plan in the United States. It represents more than 1.6 million state and local government employees in California and has assets of approximately $200 billion.
- Employee investors are employees of companies, such as Microsoft, that reward employees with stock in the companies they work for.

If you've studied stock markets at all in recent years, you might guess—correctly—that U.S. investors feel as if they've been riding a roller coaster. But studies show that they're not leaving the amusement park. Approximately 44 percent of U.S. households owned mutual funds in 2009, up from 33 percent in 2003.[45]

Despite their willingness to stay in the market, U.S. investors began the second decade of the 21st century as a fairly pessimistic public. In 2009, for example, the Gallup Index of Investor Optimism hit its lowest levels since that survey began in 1996.[46] Few investors, however, have abandoned the stock markets. "American investors are a resilient bunch," said investment analyst Dan Greenshields in 2010. "Poor market performance isn't stopping them from continuing to invest and, in some cases, investing more than last year."[47]

INVESTOR PUBLICS: FAQS

1. *What resources do investor publics have that organizations need?*
   Investors purchase stocks. Financial analysts, mutual fund managers, and journalists evaluate stocks and make recommendations to investors.

2. *What are the greatest challenges to building successful relationships with investor publics?*
   Investor publics need information and reassurance as stock markets become increasingly volatile. The growing diversity of investors means that old ways of communicating may not be effective.

3. *Where can I find more information on investor publics?*
   - Securities and Exchange Commission, online at www.sec.gov
   - New York Stock Exchange, online at www.nyse.com
   - National Investor Relations Institute, online at www.niri.org
   - The *Wall Street Journal*, published Monday through Friday by Dow Jones and Company, Inc.

Who are these resilient investors? Table 4.1 lists data on the investing public.[48]

What about would-be investors, primarily the new college-grad group that many readers of this book hope to enter soon? For the age 35 and younger group, income is the key: Only 7 percent of households in that age group with an annual income of $25,000 or less are investors; 24 percent in the $25,000 to $49,999 range; 48 percent in the $50,000 to $99,999 range; and 72 percent of the $100,000 or more range.[49] Investors ages 21–39 tend to seek investment advice from financial websites and blogs rather than from personal financial planners.[50] Some 27 percent of that age group consider themselves to be aggressive, high-risk investors, compared with a national average of 22 percent.[51]

TABLE 4.1

U.S. INVESTORS: WHO THEY ARE

- 71 percent of U.S. adults own stock: 73 percent of Asian-American adults, 72 percent of white adults, 70 percent of Hispanic adults, and 66 percent of black adults.
- 67 percent are college graduates.
- 56 percent are married.
- 70-plus percent of households with an annual income of $100,000 or more are investors; fewer than 20 percent of households with an annual income of less than $25,000 are investors.
- 47 percent are willing to accept some risk in pursuit of higher returns.
- Investors of all ages cite retirement as their top motivation, followed by reducing taxes, preparing for emergencies, and saving for education.

Although they are diverse, investors can be stable publics for public relations: The majority consider themselves to be long-term investors preparing for retirement. Most are decreasing their contacts with personal investment advisers and are conducting research on their own—a good reason for organizations to increase their investor relations efforts.[52] Above all, investors value profitability and stability.

Consumers/Customers

As Americans began the second decade of the 21st century, they faced the worst domestic economy since the Great Depression.[53] Economists might have debated the causes, but they agreed on the solution: consumer spending. "Consumer spending is considered key to recovery because it accounts for roughly two-thirds of economic activity," reported Reuters News Service in 2010.[54] In the United States, consumers spend twice as much as government and business combined.[55] "Few doubt the importance of consumer spending to the U.S. economy and its multiplier effect on the global economy," said investment analyst Meredith Whitney.[56]

Who are these big spenders, and what are they spending all that money on? Some facts:

- The average U.S. household has a before-tax income of $63,563. Its annual expenditures total $50,486. Where does the money go? Table 4.2 gives a partial breakdown.[57]
- The biggest spenders are people aged 45 to 54. Households in which the main earner falls into that age bracket spend $61,179 a year. By way of comparison, households in which the main earner is under 25 spend only $29,325 a year. For age 65 and older, the total is $36,844.
- Annual consumer spending also varies by ethnicity. Black households annually spend $36,685; Hispanic and Latino households (not including blacks and

TABLE 4.2

HOW U.S. HOUSEHOLDS SPEND THEIR AFTER-TAX INCOME

Food	$ 6,433
Housing	$17,109
Apparel and services	$ 1,801
Transportation	$ 8,604
Health care	$ 2,976
Entertainment	$ 2,835
Personal care products and services	$ 616
Alcoholic beverages	$ 444
Tobacco products and smoking supplies	$ 317

CONSUMER/CUSTOMER PUBLICS: FAQS

1. *What resources do consumer/customer publics have that organizations need?*
   Loyalty: a willingness to purchase and repurchase an organization's products. Consumers also possess the resource of publicity: Word-of-mouth cheers or jeers are a powerful force in the marketplace.

2. *What are the greatest challenges to building successful relationships with consumer/customer publics?*
   Fifty percent of shoppers report that customer service is "often dreadful." Almost one-third of dissatisfied shoppers tell others.[58] The diversity of consumers is increasing. Also, public relations must learn to coordinate its tactics with the tactics of marketing, and vice versa (see Chapter 13).

3. *Where can I find more information on consumer/customer publics?*
   - *Business Week* magazine, published by Bloomberg L.P., online at www.businessweek.com
   - U.S. Department of Commerce, online at www.commerce.gov
   - U.S. Bureau of Labor Statistics, online at www.bls.gov

whites) spend $43,052; households of Asian ancestry spend $55,430; and whites (including Pacific Islanders, Native Americans, and Native Alaskans) spend $53,773.

- Women account for approximately 83 percent of U.S. consumer spending.[59]
- Generation Y (people born between 1980 and 1994) contributes about 4 percent of annual consumer spending in the U.S. economy. According to PricewaterhouseCoopers, an international accounting and auditing agency, "Gen Y is accustomed to instant gratification and demands the latest and greatest gadgetry; a tech lifestyle is a need, not a want."[60]

Online shopping, also known as **e-commerce** (for electronic commerce), continues to soar in popularity: In 2009, total U.S. e-commerce spending jumped to $134.9 billion, an increase of 23 percent compared with 2005 e-commerce figures. Even with that dizzying total, however, e-commerce represented only 3.7 percent of total U.S. sales in 2009.[61] Thirty-four of the 40 most successful e-commerce retailers also have traditional stores, with Amazon.com being a notable exception.[62] Research by online-payment company PayPal shows that high shipping costs are the top reason online shoppers log off before making a purchase. "Sweetening the deal with free shipping, coupons, and special discounts is also a great way to encourage online shoppers to complete their purchases," said Eddie Davis, a PayPal executive.[63]

Regardless of where and how customers do their shopping, what do they value? Any survey gives you the same answer: quality at a fair price. Customers want to get what they paid for—and more.

QUICKBREAK 4.3

The Customer Is Always Right?

The reigning master of bizarre customer inquiries is the mysterious Ted L. Nancy (who just might be comedian Jerry Seinfeld).[64] Posing as a clueless customer, Nancy bedevils corporate America with inane letters that usually draw painfully serious responses.[65]

To wit: Nancy wrote to San Francisco's Pan Pacific Hotel, asking if it could accommodate his physical abnormality: "I have three legs. . . . I'll need an ottoman I can place next to the bed when I sleep."

The hotel wrote back, politely noting that "our rooms do have ottoman chairs in them."

Nancy also wrote to the Nordstrom department store chain, asking if he might purchase a store mannequin that resembled his dead neighbor.

"Dear Mr. Nancy," replied a Nordstrom representative. "Yours is one of the most interesting requests I have ever received. . . . "

Then Nancy wrote to Hanes about its underwear. . . .

Why do companies reply to such off-the-wall requests? Besides good manners, it's good business: A landmark customer-service study shows that most businesses could increase their profits 25–100 percent simply by retaining just 5 percent more of their current customers every year.[66]

Nancy has published three collections of his letters: *Letters from a Nut, More Letters from a Nut,* and *Extra Nutty! Even More Letters from a Nut.* ■

Multicultural Communities

Public relations professionals must know the so-called movers and shakers in every community in which their organizations do business. Failing to learn who wields power in a community can have catastrophic results, as the developer of a proposed landfill site once discovered:

> One private developer announced a project that soon drew surprisingly intense environmental opposition from local residents. Only months after announcing the planned facility did the developer learn that the town was home to Ralph Nader.[67]

Besides consumer activist and former presidential candidate Ralph Nader, who are the influential publics within our diverse communities? Professor Jerry Hendrix of American University offers a useful breakdown, which appears in Table 4.3.[68] Some of the worst, most expensive public relations fiascoes in recent memory have involved companies perceived as being insensitive to racial or ethnic groups—even, sometimes, to their own employees. A decade ago, the Coca-Cola company settled a racial-discrimination lawsuit for $192.5 million.[69] The class-action litigation

Booklet and Brochures

With the assistance of Valencia, Pérez & Echeveste Public Relations, the California Department of Health Services prepares these recipes and good nutrition tips for Hispanic consumers.

(Courtesy of Valencia, Pérez & Echeveste Public Relations)

TABLE 4.3

INFLUENTIAL COMMUNITY PUBLICS

COMMUNITY MEDIA

Mass media (such as newspapers and television stations)

Specialized media (such as entertainment tabloids)

Online social networks

COMMUNITY LEADERS

Public officials

Educators

Religious leaders

Professionals (such as doctors and lawyers)

Executives

Bankers

Union leaders

Ethnic leaders

Neighborhood leaders

COMMUNITY ORGANIZATIONS

Civic

Business

Service

Social

Cultural

Religious

Youth

Political

Special-interest groups

Other groups

involved approximately 2,200 black employees who alleged receiving discriminatory treatment at the hands of the world's largest soft-drink company. "This settlement sets a new standard for corporate diversity," said Cyrus Mehri, an attorney for the employees. "In short, the 'World of Coke' will be going through a 'World of Change.'[70] Douglas Daft, Coca-Cola's CEO at the time, acknowledged, "Sometimes things happen in an unintentional fashion. And I've made it very clear that can't happen anymore."[71]

Coca-Cola did change. One of the company's values now is "Diversity," which it strives to reach by being "as inclusive as our brands."[72] In a remarkable turnaround, Coca-Cola has become a repeated member of *Black Enterprise* magazine's "40 Best Companies for Diversity." In acknowledging the company's inclusion in the 2009 *Black Enterprise* list, an official statement on Coca-Cola's website linked internal diversity to improved community relations: "We're proud to be the world's largest beverage company. But it's truly an honor to be recognized for our efforts in improving the quality of life in the communities we serve."[73]

More than ever before, public relations practitioners must foster positive relationships with racial and ethnic publics within their organizations and communities. Otherwise, organizations not only may separate themselves from community goodwill, but they also risk separating themselves from potential employees, customers, investors, donors, and other publics that they depend on to survive. Although the racial/ethnic makeup of every community is different, Table 4.4 shows the U.S. Census Bureau's projections for U.S. population totals and percentages for the year 2020.[74]

TABLE 4.4

Projected U.S. Population Totals and Percentages for the Year 2020

TOTAL POPULATION	335.8 million Female: 170.7 million Male: 165.1 million
WHITE POPULATION	260.6 million (77.6 percent) Female: 131.6 million Male: 129.0 million
BLACK POPULATION	45.3 million (13.5 percent) Female: 23.6 million Male: 21.7 million
HISPANIC AMERICAN POPULATION	59.7 million (17.8 percent) Female: 29.4 million Male: 30.3 million
ASIAN AMERICAN	17.9 million (5.4 percent) Female: 9.5 million Male: 8.4 million
OTHER POPULATIONS, INCLUDING NATIVE AMERICAN	11.8 million (3.5 percent) Female: 5.9 million Male: 5.9 million

MULTICULTURAL COMMUNITY PUBLICS: FAQS

1. *What resources do multicultural community publics have that organizations need?*
   The willingness to accept an organization as a community member—to be its employees, supporters, customers, and friends.
2. *What is the greatest challenge to building successful relationships with multicultural community publics?*
   The sheer number of such groups. Organizations' resources are limited, and they usually cannot build relationships with every public within a community. Organizations must determine which relationships in a community are most essential to the fulfillment of their values.
3. *Where can I find more information on multicultural community publics?*
   - U.S. Bureau of the Census, online at www.census.gov
   - U.S. Citizenship and Immigration Services, online at www.uscis.gov
   - The *Chronicle of Philanthropy,* published weekly, online at www.philanthropy.com

As noted in Chapter 16, immigration is also changing communities in the United States. The foreign-born percentage of the U.S. population recently reached its highest level since 1930: Of today's residents, 38.1 million were born citizens of other nations—approximately 12 percent. Approximately 37 percent reside in the western United States, followed by 29 percent in the South and 22 percent in the Northeast.[75] But even in small communities in southwestern Kansas, the meatpacking industry attracts immigrants from Vietnam and Somalia.

According to the U.S. Census Bureau, 53.6 percent of today's immigrants came from Latin America, 26.8 percent from Asia, and 13.1 percent from Europe. More than one third arrived in the United States during the 1990s. Though 67 percent have at least a high school education, immigrants are more likely than nonimmigrants to be unemployed and living in poverty.[76]

In short, communities consist of diverse publics, and diversity within each public is probably increasing.

Constituents (Voters)

Not every organization considers voters to be a traditional public, although many organizations try to influence the legislative process by building relationships with eligible voters. But for public relations practitioners employed by democratically elected governments, voters often are the most important public of all.

In a sense, this group includes every citizen of a nation who is of voting age—a huge and diverse public. In countries where voting is compulsory, such as Costa Rica, a description of this public literally would be a description of the country's adult population. In the United States, however, a description of voters is somewhat easier because not every eligible citizen votes. In the 2008 presidential election, 131 million people—64 percent of those eligible—voted, approximately the same percentage as in the 2004 U.S. presidential election.[77] In voter turnout, the United States ranks 139th among the world's 170-plus democracies.[78]

CONSTITUENT/VOTER PUBLICS: FAQS

1. *What resources do constituent/voter publics have that organizations need?*
   Votes and word-of-mouth endorsements. Constituents who approve of their elected representatives can influence the opinions of other constituents.
2. *What is the greatest challenge to building successful relationships with constituent/voter publics?*
   Voter apathy, which is particularly high among voters aged 18 to 24.
3. *Where can I find more information on constituent/voter publics?*
   - The League of Women Voters, online at www.lwv.org
   - *The Almanac of American Politics,* published by the National Journal Group
   - International Institute for Democracy and Electoral Assistance, online at www.idea.int

What do we know about citizens in the United States who *do* vote? According to the U.S. Census Bureau, the most typical voter is a retired, married, female homeowner, 65 or older, with a college degree and an above-average household income. Facts from the bureau's analysis of the 2008 presidential election paint this portrait of American voters:[79]

- *Marriage counts*: 70.2 percent of married citizens voted compared with 53.5 percent of single citizens.
- *Education rules:* 77 percent of citizens with a college degree vote compared with 38.1 percent of high-school dropouts.
- *Money talks*: 78.4 percent of citizens with a household income of $100,000–$150,000 vote compared with 56.3 percent of citizens with a household income of $20,000–$30,000.

Perhaps the single greatest indicator of voting in the United States is age: Voters ages 65–74 are most likely to vote (72.4) percent. Least likely are voters ages 18–24 (48.5 percent)—the age group of many readers of this book.[80] In 2008, 32 percent of young voters (ages 18–29) identified themselves as liberal, and 26 percent identified themselves as conservative. Older voters, however, "were much more likely to call themselves conservative."[81]

Race can also be a predictor of voter turnout. In the 2008 presidential election, which was won by Barack Obama, an African American, 64.7 percent of black voters went to the polls; 64.4 percent of white voters; 49.9 percent of Hispanic voters; and 47.6 percent of Asian-American voters. As for gender at the ballot box, women voted more than men by a margin of 65.7 percent to 61.5 percent.[82]

Registered voters who don't vote offer these Top 10 reasons for not going to the polls (if you're a David Letterman fan, imagine a Top 10 Countdown):

10. Inconvenient polling place.
9. Registration problems.
8. Forgot.
7. Don't know.
6. Did not like candidates or issues.
5. Other reason.
4. Out of town.
3. Not interested.
2. Illness or disability.
1. Too busy, conflicting schedule.[83]

Businesses

Organizations have relationships with a variety of businesses. Why? Because those businesses have resources that the organizations need if they are to fulfill their values-driven goals. Such relationships involve **business-to-business communication**, often called **B2B** communication. For example, an organization may have relationships with vendor businesses that supply materials to the organization; distributor businesses that help move the organization's products to consumers; customer businesses that purchase the organization's products; and industry partners, which are in the same type of business and work with the organization to help influence legislative and regulation processes at different levels of government. That same organization has sometimes-uneasy relationships with direct competitors. With this wide-ranging focus on relationship building, the management of B2B communications is increasingly known as **partner relationship management (PRM)**.

B2B communication is big business, and it's growing. The U.S. Census Bureau reports that business-to-business transactions constitute 93 percent of U.S. e-commerce. In other words, the billions of dollars spent annually by individual online shoppers—at Amazon and iTunes, for example—still amounts to only 7 percent of e-commerce activity.[84] But partner relationship management is more than sales: As noted earlier, companies have partnerships with suppliers, distributors, and others. Recent studies by Forrester Research show that 28 percent of companies believe that PRM efforts are essential to their success. Among companies that specialize in B2B transactions, that number jumps to 45 percent.[85]

"As organizations mature, they want to enable their partners to check availability online, get smarter at pricing and deal negotiations, and better match supply and demand . . . ," said Caroline Kohout of software giant SAP. "They also want to orchestrate their business networks to be more responsive and act in synchronization."[86]

BUSINESS PUBLICS: FAQS

1. *What resources do business publics have that organizations need?*
   Vendor businesses have supplies and loyalty. Customer businesses have the willingness to purchase and repurchase an organization's products. Direct competitors have the resource of competing fairly.
2. *What are the greatest challenges to building successful relationships with business publics?*
   One surprising challenge may be the reputation of B2B communications. *Marketing* magazine reports that B2B is thought to be "the least glamorous part" of public relations.[87] Also, the sheer number of business relationships an organization has poses a challenge to relationship building.
3. *Where can I find more information on business publics?*
   - *BtoB* magazine, published monthly by Crain Communications, Inc., online at www.btobonline.com
   - *Sales & Marketing Management* magazine, published monthly by Nielsen Business, Inc., online at www.salesandmarketing.com
   - *Business Week* magazine, published weekly by Bloomberg L. P., online at www.businessweek.com

QUICK CHECK

1. What is the demographic profile of people in the United States who invest in the stock markets?
2. What age group in the United States spends the most money on consumer goods and services?
3. What does *B2B* mean? *PRM*?
4. For public relations practitioners, what important resources are possessed by investor, consumer, community, constituent, and business publics?

SUMMARY

A public is a group of people who share a common value or values in a particular situation. In other words, publics unite around their values. For employees, the core value may be job security. For an environmental group, maybe it's clean air and water. An organization forms relationships with publics that have the resources it needs to fulfill its values-driven goals. However, when the values of a public intersect with the values of an organization, a relationship—whether the organization wants it or not—is born. Resource dependency theory and social exchange theory can help explain the why and the how of relationships in public relations.

Traditional publics may vary among different organizations. For many organizations, however, long-established traditional publics include employees, the news media, governments, investors, consumers, multicultural community groups, constituents (voters), and businesses.

Publics can and do change constantly, but the questions a practitioner must answer about each public remain the same. Whether a public is latent, aware, or active, if it has the power to influence an organization, a practitioner must answer these questions:

- How much can the public influence our organization's ability to achieve our goals?
- What is the public's stake, or value, in its relationship with our organization?
- Who are the opinion leaders and decision makers for the public?
- What is the demographic profile of the public?
- What is the psychographic profile of the public?
- What is the public's opinion of our organization?
- What is the public's opinion (if any) of the issue in question?

Not until those questions are answered can public relations practitioners strive to build the relationships that will help an organization achieve its values-driven goals.

DISCUSSION QUESTIONS

1. Your authors state that the most important publics in public relations are employee publics. Do you agree? Why or why not?
2. Can you think of examples of nontraditional publics that have become—or are becoming—traditional publics?

3. Why do public relations practitioners try to identify opinion leaders and decision makers for each public?
4. Why is it important to identify a public's stake in an issue of importance to a practitioner's organization?
5. In our opening scenario, how would you classify the local Boy Scout troops? Are they a primary or a secondary public?

MEMO FROM THE FIELD

DAVID A. NARSAVAGE
Consultant; The Friday Group
Washington, D.C.

A journalism school graduate and former print journalist, Dave Narsavage has been a professional communicator for more than 35 years. Once an Army combat correspondent in Vietnam, he's held communications positions in the U.S. Senate, with a national political party, and as director of employee communications for a 26,000-employee corporation. He now consults for The Friday Group, a Washington, D.C.–based public relations agency.

It's all about publics, and messages, and desired effects. And the wheelie video. You've got to figure out who you *want* to see the wheelie video. And who you don't.

My teenaged son was lobbying me for a motorcycle. Not *my* kind of motorcycle: low-slung, no plastic in sight, a throaty "potato potato potato" idle note. Now that's a bike. No, his rocket would be clad in fiberglass, sound like a crazed bee, and hit warp speed in a nanosecond.

"Forget it," I told him. "It's a fatal attraction."

But since we were already *in* a motorcycle showroom during this discussion, I agreed there was no harm in looking. We started chatting with a young salesman, making it clear that my son had a fantasy—and I had a fear of him flying.

The salesman smiled and nodded. Knowingly, I thought. "Dudes!" he blurted suddenly, as if just hit with a truly huge idea. "You've *got* to see this video!" And he took us to a monitor, where we watched young men of little brain race my son's fantasy ride on rear wheel only, front wheel only, and no wheels only. "Isn't that *awesome*!?"

My son, no fool, looked at me and smiled. He knew: *This* was a man who had never read a word from Professors Guth and Marsh.

Know the room. Whether you call them a public or a target audience, know who those people are. Know what will move them: the hot buttons that can either bring them closer to your point of view or push them out of sight.

Remember that they'll have some selfish, self-interest issues, because that's how we humans are. But mostly it will come down to emotions.

One of my relics from a previous life as a U.S. senator's press secretary is a treasured copy of a "Shoe" comic strip, personally signed by the much-missed Jeff MacNelly.

(continued)

It shows the editor bird (just go with me on this if you're not a "Shoe" fan) holding up a sheet of paper and asking the professor bird, "Where should I file this urgent press release from Senator Belfry?" The professor replies, "File it under 'W'—for 'Who cares?' "

Who *cares* about your message? Who *doesn't* care now, and what will it take to rouse them? Because no matter how much your client/employer pays you, no matter how much you buy into his or her fervor and embrace that gospel, if your key audiences don't *care,* you're wasting good professional effort.

Public and *relations.* Of the two, I'd worry about relations. That's where the power is, where the blood, and character, and emotions are. Where the *caring* is. As you'll read in this textbook, the value of our profession comes in the building and nurturing of relationships.

You build those relationships by treating audiences with respect and by communicating with them in the same clear and direct way you would in a letter to a friend. Wait, you don't know what a letter is. In a *text* to a friend, OK? But with capitalization and punctuation.

Do the world a favor. Don't let clients insist on corporate-speak, and puffery, and inflated verbiage whose message seems to be "If you can't understand what I'm saying, then I must be *really* smart."

Have a *conversation* with your audiences. Your authors call it two-way symmetrical public relations. We call that communicating. Anything else is what my father used to call—in mixed company—a bunch of padookey dust.

I love these guys, Guth and Marsh. Not just because they gave me a podium, and as a presentation-trainer friend says, *seize* the podium as your own space, but because they share my concern for employees. Talk about an important audience. These are people who will have a long-term influence on putting meaning behind your message and people who represent a built-in grassroots network for your client.

But more than that, it's simply a basic consideration, a courtesy. People shouldn't have to read the paper or watch the news to know about changes in their work home. Bring them into the communications tent. If that helps you achieve your "values-driven goals," peachy. And even if it doesn't, you'll feel better about looking in the mirror.

I'm getting a "cut" signal from the author guys. Wrap it up.

In time, you *will* need to do some honest work. So before you fold up your "College" sweatshirt, pack your street signs, and leave those hallowed halls—why do we never hear of *un*hallowed halls?—I leave you with this:

- Remember that what seems so vital to your client, and thus to you, probably means jack to most everybody else. So find the people who care. It's better to reach the people who count than count the people you reach.
- Don't use *impact* as a verb. Genuflect before the *AP Stylebook* daily.
- You shouldn't expect any audience to understand and retain any more than about three key messages. If you can't state your position during a routine elevator trip, you need help.
- Laugh in the office every day. Avoid agencies and clients who don't know how.

- If you think you're there to do your client's blind bidding, you're in the wrong gig. If you think you're there to be your client's communications *counsel* and *partner,* welcome to the bond.
- Buy quality hand tools. The cheap stuff won't last. Hey, I'm still seizing the podium here.

What we do serves an honorable purpose: We help people tell their stories. We help them be heard. Then the key audiences have what they need to decide whether to print, buy, vote, move, change, eat, love, hate, or yawn. That's a good thing.

And *your* job is to decide: Should I show the wheelie video? ■

CASE STUDY 4.1 Big Brother Is Botching: Amazon's Orwellian Debacle

Oh, the irony.

Let's say you're a 17-year-old high school student. In fact, let's say your name is Justin G., that you live in Shelby Township, Michigan, and you're enduring a high-school rite of passage: writing a book report on George Orwell's *1984*. You remember: Big Brother Is Watching. A totalitarian government that controls all media. A protagonist employed to destroy inconvenient texts.

You're reading the book on your Amazon Kindle, scrupulously adding notes to the text and highlighting key passages. You go to bed one night, awaken the next morning—and *1984* is gone. Vanished like—well, like some inconvenient text. Your digital notes remain, but separated from their links to the text, they're almost worthless.

In this case, Big Brother was actually Amazon. In July 2009, upon discovering that it had sold electronic versions of *1984* that lacked legal copyright, Amazon reached into customers' Kindles and withdrew the book without notification. Justin G. wasn't alone. "Hundreds" of Amazon customers lost copies not only of *1984* but also of another classic totalitarian dystopia from Orwell, *Animal Farm.*[88]

"Hear that whirring?" asked SciFiWire.com, an online extension of the SyFy television network. "That's the sound of Orwell spinning . . . in his grave."[89]

It turns out that Kindles are a bit like the two-way telescreens in Orwell's *1984*. Using those devices, Big Brother not only could send; he also could receive. Almost before the clocks could strike 13 (as happens in the novel's famous first sentence), some former owners of the text consulted lawyers; but, for others, the issue went beyond legality.

"Legal or not," said one post in an online Kindle-users site, "it showed a capability on the part of Amazon that I don't wish to participate in. Amazon, I really, really wish you hadn't demonstrated your willingness to act in this manner. I will never be able to trust the Kindle now."[90]

Said *CIO*, a magazine for chief information officers, "This was a public relations disaster of the highest magnitude for Amazon."[91]

Amazon's initial response was to offer a refund. When that proved inadequate to stifle the outrage, the company upped the offer to a $30 gift certificate or check and a pledge to restore the novels.[92]

Even earlier, Jeff Bezos, the company's founder and CEO, had apologized to Kindle owners via a post in Amazon's online "Kindle Community":

This is an apology for the way we previously handled illegally sold copies of *1984* and other novels on Kindle. Our "solution" to the problem was stupid, thoughtless, and painfully out of line with our principles. It is wholly self-inflicted, and we deserve the criticism we've received. We will use the scar tissue from this painful mistake to help make better decisions going forward, ones that match our mission.[93]

Most comments that followed Bezos' post were understanding and forgiving. Others, however, were slightly Orwellian: "Thank you for respecting what shred of autonomy I have left," wrote one Kindle user. Another wrote, "While some saw this as no big deal, I saw this as electronic Breaking and Entering. You didn't have the users' permission to delete content they had paid for, but you did it anyway."[94]

Even with Bezos' apology, few observers saw the episode as a shining moment in customer relations. "The erasures . . . proved to be a public relations fiasco for Amazon," declared *Online Media Daily*.[95] *Podcasting News* added, "It's a public relations disaster for Amazon, resulting in headlines like 'Think You Own the Book You Bought for Your Kindle? You Don't, Says Amazon' and 'Whose Kindle Is It, Anyway?' "

Heightening the irony of Amazon's *1984*-ish zapping of *1984* is the wording of the company's Corporate Mission, which, above all, focuses on customer service: "We seek to be Earth's most customer-centric company for three primary customer sets: consumer customers, seller customers, and developer customers."[96] In a reference to paramilitary enforcers in *1984*, however, technology blog-ger Ken Fisher wrote, "Perhaps the ~~Thought Police~~ Amazon Customer Service team could cut off your books whenever they wanted to."[97]

As for Justin G. and his uniquely interrupted homework? He and a co-plaintiff sued Amazon and won a $150,000 payment. Terms of the settlement dictated, however, that after lawyers' fees, the remainder be donated to charity.[98] Perhaps Justin should consider the George Orwell Archives at University College London.

DISCUSSION QUESTIONS

1. What procedures, in your opinion, should Amazon have used to retrieve the improperly distributed novels?
2. Within this case study, where did Amazon succeed in meeting its Corporate Mission? Where did it fail?
3. What is your opinion of Jeff Bezos' written apology? Do you think it might have concerned Amazon's lawyers? If so, why?
4. The great majority of comments posted below Bezos' apology were understanding and forgiving. Can you think of other situations in which an organization's sincere apology had a positive impact?
5. Do you agree with the critics that this was a public relations disaster for Amazon? Why or why not? ■

CASE STUDY 4.2 Swinging for the Wall: Whirlpool Corporation and Habitat for Humanity

Baseball fans know the story well. In the 1932 World Series, Babe Ruth and the New York Yankees faced the Chicago Cubs. In game three of the fall classic, Ruth homered in an early inning. So when he came to the plate again in the fifth, Chicago fans booed mercilessly and jeered as pitcher Charlie Root zipped two strikes past Ruth.

Then Ruth made the gesture.

He pointed to the centerfield wall. And he hit the next pitch over that wall.

Home run.

In the 21st century, the Whirlpool Corporation just might think it's the Babe Ruth of corporate America. One of the world's best-known makers of home appliances, the company generates annual profits of more than $12 billion. Because Whirlpool is an ambitious company—it sells its products in more than 170 countries—it sought an ambitious new goal.[99]

Then Whirlpool made the gesture.

The company committed, in writing, to this pledge: "Every Home . . . Everywhere. With Pride, Passion, and Performance."[100]

Every home. . . . But what about homeowners who simply couldn't afford Whirlpool appliances— or any appliances for that matter? Figuratively speaking, Whirlpool had pointed to the centerfield wall. And now it had to deliver or strike out.

Whirlpool delivered. In 1999, the company vowed to donate a refrigerator and a range to every new Habitat for Humanity house in the United States.[101]

Most college students no doubt are familiar with Habitat for Humanity; many have helped build Habitat homes. Habitat for Humanity International is an organization dedicated to ending substandard housing and the lack of homeownership in low-income families. Since its founding in 1976, Habitat has built more than 350,000 houses in more than 3,000 communities for more than 1.75 million residents.[102]

Since 1999, Whirlpool has donated more than 73,000 appliances to Habitat for Humanity.[103]

"Across the board, our employees are extremely committed to our ongoing relationship with Habitat for Humanity," said Whirlpool President and CEO Jeff Fettig. "Whirlpool employees around the globe are working toward the Habitat mission of providing families with adequate, decent homes."[104]

Whirlpool prides itself on being a values-driven company. One of its core values is integrity— matching its words with actions—and the company clearly addresses values in its statements on *Corporate Responsibility* and *Vision & Strategy:*

> At Whirlpool we strongly believe in the principles of Corporate Responsibility—of achieving success in ways that honor ethical values and respect people, communities, and the natural environment. . . . Supporting those in our communities that need support provides our stakeholders with a real sense of Whirlpool's values. . . . Our employees live by the values-based strategy that has made Whirlpool the international leader that we are today. Our values represent who we are to our customers, our investors, and to each other.[105]

To help honor its value of community service, Whirlpool assists Habitat for Humanity with more than donations:

- Whirlpool offers substantial price discounts on additional appliances to Habitat homeowners.[106]
- Whirlpool has sponsored four Habitat for Humanity concert tours, headlined by country music star Reba McEntire.[107]
- Whirlpool employees have completed "Building Blocks" programs—in which Whirlpool employees "blitz build" several Habitat houses—in Nashville, Phoenix, Dallas, and Atlanta.[108]

In working to fulfill its values, Whirlpool believes that it's being more than a good corporate citizen: The company believes it's strengthening its financial future. Whirlpool's *Corporate Responsibility* statement offers this explanation: "Initiatives such as these help ensure the short-term and long-term viability of our company. . . . We firmly believe the socially responsible actions we take today will produce bottom-line benefits tomorrow."[109]

In pursuing its Every Home pledge, Whirlpool encountered a public it might not have anticipated: deserving individuals who couldn't afford their own homes and appliances. Whirlpool could have changed its goal. Or it could have ignored a public that probably wouldn't have fought back. Instead, like Babe Ruth, Whirlpool stood tall and swung for the wall.

Home run.

Or, maybe, just home.

DISCUSSION QUESTIONS

1. Should an organization establish a goal it can never realistically fulfill?
2. Do you agree with Whirlpool that its commitment to Habitat for Humanity can actually help it financially? If so, how?
3. Do you think "cause marketing" works? How can support for a worthy social cause help a company?
4. Can you name other companies involved in cause marketing? ■

NOTES

1. "Pitney Bowes Statement of Value," online, www.pitneybowes.com.

2. Norimitsu Onishi, "As Oil Riches Flow, Poor Village Cries Out," *New York Times,* 22 December 2002, online, LexisNexis.

3. Charles Babington and Philip Elliott, "Obama's Expansion of Gay Rights Draws Tepid Praise," *Lawrence Journal World,* 17 April 2010, 5A.

4. Cherie Jacobs, "More Companies Extend Benefits to Same-Sex Partners," *Tampa Tribune,* 12 August 2001, online, LexisNexis.

5. "Snapshots of Our Work," The Gay & Lesbian Alliance Against Defamation, online, www.glaad.org.

6. James E. Grunig and Fred C. Repper, "Strategic Management, Publics, and Issues," in *Excellence in Public Relations and Communication Management,* ed. James E. Grunig (Hillsdale, N.J.: Lawrence Erlbaum, 1992), 125.

7. John Ledingham and Stephen Bruning, "Managing Community Relationships to Maximize Mutual Benefit," in *Handbook of Public Relations,* ed. Robert L. Heath (Thousand Oaks, Calif.: Sage, 2001), 530.

8. James E. Grunig, "Furnishing the Edifice: Ongoing Research on Public Relations as a Strategic Management Function," *Journal of Public Relations Research* 18 (2006): 156.

9. "2009 Employee Job Satisfaction," Society of Human Resources Management, June 2009, online, www.shrm.org.

10. "The State of the American Worker, 2009," American Enterprise Institute, 21 August 2009, online, www.aei.org/publicopinion17.

11. "Work and Workplace," Gallup, Inc., August 2009, online, www.gallup.com/poll.

12. "Jobless Recovery in the U.S. Leaving Trail of Recession-Weary Employees in Its Wake, According to New Study," Towers Watson, 16 March 2010, online, www.towerswatson.com.

13. "Employee Engagement Survey," International Association of Business Communicators and Buck Consultants, 2009, online, www.iabc.com.

14. "The New Employment Deal: Insights From the 2010 Global Workforce Study," Towers Watson, 2010, online, www.towerswatson.com.

15. "Millennials: A Portrait of Generation Next," Pew Research Center, February 2010, online, pewresearch.org/millennials.

16. "2009 Employee Job Satisfaction."

17. "The New Employment Deal: Insights From the 2010 Global Workforce Study."

18. "The New Employment Deal."

19. "The New Employment Deal."

20. "Employee Engagement Survey."

21. "New Frontiers in Employee Communications: 2006," Edelman and PeopleMetrics, 16 January 2006, online, www.edelman.com.

22. "Brussels Talk," Towers Watson, Winter 2010, online, www.towerswatson.com.

23. "State of the News Media 2010: An Annual Report on American Journalism," Pew Charitable Trusts, online, www.stateofthemedia.org/2010.

24. "Media Survey," *PRWeek,* April 2010, online, www.prkweekus.com.

25. "State of the News Media 2010."

26. "State of the News Media 2010."

27. Lynne Sallot, Thomas Steinfatt, and Michael Salwen, "Journalists' and Public Relations Practitioners' News Values: Perceptions and Cross-Perceptions," *Journalism and Mass Communication Quarterly* (summer 1998): 369–370.

28. Felicity Barringer, "Editors Debate Realism vs. Retreat in Newsroom Diversity," *New York Times,* 6 April 1998, online, LexisNexis.

29. "Diversity," American Society of Newspaper Editors, April 2010, online, www.asne.org.

30. "Diversity," American Society of Newspaper Editors, online, www.asne.

31. Bob Papper, "Year of Extremes," *Communicator,* July/August 2006, online, www.rtnda.org.

32. Papper.

33. "Federal Government Civilian Employment by Function," U.S. Bureau of the Census, December 2009, online, www.census.gov.

34. *The Career Guide to Industries: 2010–2011,* U.S. Bureau of Labor Statistics, online, www.bls.gov.

35. "Federal Government Civilian Employment by Function."

36. "Federal Human Capital Survey 2008," Federal Office of Personal Management, January 2009, online, www.fhcs.opm.gov/2008/Reports; "The Best Places to Work in the Federal Government 2009," Federal Office of Personal Management, May 2009, online, http://data.bestplacestowork.org/bptw/overall/large; Ed O'Keefe, "Eye Opener: Best Places to Work 2009," *Washington Post*, 20 May 2009, online, http://voices.washingtonpost.com/federal-eye/2009.

37. "Annual Report to Congress," Federal Equal Opportunity Recruitment Program, September 2008, online, www.opm.gov/feorpreports.

38. "The 2010 Statistical Abstract," U.S. Bureau of the Census, online, www.census.gov/compendia/statab.

39. "Federal Human Capital Survey 2008," report by the U.S. Office of Personnel Management, 8 January 2008, online, www.fhcs.opm.gov/2008.

40. "2008 Public Employment Data: State Governments," U.S. Bureau of the Census, online, www.census.gov; "2008 Public Employment Data: Local Governments," U.S. Bureau of the Census, online, www.census.gov.

41. "Employment by Major Industry Sector," U.S. Bureau of Labor Statistics, December 2005, online, www.bls.gov.

42. "The 2010 Statistical Abstract."

43. "The 2010 Statistical Abstract."

44. "Grading the States 2008," The Pew Center on the States, online, www.pewcenteronthestates.org/gpp_report_card.aspx.

45. "Characteristics of Mutual Fund Investors, 2009," Investment Company Institute, December 2009, online, www.ici.org; "U.S. Household Ownership of Mutual Funds in 2003," Investment Company Institute, December 2009, online, www.ici.org.

46. Dennis Jacobe, "U.S. Investor Optimism Tumbles in June," Gallup, Inc., 1 July 2009, online, www.gallup.com/poll.

47. "Groundbreaking New Survey Compares Investor Sentiment of Younger & Older Americans," ShareBuilder Securities Corporation, 22 March 2010, online, www.prnewswire.com.

48. "401(K) Plans in Living Color: The Ariel/Hewitt Study," Ariel Investments, 7 July 2009, online, www.arielinvestments.com; "Equity and Bond Ownership in America, 2008," Investment Company Institute, 15 December 2008, online, www.ici.org.

49. "Equity and Bond Ownership in America, 2008."

50. "ING DIRECT USA's ShareBuilder Investor Study," ING Direct and ShareBuilder, January 2010, online, content.sharebuilder.com.

51. "ING DIRECT USA's ShareBuilder Investor Study."

52. "ING DIRECT USA's ShareBuilder Investor Study."

53. "U.S. Consumer Spending Up Again," Reuters, 1 March 2010, online, www.reuters.com.

54. "U.S. Consumer Spending Up Again."

55. Jeannine Aversa, "Growth Likely Slowing After Big Year-End Spurt," Associated Press, 26 February 2010, online, www.ap.org.

56. Meredith Whitney, "Credit Cards Are the Next Credit Crunch," *Wall Street Journal*, 10 March 2009, online, http://online.wsj.com.

57. "Consumer Expenditures in 2008," U.S. Bureau of Labor Statistics, March 2010, online, www.bls.gov.

58. Wendy Kaufman, "Poor Customer Service Common, Expensive," *All Things Considered*, 21 May 2007, online, www.npr.org; "Beware of Dissatisfied Customers: They Like to Blab," Knowledge@Wharton, 8 March 2006, online, http://knowledge.wharton.upenn.edu.

59. "Men Buy, Women Shop," Knowledge @ Wharton, 28 November 2007, online, http://knowledge.wharton.upenn.edu. "Consumer Expenditures in 2008."

60. "The New Consumer Behavior Paradigm: Permanent or Fleeting?" Pricewaterhouse-Coopers, 9 March 2010, online, www.pwc.com.

61. "Quarterly Retail E-Commerce Sales, 4th Quarter 2009," U.S. Bureau of the Census, 16 February 2010, online, www.census.gov.

62. Jordan McCollum, "Survey: Online Shopping Satisfies; Bigger is Better," Marketing Pilgrim, 30 December 2009, online, www.marketingpilgrim.com.

63. "New PayPal Survey Reveals Why Online Shoppers Abandon Purchases," PayPal, 23 June 2009, online, www.paypal-media.com.

64. Oliver Burkeman, "Is Jerry the Joker?" (London) *Guardian,* 3 July 2002, online, www.guardian.co.uk.

65. All examples are from Ted L. Nancy, *Letters from a Nut* (New York: Scholastic, 1997).

66. Frederick F. Reichheld, *The Loyalty Effect* (Boston: Harvard Business School Press, 1996), 33.

67. David McDermitt and Tony Shelton, "The 10 Commandments of Community Relations," *World Wastes,* September 1993, online, LexisNexis.

68. Jerry A. Hendrix, *Public Relations Cases,* 4th ed. (Belmont, Calif.: Wadsworth, 1998), 18–19.

69. "Cyrus Mehri," Mehri and Skalet PLLC, online, www.findjustice.com/sub/cyrus-mehri.jsp.

70. "Interview with Cyrus Mehri," *Corporate Crime Reporter,* 27 November 2000, online, www.findjustice.com/sub/interview-cm.jsp.

71. "Coke to Pay $192.5 Million to Settle Discrimination Suit," Associated Press, 17 November 2000, online, www.associatedpress.com.

72. "Mission, Vision, and Values," the Coca-Cola Company, online, www.thecoca-colacompany.com.

73. "Raising the Standard of Excellence," the Coca-Cola Company, online, http://www.thecoca-colacompany.com/ourcompany/awards_recognition.html.

74. "U.S. Interim Projections by Age, Sex, Race and Hispanic Origins: 2000–2050," U.S. Bureau of the Census, online, www.census.gov.

75. Luke J. Larsen, "The Foreign-Born Population in the United States: 2003," U.S. Bureau of the Census, August 2004, online, www.census.gov. Elizabeth M. Grieco, "Race and Hispanic Origin of the Foreign-Born Population in the United States, 2007," U.S. Bureau of the Census, January 2010, online, www.census.gov.

76. Larsen; Grieco.

77. "Voter Turnout Increases by 5 Million in 2008 Presidential Election," U.S. Bureau of the Census, 20 July 2009, online, www.census.gov.

78. "Voter Turnout from 1945 to Date," International Institute for Democracy and Electoral Assistance, 2004, online, www.idea.int.

79. "Voter Turnout Increases by 5 Million in 2008 Presidential Election."

80. "Voter Turnout Increases by 5 Million in 2008 Presidential Election."

81. Scott Keeter, "Young Voters in the 2008 Election," Pew Center for the People and the Press, 12 November 2008, online, http://pewresearch.org.

82. "Voter Turnout Increases by 5 Million in 2008 Presidential Election."

83. Allison Dale and Aaron Straus, "Don't Forget to Vote: Text Message Reminders as a Mobilization Tool," *American Journal of Political Science*, 53, no. 4, October 2009: 790.

84. "E-Commerce 2007," U.S. Bureau of the Census, 29 May 2009, online, www.census.gov.

85. Christopher Musico, "Partner Relationship Management: Rousing from a Slumber," *CRM Magazine*, July 2009, online, www.destinationcrm.com.

86. Denise J. Deveau, "PRM: Ready to Break Out," *E-Commerce Times*, 28 September 2009, online, www.ecommercetimes.com.

87. "PR League Tables: Why Trade PRs Are Hooked on the Net," *Marketing,* 25 May 2000, online, LexisNexis.

88. James Lewis, "Amazon Just Killed Off the Kindle's Buzz," *Podcasting News,* 17 July 2009, online, www.pocastingnews.com.

89. "Amazon Coughs Up $150K after Kindle Eats Teen's 1984 Homework," SciFi Wire, 2 October 2009, online, http://scifiwire.com.

90. Jim Milliot, "Cracks in Amazon's E-book Empire," *Publishers Weekly,* 27 July 2009, online, www.publishersweekly.com.

91. "Amazon Shows Us the Future," *CIO,* 22 July 2009, online, www.cio.com.

92. "Amazon Offers to Replace Deleted Books on Kindles," Associated Press, 4 October 2009, online, www.associatedpress.com.

93. Jeff Bezos, "An Apology from Amazon," Kindle Community, 23 July 2009, online, www.amazon.com/tag/kindle/forum.

94. "An Apology from Amazon."

95. Wendy Davis, "Amazon Sued For Erasing Orwell Books," *Online Media Daily*, 2 August 2009, online, www.mediapost.com.

96. "Corporate Mission," Amazon Investor Relations, online, http://phx.corporate-ir.net/phoenix.zhtml?p=irol-irhome&c=97664.

97. Ken Fisher, "Why Amazon Went Big Brother on Some Kindle E-books," *ars technica*, 17 July 2009, online, http://arstechnica.com.

98. "Amazon to Pay $150,000 over Kindle Eating Orwell—and Teen's Homework," *Los Angeles Times*, 1 October 2009, online, http://latimesblogs.latimes.com.

99. "Whirlpool Brand Announces 2004 Reba McEntire Tour Dates," news release issued by Whirlpool Corporation, 10 May 2004, online, LexisNexis.

100. "Vision & Strategy," Whirlpool Corporation, online, www.whirlpoolcorp.com.

101. "Whirlpool and Habitat for Humanity," Whirlpool Corporation, online, www.whirlpoolcorp.com.

102. "What Is Habitat for Humanity International?" Habitat for Humanity, online, www.habitat.org.

103. "Whirlpool Corporation and Habitat for Humanity," Whirlpool Corporation, online, http://www.whirlpool.com/content.jsp?sectionId=794.

104. "Whirlpool, Reba Deepen Commitment to Habitat for Humanity," Habitat for Humanity, 1 March 2005, online, www.habitat.org/newsroom/2005archive.

105. "Our Commitment to Corporate Responsibility," Whirlpool Corporation, online, www.whirlpoolcorp.com; "Vision & Strategy."

106. "Whirlpool and Habitat for Humanity."

107. "Whirlpool Corporation and Habitat for Humanity."

108. "Whirlpool Corporation and Habitat for Humanity."

109. "Our Commitment to Corporate Responsibility."

Photo Courtesy the White House

5

Communication Theory and Public Opinion

OBJECTIVES

After studying this chapter, you will be able to

- understand the process of communication and some of the theories of how people react to what they encounter in the mass media
- identify the forces that motivate people
- describe the power of public opinion and the process under which it develops

- recognize the differences between the use of persuasion and manipulation in public relations

KEY TERMS

active public opinion, p. 147
agenda building, p. 139
agenda-setting hypothesis, p. 137
attitude, p. 146

REAL WORLD
Growing Pains

The local state university was founded as an agricultural college in the late 19th century. At that time, it was located on farmland several miles from a small town. However, times have changed, and both the school and the community are experiencing growing pains, apparently at each other's expense.

The latest controversy involves the university's purchase of three dilapidated houses on the edge of one of the town's oldest neighborhoods. School administrators want to tear down the houses and build a much needed residence hall. The neighbors object, saying the structure will increase noise and traffic. Also opposed are members of the local historical society, who believe the dormitory would have a negative impact on a nearby historic site. It seems as if everyone has a dog in this fight, including the university, its students, the neighborhood, the historical society, the local zoning board, and even the governor, who also chairs the state historical commission.

If you were a public relations counselor to one of the many sides in this dispute, how would you proceed?

THE POWER OF PUBLIC OPINION

When Depression-era humorist Will Rogers said, "The United States is the only country ever to go to the poorhouse in an automobile," a lot of people thought that wisecrack was funny.[1] However, when CEOs of the nation's three largest automakers flew to Washington in separate private jets in November 2008 to ask Congress for $25 billion to help their financially ailing companies, very few were laughing.

"There's a delicious irony in seeing private luxury jets flying into Washington, D.C., and people coming off of them with tin cups in their hands," Rep. Gary L. Ackerman (D-NY) told the executives. "Couldn't you all have downgraded to first class or jet pooled or something to get here?"[2]

Few, if any, believed that the use of private jets was at the core of the auto industry's financial troubles. However, the symbolism of highly paid executives traveling to the Capitol in luxury to beg for taxpayer money was too much for many to stomach. Congress initially rejected the automakers' request. In an effort to prove to a skeptical public that they got the message, the next time the executives came to Washington to discuss the bailout package, they drove.

This is not simply a cautionary tale about the role of symbolism in politics. It is also about the power of public opinion and the role it plays in democratic societies. Effective communication is a key to success. So is the ability to persuade others to accept or at least respect your point of view. Both are at the heart of the practice of public relations.

SOCIAL MEDIA APPS

The Twitter Revolution

Almost 20 years to the day after the Chinese government learned that advances in communications technology had outstripped its ability to stifle public opinion, Iranian President Mahmoud Ahmadinejad was forced to swallow the same bitter pill.

The Chinese government went to great lengths in June 1989 to suppress global media coverage of its brutal crackdown on student-led pro-democracy protests, in what came to be known as the Tiananmen Square Massacre. Despite a ban on satellite transmissions, news organizations circumvented Chinese censorship by using new digital technology that allowed them to feed videotape footage as still photographs via standard telephone lines.[3]

Twenty years later, thousands swarmed into the streets of Tehran to protest alleged ballot fraud in the nation's presidential election. When a young woman protester was shot to death by government security forces, state-controlled media did not mention the incident. However, protesters captured it on a videophone and posted it to YouTube, creating worldwide condemnation of the Iranian regime.

The June 2009 Iranian election protests have been called "the Twitter Revolution" because of the microblogging service's role in keeping the opposition informed of events. *Time*'s Lev Grossman called Twitter "the medium of the movement" because it had the advantage of being easy for the average person to use but difficult for the government to control.

"When protests started to escalate, and the Iranian government moved to suppress dissent both on-line and off-line, the Twitterverse exploded with tweets from people who weren't having it," Grossman said. "While the front pages of Iranian newspapers were full of blank space where censors had whited-out news stories, Twitter was delivering information from street level, in real time."[4] ■

As we've said before and will say again, good public relations involves two-way communication between an organization and the publics important to its success. Responding to the concerns and needs of others is a big part of public relations. Ultimately, you want to create a mutually beneficial environment in which both an organization and its publics can flourish. That environment is achieved through the give and take that characterizes two-way communication. It is not enough for an organization to be a good listener. It also must be a good communicator. Successful companies and individuals excel in letting others know their values and preferences. And in today's results-oriented environment, success is often measured by one's ability to persuade others to come around to a certain way of thinking.

In this chapter's "Real World" opening scenario, local residents and university officials are at loggerheads over plans to build a dormitory. School officials see the construction as a good deal for the community. More students on campus means more money for local merchants. Construction would also remove some community eyesores. However, the residents have a different perspective. They fear a dormitory would change the nature of their neighborhood and lower their property values. As a result, each side has certain values it does not want to compromise.

Because public relations focuses on building and maintaining relationships, it is important for practitioners to understand how the processes of communication and persuasion work—and how to use that knowledge to achieve values-driven and mutually beneficial solutions.

A COMMUNICATION MODEL

Before we discuss how public opinion is formed, let's look at the process that makes it happen, communication. It is a process familiar to all and completely understood by none. Since Aristotle's day, scholars have tried to figure out how it works. They have developed what are called "communication models," graphic representations helpful in understanding the dynamics of the communication process. Some of these models are simplistic. Others look like the schematic drawing of an mp3 player. For our purposes, we have chosen a model based on the writings of David Berlo.[5] The elegance of this model is its simplicity. It breaks down the communication process into six basic ingredients: noise, source, message, channel, receiver, and feedback (Figure 5.1).

NOISE Sometimes referred to as static, **noise** envelops communication and often inhibits it. Noise can take both physical and intangible forms. It can have a physical quality, such as that experienced when a person is trying to talk with someone in a large crowd. The crowd noise can make it difficult to understand everything being said. However, noise does not have to be audible to inhibit communication. A person's state of mind can also block effective communication. An example is the mental "static" experienced by a person who is reeling from an emotional event and is not really listening to what is said. There are also times when for

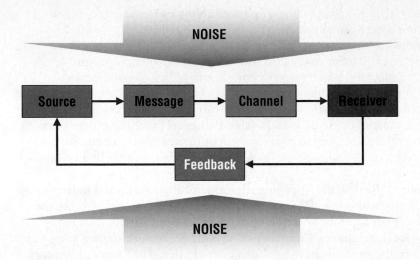

FIGURE 5.1
A Communication Model

a variety of reasons—cultural, religious, and generational among them—we erect barriers to communication. In these instances, we often generate "noise" because we don't like either the message or the messenger.

SOURCE   The **source** is where a communication originates. The source is also the first part of the coorientation model mentioned in Chapter 4. How a source views its audience—and is viewed by an audience—can help or hinder communication. Source credibility can be influenced by a variety of factors, including reputation, context, and communication ability. For example, a particular elected official was once seen as a leading advocate for strong family values. His subsequent arrest on a morals charge, however, undermined his credibility and ultimately ended his political career.

MESSAGE   The **message** is the content of the communication. To a large degree, successful formation of the message relies on knowledge of both the purpose of the message and its intended receiver. If the message is not relevant or is not in language understood by that receiver, it will probably be misunderstood or ignored. It wouldn't make sense for your professor to speak to the class in French—unless, of course, it was a French class.

CHANNEL   The **channel** is the medium used to transmit the message to the intended receiver. The selection of the most appropriate channel or channels is a key strategic decision. Like the source, the channel must be relevant and credible to the intended receiver. And much like a broadcast channel on an old-time radio, the channel can be susceptible to static. In this case, static is defined as physical and psychological forces that can make it difficult for the receiver to acquire the

Even Ronald Reagan, considered one of the best communicators to live in the White House, faced the challenge of overcoming noise in the environment when promoting his administration's policies.

(Photo by David Guth)

message. For example, many public relations practitioners have had their well-planned efforts at obtaining publicity foiled by breaking news stories that have caused reporters to focus their attentions elsewhere. One of your authors had three painstakingly planned news conferences derailed by attempted political assassinations in the same year.

RECEIVER The **receiver** is the person or persons for whom the message is intended. The receiver is also the second part of the coorientation model mentioned in Chapter 4. How the receiver views the source—and is viewed by the source—can help or hinder communication. The most effective communications are those that specifically target the intended receiver. For reasons already stated, the communicator must select the source, message, and channel with the needs of the receiver in mind. That, in turn, requires a thorough knowledge of the receiver, including its needs, values, predispositions, and communication ability. After all, what good does it do to communicate if the intended audience is not listening?

FEEDBACK **Feedback** is the receiver's reaction—as interpreted by the source—to the message. Without this final step, true communication does not occur. Feedback lets you know whether the message got through and how it was interpreted. Think of a stand-up comedian: If the audience laughs, the joke was funny. If there is silence, the joke failed. Good communicators, especially public relations practitioners, actively seek feedback. Feedback, often in the form of telephone calls, e-mails, and letters, can be spontaneous. However, that isn't always the case. Sometimes special mechanisms are established to generate feedback, such as toll-free telephone numbers, interactive websites, and public opinion polls.

As stated before, social scientists have developed a variety of communication models. However, the models all have something in common: Communication is a lot like an electrical circuit: If a short or break occurs anywhere along the wire, nothing happens. No communication takes place if the source is not seen as credible, the message is not relevant, the channel is filled with static, the receiver is not listening, or feedback is lacking.

QUICKBREAK 5.1

Mokusatsu

Communication fails when a source sends a message that cannot be understood or is misinterpreted by the receiver. Never has that fact had more tragic consequences than at the end of World War II, when the decision to use atomic bombs may have hinged on a misunderstanding over the meaning of a single Japanese word.

The decision to use the recently developed bomb against Japanese targets was not an easy one for President Harry Truman. On the one hand, the bomb might shock the Japanese military into surrendering, thus avoiding the bloody consequences of a full-scale military invasion of the island nation. On the other hand, Truman also knew that many civilians would be killed in an atomic attack. However, the signs coming out of Tokyo were not good. Although the Japanese military had been crushed as a result of three years of terrifying and unrelenting warfare, its leaders said Japan would never surrender.

Truman decided to give the Japanese one last chance before unleashing the bomb. In what has become known as the Potsdam Declaration, Truman told the Japanese that they had to surrender unconditionally or face unspecified consequences. Japanese Prime Minister Kantaro Suzuki, an aging civilian aristocrat, wanted to negotiate peace quickly with the Americans. But Suzuki also knew that the military, which dominated the government, would not let him.

When asked by the military press for his response to the Potsdam Declaration, the prime minister said, "We *mokusatsu* it." Suzuki thought he had been clever. *Mokusatsu* is a Japanese word that has a variety of interpretations, largely dependent on who is perceived as its source. In saying "We *mokusatsu* it," Suzuki was speaking for himself and asking the Americans to keep negotiations open and make another peace offer. However, Truman believed the prime minister was speaking on behalf of the military. In that context, *mokusatsu* was interpreted as meaning "hold in silent contempt."

Believing that the Japanese had rejected the United States' last olive branch, Truman authorized the use of atomic bombs. Hiroshima was attacked on August 6, 1945. An estimated 92,000 people were killed and an unknown number suffered long-term effects from radiation. Another 40,000 people died three days later in the atomic bombing of Nagasaki. One week later, the Japanese surrendered. ∎

A breakdown in the communication process was evidenced by the March 2002 introduction of the Homeland Security Advisory System. The five-level, color-coded system was designed to alert the nation about possible terrorist attacks. In theory, it was a good idea. In practice, it became confusing. For example, when the alert condition escalated from yellow to orange in February 2003, people were not certain what it meant and what they were supposed to do. When government officials suggested people take precautions against a potential terrorist gas attack, stores nationwide reported a near-panic run on duct tape and plastic sheeting:[6] The officials hadn't meant to imply that a gas attack was imminent, but their message was misunderstood.

 **QUICK CHECK**

1. What are the six elements of the communication model used in this text?
2. What are some of the things that can block communication?
3. Why is listening essential to good communication and effective public relations?

MASS COMMUNICATION THEORIES

Public relations practitioners are, in some respects, the race car drivers of mass communication. Aside from the obvious comparisons—that speed, accuracy, and winning are desired—there's also a critical need to know what makes things work. Drivers know what makes their machines tick. That knowledge gives them the edge they need to gain maximum performance from their cars. For the same reason, practitioners need to understand the processes of mass communication, what makes it tick. Over the past century, a variety of mass communication theories have evolved for just that reason.

The Magic Bullet Theory

World events had a great influence on early theories of mass communications. As you may remember from the history chapter of this book, research interest in persuasion and public opinion heated up in the wake of the use of propaganda techniques during World War I. The growth of fascism in Europe and Asia during the 1930s largely paralleled the growth of the first electronic mass medium, radio. Out of these developments came the first mass communications theory, the **magic bullet theory** of mass communications. This theory, illustrated in Figure 5.2, is grounded in a belief that the mass media wield great power over their audiences. It was thought that if a sender developed

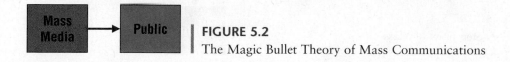

FIGURE 5.2
The Magic Bullet Theory of Mass Communications

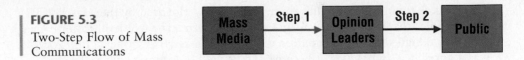

FIGURE 5.3
Two-Step Flow of Mass
Communications

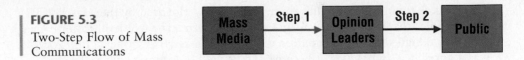

just the right message, the so-called magic bullet, people could be influenced to do almost anything. The problem with this approach to mass communications is that it supposes that people are weak-willed robots unable to resist finely sculptured appeals.

The Two-Step Theory

By the end of World War II, the magic bullet theory had been largely discredited. Social scientists began to understand better the role of intervening publics in influencing public opinion. From this realization evolved the **two-step theory** of mass communications, the foundation of which is the belief that the mass media influence society's key opinion leaders, who in turn influence the opinions and actions of society itself (Figure 5.3). These key opinion leaders were said to include elected public officials, powerful business executives, and religious figures. Although the opinion leaders were seen as powerful, this theory remained based on the belief that the mass media were powerful forces in molding public opinion.

The N-Step Theory

Recognizing that different people might be credible in different contexts, communication researcher Wilbur Schramm developed the **n-step theory** of mass communications (Figure 5.4). It was similar to the two-step theory in that it stressed the role of opinion leaders. However, under the n-step theory, key opinion leaders may vary from issue to issue. For example, you may turn to Peyton Manning if you want to

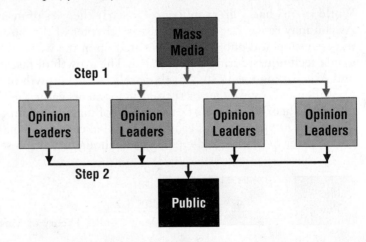

FIGURE 5.4
N-Step Flow of Mass
Communications

learn how to throw a football. However, it is more likely that you would seek insight from a finance expert if you actually wanted to buy a football team.

Diffusion Theory

Unlike its predecessors, the **diffusion theory** of mass communications was based on a belief that the power of the mass media is not as much to motivate people as it is to inform them (Figure 5.5). Under this theoretical view of mass communications, people have the power to influence members of their own peer groups. Agricultural extension agents have followed this approach for decades. The agents provide farmers with information on how they can improve their crop yields. If a farmer adopts an approach that works, he or she spreads the word of this success to other farmers. In other words, the idea is passed along through a diffusion process. In a sense, everyone can become an opinion leader.

The Agenda-Setting Hypothesis

The most significant and widely accepted view of how the mass media interact with society is currently the **agenda-setting hypothesis.** It is based on the simple principle that the mass media tell people not what to think, but what to think about. In other words, the media set the public agenda (Figure 5.6).

We see examples of the agenda-setting hypothesis at work in every morning's newspaper. Have you ever noticed how one issue can dominate the newspapers—and public debate—for several weeks, only to be replaced by another? Just ask public relations practitioners for Louisville-based Yum Brands. The company's Taco Bell restaurants received intense media scrutiny—and became the target of late night comedians—when an *E. coli* outbreak sickened 71 customers in the northeastern United States during November 2006. This launched a flurry of news stories about food safety. The company engaged in two weeks of damage control, and by mid-December, the media turned their attention to other matters.[7] However, the company returned to the media's crosshairs in February 2007 when a New York television station videotaped dozens of rats running around a Greenwich Village

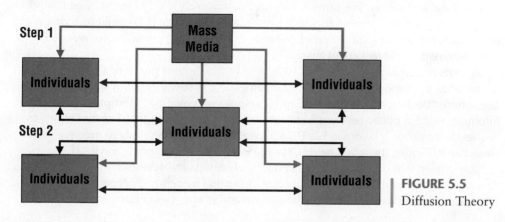

FIGURE 5.5
Diffusion Theory

FIGURE 5.6
The Agenda-Setting Hypothesis

KFC/Taco Bell. Within hours, more than 1,000 blogs had cited the story or posted the video. Food safety was again at the center of public debate.[8]

If you take the agenda-setting hypothesis to its next logical step, it raises an important question: If the media tell us not what to think but what to think about, who tells the media what to think about?

QUICKBREAK 5.2

Why Public Relations Is Not Propaganda

Few words in the English language are as emotionally and ethically charged as *propaganda.*[9] That's why public relations practitioners bristle when people—especially journalists—suggest that public relations and propaganda are one and the same.

The problem is that propaganda, just like public relations, is hard to define. Historian Brett Gray wrote, "Propaganda as a label suffered (and suffers) from a certain imprecision; it is not unlike Justice Potter Stewart's fabled definition of pornography: 'I don't know how to define it, but I know it when I see it.'"[10]

Many see propaganda as an umbrella covering all forms of persuasive communication, including advertising and public relations. Even the man considered the father of modern public relations, Edward L. Bernays, gave credence to this interpretation when he defined *public relations*—the term he coined in *Crystallizing Public Opinion*—as "the new propaganda."[11]

Some researchers lump all persuasive communication into two broad categories. One is *revealed propaganda,* messages that are overt in their effort to persuade, such as those in conventional advertising. The other is *concealed propaganda,* such as publicity generated from the distribution of news releases. However, if this approach is followed to a logical conclusion, it could be argued that *all* communication is propaganda.[12] One wonders how journalists would feel about that.

Since its earliest days, practitioners have tried to differentiate public relations from propaganda by placing it within an ethical framework. That was certainly the intent of Ivy Lee, whose "Declaration of Principles" in 1906 spoke of providing "prompt and accurate information.[13] But public relations historian Scott M. Cutlip wrote that Bernays' efforts to further define public relations in his 1928 book *Propaganda* served only to muddy the waters and "handed the infant field's critics a club with which to bludgeon it."[14]

Gray argued that propaganda should not be confused with advertising and public relations. "For my part, I try to maintain that distinction by defining propaganda as the organized manipulations of key cultural symbols and images (and biases) for the purposes of persuading a mass audience to take a position, or move to action, or remain inactive on a controversial matter," he wrote.[15]

Propaganda researchers Garth S. Jowett and Victoria O'Donnell prefer an even narrower definition. "Propaganda is the deliberate, systematic attempt to shape perceptions, manipulate cognitions, and direct behavior to achieve a response that furthers the desired intent of the propagandist."[16] In contrast, they argue that persuasion "is interactive and attempts to satisfy the needs of both the persuader and persuadee."[17] These interpretations are in line with more widely accepted definitions of public relations that stress two-way communication as well as the building and maintaining of mutually beneficial relationships.

As is discussed at the end of this chapter, there's a big difference between persuasion and manipulation. Public relations practitioners know this. ■

One answer is **agenda building,** the process through which journalists emphasize certain events, issues, or sources over others. As communication researcher Matthew Nisbet notes, "News coverage is not a reflection of reality, but rather a manufactured product, determined by a hierarchy of social influences." Among the influences Nisbet cites are economic conditions; cultural and ideological variables; media ownership structure; and media trends. He also writes that journalists' socioeconomic, political, and psychological orientations also influence agenda building.[18] The challenge for public relations practitioners—in fact, for anyone wishing to influence the public agenda—is to recognize and address those influences and orientations.

Uses and Gratifications Theory

This brings us to yet another evolution in communications theory. In recent years, theorists have noted that the agenda-setting hypothesis is based on a model in which the receiver is seen as a passive participant in the communication process. If this model is correct, theorists point out, then the source has the ultimate power of persuasion over the receiver. However, this concept of a passive receiver is being challenged by what is known as the **uses and gratifications theory.** The technological advances of recent years have resulted in an explosion of available mass communications channels. Researchers say that the real power now rests in the ability of receivers to pick and choose their channels of information. Although many communicators may seek to persuade the audience to take a particular course of action, the audience serves as a gatekeeper, in effect, deciding to whom it will grant influence (Figure 5.7).[19]

A Two-Way Process

Mass communications theory appears to have undergone a complete reversal. It has evolved from a belief that people are powerless to resist the mass media to an acknowledgment of the public's supremacy over media. This new view suggests that persuasion,

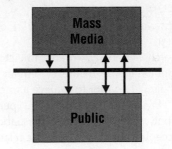

FIGURE 5.7
Uses and Gratifications Theory

like communication, is a two-way street. According to *Excellence in Public Relations and Communication Management,* a publication of the IABC Research Foundation, "The concept of negotiation, rather than domination or persuasion, is the key to understanding the effects of communication and programs."[20]

Let's go back to the opening scenario of this chapter. Each side of the dormitory debate has its merits. The university says construction will bring important economic benefits to the community as well as remove unwanted, dilapidated housing. Opponents of the plan fear it will disrupt the peace and quiet of their neighborhood and possibly harm a historically significant site. If each side enters the debate unwilling to listen to the other, sparks will, no doubt, fly. Eventually, one side will win and the other side will lose. But the controversy will not end there. The lingering effects of the ill will created by such a controversy could have political, social, and economic ramifications for years. However, if the two sides enter the discussion willing to listen to each other's concerns, a compromise is possible. Neighborhood preservation and campus growth are not necessarily mutually exclusive concepts. However, the key to keeping the peace is two-way communication.

 QUICK CHECK

1. What is diffusion theory?
2. What is the agenda-setting hypothesis?
3. What is the difference between public relations and propaganda?

MOTIVATION

Having discussed the communication process and the various theories on how mass communications influence people, we now focus on the individual. What motivates a given individual to do something? What forces are in play when we try to influence someone's behavior? What kind of appeals can spark action? These are questions psychologists and sociologists have pondered for centuries.

Although many theories explain why people do the things they do, one simple explanation is best: People usually act in their own self-interests. This may not seem, on the surface, to be an earth-shattering revelation. However, this simple truth is at

QUICKBREAK 5.3

Spinning, Framing, and Priming

As already noted several times in this book, many find public relations a difficult concept to define. That's why one often hears practitioners referred to by a variety—and sometimes unflattering array—of nicknames. They have been called press agents, flacks, mouthpieces, fronts, shills, and a few names of which your mother would not approve.

However, public relations practitioners were given a new handle in an October 21, 1984, *New York Times* editorial: **spin doctors.** Editorial writer Jack Rosenthal coined the phrase on the eve of that year's second presidential campaign debate:

> Tonight at about 9:30, seconds after the Reagan–Mondale debate ends, a bazaar will suddenly materialize in the press room of the Kansas City Municipal Auditorium. A dozen men in good suits and women in silk dresses will circulate smoothly among reporters, spouting confident opinions. They won't be just press agents trying to impart a favorable spin to a routine release. They'll be the Spin Doctors, senior advisers to the candidates, and they'll be playing for very high stakes. How well they do their work could be as important as how well their candidates do theirs.[21]

In his book *New Political Dictionary,* political columnist William Safire defined **spin** as "deliberate shading of news perception; attempted control of political reaction."[22] In essence, spin doctors try to influence perceptions by emphasizing certain aspects of events that reinforce their point of view. An example of spin would be the classic difference between a pessimist and an optimist: The pessimist sees the glass half empty whereas the optimist sees the glass half full.

Although *spin* is the popular term-of-art, a more appropriate word to describe this kind of activity is **framing.** It is a concept first articulated by Canadian sociologist Erving Goffman in 1974. In his book *Frame Analysis: Essays on the Organization of Experience,* Goffman wrote that all of us "actively classify and organize our life experiences to make sense of them."[23] Researcher Robert Entman has defined framing as communicating an idea in such a way that an audience is influenced, either intentionally or unintentionally, by the way it is expressed.[24]

Regardless of whether it is called spinning or framing, its real purpose is **priming.** According to priming theory, people make judgments about complex issues based on bits and pieces of easily accessible memory. By framing issues in the simplest of terms, politicians and other advocates prime the memories of their audiences, thus leading these publics to see matters in the most favorable light.[25]

At this point, you might question whether spinning, framing, and priming are things ethical public relations practitioners do. The answer is yes—if done in an appropriate manner. Using accurate Information within a proper context is no different from articulating mutual interests and values. It is only when one attempts to distort, hide, or mislead that the use of these tactics comes into question. ■

the heart of molding public opinion. But how do people determine their self-interests? You can look to an older generation for the answer.

As strange as it may seem, your parents and grandparents were once teenagers. If they grew up in the late 1960s and early 1970s, it is very possible that they owned bell-bottom jeans, wore long hair, and spoke of a desire for a peaceful world governed by a loose-knit philosophy known as "flower power." At the center of this popular culture was the most successful rock band the world had ever known, the Beatles. John, Paul, George, and Ringo had a generation believing that if you sought peace and tranquillity, "all you need is love."

If only it were that simple. Unfortunately, the Beatles were wrong.

Maslow's Hierarchy of Needs

Long before the Fab Four sang that love is the central force behind everything, psychologist Abraham Maslow developed a theory to explain how people determine their self-interests: **Maslow's Hierarchy of Needs** (Figure 5.8). The basis of the theory is that some needs are more basic than others and, therefore, must be fulfilled first.[26] On Maslow's list, love comes in only third.

According to Maslow, the lowest (most basic) order of needs is our *physiological* needs. These are the biological demands our bodies make for food, water, rest, and exercise. He included sex among our most basic needs but only as it related to the continuation of our species. Love and romance had nothing to do with it. By Maslow's way of thinking, if humans do not fulfill their physiological needs, little else matters.

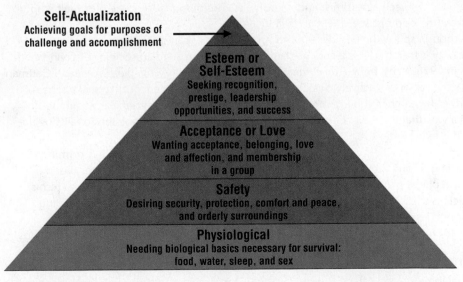

FIGURE 5.8
Maslow's Hierarchy of Needs

According to Maslow, *safety* is the next order of need. By "safety needs," he means things such as personal security, comfort, and orderly surroundings. To understand Maslow's ranking, assume for a minute that you are in a shelter in the middle of a war zone. Bombs and bullets are flying all around you. The shooting is expected to last for weeks. As long as you stay in that shelter, you are safe. However, suppose that shelter has no food or water. Maslow believed that, eventually, you will leave that shelter and forgo personal safety to fulfill your physiological needs. Otherwise, you will die anyway.

The third order of need is *acceptance,* or what Maslow referred to as love and belongingness. This is where the Beatles come in. At this level, we seek out love, a sense of belonging, an affiliation with others through group memberships. Still, this is only third on the list. Pretend that you have entered our imaginary bomb shelter only to find that it is filled with people you do not like and vice versa. Under Maslow's hierarchy, you are willing to endure any annoyance and indignity that might occur from these uncomfortable arrangements because of the safety the shelter provides.

Next on Maslow's Hierarchy of Needs is *self-esteem,* for which we strive to earn recognition and view ourselves as being successful. Everyone wants to be seen as a winner. However, people are often willing to let their self-esteem suffer if doing so provides some measure of acceptance. That is why some people choose to remain in abusive, unhealthy relationships. It isn't until the victim understands that this isn't true acceptance or that physiological or safety needs are threatened that the abusive relationship ends.

The highest order is *self-actualization* needs. We reach self-actualization when we achieve a goal just for the sake of achieving that goal. Climbing a mountain "because it is there" is an expression of self-actualization. Some people never achieve self-actualization because they haven't fulfilled the requirements imposed by lower-order needs. In some ways, self-actualization is like the Great American Novel that many people say they will write but never do because their attention is constantly focused on more pressing needs.

Examples of Maslow's Theory at Work

Just a guess: You are not reading about Maslow's Hierarchy of Needs as an expression of self-actualization. Your motivation is probably a result of a need to fulfill your safety needs: Failure to read the material assigned by your professor could well put your grade at risk! However, there is more to this stuff than just passing your next test. Maslow's theory figures prominently in the practice of public relations.

We can see Maslow's theories at work by looking at U.S. politics. The September 11, 2001, terrorist attacks pushed national security (survival) concerns to the top of the national political agenda and made it the leading issue of the 2004 presidential campaign. However, by the 2008 election, the ailing U.S. economy (safety) had replaced national security as the leading public issue. There it remained until Christmas 2009, when a failed bombing attempt aboard a U.S. airline elevated concerns for survival back to the top of the national political agenda.

We can see the practical use of Maslow's theory in other ways. When environmental groups such as Greenpeace seek public support, their messages focus on physiological needs—specifically, the survival of the planet. When social service organizations seek additional funding, they realize that an appeal to the public's unfulfilled safety needs will be more effective than one based in either acceptance or self-actualization. By the same token, an appeal to personal self-esteem will have a greater chance of success among affluent audiences, whose physiological and safety requirements have been met, than among lower-income audiences struggling to fulfill basic needs.

Do people stop and think, "What would Maslow have me do under these circumstances?" Of course not. However, we instinctively follow Maslow's model. Self-interest is at the heart of motivation. Understanding the needs of the public being targeted is the key to successful communication and persuasion.

QUICKBREAK 5.4

Monroe's Motivated Sequence

In an era in which change is the only constant, it is refreshing to see an idea that has stood the test of time. In the mid-1920s, Purdue University Professor Alan H. Monroe developed an organizational pattern for persuasive messages that has come to be known as **Monroe's Motivated Sequence**.[27] More than 80 years later, it remains a standard for persuasive communication.

Building persuasive messages using Monroe's Motivated Sequence involves a five-step process. Let's look at that process, using a real-world example: a company executive trying to motivate employees to improve quality by reducing workplace errors:

1. *Attention.* Get the attention of the audience through a dramatic story, quote, or statistic. Tell the audience why the topic is important to it.

   "One of our competitors has been forced to cut back production and lay off some of its employees. Its sales have dropped because of consumer complaints of shoddy products. We can't afford to have that happen here."

2. *Need.* Show that a significant problem exists and that it won't go away by itself. Document the need with relevant examples.

   "There is a great deal of competition in today's global economy. Consumers are demanding quality. If they don't get it from us, they have plenty of other options."

3. *Satisfaction.* Now that a need has been shown, offer solutions. They should be reasonable solutions that adequately address the need.

   "By working together, the management and employees of this company can develop reasonable training programs to improve the quality of our products and reduce production-line errors."

4. *Visualization.* Tell what will happen if nothing is done to solve the problem. Explicitly tell the audience the consequences of its choices.

"In recent weeks, our research department has noticed an increasing number of consumer complaints. We are headed down the same road as our competition. If we don't make changes, it is likely that some of us will lose our jobs."

5. *Action.* Tell the audience members what they, personally, can do to solve the problem. It is important that the actions requested are explicitly stated.

"I am asking you to make a personal commitment to quality. Don't be afraid to share your ideas for improving our products. Volunteer to serve on the various committees we are establishing to examine this issue. Help make this company's mission statement—'providing quality products and services'—a reality."

It is not a coincidence that the example cited here is closely linked to the company's mission statement. Values should serve as the foundation of all persuasive communication.

In today's world of the six-second sound bite, the art of persuasive speaking may seem irrelevant. But it is just as important today as it was in Monroe's time. Monroe's Motivated Sequence is a tried-and-true method of making one's points in a logical and persuasive manner. ■

PERSUASION AND PUBLIC OPINION

Since the beginning of recorded history, people have pondered the question of how to persuade others to take a desired course of action. And it is a very important question. The persuasion of others and the molding of public opinion are central to our concept of a society, the manner in which people choose to organize themselves.

In democratic societies, we organize ourselves around a core belief in fulfilling the will of the people. However, history has shown us that democratic societies operate best when there is a willingness to seek consensus on matters of importance to all. That, in turn, requires a willingness among the members of these societies to engage in public debate. It is during this debate that we either persuade others to come over to our point of view or are persuaded to accept the opinion of someone else. A measure of these ongoing discussions is what we commonly refer to as public opinion.

Persuasion and public opinion are vital elements in the practice of public relations. As has been stressed in many places throughout this textbook, public relations is a two-way process of both communicating and listening. Sometimes the need to convince others about the advisability of a certain course of action arises. In that situation, we try to persuade others to adopt our point of view. However, we must also be sensitive to public opinion and the concerns of others. At its best, public relations is not about winning or losing. Instead, it is about building and maintaining mutually beneficial relationships. That is why understanding the dynamics of persuasion and public opinion is so critical to successful public relations.

Aristotle, Persuasion, and Public Relations

Aristotle said that **persuasion** takes three forms: **logos,** or an appeal to reason; **pathos,** or an appeal to emotions; and **ethos,** or an appeal based on personality or character. He said that a persuasive argument may use one of these forms exclusively or in any combination with the others.

Aristotle believed the decision to choose one form of persuasion over another depended on several factors: the circumstances in which the appeal is made, the specific nature of what is being argued, and the makeup of the audience being addressed.[28] To state this concept in simpler terms: The selection of an appropriate persuasive appeal depends on determining what you are saying, where and when you are saying it, and to whom you are saying it. This concept should sound familiar to you. It is pivotal to the practice of public relations.

Aristotle believed that ethos, the persuasive value of a communicator's character, is often the most powerful of the three modes of persuasion. In his classic book *Rhetoric,* he said that a communicator's character "may almost be called the most effective means of persuasion he possesses."[29] That's one reason practitioners should strive to practice ethical, values-driven public relations: Their well-earned good name can help build the relationships that are essential to their organization's success.

Aristotle's analysis of persuasion raises an important question that is currently being debated within professional and academic circles: Is persuasion an appropriate activity for public relations practitioners? Some people believe that the goal of persuasion is inconsistent with the two-way communication requirement for effective public relations. Two-way communication, by definition, implies a willingness to listen to the needs and concerns of the targeted public and act accordingly. Persuasion linked to one-way communication tends to ignore a central tenet of motivation, that people act in their own self-interests. Any effort at persuasion that does not first take into account the public's point of view is poor public relations and probably won't work. However, when practiced at its highest levels, public relations identifies common interests and promotes actions that are mutually beneficial. Therefore, in that context, persuasion is a **compliance-gaining tactic** appropriate for public relations practitioners.[30]

Public Opinion Defined

In much the same way that an atom is the basic building block of matter, **belief** is the basic building block of public opinion. A belief is one's commitment to a particular idea or concept based on either personal experience or some credible external authority. For example, many people who have traveled to and experienced Paris believe that it is the most beautiful city in the world. However, others who have never been to France may feel the same way because they have heard it from sources they consider credible, such as friends, travel guides, and popular culture.

When a belief starts affecting the way we behave, it creates an **attitude.** To put it another way, an attitude is a behavioral inclination. For example, if a belief that Paris is a beautiful city causes you to start reading about Paris, encourages you to enjoy French cuisine, or just encourages you to look positively upon all things Parisian, you have developed an attitude.

If that attitude is strong and inspires you to share it with others, you have developed an **opinion.** By definition, an opinion is an expressed behavioral inclination. That opinion can be expressed verbally, by telling others how much you admire Paris, or nonverbally, by adopting French fashion as your own preferred style.

That takes us to **public opinion,** the average expressed behavioral inclination. Public opinion takes into account a wide range of positions that people may have on the same issue. For example, a majority of people may feel that Paris is a beautiful city. A small minority may disagree. Yet another group may have no opinion at all. Together, those three groups constitute public opinion on the issue of the beauty of Paris.

As noted in Chapter 4, the publics of public relations can be divided into what are known as latent, aware, and active publics. Which one of these defines a particular public depends on the degree to which the public realizes and cares about the intersection of its values with an issue. The same can be said for public opinion. **Latent public opinion** is the result of people having varying degrees of interest in a topic or issue but being unaware of the interests of others. **Aware public opinion** occurs when people grow aware of an emerging interest. **Active public opinion** occurs when people act—formally or informally and, often, not in unison—to influence the opinions and actions of others.

The Evolution of Public Opinion

Although persuading one person to adopt a particular point of view can be difficult, the true challenge is to persuade large numbers of people. That is the essence of decision making in a democratic society—a public debate that leads to a public consensus and, eventually, to public policy. The evolution of public opinion can be outlined as follows:[31]

1. Public opinion starts with an *already present mass sentiment,* a consensus that developed as a result of earlier public debates.
2. Public opinion begins to evolve when an *issue* is interjected into that consensus. For something to be considered an issue, it has to affect a variety of groups and be seen as evolving.
3. Like-minded individuals coalesce into a *public.* Often these publics can be characterized as being either pro or con. However, many issues are complex and have more than two sides.
4. The various publics engage in *public and private debate* over the issue. This debate can take many forms. It is at this stage that the practice of public relations has its greatest influence among publics that have not yet formed a strong opinion.
5. There is an unspecified period of *time* during which the debate occurs and people make up their minds. The amount of time needed for this to happen varies from issue to issue. With some issues, such as gun control and abortion, the debate seems never to end.

QUICKBREAK 5.5

A Public Opinion Checklist

Volumes have been written about how to influence public opinion, but here are 10 key guidelines you should remember:

1. *You might not be the best judge of public opinion.* Don't trust hunches or gut reactions. They could be wrong. Base your decisions on solid research and analysis.
2. *People resist change.* Change is often viewed as a threat. For that reason, do not assume that a targeted public understands the benefits of a proposal. Spell them out.
3. *WIIFM (What's In It For Me?).* Social psychologist Hadley Cantril wrote, "Once self-interest is involved, opinions are not easily changed."[32] Don't tell targeted publics why something is good for you. Instead, describe how the desired action benefits them.
4. *People believe what they want to believe.* When people have their minds made up on an issue, they tend to seek out information that reinforces their position. They also tend to avoid or block out what social scientists call **cognitive dissonance**—the mental disturbance resulting from encountering information that runs contrary to their beliefs.
5. *Plant seeds in fertile ground.* It is easier to provide information than it is to shape an opinion. It is also easier to shape an opinion than it is to change an opinion. You can't afford to waste limited time and resources on those who have already decided against you. You can achieve greater success by directing public relations efforts to those who are already on your side and those still willing to listen.
6. *KISS (Keep It Simple and Straight).* In the clutter that makes up mass communications, it is the simplest of messages that are most likely to get through and register with a public. Symbolism is often more effective than a complex explanation of concepts.
7. *Demonstrate knowledge of the issue.* When public opinion is undecided or running against you, presenting all sides of the issue tends to be the most effective approach. It also provides an opportunity to demonstrate the comparative strength of your position.
8. *When among friends, preach to the choir.* When public opinion is on your side, stick to your message. In this case, usually, no need arises to discuss the other side of the issue. Your job isn't so much to change public opinion as to solidify it into action.
9. *Actions speak louder than words.* People are impressed when you actually do what you say you are going to do. Empty promises breed mistrust; keeping your word builds credibility.
10. *Get in the last word.* When there is little to choose from between opposing views, a determining factor tends to be the argument heard last. ■

6. Eventually the debate leads to a consensus, which is known as *public opinion*.
7. In turn, that public opinion precipitates some form of *social action,* such as a policy change, an election, or the passing of a new law.
8. At this point, the issue evolves into a *social value;* this, in turn, becomes part of the already present mass sentiment, and the public opinion process begins anew.

You can see the public opinion process at work as public safety officials address the danger posed by distracted drivers. Since the late 1980s, state and federal lawmakers have written a variety of laws prohibiting people from talking on cellular telephones while driving (*an already-present mass sentiment*). As text messaging and e-mail caught on at the turn of the century, officials confronted new challenges (*an issue*). Although everyone is in favor of safe driving, opinions differed on the best ways to restrict texting and e-mailing while driving (*like-minded individuals coalesce into publics*). Various approaches were studied and discussed (*public and private debate*) over the following months and years (*time*). A consensus was eventually reached (*public opinion*) and by January 1, 2010, 18 states had enacted bans on the sending or reading of text messages or e-mails while driving (*social action*).[33] As other states join in the ban, the issue will evolve into a *social value*. In turn, it will become part of the *already present mass sentiment*, and the public opinion process will begin anew.

The dynamics of the public opinion process point out the need for companies and organizations to conduct ongoing programs of public relations. Because public opinion is always evolving, one-shot efforts at influencing it are rarely effective. Sometimes public opinion crystallizes very quickly, as it did following the 9/11 terrorist attacks. Public opinion is also very fluid and can evolve over time, as with the dramatic change in public attitudes toward civil rights since the early 1960s. Public relations practitioners need to keep their fingers constantly on the pulse of public opinion. Only then are they properly prepared to guide their organizations through potentially stormy seas.

VALUES STATEMENT 5.1

APCO Worldwide

APCO Worldwide is a Washington-based global communication consultancy. Listed among its nearly two dozen services are coalition building and grassroots advocacy, communication for governments, crisis management, and issue management and public information campaigns.

Vision & Values

At APCO we encourage an entrepreneurial spirit where employees have the freedom to push the boundaries of communication and provide innovative solutions for clients.

(continued)

APCO is a global company providing employees with enriching experiences working with colleagues of diverse backgrounds, both professionally and culturally. Our culture fosters a collegial work environment where everyone feels valued for his or her contributions to client successes and the firm.

Spanning the globe, the glue that binds us is a commitment to living APCO's values. Values are the cornerstone of the company's culture and work environment. The values provide direction on what is important to the company and to each other, and serve as a guide to how we make business decisions and influence interactions with staff and clients. Our values transcend geographical boundaries and are apparent in any APCO office regardless of city, country or continent.

Our Values
- Client service is our measure of achievement.
- Push the boundaries with innovative solutions.
- Tell the truth.
- Empower great people to do great work.
- Nurture an organization where everyone is valued.
- Rely on one another in achieving our personal potential.
- Provide global service culture by culture.
- Building relationships is the best business development.
- Business success assures our future.

—APCO Worldwide www.apcoworldwide.com ■

Persuasion versus Manipulation

Understanding the dynamics of public opinion is essential to the practice of public relations. However, as is true with most things in life, it is possible to get too much of a good thing. Although it is often desirable to win people over to a particular point of view, there is a great temptation to try to manipulate public opinion to achieve one's goals. Such an effort came to light in December 2005, when it was learned that the news articles written by U.S. military public affairs officers had been placed in Iraqi newspapers by Lincoln Group, a Washington-based public relations agency, as paid advertisements. The purpose was to counter negative stories spread by opponents of the U.S. occupation. However, in many instances, the articles were not properly identified as advertisements. Defending the practice, agency spokeswoman Laurie Adler said, "Lincoln Group has consistently worked with Iraqi media to promote truthful reporting across Iraq." However, that explanation didn't satisfy some on Capitol Hill. Politicians from both sides of the aisle said the disclosure could undermine U.S. efforts in Iraq and called into question the notion that U.S. troops had been received in that nation as liberators.[34]

This incident illustrates two valuable lessons for public relations practitioners. First, it suggests the need to draw the line between influencing and manipulating public opinion. **Manipulation,** by its very nature, suggests something underhanded. It is true that one may reap short-term gains by telling half-truths or by putting narrow interests ahead of broader ones, but it is also true that those gains are short-lived. Manipulation, whether real or perceived, comes with a cost: credibility. No one likes to feel as if he or she has been used. Manipulation also runs contrary to the ideal of public relations as a problem-solving discipline whose practitioners seek alternatives that are mutually beneficial to all parties concerned.

A second valuable lesson is that those who seek to master public opinion often become a slave to it. This results in a lack of leadership. A common complaint we hear these days about politicians and corporate executives is that they are too often driven by public opinion polls. Instead of acting on what they believe, they seek to do what is popular. Although public opinion is important in democratic societies, so are values. It is often necessary to forgo what is popular for what is right. Think how different human history would be if certain special individuals had not, at critical moments, put their values ahead of public sentiment. Public relations is a values-driven discipline. Those values are determined by what we believe, not necessarily by what is popular.

QUICK CHECK

1. What are the three kinds of persuasive appeals identified by Aristotle?
2. How does public opinion develop?
3. What is the difference between manipulation and persuasion?

SUMMARY

History has shown us that communication is a fragile process. It can fail in a variety of ways, including a lack of source credibility, an irrelevant message, an inappropriate channel, an inattentive receiver, the absence of feedback, or the presence of physical or psychological noise.

With the growth of communications technology in the 20th century, people initially feared that mass media could dominate public opinion. This fear led to the development of what came to be known as the magic bullet theory. However, as the technology of mass communications evolved, so did our understanding of mass media. Now we realize that mass media do not tell us what to think, but rather influence what we think about. That concept is known as the agenda-setting hypothesis. However, even that theory is evolving. According to uses and gratifications theory, the *real* power to persuade resides with individuals who can pick and choose from thousands of information sources and are driven by their own self-interests—especially by their need to survive.

The evolution of public opinion is a dynamic process that never ceases; for this reason, organizations need to stay attuned to changes in public attitudes and conduct ongoing programs of public relations.

Although efforts to win people over to a point of view are legitimate, manipulation of public opinion by underhanded means is counterproductive. Those who engage in manipulation lose credibility and can become slaves to the public mood.

DISCUSSION QUESTIONS

1. Can and should public relations practitioners try to influence public opinion? Should our ability to persuade have any limits?
2. Describe the process of communication. What are some factors that can cause communication to break down?
3. Does an explanation exist for why some things serve as stronger motivations to action than others?
4. To what degree do you think mass media influence you? How does your personal experience relate to the various theories of mass communication?
5. What would be a good example of an issue that has undergone a rigorous public debate and emerged as a social value? Describe the process by which this happened.

MEMO FROM THE FIELD

JANE HAZEL
Director General of the Marketing and Consultation Directorate; Health Canada
Ottawa, Ontario

Jane Hazel is the director general of the Marketing and Consultation Directorate of Health Canada. Health Canada is the Canadian federal department responsible for helping the people of Canada maintain and improve their health. Based in Ottawa, Ontario, the Marketing and Consultation Directorate is the departmental focal point for strategic advice; planning and implementation of social marketing; Health Canada's Internet; public opinion research and evaluation; and policy lead for corporate consultation. Hazel's publications include coauthorship of "Social Advertising and Tobacco Demand Reduction in Canada" in the textbook *Social Marketing: Theoretical and Practical Perspectives.*

As a longtime communications professional, I rely heavily on public opinion research (POR) to inform my work. It gives me critical insight into my audience: It helps me understand people's views, attitudes, and perceptions; what they are thinking and feeling and why; what's important to them and how they feel about my organization. This information forms the base of all my communications efforts.

Typically I tend to use POR in 2 specific ways:

1. CAMPAIGN DEVELOPMENT

Working for the health department, a key aspect of my job is to design social marketing campaigns to encourage people to be healthy, e.g., quit smoking, eat better, and be more active. This type of behavior change depends heavily on an in-depth understanding of people's knowledge, awareness, and behaviors. POR helps:

- understand who engages in the behavior
- identify the triggers to starting and the barriers to quitting
- identify role models and credible voices
- determine what information people want and need
- identify where people would go to get information
- determine what would motivate change

We also use POR to pre-test our creative material before production (ads, brochures, posters, and so on) and to evaluate the campaign's effectiveness post launch.

2. ISSUE MANAGEMENT

Another key role POR plays in our organization relates to issue management. Using surveys, we track issues percolating in the media to see if they become part of public debate. This helps us proactively position ourselves to provide accurate information in a timely manner and to plan strategically.

Typically there is a 4-step approach to tracking public opinion to support issue management:

1. First assess the "salience" of the issue.
   - Are people aware of the issue? Have they talked about it in the recent past?
   - Ask "Have you read, seen, or heard anything about X?"
2. Then try to put the issue in context.
   - Issues can be exaggerated if looked at in isolation.
   - Ask "What have you read, heard, seen about X?"
3. Next, assess the impact of what people learn related to your organization.
   - Ask "Did what you read, see, or hear about X leave you feeling (more or less positive) toward organization Y?"
4. Then find out what people think of your reaction.
   - The real question is how well you are seen to be managing the issue.
   - The initial reaction to most issues is negative.
   - Ask "Do you (strongly approve, somewhat approve, somewhat disapprove, or strongly disapprove) of the performance of organization Y in responding to issue X?"

This approach worked well in 2003 when SARS hit Toronto. In that case, we supplemented tracking with surveys and focus groups to develop, tailor, and adjust our communication strategy. Nightly rolling polling assessed people's evolving understanding of this epidemic, what

(continued)

information they received, and how they received it. This allowed us to tailor our daily media briefings, to ensure that we were providing relevant information, to immediately correct any misinformation, and to use the right channels with our communications strategy overall.

3. TWO THINGS TO REMEMBER

1. Be survey savvy: In an environment where every newspaper headline proclaims a startling new survey result, take the time to understand and interpret surveys. Methodological rigor and quality control are important, but numbers can also suggest a false or exaggerated sense of accuracy. Be critical.
   - Who sponsored the survey?
   - Examine question wording and where questions are placed in the survey.
   - Compare how many people were asked to participate versus how many did. If the gap is large, is there something different about those who did not respond?
   - How were the data interpreted (was "very good" grouped with "good"?)
   - Remember people are usually doing other things when a survey call comes in. They answer based on their top-of-mind values, core attitudes, and experiences, and usually not on a reflective consideration of all options.

2. Let research be your guide, not your master.
   - Use POR to help your judgment, not as a substitute for it.
   - Plan, plan, plan, and pre-test. Know why you need the data and what you will do with it. The saddest words I hear are "If only I'd asked X!"
   - Find the resources to hire a professional to help you.
   - Leave maneuvering room: Interpret with common sense; don't tie yourself to a decision based on a single source.
   - Seek first to understand. The reasons behind the numbers are more important than the numbers themselves.

All good communication strategies start with a full understanding of the audience. Public opinion research is the first step to that understanding and is critical to anyone working in the field of PR. ■

CASE STUDY 5.1 Broken News

At the time, it was called "breaking news." However, it didn't take long for journalists to realize that the news wasn't breaking—it was broken.

A man who identified himself as U.S. Chamber of Commerce spokesman Hingo Sembra stunned reporters at the National Press Club in Washington when he announced that the Chamber was dropping its opposition to federal climate change legislation. The Chamber had been in a widely publicized battle with the Obama administration over the bill. In fact, the Chamber's stance had caused several of its members, including Apple, Pacific Gas and Electric, and Exelon, to withdraw from the organization.[35]

"Breaking news, right now, the Chamber of Commerce saying it will reverse its position on the climate-change bill," one Fox Business News anchor reported. Then, he paused, listened intently to an off-screen producer, and announced, "Apparently we just called the Chamber of Commerce, and they're denying that they are changing their position." After more discussion with his producer, the anchor sheepishly explained, "It's live TV, folks."[36]

More than just "live TV," the October 2009 announcement was a hoax perpetrated by the Yes Men, a group with a long history of scamming reporters. Fox Business News wasn't the only media outlet taken in by the stunt. The Reuters newswire issued a bulletin based on the bogus announcement, which subscribing news organizations, including the *New York Times* and *The Washington Post*, promptly posted on their websites.

It was a convincing performance. The news conference included fake handouts on Chamber letterhead, a lectern adorned with the Chamber's logo, and several phony reporters. There was even an authentic-looking website with a plausible URL, chamber-of-commerce.us, instead of the real Web address, uschamber.com.[37]

Not until 20 minutes into the news conference was the hoax was unveiled. "This is not an official U.S. Chamber of Commerce event," shouted Eric Wohlschlegel of the *real* Chamber of Commerce as he burst into the room. "This is a fraudulent press activity and a stunt."[38] As *The Washington Post* reported the next day, "What followed was a spectacle not usually seen in the John Peter Zenger Room at the National Press Club: two men in business suits shouting at each other, each calling the other an impostor and demanding to see business cards."[39]

This wasn't the first time the Yes Men punked the news media. An estimated 15,000 people died as a result of a poisonous gas leak from a Union Carbide pesticide plant in Bhopal, India, in 1984. On the 20th anniversary of the tragedy, a bogus

website announced that Dow Chemical, the new owners of the plant, had established a $12 billion fund to compensate the victims. Media outlets, including the BBC and CNBC, reported the news. The price of Dow stock plummeted until the hoax was revealed. Exxon, Halliburton, and the U.S. Department of Housing and Urban Development have also been Yes Men targets.[40]

The Chamber did not find much humor in the stunt, immediately filing a federal civil lawsuit over copyright and trademark infringement. Yes Man Andy Bichlbaum, who identified himself as Hingo Sembra and who the *New York Times* said is *really* Jacques Servin, responded by saying "powerful business lobbies and their massively funded PR campaigns are subverting the media every day."

Bichlbaum/Sembra/Servin added, "It's shameful that the Chamber has decided to lash out at a public interest group like ours for trying to push back and call attention to the Chamber's outrageous positions."[41]

DISCUSSION QUESTIONS

1. Do you agree or disagree with the tactics of the Yes Men? What concepts in the chapter that precedes this case support your position?
2. In what way, if any, do values relate to the Yes Men's tactics?
3. What degree of culpability do you believe news organizations have in the success of Yes Men hoaxes?
4. If your organization were confronted by a hoax similar to that faced by the U.S. Chamber of Commerce, how would you respond? ■

CASE STUDY 5.2 Flying Against the Wind

Many cities have a love–hate relationship with their airport. On the one hand, it is a gateway to a world of possibilities. On the other, it can be a noisy and intrusive neighbor.

That was the challenge facing the San Diego International Airport, known locally as Lindbergh Field. Conveniently located in downtown San

Diego, it has been consistently ranked as one of the best in nation in terms of passenger satisfaction and customer service. However, it is landlocked into a bay-front location with no room to grow. It is the nation's busiest single-runway airport, serving more than 18.3 million passengers in 2007.[42] When given the option of moving the airport to an alternative site in November 2006, San Diego County residents rejected the ballot measure by a 62 percent to 38 percent margin.[43]

Left with few other options, the San Diego County Regional Airport Authority decided to develop a master plan to expand airport operations in the existing 661-acre site. That, in turn, would require Authority Board approval of an Environmental Impact Report (EIR), a requirement under California's stringent environmental laws.[44] It should also be noted that the airport's environmental mission statement is "to lead the airport industry in the development and implementation of comprehensive programs and practices designed to minimize the airport's environmental footprint and to ensure a safe operating environment throughout the airport and the surrounding communities."[45]

At this point, the Authority public affairs team partnered with public relations agency Porter Novelli. During the summer and fall of 2007, the agency conducted four focus groups, two with voters living within five miles of the airport and two with people living in other areas of the county. Porter Novelli targeted people "most likely to voice their opinions about a public project," especially targeting those who had opposed prior expansion of the airport. Agency practitioners also interviewed 28 community opinion leaders from diverse industry sectors. This research revealed low public awareness of the airport's expansion plans, that people wanted to be kept informed of these plans, and that people who knew the details overwhelmingly supported airport improvements.[46]

In addition to a series of public hearings required by state law, the Authority and the agency sent direct-mail business reply cards to airport neighbors, asking them to sign up for a "keep informed" list. Airport tours, a monthly e-mail newsletter,

advertising, a project video, and a website were used to publicize the airport's proposed master plan. A speaker's bureau was created to take the message to influential community groups. Porter Novelli also engaged in an aggressive media relations campaign that included media briefings and tours, op-ed pieces, and a steady stream of news releases.

Just days before the Authority Board was scheduled to consider the EIR, San Diego City Councilman Kevin Faulconer organized a protest just across the street from the airport. Faulconer and 40 other area residents opposed the construction of a five-story parking garage—a key element of the master plan—that they said would create traffic gridlock on one of the city's busiest streets. They sought to delay a decision on the master plan.[47] In response, airport and agency officials produced evidence of public support for airport expansion in the form of 200 support cards from residents favoring the plan, as well as 313 letters of support from individuals and businesses.

The Airport Authority Board unanimously approved the EIR and adopted the master plan on May 1, 2008. In doing so, the board praised the public affairs staff for its outreach efforts.[48]

DISCUSSION QUESTIONS

1. What kind of research was used in support of this campaign?
2. Who were the stakeholders in this case, and what tactics were used to reach them?
3. What role did values play in this case study?
4. Why is it appropriate or inappropriate for a public agency such as the San Diego County Regional Airport Authority to contract with a public relations agency in an effort to influence public policy? ∎

NOTES

1. *Webster's New World Dictionary of Quotations* (Hoboken, N.J.: Wiley, 2005), as cited online, www.yourdictionary.com.
2. Dana Milbank, "Auto Execs Fly Corporate Jets to D.C., Tin Cups in Hand, *Washington Post*, 20 November 2008, online, www.washingtonpost.com.
3. Jay Sharbutt, "Shots Seen 'Round the World via Phone Lines," *Los Angeles Times*, 7 June 1989, via LexisNexis.

4. Lev Grossman, "Iran Protests: Twitter, the Medium of the Movement," *Time,* 17 June 2009, online: www.time.com.

5. David Berlo, *The Process of Communication: An Introduction to Theory and Practice* (New York: Holt, Rinehart and Winston, 1960).

6. Jeanne Meserve, "Duct Tape Sales Rise Amid Terror Fears," CNN, 11 February 2003, online, www.cnn.com.

7. Chris Cobb, "Taco Bell *E. Coli* Outbreak: Calming Public Fears during Food-Borne Illness Scares," *Public Relations Tactics,* February 2007, 11.

8. Kate MacArthur, "Taco Hell: Rodent Video Signals New Era in PR Crises," *Advertising Age,* 26 February 2007, 1.

9. This QuickBreak is based on the academic paper, "Propaganda v. Public Diplomacy: How 9/11 Gave New Life to a Cold War Debate," by David W. Guth, presented at the annual conference of the Association of Educators in Journalism and Mass Communications, August 2003, Kansas City, Mo.

10. Brett Gray, *The Nervous Liberals: Propaganda Anxieties from World War I to the Cold War* (New York: Columbia University Press, 1999), p. 8.

11. Scott M. Cutlip, *The Unseen Power: Public Relations, A History* (Hillsdale, N.J.: Lawrence Erlbaum, 1994), 82–183.

12. Gayle Mertz and Carol Miller Lieber, *Conflict in Context: Understanding Local to Global Security,* Educators for Social Responsibility, 1991, online, www.esrnational.org/whatispropaganda.htm.

13. Cutlip, 45.

14. Cutlip, 182.

15. Gray, 8.

16. Garth S. Jowett and Victoria O'Donnell, *Propaganda and Persuasion,* 3rd ed. (Thousand Oaks, Calif.: Sage Publications, 1999), p. 6.

17. Jowett and O'Donnell, 1.

18. Wolfgang Donsbach, ed., *The International Encyclopedia of Communication,* 2008, as cited online, www.communicationencyclopedia.com/public/.

19. James E. Grunig et al., eds., *Excellence in Public Relations and Communication Management* (Hillsdale, N.J.: Lawrence Erlbaum, 1992), 165.

20. Grunig.

21. Jack Rosenthal, "Spin Doctors," *New York Times,* 21 October 1984, as quoted by "Present at the Creation: Spin," National Public Radio, 4 November 2002, online, www.npr.org/programs/morning/features/patc/spin/index.html.

22. "Present at the Creation: Spin."

23. Erving Goffman, *Frame Analysis: Essays on the Organization of Experience* (New York: Harper & Row, 1974), 21.

24. Robert Entman, "Framing: Toward Clarification of a Fractured Paradigm," *Journal of Communication* 43, no. 3 (December 1993): 51–58.

25. Shanto Iyengar and Donald R. Kinder, *News That Matters* (Chicago: University of Chicago Press, 1987), 63–72.

26. Abraham Maslow, *Motivation and Personality* (New York: Harper & Row, 1954), 9.

27. Raymie E. McKerron, Bruce E. Gronbeck, Douglas Ehninger, and Alan H. Monroe, *Principles and Types of Speech Communication,* 14th ed. (Boston: Allyn & Bacon, 2000), 153–164.

28. Edward P. J. Corbett, *Classical Rhetoric for the Modern Student* (New York: Oxford University Press, 1971), 50.

29. Aristotle, *Rhetoric,* trans. W. Rhys Roberts (New York: Modern Library, 1954), 25.

30. Grunig, 331.

31. Based on Lang and Lang's *Collective Dynamics,* cited in *PRSA Accreditation Study Guide* (New York: Public Relations Society of America, 1993), 38.

32. Hadley Cantril, *Gauging Public Opinion* (Princeton, N.J.: Princeton University Press, 1972), 226–230.

33. "New Traffic Laws for 2010 to Go into Effect Friday," *Chicago Sun-Times Media Wire,* 28 December 2009, online: www.suntimes.com/news/transportation.

34. Eric Schmitt, "Military Admits Planting News in Iraq," *New York Times,* 3 December 2005, online, www.nytimes.com.

35. David A. Fahrenthold, "Apple Leaves U.S. Chamber over Its Climate Position,"

Washington Post, 6 October 2009, online: www.washingtonpost.com.

36. "The News Is Broken," *Washington Post*, 20 October 2009, A2.

37. "The News Is Broken."

38. "The News Is Broken."

39. David A. Fahrenthold, "Pranksters Stage Chamber of Commerce Climate Change Event," *Washington Post*, 19 October 2009, online: www.washingtonpost.com.

40. Stephen Holden, "All Suited Up for Mischief, to Rumple Stuffed Shirts," *New York Times*, 7 October 2009, C9.

41. Andy Bichlbaum, "Yes Men Statement on Chamber Lawsuit," 28 October 2009, the Yes Men website, http://theyesmen.org/statement.

42. "Final Environmental Impact Report for San Diego International Airport Mast Plan Now Available," news release, San Diego County Regional Airport Authority, 18 April 2008.

43. Jeff Ristine, "Vigorous 'No' for Miramar Airport," *San Diego Union-Tribune*, 11 December 2006, B1.

44. "Public Affairs Campaign for San Diego County Regional Airport Authority's Master Plan Environmental Impact Report," Silver Anvil Case Study 6BE-0906C04, Public Relations Society of America, online: www.prsa.org.

45. San Diego International Airport website, www.san.org.

46. "Public Affairs Campaign for San Diego County Regional Airport Authority's Master Plan Environmental Impact Report."

47. Steve Schmidt, "Garage Plans Draw Protest," *San Diego Union-Tribune*, 30 April 2008, B1.

48. "Public Affairs Campaign for San Diego County Regional Airport Authority's Master Plan Environmental Impact Report."

6

Ethics and Social Responsibility in Public Relations

OBJECTIVES

After studying this chapter, you will be able to

- define what is meant by the word *ethics*
- specify categories of ethics codes
- understand the most common ethical challenges
- describe the ethics codes of important philosophers from Aristotle to John Rawls

- use the Potter Box to analyze ethical dilemmas

KEY TERMS

categorical imperative, p. 170
cause branding, p. 172
cause marketing, p. 172
civil disobedience, p. 166
corporate social responsibility (CSR), p. 171

REAL WORLD
Choose and Lose

You are an upper-level public relations practitioner for an international manufacturing company. Your primary duty is internal (employee) public relations. Three days ago, the CEO of your company told the news media that a much-publicized though minor environmental hazard in your company's production process had been eliminated. The person responsible for eliminating the hazard is one of your best friends. And right now, she really needs your friendship: Because of a death in her family, she's going through a rough time.

As your concern for her grows, you learn, by accident, that she hasn't eliminated the environmental hazard; it still exists. In her distraught condition, she doesn't even realize that she hasn't corrected it. You're afraid that telling her will damage your friendship, one of the few positive things in her life right now. But if the CEO discovers the oversight, he might fire her—which, you fear, would deepen her depression. And, of course, you're concerned that the news media will find out that they were given, albeit unintentionally, false information.
What do you do?

WHAT ARE ETHICS?

In the old comedy *Bill and Ted's Excellent Adventure,* two young slackers travel through time to learn about history. If you could do the same (not that you're a slacker), you could round up some of the great minds of philosophy to help you learn about ethics. Imagine bringing Aristotle, Immanuel Kant, and John Stuart Mill to your local pizza joint.

"We don't seem to agree on much about ethics," Mill says.

"I disagree," says Kant as Aristotle rolls his eyes. "We agree on a lot."

"The truth is somewhere in the middle," says Aristotle. "We *do* agree that more than anything else, human beings want happiness. Pass the pizza."

"Right," says Kant. "And we agree that unless we're ethical, we can never be truly happy."

"And we agree that being ethical means knowing and acting on our values," Aristotle says. "Ethics are values in action."

"Perfect," says Mill. "But we disagree on how to find those values."

"But we agree that Aristotle eats too much pizza," Kant shouts, banging his fist on the table.

QUICKBREAK 6.1

The Ethics Code of PRSA

Members of the Public Relations Society of America pledge to abide by that organization's Code of Ethics. Based on the values of advocacy, honesty, expertise, independence, loyalty, and fairness (see p. 528), the PRSA ethics code specifies six "Core Principles," including the following two:

- Free flow of information: Protecting and advancing the free flow of accurate and truthful information is essential to serving the public interest and contributing to informed decision making in a democratic society.
- Safeguarding confidences: Client trust requires appropriate protection of confidential and private information.

Each core principle includes guidelines that define in greater detail the principle's intent. For example, the following list reproduces the guidelines for the "free flow of information" principle.

A member shall:

- Preserve the integrity of the process of communication.
- Be honest and accurate in all communications.
- Act promptly to correct erroneous communications for which the practitioner is responsible.
- Preserve the free flow of unprejudiced information when giving or receiving gifts by ensuring that gifts are nominal, legal, and infrequent.

The complete text of the PRSA ethics code can be found in the appendix of this book. ■

And the debate would go on. But you've probably read enough philosophy in your other classes to know that this fantasy is fairly accurate: **Ethics** are values in action. And without ethics, philosophers say, we cannot achieve our goal of happiness. Consider the ethics scandals of recent years: religious leaders forsaking their vows; a famous golfer involved in extramarital escapades; Wall Street executives overcome by greed. None seemed to lead to happiness for those involved.

Being ethical means identifying our values and acting on them. The late John Ginn, a journalism professor at the University of Kansas, often told his students, "Ethics are not just something that we *have*. They're something that we *do*." Ideally, once we decide what our values are, we embrace guidelines for behavior that will help us reach those values. Those guidelines become our ethics code. In other words, ethical behavior isn't a distant goal. Rather, it's part of daily life.

Ethics Codes for Values-Driven Public Relations

Ethics codes identify core values. They also specify ways of acting to help us achieve those values. Therefore, ethics codes offer guidelines for values-driven actions. Public relations professionals live their lives under the guidance of several ethics codes: international codes, societal codes, professional codes, organizational codes, and personal codes. Let's look at examples of each.

INTERNATIONAL CODES As more organizations build relationships with publics in other nations, international codes of business ethics are emerging. For example, the Global Alliance for Public Relations and Communication Management, a consortium of public relations professional organizations throughout the world, bases its ethics code on these core values: cooperation and teamwork; professionalism and credibility; integrity; innovation and change; and openness and dialogue. The Global Alliance's code is online at www.globalalliancepr.org.

SOCIETAL CODES The Ten Commandments, a foundation of Judeo-Christian culture, are an example of a societal ethics code that influences the lives of millions of people throughout the world. Other religions, of course, have codes to help their believers act on core values. Eighteenth-century historian Edward Gibbon said of the Koran, the holy book of Islam, "From the Atlantic to the Ganges, the Koran is acknowledged as the fundamental code, not only of theology, but of civil and criminal jurisprudence."[1]

PROFESSIONAL CODES Unlike members of some professions, public relations practitioners have no central, binding code of ethics. We're not licensed by a central organization, as are doctors and lawyers. Many public relations practitioners, however, voluntarily join organizations that do have binding ethics codes. The two largest such organizations in the world are the Public Relations Society of America (PRSA) and the International Association of Business Communicators (IABC). Unfortunately, not everyone is familiar with public relations ethics codes. "Recently," say public relations scholars Hugh Culbertson and Ni Chen, "we commented to a journalist friend that we'd been asked

Truett Cathy, founder of the Chick-fil-A restaurant chain, follows his personal ethics code by sponsoring more than 100 foster children. They call him Grandpa.

(Courtesy of Chick-fil-A, Inc.)

to write a paper on public relations ethics. 'There aren't many,' he joked. 'Your paper ought to be quite brief.' "[2] Ouch.

ORGANIZATIONAL CODES   Many organizations have ethics codes that employees are asked to read, sign, and follow. Often, members of an organization's public relations staff are asked to help draft, evaluate, and revise these codes. In *The 18 Immutable Laws of Corporate Reputation,* author Ronald J. Alsop notes that when Philip Morris Companies Inc., whose holdings included several cigarette companies, wanted to improve its public image, it not only changed its name to the Altria Group; it also adopted a new ethics code.[3]

PERSONAL CODES   Truett Cathy, founder of the Chick-fil-A restaurant chain, closes his 1,400-plus restaurants on Sundays. The company's website makes it clear that the policy stems from Cathy's personal values:

> Our founder, Truett Cathy, wanted to ensure that every Chick-fil-A employee and restaurant operator had an opportunity to worship, spend time with family and friends, or just plain rest from the work week. Made sense then, still makes sense now.[4]

Cathy's son Dan, president of the company, said that his father "didn't want to have to wash dishes on Sunday afternoon like he had to when he was a kid in a boardinghouse, and he didn't want to ask others to do what he didn't want to do himself."[5]

OBJECTIVITY VERSUS ADVOCACY: A MISLEADING ETHICS DEBATE

In addition to identifying specific ethics codes, we can learn more about ethics in public relations by studying the values of related professions. However, an enduring debate in public relations ethics comes from comparing public relations practitioners with lawyers and journalists. At the heart of this debate lies this question: Are public relations practitioners objective communicators, like journalists, or are we advocates, like lawyers?

Some practitioners charge that total objectivity would lead us to tell the truth but ignore the consequences of what we say. Imagine, for a moment, the consequences of telling every public everything you know about the organization you represent. Surely, not every public has a right to know everything. Legally, some information, such as employee health records, must be confidential. And surely you wouldn't betray strategic secrets that help your organization stay competitive. Advocacy, with its focus on the consequences of communicating, can seem more suitable than objectivity for public relations.

If, however, we choose to operate solely as advocates, we soon encounter the sticky issue of selective truth. In attempting to build relationships with publics, are we allowed to withhold damaging information that certain publics have a right to know? Sometimes we can withhold such information legally—but can we do so ethically? Some scholars actually say yes. They maintain that our society has become adversarial, like a courtroom. Public relations practitioners engaged in a debate, they say, need present only the facts that help them, trusting that opponents will present other facts and that a judge—the public—will decide the truth of the matter.[6]

A Relationship-Management Solution

In recent years, public relations practitioners have worked hard to develop an ethical solution to the misleading "are we journalists or lawyers" question. Perhaps the answer is "neither." Many practitioners respond to the debate by saying that public relations practitioners are, first and foremost, relationship managers. Their priority is building honorable, ethical relationships between an organization and the publics that are essential to its success. Sometimes relationship management calls for delivering unpopular truths, either to a public or to the organization itself. And sometimes relationship management involves being an advocate, even if that means advocating the viewpoint of an important public within your own organization. In all their actions, however, public relations practitioners are acting for the good of the relationships that sustain an organization.

 QUICK CHECK

1. What does the word *ethics* mean?
2. Besides the international level, at what levels do we find ethics codes?
3. What solution does this chapter offer for the misleading "journalist or lawyer" role-model debate?

CHALLENGES TO ETHICAL BEHAVIOR

Identifying our values is one thing; acting on them is another. Many kinds of challenges stand in the way of ethical behavior. For one thing, some ethical questions aren't easy. They can keep you lying awake at night, staring at the ceiling and trying to select the right course of action amid four or five unappealing options. Also, overwork sometimes conceals ethical problems while the damage has already begun. Still another challenge is the mistaken assumption that something legal is always ethical. Or perhaps the business practices of an international client lead you into unfamiliar cross-cultural ethical territory. Or perhaps the challenge lies in the dangers of short-term thinking, or of working in a so-called virtual organization in which values clash. Let's discuss each of these challenges.

Dilemmas

Some ethical challenges are called *dilemmas,* meaning difficult quandaries in which important values clash and every potential solution will cause pain. A dilemma isn't simply a problem; it's a problem that lacks a good, painless solution. The Choose and Lose scenario that opens this chapter is an example of a dilemma. No matter which course of action you select, you seem to hurt or betray someone who trusts you: your CEO, your friend, the news media, or the publics that might suffer from the environmental hazard.

In real life, PepsiCo, Northwest Airlines, and other large international companies encountered clashing values when the government of Myanmar, a country (formerly known as Burma) in which the companies operated, began a series of increasingly brutal crackdowns on opposition political parties. Should the companies honor the value of justice and leave the country, refusing to help the government through taxes? Or should they honor the value of supporting their local employees, who desperately need their jobs, and stay? By

QUICKBREAK 6.2

Aristotle, Confucius, and the Golden Mean

Is it all right to tell a lie? If we answer quickly, most of us will probably answer no. Telling a lie, we will say, is wrong. It's unethical.

Let's complicate the situation. Is it unethical to tell a lie to save someone's life? Here's a classic ethical question: If you were hiding an innocent victim of political persecution in your attic and representatives of the corrupt regime asked whether you were hiding that individual, would you lie? Or would you tell the truth and betray an innocent person?

Moral absolutes can be troublesome. We can almost always think of exceptions to the moral guidelines we generally follow. Those exceptions can help us understand the concept of the **golden mean,** developed by the Greek philosopher Aristotle (384–322 BC).

Aristotle believed that ethical conduct existed at a point of balance and harmony between the two extremes of excess and deficiency. That point of balance is the golden mean. For example, Aristotle would contend that it's unethical *never* to lie (one extreme), just as it's unethical *always* to lie (the opposite extreme). The challenge of the golden mean lies in answering the crucial question *when:* When is it all right to lie? In what specific circumstances could lying be considered an ethical course of action?

A century before the birth of Aristotle, the Chinese philosopher Confucius (551–479 BC) established much the same principle with his *Doctrine of the Mean:* "The superior man . . . stands erect in the middle, without inclining to either side."[7]

Finding the golden mean isn't easy. But as we seek the ethical course between absolutist extremes, we learn more about the values that govern and will govern our lives. ■

2009, PepsiCo, Northwest Airlines, Tommy Hilfiger, Walmart, and nearly 100 other international companies had made the difficult decision to leave Myanmar.[8]

Overwork

Is it possible to work too hard? Yes, if doing so clouds your judgment. You, and your organization, have an ethical obligation regarding workload: You should shoulder only the work you can handle effectively in a typical 40- to 50-hour workweek. Hard work is a value within most organizations—but so are quality and accuracy. You have an ethical obligation to control the quality of your work. Overwork can also rob you of time you ideally would devote to self-analysis—that is, to thinking about your organization's values and your own values and checking to see whether all your actions are working toward those values.

Legal/Ethical Confusion

What is legal isn't always ethical—and, to a lesser degree, what is ethical might not always be legal. For example, does any law prevent you from remaining silent when you're mistakenly praised for someone else's work? Your silence wouldn't be illegal—but, by most standards, it would be unethical. Or perhaps your supervisor asks you whether a particular project is done. You're a little behind, but you're certain you can finish it this afternoon. Because you know she won't ask for it until tomorrow, you say it's done. The small lie isn't illegal, but is it a breach of your personal ethics code? Probably. Simply following the law isn't enough to guarantee ethical behavior.

A continuing debate at the University of Wisconsin-Madison, for example, addresses the ethics of conducting experiments on monkeys in the campus's Wisconsin National Primate Research Center. At a 2009 meeting of the university's All-Campus Animal Care and Use Committee, one member, after considering many sides of the issue, acknowledged that "the mere fact that research is common, legal, and has an oversight system in place does not necessarily mean that it's ethical."[9]

On the other hand, can something illegal be ethical? Can doing the right thing involve breaking the law? Activists ranging from college students to a 90-year-old woman recently climbed oak trees owned by the University of California-Berkeley to prevent the trees from being cut down to clear space for a new athletics training center. Said one organizer, "We think a university that has produced 27 Nobel laureates ought to be able to figure out how to build a gym without destroying this precious natural resource."[10] The concept of **civil disobedience** involves peaceful, unlawful actions designed to help change government policies.

Cross-Cultural Ethics

Let's say you're doing business overseas and you're given an expensive vase by one of the many companies seeking to establish a partnership with your organization. Giving gifts to new acquaintances is standard in the culture you're visiting. Can you ethically accept the gift? Or do you reject it as a bribe?

Professor Thomas Donaldson of the Wharton School of Business notes two extremes in the range of your possible responses to the gift: **cultural relativism** and **ethical imperialism.** Both, he says, are wrong. Cultural relativism involves the belief that no set of ethics is superior to any other set. With cultural relativism, you could accept the gift, saying, "It may violate my sense of ethics, but I'm just honoring the ethics of my host nation." Ethical imperialism is the belief that your system of ethics has no flexibility and no room for improvement; your system overrules every other system. With ethical imperialism, you would quickly reject the gift, saying, "Sorry, but this looks like a bribe to me."

SOCIAL MEDIA APPS

Ethics and Social Media

New media can present new ethics challenges. A decade ago, for example, cell phone cameras powerfully increased our ability to embarrass one another. So what seem to be the top ethics challenges presented by social media?

In a recent survey of public relations and marketing professionals, 21 percent said their organizations had created bogus consumer reviews of their own products. Eleven percent said they had removed negative comments from various social media, and 11 percent had offered gifts or other payment for favorable comments in blogs (see Chapter 15). Almost 60 percent said they had not engaged in such activities.[11]

In terms of ethos, or the credibility that comes from having a reputation for trustworthiness, social media lag significantly behind traditional media. Eighty percent of respondents to a recent survey said they expect traditional news media "to be honest, tell the truth and be ethical." Only 41 percent said the same of social media.[12]

Bob Pearson, chief technology and media officer for the WeissComm Group public relations agency, recommends asking these questions to help ensure ethical use of social media:

Do you have a clear policy on social media that everyone who works for you adheres to? Do you have clear rules of the road for how one should represent your brand online? Do you know what the best practices are for the industry?

And if the answers are "yes," Pearson recommends a final question: "Are you sure?"[13] ■

Like Aristotle, Donaldson suggests a middle ground:

When it comes to shaping ethical behavior, companies should be guided by three principles:

■ Respect for core human values, which determine the absolute moral threshold for all business activities.
■ Respect for local traditions.
■ The belief that context matters when deciding what is right and what is wrong.[14]

In other words, be clear on your own beliefs but willing to explore the beliefs of others. Is that lavish gift a bribe—or is it a genuine gift of friendship, an important part of the culture you're visiting? If it's clearly a bribe, you politely but firmly explain that you can't accept it. If it's a genuine gift, perhaps your organization's policy allows you to accept it on behalf of the company. Maybe you can donate it to charity when you return home.

Short-Term Thinking

The classic example of someone engaged in short-term thinking is the person who plugs a leaking dam with a lit stick of dynamite. The short-term problem is solved, but at too high a cost. A public relations practitioner who deceives members of any public, from reporters to employees, is guilty of short-term thinking. Eventually, the deception might be revealed, damaging the long-term relationship between the practitioner and the public.

Virtual Organizations

An emerging threat to ethical behavior comes from **virtual organizations,** which are temporary organizations formed by smaller, independent units or people to complete a specific job. For example, a public relations consultant might team up with an architect and a developer to try to persuade a community that it needs a new shopping center. These different units would consider themselves part of one organization for the duration of the project; when the project ends, so does the organization.

Dramatic improvements in communications technology have spurred the growth of virtual organizations, allowing them to include partners from different locations throughout the world. But unfamiliar partners or a lack of internal communication can lead to clashing values and ethics. For example, it's unlikely that a virtual organization would have a written values statement or a written ethics code. An organization that doesn't know and act on its values probably is an organization headed for trouble.

Specific Ethics Challenges

Studying the specific ethics challenges faced by today's practitioners is another way we can prepare ourselves for an effective career in public relations. To support its Code of Ethics, the Public Relations Society of America issues Professional Standards Advisories. PRSA issues a Professional Standards Advisory when a particular ethics

TABLE 6.1

ETHICS CHALLENGES IN PUBLIC RELATIONS: PRSA PROFESSIONAL STANDARDS ADVISORIES

PS-1:   Disclosure of Employment Status of Client-Based PR Agency Staff (May 2004)

PS-2:   Overstating Charges, Fees and/or Compensation (May 2004; revised August 2007)

PS-3:   Representation of Front Groups with Undisclosed Sponsors (July 2004)

PS-4:   Reporting Unethical Behavior or Unprofessional Performance (August 2004)

PS-5:   Telling the Truth, Especially in War Time (January 2005)

PS-6:   Disclosure by Expert Commentators and Professional Spokespersons of Payments or Financial Interests (April 2005)

PS-7:   Deceptive Practices While Representing Front Groups (October 2006; revised, October 2008)

PS-8:   Deceptive Online Practices and Misrepresentation of Organizations and Visuals (October 2008)

PS-9:   Pay for Play: Secretly Paying Journalists to Publish Stories (October 2008)

PS-10: Phantom Experience: Inflating Résumés, Credentials and Capabilities (July 2009)

PS-11: Professional Conflicts of Interest (October 2009)

PS-12: Questionable Environmental Claims (October 2009)

PS-13: Use of Video News Releases as a Public Relations Tool (October 2009)

PS-14: Expropriation of the Intellectual Property of Others (February 2010)

Note: Full text of PRSA Professional Standards Advisories is online at www.prsa.org.

challenge emerges as a widespread concern within the profession. From the adoption of its revised Code of Ethics in 2000 to late 2010, when this book went to press, PRSA had issued 14 Professional Standards Advisories. Table 6.1 lists those ethics challenges.[15]

THE REWARDS OF ETHICAL BEHAVIOR

Let's ask a blunt question: What's the payoff for ethical behavior? What's in it for you?

Payoffs for ethical behavior, of course, are many, but among the most important is simply the deep satisfaction of doing the right thing. As different as Aristotle, Kant, and Mill are, they do agree on one point: You can't be truly happy unless you strive to honor your deepest values. (Unfortunately, they also agree that, though indispensable, ethical behavior may not be enough to guarantee happiness.) Still, this chapter is based on the assumption that you want to be an ethical person who works for an ethical organization.

Besides helping to create a happy life, ethical behavior can have some bottom-line bonuses—compensation, perhaps, for the sheer difficulty of behaving ethically. There's growing evidence that ethical behavior can lead to promotion within your organization. A Harvard University study of successful leaders concluded that a powerful correlation exists between leadership and "strong personal ethics."[16] Many public relations practitioners believe that good ethics positively affect an organization's financial success. A 2006 survey showed that corporations well known for ethical behavior, including Starbucks, Timberland, and Whole Foods, earn profits almost 400 percent higher than companies with average reputations.[17] And ethical companies may have superior employees: One recent survey showed that 65 percent of U.S. employees felt truly loyal to employers who "subscribed to ethical practices."[18] However, a recent National Business Ethics Survey of U.S. companies concluded that a code of ethics alone has no effect on profits. Instead, values-based ethics must truly be part of an organization's culture.[19] "If you are going to have a values statement and not follow it," says Shane McLaughlin of the Best Practices in Corporate Communications organization, "it does much more damage to a company than not having a values statement at all."[20]

Not everyone is persuaded by the many studies that tie an organization's profits to its good ethics. "Ultimately, trade-offs must be made between the financial health of the company and ethical outcomes," says Deborah Doane, former director of the Corporate Responsibility Coalition. "And when they are made, profit undoubtedly wins over principles."[21]

QUICKBREAK 6.3

Immanuel Kant and the Categorical Imperative

The German philosopher Immanuel Kant (1724–1804) contributed the concept of the "categorical imperative" to the study of ethics. Despite the fancy name, the concept is fairly simple. Let's say that you're experiencing an ethical crisis that has several possible solutions. Kant would tell you to imagine that a universal maxim—a clear principle designed to apply to everyone in the world—will be the outcome of whichever course of action you choose. For example, one course of action might be for you to make a promise that you know you can't keep. Kant would ask you to imagine such an action becoming standard behavior for everyone—and he would ask you to answer two important questions:

1. Could such a world work?
2. Even if such a world could function, would you want to live in it?

In *Fundamental Principles of the Metaphysic of Morals,* Kant writes, "Act only on that maxim whereby thou canst at the same time will that it should become a universal law."[22] When you discover a course of action that could and probably should be a universal law, that is a **categorical imperative.** And a categorical imperative, says Kant, is a course of action that you must follow.

How would you apply Kant's theory of categorical imperatives to the scenario that opens this chapter? You would imagine that each possible course of action created a maxim that everyone in the world would follow. You would then reject any course of action that could lead to undesirable behavior if it were truly adopted by everyone. For example, one such maxim might be "It's all right to deceive the news media to protect our employees." Would that be a categorical imperative you'd want the world to follow every day? ■

At the very least, we can say that good ethics are probably good for business—and that bad ethics are probably bad for business. The odds favor doing the right thing.

 QUICK CHECK

1. What is a golden mean? How does that concept apply to ethics?
2. How is a dilemma different from a problem?
3. Is legal behavior always ethical? Is illegal behavior always unethical?
4. In the business world, is ethical behavior financially profitable?
5. What is a categorical imperative?

TRUST AND CORPORATE SOCIAL RESPONSIBILITY

The business scandals of the early 21st century have damaged an essential ingredient for ethical relationships: trust. Professors Gene Laczniak and Patrick Murphy say trust is the logical outcome of ethical behavior.[23]

Additionally, in a 2009 report titled "The Dynamics of Public Trust in Business," top U.S. business and public relations leaders acknowledged that "the issue of public trust in business has never been more urgent or consequential than it is today. In many ways, the current global economic downturn is, at its core, a crisis of trust."[24]

Unfortunately, the 2010 Edelman Trust Barometer, an annual survey of public attitudes toward businesses, reported that, worldwide, trust in business is "tenuous"; nearly 70 percent of respondents believed that businesses' behavior would worsen when the international economic recession eased.[25]

In their "Dynamics of Public Trust in Business" report, business and public relations executives concluded that solving the crisis of trust would require a solution familiar to readers of this book: values-driven public relations. The report's top two recommendations for business leaders were:

1. Create a set of values that define and clarify what the enterprise and its people are at root and work to ensure that these values are adhered to consistently across your enterprise.
2. Build and manage strong relationships based on mutual trust.[26]

As you know from Chapter 1, a values-driven public relations approach to rebuilding public trust would involve two key public relations philosophies: two-way symmetry, with its focus on building mutually beneficial relationships; and the reflective paradigm, with its emphasis on bolstering an organization's social legitimacy.

Corporate Social Responsibility

One way that public relations can help build trust over time involves a philosophy known as **corporate social responsibility,** or CSR. Organizations that embrace CSR are "a positive force for change to help improve the quality of people's lives" in the words of the International Business Leaders Forum. In other words, such organizations are good corporate citizens. According to the Corporate Social Responsibility Forum, corporate social responsibility strives for high standards in seven areas:

1. human rights, labor, and security
2. enterprise and economic development
3. business standards and corporate governance
4. health promotion
5. education and leadership development
6. human disaster relief
7. environment[27]

Organizations that address particular social needs though ongoing support and publicity programs engage in a practice known as **cause marketing** or **cause branding;** that is, they identify themselves with a worthy cause. More than 90 percent of U.S. women—the nation's primary shoppers—"said it was important for companies to support a cause," according to research conducted by *PRWeek* and Barkley, a full-service strategic communications agency. "It's only natural that the baby boomers and younger generations, as they begin to move into power structures, take their values with them," said Mike Swenson, a Barkley founder.[28]

Around the world, publics increasingly expect organizations to be good citizens, contributing to the social well-being of their communities—contributing, that is, to a fully functioning society. **Fully functioning society theory** involves the belief that, through public relations, organizations should help address important social needs by using wide-ranging two-way communication to build consensus and discover shared goals. Essentially, in a society that functions at its best, organizations act as citizens who seek the common good. In case this sounds too good to be true, proponents of the theory also point out that a fully functioning society would be good for business.[29] Additionally, corporate social responsibility can help an organization achieve the social legitimacy emphasized in the reflective paradigm of public relations (Chapter 1).

As a values-driven, relationship-oriented philosophy, corporate social responsibility fits perfectly into the broad profession of public relations. A generation ago, Harold Burson, founder of the Burson-Marsteller public relations agency, offered these thoughts on CSR and public relations in a speech at Columbia University: "My subject pertains to the relationship between public relations and corporate social responsibility. I do not believe there is a relationship between the two. They are not cousins or even siblings. They are even closer than identical twins. They are one and the same."[30]

BEYOND CSR: STRENGTHENING ETHICAL BEHAVIOR

Ethical behavior and CSR in an organization must start with top management. Public relations practitioners can monitor and counsel on ethical matters, but ultimately an organization's top managers must lead by example. A whopping

95 percent of respondents to a *Fast Company* magazine survey on business ethics responded "Absolutely" or "Yes" to this question: "Do the ethics of the CEO play a meaningful role in the way the business gets done?" Said one respondent, "Great leaders inspire by example. The behavior of ethical CEOs trickles all the way down into an organization." Another respondent was more concise: "A fish rots from the head."[31]

Top executives, with the assistance of public relations counsel, should create an environment that helps the organization to focus constantly on the importance of ethical behavior in its relationships with others. Creating this environment involves CSR and more:

- periodic ethics audits to help you assess the current state of affairs in your organization
- integration of values into the four-step public relations process (described in Chapter 1)
- a system such as the Potter Box (see p. 177) for analyzing ethical challenges when they do occur

Corporate Social Responsibility

Professional Golfers' Association Tour Commissioner Tim Finchem, right, and Dan Nevins, the PGA Tour's community outreach manager, welcome wounded military veterans and their families to a "Birdies for the Brave" event in Washington, D.C. Like traditional for-profit companies, organizations such as the PGA engage in corporate social responsibility.

(Courtesy of Army Staff Sgt. Michael J. Carden and the U.S. Department of Defense)

Ethics Audits

An audit is a process of examination, evaluation, and recommendations. Most of us, probably, have heard of financial audits, in which a professional auditor examines an organization's income and expenditures and makes recommendations for improvement. In an **ethics audit,** we should ask and answer six basic questions:

1. What is our organization's ethics code?
2. How do we communicate that code to ourselves and others?
3. What do key publics, including employees, know about our ethics code?
4. What successes in ethics have we recently had, and why?
5. What setbacks in ethics have we recently had, and why?
6. What can we do to bolster strengths and reduce weaknesses in our ethics?

Periodically answering these questions and correcting any seeming deficiencies can help your organization build the necessary foundation for ethical behavior. However, because ethics audits can deal with sensitive matters—who really wants to criticize the ethics of a colleague or a boss?—organizations often hire outside consultants for such audits.

Integrating Ethics into the Public Relations Process

As we'll discuss in Chapter 12, the best time to solve a problem is before it starts. That's certainly true of challenges to ethical relationships: The best time to solve them is before they become problems. How can you attempt to do that? By ensuring that a focus on values is at the heart of your four-step public relations process.

In the *research* phase, as you scan the horizon searching for issues that may affect your organization, you should be well aware of your organization's written values. When you begin to research a particular issue, you should both remind yourself of those values and gather information on the values of the involved publics. Any clashes among those sets of values should alert you to a potential ethics problem.

In the *planning* phase, you should test every proposed action against your organization's values and against the values of involved publics.

In the *communication* phase, you should implement every action with a clear understanding of how it reflects the values of your organization and the involved publics.

In the *evaluation* phase, you should study whether your completed actions were indeed consistent with your organization's values. You should also consider the impact of the actions on the values of the involved publics. Any lapses or clashes should initiate a study to see whether problems stemmed from the actions or from your organization's values.

The Potter Box

With CSR, periodic ethics audits, and your values-driven public relations process, you've established a foundation. But let's be realistic: Some challenges, like the

"Real World" scenario that begins this chapter, appear out of the blue. We can't predict them. All we can do is try to react effectively and ethically. A helpful tool in such situations is the **Potter Box.** Designed by Ralph Potter, a former professor of divinity, the Potter Box helps people analyze individual ethical crises.[32] It derives its name from its boxlike format (see Figure 6.1).

To analyze and address an ethical problem with the aid of the Potter Box, you follow a six-step process:

1. *Definition box:* Define the situation as objectively as possible. What *don't* you know? Would anyone define the situation differently? Who and why?
2. *Values box:* State the different values involved in the situation and compare the merits of the differing values. Do particular values suggest particular courses of action?
3. *Principles box:* Consider traditional ethics principles and approaches from relevant ethics codes and from this chapter's QuickBreak philosophers: Aristotle, Kant, Mill, and Rawls. How might they help you act on the values you've just identified? For example, what courses of action do Aristotle's principles suggest? Do these principles suggest any new values?
4. *Loyalties box:* Identify all the stakeholders. What obligations do you have to each? Who most deserves your loyalty? Do these loyalties suggest new principles and values that you haven't considered? What courses of action do your top loyalties suggest? Do the actions you've already considered honor your top loyalties?
5. Select a course of action that embraces the most compelling values, principles, and loyalties. Examine it in the light of your definition. If it still seems to be the best choice, implement it. Again, this is not easy. But in each possible course of action, you can now see which values, principles, and loyalties you're honoring.
6. Evaluate the impact of your decision.

This six-step process won't automatically tell you what the most ethical course of action is. But it can help you dissect the situation so that you can act on your top values, principles, and loyalties and justify your decision to yourself and to others. The Potter Box can help you practice values-driven public relations.

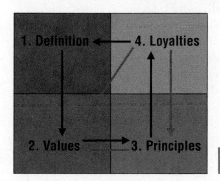

FIGURE 6.1
The Potter Box

VALUES STATEMENT 6.1

Goodwill Industries of Orange County

Goodwill Industries of Orange County, California, helps people with disabilities find rewarding employment that benefits employers and employees alike. Founded in 1924, Goodwill Industries of Orange County is accredited by Goodwill Industries of America, Inc.

Mission

The mission of Goodwill Industries of Orange County is to provide people with disabilities the opportunity to achieve their highest levels of personal and economic independence.

Vision

We envision a world where all individuals with disabilities and other barriers to employment will have opportunities to enjoy the full benefits of competitive employment. Goodwill will focus on being the leader in providing quality education, training, and employment services. The core of Goodwill programs will empower individuals to be productive and independent, based on their abilities and interests.

Values

We believe in the inherent value of work; work has a greater value than charity. We trust and respect the dignity and creative potential of every person.
  We strive for superior quality in our programs and services.

—Goodwill Industries of Orange County website ■

The Potter Box at Work

Let's apply the Potter Box to Choose and Lose, the "Real World" scenario that opens this chapter:

1. *Definition box:* Three days ago, the CEO of my company told the news media that a much-publicized environmental hazard in our company's production process had been eliminated. The person responsible for eliminating the hazard is one of my best friends. Right now, she really needs me because she's going through a rough time dealing with the death of her oldest child. Yesterday I learned that she hadn't eliminated the environmental hazard; it still exists. In her condition, she doesn't even realize that she hasn't corrected it. I'm afraid that telling her will damage our friendship, which is one of the few positive things in her life right now. But if our CEO discovers the oversight, he might fire her—which, I'm afraid, could deepen her depression to a dangerous level.
2. *Values box:*
   A. Caring for my friend
   B. Duty to CEO and company
   C. Protecting the environment
   D. Honesty with news media

Ethics Helpline Poster

Mired in an ethics dilemma? If you're an employee of Sprint Corporation, help—or at least understanding— may be just a phone call away.

(Courtesy of Sprint Corporation)

3. *Principles box:* Using Aristotle's excess–deficiency principle, you might decide that caring for your friend—the first value you've listed—could be taken to an unethical extreme. You might decide that the true value of caring for your friend cannot involve deceiving both your company and the news media. You will still honor the value of caring—but not to that unethical extreme.

Now you ask whether other, standard ethical principles apply. Kant's categorical imperative (QuickBreak 6.3)? Mill's principle of the greatest good for the greatest number (QuickBreak 6.4)? John Rawls' demand for unbiased social justice for all, with special consideration for society's least powerful (QuickBreak 6.5)? Do the ethics codes of your organization, PRSA, and other relevant organizations offer guidelines for action?

Mill and Rawls help you realize that you've left out a key value: the health and welfare of people who may be affected by the uncorrected environmental hazard. You now use your company's ethics code plus the principles of Kant and the other philosophers to ponder how you might act on this value.

At this point, perhaps the Potter Box has shown you that caring for your friend does have limits (Aristotle); that you don't want to live in a world in which companies deceive important stakeholders (Kant); that the greatest good for the greatest number involves quickly fixing that environmental hazard (Mill); and that your solution needs to be as compassionate as possible to your friend as well as to the citizens affected by the hazard (Rawls). Among the many options, perhaps you're starting to formulate a decision that involves several actions and addresses several publics.

QUICKBREAK 6.4

Jeremy Bentham, John Stuart Mill, and Utilitarianism

The English philosophers Jeremy Bentham (1748–1832) and John Stuart Mill (1806–1873) helped develop the philosophy of utilitarianism. **Utilitarianism** holds that all our actions should be directed at producing the greatest good for the greatest number of people.

The obvious question here is What is the greatest good? According to utilitarianism, the greatest good is the action that produces the greatest happiness. "Actions are right in proportion as they tend to promote happiness, wrong as they tend to produce the reverse of happiness," writes Mill in *Utilitarianism*.[33] Bentham and Mill don't mean cheap, momentary, sensual happiness. They mean profound, lasting happiness, the kind produced by justice and love.

Utilitarianism asks us to consider courses of action that may not benefit us. "As between [a person's] own happiness and that of others," writes Mill, "utilitarianism requires him to be as strictly impartial as a disinterested and benevolent spectator."[34]

You might consider utilitarianism when you face a dilemma—that is, when you face an ethical problem in which every option has a downside. Utilitarianism would suggest that you select the solution that creates the greatest happiness—or perhaps the least unhappiness—for the greatest number of people.

How might you apply utilitarianism to the "Real World" scenario that opens this chapter? Simply put (though hard to do), you would examine which course of action creates the greatest good for the greatest number of people. ■

4. *Loyalties box:* Reviewing the situation, you determine that there are six primary stakeholders:
   A. your friend
   B. the CEO and the company
   C. the environment
   D. the news media and their audiences
   E. people affected by the environmental hazard
   F. yourself

   As you strive to determine the most ethical action in this situation, you begin to see that if you remain loyal only to your friend and say nothing, you're damaging the environment, hurting your company's important relationship with the news media, hurting those affected by the hazard, and perhaps hurting your future with the company. You realize that such damage will affect your organization's ability to reach its goals. Failure to reach those goals will affect your coworkers' ability to send children to college, to plan for retirement, to assist elderly parents, and other important concerns.

5. *Decision and action:* You decide that the value of caring for your friend does not outweigh the competing values of duties to the CEO, your company, the news media, and citizens affected by the hazard. Utilitarianism's philosophy of

QUICKBREAK 6.5

John Rawls and Social Justice

What do we owe to those less fortunate than we are? In decision-making processes, who speaks for the powerless who may be affected by the decisions? These questions concern advocates of social justice such as John Rawls.

In his book *A Theory of Justice,* Rawls urges decision makers to recognize and consider the values of all affected publics, not just those who have the power to influence decisions. Rawls recommends two particular techniques for an ethical decision-making process:[35]

1. Rawls suggests that before a decision is made, decision makers figuratively pass through a **veil of ignorance** that strips away their rank, power, and status. The veil of ignorance strategy asks decision makers to examine the situation objectively from all points of view. In particular, it asks them to imagine lifting the veil of ignorance only to discover that they are now a member of one of the affected publics instead of the decision maker.
2. Rawls suggests that to redress social injustice, the most disadvantaged publics in a situation should receive the most consideration. In other words, those in positions of power and advantage should justify their status by using their advantages to help those who have had fewer opportunities or more misfortunes, including forms of discrimination.

Rawls' theory of social justice may sound extreme, but it shares some similarities with values-driven public relations. It asks us to identify, respect, and build relationships with the publics whose values come into contact with the values of our organizations. ∎

the greatest good for the greatest number of people has urged you to honor the values that involve those other key publics. The philosophy of Rawls has helped you realize that, although you can't protect your friend as much as you'd like, you can still find ways to help her. You decide to tell the CEO, help correct the problem, and inform the news media. You approach an official in the company's human resources department with the following plan:

A. You will gently inform your friend of the problem and help her correct it.
B. The human resources official will inform the CEO of the death in your friend's family and the consequent depression your friend is experiencing. The official will inform the CEO that your friend needs to meet with him on an important matter, but the official will not reveal the failure to correct the environmental hazard. Your friend will do that.
C. Along with the official from the human resources department, you will accompany your friend to the CEO's office, and she will tell him of the omission and of her corrective actions.

D. You will help prepare a news release to be sent to all appropriate news media. In that release, the company will announce the error and state what it is doing to ensure that such temporary inaccuracies never happen again. Your strategy is to explain that the uncorrected problem was the result of an inadvertent human error and that steps are being taken to correct the possibility of a recurrence.

E. You will increase your efforts to support your friend and, with the official from human resources, will explore what company policies and programs are available to help her.

6. *Evaluation:* Most publics, including the news media, are impressed by honesty and will forgive unintended errors. But you'll still evaluate the reaction of important publics such as employees and journalists. You'll also evaluate your friend's progress in dealing with her grief. Your evaluation of this episode will also, no doubt, lead you to establish procedures to verify information before it is distributed throughout your company and to the news media.

 QUICK CHECK

1. What is CSR?
2. In the four stages of the public relations process, where should we consider values?
3. What is an ethics audit? What questions should we ask in the course of an ethics audit?
4. What ethical principle is the foundation of utilitarianism?
5. In order, what are the four quadrants of the Potter Box?
6. What is meant by the veil of ignorance? How can it assist ethical decision making?

SUMMARY

No thinking person will ever say that living an ethical life is easy. But the rewards of ethical behavior are substantial. We can attain those rewards by constantly examining our values and how well our actions live up to our high standards. Sometimes our only reward is the satisfaction of knowing that we analyzed a tough situation and followed the most ethical course of action. Hardly a day goes by, on the other hand, without a new story about unethical behavior in the business world. The penalties for unethical behavior can be substantial, leading to lost profits and, often, lost jobs. And for public relations practitioners, unethical behavior can mean the loss of credibility, which is one of our most valuable possessions.

The ethics that affect public relations come from five general sources: international codes, societal codes, professional codes, organizational codes, and personal codes. Practitioners must know these codes and should be familiar with ethical decision-making processes such as the Potter Box if they hope to successfully tackle traditional ethical challenges that arise from dilemmas, overwork, legal/ethical confusion, values of other cultures, short-term thinking, and virtual organizations. Practicing CSR and examining your organization's values, as well as those of important publics, at every stage of the public relations process can help you achieve ethical, values-driven behavior.

It's hard to write about ethics and not sound preachy. That's not our purpose in this chapter. But ethical behavior is indispensable in values-driven public relations. For our society, for our organizations, for our important publics, and for ourselves, we should strive for nothing less.

DISCUSSION QUESTIONS

1. Where do you stand in public relations' objectivity–advocacy ethics debate? Should practitioners always tell 100 percent of what they know? Or is selective truth telling acceptable? If so, when?
2. What organizations have news media recently featured for ethical behavior? For unethical behavior?
3. Imagine that you're counseling an organization on the wisdom of ethical behavior. How would you work the following concepts into your presentation: resource dependency theory, two-way symmetry, the reflective paradigm, trust, and the Potter Box?
4. Are John Rawls' theories of social justice unrealistic for profit-making businesses? Why should for-profit businesses care about powerless, disadvantaged publics?
5. What companies are well known for CSR? Do their reputations affect your purchasing decisions?

MEMO FROM THE FIELD

MIKE SWENSON
President; Barkley PR/Cause
Kansas City, Missouri

Mike Swenson is an internationally recognized leader in the concept of cause branding. As a moving force behind the annual Barkley/*PRWeek* Cause Survey, Swenson has helped create cause-branding initiatives and other strategic communication programs for clients that include Lee Jeans, Sonic Drive Ins, H&R Block, and L'Oreal Paris. Barkley also works with well-known nonprofit brands, including March of Dimes, Komen for the Cure, and the Entertainment Industry Foundation.

Swenson volunteers for several organizations, including the Kansas City Zoo and Harvesters Community Food Bank. He also served as chair of the 2010 March for Babies, which benefited March of Dimes.

(*continued*)

Swenson was press secretary for former Kansas Governor John Carlin and has worked as a news reporter, director, and producer for an NBC-TV affiliate. He is past president of IPREX, a global corporation of more than 70 independent public relations firms. His Citizen Brand blog (www.citizenbrand.typepad.com) champions companies, nonprofits, and individuals that lead as Citizen Brands within their communities.

It's often difficult to improve upon the wisdom of popular sayings. A perfect example is the one that goes "If you talk the talk, you had better walk the walk." If everyone followed this advice, there would be little need for public relations professionals. But since individuals and organizations of every type frequently talk a better game than they actually walk, there will always be a need for people like us.

Ethics and social responsibility must be the foundation for good public relations. As professionals-to-be, you need to learn not only the techniques and tactics of PR, but also come to understand why we do them. The principal reason behind any public relations strategy for an organization is to improve its reputation. A reputation is a moving target. It is always changing. Our job as PR professionals is to make sure the change is always positive.

The explosion of technology and the proliferation of information make the spotlight shine brighter than ever on organizations today. When bad things happen, we find out about them faster, and we learn more than we have before. Often, more than we need to know. This is the environment PR pros work in now.

Gone are the days when companies could put a shroud over their business and avoid scrutiny. Our role is to show these organizations that open and transparent communication is a good thing. It is good because if a company practices it, then the company is likely a socially responsible organization acting in an ethical way.

One of the best ways for organizations to exhibit social responsibility is cause branding. It is also rapidly becoming one of the best business strategies for growth and enhancement of a brand. Consumers expect companies to give back to society. They want to do business with companies that show they care.

Our Barkley/*PRWeek* cause research has consistently shown growing consumer support for companies that support causes. This is particularly true among women—who account for more than 80 percent of household spending. That statistic should matter to public relations pros as well as to marketing leaders. Two of three women have purchased a brand because it supports a cause they believe in, and three of four have recommended a brand to others for the same reason.

Socially responsible companies that do cause branding will also attract and retain the best employees. We all want to work for organizations that care. Our research tells us that two out of three corporate leaders said their cause programs resulted in improved employee morale and retention. Good morale among employees will result in better work and improved results. Cause branding is one important way for an organization to show it is walking the walk.

Consumers and employees represent two of the most important stakeholders for any organization, but there are others. Public companies have to be responsive to shareholders. Nonprofits have to be responsive to their boards, donors, and volunteers. And all organizations have to be mindful of governmental stakeholders on some level. Acting in a socially responsible manner will improve the reputation of any organization with all of these important stakeholders.

I am often asked whether I believe cause branding will eventually die out because there is too much of it. I believe that notion is ridiculous. Why would any of us grow tired of seeing people being helped and good causes being supported? Instead, I think the question that should be asked is why a company would not want to be engaged in helping to better society.

Because of the heightened importance being put on social responsibility in business, this is an exciting time to be entering the public relations profession. Besides learning as much as you can in class, get out into the world now and get involved. Volunteer with a local charity either in your college town or your hometown. Apply for internships with companies that practice social responsibility and see it in action from the inside. And read as much as you can about corporate social responsibility, cause branding, and business ethics.

We all are looking for ways to make a difference. You can make a difference and have a successful career at the same time in public relations. Most important, you will be a person who not only talks the talk, but one who definitely walks the walk. ■

CASE STUDY 6.1 Canada's Family Channel Battles Bullies

A recent worldwide survey asked 26,000 adults to name the friendliest nation on Earth. The top answer? Think hockey, maple leaves, and maybe even actors Jim Carrey and Mike Myers. Think Canada.[36]

Even the world's friendliest nation, however, can contain an oddly discordant note: Think bullies. Research shows that 20 percent of Canadian youths ages 4 to 19 have been bullied continually for two or more years.[37]

"Bullying is about behavior," says middle school teacher Bill Belsey, president of Bullying.org Canada. "And we can change behavior."[38]

Although changing a public's behavior may not be as easy as Belsey thinks (see Chapter 8), he has good reason for optimism: His partner in the crusade to end bullying is a media giant—Canada's Family Channel, a subsidiary of Astral Media that reaches more than 5 million homes in that nation.

Why would a for-profit media outlet join a grassroots organization to combat a problem that could hardly affect its bottom line?

In a word, values.

"If it's important to kids, it's important to us," says Joe Tedesco, vice president and general manager of the Family Channel. "The majority of

our viewers are Canadian kids, and bullying is an issue that faces every kid at one time or another."[39]

In "The Way We Do Business: Our Guide to Ethical Business Conduct," Astral Media specifies its commitment to corporate social responsibility:

We are committed to being a responsible corporate citizen of the communities in which we reside. We will strive to improve the well-being of our communities through the encouragement of employee participation in civic affairs and through corporate philanthropy.[40]

In 2005, additional research by the Family Channel and the Canadian Initiative for the Prevention of Bullying noted that the presence of observers can reduce bullying:

- When an observer objects, bullying stops within 10 seconds in 57 percent of incidents.
- In 85 percent of bullying situations, observers are present.
- When observers are present in a bullying situation, they object only 25 percent of the time.[41]

"Family Channel and Bullying.org are trying to change 'bystander' behavior by showing kids examples of how they can act differently and defuse bullying situations," says Belsey. "We are not asking kids to get involved in a physical way but rather to reach out to victims and show bullies that their actions will not be tolerated."[42]

At the center of the intervention strategy is a pledge that the Family Channel and Bullying.org encourage young Canadians to take:

> This is for me, my friends today, and my friends tomorrow. I think being mean stinks. I won't watch someone get picked on, because I am a do-something person—not a do-nothing person. I care. I can help change things. I can be a leader. In my world, there are no bullies allowed. Bullying is bad. Bullying bites. Bullying bothers me. I know sticking up for someone is the right thing to do. My name is _____. And I won't stand by. I will stand up.[43]

To promote the pledge and encourage intervention in bullying situations, the Family Channel has helped implement the following public relations tactics:

- a National Bullying Awareness Week, launched in 2003
- a Bullying.org website where youths can take the pledge and share advice
- television public service announcements showing youths intervening in bullying situations and taking the pledge
- a video news release showing the launch of Bullying Awareness Week at an elementary school in Ontario

- media interviews with young stars of Family Channel shows such as *Radio Free Roscoe*
- news releases announcing National Bullying Awareness Week

In the first National Bullying Awareness Week, 55,000 Canadian youths took the pledge. "The message of the pledge," says Belsey, "is to encourage kids to be leaders and not followers and set an example that bullying is not cool."[44]

In 2005, the Canadian Public Relations Society honored the Family Channel and its anti-bullying campaign with the Award of Excellence for Community Relations.

"As long as they're bringing it to the forefront for people to hear and learn about...," says Ali Mukaddam, a star of *Radio Free Roscoe,* "then it's just a good thing."[45]

DISCUSSION QUESTIONS

1. Family Channel and Bullying.org want to change a public's behavior. What does public relations research say about their chances of success?
2. In addition to the tactics used by the Family Channel to promote the pledge and encourage intervention in bullying situations, what other tactics would you recommend?
3. If you were public relations director of the Family Channel, how would you answer possible stockholder concerns about using corporate resources for charitable activities that don't directly boost the bottom line?
4. Do you believe that ethical companies benefit financially? Do you prefer to do business with ethical companies? ■

CASE STUDY 6.2 A Dirty Campaign for Clean Coal

You've probably heard a professor say these words in defense of a particular assignment: "Hey, life is a group project."

With all the attendant advantages and disadvantages, life—including public relations—generally *is* a group project. But when group members don't

share the same values, disaster lurks on the horizon. Just ask the American Coalition for Clean Coal Electricity.

The American Coalition for Clean Coal Electricity (ACCCE) is "a partnership of the industries involved in producing electricity from coal."[46] In 2009,

ACCCE began a campaign—a group project—to persuade Congress to defeat the American Clean Energy and Security Act, which would, in part, regulate emissions from coal-powered electrical plants.

ACCCE hired the Hawthorn Group, a strategic communications agency, to enlist like-minded groups for ACCCE's lobbying efforts against the legislation. In turn, the Hawthorn Group hired Bonner & Associates, which specializes in building grassroots campaigns, to help locate such groups and persuade members to write letters to Congress. And Bonner & Associates hired an employee who—well, let the *Charlottesville* (Va.) *Daily Progress* tell the story: "As U.S. Rep. Tom Perriello was considering how to vote . . . , the freshman congressman's office received at least six letters from two Charlottesville-based minority organizations voicing opposition to the measure. The letters, as it turns out, were forgeries." The writer of at least one of the letters, the newspaper reported, "was employed by a Washington lobbying firm called Bonner & Associates."[47]

Perriello was furious—at both the forgery and the apparent silence of Bonner, Hawthorn, and ACCCE, any of which might have informed him of the deception before he voted on the bill. In Congressional testimony, Perriello declared:

> While politics has never been pretty, there are certain lines you just don't cross, like the forging of letters. . . . A letter from [community group Creciendo Juntos] informed me that a partner with the lobbying firm Bonner and Associates had contacted Creciendo Juntos to inform them that an employee . . . had faked a letter claiming to be from Creciendo Juntos. . . . This was the first my office was told of this or any other faked letter, despite the fact that it is now known that Bonner and Associates and the American Coalition for Clean Coal Electricity that had hired them knew about the forged letter before the final vote on this crucial energy legislation.[48]

Soon after news of the first forgeries broke, *Roll Call*, a Capitol Hill newspaper, reported that "[s]o far, ACCCE has verified that 12 falsified letters were sent" to members of Congress.[49]

The problem apparently started with an employee hired by Bonner & Associates, which, in turn, was hired by the Hawthorn Group, which was hired by ACCCE, which was created by a coalition of more than 30 companies and organizations. Within that complex group, finger-pointing began as the members began to edge away from one another. Bonner & Associates distanced itself from the forger—who, according to founder Jack Bonner, was a "temporary employee who worked for us for 7 days [and] acted alone. . . . [I]t was through our quality control efforts that we found the problem and fired the employee on the same day we discovered it."[50]

The Hawthorn Group then distanced itself from Bonner & Associates. In a news release, an agency representative said, "This [situation] violated Bonner's own quality control and verification process that we understood was in place before we hired [the agency]. Hawthorn immediately terminated our work with Bonner."[51] In comments to the *Washington Post*, however, Jack Bonner denied the termination, stating that his agency had completed its contract with Hawthorn.[52]

Although ACCCE did not fire the Hawthorn Group, the coalition made it clear who had hired Bonner. "We are outraged at the conduct of Bonner and Associates," said ACCCE's president. "Bonner and Associates was hired by the Hawthorn Group—our primary grassroots contractor—to do limited outreach earlier this year."[53]

As environmental groups and members of Congress demanded a Justice Department investigation, a representative of ACCCE told *Roll Call*, "We are clear that No. 1, we believe that we have very high standards with regard to our grassroots program at this point."[54]

In the offices of Creciendo Juntos, however, a different viewpoint prevailed. "It's this type of activity that undermines Americans' faith in democracy," a representative said.[55]

DISCUSSION QUESTIONS

1. Can you find an ACCCE ethics code on the group's website (www.cleancoalusa.org)? What do the results of your search indicate?

2. In your opinion, does ACCCE bear any responsibility for the actions of Bonner & Associates? Does the Hawthorn Group?

3. Bonner & Associates did notify Creciendo Juntos of the deception. In your opinion, should it also have notified Representative Perriello?

4. How might ACCCE prevent similar problems in future lobbying efforts? ■

NOTES

1. *New Standard Encyclopedia*, vol. 5 (Chicago: Standard Education Society, 1947).

2. Hugh N. Culbertson, Ni Chen, and Linzhi Shi, "Public Relations Ethics: Some Foundations," *Ohio Journalism Monographs*, no. 7 (January 2003): 2.

3. Ronald J. Alsop, *The 18 Immutable Laws of Corporate Reputation* (New York: Free Press, 2004).

4. Chick-fil-A, online, www.chick-fil-a.com.

5. L. M. Sixel, "Five Questions with Dan Cathy," *Houston Chronicle*, 25 June 2004, online, LexisNexis.

6. Ralph D. Barney and Jay Black, "Ethics and Professional Persuasive Communication," *Public Relations Review* 20, no. 3 (fall 1994): 189.

7. Confucius, *The Doctrine of the Mean*, online, http://classics.mit.edu/Confucius/doctmean.html.

8. Free Burma Coalition, online, www.freeburmacoalition.org; John Lanchester, "Walled Off," *The New Yorker*, 11 December 2006, online, LexisNexis Academic.

9. Todd Finkelmeyer, "When Pushed, UW Panel Insists the School's Existing Standards for Primate Research Are Sufficient," *Capital Times* (Madison, Wis.), online, LexisNexis Academic.

10. Jesse McKinley, "A Dose of Maturity for a California Protest," *New York Times*, 22 January 2007, online, LexisNexis; John Ritter, "Berkeley Protest Branching Out," *USA Today*, 11 January 2007, online, LexisNexis.

11. Social Media Survey 2009," *PRWeek* and MS&L Worldwide, October 2009, online, www.prweekus.com.

12. Donald K. Wright and Michelle D. Hinson, "An Updated Look at the Impact of Social Media on Public Relations Practice," *Public Relations Journal* 3, no. 2 (Spring 2009), online, www.prsa.org.

13. Bob Pearson, "Strong Ethics or Strong Regulation—Our Choice," *E-Commerce Times*, 30 September 2009, online, www.ecommercetimes.com.

14. Thomas Donaldson, "Values in Tension: Ethics Away from Home," *Harvard Business Review*, September–October 1996, online, LexisNexis.

15. "Ethics Resources," Public Relations Society of America, online, www.prsa.org/aboutUs/ethics.

16. Bodo Schlegelmilch, *Marketing Ethics: An International Perspective* (London: International Thomson Business Press, 1998), 145.

17. "Quick Study: PDA Users Report E-mail Overload; Ethical = Profitable; Executive Pay-for-Performance Model PR News," *PR News*, 4 December 2006, online, LexisNexis.

18. "National Workplace Study Shows Employees Take Dim View of Current Leadership Ethics," news release issued by Walker Information, 1 September 2003, online, www.walkerinfo.com.

19. Shane McLaughlin, "A New Era for Communicating Values," *The Public Relations Strategist* (winter 2003): 10.

20. Thomas Donaldson, "Adding Corporate Ethics to the Bottom Line," *Financial Times*, 13 November 2000, online, LexisNexis.

21. Deborah Doane, "The Myth of Corporate Social Responsibility," *Stanford Social Innovation Review* 3, no. 3 (fall 2005): 24.

22. Immanuel Kant, *Fundamental Principles of the Metaphysic of Morals*, in *Harvard Classics*, vol. 32 (New York: P. F. Collier and Son, 1910), 352.

23. Gene Laczniak and Patrick Murphy, *Marketing Ethics: Guidelines for Managers* (Lexington, Mass.: Lexington Books, 1985).

24. "Special Report: The Dynamics of Public Trust in Business—Emerging Opportunities for Leaders," a report issued by the Arthur W. Page Society and the Business Roundtable Institute for Corporate Ethics, 2009, p. 8.

25. "Trust in Business Rises Globally, Driven by Jumps in U.S. and Other Western Economies," Edelman, online, www.edelman.com.

26. "Special Report: The Dynamics of Public Trust in Business—Emerging Opportunities for Leaders," p. 28.

27. Ronald Alsop, "Ranking Corporate Reputation," *Wall Street Journal,* 6 December 2005, online, http://online.wsj.com.

28. Tonya Garcia, "Committed to the Cause: Cause Survey 2009," *PRWeek*, November 2009, online, www.prweekus.com.

29. Robert L. Heath, "Onward into More Fog: Thoughts on Public Relations' Research Directions," *Journal of Public Relations Research* 18, no. 2 (2006).

30. Harold Burson, "Social Responsibility or 'Telescopic Philanthropy': The Choice Is Ours," speech to the Columbia University Graduate School of Business, 20 March 1973.

31. "The 'Fast Track Leadership Survey' on Business Ethics and Integrity," report issued by *Fast Company* magazine, August 2005, 17.

32. See Clifford Christians, Mark Fackler, Kim Rotzoll, and Kathy Brittain McKee, *Media Ethics: Cases and Moral Reasoning,* 5th ed. (New York: Longman, 1998).

33. John Stuart Mill, *Utilitarianism*, ed. Oskar Priest (New York: Bobbs-Merrill, 1957), 10.

34. Mill, 22.

35. John Rawls, *A Theory of Justice* (Cambridge, Mass.: Harvard University Press, 1971).

36. "It's Official—Australia Is All About the Food, Footy, and Fame," news release issued by Global Marketing Insight, 22 February 2006, online, LexisNexis.

37. "Survey Finds That Children Are Often Bullied for an Extended Period of Time," Family Channel news release, 14 November 2005, online, LexisNexis.

38. Todd Saelhof, "Bully Effort Scares Up Help," *Calgary Sun,* 16 November 2004, online, LexisNexis.

39. "Family Channel Takes a Stand against Bullying," Family Channel news release, 8 November 2004, online, LexisNexis.

40. "The Way We Do Business: Our Guide to Ethical Business Conduct," Astral Media, online, www.astralmedia.com.

41. "Survey Finds That Children Are Often Bullied for an Extended Period of Time."

42. "Family Channel Takes a Stand against Bullying."

43. Stephanie McGrath, "Fighting Words," *Toronto Sun,* 21 November 2004, online, LexisNexis.

44. "Family Channel Takes a Stand against Bullying."

45. Saelhof.

46. American Coalition for Clean Coal Electricity, online, www.cleancoalusa.org.

47. Brian McNeill, "Forged Letters to Congressman Anger Local Groups," *Charlottesville* (Va.) *Daily Progress,* 31 July 2009, online, America's Newspapers.

48. "House Energy Independence and Global Warming Committee Hearing," 29 October 2009, online, http://globalwarming.house.gov/files/HRG/102909Letters/periello.pdf.

49. Anna Palmer, "Coal Caught in Dust-Up," *Roll Call,* 5 August 2009, online, LexisNexis Academic.

50. David A. Fahrenthold, "Coal Group Reveals 6 More Forged Lobbying Letters," *Washington Post,* 5 August 2009, online, LexisNexis Academic.

51. "Statement of Michael Coe, Chief Operating Officer of the Hawthorn Group, Regarding Falsified Constituent Letters sent to Congressional Offices by Bonner and Associates," Hawthorn Group, 3 August 2009, online, www.hawthorngroup.com/NewsReleases/8.3.09news_release.html.

52. Fahrenthold.

53. "ACCCE Statement Regarding Falsified Constituent Contacts Made to Congressional Offices by Bonner and Associates," American Coalition for Clean Coal Electricity, 3 August 2009, online, www.americaspower.org/News/Press-Room/Press-Releases.

54. Palmer.

55. McNeill.

7

Research and Evaluation

OBJECTIVES

After studying this chapter, you will be able to

- describe the value of research and evaluation in the public relations process
- recognize the differences between formal and informal research
- develop a strategy for conducting research
- explain the basics of conducting the five most common forms of public relations research
- glean valuable information through effective analysis of survey results

KEY TERMS

REAL WORLD

Don't Drink the Water?

You have just had one of those "I can't believe they are asking me to do this" moments. As public information officer for a metropolitan county government, you have communicated with citizens on a wide range of issues. Many times, you have asked the public to take some sort of action to promote the community's best interests. But this one takes the cake: Your boss wants you to convince the people of your county that it is safe to drink sewer water.

To be more accurate, this is recycled and purified sewer water: as clean—if not cleaner—than bottled water found on grocery store shelves. Local water and sanitation engineers developed the idea in response to severe water shortages. The county sits in an arid region subject to drought. Water is pumped in from hundreds of miles away at great expense. As the

community's population grows, so does the strain on the region's water supply. In addition to conservation measures, county officials believe that blending the purified sewer water with traditional water sources will significantly ease the problem. However, construction of the water purification plant will be costly, and the thought of having people drink recycled sewer water may be one they find, well, hard to swallow.

Your county is ethnically and economically diverse. Dozens of stakeholder groups regularly lobby county government, many of them in Spanish. Local business and industry groups will likely be heard.

"We need the public's support," your boss says. "The future of our county depends on this."

You ask yourself, "What is the first thing I should do?"

DUE DILIGENCE

Although the concept emerged in the business world more than a century ago, **due diligence** has taken a prominent place in the lexicon of 21st-century public relations. The term, which has its origins in legal and financial circles, refers to the research and disclosure obligations individuals face during the course of business transactions. Simply put, parties doing business with one another are expected to investigate and disclose all aspects of the transaction—positive or negative—prior to closing the deal. However, in a world dominated by buzzwords and new lingo, *due diligence* has taken on a different meaning. When public relations practitioners speak of doing their "due diligence," they mean conducting research and analysis, the first step in the public relations process.

It is hard to find a practitioner who does not believe in doing due diligence. However, recent studies suggest this doesn't always happen. The failure to conduct adequate public relations research often involves the usual suspects: a lack of time and a lack of money. However, Australian scholar Jim Macnamara identifies a more basic reason for this shortcoming. "Most PR practitioners do not proactively use research to measure, either for planning or evaluation, because in their worldview they do not see it as relevant," he said. "When one focuses on and sees one's job as producing outputs such as publicity, publications, and events, measurement of effects that those outputs might or might not cause is an inconsequential downstream issue – it's someone else's concern."[1] Or is it? Even before the Great Recession of 2008, clients and employers were asking a tough question: For what I spend on public relations, am I getting my money's worth?

Here's where many practitioners get into trouble. When they say that you can't measure the value of public relations, employers and clients ask, "why not?" They want hard numbers, much like they get from advertising sales representatives and marketing managers. In response, public relations practitioners and educators have created several complex equations that place a numerical value on intangible concepts such as relationships. However, to many a skeptical client, these formulas seem little more than smoke and mirrors.

In an era of economic downsizing and consolidation, practitioners must turn to research and evaluation to answer the same question asked of Edward L. Bernays in the previous century: Are we getting a big enough bang for our bucks?

Measuring Intangibles

It is not as if practitioners have only recently had an epiphany about the importance of research and evaluation in public relations. From its infancy in the days of Ivy Lee, Edward Bernays, and Arthur Page, the profession has evolved into a social science. An important milestone in this transformation was the creation of the Foundation for Public Relations Research and Education in 1956. Known today as the Institute for Public Relations (IPR), the organization promotes itself as the "science beneath the art of public relations." A report commemorating IPR's 50th anniversary said its founders understood "that no occupation attains the status of a profession without a substantial body of codified professional knowledge and educational systems designed to help create and disseminate that knowledge."[2]

Although organizations such as IPR, PRSA, and IABC historically have promoted increased sophistication in research and evaluation, the profession also is reacting to pressure from businesses and organizations for increased accountability. That is especially true at the start of the second decade of the millennium, as globalization and the move toward a digital economy create new challenges. According to Mark Weiner, CEO of PRIME Research in North America, "While the current environment presents challenges to all forms of business activity, it underscores public relations' most ubiquitous challenges: proving PR value and connecting PR performance with business outcomes."[3]

Among the most notable attempts to make public relations outcomes more tangible was 1999's *Guidelines for Measuring Relationships in Public Relations* by Linda Childers Hon and James Grunig (see QuickBreak 7.3). It marked the first serious attempt to quantify the strength of the relationships an organization has with its key stakeholders.[4] Recently, much of this academic theory has been put to practical use. Katie Delahaye Paine, a noted public relations research guru, noted in 2009 that the Hon–Grunig guidelines for measuring relationships also were ideal for measuring the success of social media relationships.[5]

Research and Evaluation

Research and evaluation are cornerstones of good public relations practice. They lead us to explore two areas essential to success in any public relations effort:

1. *What we think we know:* Do our assumptions hold up under closer examination? If nothing else, research and evaluation can remove lingering doubts by validating the accuracy of information.
2. *What we don't know:* Are pieces missing from the puzzle? By exploring terra incognita—unknown territory—we can open doors of opportunity that might otherwise remain closed.

Why not have separate chapters on research and evaluation? We link those parts of the public relations process in this chapter for two reasons. First, as we noted in Chapter 1, public relations is a dynamic, nonlinear process. The traditional four-step process implies a straight-line approach: research, followed by planning, followed by communication, followed by evaluation. However, public relations does not work that way. The four steps are intertwined. Research and evaluation occur at every phase of the public relations process. It's not unusual for practitioners, in the midst of planning, to decide they need more information. Nor is it unusual for public relations professionals to adjust strategy in the midst of its execution based on either feedback or new information.

The second reason we combine the two steps here is that the processes of research and evaluation are closely related. Both involve using similar methods to gather information. It could be said that research is gathering information before the fact and evaluation is gathering information after the fact. That notion has an element of truth,

QUICKBREAK 7.1

ROI, AVE, and WMC

Now more than ever, organizations expect public relations practitioners to demonstrate a **return on investment (ROI)** to show that their efforts have added to the bottom line.

Some practitioner associations, such as the Institute for Public Relations, believe that ROI is not the best measure. A 2004 IPR survey showed that a majority of communications directors believe it is possible to show that public relations efforts can make more money for an organization than they cost. However, only one-third of those surveyed said they actually consider public relations budgets in ROI terms.[6]

Facing pressures to demonstrate public relations ROI, many practitioners have turned to **advertising value equivalency (AVE),** a calculation based on advertising rates and the amount of media coverage. For example, suppose a public relations agency distributed a news release that generated a story that took up 10 column-inches of space in the local newspaper. If the newspaper charges $100 per column inch, the math would be simple: 10 inches times $100 equals an AVE of $1,000.

Because of third-party endorsement, some note that publicity is more credible—and therefore more valuable—than advertising. They argue that there should be a multiplier in the AVE formula to account for publicity's added value. For example, the Texas Commission on the Arts advises its stakeholders that "a good rule of thumb is to mark up the advertising value by a factor of three for a general story."[7] Using this formula, the AVE of our news story would balloon to $3,000.

You may be asking yourself how this credibility multiplier was determined. That's the heart of the controversy. "There is no scientific evidence to demonstrate that a six-inch ad has the same impact as a six-inch story in the same publication," wrote Katie Delahaye Paine of KD Paine & Partners.

The use of AVE raises other issues such as comparing the value of local versus national publicity, the effect of negative news coverage, and the failure to measure publicity outcomes. There also is the ethical question of telling journalists that a news release contains news and then using advertising rates to measure its value.

IPR's Commission on Public Relations Measurement and Evaluation rejected the use of AVE "as a media measurement concept and practice" in October 2009.[8] In its place, the commission threw its support behind a new concept, **weighted media cost** (WMC). Instead of placing a dollar amount on public relations outcomes based on advertising rates, WMC employs a comparative index created over time. The researchers who created WMC say the number generated by this analysis "has no meaning or value beyond that of any index used for comparisons of any kind."[9] And there's the rub: Although many believe WMC is a more accurate tool for evaluation, others are attracted to AVE's more tangible outcomes. ■

but it's an oversimplification. Instead, we constantly gather information, evaluate it, and seek new information to test a developing hypothesis. Remember your first school dance? You probably picked a dance partner based on an ongoing process of research and evaluation. At first glance across a dimly lit gymnasium, you may have been interested in dancing with a particular person. However, on closer inspection, appearance and behavior might have changed your mind. You may then have sought new information on someone else. Several cycles of research and evaluation may have occurred before you took that big step and ventured onto the dance floor. Public relations is no different—although it is often less traumatic.

No one, certainly not the authors of this book, expects you to become an expert researcher based on the information you find in this chapter. Later in your career, it may be that you rarely do in-depth research—it may be someone else's job to do it for you. Nevertheless, it is important that you know enough to be a good consumer of research.

"As communicators, we need to learn how to measure," said Julie B. Chughtai, director, executive communication, DePaul University. "Unfortunately, I had to learn on the job. We should be teaching the next generation of communicators both the art and the science of what we do."[10]

And that's *exactly* what we are going to do.

QUICKBREAK 7.2

Issues Management

If you think it is difficult for public relations practitioners to measure what has happened, think of how hard it is for them to predict the future. When they do, they are engaged in **issues management,** a process of predicting and managing *future* issues and concerns.

Issues management often begins with **scanning,** which is short for "scanning the horizon." In the days before satellites and radar, scanning the horizon was the only way to determine if there were any potential threats approaching. This is the concept behind issues management: Through a process of analyzing emerging trends and issues, practitioners can prepare their organizations to respond in a timely and appropriate manner.

That's what the U.S. cattle industry did in 2001 when an outbreak of foot-and-mouth disease in European cattle created a panic among consumers. During that crisis, poor media relations had made a bad situation worse. Learning from Europe's mistakes, Dairy Management, Inc., a marketing coalition created to build demand for U.S. dairy products, launched a proactive campaign of food-safety education and training. Tactics included the creation of a website, called the Dairy Response Center, designed to go online at a moment's notice.[11] At about the same time, the National Cattlemen's Beef Association conducted its own research and developed a crisis response plan. Much like DMI, the NCBA focused its efforts on creating online resources and conducting extensive media training for staff and industry opinion leaders.[12]

(continued)

When a single case of mad cow disease was detected in Washington state in 2003, the dairy and beef associations activated their crisis plans. Although the industry lost an estimated $1.3 billion because of the outbreak, things could have been much worse.[13] A January 2005 survey showed that consumer confidence in U.S. beef was higher than before the outbreak.[14] Observers credited the cattle industry's proactive crisis planning with softening the blow.[15]

The goal of any issues management program is to scan for issues and trends with a potential impact—either positive or negative—on the organization. Once an issue is identified, active **monitoring** should begin. By keeping track of the latest developments, organizations can plan responses consistent with their values. And this is where the *real* value of issues management is demonstrated: giving an organization time to act in a manner that allows it to dictate its own course rather than having its response dictated by events. ■

QUICK CHECK

1. Why is research an essential part of the public relations process?
2. What are ROI, AVE, and WMC?
3. What is issues management?

DEVELOPING A RESEARCH STRATEGY: WHAT DO I WANT TO KNOW?

A quirky but entertaining show called *Mythbusters* premiered on the Discovery Channel in January 2003. The premise of the program involves two former Hollywood special effects artists creatively blending science and show business wizardry to test the validity of urban legends. For example, in episode four they challenged the conventional wisdom that a penny thrown from the top of a skyscraper can kill a pedestrian on the street below. By creating an experiment using a dummy and a staple gun modified to fire pennies, the Mythbusters proved that a penny dropped from a tall building lacks sufficient speed and mass to be lethal. (But it sure can hurt!)

So what does all this have to do with research and evaluation? Perhaps more than you may think. When the Mythbusters designed an experiment to simulate the conditions of a real penny drop, they engaged in a process social scientists call *operationalization*. In effect, they developed a strategy to find out what they wanted to know. The Mythbusters also illustrate another important lesson: Creativity is important at every step of the public relations process.

Getting started in almost any endeavor can be difficult. Research is no different. Before setting out on any journey, it is important to know the destination. A journey into research is no different. That is why the first step when you embark on a research project is to develop a **research strategy**. Just like the Mythbusters, that involves asking yourself two important questions:

1. What do I want to know?
2. How will I gather that information?

By answering these questions, you develop a research strategy. Your research strategy, in turn, begins to lay the foundation for a successful public relations program. Let's take a closer look at how we might answer the first question.

What we need to know in public relations research falls into one of four categories: client research, stakeholder research, problem–opportunity research, and evaluation research. Quite often, research findings can fit into more than one category. However, the information itself is far more important than how it is categorized.

Client Research

Client research focuses on the individual client, company, or other organization on whose behalf the practitioner is working. Efforts are geared toward discovering an organization's size; the nature of the products or services it offers; and its history, staffing requirements, markets and customers, budget, legal environment, reputation, and beliefs about the issue in question. It is also essential to understand a client organization's mission and consequent goals. As noted in Chapter 1, an organization's mission statement is based on the organization's core values. Goals are general statements indicating the direction the organization wants to take and are consistent with an organization's values and mission statement.

Stakeholder Research

Stakeholder research focuses on identifying the specific publics important to the success of the client. These various constituencies are known as stakeholders, for each has a different stake in how the organization responds to various issues. The people important to your organization are not a homogeneous mass. They are a wide range of constituencies, each having its own values, attitudes, concerns, needs, and predispositions. How these stakeholders relate to an organization can change from issue to issue. For example, a teachers' union may oppose proposed tax increases for new roads but favor higher taxes for educational programs. Also, people are often members of more than one stakeholder group. Building on the prior example, a member of the teachers' union may favor new road taxes if the funds are earmarked for the area in which that member lives. Stakeholder research helps you better target the message and the media for that message to the needs of each constituency.

Problem–Opportunity Research

Put in the simplest terms, **problem–opportunity research** is research designed to answer two critical questions: What is at issue, and what stake, if any, does our organization have in this issue? Problem–opportunity research develops background information on a particular topic or issue. It also identifies related trends that might have developed. Ultimately, problem–opportunity research answers a key question: Why is it necessary—or unnecessary—for our organization to act? Sometimes organizations are reactive, responding to events that could shape their destiny. Other times they are proactive, launching those destiny-shaping events. There are even times when doing nothing is the best course of action. Problem– opportunity research helps the organization decide whether and how to act.

Evaluation Research

Although evaluation is listed last among the four steps in the traditional public relations process, today's climate demands attention to **evaluation research**—procedures for determining the success of a public relations plan—from the very beginning. With practitioners facing greater demands for accountability, every public relations plan must achieve an impact that is measurable.

Just how important is evaluation? According to a 2006 survey of 1,493 public relations practitioners, 39 percent said that "universalizing our ability to demonstrate a clear Return-on-PR-investment, thereby proving the value of

VALUES STATEMENT 7.1

Institute for Public Relations

The Institute for Public Relations (IPR) was founded in 1956 as the Foundation for Public Relations Research and Education. Located at the University of Florida, IPR is dedicated to improving the professional practice of public relations around the world and encouraging academic and professional excellence in the field of public relations.

The Institute for Public Relations: Our Purpose

No real profession attains that status without a substantial body of codified professional knowledge, as well as educational systems to help create and disseminate that knowledge. This is as true of public relations as it is of medicine, law, accounting or teaching. There is science underlying the art, and it is the working knowledge of that science combined with creativity that marks the best professionals.

The Institute for Public Relations is focused on the science beneath the art of public relations. We exist to expand and document the intellectual foundations of public relations, and to make this knowledge available and useful to all practitioners, educators, researchers and client organizations.

—IPR website ■

QUICKBREAK 7.3

Measuring Relationships

A reason so many people enjoy watching sporting events is that, at the end of the day, a final score determines success. In the real world, things are not always so black and white. That is especially true of public relations, in which practitioners often struggle with the question of how best to measure success.

For example, how does one measure the success of a news release? Sometimes we measure **outputs,** such as the number of news releases we send to the media. Other times, we measure **outcomes,** which, in a limited sense, might mean only the amount of media coverage generated. However, neither approach tells us whether the target audience acted in the desired manner. Both also have a short-term focus.

Missing is an understanding of the long-term effects a public relations program has on relationships with key publics.

To address this broader issue, the Institute for Public Relations, based at the University of Florida, established a panel of educators and professionals to search for more meaningful ways to measure the effectiveness of public relations. One of its reports recommends a process through which practitioners measure the quality of important relationships.

Linda Childers Hon of the University of Florida and James E. Grunig of the University of Maryland wrote that the evaluation of long-term relationships rests on examining six key **components of relationships:**[16]

1. **Control mutuality:** the degree to which parties agree on who has the power to influence the actions of the other. In an ideal relationship, the parties share a degree of control.
2. **Trust:** the willingness of one party to open itself to the other. This depends on perceptions of each party's integrity, dependability, and competence.
3. **Satisfaction:** the degree to which the benefits of the relationship outweigh its costs.
4. **Commitment:** the extent to which each party feels the relationship is worth the time, cost, and effort.
5. **Exchange relationship:** the giving of benefits to one party in return for past benefits received or for the expectation of future benefits.
6. **Communal relationship:** the provision of benefits to each other out of concern and without expectation of anything in return.

Hon and Grunig believe that by administering a questionnaire that includes agree–disagree statements focusing on these six aspects of a relationship, practitioners will have a more meaningful measure of the effectiveness of public relations programs. Trent Seltzer of Texas Tech University has taken this process a step further. He suggests an approach using coorientation (discussed in Chapter 4), measuring the perceptions of both the organization and its publics. "Applying these measures within a coorientational model," he explained, "will indicate the degree of agreement and accurate perceptions between the organizations and their publics when assessing important relationship dimensions."[17] Others, no doubt, will add new twists as the profession struggles to measure its impact in tangible terms. ■

public relations" was the greatest challenge facing the profession. That was second only to the 41 percent who said that upholding the credibility of the profession was its greatest challenge.[18] However, a global survey of public relations practitioners unveiled at the European Summit on Measurement in Berlin in 2009 placed the profession's challenge in sharp focus. Whereas 88 percent of the practitioners questioned said they believe measurement is an integral part of the public relations process, the survey results also showed a lack of consensus on the best ways to do it. The respondents said newspaper clippings were their most popular method of measurement (77 percent), followed by media evaluation tools (66 percent). These methods, especially the use of the controversial Advertising Value Equivalent (AVE), have their detractors (see QuickBreak 7.1).

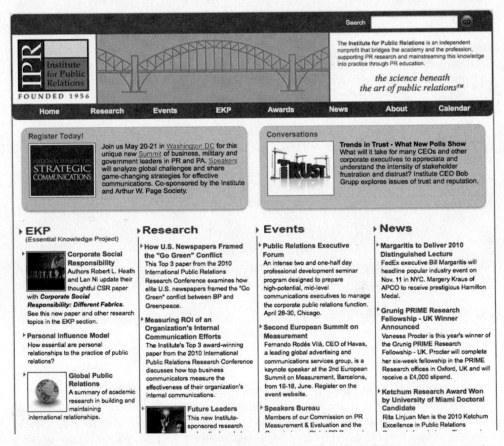

Through its website (www.instituteforpr.org), the Institute for Public Relations provides both scholars and practitioners with the latest research into a wide range of topics important to the profession.

(Used with permission, Institute for Public Relations)

Other popular methods of evaluation mentioned included opinion surveys (61 percent), benchmarking (61 percent), focus groups (59 percent), and internal reviews (59 percent).[19]

In an effort to find agreement on standardized methods of measurement, PRSA announced a series of recommended approaches for evaluating public relations' influence on key business outcomes later that year. The recommendations focused on measuring four types of program goals: financial; reputation and brand equity; employees and other internal publics; and public policy. "Our fundamental goal is to change how the industry talks about what public relations accomplishes," said PRSA Chair and CEO Michael G. Cherenson. "Instead of meaningless catch phrases, such as 'create buzz,' our recommended approach focused on identifying meaningful expressions of business performance, suggesting more appropriate measurement metrics and recommending proven tools for demonstrating how those metrics were impacted."[20]

QUICK CHECK

1. What are the six key components of relationships?
2. When developing a research strategy, what two questions should you ask yourself?
3. What are the four major categories of public relations research?

DEVELOPING A RESEARCH STRATEGY: HOW WILL I GATHER INFORMATION?

First we asked the initial question, "What do I want to know?" Having done that, our next major strategy decision has to do with the methods we will use to gather information. To a large degree, the answer to the question "How will I gather that information?" depends on the time and resources at our disposal. Those factors, in turn, determine whether the research we are planning to conduct will present a reasonably accurate picture of reality or just a snapshot of some smaller aspect of it.

Using the vocabulary of researchers, this is the essential difference between **formal research** and **informal research**. Formal (also known as quantitative or scientific) research presents an accurate picture. That is because it uses scientific methods designed to create a representative picture of reality. In public relations, formal research generally is used to create an accurate portrayal of a stakeholder group. On the other hand, informal (also known as nonquantitative or nonscientific) research describes some aspect of reality but doesn't necessarily develop an accurate picture of the larger reality as a whole. In public relations, informal research is very useful, but it should not lead us to conclusions about an entire stakeholder group.

Now, back to the question at hand: How will I gather the information I need? Public relations practitioners commonly employ five research methods, some of which are already familiar to you: secondary (library) research, feedback research, communication audits, focus groups, and survey research.

Secondary (Library) Research

Secondary research is probably a research method you know well. It uses materials generated by others—sometimes for purposes entirely different from your own. The alternative to secondary research is **primary research,** which is new research you generate from scratch. Sources used in secondary research include:

- *Published materials,* such as newspaper and magazine articles, library references, various directories, and trade association data. This also includes information available through online databases and services such as Lexis-Nexis, Factiva, and various sites on the Web.
- *Organizational records,* such as annual reports, statistics, financial reports, and other disclosures that organizations with publicly held stock are required by law to release. For example, check out the disclosure documents that have been filed with the Securities and Exchange Commission and are available online through the EDGAR search engine at www.sec.gov.
- *Public records generated by governments:* With few exceptions, government agencies in the United States are required to operate in the open. These agencies often generate a wealth of useful information, such as the U.S. census and monthly reports on the nation's economy. Much of this information is available online as well as through federal and state depository libraries located in communities and on college campuses around the country. For example, check out the FedStats database at www.fedstats.gov.

Secondary research is especially valuable in providing information you might never have the means to gather on your own.

Feedback Research

Feedback research enables an organization to receive tangible evidence—often unsolicited—of stakeholder groups' responses to its actions. This evidence can manifest itself in many forms, most commonly through letters and telephone calls to the organization. For example, every time the president of the United States speaks on television, White House operators keep a running tally of the number of calls expressing support for or disapproval of what was said. Proactive organizations monitor all media, including the Internet, to track what others say about them. Web-monitoring products include eWatch, CyberAlert, Cison, and Vocus. Organizations also encourage feedback through a variety of tactics, including point-of-sale surveys and e-mail links on their websites. Although feedback research is not a formal research method, it can give very strong indications of the public relations environment.

SOCIAL MEDIA APPS

Monitoring Social Media

The use of social media for research purposes is in its infancy, and the reviews are mixed. One of the most promising applications is in the area of monitoring. *Public Relations Journal* reported in 2009 that 45 percent of the companies surveyed hired "external agencies" to keep track of what is being said about them online. Another 34 percent indicated they conducted this monitoring in-house.[21] However, a second survey, released simultaneously by Econsultancy, an online community of digital marketing and e-commerce professionals, painted a different picture. According to its survey, "only a quarter of companies using social media are tapping its potential for customer feedback."[22] In yet another survey, only 14 percent of respondents said they were interested in incorporating social-networking data into their current data analysis.[23]

Although the degree to which public relations practitioners use social media may be debatable, there appears to be little doubt that others are using social media for research and monitoring purposes. A study released in early 2010 said that nearly 70 percent of journalists are using social networking sites to gather and disseminate the news.[24] And there is another study that students reading this book should especially note: Nearly half of the companies surveyed said they use search engines and/or social networking tools to recruit and evaluate potential employees.[25] Maybe this will give you cause to watch what you Tweet. ■

The Communication Audit

Communication audits are evaluative procedures used to determine whether an organization's communications are consistent with its values-driven mission and goals. In completing a communication audit, we review an organization's communications and records, and we conduct interviews with key officials.

Rebecca Hart, founder of the Florida-based Hart & Partners, said communication audits are especially useful during times of organizational change. "Communication audits are recommended after management (or board leadership) changes, mergers and acquisitions or whenever significant cost-cutting or re-engineering corporate policies and structures are being revised," Hart said. She also said communication audits provide useful insights following a product or service rollout and in crisis communication situations.[26]

Although there are a variety of ways to conduct communication audits, each method should answer these five questions:

1. What are the organization's stated goals in relation to its stakeholder groups?
2. What communication activities has the organization used to fulfill those goals?

3. Which communication activities are working well and are consistent with those goals?
4. Which communication activities are not working well toward the achievement of those goals?
5. Given the findings of this audit, what revisions in goals or communication activities are recommended?

THE COMMUNICATIONS GRID   One illustrative method of conducting a communication audit is a **communications grid**. The various media used by an organization are listed on one axis. Stakeholders important to the organization are listed on the other. An X is placed everywhere a particular stakeholder is reached by a particular medium. This exercise graphically illustrates where efforts have been directed and which stakeholders might have been overlooked.

Figure 7.1 shows a simplified version of a communications grid using the scenario that opened this chapter. Each mark on the grid represents communication between the county and a key stakeholding public. We know from the scenario that county officials need to convince local residents that recycling sewer water for use as drinking water is safe. We also know that the community is diverse and bilingual. For the purposes of this example, we assume that there are only seven stakeholder groups and six channels of communication. In real life, there would be many more of both.

The grid illustrates that all seven publics represented here have access to the county's website. But this is a passive form of communication: the only people who see it are those who seek it out. (In reality, some residents might not have Internet

	Media Used by County Government					
County Government's Stakeholders	Engineering report detailing the sewer water proposal	Media kits	English-language print/TV advertising	Spanish-language print/TV advertising	e-mail	County government bilingual website
County employees			X		X	X
Local and county officials	X		X		X	X
English-language media		X				X
Spanish-language media						X
English-speaking residents			X			X
Spanish-speaking residents						X
Health care professionals			X			X

FIGURE 7.1

County Government's Communication Channels

access.) By using only English-language media for publicity and advertising, county officials have ignored the Spanish-speaking community. And although most people may not care to read the county's engineering report, it is likely that health care professionals—an important group of potential opinion leaders—would be *particularly* interested in it, yet didn't receive it. The grid also shows that e-mail is the only direct communication county government has with its employees, another potentially influential group of opinion leaders.

In short, a communications grid is a good way to audit visually whether an organization is reaching all the publics important to its success. However, there is one significant drawback: A grid does not address the messages contained in the various media. Those can be determined only through an analysis of their content.

Focus Groups

Focus groups are an informal research method in which interviewers meet with groups of selected individuals to ascertain their opinions. Although focus group results should not be seen as representative of any particular public, they can indicate a public's knowledge, opinions, predispositions, and behavior.

Focus groups are small, informal gatherings in which participants are encouraged to discuss their concerns, attitudes, and predispositions about the subject at hand.

(Photo by David Guth)

Focus groups are a popular research method because, compared with survey research (that is, formal questionnaires), they are relatively inexpensive. They also have the advantage of giving the researcher immediate feedback. Focus groups are often used in advance of survey research. The interaction among focus group participants often raises issues that merit further study. Focus groups can even test the clarity and fairness of survey questions.

Focus group research played a key role in allowing Allstate Insurance Company to address a serious image problem. In the wake of a series of devastating hurricanes, insurance companies sought to limit their financial risks. When Allstate announced it would not renew policies on high-risk properties in eight southern New York counties, the company faced a storm of criticism. A series of focus groups pointed to the need to repair the company's reputation. The focus groups also uncovered a growing concern over teenage-driver safety. The result was an award-winning safe-driving campaign that not only won support from parents and school officials but also resulted in a 90 percent brand favorability rating in the region.[27]

HOW TO CONDUCT A FOCUS GROUP When preparing to conduct focus group research, we suggest you follow this 10-step process:

1. *Develop a list of general questions based on information needs.* The questions should usually be open-ended, avoiding simple yes–no answers.
2. *Select as a moderator someone skilled in interviewing techniques.* The moderator must be strong enough to keep the discussion on track.
3. *Recruit 8 to 12 participants.* Because of the problem of no-shows (people who promise to participate in the focus group but fail to show up), it is necessary to invite a larger number than you need. You can dismiss any extras with a small reward. As to who should be invited to attend, decide on a selection strategy. From what kind of people do you want to hear opinions? Sometimes a screening questionnaire will narrow the field. Participants are often compensated (with money, a free meal, etc.) for their time. An important rule: Avoid inviting people who have sharply divergent points of view. You are interested in gathering information; you are not interested in conducting a debate. Too much clash can stifle participants who might speak up in a friendlier environment. Even if it means conducting additional focus groups, it is best to keep people with sharply different opinions separated.
4. *Record the session.* Make certain participants know that the session is being recorded. It may be necessary to reassure them that it is being done to provide a record of what was said and will not be used for any other purposes.
5. *Observe the session.* In addition to the moderator, others should watch the focus group. They should record their impressions in notes. They do not participate in the session. Some facilities allow these observers to watch the proceedings from behind two-way mirrors. In many cases, however, observers sit quietly along the wall of the room in which the session is being held.

6. *Limit the discussion to 60–90 minutes.* When the conversation starts repeating itself, that is a sign to wrap it up.
7. *Discuss opinions, problems, and needs—not solutions.* It is very likely that participants are not qualified to discuss solutions.
8. *Transcribe the session.* This makes it much easier to analyze participants' comments.
9. *Prepare a written report on the session.* Identify participants by name, age, occupation, hometown, and any other pertinent information. Where possible, use direct quotations.
10. *Remember that focus groups are informal research.* Opinions stated in a focus group do not necessarily represent everyone else's view. At best, they serve as indicators of public opinion. However, they can be considered even stronger indicators if multiple focus groups yield the same comments.

Although these are the recommended steps for conducting focus group research, we also realize that sometimes it is necessary to bend the rules. For example, time and distance may make it difficult to get everyone together in the same room at the same time. Under those circumstances, the use of Internet technology such as Skype might provide a viable alternative.

QUICK CHECK

1. What is secondary research?
2. What is the purpose of a communication audit?
3. What are some of the reasons a researcher may choose to conduct a focus group rather than a survey?

SURVEY RESEARCH

When you are unable to gather the information you need through secondary research or informal research methods, conducting a formal survey may be your best choice. Although **survey research** can be both expensive and time consuming, it can also be a highly accurate way to gauge public opinion. Through the use of specifically worded questionnaires and a carefully selected list of people, researchers are able to make judgments about a much larger population. In essence, surveys provide a snapshot of what people are thinking on a particular subject at a moment in time.

Of course, some surveys are better than others. When the local newspaper asks its readers to vote on a "question of the day," is that a valid survey? When the local television station conducts person-on-the-street interviews, do those interviews necessarily reflect the opinions of the larger community? The answer to both questions is no. But if you change the question and ask whether any useful information can be gleaned from those two approaches, the answer is yes.

The degree to which survey results can be seen as an accurate reflection of a larger population depends on two key factors: the composition of the people you are surveying and the structure of the survey instrument.

QUICKBREAK 7.4

Worth Every Penny

Although some may question the cost of research in preparing public relations campaigns, they need only look at recent case histories to discover that research is often worth every penny.

One example comes from Down Under, where an extortionist threatened to poison candy bars. MasterFoods Australia New Zealand, which distributes the products in New South Wales, did not waste any time getting a finger on the pulse of consumers. During the seven weeks between the time the candy bars were recalled and later returned to store shelves, MasterFoods and its public relations agency conducted six surveys and 20 focus groups. The research helped them gauge whether the company's key message—that it had acted properly to protect the public—resonated with consumers. When the crisis passed, research showed that 98 percent of consumers thought that MasterFoods acted responsibly. Candy bar sales were 250 percent above average in the week the products went back on sale.[28]

About 17 percent of U.S. children under the age of 18 have a developmental disability. In half of those cases, the problem is not diagnosed until the children enter school. The Centers for Disease Control and Prevention wanted to know why. Working with the Porter Novelli Convergence Group, the CDC surveyed parents and pediatricians nationwide. What they learned was that there was a communications disconnect: The parents didn't know the warning signs, and the pediatricians didn't have the resources necessary for educating parents. The research became the impetus for a campaign called "Learn the Signs. Act Early." As a result, the number of early screenings conducted by pediatricians increased, as did the number of parent inquiries to the CDC.[29]

Sometimes, research is more than just research. It can also be the strategy. That was the case when the Minnesota Chapter of PRSA teamed with local magazine *Twin Cities Business* to conduct a survey and a series of focus groups. The purpose of the research was to engage the business community in a discussion of ethics and reputation management. It resulted in a cover story, "What Business Thinks: Minnesota's Most-Admired Companies—And How They Stay That Way." The survey and focus groups accomplished both of the chapter's goals, to raise the profile of PRSA and to launch a dialogue about reputation and reputation management in the business community.[30]

These are just three examples of why planners should think twice before skimping on the research budget. ∎

The Survey Sample

A sample is a portion of a public that we select for the purpose of making observations and drawing conclusions about the public as a whole. In other words, when we question members of a large stakeholder group, we generally don't question every member. Instead, we question a portion, or sample, of that public. A sample is said to be a **representative sample** of a targeted population when it is of sufficient size and when every member of the targeted population has an equal chance of being selected for the sample. Although surveying a representative sample provides a more accurate picture, it is not always practical because of time, cost, and personnel considerations.

For example, which would give you a better picture of U.S. public opinion regarding gun control: an informal poll of your classmates or a formal nationwide survey? Clearly, the latter would provide the more accurate picture. However, the informal poll would at least have advantages in terms of time, money, and effort. And it provides an indication of what public attitudes may be—within the limitations of the sample. In this case, those limitations are the size of your sample and the fact that not everyone in the nation has an equal opportunity of being questioned. You would not be able to say that your classroom poll was an accurate reflection of national opinion. However, if everyone in your class had the same opportunity to express his or her opinion, those results would be representative of the class's views on gun control.

How big should the sample be? No one answer is correct. Nor does a simple explanation exist. At issue here are what statisticians call **confidence levels,** the statistical degree to which we can reasonably assume the outcome is an accurate reflection of the entire population. As a general rule, the larger the sample, the more accurate the outcome is. However, there is a point where additional numbers do not significantly improve accuracy. Statistical accuracy within two or three percentage points is usually the best one can hope for.

DEVELOPING A SAMPLING STRATEGY

Developing a sampling strategy is a step critical to the administration of an accurate survey. Sampling can be as much an act of creativity as writing the survey instrument itself. However, as mentioned earlier, it is not always possible or practical to administer a formal survey. Issues such as cost, time, and staffing often come into play. Before we discuss some of the more common sampling strategies, a few definitions are in order.

- **Sample:** the segment of a population or public a researcher studies to draw conclusions about the public as a whole.
- **Sampling frame:** the actual list from which the sample, or some stage of the sample, is drawn. The sampling frame is important because the accuracy of your list will affect the accuracy of the survey. For example, using the local telephone book as a sampling frame may underrepresent the attitudes of either the very rich or the very poor. Survey results should always be reported in the context of the limitations of their sampling frame.

The U.S. Constitution requires the government to conduct a head count of everyone living in the country at the start of each new decade. The census, named after the sampling technique used in the survey, helps determine congressional districts and levels of federal funding. Residents are asked to complete a questionnaire that provides a wealth of information about who they are and how they live. Critics claim that many residents, particularly the homeless and undocumented foreign workers, are left uncounted.

(U.S. Census Bureau)

- **Units of analysis:** what or whom you are studying to create a summary description of all such units. It is important to be clear about units of analysis because you don't want to make a common error in analyzing results—comparing apples to oranges. The results of a survey of attitudes of students in your classroom should not be used to describe the attitudes of all students because the units of analysis in your sample were students in your classroom, not all students. The views of students in your classroom might not be representative of those of all students.
- **Probability sampling:** the process of selecting a sample that is representative of the population or public being studied. The sample is considered to be representative when it is large enough and when all members of that population or public have an equal chance of being selected for the sample. Usually within a few percentage points, known as the sampling error, the results of a survey of a representative sample are considered an accurate reflection of the sampling frame.
- **Nonprobability sampling:** the process of selecting a sizable sample without regard to whether everyone in the public has an equal chance of being selected.

This sampling technique is often chosen because of time, cost, or personnel considerations. This does not mean that the results are without value. To the contrary, nonprobability sampling results can give researchers an indication of public opinion. However, those results cannot be said to be an accurate reflection of the attitudes of any particular public.

It is important for you to understand these concepts because they are central to your selection of a sampling strategy. The challenge of survey research is to use a sampling technique that serves two masters: a desire for accuracy and a need to achieve it in a logistically realistic and cost-effective manner. Using some techniques, it is possible to be both accurate *and* cost effective.

NONPROBABILITY SAMPLING   In the real world of public relations, practitioners are often challenged to conduct survey research with little time, money, or staffing at their disposal. This often leads to using a form of nonprobability sampling known as **convenience sampling**—the administration of an informal survey based on the availability of subjects. As the name suggests, this approach has the advantage of being easy to do. However, it also sacrifices accuracy.

The so-called person-on-the-street interviews seen in newspapers and on television are examples of convenience sampling. Reporters often ask a "question of the day" to passersby in an attempt to gauge the mood of their community on a particular topic. But instead of getting an accurate picture of community attitudes, these reporters are measuring the opinions of only the people who happen to be walking by that spot at that time. A reporter standing on an inner-city sidewalk might get answers to questions about the state of the economy that differ greatly from answers obtained in a suburban shopping mall. Even the time of day can make a difference.

Does this mean that data obtained from an informal survey are useless? No, it doesn't. Data obtained from such a survey can provide an *indication* of public opinion. The more indicators you have pointing in the same direction, the greater the chance that your data are accurate.

PROBABILITY SAMPLING   When planning to conduct formal probability sampling, you have a choice of several techniques. All of them have one important element in common: *Every person within the sampling frame has an equal chance of being selected for the sample.* In other words, surveys based on these sampling techniques have a high probability of being an accurate reflection of public opinion. These are some of the most common probability sampling strategies used by public relations practitioners:

- **Simple random sampling** (Figure 7.2) is the most basic form of probability sampling. But often it is not practical. Simple random sampling involves assigning a number to every person within the sampling frame. By making a random selection of numbers, as in drawing numbers out of a hat, you develop a representative sample. However, think how tedious it would be to

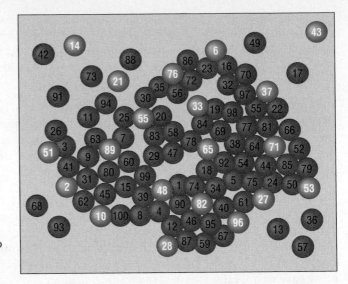

FIGURE 7.2

Simple Random Sampling

In this example, every individual is assigned a number—in this case, a number from 1 to 100. To achieve a sample of 20 individuals, 20 numbers are selected at random.

assign a number to every name in the local telephone book. Because simple random sampling can be a cumbersome process, especially with large sampling frames, this technique is seldom used in practice.

- **Systematic sampling** (Figure 7.3) is a more practical approach to probability sampling. Through a standardized selection process, it is possible to create a sample that is both representative and easy to develop. At its most basic level, systematic sampling involves the selection of every Kth member of a

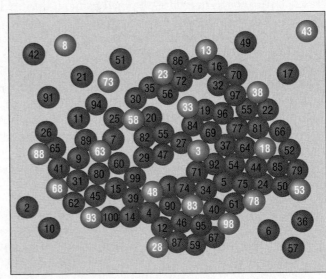

FIGURE 7.3

Systematic Sampling

In this example, we want to achieve a sample size of 20. There are 100 individuals in the sampling frame. The value of K is 100/20, or 5. Therefore, we pick every fifth individual for our sample.

sampling frame. For example, let us assume that your college or university has 25,000 students. The sampling frame for your survey is a computer printout of enrolled students. If you are seeking a sample of 250 names from a sampling frame of 25,000, then K = 25,000/250, or 100. In this scenario, you would select every 100th name from the enrollment printout for the sample. Compare this with the work involved in simple random sampling, and it is easy to see why many researchers choose to go this route.

■ It is often hard to identify a perfect sampling frame. Although a city telephone directory gives you the names of most city residents, it excludes those who do not have a land-line telephone, who tend to be poor, and those with unlisted numbers, who tend to have higher incomes. In this case, the extremely rich and extremely poor may be underrepresented. One way to overcome a flaw in a sampling frame is by using what is known as **cluster sampling** (Figure 7.4). This technique involves breaking the population into homogeneous clusters and then selecting the sample from individual clusters. For example, pretend that your sampling frame is students enrolled in public relations courses. If your school is typical of the national trend, there is a

FIGURE 7.4

Cluster Sampling

In an attempt to correct an imbalance in the sampling frame, individuals with similar characteristics are clustered. In this example, systematic sampling is used within each cluster to develop a sample containing 10 from each group.

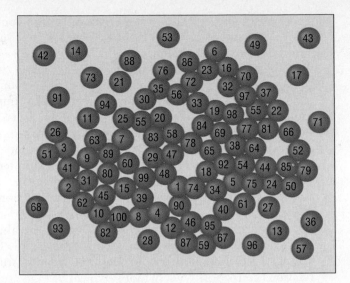

FIGURE 7.5

Census

In a census, everyone in the sampling frame is selected.

strong probability that women will easily outnumber men. To achieve a sample that is half men and half women, you group the students' names into different gender pools and select an equal number of names from each pool. Cluster sampling is generally not as accurate as simple random sampling or systematic sampling. Under certain conditions, however, it can be the most practical.

■ One way to ensure that a sample is an accurate reflection of a specific population is to survey *everyone*. That is what is known as taking a **census** (Figure 7.5)—that is, surveying every member of the sampling frame. A well-known census is the decennial U.S. census, in which an attempt is made to count and analyze every person living in the United States. Although a properly done census has the advantage of accuracy, this technique comes up short when it comes to practicality. It might be easy to administer a questionnaire to everyone in your class, but how easy would it be for you to survey everyone in your college or university?

 QUICK CHECK

1. What two elements are critical to the administration of an accurate survey?
2. How does a sample differ from a sampling frame?
3. What is the major difference between probability and nonprobability sampling?

The Survey Instrument

Creating a good survey instrument is just as important as having a good survey sample. Even if you identify a sample that is representative of the population you want to study, a faulty questionnaire can render your results meaningless. It is not just *whom* you ask, but also *how* you ask the questions that matters.

There are many considerations you need to keep in mind when developing survey questions. The questionnaire should use language that is appropriate for and readily understood by the public for whom the survey is intended. Researchers wouldn't ask elementary school students, homeowners, and nuclear scientists the same questions about nuclear power. Each group has a different level of understanding of the issue; therefore, the questions need to be tailored to the knowledge level of each group. In certain situations, it may be necessary to provide background information before asking a question.

Questions asked on surveys cannot be vague if they are to have any real meaning. Questions have to be explicit, not indirect. Ask exactly what you want to know. If respondents are guessing at what a question means, their answers cannot serve as an accurate measure of anything (except, of course, of someone's inability to write clear questions).

Use words that have clear and specific meanings. For example, let's consider a question about presidential job performance. Suppose respondents are given the choice of answering the question using these options: gnarly, groovy, super, cool, and awesome. Can these survey results have any real meaning? The problem is that what may be gnarly to one person could be groovy to another. For the survey results to have real meaning, the words used in the survey must have precise definitions. A good survey instrument also keeps the questionnaire reasonably short. The longer the survey, the more likely that people will decline to participate because they "don't have the time."

Avoid bias in the wording or ordering of questions. The manner in which a question is worded can influence the response. Even the placement of the question can influence responses to questions that follow. For example, suppose you are answering a survey that poses a series of questions about high taxes, then asks, "What is the most important issue facing government today?" Because of the earlier questions, you may be primed to answer, "High taxes, of course!"

Don't ask objectionable questions. Even the most sensitive information can be obtained if questions are worded tactfully. Also, save the toughest questions for last.

Asking the toughest questions first could abruptly end the process or bias subsequent responses. Demographic questions regarding matters such as age, income, and political affiliation can also be sensitive. Often, researchers place demographic questions at the end of the questionnaire in the belief that members of the sample won't skip them because they've already invested time in filling out the rest of the survey.

A way to avoid problems is to pretest the questionnaire. If the survey instrument has any bugs, it is best to find them before distributing surveys on a large

QUICKBREAK 7.5

Five Ways to Ask Questions

1. **Contingency questions:** Whether a respondent is expected to answer a specific question is often contingent on the answer to an earlier question. For example, if a respondent indicates that he or she doesn't like ice cream, it would make no sense to ask that person in the next question to identify his or her favorite flavor of ice cream. Therefore, the second question is a contingency question. Respondents who answer yes about liking ice cream will answer the next question. Those who answer no will be instructed to skip it.

2. **Dichotomous questions:** These are either/or questions such as true–false, yes–no, and positive–negative. They are sometimes used to set up contingency questions. In the previously cited example, a no answer would make it unnecessary for the respondent to answer the next question about favorite flavor. The respondent would be instructed to skip that question.

3. **Rating scale questions:** These questions measure the range, degree, or intensity of attitudes, something a dichotomous question cannot do. An example of a rating scale question is one that news and polling organizations often ask about the president's job performance. Respondents are asked to respond to the statement "I think the president is doing a good job." Their options are to strongly agree with the statement, agree, disagree, strongly disagree, or express no opinion. These kinds of questions can give researchers a more detailed read on public opinion than dichotomous questions can provide.

4. **Open-ended questions:** These questions don't define a range of possible answers (called a response set). In other words, the respondent is left to fill in the blank. Answers to these questions can provide detailed information. However, they are the most difficult to analyze because they can't be tabulated as quickly as answers to questions in which the response set is specifically defined.

5. **Closed-ended questions:** These are questions in which the response set is specifically defined. To put it another way, respondents are required to select their answer from a predetermined menu of options. The risk with these questions is that researchers may leave out certain options or overemphasize other options. Another problem to watch for is answers that overlap slightly. However, these questions are significantly easier to analyze than open-ended questions. ■

scale. Run a small test first to make sure that the questions are understandable, all biases corrected, and objectionable questions removed.

When it comes time to administer the survey, logistics must be considered as well. Can the personnel requirements be met? Can the survey be administered within the desired time frame? Does the survey plan fit into the budget? The people who administer the survey, the data collectors, must be trained. Will they use the telephone or meet with members of the sample face to face? Or, as is common, will you simply mail out the survey and dispense with data collectors?

ANALYZING SURVEY RESULTS

Once all the data are collected, the time has come to analyze and report the results. This is a public relations text, not a statistics text, so any attempt at this point to offer a detailed explanation of statistical analysis would not do the subject justice. However, we do not want to ignore the subject entirely. Raw data without structure or purpose are meaningless. Analysis gives data context so that their meaning can be understood.

The truth is that the overwhelming majority of public relations practitioners never conduct survey research. Instead, they pay someone else to do it for them. That's OK. But how do you know whether the research you are buying is good? That's why this discussion of sampling and questionnaire development is important. If you plan to make a career in public relations, you need to be a good consumer of this and all kinds of research.

For the purposes of this discussion, let's start with two basic definitions:

1. **Attributes:** characteristics or qualities that describe an object. In the case of an individual, attributes can be gender, age, weight, height, political affiliation, church affiliation, and so on.
2. **Variables:** a logical grouping of qualities that describe a particular attribute. Variables must be exhaustive (incorporating all possible qualities) and mutually exclusive. For example, the variables associated with the attribute of gender are female and male.

The purpose of analysis is to get a clearer picture from the data. The deeper the analysis, the clearer the picture. The most basic form of analysis is **univariate analysis**. As the name suggests, it is the examination of only one variable. An example of a univariate analysis would be the examination of responses to the question, "Do you like ice cream?" By counting the responses to that question, we would know the total number of people who said yes and the total number who said no. But that is all we would know.

If we were to examine the same question using two variables, however, the results would become more meaningful. This is what is known as **bivariate analysis**. A bivariate analysis of the question, "Do you like ice cream?" could look at two variables: whether respondents like ice cream and the respondents' gender. We might find that men answer the question differently from women. That, in turn, could affect a variety of marketing decisions.

If we turn to **multivariate analysis,** the examination of three or more variables, our survey results would have even greater depth. Carrying our example to its logical conclusion, let's add the variable of age to our analysis of the ice cream question. Such an analysis could find that younger men and older women like ice cream more than their counterparts in other age groups. If our goal is to promote the sale of ice cream, these results suggest that we need to work harder to attract younger women and older men to the frozen delight. That information is far more valuable to us than only knowing the raw numbers.

The Rest of the Story

If you thought you would hate to be the county public information officer in the opening "Real World" scenario of our chapter, think again. The scenario is based on a true story, an award-winning groundwater replenishment system community relations program in southern California. The Orange County water and sanitation districts, working with Porter Novelli, convinced the residents of a culturally diverse community that a blend of purified sewer water with traditional water supplies was safe. Their communications program was based on solid research, including secondary research, focus group data from the region's different ethnic communities, and a series of surveys. During the four years of the public information campaign, county officials were able to maintain necessary public support for construction of the multimillion dollar treatment facility. The campaign came in approximately 10 percent below its $3.6 million budget. When you think about it, that's not much to pay for providing safe drinking water for the county's nearly 3 million residents.[31]

When confronted with a difficult challenge, the practitioners in southern California did what any public relations professional should do—they started by developing a research strategy. They asked these two all-important questions:

1. What do I want to know?
2. How will I gather that information?

After developing a research strategy, they conducted client research, stakeholder research, problem–opportunity research, and evaluation research. They used both formal and informal research methods. Eventually, they developed a successful community relations plan—one that served the best interests of both the client and the people of Orange County.

That is the essence of good public relations. And it all starts with research.

 QUICK CHECK

1. When writing a survey questionnaire, what should you consider in wording questions?
2. What are some of the logistical considerations you should take into account before administering a survey?
3. What are the differences among a univariate analysis, a bivariate analysis, and a multivariate analysis? Why would you want to do any of them?

SUMMARY

At a time when all organizations and professions must do the most they can with limited resources, public relations practitioners are expected to perform due diligence: research designed to justify, enhance, and measure the effectiveness of their strategies and tactics. Research is critical to the practice of public relations. Research enables a practitioner to understand a client, the problems and opportunities facing the client, and the stakeholders important to the client's success. Evaluation research enables a practitioner to determine the success of communication strategies and the strength of relationships.

Not all research is created equal. Formal research has the advantage of providing a more accurate picture of reality. However, conducting informal research might be necessary because of time, cost, or staffing considerations. Although not as accurate a reflection of reality, informal research results still can help you piece together a picture of the world. Before embarking on research, it is important to have a clear understanding of what kinds of information you are seeking and what is the best way for you to gather it. That is known as developing your research strategy.

The five most common forms of public relations research are secondary (library) research, feedback research, communication audits, focus groups, and surveys. Secondary research is using material generated by someone else, sometimes for a purpose other than that for which it was originally intended. Feedback research involves analyzing both solicited and unsolicited communications an organization receives from its stakeholders. Communication audits indicate whether an organization's communications are consistent with its values-driven mission and goals. Focus groups are an informal research method in which a small group of people are brought together to discuss their values, concerns, needs, attitudes, and predispositions. The successful use of survey research depends on both a good sample and a good survey instrument or questionnaire. The value of survey research is that, when properly conducted and analyzed, it provides a reasonably accurate snapshot of reality. That, in turn, provides a solid foundation for a public relations plan.

DISCUSSION QUESTIONS

1. Why do some people believe efforts to base public relations measures on advertising costs are inappropriate? What do you think?
2. Which research should you ordinarily conduct first: primary research or secondary research? Why?
3. How is issues management a part of problem–opportunity research?
4. Why aren't focus groups necessarily representative of a larger public?
5. What is the difference between probability sampling and nonprobability sampling? What is the advantage of probability sampling? Is nonprobability sampling without value?
6. What are some examples of research leading to the success of a public relations campaign?

MEMO FROM THE FIELD

DR. DAVID B. ROCKLAND
Partner and Global Director of Research; Ketchum
New York, New York

Dr. David B. Rockland is a partner at Ketchum, CEO of Ketchum Pleon Change (KPC), and managing director of Global Research, where he oversees research and measurement in all Ketchum offices in the United States, Europe, Latin America, and Asia. He was chairman of IPR's Commission on PR Measurement and Evaluation in 2007 and 2008. In 2009, he also joined the board of the International Association for Measurement and Evaluation of Communication.

The career that led me to running research at Ketchum was by no means a straight path. After getting a Ph.D. in economics, I quickly morphed primarily into lobbying in Washington on natural resource issues. I wrote for many top consumer magazines while with Times Mirror Magazines, headed global communications for the world's largest copper mining company, and then eventually sold my own firm, The Rockland Group LLC, to Roper Starch Worldwide in 1998. That's how I started doing research for public relations. At first, Ketchum was a client, and then they asked me to join them to head up a research practice with a great history and an opportunity to build it into the thriving, profitable business it is today. What's neat about a career with many twists and turns is that you learn new things almost every day. Here are some things I've learned at Ketchum.

PR PROGRAMS THAT DON'T SET GOALS AND MEASURE WILL FAIL

Countless times I've had the leader of an account rush into my office asking us to measure a program long after it's done. Their client is demanding to know the results, and although they have a nice stack of clips, the client is using terms like *ROI* and *audience outcomes*. If the account leader can't show these kinds of numbers, they'll lose the account.

You have to begin any journey, including a PR plan, knowing where you are going and agreeing with your client on what success looks like. Writing good goals at the start saves lots of heartburn at the end. Answer these questions:

- What needle are you trying to move?
- Among whom?
- By when?
- How much is success?

The needle may be outputs (e.g., reach or impressions); outcomes (i.e., awareness, comprehension, attitude, and behavior); or business results such as sales. Clearly, written goals lead you to the right measurement program. And many times that measurement program already exists at the client, one such as a brand or advertising tracking system that you can measure your goals against, sometimes as is and sometimes with minor tweaking.

PAY ATTENTION TO WHAT PEOPLE SAY

I used to think focus groups were for people who couldn't write good surveys. I was wrong. Focus groups and depth interviews often give you very clear signals on what will work and what won't. One time, I did focus groups to test a new tagline for a chemical manufacturing company. The CEO loved this new tagline. And it did sound pretty good. The focus group participants all thought the tagline made great sense if you were promoting a dating service.

Another time, we were testing a new website about retirement benefits for public employees in Florida. The logo for the program was a road sign showing a fork in the road with one arrow going left and the other right. When we asked the focus group participants to find information on the website, instead of moving their mouse to the menus on the home page, they all moved their arrows to the road sign. Unfortunately, the sign or logo was only there for decoration, so nothing happened. In 10 seconds, we knew that the Web designers were going to have to change the home page fast.

Sometimes surveys give you insights you really didn't expect. Right before the 2004 elections, we did a quick national survey for a new American Kennel Club credit card with Chase Card Services. The key question was along the lines of which breed of dog do President Bush and Senator Kerry most remind you of? The survey resulted in tremendous press coverage for clients. The results (Bush a rottweiler and Kerry a French poodle) showed Kerry didn't have a chance. Apparently, French poodles don't get elected president.

AVES CAN BE VERY IMPORTANT

Many in our field think that comparing PR to advertising is wrong. I disagree, assuming you do the math right. Here are things to account for:

- PR's results are not always perfect. When you place advertising, you get to say what you want, where, and when. You have to discount the PR value to reflect how good the placement was.
- PR is not necessarily more credible or valuable than advertising. When I wrote for *Field and Stream*, readers were often more interested in the ads for new hunting and fishing equipment than in the editorial. Don't mark up the PR value unless you can document clearly that such an increase is warranted. Usually, such multipliers are just plain wrong and are based on PR practitioners desperate to exaggerate their own value.
- Use net ad rates, or the rate the client pays on the open market. Few pay the retail costs on the rate card; hence, those numbers are artificially high.
- Also, don't call it AVE. The "V" is value, and this metric is not the value of PR but the cost of comparable space or time as advertising. Weighted media cost is a much better term.

Many companies have a choice of whether to use their marketing dollars for PR or for advertising. Assuming the cost they would pay for advertising has to be worth at least as much to their business, applying such a number to a PR placement with the above modifications can make good sense. Otherwise, often, the person with the marketing budget decides to put all the dollars into advertising. If we can't speak the language of the

(continued)

marketing person, PR usually loses. But remember that it is always better to measure what advertising or PR produces in terms of audience or business change.

"NEW MEDIA" ARE STILL NEW AND UNTESTED

The PR world continues to buzz about CGM—consumer-generated media. Newspapers are dead; blogs and Twitter are here to stay. Wrong. We periodically field a national survey of America's media habits. Here are a few things we've learned.

TRADITIONAL MEDIA ARE ALIVE AND KICKING

- Americans turn to local TV and newspapers over almost anything else to form opinions and decide what to buy. This is also true of younger Americans (ages 18–24). And traditional sources are way more credible than CGM.
- Word of Mouth (WOM) is critical. Most people make decisions from talking to friends and family. PR's role in understanding WOM and affecting it is the discipline's next frontier.
- Corporations talk to themselves too much. They place too much emphasis on communicating through their websites and on their own schedules. A good communicator knows what the audience wants and what the best time to reach it is.

FINAL WORD

I have two daughters. Both majored in communications and public relations in college and now work in this field. I am very proud of them, but I do hope they approach this field as a serious discipline that can have a huge impact. Too many PR majors choose that major because they think "fashion and beauty PR would be so much fun." Three years into their careers, they are still stuffing press kits with perfume samples and booking car services for C-list celebrities. With good research and measurement skills, the PR practitioner is taken more seriously, gets a seat at the management table, and has a career that is meaningful and profitable. Otherwise, the field and the people in it will always take a second seat to other types of communications and marketing. ■

CASE STUDY 7.1 The Green Police

Many thought it was funny. Others thought it was insulting. The *New York Times* said "it put the 'mental' in 'environmental.'"[32]

What was it? It was a television commercial—in fact, the second-most watched TV ad of all time, with an estimated 115.6 million viewers.[33] The 60-second spot promoting Audi's A3 TDI clean diesel technology was broadcast during the fourth quarter of Super Bowl XLIV. The ad was also the linchpin of a multimedia advertising and public relations campaign that included its own Facebook page, a series of parody public service announcements on YouTube, and a Twitter page. The campaign was the brainchild of the San Francisco–based Venables Bell & Partners, which claimed Audi had gained one billion media impressions within a week of the game.[34]

The controversial ad depicted a time and place in which so-called Green Police could arrest ordinary citizens at the grocery store for using plastic instead of paper. The ad also showed the Green Police storming a home and arresting its owner for failing to compost an orange rind. Then there's the swimsuit-clad couple being hauled away because the thermostat on their hot tub was set too high. However, at an "eco-roadblock," the driver of an Audi is allowed to pass through quickly—presumably because the car is eco-friendly.

"It's an appeal to a new and growing demographic that isn't hard-core environmentalist—and doesn't particularly like hard-core environmentalists—but it basically wants to do the right thing," wrote David Roberts on *Grist*, a nonprofit online magazine of environmental news and opinion. Roberts said Audi's message was, "Here's a way to meet your green obligations and still have a bad-ass car!"[35]

However, not everyone viewed the commercial as enthusiastically. "Some eco-bloggers disliked the ad because it reinforces the association of undemocratic statism or PC bullying with environmentalism," wrote Tribune Media Services columnist Jonah Goldberg. "Meanwhile, some conservatives didn't like it because it makes light of what they believe is actually happening."[36]

However, there was another, even more controversial aspect to the commercial. The Green Police—the name given to Audi's eco-cops—was also the common nickname of Nazi Germany's Ordnungspolizei (Order Police), green-uniform-clad police involved in sending Jews, Poles, Gypsies, and political dissidents to concentration camps during World War II.

"The implications of Audi's choice of name for their campaign could be huge, especially since Audi is a German company," wrote blogger Danny Brown. "The first question is obvious: didn't anyone at Audi's PR or advertising arm/agency do any research?"[37]

Audi officials said they researched the term thoroughly. "We sought input and reaction from key organizations, including the Jewish community," said Jeff Kuhlman, chief communications

officer for Audi of America. "Reactions to the term are completely in line with our intent—environmental enforcement." Kuhlman added that the Israeli Ministry of Environmental Protection's enforcement division is also called the Green Police.[38]

On its website, Venables Bell & Partners says its agency philosophy is "Our intentions are good." In explaining the philosophy, the website goes on to say, "Something incredible happens when you actively work to do right by people. You become utterly unafraid. . . . This fearlessness also leads to disagreement. Lively debate. Occasionally, even awkward silence."[39]

This might be a situation in which difference between good and bad practice is in the eyes of the beholder. Nor can one say Audi and its advertising agency didn't do their research. In this case, the ad accomplished what every Super Bowl ad hopes to achieve, a buzz in the marketplace. The Green Police campaign received a large number of favorable reviews posted online by television viewers. However, other comments mirrored the thoughts of Aimee Picchi of AOL Online's *Daily Finance*, who wrote, "While the mock PSAs are humorous with a shtick that leans more toward *Reno 911!* than *Schindler's List*, it's certainly never fortuitous for a German company to bring up reminders of the Third Reich."[40]

DISCUSSION QUESTIONS

1. Do you agree that "this may be a situation where the difference between good and bad practice is in the eyes of the beholder"? Explain your reasoning.
2. This controversy came nearly 65 years after the end of World War II. Do German companies such as Audi still need to demonstrate a special sensitivity toward their nation's troubled past?
3. How can one measure the success of this or any other controversial communications campaign?
4. Was this campaign consistent with Audi's and Venables Bell & Partners' values? ■

CASE STUDY 7.2 Big Bang PR

Unless you have been trained in nuclear physics, you might believe that *quark* refers to an alien bartender on the old television series *Star Trek: Deep Space Nine.* You could also be forgiven for thinking *gluon* is something you do when you break the handle on a coffee mug. However, if you have a lot more scientific knowledge than, say, the authors of this textbook, then you know that quarks and gluons are basic particles of atomic nuclei—the building blocks for everything in the universe.[41]

Quarks and gluons may be pretty small stuff, but they are big business at the Brookhaven National Laboratory on Long Island, New York. Operated by the U.S. Department of Energy, BNL has approximately 3,000 permanent employees and hosts more than 4,000 guest researchers each year.[42] From 1993 to 2003, BNL's total local and national spending of $4.76 billion created more than 7,700 secondary jobs in New York state.[43] Because of its huge economic impact, any challenge to BNL's federal funding is viewed as a significant threat.

BNL officials learned in early 2005 that they faced an $18 million cut in the budget for their Relativistic Heavy Ion Collider (RHIC)—basically a giant atom smasher. Ironically, at the same time they learned that the program would have to be scaled back, researchers using the atom smasher made one of the most significant scientific discoveries in years. To place their findings in laymen's terms: The scientists discovered a new substance that they say resembled the state of the universe in the first 100 millionths of a second after the big bang that created the universe. To their surprise, the matter created in the RHIC—known as quark-gluon plasma—appeared to be more of a liquid than the gas they had expected.[44] In the world of science, this was big news.

It also presented BNL officials with an opportunity and a challenge. The announcement of an important scientific breakthrough would boost the program's image at the same time that their funds were on Washington's chopping block. However, the timing of the release could also be interpreted as a blatant attempt to influence congressional budget negotiations. Their concerns were well founded: Research showed that a 2000 media announcement by a European research laboratory had been widely criticized as being premature and exaggerated. In the current political environment, they could not afford to make the same mistake.

Working with M. Booth & Associates, a New York–based public relations agency, BNL officials devised a strategy for unveiling their remarkable discovery without any hint of ulterior political motives.[45] They started by researching the schedule of up-coming scientific conferences, looking for the right venue in which to make the big announcement. They chose an April meeting of the American Physical Society in Tampa—just five weeks away. They also knew that they would have to broaden the reach of the announcement beyond the Florida meeting. Through a search of national science and consumer media, they identified leading general-science reporters. After a round of telephone calls to gauge the reporters' intentions, they realized that many of the journalists they wanted to target were not planning to attend the conference.

In advance of the big day, an embargoed news release was placed on a password-protected section of BNL's website. Also available on the site were copies of scientific papers, high-resolution photographs and animation, and links to experts. BNL also reached out to journalists affiliated with media outlets used by influential people who would appreciate the importance of the announcement. These included the *New York Times, USA Today, Science* magazine, and National Public Radio. Media relations experts were assigned to both the Tampa conference and BNL headquarters to handle the anticipated flood of media inquiries. BNL also reached out to members of the nation's scientific community in the belief that they would provide third-party endorsement of the significance of the event.

Following the April 18 announcement, BNL and M. Booth & Associates got all they asked for—and more. The news received widespread coverage, with more than 700 million impressions worldwide. Many of the stories noted the irony of the big discovery coming in the shadow of projected budget cuts. Typical was the story in *USA Today,* which reported, "Despite the success of the experiments, cuts in Energy Department financing will probably reduce the program's operating time from 30 weeks to 12 weeks next year."[46] Only one columnist linked the announcement with an effort to influence the budget negotiations. Congress restored the budget cuts to the program, and President Bush included full fund-ing in the following year's budget request. At a cost of $13,400 for the entire campaign, you would have to say that BNL got a big bang for its bucks.

DISCUSSION QUESTIONS

1. What role did research play in this case study?
2. Who were the targeted publics of this public relations campaign?
3. Would you consider this case to be an example of issues management? Please explain your reasoning.
4. As a practitioner—and as a taxpayer—do you think that Brookhaven National Laboratory officials were ethical in their attempt to influence federal budget decisions? ■

NOTES

1. Jim Macnamara, "The Fork in the Road of Media and Communication Theory and Practice," June 2007, Institute for Public Relations, online, www.instituteforpr.com.
2. *Dedicated to the Science Beneath the Art: A 50-Year Report from the Institute for Public Relations,* Institute for Public Relations, 2006, online, www.instituteforpr.com.
3. Mark Weiner, "What Executives Want: Connecting PR Performance with Business Outcomes," *Public Relations Strategist* (fall 2009): 29.
4. Linda Childers Hon and James E. Grunig, *Guidelines for Measuring Relationships in Public Relations,* Institute for Public Relations Commission on PR Measurement and Evaluation, 1999.
5. Katie Delahaye Paine, "The ROI of Engagement in Social Media," KDPaine & Partners, May 2009, online, www.kdpaine.com.
6. "Return on Investment Is an Inadequate Expression of PR Value," news release issued by the Institute of Public Relations, 19 May 2004, online, www.ipr.org.uk/Nedws/stories/ 197.htm.
7. "The Power of Public Relations: A Basic Guide to Getting Noticed—Measurement/ Evaluation/Wrap-up," Texas Commission on the Arts, 1999, online, www.arts.state .tx.us/news/prpower/measure.htm.
8. Bob Grupp, "Armistice Day for AVE," Institute for Public Relations, online, www. instituteforpr.com.
9. Angela Jeffrey, Bruce Jeffries-Fox, and Brad L. Rawlins, "A New Paradigm for Media Analysis: Weighted Media Cost," Institute for Public Relations, 2006, online, instituteforpr.com.
10. John Finney, "Assessing the Value of Communication," *Communication World,* January/ February 2004, 36–40.
11. "Maintaining Confidence in Dairy During a Crisis," Dairy Management, Inc., with Weber Shandwick, Silver Anvil Award description, Public Relations Society of America, online, www.prsa.org/_Awards/silver.
12 "Protecting Consumer Confidence in U.S. Beef: A Success Story," National Cattlemen's Beef Association, Silver Anvil Award description, Public Relations Society of America, online, www.prsa.org/_Awards/silver.
13 Alwyn Scott, "Is Beef Industry Reeling? Not Exactly," *Seattle Times,* 29 February 2004, A1.

14. "Protecting Consumer Confidence in U.S. Beef: A Success Story."

15. Greg Hazley, "Beef Industry Passes Its First Run-in with Mad Cow," *O'Dwyer's PR Services Report* 18, no. 2 (February 2004): 1.

16. Hon and Grunig.

17. Trent Seltzer, "Measuring the Impact of Public Relations: Using a Coorientational Approach to Analyze the Organization–Public Relationship," 2006, Institute for Public Relations, online, www.instituteforpr.com.

18. *2006 State of the PR Profession Opinion Survey,* Public Relations Society of America and Bacon's Information, Inc., 1 February 2007.

19. "Global Survey of Communications Measurement 2009–Final Report," International Association for the Measurement and Evaluation of Communication, September 2009, 10.

20. "PRSA Seek Industry Agreement on Measurement Standards," news release, 15 September 2009, Public Relations Society of America, online, www.prsa.org.

21. Ruthann Weaver Lariscy, Elizabeth J. Avery, Kaye D. Sweetser, and Pauline Howes, "Monitoring Public Opinion in Cyberspace: How Corporate Public Relations Is Facing the Challenge," *Public Relations Journal*, 3, no 4. (fall 2009), online, www.prsa.org.

22. James Verrinder, "Few Companies Using Social media for Insight, Survey Says," *Research*, 7 December 2009, online, http://sncr.org.

23. Joab Jackson, "Survey: Social Media Not Useful for BI Yet," *Computerworld*, 12 January 2010, online, www.computerworld.com.

24. Jen McClure and Don Middleberg, "Key Findings from the 2009 Middleberg/SNCR Survey of Media in the Wired World," Society of New Communications Research website, online, http://sncr.org.

25. Nora Ganim Barnes and Eric Mattson, "Social Media in the 2009 Inc. 500: New Tools & Trends," online, http://sncr.org.

26. Rebecca Hart, "Measuring Success: How to 'Sell' a Communications Audit to Internal Audiences," *Public Relations Tactics*, April 2006, reprint inventory number 6C-040605, Public Relations Society of America, online, www.prsa.org.

27. "Safe Teen Drive Long Island," Silver Anvil Award summary 6BE-0902B21, Public Relations Society of America, online, www.prsa.org.

28. "Mars and Snickers Extortion Threat," 2006 Silver Anvil Award Campaign Profile 6BE-0611 A12, Public Relations Society of America, online, www.prsa.org.

29. "Learn the Signs. Act Early: Educating Parents and Doctors on the Warning Signs of Developmental Problems," 2006 Silver Anvil Award Campaign Profile 6BW-0605B09, Public Relations Society of America, online, www.prsa.org.

30. David Hakensen, "PRSA's Minnesota Chapter Raises Profile of PR Locally," *Public Relations Tactics,* December 2003, 21.

31. "Groundwater Replenishment System Community Relations Program, 2006 Silver Anvil Award Campaign Profile 6BW-0601C08, Public Relations Society of America, online, www.prsa.org.

32. Stuart Elliot, "In Commercials, the Nostalgia Bowl," *New York Times*, 8 February 2010, B3.

33. Stuart Elliot, "And the Recaps of the Super Bowl Spots Just Keep on Coming," *New York Times*, 9 February 2010, online, www. nytimes.com.

34. "The Mayor Gives Us Thumbs Up," Venables Bell & Partners website, posted 16 February 2010, online, www.venablesbell.com.

35. David Roberts, "Audi's 'Green Police' Ad Isn't What You Thought It Was," *Grist*, 8 February 2009, online, www.grist.org.

36. Jonah Goldberg, "Audi's Bemusing Super Bowl Ad," *Corpus Christi Caller-Times*, 13 February 2010, A7.

37. Danny Brown, "Audi and the Super Bowl Social Media (expletive deleted) Storm," *Danny Brown: Conversations in Social Media for Marketing, PR, Communications and Community*, posted 27 January 2010, online, http://dannybrown.me.

38. Sebastian Blanco, "Audi Responds to Green Police Criticisms over Super Bowl Ad," Autoblog, posted 1 February 2010, online, http://green.autoblog.com.

39. "Our Intentions Are Good," Venables Bell & Partners website, online, www.venablesbell.com.

40. Aimee Picchi, "Audi's Super Bowl Ad Blunder: 'Green Police' Have Nazi History," 29 January 2010, online, www.dailyfinance.com.

41. "Ask A Scientist Archives—Physics Index," Argonne National Laboratory, U.S. Department of Energy, online, http://www.newton.dep.anl.gov/askasci.

42. "About Brookhaven National Lab," Brookhaven National Laboratory, online, www.bnl.gov.

43. "Gov. Pataki Announces Collaborative Effort to Support Brookhaven National Laboratory," news release, U.S. Fed News, 22 May 2005, via LexisNexis.

44. "RHIC Scientists Serve Up 'Perfect' Liquid," news release, issued by Brookhaven National Laboratory, 18 April 2005, online, www.bnl.gov.

45. "RHIC Results: Perfect Fluid Creates Big Bang for Lab," 2006 Silver Anvil Award Campaign Profile 6BW-0612B01, Public Relations Society of America, online, www.prsa.org.

46. Dan Vergano, "Picking Apart the 'Big Bang' Brings a Big Mystery," *USA Today,* 20 April 2005, 6D.

8

Planning: The Strategies of Public Relations

Courtesy of U.S. Department of Defense

OBJECTIVES

After studying this chapter, you will be able to

- describe the different kinds of public relations plans
- discuss why public relations practitioners create plans
- explain the process of creating a public relations plan
- summarize the qualities of a good plan

- explain where and how values enter into the planning process

KEY TERMS

ad hoc plan, p. 229
brainstorming, p. 235
contingency plan, p. 229
executive summary, p. 244
goal, p. 237
objectives, p. 238
proposal, p. 244

REAL WORLD

The Art of Planning

You're the director of public relations and marketing for an art museum in a city in the southwestern United States. Your museum is renowned for its collection of contemporary Native American art, but the museum also has other, diverse collections and a growing national reputation.

Like many successful public relations operations, your three-person staff has a well-organized issues-management process. You're constantly scanning the environment for potential problems and opportunities. When you spot a potential issue, you monitor it to see whether action is desirable. Last week, you discovered a possible issue: One of your assistants attended a luncheon sponsored by the Hispanic American Leadership Conference. During dessert, a participant asked her why the museum didn't promote Hispanic artists. Another participant overheard the question and agreed that the museum tended to overlook Hispanic artists.

At your weekly issues-management meeting, you and your team discuss that possible perception within your city's Hispanic community. You agree to monitor the situation. Two days later, another staff member shows you an advertisement that a local corporation placed in Hispanic Plus, a national magazine that targets graduating seniors. The ad boasts of the exciting Hispanic influence on your city's cultural attractions. Your museum is not mentioned in the ad's list of cultural highlights.

You're puzzled, because the museum recently hosted a very successful exhibition on mid-20th-century Mexican artists Frida Kahlo and her husband, Diego Rivera. But you're also concerned: Almost one third of your city's residents are of Hispanic origin. If influential members of that broad public believe that your museum is not serving their interests, consequences for future attendance as well as future budgets could be disastrous. Almost 40 percent of your museum's budget comes from city tax revenues.

You assemble a focus group, and a clearer picture of the potential problem emerges. Members of the focus group loved the Kahlo–Rivera exhibition, but they were unanimous in believing that your museum does nothing to promote Hispanic artists now living and working in your city. Additional in-depth interviews with opinion leaders in the Hispanic public echo that belief.

More research turns up some startling misperceptions. You learn that almost 65 percent of your museum's small cash grants to up-and-coming artists went to city residents of Hispanic origin—but that you haven't publicized that fact. And you discover another misperception: The head curator of the museum—herself of Hispanic origin—says to you, "I think you're wrong. There's no problem here."

On the wall in your office is a poster that contains the museum's statement of values and its mission statement. One of the values is "Diversity." Below that, part of the mission statement says, "This museum will diligently nurture the artistic interests of the residents of our city."

Given your values-based mission and the damaging misperceptions that your research has revealed, you decide that you must address this emerging problem.

What do you do?

THE BASICS OF VALUES-DRIVEN PLANNING

Flash forward 15 years.

You're a respected leader in public relations. Dozens of awards decorate your office. Organizations from Juneau, Alaska, to Johannesburg, South Africa, would jump at the chance to hire you. To quote the old Timbuk3 song, your future's so bright you gotta wear shades.

Besides hard work and a little luck, what's propelled you to the top? Odds are, a major reason for your success can be summarized in one word: planning.

Study after study shows that the top duty of public relations managers is "planning public relations programs."[1] So it doesn't take an Einstein to guess what your present self would ask your future self: How do I create effective public relations plans?

Keep reading.

Planning Follows Research

As you know from the basic public relations process, a good plan begins with research. Consider, for example, The Art of Planning, the "Real World" scenario that opens this chapter. Scanning and monitoring, which are *problem–opportunity research* techniques, have revealed the Hispanic community's belief that the museum isn't supporting local Hispanic artists. *Client research* has shown that the museum is doing a good job of supporting local Hispanic artists—but that the museum isn't publicizing that success. Last but certainly not least, *stakeholder research*—particularly coorientation (p. 97)—has identified disturbing differences in what key publics think of the situation: Leaders of the Hispanic community think there's a problem; the curator of the museum doesn't.

By this point, you (the public relations and marketing director) have studied the issue. You know what the important publics think. So you're ready to begin planning, right? Wrong. You still need to answer one more question before you begin planning: *What values-based outcome do you seek?* You're about to take action, so what results do you seek? And will those results be consistent with your organization's values, mission, and goals? In The Art of Planning, the outcome you seek is an improved, productive relationship between your museum and the Hispanic residents of your city. Is that outcome consistent with the museum's values? Indeed it is. One of your organization's stated values is "Diversity." Furthermore, the values-based mission statement poster in your office includes these words: "This museum will diligently nurture the artistic interests of the residents of our community." The improved relationship you seek definitely would help your organization fulfill its mission.

Now you're finally ready for some values-driven planning.

DIFFERENT KINDS OF PUBLIC RELATIONS PLANS

To attain their organizations' public relations goals, public relations practitioners devise different types of plans. These fall into three basic categories: ad hoc plans, standing plans, and contingency plans.

Ad Hoc Plans

The plan you will create to end the misperceptions surrounding your museum will target a temporary (we hope) situation; therefore it's called an **ad hoc plan.** *Ad hoc* is a Latin phrase that means "for this purpose only." When you and your friends make plans for a party, for example, that's an ad hoc plan. Your plan is important, but it's temporary. It's not something you're going to live with for years (unless your party is truly legendary).

Standing Plans

Because many important relationships are ongoing and long term, wise organizations have ongoing and long-term plans to nurture those relationships. A plan of this type is often called a **standing plan.** Your museum, for example, probably would devise a standing plan to maintain a positive relationship with Hispanic residents once your ad hoc plan had succeeded.

A weekly blog that a corporate CEO writes for her management team is part of a standing plan. The blog helps the organization fulfill its values-based goal of maintaining a good relationship with some very important employees. Ideally, another part of that standing plan would be frequent opportunities for those managers to express their concerns to the CEO. Remember: Successful, symmetrical public relations is built on two-way communication and on an organization's willingness to change when necessary.

One danger of standing plans is that they sometimes stand too long. The plan becomes tradition, and we continue carrying out its directives because "that's what we've always done." A plan that stands too long can become divorced from its original values-based goal. For example, the CEO may be publishing a great weekly blog for her managers, but perhaps it's no longer effective because they now need daily, not weekly, updates on some of the topics.

Conducting evaluation research can reduce the danger of obsolete standing plans. As we noted in Chapter 7, evaluation research can help us see whether our plan is meeting its goals. A communication audit, for example, is a form of evaluation research that would examine our organization's communications goals and then check to see how well our communications actions are reaching those goals. An effective communication audit would be the death of an obsolete standing plan.

Contingency Plans

A third kind of public relations plan is called a **contingency plan.** Such plans are used for "what if" scenarios. Through good scanning and monitoring, organizations often spot issues that may require action if they suddenly gather strength. If any such issue has the potential to become powerful, a smart organization prepares a contingency plan. One of the best-known examples of a contingency plan is a crisis communications plan, which is discussed in Chapter 12. Many (though not enough) organizations have a basic crisis communications plan that they practice and can quickly adapt to meet the needs of an emerging crisis.

For example, as the number of cases of H1N1, also known as swine flu, ticked upward in 2009, the U.S. National Pork Board monitored World Health Organization data before launching "Pork Is Safe," a multimedia communication campaign to reassure nervous consumers. The Pork Board's level of preparedness may have been atypical, however. "Not often enough do companies have contingency plans," said Washington, D.C.–based public relations practitioner Patrick Dorton.[2]

Despite the different natures of these three kinds of plans—ad hoc, standing, and contingency—they share many characteristics, which we'll discuss next. But one shared characteristic is so important that we'll emphasize it now as well as later: *All public relations plans should be values-driven.* Any public relations plan you propose should strive to fulfill some area of your organization's values-based mission statement. A good way to win the enthusiastic support of your organization's top managers is to show them exactly how your plan helps achieve an important business goal. It's not enough to say, "This plan is great! It's going to help us build better relationships with important publics." Instead, remind your colleagues about

QUICKBREAK 8.1

Planning for the Entire Organization

Besides creating ad hoc, standing, and contingency plans, public relations managers ideally help create plans at an even higher level: They help determine their organization's values, mission, and specific business goals.

Public relations managers should contribute to organizational planning for two important reasons:

1. Realistic values, missions, and business goals depend on a clear understanding of relationships with employees, partners, competitors, and other important publics. As you'll recall from Chapter 1, in the reflective paradigm of public relations, practitioners help ensure the social legitimacy of an organization by objectively viewing it from the outside. Ideally, reflective practitioners have an unrivaled understanding of the social environment and its many relationships.

2. A good public relations plan contributes to the fulfillment of an organization's highest aspirations: its values, mission, and business goals. An organization's public relations team, therefore, must thoroughly understand and eagerly accept those aspirations. The best way for public relations practitioners to achieve understanding and acceptance is to help the organization establish those same values, mission, and business goals. Put this in terms of your own life: You're a lot more likely to support a spring break trip if you get to help plan it.

In a well-run organization, public relations managers are part of the top management team. "It's not just about creating press releases," says Herbert Heitmann, chief communications officer for SAP, a software maker. "It's about being thought leaders."[3] ∎

resource dependency theory (see Chapters 2 and 4) and explain how your public relations plan will provide resources that help the organization achieve its goals.

QUICK CHECK

1. How do an organization's values relate to the public relations planning process?
2. What kinds of research should precede the creation of a public relations plan?
3. What are the three kinds of public relations plans? How do they differ?
4. Why should public relations practitioners help an organization establish its values, mission, and related business goals?

WHY DO WE PLAN?

Effective public relations managers spend a great deal of their time making ad hoc, standing, and contingency plans. So it's logical to ask *why?* Why is planning so indispensable to successful public relations and professional advancement? We can think of six good reasons, which we'll detail next.

To Keep Our Actions in Line with Our Organization's Values-Based Mission

As we'll discuss shortly, a good plan is a series of proposed actions designed to produce a specific result. That specific result should advance our organization toward the fulfillment of its values-based mission. Planning prevents random, pointless actions that don't promote our values or our mission. Ideally, planning helps us ensure that all our actions are ethical and goal-oriented.

Let's put this same philosophy in terms of your own life. Why are you attending college? Chances are, your presence on campus isn't a random action. Instead, your collegiate studies are part of a plan that's consistent with several values in your life: a good education, a good career, and so on. You wouldn't dream of investing so much time and money in something that took you nowhere. It's the same in public relations.

To Secure Needed Resources

In public relations, we're never far from resource dependency theory. A primary duty of public relations practitioners is to build relationships with publics that have the resources an organization needs to achieve its goals. As you know, relationship building usually requires planning. Well-run corporations, for example, have employee relations plans, media relations plans, investor relations plans, and government relations plans; in fact, name a public that has desired resources, and a well-run organization will have a relationship-building plan for that group.

To Help Us Control Our Destiny

You have surely heard the sports cliché "We control our own destiny." Planning helps an organization control its destiny by proactively managing issues rather than just reacting to them. Planning can help an organization ensure that its relationships with key publics are a source of strength, not of weakness.

To appreciate the link between planning and positive relationships, simply apply the link once again to your own life. Imagine that you'd like to spend more time with a particular someone. Are you going to call that person and, with no preparation, ask him or her to go out immediately to who knows where because you haven't yet decided? Or are you going to ask a few days in advance with a specific social agenda? Spontaneity can be fun, but a little planning is indispensable in most good relationships.

Public relations departments that create and implement ad hoc, standing, and contingency plans increase their organization's options in a constantly changing environment. In doing so, they increase their value to the organization.

To Help Us Better Understand and Focus Our Research

Planning puts our research to the test. A detailed plan can quickly show us what we know—and what we don't know. For example, before we plan a specific relationship-building action with an important public, we must know several things:

- Does the relationship really require an adjustment?
- Does our organization want to make the adjustment?
- How will the public probably react to our proposed action?
- Do we have adequate resources to implement the action successfully?

You can probably think of other questions, but note what these have in common: They force us to look closely at our research. Planning helps us ascertain what we truly know, and it identifies areas that require more research.

To Help Us Achieve Consensus

As public relations managers transform research into a plan, they seek feedback. Many people, often an organization's top managers, provide input as the plan takes shape. When the planners are satisfied, the plan often goes to the client or top management for formal approval. Thus, when the final plan is approved, there's a sense of joint ownership and consensus. The organization's decision makers and its public relations team share a commitment to the success of the plan. Consensus and commitment help an organization avoid misunderstandings regarding relationship-building activities.

SOCIAL MEDIA APPS

Monitor and Engage

24/7/365. That's the underlying reality of new social media standing plans in public relations. When should organizations monitor social media for comments, trends, and issues that might affect their success—and when should they respond? Every hour of every day of every year, if possible.

That's a tall order, but Blake Cahill, senior vice president of marketing for Visible Technologies, explains the advantages of planned engagement with social media communities:

> If the proper groundwork has been laid with not only monitoring and understanding these communities, but engaging with them through an ongoing dialogue, then product news, company updates, and big launches will feel less like "campaigns" and more like an update to a captive audience.[4]

The growth of social media standing plans can be good news for media-savvy public relations students hoping to land their first jobs. A 2009 survey of almost 300 senior communications professionals found that "48 percent of all organizations are considering adding dedicated staff" who specialize in social media.[5] A second survey shows that the top two barriers to implementing standing social media plans are a lack of time and a lack of expertise.[6]

Cahill is optimistic about the future of social media planning. "As a channel for PR activities, social media will only continue to grow as more consumers become engaged in online dialogue," he says. "So be patient, flexible, and analytical, and think about the big picture when creating PR campaigns for the social Web."[7] ■

To Allow Effective Management of Resources

Resources are finite. (Think of your own entertainment budget, for example.) Public relations managers rarely have enough time, money, equipment, and staff to pursue every public relations issue affecting their organizations. Therefore, any waste of resources is painful. Public relations practitioners create plans because they want every fraction of every resource to move the organization toward its values-driven goals.

It may seem odd that the six reasons for planning don't include the notion that we plan in order to change other people's behavior. In reality, much of public relations planning *does* seek to change the behavior of particular publics. A plan designed to motivate a public to do something that it's predisposed to do may well be successful, but research suggests that plans that seek dramatic or rapid behavioral changes rarely succeed. In the mid-1990s, the Research Foundation of the International Association of Business Communicators completed a comprehensive study of effective public relations and came to what may be a disappointing conclusion: "[C]ommunication programs seldom change behavior in the short term, although they may do so over a longer period."[8]

Behavior or even opinions *may* change, then, but it's a long process. So what do public relations practitioners do? Through research and planning, we build relationships to gain needed resources. After all, this profession is called public *relations*. Good relationships, built on trust, cooperation, and two-way communication, can gradually produce the kinds of behavior that an organization desires from its important publics. Those good relationships can even cause our organization to change its own behavior. The IABC study confirmed that when we seek partnerships with particular publics—partnerships in which both sides win—we stand the best chance of gaining those publics' cooperation as we pursue our business goals. As noted in Chapter 1, this win–win philosophy is called two-way symmetrical public relations.

Public relations planners may understand the wisdom of this relationship-building approach to planning, but there's no guarantee that the top leaders of an organization will share that understanding. They might still expect practitioners to design and implement plans aimed at producing immediate behavioral changes. When such changes are possible and ethical, we should try to bring them about. But we also need to educate—diplomatically—our organizations' top leaders. We should seek opportunities to inform them about the wisdom and legitimacy of resource dependency theory and two-way symmetrical public relations.

VALUES STATEMENT 8.1

Boeing Company

Boeing, based in Chicago, develops and produces aircraft, space systems, and missile systems for commercial and national defense purposes.

In all our relationships we will demonstrate our steadfast commitment to:

- Leadership
- Integrity
- Quality
- Customer Satisfaction
- People Working Together
- A Diverse and Involved Team
- Good Corporate Citizenship
- Enhancing Shareholder Value

—Excerpt from "Vision," Boeing website ■

HOW DO WE PLAN?

Public relations planning usually begins after an organization establishes its mission-related business goals. In an ideal setting, public relations managers help establish those business goals. Once those goals are clear, however, the focus of the public relations team shifts to the development of relationship-management plans that help the organization reach its business goals.

A public relations goal is a general statement of the outcome we want a public relations plan to achieve. The goal of our museum scenario, for example, might be *To improve our museum's relationship with Hispanic residents of this city.*

The following sections describe the phases of the planning process, from consensus building to brainstorming to the creation of a written plan.

Consensus Building

Managers of an organization must agree on the need for action before planning can proceed. In the museum scenario, do museum managers agree with the above goal? Your research has revealed that the head curator doesn't think there's a problem in the museum's relationship with Hispanic residents. Thus, before you can plan for an improved relationship, you need to persuade her, and perhaps other museum officials, that the museum indeed has a problem. Otherwise, the goal seems irrelevant.

Fortunately, you have solid research you can use to show the curator that a growing problem does exist. Is that enough to win agreement on the goal? Perhaps not. You also need to show her that fulfilling this public relations goal will help the museum fulfill its broader goals. When the curator understands that vital connection, you will probably win her enthusiastic endorsement of your goal. Again, public relations practitioners must clearly link their public relations plans to the broader goals of their organizations.

Brainstorming

Once we've achieved consensus on a goal, we move to a speculative phase in which we explore our options for action: **brainstorming.** We ask tough questions about the quality of our research. We ask which publics can help us achieve the goal. We discuss what specific actions would be the best relationship builders. A good brainstorming session might even prompt us to revise our goal. In short, we have a wide-ranging, no-holds-barred session in which we frequently ask, "Do we know that for sure?" and "What if we tried this?" One Dallas-based agency tries to ensure creative brainstorming sessions by holding them on a basketball court, mixing planning and playing as practitioners work for some slam-dunk ideas.

To guide a brainstorming session, we recommend—in addition to a basketball court—a system based on a planning grid (see QuickBreak 8.2). A planning grid is a tool public relations practitioners use to develop communication strategies. It's a systematic approach to the planning process. As a prelude to a formal, written plan, a brainstorming grid highlights five areas for discussion:

- *Publics:* Which publics are or must be involved in the issue? For each public, who are the opinion leaders and decision makers?
- *Resources:* To reach our goals, what resources do we require from each public?
- *Values:* What are each public's interests, stakes, or involved values? In other words, why does each public care about this situation?
- *Message:* What message should we send to each public? A successful message addresses a public's values and attempts to get a specified response that would help your organization achieve a particular public relations goal.
- *Media:* Note that the word *media* is plural. You're not limited to just one channel of communication when you send a message to a targeted public.

As a brainstorming session starts to generate ideas, you can write them in a grid. The beginning of a brainstorming grid for our museum scenario would articulate a clear goal:

GOAL: *To improve our museum's relationship with Hispanic residents of this city.*

In our museum scenario, one *public* we could identify would be opinion leaders within the Hispanic community; they hold the *resource* of influence with others. We might decide that from the museum's standpoint, the key *value* held by that group is seeing strong support for local Hispanic artists. Our *message* could focus on the little-publicized fact that the museum actively supports local Hispanic artists. Finally, we might discuss using face-to-face meetings and a special event as *media* to send that message.

As you brainstorm and begin to formulate a specific plan, be sure to test all the options against your organization's values-based mission statement and goals.

GOAL: To Improve our Museum's Relationship with Hispanic Residents of this City				
Public	**Resource(s)**	**Value(s)**	**Message**	**Media**
Opinion leaders in the Hispanic community.	The power to influence members of the Hispanic community.	They want support for local Hispanic artists.	The museum *is* actively supporting those artists— and it's willing to do more.	Address Hispanic Chamber of Commerce.

As we've noted before, actions that become divorced from values are counterproductive and a waste of resources.

The wonderful thing about brainstorming is that you're not yet making firm commitments. Instead, you're just thinking on paper or on a chalkboard or a flip chart. However, the brainstorming grid does provide the basic information we need for the next step: the written plan, consisting of goal(s), objectives, strategies, and tactics.

QUICK CHECK

1. Should public relations plans focus on quickly changing the behavior of a public or publics? Why or why not?
2. How can public relations practitioners win top management's support for a public relations plan?
3. What is brainstorming? Why is it useful in planning?
4. How does understanding a particular public's values help public relations practitioners create a message for that public?

Goals, Objectives, Strategies, and Tactics: The Written Plan

A written public relations plan consists of four main elements, as shown in Figure 8.1. However, practitioners often disagree on what to call those elements and how to define them. "Practitioners have almost as many different definitions of goals, objectives, strategies, and activities as we have for defining the profession itself," says Tom Hagley, a practitioner with 30-plus years of experience.[9] This book will use four commonly accepted terms:

1. a *goal* or goals
2. *objectives*
3. *strategies*
4. *tactics,* or recommended actions

The order of the four is important. Not until you've clearly established the goal and shown that it's consistent with your organization's values can you move to objectives. And not until you've specified the objectives and shown that they, too, are consistent with organizational values can you move to strategies and tactics (recommended actions), which, again, must be consistent with organizational values.

Let's look at the four main elements of planning in more detail.

GOALS. Your starting point, the **goal,** is a generalized statement of the outcome you hope your plan achieves. For example, in our museum scenario, you've diplomatically persuaded the management team that the goal is

To improve our museum's relationship with Hispanic residents of this city.

Goals often begin with infinitives, such as *to improve* or *to increase.* By beginning your plan with a verb, you place an immediate focus on action.

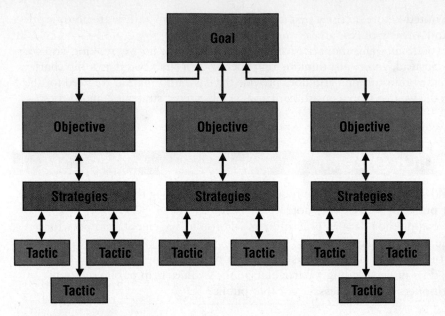

FIGURE 8.1

Goal, Objectives, Strategies, and Tactics

In a public relations plan, a goal determines the necessary objectives, which, in turn, determine the necessary strategies and tactics. In executing the plan, a public relations practitioner first executes the tactics; this leads to the fulfillment of the strategies and objectives, which, in turn, leads to the fulfillment of the goal.

OBJECTIVES.   Once you have agreement on a well-written goal, you move to the next part of a written plan: the **objectives.** Whereas goals are general statements, objectives define particular ambitions. Objectives, in the words of the PRSA Accreditation Board, are "specific milestones that measure progress toward achievement of a goal."[10] For example, we earlier mentioned an ad hoc plan for a party that you and your friends might throw. Your goal, of course, would be to throw a great party. Your objectives would include activities such as identifying and inviting guests; creating a fun, social atmosphere; and so on. You'd have to meet each of these objectives to meet your goal.

According to the Institute for Public Relations, good objectives have five qualities. They must

1. specify a desired outcome (increase awareness, improve relationships, build preference, adopt an attitude, generate sales leads, etc.).
2. directly specify one or several target audiences.
3. be measurable, both conceptually and practically.
4. refer to "ends," not "means."
5. include a time frame in which the objective is to be achieved—for example, by July 1.[11]

In the book *Using Research in Public Relations,* Professors Glen Broom and David Dozier write, "The most frequently asked question in our classes and workshops is 'How much change do you know how to call for in an objective?' The simple response is 'By researching the situation to learn what is possible.'"[12] To that solid beginning, we offer these additional pointers:

- Remember that changing a public's behavior, if it can be done at all, is a long-term process.[13] Measuring resource acquisition or the quality of relationships may be easier (see QuickBreak 7.3).
- When appropriate, consider targeting opinion leaders and decision makers with your objectives. It may be easier to create and measure results with a smaller group.
- As you enact your plan, conduct ongoing evaluation to see if your objectives were realistic. You might have time to change course.

In a public relations plan, objectives often focus on the targeted publics. If your plan involves six publics, the plan may well have six objectives—because you're seeking to build six different relationships to achieve your goal. However, it is also true that some objectives can serve more than one public. Unfortunately, no magic formula exists that can help you determine the right number of objectives for a goal. The only true test of whether your objectives are sufficient is this question: If I fulfill each objective and manage my resources wisely, will I reach the goal? If the answer is yes, you have the right number of objectives.

In our museum scenario, your objectives might look something like this:

Objective 1: To ensure that 100 percent of museum managers know of the museum-related values of this city's Hispanic residents by November 1.

Objective 2: To increase the number of Hispanic artists contacted by 30 percent by December 1.

Objective 3: To increase the Hispanic community's knowledge of the museum's programs by 20 percent by February 1.

If you can fulfill these objectives, you'll surely meet your goal. One of your challenges, however, might be measurability. To commit to specific increases, you'll need to know current levels of knowledge and activities. For example, before you plan to increase the Hispanic community's knowledge of museum programs by 20 percent, you'll need to conduct research to specify the current level of knowledge and to understand what degree of improvement is actually possible.

The specificity of your objectives will, in all likelihood, be familiar to top managers within your organization. Many organizations practice a philosophy called management by objectives, or MBO for short. MBO involves having managers commit to specific performance objectives for their particular departments. MBO is also used in performance evaluations for employees. Public relations plans that focus on goals, objectives, strategies, and specific tactics are clearly part of the MBO philosophy favored by many of today's organizations.

QUICKBREAK 8.2

The PRSA Planning Grid

Ready for a healthy dose of alphabet soup? The Accreditation Board of the Public Relations Society of America recommends that you use PIPP, POST, and TASC grids as part of a three-step planning process.[14]

PIPP, POST, and TASC are memory aids to help you complete three fill-in-the-blank planning grids. The PIPP acronym stands for a process that helps you identify and define the publics your goal-oriented plan may target. It stands for **P**ublic, **I**mportant Segments, **P**rofile, and **P**riority. A PIPP grid looks like this:

Public	Important Segments	Profile	Priority

For each public you identify, you note the important segments of that public, such as influential members and decision makers, that may require special attention. You then profile each public: You describe its "unique issues, needs, concerns, special demographics, . . . etc."[15] Profile information helps you determine what communication tactics you'll recommend for that specific group. Finally, you assign each public a priority: Which of the identified publics is the most important to your organization? Which is least?

After PIPP comes POST, which helps you develop specific communication actions. The acronym stands for **P**ublic/Segment, **O**bjectives, **S**trategies, and **T**actics. A POST grid looks like this:

Public/ Segment	Objectives	Strategies	Tactics

You begin by naming the identified segments of the key publics. For each segment, you then specify objectives, strategies, and tactics. Objectives are measurable results you hope to achieve with each public. Strategies are general descriptions of the actions you'll take to reach each objective. Tactics are specific actions that help you fulfill your strategies.

Tactic	Amount	Schedule	Coordinator

Having worked through PIPP and POST, you're ready to move to the final step of the three-phase process: outlining the logistics of each tactic. The third acronym, TASC, stands for **T**actic, **A**mount, **S**chedule, and **C**oordinator. A TASC grid looks like this:

For each tactic, you list the amount it will cost, when it is scheduled to occur, and who will coordinate its implementation.

From the identification of key publics to the naming of a coordinator for a specific action, the three-part PRSA planning grid can help you assemble the information you need for an effective public relations plan. ■

STRATEGIES. Strategies help you move from specific objectives to specific recommended actions. Based on good research, a **strategy** is a general description of the kind and tone of actions (tactics) you'll implement to fulfill an objective. Professor Robert Kendall writes that strategies "indicate the conceptual approach in selecting specific actions to be taken to achieve objectives and reach the goal."[16] For example, given our objective of increasing the Hispanic community's knowledge of our museum's programs, our research might show that a strategy of informative, face-to-face communication with community leaders would be best. Our consequent strategy might read: "Seek face-to-face opportunities to inform Hispanic community opinion leaders about our museum's support for local Hispanic artists." Strategies begin with active verbs; they resemble general commands.

TACTICS. When you're satisfied with your goal(s), objectives, and strategies, it's time to suggest specific tactics. **Tactics,** or recommended actions, make up the fourth and final part of a written plan; they are how you enact each strategy. To fulfill each objective, you need to take specific actions. Thus, you can list recommended actions under each strategy. That placement is important. You don't gather all your tactics together and place them at the end of the plan. Instead, you put

QUICKBREAK 8.3

Getting Strategic

In a public relations plan, strategies describe the general kind and tone of the tactics designed to fulfill a particular objective. Recent public relations research has shown that practitioners tend to choose from seven basic kinds of strategies:[17]

1. Informative: the delivery of accurate information designed to prompt a reaction
2. Persuasive: the direct appeal to a public's values and self-interests
3. Facilitative: the delivery of resources to help a public act on an existing inclination
4. Cooperative problem solving: the creation of partnerships to identify and solve problems
5. Promise and reward: the assurance of benefits for cooperative behavior
6. Threat and punishment: the assurance of penalties for uncooperative behavior
7. Bargaining: the direct negotiation of trading resources for resources

Research has revealed that the most-used strategies are persuasive and informative; the least used are promise and reward, threat and punishment, and bargaining. Practitioners believe that, in general, the most effective approaches are, in order, the informative, persuasive, facilitative, and cooperative problem-solving strategies.

So how do you select the best strategy for a particular public? You know the answer to that.

Research. ■

strategies and recommended actions under each objective to show how you plan to achieve that specific ambition.

Unlike goals and objectives, tactics don't begin with infinitives. They begin with active verbs; they're commands. Thus, in the museum scenario, your first tactic under your third objective might be something like this:

Objective 3: To increase the Hispanic community's knowledge of the museum's programs by 20 percent by February 1.

Strategy: Seek face-to-face opportunities to inform Hispanic community opinion leaders about our museum's support for local Hispanic artists.

Tactic 1: Address the January meeting of the city's Hispanic Chamber of Commerce.

That tactic is a good command, but it's not very complete. Who should address the Hispanic Chamber of Commerce? When is the meeting? How can you get on the meeting's agenda? What presentation materials will the speaker use? Besides being expressed as a brief command, each tactic should provide enough specific details to enable someone to implement it. It's common under each tactic to give the following information:

- *Brief description* (specifying only what is essential for the action to be executed)
- *Deadline*

Public Relations Tactic (Special Event)

Some relationship-building actions are more explosive than others. At Fort Vancouver National Historic Site, the firing of a mountain howitzer is a popular tourist attraction.

(Courtesy of Fort Vancouver National Historic Site and the National Park Service)

■ *Budget*
■ *Special requirements* (specifying anything out of the ordinary, such as a need for unusual technology or required permits or permissions)

QUICKBREAK 8.4

The SWOT Analysis

Imagine the success you would enjoy as a public relations professional if you could create relationship-building plans that helped your organization or clients

- improve strengths
- diminish weaknesses
- seize opportunities
- avoid threats

SWOT analysis can help you achieve that ambition.

SWOT is an acronym for strengths, weaknesses, opportunities, and threats. For an organization, those qualities can be internal or external.

- *Strengths* are an organization's current assets, including issues and social conditions, that can help the organization achieve its goals. Strengths can include employee expertise, public opinion, and new legislation.
- *Weaknesses* are an organization's current disadvantages, including issues and social conditions, that can prevent the organization from achieving its goals. Weaknesses can include a lack of internal resources and a public scandal.
- *Opportunities* are emerging assets, issues, and social conditions that, in the future, could help the organization achieve its goals. Opportunities can include new products and services the organization is developing, pending legislation, and new international markets.
- *Threats* are emerging disadvantages, issues, and social conditions that could prevent the organization from achieving its goals. Threats can include the upcoming retirement of key employees, growing competition in the marketplace, and pending legislation.

A SWOT analysis is a bridge between research and planning. Listing and considering strengths, weaknesses, opportunities, and threats helps sort out your data about an organization and the social environment in which it operates. Using specific information from a SWOT analysis, public relations practitioners can create plans to boost positives and reduce negatives. A highly focused SWOT analysis that identifies the strengths, weaknesses, opportunities, and threats in a particular situation can serve as a situation analysis for a proposal (p. 244).

Whether broad or narrow in scope, a SWOT analysis must be factual. Avoid opinions and the temptation to overstate positives and understate negatives. Be realistic. Be objective.

And be ready to bring SWOT analysis into the planning process. ■

- *Supervisor* (name of the person in charge of seeing that the action is executed)

Our tactic might now look something like this:

Tactic 1: Address the January meeting of the city's Hispanic Chamber of Commerce.

- *Brief description:* Request permission for curator to give a 10-minute presentation on the museum's support for local Hispanic artists. Permission is generally granted if we provide two weeks' advance notice. Use handouts and computer-generated slides to show the scope of the museum's support for local Hispanic artists. To demonstrate our willingness to change and to be accommodating, the curator should begin her presentation in Spanish (which she does speak) before switching to English. Handouts and slides should be in Spanish and English.
- *Deadline:* Contact Hispanic Chamber of Commerce by December 15. January meeting date is January 21.
- *Budget:* $100 for preparation of handouts and computer graphics.
- *Special requirements:* Take grant-application forms to the meeting so that Hispanic Chamber of Commerce members can help distribute them to local Hispanic artists. Ensure that forms are written in Spanish and English.
- *Supervisor:* Public relations director.

Having supplied this much detail, you're ready to move on to your next tactic under your face-to-face informative strategy.

Fleshing out each tactic helps give us the road map we need to reach our goal. When we're finished, we have a highly detailed, realistic, workable plan—in writing.

EXPANDING A PLAN INTO A PROPOSAL

Even with your written plan completed, your writing might be unfinished. Some plans exist alone as plans. Sometimes, however, you need to "sell" your plan to a client or a supervisor who might want a greater amount of background information. Often, therefore, a plan becomes part of a larger document called a **proposal.** Agencies often prepare proposals for their clients, and even within corporations public relations practitioners often prepare proposals for top management. A public relations proposal generally contains, in order, these sections:

1. A title page
2. An **executive summary** that briefly, in one page, describes the problem or opportunity, identifies the targeted publics, lists primary tactics for addressing the situation, and includes a budget summary
3. A **situation analysis** that accurately and fairly describes the current situation in such a way that action seems advisable
4. A concise **statement of purpose** announcing that the proposal presents a plan to address the described situation

5. A list and description of publics that the plan targets
6. A plan that specifies your goal(s), objectives, strategies, and tactics
7. Other sections as appropriate, such as
   - campaign theme and key messages
   - line-item budget
   - timetable
   - evaluative measures
   - supporting documents (usually in the appendices)

A proposal, as you can see, can be an extensive document. But at its heart is a clear plan consisting of a goal or goals, objectives, strategies, and tactics.

 QUICK CHECK

1. How is a goal different from an objective?
2. What are the qualities of a well-written objective?
3. What are tactics? What is their relationship to strategies?
4. How is a plan different from a proposal?

QUALITIES OF A GOOD PLAN

We've covered why we plan and how we plan, and we've seen how a plan can be incorporated in a proposal. Let's turn now to the qualities of a good plan. We've already mentioned some: A good plan seeks measurable results, and it has specific deadlines. What other qualities should a good plan have?

- *A good plan supports a specific goal of your organization.* As we've said before, don't take for granted that your organization's leaders automatically recognize the value of good public relations. Show them how your plan can help the organization reach a specific business goal.
- *A good plan stays goal-oriented.* Remember the problem with some standing plans? They stand for so long that we forget why we're following them; instead, we just execute the tactics, such as an employee newsletter, because we've always done them. That won't happen if we stay goal-oriented, finding ways to remind ourselves of why we're executing these particular actions.
- *A good plan is realistic.* Don't promise more than you can achieve. It's OK to dream an impossible dream, but you should plan for an achievable reality. Unrealistic goals and objectives often involve quickly changing a public's behavior. That's not necessarily always impossible, but public relations is much better at building the open and honest relationships that foster gradual changes. Unrealistic tactics include those that require more resources or expertise than your organization can supply.

■ *A good plan is flexible.* Things change. Sometimes important elements of a situation change just as you're launching a plan. If you constantly evaluate the situation, as you should do, you may need to adjust your plan to fit the new circumstances.

■ *A good plan is a win–win proposition.* Whenever possible, the success of your plan should benefit the target publics just as much as it benefits your organization. Forcing a public to change against its will is rarely possible and is almost always bad public relations; there's a reason the "threat and punishment" strategy is ineffective and unpopular (QuickBreak 8.3). A good plan tries to honor each important public's values. When that's not possible, a good plan seeks to minimize damage to important relationships.

■ *Finally, and most important, a good plan is values-driven.* As we've noted more than once, if your plan isn't helping your organization achieve its values, it's counter-productive. It's wasting resources. A good plan resonates with the well-known values of your organization.

SUMMARY

Plans usually fit into one of three categories: ad hoc, standing, or contingency. Successful public relations plans have many qualities, but they share one in particular: They must be clearly tied to an organization's goals. In other words, public relations practitioners must show an organization's top managers how a proposed relationship-building plan aligns with the organization's values and mission. If that connection is not established, the plan will probably die for lack of consensus and approval.

Good public relations plans consist of a general goal or goals; measurable objectives; strategies; and specific tactics, or recommended actions. Often, a written plan becomes part of a larger document called a proposal, which practitioners use to present a plan to a client or to their organization's top management.

Good, creative planning is an art—but it's an art based on science. A good plan is goal directed and research based. It is realistic and flexible, and it aims for a win–win outcome. Above all, a good public relations plan helps an organization fulfill its values.

DISCUSSION QUESTIONS

1. At what specific points do values enter the public relations planning process?
2. What unique characteristics differentiate ad hoc plans, standing plans, and contingency plans from one another?
3. Can you think of examples—in public relations or otherwise—of standing plans that have stood too long?

4. Why should you go to the effort of producing a written plan if you've already completed a planning grid? If you have a written plan, when should you consider expanding it into a proposal?

5. Why are measurable objectives important to the evaluation phase of the public relations process? What are the advantages of measurable objectives? What are the disadvantages?

MEMO FROM THE FIELD

TIMOTHY S. BROWN, APR, PH.D.

Director of Communications; Alstom
Washington, D.C.

Timothy S. Brown is an accredited public relations professional with more than 20 years of communications experience in public relations, public affairs, and marketing communications. Brown currently serves as director of communications for Alstom, an international power-generation and transportation company. Brown also taught a business writing course at Wesley College in New Castle, Delaware. He holds a Ph.D. in English and rhetoric from the University of Maryland at College Park, a master's degree in English from George Mason University, and a bachelor's degree in journalism from Pennsylvania State University. Brown lives in Newark, Delaware—a great college town, he says—with his wife and two children.

When I was in college, sitting where you are, one of my favorite professors began one of my favorite classes by writing a time line on the board. The time line charted the length of time between major technological advances in the history of man—from the invention of simple tools, to the domestication of fire, to the use of the wheel, and so on up to modern times. My favorite professor's point was that the pace of change had accelerated dramatically over time. Whereas it had been thousands of years between the domestication of fire and the invention of the wheel, these days major technological changes are measured in years, if not months or weeks. Such well-known history is behind the well-known maxim that life is change.

This chapter offers a wealth of valuable advice on public relations planning. It explains why planning is important, lays out a sensible approach to planning, offers useful examples of effective plans, and defines the qualities of a good plan. One particular point the authors made in the last section struck a chord with me. They note that "a good plan is flexible" because "things change," making it important for you to "constantly evaluate the situation . . . [so you can] adjust your plan to fit the new circumstances."

If I were you, I'd underline, highlight, and asterisk that passage. My 20 years of experience as a communications professional has underscored the power behind the simple truth that "things change." I've seen the electric industry where I now work change dramatically with the onset of "deregulation." I've seen dozens of executive leaders come and go. I've seen one organization significantly change its business strategy three times in six years. Such experiences have left me convinced that the best public relations plans must both anticipate and accommodate change.

(continued)

Let me give you an example that illustrates the importance of adapting your public relations plans to accommodate change. In a previous job, I coordinated the strategic communications planning process for a Fortune 500 energy-delivery company. My colleagues and I grounded that planning process in the needs of the business units that we supported. We also factored in what was happening in our industry and the broader environment in which we did business. All of these elements combined in a matrix that identified the goals, objectives, strategies, messages, and tactics that we used to execute our plan over the next several years.

I'm sure you can guess the flaw in that process. You got it: Things change. Before long, for example, that company was hit by a major hurricane that disrupted service to nearly one million of its 1.8 million customers. Those customers had questions and issues that weren't anticipated in our plan. To address those new public relations challenges, we had to adapt our well-established plans.

We followed the basic process that we used in developing the initial plan. We conducted research, including surveys and focus groups with customers that had been hardest hit by the hurricane. Based on that research, we reformulated our strategies and objectives for our matrix communications plan. Those new strategies, in turn, translated into adaptations of previously planned communications tactics. For example, we modified a long-running advertising campaign to reflect the lessons of the hurricanes, including, especially, the desire for more information about when power would be restored, which customers expressed via our research. This process resulted in a "new and improved" version of our matrix communications plan that we implemented.

You will likely find in your career that you will have to accommodate similar new developments. If anything, change will be even more of a constant for you. You will be judged in large part by how well you adapt to such a climate in which change is the norm. It will of course be important for you to follow the sound advice that you have received about planning in this chapter and this course. But it will be equally important for you to be adaptable enough to adjust those plans to the ever-changing conditions that will be a constant reality in your public relations career.

Unfortunately, I can't tell you exactly how to do that. You will need to develop the experience, expertise, and judgment to know when and how to adapt your plans based on changing conditions. Doing so will be one of the most challenging and yet satisfying aspects of your career.

There is, however, one piece of advice with which I would leave you. No matter how much you have to change your *plans* to adapt to new challenges, you should not feel that it is necessary to change your *values*. As the title of this textbook suggests, your public relations practices must ultimately be grounded in the values that define you and your organization. In fact, it is only by identifying the values that most matter to you and your organization that you can decide how to adapt existing public relations plans most appropriately in the face of inevitable changes.

Hopefully, as you look back on your own college experience in the future, you'll consider this class to be part of the formative process of the way you approach public relations. If so, I'll hope you'll agree with the importance of always being ready to change your plans but never being too quick to change your values. ■

CASE STUDY 8.1 Grape Expectations: Planning to Save California Wines

If you're a video-gamer, the glassy-winged sharpshooter might sound like one of those archvillains that haunt a game-level's conclusion. One of the sharpshooter's sworn foes, in fact, is the Terminator himself—California Governor Arnold Schwarzenegger. But the sharpshooter isn't a digital fantasy: It's a half-inch-long insect that threatens California's $45 billion wine grape industry.

In 2001, California's wine grape growers voted to create the Pierce's Disease and Glassy-Winged Sharpshooter Board to combat the insect. Overseen by the state's Department of Food and Agriculture and funded by mandatory contributions from the state's wine grape growers, the board sought to eradicate Pierce's disease, spread by the sharpshooter and devastating to vineyards. But authorization for the funding was set to end in 2006. The only way to extend the board's life to 2011 was for growers to vote again to fund its mission. And that was a problem.

"It's tough," said grower Brad Lange, who chairs the board. "Some of my colleagues may feel that they can't afford it, or they may forget to vote. But if we don't continue this, the industry will lose control of the sharpshooter, and [Pierce's disease] will start showing up in our vineyards."[18]

"We're concerned that the program might become a victim of its own success," added grower Paul Kronenberg. "Growers might say, 'Hey, it's OK. We haven't had a problem in a long time, so why should I pay this?' Things aren't OK."[19]

Concerned that it would lose the vote and its funding, the board turned to Brown-Miller Communications (BMC), a public relations agency based in San Martinez, California. BMC's initial research confirmed the board's fears: Surveys and personal interviews showed that many growers doubted the effectiveness of continued funding. The board's inadequate communications efforts had failed to spread the word of its dramatic successes.[20]

BMC's research also showed that the most credible sources for California's wine grape growers were other growers, not government officials. Based on its research, BMC crafted a public relations plan with the goal of increasing grower support for the board's continuation. The plan's objectives included:

- increasing grower recognition of the board's identity and messages by at least 25 percent
- increasing grower awareness and support for the board's goals and activities by 50 percent
- securing the support of at least 50 percent of the state's key intervening publics (grower associations and wineries) to echo the board's messages[21]

BMC recommended an overall strategy of using respected growers who supported the board as the primary spokespeople for the campaign. Particular tactics included speaker kits with talking points for the selected growers, increased involvement in trade shows and special events, a quarterly newsletter to growers, news releases, a news conference, and editorials written by respected growers.[22]

In one such tactic, three respected growers wrote a letter to the editor of the *San Francisco Chronicle* in which they declared, "We urge every grower to demonstrate their support for continuing the research and control efforts by voting 'Yes' on the referendum. For hundreds of thousands of Californians whose jobs or lifestyles are benefited by the wine industry, we hope that you'll work to persuade growers to support continuance of important research and control programs."[23]

BMC's strategy of using respected intervening publics to influence individual growers was also evident in the comments of the president of the Sonoma County Grape Growers Association: "The industry and state have done a remarkable job of containing this threat so far, but we have to remain vigilant and search for an answer.

Passage of the referendum is the best way to ensure that."[24]

The growers voted yes in overwhelming numbers: Almost 90 percent of the 4,000-plus growers who voted supported the continued funding. Virtually 100 percent of the targeted intervening publics supported the board, and the amount of media coverage of the sharpshooter threat increased by 800 percent.[25]

"Anytime a measure passes with almost 90 percent of folks marking their ballots with a yes vote, you know voters are deeply concerned," said grower Jim Richards.[26]

For its impressive success in helping the board win approval of continued funding, Brown-Miller Communications won a top public relations prize: a 2006 Silver Anvil Award from the Public Relations Society of America.

In honoring the year's many Silver Anvil winners, David Imre, chair of the awards competition, singled out BMC's superior planning. "We congratulate Brown-Miller Communications for its public relations programs that incorporated measurable and sound research, planning, execution and evaluation," he said. "These programs contribute to the best practices of our industry."[27]

DISCUSSION QUESTIONS

1. How does the Brown-Miller Communications plan show a general goal, specific objectives, general strategies, and specific tactics?
2. Besides the ad hoc plan that BMC developed, can you think of a standing plan that it might have developed? Can you think of a contingency plan it might have developed?
3. How does this case demonstrate the value of opinion leaders and intervening publics?
4. Why do you think the Pierce's Disease and Glassy-Winged Sharpshooter Board chose to use public relations rather than advertising? ■

CASE STUDY 8.2 Good Intentions, Bad Planning: The Breast Cancer–Screening Debate

Take your pick of firestorms: For *USA Today*, the event created "a news media firestorm." For the *New York Times*, it was a "political firestorm." CNN branded it "a firestorm of confusion." In the pages of the *Bakersfield Californian*, it became a "firestorm of protest." For the *Chicago Tribune* and the *Seattle Times*, it was an ordinary "firestorm," although both newspapers used the word in headlines. Dozens of other news media, including Fox News, the *Washington Post, Newsday*, and the *Philadelphia Inquirer,* labeled the event, yes, a "firestorm."[28] In all this incendiary language, two things seem certain: Journalists love the word *firestorm*—and whatever the event was, it must have been important.

It was. The event, in fact, involved a matter of life and death. In November 2009, a little-known federal agency, the U.S. Preventive Services Task Force, published an article in a little-known journal, *Annals of Internal Medicine*. The article contained the federal task force's recommended revisions for breast cancer screenings. After painstaking analyses of studies of more than 800,000 women, the task force, which consists of "independent . . . experts in primary care, epidemiology, and prevention," recommended that women in their 40s should no longer have annual mammograms and that teaching women to conduct breast self-examinations should be discontinued because it had been ineffective.[29] "We're not saying women shouldn't get screened. Screening does save lives," said a task force member. "But we are recommending against routine screening. There are important and serious negatives or harms that need to be considered carefully."[30]

And, as the news media reported, the firestorm began.

"The scientists who surveyed the mammogram studies did their job honorably," wrote national columnist Ellen Goodman. "[But] they dropped these guidelines onto an unprepared public like leaflets from a helicopter of experts who didn't understand the conditions on the ground. . . . [T]he end result was a kind of tone-deaf naïveté."[31]

Ironically, the Preventive Services Task Force had used what often is the most effective strategy in public relations planning: the informative strategy, simply delivering well-researched information to an appropriate public (see QuickBreak 8.3). So what went wrong?

Part of the public relations planning process involves studying the environment into which messages will be sent. And this particular environment had an emotionally charged history. "Women have been told as a matter of holy medical writ for years now that [breast cancer] screenings should occur routinely beginning at age 40," wrote journalist Ricardo Pimentel.[32] Further, although the task force presented compelling evidence that early mammograms might do more harm than good, women who had been saved by early mammograms were quick to come forward. "If I had waited until I was 50, I wouldn't be here," said breast cancer survivor Lillie Shockney, director of the Johns Hopkins Avon Foundation Breast Cancer Center.[33]

Yet another part of the planning process involves understanding that a message meant for one public can reach another. In publishing an article in *Annals of Internal Medicine,* the task force acted as one group of medical professionals speaking to a similar group. But that article also entered an environment obsessed with health care: A deeply divided Congress was wrestling with far-reaching health-care legislation, and Americans from all walks of life were watching intently. Said physician Val Jones, CEO of Better Health, a network of health-care bloggers:

[I]t's almost amusing how bad the timing of the . . . guidelines really was. The country was in the midst of trying to pass our country's first serious healthcare reform bill in decades . . . and opponents of the bill had already expressed vehement concern about arbitrary government rationing of healthcare services. . . . [I]t violates Public Relations 101. . . .[34]

Some opponents of the emerging congressional legislation pounced upon the task force findings, claiming they were the first shot in a federally engineered reduction of health-care services.

Because Dr. Jones linked the task force's well-meant but ill-fated communications to public relations, she earns the final word in this cautionary tale—and the word seems to be *planning*.

The new . . . guidelines for mammogram screenings debacle serves as a perfect public relations case study in what not to do in advancing healthcare reform. It was the perfect storm of high-profile subject, bad timing, poor argument preparation, and lack of back-up planning.[35]

DISCUSSION QUESTIONS

1. What would you answer if a member of the U.S. Preventive Services Task Force said, "We're just scientists delivering our findings. How was this bad planning? We're not public relations professionals"?
2. What other publics, besides the readers of *Annals of Internal Medicine,* might the U.S. Preventive Services Task Force have approached with its recommendations?
3. What strategy might the task force have used for each of those publics?
4. What specific tactics might the task force have used for each of those public-based strategies?
5. Chapter 5 includes a discussion of the ethos, logos, and pathos strategies of persuasion. How might the task force have used those strategies? ■

NOTES

1. Elizabeth L. Toth, Shirley Serini, Donald Wright, and Arthur Emig, "Trends in Public Relations Roles: 1990–1995," *Public Relations Review* (summer 1998): 145–163; Anne Gregory, "Competencies of Senior Communication Practitioners in the UK," *Public Relations Review* (September 2008): 215–223.

2. Matthew Murray, "Pork Industry Tries to Cure Swine Flu," *Roll Call*, 4 May 2009, online, LexisNexis Academic.

3. Andrew Gordon, "SAP Retools Global Comms," *PRWeek,* 9 August 2004, 1.

4. "How Can Social Media Monitoring Assist in Planning PR Campaigns?" *PRWeek*, 1 August 2009, online, www.prweekus.com.

5. "Digital Readiness Report: Essential Online Public Relations and Marketing Skills," a report by iPressroom, Trendstream, Korn/Ferry International, and Public Relations Society of America, 2009, online, www.ipressroom.com.

6. "Social Media Survey 2009," *PRWeek* and MS&L Worldwide, October 2009, online, www.prweekus.com.

7. "How Can Social Media Monitoring Assist in Planning PR Campaigns?"

8. James E. Grunig, "Communication, Public Relations, and Effective Organizations: An Overview of This Book," in *Excellence in Public Relations and Communication Management,* ed. James E. Grunig (Hillsdale, N.J.: Lawrence Erlbaum, 1992), 14.

9. Tom Hagley, "Lead with Integrity," *Public Relations Strategist* (winter 2003): 40.

10. *Accreditation Study Guide, 1993* (New York: Public Relations Society of America, 1993), 81.

11. "Guidelines for Setting Measurable Public Relations Objectives," Institute for Public Relations Commission on PR Measurement and Evaluation, 1999, online, www.instituteforpr.com/printables/objectives.htm.

12. Glen M. Broom and David M. Dozier, *Using Research in Public Relations: Applications to Program Management* (Englewood Cliffs, N.J.: Prentice Hall, 1990), 40.

13. Grunig, 14.

14. *Accreditation Study Guide, 1993,* 89.

15. *Accreditation Study Guide, 1993,* 90.

16. Robert Kendall, *Public Relations Campaign Strategies,* 2nd ed. (New York: Harper-Collins, 1996), 250.

17. Kelly Page Werder, "Responding to Activism: An Experimental Analysis of Public Relations Strategy Influence on Attributes of Publics," *Journal of Public Relations Research* (October 2006): 335–356.

18. Jon Ortiz, "Pinot Pest Growers Grapple with Extending a Fee to Fight Vine Infestation," *Sacramento Bee,* 21 March 2005, online, Lexis-Nexis Academic.

19. Ortiz.

20. "Creating an Identity to Rally Winegrape Growers Around," report by the Public Relations Society of America, 2006, online, www.prsa.org.

21. "Creating an Identity to Rally Winegrape Growers Around."

22. "Creating an Identity to Rally Winegrape Growers Around."

23. Ben Drake, Jim Richards, and Bobby Koch, "Pest Requires Vigilance," *San Francisco Chronicle,* 12 May 2005, online, LexisNexis Academic.

24. "Grape Growers Support Referendum," *Western Farm Press,* 7 May 2005, online, LexisNexis.

25. "Creating an Identity to Rally Winegrape Growers Around."

26. "New Report on PD," news release issued by Family Winemakers of California, 25 July 2005, online, LexisNexis Academic.

27. "California Firm Captures Nation's Highest P.R. Honor," Avenue Vine: Wine News and Information Magazine, 19 June 2006, online, www.avenuevine.com.

28. Nancy G. Brinker, "With Breast Screenings, Every Woman Counts," *USA Today*, 7 December 2009, online, America's Newspapers; Gina Kolata, "Mammogram Debate Took Group by Surprise," *New York Times,* 20 November 2009, online, America's Newspapers; "CNN Newsroom," CNN, 2 December 2009, online,

LexisNexis Academic. "New Breast Cancer Screening Guidelines Are Wrong," *Bakersfield Californian*, 22 November 2009, online, America's Newspapers; Judith Graham, "Mammogram Guidelines Are Sparking a Firestorm," *Chicago Tribune*, 17 November 2009, online, America's Newspapers; Kyung M. Song, "Cancer Guidelines Touch Off Firestorm," *Seattle Times*, 18 November 2009, online, America's Newspapers; "Fox News Watch, Fox News, 21 November 2009, online, LexisNexis Academic; Douglas Kamerow and Steven Woolf, "Parsing the Mammogram Guidelines," *Washington Post*, 20 November 2009, online, America's Newspapers; "Docs' 2nd Opinion Panel Says Mammograms Fine for Women in 40s Task," *Newsday*, 4 December 2009, online, America's Newspapers; Marie McCullough, "The Mammogram Storm: Benefits vs. Risks," *Philadelphia Inquirer*, 20 November 2009, online, America's Newspapers.

29. United States Preventive Services Task Force, online, www.ahrq.gov/CLINIC/uspstfix.htm.

30. Rob Stein, "Breast Exam Guidelines Now Call for Less Testing," *Washington Post*, 17 November 2009, online, America's Newspapers.

31. Ellen Goodman, "Poor Communication Created a Backlash of Mistrust," *Contra Costa Times*, 1 December 2009, online, America's Newspapers.

32. O. Ricardo Pimentel, "Cold Numbers by Themselves Aren't Enough," *Milwaukee Journal Sentinel*, 29 November 2009, online, America's Newspapers.

33. Kelly Brewington, "New Mammogram Guidelines Fuel Contradiction, Confusion," *Baltimore Sun*, 17 November 2009, online, America's Newspapers.

34. Val Jones, "The Mammogram Post-Mortem," 15 December 2009, Better Health: Smart Health Commentary, online, http://getbetterhealth.com.

35. Jones.

9

Communication: The Tactics of Public Relations

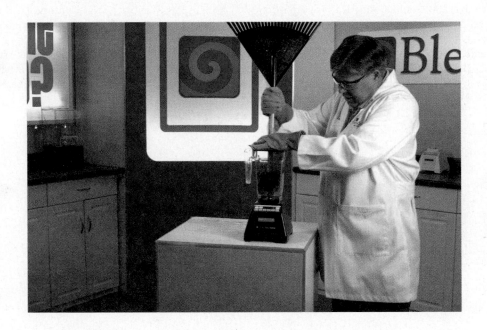

OBJECTIVES

After studying this chapter, you will be able to

- understand what makes a tactic effective
- discuss traditional and social media tactics in public relations
- select tactics that seem particularly appropriate for specific publics
- describe how to carry out tactics efficiently and effectively

KEY TERMS

actualities, p. 271
annual meeting, p. 275
annual report, p. 276
association magazines, p. 274
backgrounder, p. 268
blogs, p. 261
b-roll, p. 270
cause branding, p. 278
cause marketing, p. 278
coalition building, p. 278

REAL WORLD

Canada to Costa Rica

You are assistant director of public relations for a small but profitable international manufacturing firm based in California. Your company is publicly held; that is, it sells shares of ownership to stockholders throughout the world. Today you helped other members of the management team make a decision that's good news for some of your publics and bad news for others: To save money, your company is going to move a factory from Toronto, Canada, to San José, Costa Rica.

During the decision-making process, you advised the company's leaders about the move's impact on different publics. You suggested specific public relations tactics to be deployed if the company did vote to move the factory to Costa Rica. You even pointed out that some publics would be bitterly disappointed no matter what kinds of relationship-building tactics your company undertook. The best your company could do in those situations, you said, would be to minimize the unavoidable damage to these relationships.

After voting to move the factory, the leaders praised your assistance in helping them understand the wide-ranging impacts of such a decision. Now they've asked you to draw up a plan that recommends specific relationship-building tactics for each affected public. And they've asked you to hurry. The move will be announced next week.

Time to get started. Who are the relevant publics, and what relationship-building tactics do you suggest for each one?

TACTICS, FUN, AND VALUES

Let the fun begin.

Actually, we hope the fun has already begun with the challenges and rewards of public relations research and planning. But almost every practitioner loves to create **tactics**—the actions that we devise and undertake to influence relationships with particular publics.

The process of accomplishing the tactics—often called communication—is the third phase of the public relations process, the logical follow-up to research and planning. In public relations, tactics unavoidably shine the spotlight on values. Because people often judge us by our actions, tactics tend to show our true values as well as our knowledge of our targeted publics' values. Therefore, in this chapter, we'll do more than study the tactics of public relations—everything from low-tech bulletin boards to high-tech blogs. We'll also examine *how* you can accomplish values-driven tactics to improve their effectiveness and efficiency. It's hard to have fun standing in the smoldering ruins of poorly executed tactics.

TACTICS AS MESSAGES AND CHANNELS

In Chapter 5, as you'll recall, we presented a basic communication model, which looks like this:

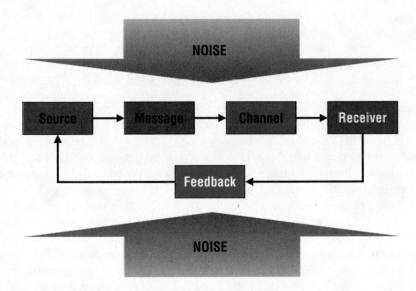

Social media, such as Wikipedia and Facebook, can turn this model on its head, with traditional receivers reversing the flow and becoming sources. For example, you've been both a source and a receiver if you've both watched and posted videos on YouTube.

Public relations tactics focus on the middle of this communication model: Tactics generally are a combination of message and channel. Messages have tactical value because they can influence a relationship. In this chapter's Canada to Costa Rica scenario, for example, management (source) could refuse to help (message) the unhappy workers in Toronto (receivers). That message certainly would influence the relationship. On the other hand, management could send a message that it will help the workers find new jobs. That message probably would have a different, more beneficial impact on the relationship. Because public relations tactics are designed to influence relationships, messages definitely are tactics.

More commonly, however, tactics are thought of as channels. A presentation from your company's top official in Toronto to the unhappy workers would be a channel—a tactic—designed to deliver a message and influence the relationship. A website that specifies exactly what the company will do for the Toronto workers could be another channel. Sometimes channels and messages are so intertwined that the channel becomes the message. For example, let's say your message to the unhappy workers in Toronto is *We'll help you find new jobs*. One channel for that message could be the creation of a training and placement center to help the employees polish their résumés and brush up on new job skills. In this case, the channel (the training and placement center) is so intertwined with the message (*We'll help you find new jobs*) that the two become indistinguishable.

If this seems overly complicated, let's remember our definition of a tactic: a public relations action designed to have a particular effect on an organization's relationship with a particular public. The messages we create can affect relationships; so can the channels we use to send messages. Thus, both messages and channels can be tactics. Generally, a tactic is a channel with a message.

Successful messages and channels must respect the receiver's needs and preferences. An effective message, as we noted in Chapter 8, clearly addresses the receiver's values and interests. Likewise, an effective channel is one that appeals to the receiver. We can't rely exclusively on the channels that are cheapest or easiest, though that may be very tempting. Instead, our messages must flow through channels that our targeted receivers prefer.

How do we know which messages to send and which channels to choose? The planning grids discussed in Chapter 8 (Planning: The Strategies of Public Relations) help you create messages and select channels that effectively address targeted publics and their values. This chapter will help you identify traditional and nontraditional channels, everything from news releases to podcasts. Generally speaking, however, two kinds of channels exist: controlled media, such as podcasts, and uncontrolled media, such as the news media. As channels become more interactive, however, the differences between controlled and uncontrolled media are diminishing.

Controlled Media

Media channels send words and images to the receiver. Some media channels, such as newspapers and television news programs, are beyond the direct control of public relations practitioners; we can only give their editors information and hope that they use it. But with other media channels, such as various forms of advertising,

Special Event

Sponsored by the Canadian Dermatology Association, the Raywatch safe-sun team hosts product giveaways on beaches in hopes of reducing the incidence of skin cancer among Canadian teens.

(Courtesy of Canadian Dermatology Association and GCI Group)

employee newsletters, speeches, podcasts, brochures, and websites, we control the message. Such media are called **controlled media.** In controlled media, not only do we control the words and images; we also control when the message is sent and how often it's repeated.

In the Canada to Costa Rica scenario, for example, you could create a training and placement center to help workers prepare for new jobs with other employers. Such a tactic would help send this message to your Canadian employees: *We appreciate all you've done for us, and we'll help you find new jobs.* Because the center would be a planned occurrence of limited duration, it would be considered a **special event.** And within that event, you could include other controlled media: You might inaugurate the center with a speech from your company's district manager. In that speech, he or she could reassert the core message of the center itself: *We appreciate all you've done for us, and we'll help you find new jobs.* You might also produce and distribute a brochure that describes the extended-salary policy as well as the features of the new training and placement center.

QUICKBREAK 9.1

Two-Way Tactics: User-Generated Media

User-generated media. Consumer-generated media. User-generated content. Call it what you will, but here's how PCMag.com defines it:

> The production of content by the general public rather than by paid professionals and experts in the field. Also called "peer production," and mostly available on the Web via blogs and wikis, user-generated content refers to material such as the daily news, encyclopedias and other references, movie and product reviews as well as articles on any subject, all of which have been traditionally written by editors, journalists, and academics in the past.[1]

Some forms of user-generated media demonstrate the continuing relevance of the basic communication model (p. 256). The traditional sender might still supply the channel (such as a blog), but traditional receivers can use that channel to send their own messages (such as a comment with links to other sites). Such a message might be feedback, or it might be a new topic altogether. If the channel involves a wiki, the receiver can become a co-creator of the message.

User-generated media illustrate the increasingly vague boundary between controlled and uncontrolled media. Public relations and marketing professionals can partially control some user-generated messages by designing and hosting websites, wikis, blogs, and other forms of interactive media that request input from members of key publics. But the professionals have little control—short of deleting messages—over what those highly visible responses will say. For example, when Honda launched a Facebook page to promote its new Crosstour, one commenter called the vehicle "a pig of a car." Honda scored points, however, by using the same Facebook page to reply to such concerns.[2]

In our digital world, user-generated media are here to stay. Public relations and marketing practitioners should continually search for mentions of their products, services, brands, and organizations and be prepared for rapid response. ■

You could also use controlled media to manage your relationships with several other affected publics. You could send letters from the chief executive officer to all your stockholders, explaining how they'll benefit from the move. You could place articles in employee newsletters in your other factories around the world, telling employees there that their jobs are not in danger. You could place advertisements in the news media in San José, Costa Rica, notifying residents of the move and seeking employment applications. Such nonproduct advertising is often considered to be part of public relations. Additionally, you could create special sections of your website for different publics. Those messages could help you manage relationships with publics that initiate contact with you rather than vice versa.

No media, of course, can ever be wholly controlled. The inauguration of your training and placement center, for example, could be disrupted by a power outage or even an employee protest. As you know from the previous chapter, effective public relations involves planning for success as well as preparing for what might go wrong. However, the consistent delivery of values-driven tactics and compassionate messages may, in the long run, protect important relationships that your company still has within Canada.

Uncontrolled Media

Not all media, of course, are controlled. We can't tell television and radio stations which news stories to broadcast. We can't tell bloggers what to write about our organization. Yet those media can be valuable channels in our quest to send messages to our targeted publics. By **uncontrolled media,** we often mean the news media: newspapers, radio and television stations, magazines, and online news providers. Each of those news providers employs individuals who act as gatekeepers—that is, editors who decide which stories to include and which stories to reject. Even if the gatekeepers decide to publish or broadcast our story, we can't control exactly what information they'll use or what other sources of information they'll seek out. Nor can we control when or how often they will publish or broadcast our story. In recent years, uncontrolled media have grown to include blogs, content communities, wikis, and social networks.

Furthermore, uncontrolled media can initiate a story against your wishes. For example, perhaps a television station in Toronto has learned about your factory's planned move to Costa Rica before you're ready to announce it. The station sends a camera crew to your California headquarters with a request to interview the CEO. Should the CEO tell the reporters about the move? Ideally, you've planned for this possibility, and you have a tactic ready. For example, the CEO might simply say, "We'll be making an announcement about that in a few days." That won't satisfy reporters, but at least you haven't allowed a definite message to reach your publics ahead of schedule; just as important, you haven't violated your values by lying. Because the reporters will keep digging, you'd be wise to speed up your timetable to make the announcements as soon as possible.

Again, not every form of media is easily classified as controlled or uncontrolled. Sometimes a channel can be both. For example, suppose your organization's director of investor relations has a blog that invites readers to post comments. Blogging etiquette would allow her to delete obscene or abusive feedback—but not comments that simply disagreed with her. Although she can control the content of her blog and the wording of her responses to comments, she has chosen not to control the comments. Although her blog is basically a controlled medium, it actually doesn't fit neatly into either category: Some portions are controlled whereas others are uncontrolled.

Controlled versus Uncontrolled Media

So which are better: controlled or uncontrolled media? Neither. Each has its own advantages and disadvantages. The advantages of controlled media include your ability to select the exact words and images that get sent. A possible disadvantage is a lack of credibility. Receivers know that you're controlling the message, and they may wonder whether you're telling the whole truth. Another disadvantage of controlled media is cost: Generally, you pay for control, especially when using advertising to send a message. Unlike public relations, advertising purchases space or time in the news media; and, within legal limits, advertising controls the content of its messages.

SOCIAL MEDIA APPS

The Tactics of Social Media

Social media now present an array of tactics for public relations practitioners:

Blogs. Short for *Web log,* a blog is an online journal that offers the author's opinions about politics, entertainment, marketing—whatever. Most blogs allow and encourage reader comments, which bloggers post below their own comments. Not content with print, some bloggers have moved to video, creating *vlogs.*

Microblogs. As the name suggests, microblogs are concise blogs. For example, the Twitter microblogging service limits postings to 140 or fewer characters.

Social networks. Chances are strong you know all about these: Facebook and LinkedIn are examples. Social networks link small personal websites, often called "profiles," within a larger website.

Content communities. YouTube is perhaps the most famous example of a content community. These websites seek particular kinds of input from individuals or organizations. YouTube hosts videos and encourages feedback. Flickr primarily hosts photographs and encourages comments.

Wikis. Wikis are websites or online multimedia documents that allow individuals to contribute and edit the content; they're often perpetual works in progress. The word *wiki* is Hawaiian for "quick."

Podcasts. A podcast is a downloadable audio program—a movie review, for example. Video versions are called *vodcasts,* although increasingly *podcast* now covers both audio and video.

Social bookmarking services. In the words of Wikipedia (not always the world's most reliable source), social bookmarking "is a method for Internet users to share, organize, search, and manage bookmarks of web resources." Delicious.com, for example, is a searchable website that allows users to bookmark favorite websites and share those bookmarks with others.

(continued)

Social media news releases. Social media practitioners—especially bloggers—have made it clear they have little use for traditional news releases and media kits.[3] Although public relations practitioners can write blogs, they can also seek the third-party endorsements that other blogs and social media offer. Few social media reproduce long narratives; rather, they use snippets—a quote here, a fact there, a brief video and links to more information. Social media news releases, therefore, aren't news stories. They contain enough snippets—quotes, facts, videos, and links—to create a news story, but they leave the selection of snippets to the blogger. In that sense, social media news releases resemble b-roll in a video news release. They supply raw materials for others to arrange. ■

Credibility and costs are lesser problems with *un*controlled media. Receivers know you're not controlling the message; that key fact tends to give the message more credibility. As we've noted before, one reason media relations is such an important part of public relations is that the news media can provide a **third-party endorsement** or **independent endorsement** of a news story. In public relations, news media are third parties—neither the sender nor the receiver—that can implicitly offer independent verification of a story's newsworthiness.

Sending messages through uncontrolled media usually costs less than doing so through controlled media. Using uncontrolled media may call for a written news release or a time-consuming meeting with a reporter, so it's not fair to say that uncontrolled media are free, but they generally are significantly less expensive than controlled media.

The disadvantage of uncontrolled media is clearly stated in their name: *uncontrolled.* Public relations practitioners can do their best to ethically influence the messages sent through uncontrolled media, but ultimate control of the message rests with others.

Public relations campaigns generally use both controlled and uncontrolled media. The trade-off is that controlled media ensure precise messages; uncontrolled media are less expensive and offer stronger credibility.

TACTICS AND TRADITIONAL PUBLICS

Public relations tactics range from low-tech, such as face-to-face meetings, to high-tech, such as wikis. However, successful public relations tactics have several qualities in common:

■ Successful tactics are part of a written, approved public relations plan that is tied to an organization's values-based mission.
■ Successful tactics target one public at a time. What works for one public might be completely inappropriate for another. However, if a tactic would be effective with more than one primary public, using it for all the appropriate publics could save time and money. A newsworthy special event, for example, could

target event participants while also targeting other publics through the intervening public of the news media.

- Successful tactics are based on research about the targeted public's values, interests, and preferred channels of communication.
- Successful tactics send a clear message that targets a public's values and interests even as it strives to achieve an organization's objective. In other words, successful tactics try to create win–win situations in which both the sender and the receiver benefit.
- Successful tactics are specific. As we noted in the previous chapter on planning, a *strategy* is a general description of a group of communications actions—informative face-to-face meetings, for example. A related *tactic,* however, would propose the details of one specific face-to-face meeting: a question-and-answer session with an employee group, for example.
- Successful tactics are evaluated as they're performed and after they're executed.

It would be impossible—and unwise—to create a list of standard public relations tactics to fit every situation. Every public relations challenge is different and requires special, even sometimes unique, tactics. But there are traditional tactics that every practitioner should know. Because successful tactics are directed toward specific publics, we'll organize a discussion of traditional tactics around the publics that they might target. Table 9.1 presents a capsule summary of the discussion that follows, beginning with a list of social media tactics.

Employees

We'll start with employees, who usually constitute one of every organization's most important publics. If employees aren't well informed and motivated, the quality of an organization's relationships with other publics might not matter; the organization is in danger of collapse.

FACE-TO-FACE MEETINGS   Virtually every study of internal communications shows that employees' favorite channel for receiving information about their organizations is face-to-face meetings with their immediate supervisors. To use this channel, you might need to work with your organization's human resources or personnel department to create communication training programs for supervisors. Perhaps your organization could use the approach known as MBWA—management by walking around. Managers who aren't "chained" to their desks can initiate spontaneous face-to-face meetings with employees. However, as more organizations allow employees to work at home and telecommute by computer, organizing face-to-face meetings with immediate supervisors is becoming more difficult.

NEWSLETTERS   Newsletters are generally inexpensive, and they have the virtue of putting a message in writing so that employees can review it. Like blogs, newsletters should be frequent; if they appear infrequently, they run the risk of delivering

TABLE 9.1

TACTICS FOR TRADITIONAL PUBLICS

Social Media
blogs
microblogs
wikis
content communities
social networks
podcasts/vodcasts
social bookmarking
social media news releases

Employees
face-to-face meetings
newsletters
magazines
videos
bulletin boards
speeches
intranets
e-mail
instant messaging
special events

News Media
news releases
media kits
fact sheets
backgrounders
photo opportunity sheets
media advisories
pitches (letters, e-mail, and
    telephone)
video news releases
actualities

digital newsrooms
news conferences
public service announcements
guest editorials and commentaries
letters to the editor and comments
interviews
satellite media tours
stories for trade or association
    magazines

Investors
newsletters
magazines
letters and e-mails
annual meetings
annual reports
websites
facility tours
conference calls
news releases to financial
    news media
media advisories to financial
    news media
webcasts

Community Groups
volunteering
donations
sponsorships
cause marketing/cause branding
speeches
open houses and tours
face-to-face meetings

Governments
lobbies
grassroots lobbying
political action committees
soft money
disclosure documents

Customers
product-oriented news
    releases
product-oriented media kits
special events
open houses and tours
responses to customer
    contacts
cell phone text messaging
mobile marketing

Constituents (Voters)
letters and e-mails
newsletters
news releases
media advisories
news conferences
speeches
face-to-face meetings
websites
responses to constituent
    contacts

Businesses
stories in trade magazines
extranets

old news—which means, of course, that they won't be read. Newsletters needn't be limited to paper. Online newsletters can include videos, sound clips, links to other sites, and an archive of former issues.

MAGAZINES Because they're more difficult than newsletters to produce, magazines usually aren't used to communicate breaking news stories to employees. Instead, magazines contain less time-sensitive stories, such as broad overviews of the organization's values and goals, stories about key employees, and updates on continuing issues. Some organizations mail their magazines to employees' homes, hoping other family members will read them and feel goodwill toward the organization. Like newsletters, magazines can also exist online.

VIDEOS   A message-bearing video can be used in several ways. Special videos or video newsletters might be shown on monitors in employee cafeterias and break rooms. Online videos and DVDs can easily reach employees around the world.

BULLETIN BOARDS   Low-tech doesn't mean ineffective. Some organizations use controlled-access bulletin boards—often with the messages under a locked glass cover—to deliver daily news to employees. Some large organizations place the cafeteria's daily lunch menu on the bulletin board. Employees checking out the daily desserts just may stop and read other important announcements. Bulletin boards can help organizations meet legal requirements to post information regarding new labor laws or changes in employee benefits.

SPEECHES   Employees generally like to see and be seen by the big boss. If an organization's leader is a good speaker, a face-to-face speech containing an important message can be highly effective as well as complimentary to an organization's employees. Such a speech means that the leader cares enough to look employees in the eye and tell them about the future of their organization. Copies of speeches can be distributed to specific employees; short speeches and excerpts of longer speeches can also be reprinted in employee newsletters and posted online.

INTRANETS   An **intranet** is an organization's controlled-access internal computer network. A well-designed intranet not only provides e-mail processing; it includes an internal website with department descriptions, links to other websites, an area for the latest news, and maybe even a social network similar to Facebook. As noted above, it also can contain newsletters, magazines, and videos.

E-MAIL   According to recent studies, **e-mail** usage has soared to become organizations' most-used employee communications tactic. However, employees still consider face-to-face meetings more effective.[4] Employees report feeling overwhelmed by the volume of e-mail—and they know that it allows supervisors to relay bad news without the awkwardness of a face-to-face meeting. E-mail's convenience can also be its danger: Misunderstandings—or worse—can arise if one doesn't think before posting a message.

INSTANT MESSAGING   As most teenagers and young adults know, **instant messaging** is a network-based computer system that allows several individuals to exchange typed messages instantly with one another. For example, five employees in different locations could conduct an instant messaging meeting on an important project.

All five employees could see and respond to messages from one another. As with e-mail, users of instant messaging should not sacrifice clarity and diplomacy for speed and convenience.

SPECIAL EVENTS Special events for employees can range from company picnics to special nights at sporting events to more complex tactics such as the hypothetical training and placement center for your former employees in Toronto. Remember: Controlled media such as brochures can often emphasize the message sent by a special event. For example, a groundbreaking ceremony for your new factory in Costa Rica would be a special event for government officials and the news media. A short speech, ideally in Spanish, by your CEO could be a controlled medium within that special event to help ensure that participants and observers receive the message that your company pledges to be a good corporate citizen.

When public relations practitioners create a special event designed only to attract the attention of the news media, some practitioners call it a **pseudoevent.** However, that term may be misleading. Public relations practitioners do not have the final say in what is news. Journalists who cover special events determine what is pseudo and what is not—and what is news and what is not.

 QUICK CHECK

1. What is a public relations tactic? In what stage of the public relations process do tactics play a role?
2. What's the difference between a message and a channel? When are they the same? When are they different?
3. What are the differences between controlled media and uncontrolled media?
4. What are examples of social media?

News Media

Public relations practitioners generally target the news media as an intervening public—that is, as a go-between public that helps carry a message to a primary public. To place a message in the news media, practitioners use a variety of tactics to appeal to the media's so-called gatekeepers: the editors and producers who decide which stories to report and which to reject.

NEWS RELEASES The **news release** is one of the most important yet misused documents in all of public relations. A traditional news release, ideally, is an objective, straightforward, unbiased news story that a public relations practitioner writes and distributes to appropriate news media. For example, in our Canada to Costa Rica scenario, you would issue news releases to news media in Costa Rica, in Toronto, in your hometown in California, and in any other cities where your organization has operations. In addition, because you have stockholders, you would issue news

QUICKBREAK 9.2

"Die! Press Release! Die! Die! Die!"

"Die! Press Release! Die! Die! Die!" Give Tom Foremski, owner and publisher of Silicon-ValleyWatcher, credit for a catchy title for his article condemning public relations news releases. He even included an illustration of a bloody knife stuck through a news release and pinned to the dirt beneath a tombstone that read "Press Release."[5]

Actually, Foremski didn't want news releases to die. He wanted them to evolve into a user-friendly format for bloggers and other online journalists. In other words, he wanted social media news releases.

News media that publish and broadcast narratives, however, still need the who-what-where-when-why-how approach of traditional news releases. Journalism professor Linda Morton has conducted several national studies of what journalists seek in news releases, and she offers this advice:[6]

- Write in a simple style. Use short sentences and paragraphs and common words.
- Avoid unattributed opinions. Be objective. Write like a reporter.
- Focus your news release on one of the four topics that succeed best with editors: consumer information, a coming event, interesting research, or a timely issue.
- Localize the news release. Practitioners often call such news releases "hometowners" because they clearly target an editor's specific audience.
- Above all else, serve the editor's audience. Research the information needs of each editor's audience, find a way in which your organization can address those needs, and then write an objective news story on that crucial link.

Morton's research shows that public relations practitioners who follow these basic guidelines place almost one third of their news releases. That's about 700 percent better than the success rate of practitioners who ignore the needs of journalists and their audiences.

Social media news releases can link to traditional versions. Traditional news releases can link to social media versions. It's just a matter of addressing the values and needs of the target public, whether journalists, bloggers, or others. ■

releases to the major financial news media around the world. News-release distribution services such as PR Newswire and BusinessWire could help circulate the news releases, and you could post the stories on your organization's website as well.

Why do we say that news releases are among the most misused documents in public relations? Studies show that gatekeepers throw away more than 90 percent of the traditional news releases they receive. Many news releases commit one or both of two deadly sins: They have no local interest—that is, no appeal to a particular gatekeeper's audience—and/or they're too promotional; they lack the strict objectivity that characterizes good news reporting. An effective news release uses its headline and first paragraph to show a gatekeeper that it contains local interest.

For example, your news release to the Toronto news media would be slightly different from your California news release. And far from being promotional, the information about your organization would sound as if it were written by an objective reporter, not a public relations practitioner.

Bloggers and multimedia online journalists tend to prefer social media news releases to traditional news releases. Public relations practitioners can also prepare special broadcast-format news releases for television and radio stations, but, in general, broadcast media adapt both traditional and social media news releases for their own needs. The news media rarely publish or broadcast news releases word for word. If they use a news release, they often rewrite it, shortening it or including additional sources.

News releases reach the media in a variety of ways. They can be e-mailed, accessed through an organization's digital newsroom, sent through the mail, picked up at trade shows, or distributed through services such as PR Newswire. One of your authors once received a news release printed on the label of a full bottle of champagne (which gives new meaning to the concept of social media).

MEDIA KITS   Public relations practitioners use media kits—both digital and paper—to publicize complex stories that have many newsworthy elements. For example, television networks use media kits to publicize their upcoming programming seasons. A **media kit** packages at least one news release with other supporting documents. Two of the most common types of supporting documents are called *fact sheets* and *backgrounders*. A **fact sheet** is usually a what–who–when–where–why–how breakdown of the news release. Unlike the news release, however, the fact sheet is not written as a story; instead, it's just a well-organized list of the facts. Why include a fact sheet when the media kit already has a news release? Some journalists don't want to see your version of the story; they think you're biased. They want just the facts, and the fact sheet delivers those.

A **backgrounder** is a supplement to the news release. It contains useful background information on, for example, a person or organization mentioned in the news release. Like news releases, backgrounders usually are written as stories. Unlike news releases, however, backgrounders aren't news stories. Some feature testimonials from satisfied customers. Many others read like biographies. For example, you might choose to send media kits to Costa Rican news media so that they can learn more about your company. Your news release might announce a groundbreaking ceremony for the new factory. Your backgrounders might include a short history of the company that expands the brief description contained in your news release. Another backgrounder might be a biography of the CEO that, again, expands the briefer identification of that individual contained in your news release.

Media kits can have other documents. If the media kit is publicizing a visually attractive event, such as a groundbreaking ceremony for your new factory in Costa Rica, you might include a **photo opportunity sheet.** Photo opportunity sheets aren't meant for publication, so they can include a little bit of fact-based promotional writing designed to spark a gatekeeper's interest. Photo opportunity sheets tell what, who, when, and where. They can include special instructions for photographers as well as maps showing the location of the event.

SOCIAL MEDIA PRESS RELEASE
TEMPLATE, VERSION 1.0

CONTACT INFORMATION:	Client contact	Spokesperson	Agency contact
	Phone #/skype	Phone #/skype	Phone #/skype
	Email	Email	Email
	IM address	IM address	IM address
	Web site	Blog/relevant post	Web site

NEWS RELEASE HEADLINE
Subhead

CORE NEWS FACTS
- Bullet-points preferable

 LINK & RSS FEED TO PURPOSE-BUILT DEL.ICIO.US PAGE
The purpose-built del.icio.us page offers hyperlinks (*and PR annotation in "notes" fields*) to relevant historical, trend, market, product & competitive content sources, providing context as-needed, and, on-going updates.

PHOTO e.g., product picture, exec headshot, etc.	MP3 FILE OR PODCAST LINK e.g., sound bytes by various stakeholders	GRAPHIC e.g., product schematic; market size graphs; logos	VIDEO e.g., brief product demo by in-house expert

MORE MULTIMEDIA AVAILABLE BY REQUEST
e.g., "download white paper"

PRE-APPROVED QUOTES FROM CORPORATE EXECUTIVES, ANALYSTS, CUSTOMERS AND/OR PARTNERS
Recommendation: no more than 2 quotes per contact. The PR agency should have additional quotes at-the-ready, "upon request," for journalists who desire exclusive content. This provides opportunity for Agency to add further value to interested media.

LINKS TO RELEVANT COVERAGE TO-DATE (OPTIONAL)
This empowers journalist to "take a different angle," etc.
These links would also be cross-posted to the custom del.icio.us site.

BOILERPLATE STATEMENTS

 RSS FEED TO CLIENT'S NEWS RELEASES

"ADD TO DEL.ICIO.US"
Allows readers to use the release as a standalone portal to this news

 TECHNORATI TAGS/"DIGG THIS"

Social Media News Release Template
Shift Communications, an award-winning, Boston-based public relations agency, has developed a popular template for social media news releases.

(Courtesy of Shift Communications)

Media kits can also include brochures, product samples, and any other document or item that can help gatekeepers make well-informed decisions about the newsworthiness of the story.

Media kits—both paper and digital—can be mailed or e-mailed to the news media. E-mail or text messages to well-chosen, specific journalists can also alert them to the presence of a useful media kit in an organization's digital newsroom; journalists can even subscribe to automatic updates to an organization's digital newsroom. Of course, your best chance of winning journalists' attention involves developing individual relationships with them and learning about their preferred channels of communication.

MEDIA ADVISORIES　Some newsworthy stories take shape so quickly that there's not time to write and distribute a news release. In such situations, public relations practitioners often issue a **media advisory.** Media advisories are also issued to remind the news media about events they may want to cover. Like a fact sheet, a media advisory isn't written as a story; instead, it simply lists the necessary information about what, who, when, where, why, and how. Media advisories are generally faxed or e-mailed to the news media.

PITCHES　A **pitch** is a specific, persuasive message to a specific journalist; a recent survey found that 80 percent of journalists prefer to receive pitches via e-mail as opposed to phone calls, letters, faxes, or social media messages such as Facebook comments.[7] An e-mail pitch begins with selecting a particular journalist (don't pitch a teen fashion story to a sportswriter, for example). Next comes an accurate, attention-grabbing subject line for the e-mail. Finally, the pitch itself: a concise, compelling description of a story you hope the journalist will write, plus your offer of assistance with interviews and additional information. Effective pitches often offer the story to only one journalist in a market—for example, one journalist in Dallas, one in Denver, one in Des Moines, and so on. Such exclusive offers include a polite deadline for response. If a well-written pitch truly might appeal to a well-chosen journalist, it's alright to send a follow-up e-mail and even make a follow-up telephone call. But if the pitch is poorly written—or if the sportswriter received the teen fashion pitch—be prepared for some colorful language, a hang-up, and a damaged relationship. Companies such as Vocus offer databases of journalists and bloggers and the areas they cover.

VIDEO NEWS RELEASES　**Video news releases,** commonly called **VNRs,** are distributed to television stations and online news media. Video news releases are designed to look like television news stories. Like news releases, VNRs ideally are finished products; they're ready to broadcast. However, most VNRs include a section called **b-roll,** which contains unedited video footage of the news story. Many television stations prefer to create their own version of the story, using b-roll instead of the finished VNR. B-roll, they believe, gives them more control over the presentation of the story.

VNRs are distributed via videocassette, DVD, websites, and satellite. A VNR can be beamed to a satellite at a particular time and downloaded by interested television stations, which have been notified, often by media advisories, about the timing and the correct satellite coordinates. Unlike print news releases, VNRs are expensive to produce and distribute. They should be used only for highly visual, highly newsworthy stories.

ACTUALITIES **Actualities** are sound bites for radio stations and websites. They're catchy quotes and sometimes accompany written news releases. Actualities can be distributed via satellite, websites, CDs, telephone links, and even old-fashioned cassette tapes.

DIGITAL NEWSROOMS A digital newsroom is an organizations' online, multimedia news center for journalists. It contains news releases, video news releases, media kits, photos, videos of significant events such as news conferences, histories of the organization, biographies of key officials, and more. A good digital newsroom is easily accessed from the website's home page, is searchable, and has both a site map and archives of older documents.

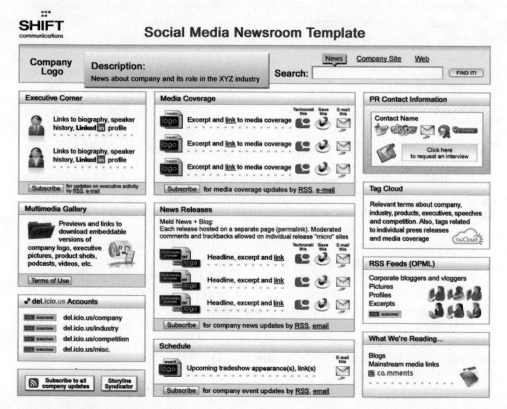

Digital Newsroom Template

Shift Communications, an award-winning, Boston-based public relations agency, has developed a popular template for digital newsrooms.

(Courtesy of Shift Communications)

NEWS CONFERENCES News conferences are like dynamite. They should be used only when necessary—and even then with caution. A **news conference** is a scheduled meeting between an organization's representative(s) and the news media. Your organization should consider scheduling a news conference when—and *only* when—three conditions exist:

1. You have a highly newsworthy breaking story. A breaking story is extremely timely; it can't wait for a news release, media kit, or VNR.
2. It is advantageous to meet with reporters as a group instead of individually.
3. You know that journalists will be glad they came; the story is that good.

If your story meets these three criteria, no problem; your news conference is a productive media relations tactic. But if your story *doesn't* meet those criteria, get ready for trouble: Either journalists will be angry that you didn't use a different communication tactic that shows more respect for their time—or they simply won't come, damaging your reputation as a public relations practitioner. If journalists can get the same information in another form—such as a VNR or a media kit—without being disappointed, use that other form instead of a news conference.

News conferences should be used with caution because they are the ultimate experience in uncontrolled media. You can try to set the agenda with an opening statement, but following that, reporters generally get to ask questions—and there is no guarantee that they'll ask questions you want to answer.

When a news conference definitely is the media relations tactic to use, however, consider these guidelines:

■ Invite news media to the news conference with media advisories and follow-up telephone calls.
■ Schedule the news conference strategically. By this we mean that you should balance your organization's interests against those of the news media. Traditional news media generally prefer a mid-morning schedule. That's the best time for TV journalists who want to broadcast the story on the evening news, and it benefits newspaper journalists with late-afternoon deadlines for the next morning's paper. A mid-*afternoon* news conference, on the other hand, limits immediate media coverage of the story to your organization's message; it reduces journalists' time for investigation. In scheduling a news conference, you must balance the needs of your organization against the value of a good relationship with the news media.
■ Rehearse your presenters. Ask them the toughest questions that reporters may pose, and help them develop honest, credible answers.
■ Have very few presenters—ideally, just one. Don't muddle the news conference with several speakers.
■ Hold the news conference in a location that's easily accessible and has plenty of parking spaces.
■ Hold the news conference in a room that has plenty of electrical outlets for television crews and photographers.
■ Begin with a prepared statement; have copies available. After that, accept questions from journalists. Avoid answering, "No comment." If you can't or won't answer a question, explain why.

- Don't let the news conference run more than one hour.
- Distribute media kits that reinforce and supplement the news story.
- Film and record the conference to provide video- and audiotapes to TV and radio stations that couldn't attend. These recordings also allow you to keep a record of exactly what was said.

PUBLIC SERVICE ANNOUNCEMENTS   **Public service announcements,** often called **PSAs,** are advertisements created by nonprofit organizations to publicize their services. The news media do not charge for PSAs as they do for commercial announcements. PSAs for the broadcast news media exist in a variety of formats. A broadcast PSA might be simply a short script for a radio announcer to read, or it might be produced like a commercial and distributed via **DVDs** and digital newsrooms. Radio and television stations broadcast PSAs to meet legal public service requirements. Just as with news releases, however, there's no guarantee that the media will use your PSA.

PSAs also target the print media, where they're sometimes called *public service advertisements* or *public service messages.* In newspapers and magazines, PSAs are similar to print advertisements. Organizations provide them in standard advertising sizes and camera-ready, which means ready to be downloaded into the digital pre-press version of the magazine.

PSAs also exist for websites. In the United States, the Ad Council, a group of corporations and other organizations that creates and distributes PSAs, offers animated graphics and thin horizontal online advertisements called banners that promote Smokey Bear, seat-belt safety, education, and other social needs. Organizations wanting to support those causes can, with permission, download a banner from the Ad Council's website and place it on their own website.

GUEST EDITORIALS/COMMENTARIES   Most news media, especially newspapers and bloggers, are willing to consider guest editorials or commentaries on issues important to the medium's audience. In this chapter's Canada to Costa Rica scenario, for example, you might consider having your chief executive officer prepare an editorial for a Toronto newspaper. The editorial could defend the move, describing the actions your company took to try to stay in Toronto and explaining why those efforts failed. In reality, the CEO might ask you to write the editorial. He or she might then make a few changes, and the editorial would be sent to the newspaper under the CEO's name.

Unlike news releases, guest editorials or commentaries aren't sent to several news media at once. Instead, news media are approached one at a time and asked whether they would be interested in such an editorial. Editorials are offered as exclusives. Editors and producers can be contacted by a business letter or e-mail message that's quickly followed up with a phone call.

A related tactic involves meeting with a news medium's editorial board. That board doesn't exist to do favors for your organization, but it should be interested in fairness and fact-based opinions. Some news media have community editorial boards in which selected nonjournalists help a news medium formulate the editorials it publishes or broadcasts. Members of such boards occasionally write the editorials themselves.

LETTERS TO THE EDITOR AND COMMENTS   Like a guest editorial or commentary, a letter to the editor allows a member of your organization to express an opinion on an important issue. Unlike an editorial, however, a letter to the editor doesn't require you to contact the news medium first. You simply send a well-written letter or e-mail message and hope for the best. Though most of us think of sending letters to print media such as newspapers and magazines, radio stations and television stations also sometimes read, on air, messages from members of their audiences. For example, the show *All Things Considered,* on National Public Radio, reads messages from its listeners every Thursday afternoon.

Most blogs and online newspapers also invite comments on recent postings and articles. Usually placed below the original content, the comments section can be an uncertain environment. Some blogs have well-respected comments sections that expand and clarify the original posting. Readers of this book, however, probably have had some experience with a "troll," defined by the online *Urban Dictionary* as "one who posts a deliberately provocative message to a newsgroup or message board with the intention of causing maximum disruption and argument." Some online newspapers have become so bedeviled by trolls that they have considered closing their comments sections.

INTERVIEWS   Yet another way for your organization to publicize its point of view is to offer a high-ranking official to different news media for interviews. Occasionally, interviews for television stations can involve a tactic called a **satellite media tour (SMT)**. During a satellite media "tour," your organization's official actually never leaves a local television studio. Instead, he or she links one at a time, via satellite, with television stations around the world for live or recorded interviews. In the Canada to Costa Rica scenario, for example, your organization's CEO could offer individual interviews to the major television stations in Canada and Costa Rica without ever leaving California. Satellite media tours often are publicized by means of media advisories or phone calls to specific television stations.

STORIES FOR TRADE OR ASSOCIATION MAGAZINES   If your organization is known for its expertise in a particular area, trade or association magazines may well be interested in publishing a story written by one of your experts. **Trade magazines** target members of particular trades and professions: construction companies, farmers, veterinarians, and so on. **Association magazines** are similar, being a benefit of belonging to an organization such as the American Library Association. If your organization offers a product or service that might benefit members of a trade, profession, or association, you can contact these magazines' editors with story ideas. You can also offer your experts if the magazine editors have story ideas for which they're seeking writers. Unlike news releases, such stories are not distributed to several magazines at once. Instead, the story is an arrangement between your organization and one particular magazine.

Investors

Investors are an important traditional public in public relations. By purchasing stock, they represent a source of capitalization for an organization—and because they own stock, they technically are the organization's owners. As we note in Chapter 4, investors include individual stockholders; institutional investors, such as the huge California Public Employees Retirement System; investment analysts; mutual fund managers; and the financial news media. We now know the traditional ways to communicate with the news media, but what are the standard tactics for other members of the investment community? A warning before we proceed: As we discuss in Chapter 15, communications with the investment community are closely regulated by such organizations as the Securities and Exchange Commission and the major stock exchanges.

WEBSITES   Websites are an excellent way for companies to communicate with their investors. Live **webcasts** regarding important announcements can be broadcast; Web-based applications such as Skype can unite geographically diverse individuals through video conferencing. Stock prices can be updated continuously; e-mail links can be provided; news releases can be indexed; video tours can be offered; the text of recent speeches can be featured; and the annual report (pp. 276–277) can be included, as can the quarterly updates filed with the SEC. A good, interactive website can function as a daily newsletter for investors, investment analysts, and the financial news media. Just as many organizational websites have a digital newsroom, they can also include a digital investor relations information center.

NEWSLETTERS AND MAGAZINES   Some companies have periodic publications that they distribute to investors. Such publications can discuss company goals, changes in leadership, new product lines, or anything else that might affect the performance of the company's stock. The publications also can steer investors to the company's website or its investor relations office for more current information.

LETTERS AND E-MAIL MESSAGES   Databases allow companies to send personal messages to stockholders, addressing them by name and noting the number of shares they have as well as how much they're earning in dividends. These messages can be more intimate than comparatively impersonal newsletters and magazines. A company might use personal letters for sensitive situations, as in an effort to get minor shareholders either to buy more of the company's stock or to sell their few shares back to the company.

ANNUAL MEETINGS   The Securities and Exchange Commission requires every U.S.-based company that sells stock to hold an annual meeting for its stockholders. Most stock exchanges also require annual meetings as a prerequisite for membership. Not only stockholders but investment analysts and members of the financial news media attend annual meetings. The **annual meeting** can be an excellent channel to investors; it allows a company to use controlled media tactics such as speeches, videos, and printed materials.

Not every element of an annual meeting is controlled, however. Question-and-answer periods with investors can rattle even the toughest executives. Some investors, known as gadflies, buy a few shares of a company's stock just to earn the right to attend the annual meeting, where they ask confrontational questions. In the Canada to Costa Rica scenario, for example, you should prepare for the possibility that former employees or other residents of Toronto who own shares in your company may attend your next annual meeting and launch emotional attacks on your rationale for the move.

ANNUAL REPORTS   Like annual meetings, annual reports are required by the Securities and Exchange Commission and by most stock exchanges. Anyone who owns even a single share of stock in a company receives its annual report, which often looks like a glossy magazine but can also exist in a second, complementary form such as a video, DVD, or website. By law, an **annual report** features recent financial information, a year-to-year comparison of financial figures, a description of

VALUES STATEMENT 9.1

Johnson & Johnson

Johnson & Johnson is a manufacturer and provider of health-care products and services. The company was founded in 1886 and is headquartered in New Brunswick, New Jersey.

Our Credo:

We believe our first responsibility is to the doctors, nurses and patients, to the mothers and fathers and all others who use our products and services. In meeting their needs everything we do must be of high quality. We must constantly strive to reduce our costs in order to maintain reasonable prices. Customers' orders must be serviced promptly and accurately. Our suppliers and distributors must have an opportunity to make a fair profit.

We are responsible to our employees, the men and women who work with us throughout the world. Everyone must be considered as an individual. We must respect their dignity and recognize their merit. They must have a sense of security in their jobs. Compensation must be fair and adequate, and working conditions clean, orderly and safe. We must be mindful of ways to help our employees fulfill their family responsibilities.

We are responsible to the communities in which we live and work and to the world community as well. We must be good citizens—support good works and charities and bear our fair share of taxes. We must encourage civic improvements and better health and education. We must maintain in good order the property we are privileged to use, protecting the environment and natural resources.

Our final responsibility is to our stockholders. Business must make a sound profit. We must experiment with new ideas. Research must be carried on, innovative programs developed and mistakes paid for. New equipment must be purchased, new facilities provided and new products launched. Reserves must be created to provide for adverse times. When we operate according to these principles, the stockholders should realize a fair return.

—"Our Credo," Johnson & Johnson website ■

the organization's upper-level management, and a letter from the company's leader that discusses the organization's health and direction.

Annual reports are also sent to investment analysts, mutual fund managers, the major financial news media, and any potential investor who requests a copy. Many organizations post their annual reports on their websites.

OTHER TACTICS FOR INVESTMENT ANALYSTS, MUTUAL FUND MANAGERS, AND THE FINANCIAL NEWS MEDIA   Investment analysts, mutual fund managers, and financial journalists don't like to be surprised. They require current information on a company and immediate updates about any events that might affect the company's financial performance. Investor relations practitioners can ensure rapid, frequent communication through such tactics as live webcasts, factory or other facility tours, telephone conference calls, e-mail updates, and letters. News releases and media advisories can be distributed to the financial news media, often through services such as PR Newswire and BusinessWire, which can electronically transfer these documents to news media throughout the world. Often, news releases regarding important developments are required by the SEC and the major stock markets (see Chapter 15).

 QUICK CHECK

1. How is a traditional news release different from a social media news release? From a media advisory? From a backgrounder? From a fact sheet? From a VNR?
2. What advice would you have for a friend who wants to hold a news conference?
3. What is an annual report? What publics does it target?

Community Groups

Community groups include churches, schools, professional organizations, clubs, chambers of commerce, and other local groups whose values somehow intersect with those of an organization. Relationship-building tactics for such groups can be high-tech; more often, however, community relations tactics fall into the roll-up-your-sleeves-and-get-involved category.

VOLUNTEERING   Many organizations encourage employees to volunteer at schools, churches, hospitals, senior centers, libraries, and other important local institutions. Some organizations allow time off for volunteer activities, and others make cash donations to community groups based on how many volunteer hours their employees donate. Volunteerism is a powerful, rewarding way to build positive relationships with community groups.

DONATIONS AND SPONSORSHIPS   After organizations have rolled up their sleeves and volunteered, they sometimes open their wallets and donate. Sometimes those donations take the form of sponsorships—for example, paying the bills for a local literacy program's fundraising carnival. Such generosity can create goodwill for an organization, but letting someone else spend your money sometimes leads to unpleasant surprises. Be sure to specify in writing exactly what the donated money is for, and then monitor the situation to ensure that your donation was spent correctly. Instead of money, some organizations donate goods or services or even the expertise of their employees. For example, a community bank might lend a tax expert to a local nonprofit organization to help it prepare its tax exemption forms.

Cause Marketing/Cause Branding Organizations sometimes devote money, goods, services, and volunteerism to particular social needs such as literacy or cancer research. In a sense, the organizations adopt a particular social need as their primary philanthropy. Such a community relations tactic is called **cause marketing** or **cause branding.** Like special events, cause marketing often addresses more than one public. As a form of social responsibility (Chapter 6), cause marketing certainly addresses people affected by the social need; most organizations that adopt a cause genuinely want to help. But the tactic also is designed to create goodwill among government officials, consumers, current and potential employees, and other important publics that can help the organization achieve its goals. Cause marketing can help brand an organization as being associated with a worthy cause.

Speeches Professional and civic groups such as the Kiwanis Club, the Rotary Club, and the League of Women Voters often seek community leaders to speak on current issues at weekly or monthly meetings. If an organization has a stake in a local issue, a speech followed by a question-and-answer session can promote the organization's point of view and collect information about how other people feel.

Open Houses/Tours Organizations that produce interesting goods or services can build goodwill in the community by sponsoring open houses and offering tours of company facilities. Open houses and tours often provide opportunities to use controlled media such as speeches, brochures, and videos. They also provide opportunities to distribute so-called specialty advertising products such as coffee mugs, Frisbees, ball caps, and other items that feature an organization's name and logo.

Face-to-Face Meetings Community groups sometimes are activist groups. For example, an environmental group in Costa Rica may wonder how your company's new factory will dispose of toxic waste. At the first sign that such a group is studying your organization—or even before—it's vital for you to open lines of communication with its members, ideally through face-to-face meetings. Many activist groups gather their research before they assume a firm public stance; in other words, they are *aware publics* (p. 91). If you can demonstrate your organization's good intentions before the activist group solidifies its position, you may defuse a crisis before it begins.

In community relations, face-to-face meetings need not be limited to activist groups. An organization can conduct such meetings with a variety of neutral or friendly community groups in hopes of paving the way for alliances or partnerships on future problems or opportunities. Such a process is called **coalition building.**

Governments

Governmental action at any level—federal, state, county, or city—can profoundly affect an organization. Public relations practitioners thus use a portfolio of tactics to make their organizations' voices heard in the halls of government.

Just like investor relations, some aspects of government relations are highly regulated by ever-changing legislation. Government relations practitioners, therefore, must keep pace with those changes. In 2010, for example, the U.S. Supreme Court, in *Citizens United v. the Federal Elections Commission,* struck down federal legislation "which prohibits, in part, corporations and labor organizations from making electioneering communications and from making independent expenditures—communications to the general public that expressly advocate the election or defeat of clearly identified federal candidates."[8]

LOBBIES AND LOBBYISTS   A **lobby** is a special-interest group that, among its functions, openly attempts to influence government actions, especially federal and state legislative processes. One of the most effective lobbies in recent decades, for example, has been AARP, formerly the American Association of Retired Persons, which advances the interests of people age 50 and older. A *lobbyist* is someone who, acting on behalf of a special-interest group, tries to influence various forms of government regulation. Lobbies and lobbyists generally pass persuasive information along to government officials. They host educational events for officials and their staffs, and they often respond to government officials' requests for information on particular issues.

At the federal level in the United States, lobbies and lobbyists are regulated by the Lobbying Disclosure Act, which mandates that people who are paid to lobby Congress or the executive branch of the federal government must register with the government. Paid lobbyists must specify whom they represent and how much they are being paid.

GRASSROOTS LOBBYING   Not all lobbyists must register with the federal government. If you write a letter to your congressional representatives asking them to increase funding for student loans, you're acting as a lobbyist for a special interest, but you need not register. Such informal, infrequent, "unprofessional" lobbying is often called **grassroots lobbying,** especially if you're acting with others to show legislators broad support for your opinion. Because grassroots lobbying is the "voice of the people," it can be highly influential with elected government officials. (For an example of the abuse of grassroots lobbying, see Case Study 6.2.)

POLITICAL ACTION COMMITTEES   **Political action committees,** often called **PACs,** have one purpose: to donate money to candidates and political parties. Two types of PACS exist: separate segregated funds (SSFs) and nonconnected committees. SSFs are sponsored by corporations, labor unions, special-interest groups, and other formal organizations. They can collect voluntary donations only from members. Nonconnected committees are not sponsored by groups and can collect money from almost anyone. Both kinds of PACs must register with the federal government if they donate to candidates for federal offices. State governments have similar laws.

SOFT MONEY   So-called **soft money** was money donated to political parties to be spent not on individual candidates but on noncandidate projects such as get-out-the-vote drives, voter education, and issues-oriented advertising. Critics of soft money contended that political parties often illegally used it to support candidates. In 2002, Congress passed legislation that stopped the flow of soft money to political parties. Proponents and opponents of soft money alike attacked the legislation. Proponents claimed it violated First Amendment guarantees of freedom of speech. Opponents of soft money claimed the legislation left open many loopholes, including hefty donations to national political conventions, local branches of political parties, and special-interest groups. Proponents and opponents of soft money also agree that the legislation will change in the future. Public relations practitioners who specialize in government relations are well advised to monitor the legality of soft money.

DISCLOSURE DOCUMENTS   In the United States, companies that sell stock must, by law, communicate with the government. Often, investor relations practitioners help write and file a comprehensive annual report—called a Form 10-K—with the federal Securities and Exchange Commission. Other SEC forms that practitioners often help prepare or review are the Form 10-Q (quarterly financial report) and the Form 8-K (used to announce an event that might affect the price of the company's stock). Disclosure law is covered more fully in Chapter 15.

Customers

Customer relations is where public relations overlaps with marketing (see Chapter 13). Marketing, simply put, is the process of getting a customer to buy your product or service. Most marketing tactics lie outside the boundaries of traditional public relations; marketing tactics include advertising, direct-mail letters, coupons and other sales promotions, and face-to-face sales encounters. But public relations can add several tactics to what is called the *marketing mix*.

PRODUCT-ORIENTED NEWS RELEASES AND MEDIA KITS   We discussed news releases and media kits earlier in this chapter. When news releases or media kits focus on a newsworthy aspect of a product or service, they target customers and are part of the marketing mix. The news media become an intervening public between an organization and the customers it's hoping to reach.

SPECIAL EVENTS   There's no telling who the next fictional hero for young readers will be. We've already seen a wizard named Harry and a school principal who can become Captain Underpants. One thing is certain: Whoever or whatever the next heroes are, costumed actors who portray them will visit our bookstores. Such a visit is a special event, which is any out of the ordinary occurrence designed to build relationships with targeted publics.

OPEN HOUSES/TOURS   An organization with interesting products or services or unusual production technology can attract customers by inviting them to tour its facilities. During open houses and tours, customers often get to sample or test products or services. Wineries, for example, often offer tours and free samples to visitors of legal drinking age.

Content Community Video
Blendtec "Will It Blend?" videos, starring company CEO Tom Dickson, are among the most popular postings on the content community YouTube.

(Courtesy of Blendtec)

RESPONSES TO CUSTOMER CONTACTS Smart organizations respond quickly to phone calls, letters, e-mails, and texts from customers and potential customers. Such two-way communication not only builds customer loyalty; it also helps an organization know what its customers are thinking.

CELL PHONE TEXT MESSAGING AND MOBILE MARKETING Organizations can use **text messaging** to notify customers of special offers—even using global positioning devices and satellites to contact customers as they near favorite stores. **Mobile marketing** is the delivery of a sales-related message through any kind of wireless communications device.

Constituents (Voters)

As we noted in Chapter 4, many organizations try to influence the legislative process by building relationships with eligible voters. But for public relations practitioners employed by democratically elected governments, voters may be the most important public of all. We're already familiar with many of the tactics government practitioners use to build productive relationships between elected or appointed officials and their constituents: interactive websites; blogs; letters and newsletters; news releases, media advisories, and news conferences; speeches; digital newsrooms; and face-to-face meetings.

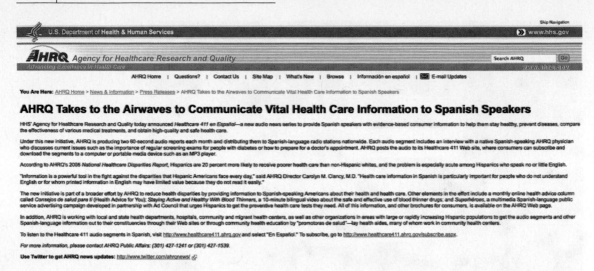

Online News Release

The United States Department of Health and Human Services uses news releases to promote its Spanish-language series of health-related radio public service announcements. For a Spanish-language version of this news release, please see p. 445.

(Courtesy of the Department of Health and Human Services)

Although every organization should respond quickly to messages from members of important publics, such responses are particularly significant in the relationship between elected or appointed government officials and voters. A quick, personalized reply, even if a more detailed follow-up response is necessary, is one of the most important tactics in constituent relations. These responses encourage constituents to feel connected to and valued by their representatives. Members of Congress, for example, have staff members who spend the majority of their working hours addressing constituent concerns. Contacts from constituents can also be an excellent source of research data regarding issues that concern potential voters.

Businesses

Business-to-business communication is big business. If organizations are to reach their goals, they must use a variety of tactics to build relationships with other businesses that have needed resources: suppliers and business customers, for example. Just like tactics for individual customers, business-to-business tactics sometimes more closely resemble marketing than public relations. Such tactics include personal selling, price discounts, trade shows, and direct-mail advertising. But some business-to-business tactics are pure public relations.

EXTRANETS   Extranets are controlled-access computer networks, similar to intranets. At a minimum, they usually include websites and e-mail capabilities. Unlike intranets, extranets are for businesses outside the host business. For example, wine-maker Robert Mondavi purchases NASA satellite photos of

QUICKBREAK 9.3

Sticky Situations

As we said earlier, a tactic is a fusion of message and channel. Much of this chapter focuses on traditional and social media channels. But what about messages? We know they should be values-driven and goal-oriented. But what makes a message effective? What makes it memorable? What makes it, in a word, "sticky"?

Brothers Chip and Dan Heath, authors of the book *Made to Stick: Why Some Ideas Survive and Others Die,* believe they know the answer. Their research shows that a sticky, memorable concept comes from having one or more of six qualities: simple, unexpected, concrete, credible, emotional, and story. Bonus points if you see the acronym SUCCES(S) there.[9] (Maybe the last "S" can be for *sticky.*)

If that memory trick seems too cute, *Time* magazine noted that the Heath brothers support their findings with "an avalanche of social-science research."[10] The Heaths maintain that with a little work, you can make your ordinary message sticky by seeking the elements of SUCCESS.

The book illustrates successful stickiness with specific examples, among them the famous anti-litter "Don't Mess with Texas" campaign and presidential candidate Bill Clinton's "It's the Economy, Stupid" sign to help him stay on message. Then there's the stickiest idea of all: Jared, the slim spokesman for the Subway restaurant chain. Jared's tale of weight loss by eating fast food scores a six of six on the SUCCESS scale.

So what makes a message effective? The explanation gets a little sticky. ■

---

vineyards and posts them on its extranet so that its independent grape suppliers can spot problems before they become serious.[11]

MAGAZINES   Businesses that offer products to other businesses sometimes publish glossy magazines with articles that feature product applications. Targeted customers receive the magazines at no charge.

STORIES IN TRADE MAGAZINES   Businesses can attract new customers as well as new suppliers by writing and submitting stories to trade, or professional, magazines. Often, such stories present a company official as an expert on a particular topic. Many magazines focus on trades or professions such as law, carpentry, and farming. Those magazines accept and publish well-written stories of interest to their readers. Such magazines also publish news releases, which generally are shorter than featured stories and do not include a byline.

ACCOMPLISHING THE TACTICS

Most of the research has been done. The plan has been written and approved. Now it's time to carry out the tactics. Though this section appears near the end of the chapter, it is, in reality, the center of gravity, the focus of this chapter. Simply selecting a tactic does not create communication. Rather, communication begins when the tactic is executed. High standards are essential at this point of the public relations process. No amount of research or planning can overcome sloppy communication efforts. Public relations practitioners, therefore, tend to stress six key factors as they execute a plan's tactics: delegation, deadlines, quality control, communication within the team, communication with clients and supervisors, and constant evaluation.

1. *Delegation.* Delegate the responsibility for a tactic's execution to a particular individual. With every tactic in a written plan, include the responsible individual's name. For example, in the Canada to Costa Rica scenario, your plan would charge one individual with the responsibility of creating a job-training and placement center. That individual wouldn't have to act alone—but he or she, ultimately, would bear the responsibility of creating the center. Naming names in this manner helps ensure successful results: No one wants to be the highly visible manager of a failed tactic.

2. *Deadlines.* In the written plan, establish a deadline for the completion of each tactic. For example, each local-interest news release necessary in the Canada to Costa Rica scenario would have a distribution deadline. The named manager of each tactic would be responsible for meeting that deadline.

3. *Quality control.* Conduct quality control. Have more than one editor and proofreader examine every message. Attend photo shoots to ensure that photographers are getting the picture you planned. Visit printing companies to ensure that the colors of your brochures and magazines are correct. (You may even get to shout, "Stop the press!") Look over a lot of shoulders as the tactics progress. In public relations for the move to Costa Rica, part of quality control would include double-checking the quality of Spanish-language news releases and podcasts. And because the Spanish of Costa Rica is different from the Spanish of Spain, you would be wise to seek the assistance of native Costa Rican public relations professionals.

4. *Communication within the team.* Encourage communication among the practitioners who are executing the tactics. Frequent short meetings in which teammates update one another can be a good idea. For example, the manager of one of the news releases on the Costa Rica move may need to know that the job-training and placement center will indeed open on a particular date; it may be an important point in her news release. Good communication within your team can ensure that the tactics of your plan complement one another as they are accomplished.

5. *Communication with clients and supervisors.* Communicate frequently with the clients and/or supervisors as the execution of the tactics progresses. Be sure to inform them of any problems, and try to present realistic solutions. In our scenario, perhaps a company executive phones you at the last moment, wanting to change some of the job-training and placement brochures from two colors to full color. You will need to communicate as quickly as possible with your supervisor, detailing the impact of the proposed change on budget and scheduling.

6. *Constant evaluation.* Evaluate the process as it progresses. Are news releases, videos, and websites professional in every respect? Are people downloading

podcasts? Are deadlines being met? Do any sudden changes within your targeted publics or within the social or political environment require a change of tactics? Perhaps a video news release prepared for San José television stations, for example, doesn't run because, as you later discover, the stations wanted a longer Spanish-language question-and-answer session on the VNR's b-roll. If your plan calls for a second VNR, you can remedy that situation in hopes of improved media coverage.

Carrying out the tactics of a public relations plan is exciting. You've worked hard to create a realistic, effective plan, and now you're giving it your best shot. But even after the tactics are completed and you heave a heartfelt sigh of relief, the public relations process isn't over. Now it's time to evaluate the impact of the tactics. It's time to see whether your plan met its objectives and goals.

 QUICK CHECK

1. What is cause marketing, also known as cause branding?
2. What are the differences between a lobby and a political action committee?
3. What makes a message sticky?
4. What can you include in a written plan to help ensure that tactics are completed on schedule?

SUMMARY

Accomplishing the tactics—often called communication—is the third phase of the public relations process, coming after research and planning. During this phase, practitioners complete well-defined actions to achieve a written plan's objectives. Each tactic targets a particular public and sends a message that does two things: appeals to the receiver's values and promotes the sender's objective. An effective tactic helps build a relationship that benefits a message's receiver as well as its sender.

A wide range of effective tactics can help organizations communicate with their publics: employees, the news media, investors, community groups, governments, customers, constituents (voters), businesses, and others. Ranging from low-tech face-to-face meetings to high-tech wikis, such tactics strive to create win–win situations that benefit both an organization and the targeted public.

As public relations professionals execute the tactics of a plan, they are guided by the principles of delegation, deadlines, quality control, communication within the team, communication with clients and supervisors, and constant evaluation.

Public relations tactics, after all, are values in action. An organization's values lead to a mission statement. That mission statement leads to goals. Those goals lead to objectives. And those objectives lead to strategies and tactics. Tactics are actions that allow an organization to strive toward its highest values.

DISCUSSION QUESTIONS

1. In the Canada to Costa Rica scenario, what publics besides employees, stockholders, investment analysts, and the news media would you target with a public relations plan?
2. What message would you send to each public you identify in your answer to question 1? Can you create win–win messages?
3. What tactics could you use to send the messages that you described in your answer to question 2?
4. Why should tactics be evaluated as they're being implemented?

MEMO FROM THE FIELD

JOSHUA DYSART
Manager of Corporate Communications; Draftfcb
Chicago, Illinois

Joshua Dysart is a manager of corporate communications at Draftfcb, one of the world's largest holistic marketing communications agencies. In addition to working on a variety of internal and external communications for the agency, he is responsible for managing the agency's social media tools, including developing strategy and leading execution across all channels. He is a graduate of the University of Kansas, where he earned his bachelor's degree in strategic communication from the School of Journalism.

If only the answers were as simple as the questions themselves:

> *Are journalists bloggers?*
> *Are bloggers journalists?*

Ask ten different people, and I'm willing to guess that you'd find quite a number of varying perspectives. For public relations practitioners, however, the answers are irrelevant. Regardless of designation, we have to treat journalists as bloggers and bloggers as journalists. Your target audiences are spending just as much time, if not more, reading blogs, checking their Facebook pages, and catching up on their Twitter streams. They're learning about current events in places other than traditional news sources, and as a result, the line separating traditional journalism and social media journalism is practically gone. They're all just reporters.

TECHNOLOGY + ANONYMITY = A RECIPE FOR TROUBLE

Every morning, I follow the same routine. I read my e-mails on the bus heading in to work. I check to find out what's in the news by visiting traditional news sources such as *Ad Age* and *Adweek*. And, finally, I go read blogs, and I search Twitter to see what other industry news is breaking and what, if anything, is being said about our agency. I typically find two types of news: "reported" news such as new creative campaigns, personnel changes, and major new business wins; and "rumored" news that spans each of the aforementioned categories. It's all fair game, and it all has the opportunity to negatively impact you and your company if taken out of context or if consumed by an unintended audience. Whether you realize it or not, the internal memos and newsletters that you distribute and the comments that employees share via social media have the potential to be passed on to reporters and bloggers alike. More than likely, they are.

It can't be overstated, especially in our profession, but technology has simplified everything. It's made it easier for anyone with journalist aspirations to publish content, and it's given everyone the ability to engage directly with representatives from their favorite companies. It is because we now have easier access than ever to each other that we freely share news and information without considering whom we are sharing the news with and the ultimate repercussions of the pass-along.

WORKING WITH SOCIAL MEDIA JOURNALISTS

As the spokesperson for a company, we are ultimately responsible for engaging reporters and other individuals to share accurate and timely information about the organization. If an employee is excited about a recent new business win and shares the not-yet-published announcement with a blogger who in turn calls you, you must be ready to respond to that inquiry just as you would to a traditional journalist. In my experience, however, this isn't a bad thing. It's true that social media journalists might not typically be held to the same standards as traditional journalists—and as a result, posts can be biased—but by working with reporters of all types, you help build your personal relationships and increase the reputation of your organization. Social media journalists are fighting for the same rights and privileges as traditional journalists; they're fighting to earn credibility as legitimate news sources.

As I write this, Draftfcb has an active social media presence across Facebook, LinkedIn, Twitter, and Flickr. We have an ongoing podcast series and an agency blog (DRAFTFCBlog), and we make sure the agency and its executives are represented on Wikipedia. It is only to be expected that our employees are equally active in the social media landscape, and trust me, they are. In addition to all of the above, they use tools such as Yammer and Foursquare (and about a dozen other tools I'm sure I'll learn next week). We took a stance long ago that we wouldn't police what everyone says on their personal blogs and social media profiles, and instead, we simply instructed them to "think twice before you post . . . and then think again." Remember, whether you're blogging, tweeting, or managing other social media tools on the behalf of your company or from your own personal account, we are now living in an era in which you are representing not only yourself but your organization 24 hours a day, seven days a week. Right or wrong, it's the world we live in, and you have to be equipped to work with reporters in the social media landscape just as you would traditional journalists.

The decision to make isn't *if* you work with social media journalists, but *how*. ■

CASE STUDY 9.1 Fleishman-Hillard Prompts Young Singles to Shout Yahoo!

In retrospect, doing the downward dog in front of national news media and millions of viewers might not have been the best idea, but scheduling nine romantic dates in three days can scramble the best of brains.

The dog (a yoga position) and dates were part of a special event designed to attract media attention to Project: Real People, an advertising campaign for Yahoo! Personals, an online dating service hosted by the popular Web portal. The ad campaign would feature 50 real subscribers to Yahoo! Personals. To launch the campaign, public relations agency Fleishman-Hillard helped Yahoo! create a special event: Julie Koehnen, a 39-year-old Hollywood screenwriter who was one of the 50 subscribers featured in the ads, would live—and date—for three days under a billboard on Los Angeles' Sunset Boulevard.

While living on an elevated platform beneath the billboard, which featured her photograph and the confession that she was "looking for a few good dates," Koehnen would go online and select eight Yahoo! Personals subscribers for dates, inviting her favorite back for a ninth date. And the world could watch it all via a live webcast on Yahoo!

The Yahoo! team did show some mercy: Koehnen could depart for her real home at night. But from 7 a.m. to 7 p.m. for three days, she would eat, go online, date, work, date, exercise, be interviewed, date, doze, and date for all the world to see.

"The immediate interaction with people was amazing," Koehnen said of her three-day marathon. "They'd e-mail me while I was up there and respond as fast as I read their messages on the webcam. The Internet is so fast and visceral."[12]

If the Internet was fast and visceral, the traditional media weren't far behind. On day one of the special event, TV trucks from local stations and national networks arrived in the predawn

darkness. "I got a phone call at 4:30 in the morning that the trucks were there and I had to get ready for interviews right away," Koehnen said. "I thought I'd just be hanging out with the Yahoo! people, but this was really huge."[13]

To promote the special event, Fleishman-Hillard used other public relations tactics. Before the event, it prepared video b-roll footage, distributing it to local and national media via satellite and disk. It also prepared and distributed a media advisory/photo opportunity sheet headlined "Los Angeles Single Searches for Love on Yahoo! Personals atop Sunset Strip Billboard." Finally, the agency helped sponsor a contest on a Los Angeles radio station, with the winner gaining one of the eight dates.

Although it called the special event "a live ad," Adweek magazine noted the importance of public relations in attracting news media: "Because PR determines the success of a live ad, novelty and originality are crucial."[14]

Not only did novelty, originality, and romance flourish—among Koehnen's billboard dates were a police officer, a surfer, and a race-car mechanic—so did media coverage and activity on the Yahoo! Personals site. The special event generated almost 350 stories in 100 U.S. media markets, gaining exposure to a potential audience of 126 million. Traffic on the dating website jumped almost 20 percent from the previous two-week period; subscriptions jumped 27 percent during the same period. The webcast recorded more than 500,000 hits.[15] Promo magazine named the billboard extravaganza its Campaign of the Year,[16] and the Public Relations Society of America honored Fleishman-Hillard with a Silver Anvil, the society's top award, in its special events category.[17]

And the downward dog? It was a yoga position that Koehnen assumed during an early-morning workout—a position that involved inadvertently aiming her posterior at the news media. "I don't think I'll do that again," she told a reporter from Reuters, an international news service.[18]

On a brighter note, the story might have a Hollywood ending for screenwriter Koehnen: She and the winner of the ninth date are still together.[19]

DISCUSSION QUESTIONS

1. Recall the discussion of special events and so-called pseudoevents. Was the Yahoo! billboard tactic a pseudoevent?

2. *Adweek* magazine called the special event "a live ad." Was the event an advertisement? Would that mean it wasn't public relations?

3. If you had been able to help Fleishman-Hillard promote the special event, what tactics besides the b-roll, media advisory, and radio contest might you have used?

4. Using the communication model described in this chapter and in Chapter 5, can you describe source, message, channel, receiver, feedback, and noise for this special event? ■

CASE STUDY 9.2 "Lying Is a Whole Different Thing": An April Fools' News Release

The news release carried the date April 1, 2010. That should have provided the first clue: April Fools' Day.

The second indication that the release might be a hoax was the subject matter. Issued by the Eugene Emeralds, a minor league baseball team in Eugene, Oregon, the release said that the former quarterback of the University of Oregon Ducks—suspended for a season after pleading guilty to second-degree burglary—"will be keeping his arm fresh by pitching for the Ems this upcoming season."[20] Would the Emeralds and the quarterback really seek such a high-profile relationship?

"For obvious reasons, we here at KEZI 9 News were skeptical," said Michelle Dapper, sports director for Eugene's ABC-TV affiliate. So she phoned the Emeralds' director of media relations to ask whether the news release was an April Fools' joke. "The PR spokesperson said no," Dapper reported. KEZI broadcast the story.[21]

A reporter from KVAL, Eugene's CBS-TV affiliate, also phoned the Emeralds to ask whether the team was kidding. "The media relations director . . . said no, it was serious," the station reported. KVAL broadcast the story.[22]

A reporter from KMTR, Eugene's NBC-TV affiliate, phoned the Emeralds to question the news release. And—you guessed it: "A spokesperson for the Ems

confirmed the announcement Wednesday night to NewsSource 16." KMTR broadcast the story.[23]

Hours later, when the Emeralds announced that the news release was an April Fools' joke, Eugene's television stations did not respond with laughter.

"Eugene Emeralds Lie About [the Quarterback] Playing for the Ems" was the headline on KEZI's website.

"An April Fools' joke is one thing," said Sean Schoppe, the station's assistant news director. "But lying is a whole different thing."[24]

Other media joined the condemnations. "The Ems have crossed a line here, by making a joke out of something that has been so sad, on so many levels," wrote Ron Bellamy, a columnist for Eugene's *Register-Guard* newspaper. The Emeralds' director of media relations, he added, "has flushed her credibility down the toilet."[25]

How did things go so wrong? Poor planning played a role. An Emeralds representative explained that the news release was a last-minute idea, distributed at 10 p.m. March 31 in hopes of catching the attention of the next morning's "East Coast radio shows and ESPN." Instead, the timing was just early enough to allow local TV stations to scramble, confirm, and squeeze the story into their news programming.[26]

The Emeralds' director of media relations conceded that the calls from local journalists caught her by surprise. "I didn't anticipate getting those," she said.[27]

But why not tell the truth?

"If we had told the truth," said the Emeralds' general manager, the news release "wouldn't have gotten any play."[28]

When a TV reporter told the Emeralds' media director that the bogus news release combined with the false confirmation "makes it pretty tough for us to believe you from here on out," she responded that minor league baseball played by a different set of media relations rules: "Minor league baseball teams do this across the country. I realize it's new here in Eugene—and hopefully, you know, April 1 is only once a year."[29]

The Emeralds' media relations director didn't improve her credibility when, on April 1, she told a KEZI news team that, in Michelle Dapper's words, "someone at the [University of Oregon] knew about it ahead of time and signed off on it." Dapper reported that the Emeralds' general manager later called KEZI to say that the media director's statement was inaccurate: No one at the university had agreed to the prank.[30]

The Public Relations Society of America takes a dim view of misleading the news media, whatever the intent might be. Members of that organization pledge to "maintain the integrity of relationships with the media" and to "deal fairly with clients, employers, competitors, peers, vendors, the media, and the general public."

Among its descriptions of improper conduct, PRSA includes this example: "A member discovers inaccurate information disseminated via a website or media kit and does not correct the information."[31]

"It's a major breach of trust between local media and a professional sports team," said Jenny Kuglin, news director at KVAL. "I think it will affect how we treat information we receive from the Ems in the future."[32]

DISCUSSION QUESTIONS

1. In your opinion, did the Eugene TV stations overreact? Was the April Fools' joke just a harmless prank?

2. If you had been the Emeralds' media relations director, how would you have responded when TV reporters called to ask whether the news release was true?

3. Did the Emeralds' general manager do the right thing when he telephoned reporters and revised what his media relations director had earlier said about the University of Oregon's agreeing to the prank? Why or why not?

4. Minor league baseball teams do have a tradition of unusual promotions. Should they be judged by a less stringent set of media-relations standards?

5. Do you agree with the PRSA standards regarding media relations? Or do you think they're too strict? ■

NOTES

1. "User-Generated Content," PCMag.com Encyclopedia, online, www.pcmag.com/encyclopedia.

2. Dan Gearino, "Unleashing a Monster," *Columbus Dispatch*, 21 February 2010, online, www.dispatch.com.

3. "Blog to the Chief: The Impact of Political Blogs on the 2008 Election," panel discussion sponsored by the Dole Institute of Politics, University of Kansas, 13 February 2007.

4. "New Survey Shows High Trust Levels among New Jersey Employees," news release issued by the New Jersey Chapter of the International Association of Business Communicators and Berry Associates Public Relations, 4 December 2003, online, LexisNexis.

5. Tom Foremski, "Die! Press release! Die! Die! Die!" *SiliconValleyWatcher*, 27 February 2006, online, siliconvalleywatcher.com.

6. Linda Morton, "Producing Publishable News Releases: A Research Perspective," *Public Relations Quarterly* 37, no. 4 (22 December 1992), online, LexisNexis.

7. "Media Survey 2009," *PRWeek*, 6 April 2009, online, www.prweekus.com.

8. "FEC Statement on the Supreme Court's Decision in *Citizens United v. FEC*," Federal Elections Commission, 5 February 2010, online, www.fec.gov.

9. Chip Heath and Dan Heath, *Made to Stick: Why Some Ideas Survive and Others Die* (New York: Random House, 2007).

10. Barbara Kiviat, "Are You Sticky?" *Time*, 29 October 2006, online, www.time.com.

11. Andy Reinhart, "Extranets: Log On, Link Up, Save Big," *Business Week*, 22 June 1998, online, LexisNexis.

12. Betsy Spethman, "Getting Personal," *Promo*, 1 December 2004, online, LexisNexis.

13. Spethman.

14. Joan Voight, "Living It Up," *Adweek*, 26 September 2005, online, LexisNexis.

15. Fleishman-Hillard, "Yahoo! Personals Takes Online Dating to New Heights," Silver Anvil 2005 competition entry, online, www.prsa.org.

16. Spethman.

17. Fleishman-Hillard.

18. "Love Writ Large," *Sydney Morning Herald*, 9 January 2004, online, LexisNexis.

19. Spethman.

20. "Ducks QB . . . to Pitch for the Emeralds," a news release issued by the Eugene Emeralds, 1 April 2010, online, images.bimedia.net.

21. Michelle Dapper, "Eugene Emeralds Lie about . . . Playing for the Ems," KEZI, 1 April 2010, online, http://kezi.com/ news/local/168388.

22. "Minor League Baseball Team Scams Local Media," KVAL Sports, 1 April 2010, www.kval.com/sports/89666092.html.

23. "Ems Admit . . . Announcement Was an April Fools' Day Joke," KMTR, 1 April 2010, online, http://www.kmtr.com.

24. Steve Mims, "TV News Whiffs on Ems' Prank, *Register-Guard*, 2 April 2010, online, www.registerguard.com.

25. Ron Bellamy, "Emeralds' Credibility Is the Joke," *Register-Guard*, 2 April 2010, online, www.registerguard.com.

26. "Minor League Baseball Team Scams Local Media."

27. "Minor League Baseball Team Scams Local Media."

28. Dapper.

29. "Interview: Ems Marketing Director Talks About . . . Hoax," YouTube, 1 April 2010, online, http://www.youtube.com/watch?v=0hUxVxGsGZ0&feature=player_embedded.

30. Dapper.

31. "PRSA Code of Ethics: Ethical Guidance for Today's Practitioner," online, www. prsa.org.

32. Mims.

10

Multimedia Message Development

OBJECTIVES

After studying this chapter, you will be able to

- describe the message-development process
- explain the processes for critical thinking
- discuss the processes for creative thinking
- describe fundamentals of inclusive, multimedia messages
- explain a writing process that begins with research and ends with evaluation

KEY TERMS

active voice, p. 308
AIDA, p. 300
attribution, p. 312
causal analysis, p. 297
creative thinking, p. 299
critical thinking, p. 296
dialectic, p. 296
ethos, p. 300
feedback, p. 315

REAL WORLD

Publicizing Volunteer Clearinghouse

A college internship has led to your first job: You're now an assistant account executive with a public relations agency. As an intern, you impressed the agency's partners with your character, work ethic, team spirit, and writing abilities. At the end of your internship, the partners asked you to stay in touch, which you did, occasionally sending them class projects and successful assignments from other internships. One week before you graduated, the partners rewarded your talent and persistence with a job offer, which you accepted.

Your first task at the agency involves helping Volunteer Clearinghouse, which coordinates volunteer recruitment for nonprofit social-service agencies in your county. Volunteer Clearinghouse is one of your agency's pro bono clients, meaning the agency doesn't charge for its services. Offering unpaid services to Volunteer Clearinghouse helps your agency honor one of its founding values: a commitment to building a better community through social responsibility.

The board of directors of Volunteer Clearinghouse has just named a new executive director. Her name is Elaine Anderson, and she succeeds Phil Connors, who accepted a similar position in another state. The board of directors would like your agency to let the community know about Anderson's hiring. The account executive who serves as a liaison to Volunteer Clearinghouse volunteers your services.

It's 3 p.m., and the account executive would like some ideas by 10 a.m. tomorrow.

It's the first assignment of your new job, and you want to do well. How and where do you start?

THE CHALLENGE OF NEW MEDIA

The young man shook his head in frustration. The media were changing so quickly that he questioned the value of his education. New and powerful media were rapidly displacing the old, and no one knew where it all would end. But even his favorite professor seemed out of touch, scoffing at the new media and vigorously defending the old. In the midst of such overwhelming change, did nothing stay the same? How could he possibly prepare himself for success in such a turbulent media environment?

Sound familiar?

Facebook, Twitter, wikis, blogs, podcasts, Flash ads, YouTube, viral videos, mobile marketing, word-of-mouth marketing, iPads, search engine optimization, interactive Web TV, the decline of newspapers, and more and more. A generation ago, as communication experts foresaw the coming revolution, media philosopher Marshall McLuhan compared the media world to a maelstrom, a violent whirlpool that could batter and defeat the unprepared. From your own viewpoint within the current whirlpool, you might feel just like the frustrated student in the first paragraph.

Fortunately for us, that frustrated student was Aristotle, owner of perhaps the greatest analytical mind in Western civilization. The new media, believe it or not, were the Greek alphabet and the birth of written documents, a combination that created an explosion of literacy and undermined the dominance of an old medium: oral communication. Even today, communication scholars still call it the greatest new-media upheaval in history. And that old, out-of-touch professor? It was Plato, who—though he himself wrote—disparaged and feared writing, preferring the immediate give and take of conversation.

As he tumbled around in that ancient media maelstrom, Aristotle set out to discover what qualities of successful communication remained the same: What qualities of message development, he wondered, stood steadfast despite the relentless onset of new media? More than two millennia later, his answers still provide a reassuring roadmap for successful communication in a turbulent media environment.

THE *IDEA* IDEA

Aristotle believed that successful message development consisted of four parts: idea generation (discovering the right message); arrangement (organizing the message); expression (finding the best words and images); and delivery (selecting the most effective media). Idea generation, arrangement, expression, delivery: If we alter the order, we can easily remember the four parts by using the acronym **IDEA**. In fact, changing the order helps emphasize an important truth about IDEA: Each of the four parts can influence and change the others; the IDEA process is not rigidly linear. For example, if the best method of *delivery* is a podcast, that tells us something about *expression*: We can't use long sentences; most listeners prefer concise, informal, easy-to-follow comments. Similarly, if the basic message created in the *idea-generation* stage will be unpopular with a particular public, we know that *arrangement* becomes very important: We'd better build up to the unpopular message, carefully preparing the public to receive it.

This chapter is devoted to helping you master the IDEA process so that you know how to discover, arrange, express, and deliver effective messages to important publics. But it has a secondary purpose: reassurance. As you prepare for a career within the ever-changing media maelstrom, remember the IDEA idea: Your choice of media—whether a Twitter tweet, an old-fashioned paper news release, or both—is just one part of the process. What *doesn't* change is the process itself: Find the right idea, organize it, express it, and use appropriate media to deliver it: IDEA. Additionally, the next chapter, Cyber-Relations in the Digital Age, can further your understanding of how to integrate technology into the message development process.

QUICKBREAK 10.1

Love Affairs and Multimedia Messages

The class for which you're reading this book (thank you, by the way) models an important part of message development: the power of multimedia. You're reading the book; your professor lectures; your course might have a website; your professor might use PowerPoint with occasional YouTube links; maybe there's time for a guest lecturer or two.

Why? You're the target public, and studies show that students often prefer multimedia communication.

Because public relations employers insist on hiring good writers, much of this chapter focuses on perfecting written messages. However, your generation more than any other understands the power of multimedia. As you craft a relationship-building message, ask yourself the following questions:

1. What photographs, illustrations, or diagrams might clarify the message?
2. What audio clips might enhance the message?
3. What video clips might strengthen the message?
4. What interactive elements, such as online hypertext, might improve the message?

And now the tough question:

5. Are you in love (with particular media)? Are you choosing delivery methods based on what *you* want rather than what your target public wants?

In developing relationship-building messages, be guided by the wants and needs of your target public. Don't use multimedia just because you can or because you want to. In the words of an old song, don't be a fool for love. ■

In this chapter, we'll certainly review tips for good writing: Good writing remains the no. 1 skill public relations employers seek in new employees. They know that good writers are good thinkers.[1] However, effective communication involves more than good writing. It involves a message-development process that begins with idea generation and moves through arrangement and expression to the delivery of the message to the appropriate publics. Let's begin at the beginning, with idea generation.

IDEA GENERATION: THE "I" OF IDEA

Where do ideas come from? You know the answer. Research. Research. Research. And more research. In Chapter 7, we presented four key areas of research for public relations practitioners: client research, stakeholder research, problem/opportunity research, and evaluation research. In researching these broad areas—and, in turn, thinking about that research—public relations professionals generally rely on two complementary ways of thinking: critical thinking and creative thinking. The dividing line between critical thinking and creative thinking can be fuzzy, so let's examine both basic systems.

Critical Thinking

The American Philosophical Association has a good but long—very long— definition of critical thinking:

> The ideal critical thinker is habitually inquisitive, well-informed, trustful of reason, open-minded, flexible, fair-minded in evaluation, honest in facing personal biases, prudent in making judgments, willing to reconsider, clear about issues, orderly in complex matters, diligent in seeking relevant information, reasonable in the selection of criteria, focused in inquiry, and persistent in seeking results which are as precise as the subject and circumstances of the inquiry permit."[2]

If we reduce that definition to its essentials, we discover that **critical thinking** is a goal-oriented, objective, comprehensive, systematic mental exploration of a subject—of a particular problem or a particular public, for example. You can use the acronym COGS to remember this approach: *C* equals *comprehensive* (drawing from diverse sources); *O* equals *objective* (recognizing others' biases as well as your own); *G* equals *goal-oriented* (seeking to understand a particular situation or solve a particular problem); and *S* equals *systematic* (thinking about the situation or problem in a logical, structured way).

That's a nice, broad beginning; but how, exactly, do we think critically? Almost 2,500 years ago, Aristotle's teacher, Plato, asked the same question. Plato's critical thinking system, still widely used today, is known as Platonic dialectic. (A **dialectic** is a truth-seeking conversation.) A dialectic can be external (you and others) or internal (a conversation with yourself). Platonic dialectic has six basic steps.

1. *Specify the goal:* Be clear about what you want your thinking to accomplish. For example, why are you researching a particular public? What is the desired outcome of your research?
2. *Define key terms and concepts*—and challenge your definitions. For example, what *is* that public you're researching? How is it different, demographically and psychographically, from all others? How would you define a successful relationship with that public?
3. *Analyze:* Break the big picture down into specific parts. For example, what exactly does that public consist of? Who are its members? What are their common values? What do they think of your organization and the issues that have brought you together? What do you really know for sure?

4. *Synthesize:* With your goal in mind, start pulling together the legitimate facts that emerged in your analysis. What information is most relevant? What goal-related, evidence-supported conclusions can you draw from your analysis?

5. *Evaluate:* Challenge and justify your conclusions. Modify them if necessary.

6. *Summarize:* Decide what solid, evidence-based, relevant facts, trends, conclusions, and other findings have emerged. For example, what do you know for certain about the particular public that is relevant to your goal?

Of all these steps, Plato believed that defining and analyzing were the most important. His top student, Aristotle—history's most famous teacher's pet—developed a define-and-analyze procedure that scientists and philosophers still use today: Aristotelian **causal analysis** (with *cause* simply meaning "What causes this thing to be the way it is?"). Aristotelian causal analysis involves asking four questions:

1. *What is the subject?* Define the subject by putting it into a logical category. Then list the qualities that distinguish the subject from everything else in that category. For example, we could place public relations in the category of professions. It differs from other professions through its focus on building relationships with groups essential to an organization's success.

2. *Who and/or what made the subject?* What people? What technologies? What processes? What organizations? What social forces? For example, what made public relations? We could start with people such as Edward Bernays and Doris Fleischman, and we could include an organization's need for social legitimacy, which is emphasized by the reflective paradigm of public relations.

3. *What are the subject's ingredients?* What is the subject made of? Remember that ingredients don't need to be tangible: The ingredients of a particular public, for example, can include adherence to particular values. For example, the ingredients of public relations include its practitioners, its values, its process of research, planning, communication, and evaluation—and much more.

4. *What are the subject's purpose(s)*—and has it achieved those purposes? For example, we might say that the purpose of public relations is to build relationships with publics essential to an organization's success. Additionally, has the subject achieved unintended things? For example, some public relations tactics have unexpected results: A viral video that you distribute might be downloaded and re-edited into a parody by a group that opposes your organization. Unintended outcomes of public relations could include unexpected results of relationship-building activities.

As you apply this four-step critical-thinking process to analyzing particular publics, recall the key questions listed in Chapter 4, including "Who are the decision makers and leaders?" and "What are the demographic and psychographic profiles of this public?" And, as you've no doubt realized, answers to Aristotle's four questions can overlap. Something that helps define the subject, for example, can reappear in your exploration of ingredients.

Journalists, of course, have their own effective variation of this define-and-analyze process: what, who, where, when, why, and how? What is the subject? Who is involved? Where is it? When did it begin or happen? Why: What caused it to happen? How: In what ways does it function?

Advertisers have developed their own critical-thinking tool to generate message ideas and content. Despite a variety of names—including creative work planner, creative platform, and copy platform—the process itself is fairly standard among advertising agencies. Your authors call it the strategic message planner, and it's described in QuickBreak 10.2.

QUICKBREAK 10.2

And Now a Word from Advertising

Maybe you'll be a public relations practitioner who never has to write an advertisement—but you'd be the first. As we have noted elsewhere, advertising and public relations often work together to build relationships with customer and consumer publics. Advertisers use a creative-thinking tool called a **strategic message planner** (also called a creative work plan, a copy platform, and a host of other names) to systematically develop a compelling, research-based message.[3] A strategic message planner (SMP) consists of 10 basic questions:

1. Who is our client? And what key facts do we know about it? What is our product? And what key facts do we know about it?
2. Who is our target audience for this ad? What do we know about it?
3. What aspects of client and product will appeal to our target audience?
4. What is our current brand image with the target audience?
5. What do we wish our current brand image were?
6. Who are our direct competitors, and what are their brand images?
7. Who are our indirect competitors (not in our product category), and what are their brand images?
8. What is the goal of this ad? (This involves more than just "We want to increase sales." Rather, what impact do we want the ad to have on the target audience?)
9. Given all of the above, what should be the basic, concise theme of our strategic message? (We don't seek the ad's exact wording here; that's the job of the copywriters. Rather, we seek a description of what the ad's key message must be.) That concise message idea should appeal to our target audience; help us achieve our desired brand image; differentiate us from direct and indirect competitors; and help us achieve our ad goal.
10. What information should we include to support and clarify the idea identified in step 9?

Public relations practitioners who specialize in consumer relations often use the strategic message planner for tactics that don't involve advertising. Like all good critical-thinking tools, the SMP uses a systematic method to build to a research-supported idea. ■

Creative Thinking

All by itself, critical thinking certainly can generate new ideas for messages. Combined with creative thinking, however, it becomes a partner in a powerful, almost magical idea-generation process. **Creative thinking** is the generation of unique and compelling ideas. Like critical thinking, creative thinking embraces the COGS process by being goal-oriented, comprehensive, systematic, and objective. One of the first scholars of creative thinking was advertising executive James Webb Young, who, after studying innovative, effective advertising campaigns, determined that creative thinking often is a five-step process:[4]

1. **Gather**: Gather raw materials (information). Your critical thinking processes have generated an impressive array of reliable facts. But for breathtaking creativity, that's not enough. Creative people also stock their minds with knowledge from wildly diverse areas: sports trivia, music lyrics, embarrassing limericks, foreign languages—just about anything and everything. To be creative, stock your mind. Live your life: Go to operas and NASCAR races. Read Shakespeare and comic books.

2. **Percolate**: "Work over" the raw materials in your mind. Some philosophers believe that wit is the ability to see similarities in dissimilar things and that judgment is the ability to see differences in similar things. Regarding the subject for which you need a creative message, how is it different from similar things? How is it similar to seemingly different things? Review your extensive research about your subject until you seem to have it memorized.

3. **Incubate**: Quit reviewing your research, and move on to a different project. Research shows that your subconscious keeps noodling away at challenges even when your conscious thoughts have moved on. So take a break. On the back burners of your mind, the creative process is warming up. Your unconscious mind is matching your new research to the diverse inventory of knowledge that you've gathered over the years.

4. **Await Eureka!**: Await the moment of discovery. Have faith. The idea will come, often when you're physically engaged in something else: mowing the lawn, walking the dog, taking a shower, and so on. When the moment comes . . .

5. **Reflect**: Celebrate, of course—but massage the idea into practical usefulness. Does it meet the original goal? Creativity is great, but unless you can apply it in the real world, it can land in the scrap heap.

To Young's creative process, we would add an additional step: **Share.** Colleagues might push your brilliant idea even further—or they might spot an embarrassing downside that hadn't occurred to you.

How does this magic work? Many creativity experts agree with Young that an original idea "is nothing more nor less than a new combination of old elements"[5]— thus the importance of a wide-ranging collection of raw materials. If Young is correct, then a brainstorming process in which several people try to link the research to similar and different elements can be effective. But whether solo or enhanced by group participation, Young's creative process, like critical thinking, meets the COGS approach, particularly in being goal-oriented, comprehensive, and systematic.

Far be it from your authors to discourage the creativity that Young's process can unleash—but remember, as we saw in Chapter 8, that the most effective message strategy in public relations is the simple, informative approach. Sometimes, the intense research processes of critical thinking alone lead you directly to the best idea for your message.

If you opt for a persuasive—as opposed to informative—approach, another research-based decision awaits. Among **ethos, pathos,** and **logos** (Chapter 5), which strategy or combination of those strategies would best suit your message? Much of your answer, of course, will depend upon your target public.

Wherever it comes from, however, and whatever strategy it adopts, your message needs an effective organization.

 QUICK CHECK

1. What does the critical-thinking acronym COGS stand for?
2. What are the four questions of Aristotelian causal analysis?
3. What are the steps of James Webb Young's creative-thinking process?
4. According to Young, an original idea is a new combination of—what?

ARRANGEMENT: THE "A" OF IDEA

Guess what? Your third-grade teacher was right: Effective message development generally requires an outline. Good organization strengthens the impact of a strategic message. And organizing your idea will make the next stage, expression, easier.

There's no single best organization for an effective message. Organization depends on your purpose, audience, medium or media, and strategy (informative, persuasive, and so on). Because research shows that the top two message strategies in public relations are the persuasive and informative approaches, let's examine standard organizational schemes for both. Once again, however, the dividing lines can get a little fuzzy: Persuasive strategies can include informative elements; and, conversely, informative strategies can include persuasive elements.

Persuasive Organizational Schemes

Something about message development tends to create acronyms: IDEA and COGS, for example. Another memory trick, one that can help you remember a standard organizational scheme for persuasive messages, is **AIDA:**

A = *Attention:* Using your knowledge of your target public and its values, begin your message with words or images (or both) that will capture your target's attention. Your attention-getting opening must be logically related to your message, however, or your audience will cry foul.

"Good writing, like a good house, is an orderly arrangement of parts."

Mortimer Adler

Good writing is the core of effective corporate communication. Whether delivered in the form of a presentation, video, newsletter, annual report or other medium, most messages begin on a sheet of paper.

At Schaffner Communications we believe that good business communication belongs in the hands of skilled professional journalists, not of advertising copywriters who may sacrifice clarity for design, or aspiring novelists who could confuse the message with the medium.

Our clients agree. They recognize the need not only to master and tame the English language, but to conduct accompanying research, interviews and red pencil reviews that provide the framework for effective presentations. That's our style at Schaffner Communications.

Business communication, Schaffner-style, relies on pairing a client's message with the medium that's most appropriate for the audience and intent. Words are the heart of those messages, whether applied to printed, visual or audio materials.

Tools of the Trade

Good writing is at the core of effective communications programs, including all of the following:

Advertisements
Annual Reports
Books
Brochures
Columns
Correspondence
Documentation
Feature Stories
Flyers and Leaflets
Letters to the Editor
Magazine Articles
Manuals and Handbooks
Newsletters
Press Releases
Proposals
Public Service Announcements
Radio Copy
Scripts
Speeches and Presentations
Video News Releases

Brochure

Chicago-based Schaffner Communications wins and keeps clients with its intense focus on good writing.

(Courtesy of Schaffner Communications)

I = *Interest:* Keep your target's attention by delivering details that interest its members; directly address their values, concerns, fears, or desires. Clearly, interest must be sustained throughout your message, not just in this second stage.

D = *Desire:* Fill the target public with the desire to act by presenting potential benefits that await. Often, such benefits involve the gain of pleasure or the avoidance of pain—or even a combination of the two. Who wouldn't desire that?

A = *Action:* Reveal the action that will lead to the desired benefits. In other words, what exactly should the target public do to increase the pleasure or reduce the pain?

AIDA is the basis of the more sophisticated Monroe's Motivated Sequence, presented in Chapter 5. In the Monroe scheme, Attention is followed by Need (the identification of a problem); then by Satisfaction (the offering of solutions); then by Visualization (the discussion of the consequences of inaction); and, finally, Action (specification of the desired action).

Informative Organizational Schemes

Informative organizational schemes often depend on the nature of the news being delivered: neutral, good, or bad. Bad news organization can be so complex that it earns its own sidebar: QuickBreak 10.3.

NEUTRAL MESSAGES   The most common organizational scheme for neutral messages is the **inverted pyramid** (see Figure 10.1), which is used for traditional news releases and basic news stories. In the inverted pyramid, you present the most important information first; as the message continues, the information becomes progressively less important. Generally, the first paragraph covers the most important aspects of *who, what, where, when, why,* and *how.* In fact, the ideal first sentence of a news release specifies *who, what,* and *when,* with *where* being in the dateline.

FIGURE 10.1

The Inverted Pyramid

The inverted pyramid represents the traditional organization of a news story. Where the pyramid is widest, the information in the story is most important. The narrowing of the pyramid represents the decreasing importance of information as a news story progresses toward its ending. Thus, a traditional news story places the most important information at the beginning, which journalists call "the lead." In public relations, traditional news releases use the inverted pyramid organization.

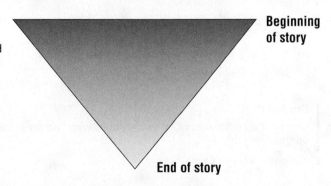

Beginning of story

End of story

The dateline, followed by a dash, is the name of the city in which news occurred; it precedes the first sentence.

GOOD-NEWS MESSAGES   As you might guess, good-news messages aren't quite as organizationally complex as their bad-news counterparts. With a four-part good news organization, you can be more direct, moving straight to the good news:

1. State the good news. Often, brief congratulatory comments accompany this portion of the message.
2. Explain any details. For example, if a member of an important public has won an award, what does it involve? What is the award? When and where does she receive it?
3. Briefly discuss what the good news means to you. For example, you might discuss why you're particularly pleased that this particular individual won the award. Or you might describe particular reasons for her success.
4. Specify the desired action—and close with congratulations. For example, you might ask the award recipient to contact you as soon as possible.

Like the bad-news organization, the good-news organization is particularly effective in face-to-face conversations, speeches, e-mails, and business letters.

Of course, many more organizational schemes exist. In brochures and feature stories, the concluding information often is just as important and compelling as the introduction. Speeches often follow the "tell 'em what you're going to say; say it; and tell 'em what you've said" organization. As always, let audience, purpose, media, and strategy be your guides.

QUICKBREAK 10.3

Damage Control: Organizing Bad-News Messages

Bad news can be delivered in a variety of organizational schemes. One of the most common bad-news arrangements, however, takes advantage of the power of beginnings and endings—and the weakness of middles.

In most forms of communication, a beginning (whether of a document, a paragraph, or a sentence) gains emphasis because it breaks a silence or a pause. Likewise, endings (whether of a document, a paragraph, or a sentence) gain emphasis because they echo into a silence or a pause. Middles, however, lose emphasis because they neither break nor echo into a silence. As readers or listeners, we tend to flow right through middles without a pause. Therefore, the traditional bad-news organization places the bad news in the middle of a paragraph, and that paragraph occurs in the middle of the document—a double-dose of low emphasis.

(*continued*)

The traditional bad-news organization consists of five parts:

1. Begin courteously, often focusing briefly on something neutral or positive in the relationship. In this opening, do not mention the bad news. For example, if a journalist has e-mailed you to request a face-to-face interview with your CEO, you might quickly comment that it's good to hear from her again and that you enjoyed her recent story on wireless widgets.

2. Explain the reasons for the upcoming (and as yet unmentioned) bad news. For example, you could begin this section by acknowledging the journalist's request and noting that your CEO will be in France at the time of the requested interview. This explanation often is the beginning of the second paragraph.

3. In the same paragraph as the explanation, state the bad news in one clear sentence. For example, you could tell the journalist, "Therefore, our CEO will not be able to meet with you Jan. 18." Ideally, the previous explanation softens the blow of the bad news: The target public at least knows why you've had to deliver such a message.

4. Still in the same paragraph, cap the bad news with something neutral or positive. For example, you could offer to arrange a face-to-face interview with your organization's executive vice president or director of investor relations. (Note how this section prevents the bad news from gaining emphasis by closing the paragraph.)

5. In a new paragraph, close courteously, again briefly focusing on something neutral or positive—perhaps how you look forward to working with the journalist to schedule an interview. Do not refer the bad news again. Do not apologize.

Voilà! You've courteously and informatively built up to the bad news, and you've clearly delivered it at the point of least emphasis in the entire message. ∎

 ## QUICK CHECK

1. What does the acronym AIDA stand for?
2. What is the inverted pyramid?
3. In a bad-news organizational scheme, where do we announce the bad news?
4. In a good-news organizational scheme, where do we announce the good news?

EXPRESSION: THE "E" OF IDEA

In this third stage of the IDEA message-development process, you clothe your idea in words and images, with images broadly defined as any elements that appeal to the senses. Within a strategic message, an image could be a photograph, an illustration, an audio clip, or even a video. Which forms of expression are best? Just as with Arrangement, that depends on purpose, audience, medium, and strategy.

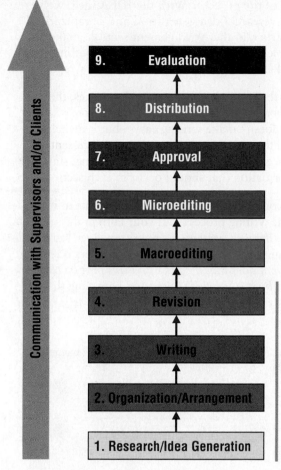

FIGURE 10.2

The Writing Process

Successful public relations writing begins with research and ends with evaluating the success of the written document. The nine stages of the writing process should be followed in order: Research comes before organization, which comes before writing, and so on. As the document progresses, the writer should discuss problems or new ideas with supervisors, clients, or both.

Because strong writing skills are essential for success in public relations, much of this section will focus on the challenging task of putting the best words in the best order. Let's begin, however, with the big picture: the writing process (Figure 10.2).

The Writing Process

Envisioning writing as a process can help you cope with the intimidation that sometimes accompanies important message-development assignments. The **writing process** can help you avoid procrastination because it eases you into the actual writing; moving from research to a final evaluation of results, it helps you approach an assignment with confidence. The writing process even prevents you from wasting your time (and others' time) by jumping in too quickly and trying to write without adequate preparation. In other words, the writing process helps you tackle a writing assignment in a logical, productive fashion.

So what are the different stages of the process? With the IDEA idea, we've already covered the first two stages: research/idea generation and organization/arrangement. One tip: As we said earlier, in the Arrangement section, make an outline—even if it's just notes scribbled on a restaurant napkin. An outline is a powerful stress reducer for the third stage of the writing process: the writing itself.

WRITING   Because you've completed the research and organization stages, the question that faces you now isn't *What should I write?* Instead, it's *How should I express what's in my outline?* The difference doesn't make writing easy—but it makes it easier. Two more tips: At this stage in the process, don't try to make each sentence perfect; that comes later. And if the beginning just seems too intimidating, start elsewhere: Your outline specifies the information that should occur in each section.

REVISION   In the previous stage, you completed a first draft. Now it's time to make good writing better. In this stage of the writing process, put your faith in the secret motto of successful writers: Good writing isn't written; it's rewritten. Poet and novelist Robert Graves recommended imagining that one of your intended readers is leaning over your shoulder and saying, *But what does that mean? Can't this part be clearer? What's in this for me? What do I gain by reading this?* Instead of banishing this annoying reader, do your best to satisfy his or her demands. Engage in a true *revision*.

U.S. President Barack Obama reviews an edited copy of a speech that he will deliver to a joint session of Congress.

(Official White House Photo by Pete Souza)

MACROEDITING   Rule no. 1 of editing your writing: Don't be the only editor; other qualified professionals should review your work carefully. But you should be the first and best editor. Your goal is to deliver a flawless message to the next editor. Editing consists of two levels: macroediting and microediting. The **macroediting** stage addresses the big-picture questions: Is the entire message clear, complete, and fair? Does it address the target public's values? Does it fulfill the goal? Does it successfully express your core idea? Does it avoid off-message tangents? Is the organization logical and graceful?

MICROEDITING   Now it's time to get picky. The **microediting** stage involves a sentence-by-sentence double-check of accuracy, spelling, grammar (including punctuation), and style. Oddly, doing this backward—beginning with the last sentence, then moving to the second-to-last sentence, and so on—can be helpful. Moving

SOCIAL MEDIA APPS

Writing for the Web

Here's a sure recipe for failure: To write for the Web and social media, just move print documents online with no changes. Some newspapers, unfortunately, still do that.

Different media, different writing styles. Studies show that we read computer screens more slowly than we do print documents. And we're less likely to read long passages. Readers have different expectations for Web writing, including searchable text and links to other material. Whether your online writing is for a social media news release, a blog, or a website page, marketing professional Bonnie Poovey Short recommends these tips:[6]

- Information must be current. Web pages in particular should immediately reflect any changes in important facts and figures.
- Web writing should include highlighted links to other sites or other pages within a website. Bloggers often link to other blogs. Social media news releases can link to videos and background information.
- Sentences on Web pages should be concise, with one idea per sentence. (The conversational nature of blogs can make them an exception to this guideline.) Paragraphs also should be short, rarely running to more than three sentences.
- Successful Web pages effectively use headlines and captions. Studies show that readers often examine those items first. Headlines, followed by a brief article summary, often link to the full article located on a separate page.
- Successful websites incorporate graphics, of course—but eye-movement studies show that readers prefer concise text to graphics.

Finally, Web writers and their organizations are accessible. Interactive websites offer contact information that includes e-mail addresses, telephone numbers, and street addresses. Responding to reader questions and comments should be a priority. ■

through the entire message backward breaks up the familiar flow and helps you focus on each sentence in isolation.

APPROVAL   Often, many colleagues will want to review the supposedly finished message before distribution to the target public: your supervisor, your client, anyone who is quoted, anyone who supplied importantinformation—the list can seem endless. If you're in charge of the approvals process, be sure to keep a chart that specifies to which reviewers the message was sent, when it was sent, when it was returned, and what revisions were requested. Often, your supervisor will make the final decisions on suggested revisions.

DISTRIBUTION   We'll discuss Distribution in a moment as the final step in the IDEA idea. But one more tip: Even when others take charge of distribution, you might unobtrusively and diplomatically observe their progress. A sad truth is that the best writer and the most polished message in the world can be defeated by faulty distribution.

EVALUATION   Just as the four-step public relations process involves evaluation, so does the writing process. And just as with the public relations process, don't wait until the end; evaluate your success during the process as well as after the message has been distributed. What didn't go well, and how will you avoid that in the future? What went well that you can repeat and build on?

Tips for Writing Better Sentences

From choosing the right word to reading aloud, the following tips can help you craft sentences with maximum impact and minimum clutter.[7]

- *Challenge "to be" verbs.* Challenge *is, are, was, were, will be,* and every other form of the verb *to be.* Often, you can find a stronger, more descriptive verb that might also shorten the sentence.

Original	Revision
He will be a good communicator.	He will communicate effectively.
We are inviting you . . .	We invite you . . .

- *Use active voice.* In **active voice,** the subject of the sentence does the action. In **passive voice,** the subject receives the action.

Passive Voice	Active Voice
Our profits were affected by a sales slump.	A sales slump affected our profits.

  Passive voice can seem timid, and it requires a *to be* verb. Active voice is confident and concise.

■ *Challenge modifiers.* **Modifiers** (adjectives and adverbs) can strengthen a sentence by sharpening your meaning. But sometimes they prop up weak words, especially nouns and verbs. A precise, well-chosen word needs no modification.

Original	Revision
We are very happy.	We are ecstatic.
She ran fast.	She sprinted.

■ *Challenge long words.* If a long word or phrase works best, use it. Otherwise, use a shorter option.

Original	Revision
utilize	use
prioritize	rank

■ *Challenge prepositional phrases.* Avoid strings of prepositional phrases:

Original	Revision
We will meet on Thursday in Centerville at the Lancaster Hotel, on McDaniel Street.	We will meet Thursday at the Lancaster Hotel, 1423 McDaniel St., Centerville.

Some prepositional phrases can be tightened into adjectives:

Original	Revision
I will present the report in the meeting on Thursday.	I will present the report in Thursday's meeting.

■ *Challenge long sentences.* How long should a sentence be? Long enough to make its point effectively—and no longer. Challenge any sentence that exceeds 25 words. Eliminate *to be* verbs and tighten prepositional phrases when possible.

■ *Avoid overused expressions.* Clichés such as "It has come to my attention" and "I regret to inform you" lack original thought. They also sound insincere.

■ *Avoid placing important words or phrases in the middle of a sentence.* The beginning of a sentence breaks a silence and calls attention to itself. The last words of a sentence echo into a brief silence and gain emphasis. The middle of a sentence generally draws the least attention.

■ *Keep the focus on the reader.* Tell readers what they want and need to know—not just what you want them to know. Keep the focus on how they benefit from reading your document.

■ *Read your sentences aloud.* Or at least whisper them quietly to yourself. That's the surest way to check for effective sentence rhythms.

The Two-Step Tighten-Up

You may have heard Abe Lincoln's joke about his long legs. When an annoying inquisitor asked, "How long *should* a man's legs be?" Lincoln responded, "Long enough to reach the ground." A similar logic applies to your sentences. How long should they be? Long enough to do the job gracefully and effectively—and not one word more.

An effective method for trimming your sentences involves enforcing two tips from the previous section: eliminating *to be* verbs and prepositional phrases. In his excellent book *Revising Business Prose*, Professor Richard Lanham demonstrates that sentence flab hides in those two areas. Eliminating *to be* verbs and prepositional phrases, when possible, produces crisper, more attractive sentences.

Figures of Speech

Clear, concise sentences need not be graceless. How about a little *antimetabole*, as in "Ask not what your country can do for you; ask what you can do for your country"? Or some *asyndeton*: "Friends, Romans, countrymen . . ."? The website "The Forest of Rhetoric" at Brigham Young University (http://rhetoric.byu.edu) has an alphabetical list of hundreds of such devices, each one potentially a striking embellishment for your message.

Such devices often are called **figures of speech,** although the term originally meant only devices that had figurative, not literal, truth—devices such as similes ("Life is like carousel") and metaphors ("Life is a carousel"). Despite the fun of studying and using figures of speech, you should use them wisely and sparingly. Messages with excessive figures of speech are like PowerPoint slides with excessive special effects: All the fireworks become annoying; they distract us from the true message.

VALUES STATEMENT 10.1

Kellogg Company

Based in Battle Creek, Michigan, the Kellogg Company produces breakfast cereals, toaster pastries, frozen waffles, bagels, cereal bars, and other food products. The Kellogg Company values statement includes this passage:

Integrity and Ethics

Integrity is the cornerstone of our business practice. We will conduct our affairs in a manner consistent with the highest ethical standards. To meet this commitment, we will:

Engage in fair and honest business practices.
Show respect for each other, our consumers, customers, suppliers, shareholders and the communities in which we operate.
Communicate in an honest, factual and accurate manner.

—Kellogg Company website ■

Writing for the Ear

We've seen how the writing process works for documents designed to be read, such as news releases. But the writing process works equally well for documents designed to be *heard,* such as speeches and podcasts. Documents designed to be heard, however, require special writing techniques to ensure that targeted publics easily comprehend the speaker's meaning. After all, unlike readers, listeners can't simply reread a paragraph or pause to decipher a challenging passage. Professional speechwriters, broadcast news writers, and other professionals who write for the ear have developed several guidelines for effectively conveying meaning to their listeners:

- *Remember that the speaker has to breathe.* Use short sentences. Short sentences create frequent pauses, which allow the speaker to breathe. The pauses also give listeners a moment to consider the previous sentence. An average effective spoken sentence contains 9 to 10 words.
- *Limit each sentence to one idea.* Avoid linking clauses together with coordinating conjunctions such as *and* and *but* or with subordinating conjunctions such as *because* and *although.* By the time listeners receive the closing idea of a multiclause sentence, they may have forgotten the idea at the beginning.
- *Use concrete words and images, not abstractions.* Clear, explicit language helps your listeners stay focused. They won't pause to try to decipher the meaning of vague, abstract language. Charles Osgood of CBS-TV and CBS Radio so believes in the power of concrete, evocative language that he ends his television broadcasts with these words: "*See* you on the radio."
- *Use precise nouns and verbs.* An imprecise verb needs an adverb to clarify its meaning. A vague noun needs an adjective to make it accurate. Choosing exactly the right word helps you create short, precise sentences. Avoid excessive use of *to be* verbs such as *am, is, was,* and *were.* Such verbs don't convey precise images to listeners.
- *Challenge every word in every sentence.* Is each word necessary? Can a more precise noun eliminate the need for an adjective? Can you replace a long word with a shorter word without losing meaning? Spoken language is not the place to impress an audience with your knowledge of sesquipedalian (long) words.
- *Spell out big numbers and give phonetic spellings for hard-to-pronounce words.* If the speaker stumbles, so do the listeners. Assist the speaker by providing pronunciation cues for big numbers and difficult names or words. For example, broadcast writers often write the number 5,200 as "52–hundred."
- *Use traditional syntax (word order).* In the English language, the simplest sentences begin with a subject, which is followed by a verb, which in turn is sometimes followed by a direct object and perhaps an indirect object. Traditional word order offers the fewest roadblocks to understanding.
- *Link sentences and paragraphs with clear transitions.* Often, you can create a clear **transition** by making the direct object of one sentence the subject of the following sentence. Note how objects become subjects in the following example: *In 1863 Abraham Lincoln wrote his greatest speech: the Gettysburg*

Address. *The Gettysburg Address expresses principles that still guide us today. The most important of those principles is contained in the words "government of the people, by the people, and for the people."*

■ *Attribute direct quotations at the beginning of a sentence.* In written English, we often place the **attribution**—the *said Abraham Lincoln*—in the midst or at the end of a direct quotation. But listeners can't see quotation marks. Placing the attribution at the beginning of a quotation is the only way to signal clearly that the speaker is citing someone else's words.

■ *Introduce important points with general, descriptive sentences.* Let listeners know that an important point is coming. If a speaker simply says, *Sixty percent of our employees want better communication with top management*, listeners may not retain the percentage as they absorb the rest of the sentence. We can assist our listeners by writing, *A high percentage of our employees want better communication with top management. Sixty percent of our employees say that top management should communicate with them more often.*

■ *Gracefully repeat main points.* Know the main points that you hope to convey, and seek opportunities to state them more than once.

DRAFT PUBLIC SERVICE ANNOUNCEMENTS

TITLE: Breathing Year-Round

LENGTH: 60

LIVE READ RADIO PSA

Heart disease claims millions of lives.

Asthma impairs the health of so many children and adults.

Air pollution, especially particles, aggravates heart disease and lung disease. In fact, it can be deadly for some people. And it can be damaging for older adults, and children.

Particle pollution tracking and Air Quality Index forecasts are now available every day throughout the year. It's one of the most effective ways for you to manage your health year-round.

The Air Quality Index is now a "forecast to breathe by."

Want to know more? Check out Air Quality Index forecasts on your local television weathercasts, radio stations, and newspapers, and at this Web site at: www.epa.gov/airnow.

Public Service Announcement

Radio public service announcements demonstrate how writing meant to be read aloud differs from ordinary print writing. Note the brevity of the sentences.

(Courtesy of the U.S. Environmental Protection Agency)

■ *Avoid closing with "In conclusion."* Readers can see the end of a document coming. But how do listeners identify an upcoming conclusion? A return to the broad theme of the document—a restatement of the main point—can signal that the end is near.

■ *Break any of these guidelines when doing so will assist the listener.* These are only guidelines, not rigid laws. Usually, these guidelines help convey meaning to the listener. When they interfere with meaning, discard them.

Tips for Inclusive Expression

Public relations writing builds relationships. The careless use of language, however, can inadvertently exclude valuable members of important publics. To create inclusive documents, consider the following guidelines:[8]

■ In documents that cite individuals as sources, draw on diverse individuals. In many organizations and publics, it's easy to rely on a steady stream of white Anglo-Saxon males in their 40s and 50s. Not all qualified sources are of that race, ethnicity, gender, or age.

■ Balance personal pronouns. For unnamed, generic individuals such as a supervisor or senator, balance the use of *he* and *she*. Don't, however, include illogical shifts. A hypothetical supervisor shouldn't change gender within a paragraph. Another solution is to use plural nouns—*supervisors* and *senators*—that can be replaced by *they*.

■ Avoid words that describe particular relationships: *your wife, your husband, your boyfriend, your girlfriend, your parents, your children.* Female readers generally are excluded by *your wife,* just as male readers generally are by *your husband.* Let your targeted public be your guide as to what is appropriate.

■ Know the dates of major religious holidays. When is Rosh Hashanah? When is Ramadan?

■ Don't describe individuals by race, ethnicity, religion, age, sexual orientation, or physical or mental disability unless the information is relevant to your document's purpose. If an individual must be so described, consider applying the same exactness of description to every other individual mentioned in your document.

■ If you are responsible for a document's design, apply your quest for inclusiveness to photographs and other visual representations of individuals. Even if you're *not* in charge of the design, don't hesitate to point out lapses of diversity.

Words and images have power. They can include—or exclude. Use them wisely.

 QUICK CHECK

1. What do your authors say is the secret motto of successful writers?
2. What are the basic steps of the writing process?
3. What is passive voice?
4. How does writing for the ear differ from writing for the eye?

DELIVERY: THE "D" OF IDEA

Other portions of this book discuss the delivery of messages—for example, the discussion of tactics in Chapter 9 (face-to-face communication, websites, and more) and the discussion of new communication technologies in Chapter 11 (viral marketing, texting, and more). So we'll keep this short by offering a few basic reminders.

As QuickBreak 10.1 notes, your personal media preferences have little to do with successful message delivery. The biggest influence on delivery is the target public: What are *its* preferred media? Which media would be most convenient and most effective for *its* members? Next in terms of influence is message content: Would your message work best in print? Or audio? Or as a multimedia, interactive message?

Another reminder: the importance of feedback. Successful communication looks more like a circle than a line. In public relations, of course, we communicate to form productive relationships, and that means two-way communication. Whatever

QUICKBREAK 10.4

Conquering the Presentation Jitters

"We have nothing to fear but fear itself," said President Franklin Roosevelt. Of course, Roosevelt referred to fear created by a faltering economy, but his shrewd comment also applies to presentations. Frequently, the presentation itself is not what we fear; instead, we fear appearing nervous and uncertain in front of others. We're unnerved by the fear that our hands will shake and our voices will tremble.

Expert presenters offer this advice about fighting stage fright:

- Practice in front of others. Present to test audiences before you present to the ultimate audience.
- Deliver the goods. If you're conveying useful information to your audience, its members will think you're great.
- As you present, maintain eye contact. Don't think about yourself; think about your audience. Talk to people, not to the walls, floor, or ceiling.
- Channel your nervous energy into movement. If appropriate, walk around as you speak. Address different sections of the room. Use hand gestures that complement your words.
- Realize that you are your own worst critic. Few people in the audience are evaluating your performance. Instead, they're evaluating the quality of the information they're receiving—so, again, deliver the goods.
- After a presentation, reward yourself with a special purchase or some other treat. Be grateful to the presentation for giving you the excuse for a minor extravagance.

One last bit of advice. Attack your fear. Seek opportunities to do presentations. Franklin Roosevelt *didn't* say, "Practice makes perfect"—but, once again, the phrase applies to presentations. ■

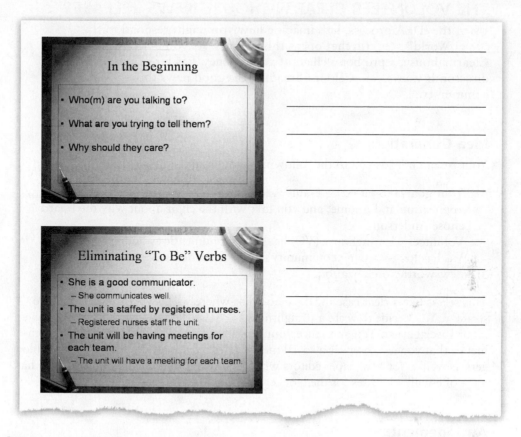

Presentation Handouts
Copies of presentation visuals can help audience members take notes and focus on a speaker's message. Most slide-creation programs have special print functions for handouts.

your messages are and however they're delivered, be sure that they encourage **feedback,** a receiver's communicated response to your message. Do your news releases have a "For More Information" section? Do your blogs encourage and post comments? Do your websites have highly visible "Contact Us" links? Make it easy for the target public to reply.

QUICK CHECK

1. According to the authors, what should most influence your choice of message-delivery media?
2. In what sense is successful communication more like a circle than a line?
3. What are some techniques for conquering the presentation jitters?

THE VOLUNTEER CLEARINGHOUSE NEWS RELEASES

Using the IDEA process, let's imagine how you might respond to the "Real World" scenario that opens this chapter. As you'll recall, Volunteer Clearinghouse, a pro bono client of your agency, has hired a new executive director. It wants your help in spreading the good news throughout the community.

Idea Generation

Your research leads you to the following findings and conclusions:

- Your goal is to publicize Elaine Anderson's hiring. You read Anderson's application and résumé, and you talk with the chair about why the board chose Anderson.
- Volunteer Clearinghouse (VC) has no communications budget.
- VC has long-standing community support; residents believe that it's a newsworthy organization.

This seems like a clear case for the who-what-where-when-why-how informative strategy. You decide to write a straightforward news release—much cheaper than an ad or special event. You announce your decision to an older colleague who recommends that you also prepare a social media news release for community-events bloggers as well as for newspaper editors who might want multimedia elements. She has a list of e-mail addresses for the bloggers.

Arrangement

In our Volunteer Clearinghouse scenario, the research you conducted in the previous stage of the writing process can now help you create an outline. You know that your targeted public consists of news editors and bloggers, and you know they want the news. Therefore, you decide to organize your traditional news release in the inverted pyramid style of a news story, with the most important information at the beginning and the least important at the end (see Figure 10.1). You review the most important details in the areas of who, what, when, where, why, and how, and you organize the details in terms of importance. You decide that your first paragraph needs to announce the most important news: The board of directors has hired Elaine Anderson to be the new executive director of Volunteer Clearinghouse. You decide that it's also important to describe briefly who Anderson is and when she'll begin her new job.

In your research, you obtained a quotation about Anderson's abilities from the chairman of the board, but you decide to place that after your lead paragraph. Although it's a good quotation, you decide it's just not as important as the announcement of Anderson's hiring and the details about her qualifications for this new job.

close window ⊠

CAROL CONE JOINS EDELMAN

April 05, 2010, -- Carol Cone, thought leader, speaker and nationally recognized "mother of cause marketing," today joins Edelman, the world's largest independent public relations firm.

Carol will provide strategic counsel to clients on the development of corporate and brand citizenship, cause and public engagement strategies. Carol also will work with the firm's leadership in the ongoing effort to apply insights from Edelman's annual goodpurpose™ Consumer Study and its Trust and Health Engagement Barometers.

Carol was previously the Founder and Chairman of Cone, Inc., where she led the development of signature cause branding programs for a host of Fortune 500 companies and nonprofits, including the Avon Breast Cancer Crusade, ConAgra Foods' Feeding Children Better, PNC Grow Up Great, the American Heart Association's Go Red for Women movement, ITT Watermark, Western Union's Our World, Our Family initiative and Reebok's Human Rights program. She also created groundbreaking research reports to advance the strategic practice of social issues engagement. In 2007, PR Week called her "arguably the most powerful and visible figure in the world of cause branding."

Global CEO and President Richard Edelman said: "In this new era of public engagement, clients look to us for counsel to activate brands around social purpose that will resonate in a stakeholder society. Carol has been a part of developing some of the most influential movements and causes at the intersection of business, brands and society. Her addition to the agency brings a powerful new dimension to our client service capabilities."

Mitch Markson, Chief Creative Officer and founder of Edelman's goodpurpose™ initiative, commented: "As we have seen through Edelman's annual goodpurpose™ study, social purpose is becoming a key driver in building both brand equity and dynamic consumer relationships. In Carol, our clients will have a world class resource who has spent her career focusing on this shift and helping companies and brands stay ahead. She will also be instrumental in helping build a stronger bridge between CSR and brand marketing."

Online News Release

The Edelman public relations agency announced the hiring of cause branding expert Carol Cone with a news release that, in Edelman's digital newsroom, linked to a video of Cone discussing the importance of social responsibility.

(Courtesy of Edelman)

Your final outline might look something like this:

Paragraph 1:   Anderson hired for new exec director.
Brief note on who she is.
Brief note on what Volunteer Clearinghouse is.
Note when she starts.

Paragraph 2:   Quote from board chairman.

Paragraph 3:   Anderson's biography.

Paragraph 4:   She succeeds Phil Connors. Note where he's gone.

Paragraph 5:   Note that anyone interested in volunteering with community service agencies can call the Volunteer Clearinghouse. List phone number and address.

For your social media news release (see p. 269), you decide to offer a series of bullet points under these headings: News Facts, Quotations, Multimedia, Related Links, Link to Traditional News Release, About Volunteer Clearinghouse, and For More Information. In researching what you might include for Multimedia, you strike it rich: You discover that Volunteer Clearinghouse has 45 seconds of video of Elaine Anderson helping to paint a mural inside VC headquarters last year. You decide to link to the video as well as to photographs of Anderson and of the VC board of directors.

Expression

Because you've completed the research and organization stages of the writing process, the question that faces you now isn't *What should I write?* Instead, it's *How should I write what's in my outline?* As we noted earlier, the difference doesn't make writing easy, but it certainly makes it easier.

Just to break the ice, you look at your outline for the traditional news release and write this opening sentence:

> The board of directors of Volunteer Clearinghouse has announced that Elaine Anderson, formerly with the Coxwold County Red Cross, will be Volunteer Clearinghouse's new executive director.

Not bad. But you quickly identify some points in your lead that you don't like:

- The sentence seems too long: 26 words. It doesn't move concisely to the announcement of a new director. Your examination of previous Volunteer Clearinghouse news releases shows that it's OK to delete the reference to the board of directors in the first sentence.
- The lead doesn't include Anderson's starting date (a question of *when*).
- The lead assumes that readers know what Volunteer Clearinghouse is (a question of *who*).

With the problems identified, you're ready to eliminate them. Your second draft might look like this:

> Volunteer Clearinghouse has named Elaine Anderson the organization's new executive director. Anderson, formerly with the Coxwold County Red Cross, will begin her new duties May 29. Volunteer Clearinghouse recruits and trains volunteers for Coxwold County United Way agencies.

That's better. There's still room for improvement, but your first paragraph is now good enough to justify moving on to another section of your document. You'll get another chance to polish the document in the next stage of the writing process: revision.

After setting your finished draft aside for about 45 minutes just to clear your head, you return to it and begin the revision process. You even imagine that the editor of a local newspaper is leaning over your shoulder. Because she's a journalist, she immediately tells you, *Give me specific details!*

In your second sentence, you are specific about *when*, but Anderson's former job at the Red Cross seems vague. So to satisfy your target public's interest in exact details, you revise the sentence: *Anderson, the former supervisor of the Coxwold County Red Cross, will begin her new duties May 29.*

After revising and polishing your news release, you're ready for the macroedit (p. 307) and the microedit (p. 307). As you move backward through your document, your first sentence would be the last to undergo a microedit: *Volunteer Clearinghouse has named Elaine Anderson the organization's new executive director.* Stifling a yawn, you double-check the spelling of Elaine Anderson's name against her résumé—and your yawn turns into a gasp. Her first name is spelled *Elayne*. As you type in the correction, you're grateful that you edited the document yourself before submitting it to another editor. Good microediting helped save your credibility as a writer.

And now it's time to tackle that social media news release . . . .

Delivery

Your colleagues at the agency clue you in on how area reporters like to receive news releases. Most prefer e-mail pastes, but one newspaper reporter still likes old-fashioned paper releases. You also e-mail the local community-events bloggers with a link to the social media news release; one prefers text messages, so you text her the link. As a pièce de résistance, you help Volunteer Clearinghouse post the traditional news release—with photo and a link to the video—on the homepage of the organization's website.

Your reward for a job well done? It just might include hearing Elayne Anderson tell your supervisors they made a great decision in hiring you.

SUMMARY

The dazzling array of new media for public relations practitioners can be both exhilarating and scary. Much of it is fun, but who can possibly keep up with and master each new medium? We hope you'll find it reassuring that Aristotle, who was no dummy, had the same concerns and found comfort in the IDEA idea. Delivery and media choices are important, but they're only one part of successful messages: Just as important—probably more important—are idea generation, arrangement, and expression.

Despite the undeniable significance of new media, public relations employers still insist, first and foremost, on hiring graduates who can write well. Those employers know that good writers are good thinkers. Media will continue to change, but most will continue to rely on good writing. Even a podcast requires good, clear language.

A final word of advice for successful message development: Stay focused on your organization's values as well as those of the publics with whom you want to build relationships. By staying true to its values, your organization can become a known and trusted source of effective messages. And messages that address the values of target publics usually gain an audience. A values-oriented message can sometimes overcome a flawed delivery method. On the other hand, even brilliant use of new media cannot add much beneficial content to a weak message.

DISCUSSION QUESTIONS

1. Apply Aristotle's four causal-analysis questions to your college or university. What is it, and what makes it different from all others? Who and what created it? What does it consist of? What is its purpose?

2. Have you had a creative-thinking experience similar to what James Webb Young describes—in which, after research, the idea just came to you? Was the new idea a combination of other ideas?

3. How might you use the AIDA organizational strategy to create a message for high-school seniors considering attending your college or university? What would attract their attention? How would you keep their interest? How would you fill them with a desire to act? What action should they take to find out how to apply?

4. Given your knowledge of high-school seniors, what media might you use to send the message that you developed for discussion question 3?

5. Do you face any personal barriers to creating effective messages? If so, what are they? Procrastination? Reluctance to *really* create an outline? Knowledge of grammar? What can you do to overcome those barriers?

MEMO FROM THE FIELD

REGINA LYNCH-HUDSON
President; The Write Publicist
Atlanta, Georgia
Regina Lynch-Hudson is founder and president of The Write Publicist in Atlanta. Self-described as "the quintessential American mutt," Lynch-Hudson has a 15-year track record of conceptualizing print media campaigns for people, places, products, and performances.

Lynch-Hudson has launched and syndicated columns about public relations, travel, business, and other topics. She has been profiled in the magazines *Entrepreneur* and *Black Enterprise*.

Admittedly, when I was asked to contribute to this public relations textbook, I wondered what I would communicate to wide-eyed, idealistic students, when my own career path has not been conventional. But then *public relations* is such an ambiguous term.

I regard public relations as an art form, combining some theory and a great deal of impressionism. From the subliminal theatrics required to deliver memorable presentations to the gut spontaneity of merging words that evoke reaction—a wordsmith's success isn't tied to academia alone. My own college years were short-circuited due to a family tragedy. NEWS FLASH: Kidney dialysis patient brutally murdered leaving hospital. *Victim's daughter turns to writing for solace.*

Ongoing courses in consumer behavior, body language, and psychology melded with world travel, and an oftentimes nontraditional mélange of seminars, workshops, and lectures enhanced my perspective. I relied on creative ripeness and ravenous "literary consumption" to whet my writing skills.

You should also develop a penchant to read anything you can get your hands on—newspapers, magazines, menus, billboards, and direct mail. You never know when you'll be writing about an automotive manufacturer; a software company; a humanitarian organization; or a corporation with international reach. Subconsciously, we all plunder our past for material—and in the profoundest, most unexpected way, up pops a tidbit of knowledge precisely when needed. Somewhere between writing's structure, public relations' principles, and imagination's abstractions, you'll discover a definite and confident style.

Be prepared to undergo years of clarifying and deepening your personal vision, of focusing your energies, of developing patience, just to objectively identify where *you* fit. Discovering one's strengths and weaknesses, maintaining one's commitment and capacity for learning, and perfecting one's craft are imperative in this business.

It's been said that life is a costume party and that we keep changing and changing and changing until we find the outfit that fits best. Some public relations practitioners blossom into world-class event coordinators. Many of us PR'ers are the "idea geniuses" who pen attention-grabbing news releases. Other PR types possess a gift for gab and are better suited to "pitch" to editors or to deliver persuasive speeches. Tailor your career around a specialty that's a "fit," rather than with what the market seemingly needs. The market can be quite capricious. Embracing those skills that spur passion and inner solace, and daringly carving out a niche based on talents and interests, are not only necessary for productivity but are also necessary for longevity.

Poignancy sells. Regardless of the company or target audience, ability to elucidate a client, on paper, verbally, and even in your body language during oral presentations, requires varying degrees of ardor—delivered enthusiastically, succinctly, and with sincerity. Frankly, one must, to a certain extent, psychologically bond with the client's product or service to promote it. Genuineness is not easily feigned unless you minor in drama and acting. And even then, audiences are not easily fooled over the long haul.

Originality rules. Oftentimes, originality implies being bold enough to go beyond accepted norms. It's how you pen (or peg) your clients as *distinct* that will brand them in the psyche of target audiences. Whether you are penning a proposal to reap sponsorship for an event, a speech to lure voters to a politician, or a script for a videotape to be used as a sales tool for a luxury resort, communicating what's "different" is fundamental. Knowing your clients enables you to gauge how demonstrative you can be in your written, verbal, or pictorial personification of them. A bank or a life insurance company may require black-and-white doses of realism, whereas in promoting tourism, the arts, or food, you may add splashes of wit and whimsy.

Don't be afraid to stroke with a broad brush, to try new techniques, to make mistakes. Mistakes are the catalysts that germinate genius. There are no paint-by-number strategies for mastering public relations. The Web and the 2000 Census reflect dramatic change in not only *how* we communicate but in the profile of who *we* are.

There's a big canvas out there, and, as Van Gogh illustrated, there is more than one way to paint a sunflower. Whether you work for a *Fortune* 500 giant or as a solo practitioner—it's how you distill millions of ideas and translate them into something cohesive that breathes life into the identity of your clients. ■

CASE STUDY 10.1 Dove Soars with Real Beauty

Chances are, you've done it. After all, more than 3 million have.

If you haven't, go ahead: Direct your browser to YouTube and search "Dove Evolution." Push play, and, for one minute and 14 seconds, watch one of the most famous integrated marketing tactics of recent years.

The Dove Evolution viral video—in which a young woman digitally transforms into an impossibly perfect supermodel—is part of the award-winning Campaign for Real Beauty, sponsored by Dove, Unilever's line of cleansing and personal-care products. The goal of the Campaign for Real Beauty is impressive: "to help widen the definition of beauty and offer a more diverse representation than the stereotypical images that women and girls are bombarded with every day."[9] To achieve that goal, Unilever, ad agency Ogilvy & Mather, and public relations agency Edelman have worked together to create an array of integrated, on-message tactics.

Before the planning and tactics, however, came the research. Edelman surveyed more than 10,000 women worldwide and discovered that only 2 percent describe themselves as beautiful. Almost 80 percent wish that the media could do "a better job of portraying women of diverse physical attractiveness—age, shape, and size."[10] A subsequent survey on age and beauty found that "91 percent of the women surveyed believe the media and advertising need to do a better job of representing realistic images of women over 50."[11]

"Without having a foundation in the global research study, which showed that the image of beauty was unattainable, we wouldn't have had the credibility in creating the materials," said Larry Koffler, Edelman's senior vice president for consumer brands. "The research was critical."[12]

To build on that credibility, Unilever wanted a campaign that went beyond advertising. "We had advertising, public relations, customer marketing and consumer promotions sit down at the table at a very early stage and all think about the entire marketing communication architecture, not just our channels," Koffler recalled.[13]

The Dove Evolution viral video, for example, earned coverage on TV programs *The View, Entertainment Tonight,* and *The Ellen DeGeneres Show*, and it generated three times more visits to the IMC campaign's website than did an earlier Super Bowl commercial.[14]

Other campaign tactics included

- print, television, and billboard advertisements featuring "real women [with] real bodies and real curves."[15]
- a "Self-Esteem Fund" and "Uniquely Me!" programs that target girls ages 8 to 17 with the aim of "educating and inspiring girls who believe in a definition of beauty that doesn't include them."[16]
- the CampaignForRealBeauty.com website, which includes news releases, the Dove Evolution video, self-esteem kits for mothers and daughters, Real Beauty e-greeting cards, online discussion forums, news about the Self-Esteem Fund, and other initiatives.
- photography and essay competitions on real beauty for young girls.
- the Campaign for Real Beauty Tour, a traveling photography exhibition, featuring photographs of women by women. According to an accompanying news release, "The images, which depict confidence, individuality and character, are accompanied by an anecdote or quote that explains the photographer's vision."[17]

Advertising has played a major role in the Campaign for Real Beauty, but the success of the public relations tactics has won admiration even from advertising media. Fernando Acosta, the senior vice president of Dove, told *Advertising Age* that "although the ads are eye-catching and thought-provoking, public relations is used as the lead medium in all countries" in which Dove has launched the Campaign for Real Beauty.[18]

Advertising Age also reported that "so powerful was the [campaign's] public relations effort that paid media was light."[19]

Media response to the campaign—a success for both advertising and public relations—has helped Dove become the leading brand in promoting realistic images of beauty. As early as 2005, *PRWeek* reported that "Dove's 'Real women, real curves' campaign has had so much press that Unilever could justifiably claim stewardship of the real women demographic that everyone is now talking about."[20]

Dove may have lost count of how many national and international marketing awards the Campaign for Real Beauty has won, but to date the list includes the Silver Anvil Award from the Public Relations Society of America and the Golden World Award from the International Public Relations Association.

Perhaps the greatest testament to success, however, came from a woman who wrote to the Campaign for Real Beauty website after seeing a Dove commercial in which young girls discussed insecurities about their appearances. "I want to hug every single one of them," she wrote, "and tell them how beautiful I think they are."[21]

DISCUSSION QUESTIONS

1. Before reading this case, were you aware of Dove's Campaign for Real Beauty? If so, where have you encountered it? What are your impressions?
2. What were the advantages of doing Dove Evolution as a viral video rather than as a television commercial?
3. Dove doesn't try to sell its products on the Campaign for Real Beauty website. Is that a mistake?
4. How did Dove use research to develop the core message of the Campaign for Real Beauty? ∎

CASE STUDY 10.2 Capitalizing on Tragedy: The Marketing of a Plane Crash

This story begins in tragedy and ends with strategic messages that many found to be in remarkably poor taste. On February 17, 2010, in Palo Alto, California, a private plane struck power lines and crashed, killing three employees of Tesla Motors, a leading manufacturer of electric cars. In a company blog, a Tesla representative wrote, "Tesla is a small, tightly knit company, and this is a tragic loss for us." Within days, the posting had drawn more than 100 comments, all mourning the three deaths.[22]

The crash also prompted another online message, this one from a California-based insurance company to potential customers, e-mailed one day after the employees' deaths. The message began by calling the crash a "horror" and "expressing sincerest condolences" to the families and friends of the three. The message then concluded with this paragraph:

Prudent risk management dictates that multiple executives should never travel together, be it on a private plane or commercially. While no one likes to think about their death or how it and the deaths of others will affect a company, it's as important to address in business as it is in one's personal life. If you would like to discuss succession planning and Key Person Insurance, please contact our specialist, Fred W—.[23]

Reaction, particularly among bloggers, was fast and furious. Valleywag, a Silicon Valley blog, posted the e-mail with the comment "In terms of exploiting tragedy, this isn't as bad as exploiting the 9/11 attacks by turning them into product endorsements. But it's close. . . ."[24] Soon after, a *Wired* magazine blog linked to the Valleywag posting and added this sarcastic headline: "Tesla's Tragedy Becomes Another Business's Golden Opportunity." The *Wired* blogger added, "[T]his email, sent barely 24 hours after a terrible tragedy, . . . effectively blames Tesla and the victims for what happened, all the while implying that if they were customers somehow the outcome would have been better."[25]

As more business and technology blogs cited the Valleywag posting, reactions were consistently negative:

- In a posting titled "Disturbing Ad Following Tesla Plane Tragedy," a blogger for Infotainment News wrote, "I . . . am sickened at the nerve of this company."[26]
- In "The Corner Office Blog," marketing consultant Steve Tobak wrote, "[T]his e-mail went out the day after the incident, before the victims had even been publicly identified. Personally, I'm appalled. Professionally, I think this behavior is well beyond the realm of ethical executive and corporate conduct. . . ."[27]
- At Los Angeles' LAist blog, Zach Behrens compared the insurance e-mail to a recent, troubling public relations pitch: "When [a local school official] was kidnapped and later executed in Mexico during the holidays, LAist's phone rang—someone had a story idea for us. 'Would you like to write a story about kidnap and ransom insurance?' a young perky voice on the other end asked. She then e-mailed over a press release about the policies. The whole thing just felt super skeezy. Pass."[28]

Perhaps the only point in the insurance company's favor is that it seemed to be monitoring the social media furor. In the Comments sections of both the Valleywag and the *Wired* blogs, a company executive posted this response:

Our company sent out the above newsletter yesterday as we were deeply sadden [*sic*] about the tragic Tesla accident. Our primary reason for sending it out was not to ambulance chase or to do anything other than remind small businesses that perpetuation planning is a very difficult and often overlooked subject.

For anyone that found our newsletter offensive, distasteful or unpleasant we sincerely apologize. Our goal is to do business with integrity, and we regret if sending this newsletter caused anyone to believe otherwise.[29]

Commenters on *that* comment weren't appeased. "In an unrelated decision, [the company executive] traded his window office for a cubicle near the stairwell," wrote one. "'Our goal is to do business with integrity?'" wrote another. "Well, you failed."[30]

Finally, one commenter no doubt spoke for many in offering this concise assessment of the insurance company's misguided message: "You guys need a lesson or two in PR."[31]

DISCUSSION QUESTIONS

1. In your opinion, is the insurance company's message justified because it begins with expressions of sympathy? Why or why not?
2. Is this truly a "thumbs down" moment in public relations? After all, outrage was largely confined to the blogging community.
3. In your opinion, should the insurance company have commented on the negative blogs? Why or why not?
4. Do you think the misspelling in the company's response affected the success of its message? Why or why not? ■

NOTES

1. "Agency Career Path," *PRWeek*, 25 August 2008, online, http://www.prweekus.com/talent-concerns/article/115720/.
2. Peter A. Falcone, *The Delphi Report—Critical Thinking: A Statement of Expert Consensus for Purposes of Educational Assessment and* Instruction (Millbrae, CA: California Academic Press, 1990), 2.
3. Charles Marsh, David W. Guth, and Bonnie Poovey Short, *Strategic Writing*, 2nd ed. (Boston: Allyn & Bacon, 2009).

4. James Webb Young, *A Technique for Producing Ideas* (New York: McGraw-Hill, 2003).
5. Young, 25.
6. Marsh, Guth, and Short.
7. Adapted from Marsh, Guth, and Short.
8. Adapted from Marsh, Guth, and Short.
9. "Dove Campaign for Real Beauty Press Statement," news release issued by Unilever, 22 December 2006, online, LexisNexis.
10. Taylor Simmons, "Real Women, Real Results," *The Strategist,* August 2006, online, LexisNexis.
11. "Too Old to Be Young," news release issued by Unilever, 8 February 2007, online, LexisNexis.
12. Simmons.
13. Simmons.
14. Jack Neff, "A Real Beauty," *Advertising Age,* 30 October 2006, online, LexisNexis.
15. Simmons.
16. Laurel Wentz, "Real Beauty Gets Global Break-out via Evolution," *Advertising Age,* 8 January 2007, online, LexisNexis.
17. "Get the Picture!" news release issued by Unilever, 11 March 2005, online, LexisNexis.
18. Wentz.
19. Randall Rothenberg, "Dove Effort Gives Package-Goods Marketers Lessons for the Future," *Advertising Age,* 5 March 2007, online, Lexis-Nexis.
20. Eleanor Trickett, "When Marketing Directly Reflects Everyday Women, Brands Take on Real-Life Credibility," *PRWeek,* 22 August 2005, online, LexisNexis.
21. Campaign for Real Beauty, online, www.CampaignForRealBeauty.com, posted 13 April 2007.
22. Elon Musk, "Doug, Brian, and Andrew," 18 February 2010, online, www.teslamotors.com/blog2.
23. Valleywag, "The Terribly Tasteless Tesla Plane Crash Ad," 18 February 2010, online, http://gawker.com/5474956/the-terribly-tasteless-tesla-plane-crash-ad?.
24. "The Terribly Tasteless Tesla Plane Crash Ad."
25. David Pierce, "Tesla's Tragedy Becomes Another Business's Golden Opportunity," 18 February 2010, online, http://www.wired.com/epicenter/2010/02/teslastragedy.
26. Infotainment News, "Disturbing Ad Following Tesla Plane Tragedy," 18 February 2010, online, http://www.infotainmentnews.net/2010/02/18/disturbing-ad-following-tesla-plane-tragedy.
27. Steve Tobak, "Tragic Tesla Plane Crash Exploited by Insurance Company," The Corner Office Blog, 19 February 2010, http://blogs.bnet.com/ceo/?p=3860.
28. Zach Behrens, "Insurance Company Takes Tesla Plane Crash Too Far," LAist, 19 February 2010, online, http://laist.com/2010/02/19/insurance_company_takes_tesla _plane.php.
29. "The Terribly Tasteless Tesla Plane Crash Ad"; Pierce.
30. "The Terribly Tasteless Tesla Plane Crash Ad"; Pierce.
31. "The Terribly Tasteless Tesla Plane Crash Ad."

11

Cyber-Relations in the Digital Age

OBJECTIVES

After studying this chapter, you will be able to

- describe the changes occurring through the development of digital communications technology as well as the implications of those changes
- recognize the opportunities and challenges confronting public relations practitioners in the Digital Age

- identify the challenges and opportunities facing practitioners with the creation of social media and nontraditional online social networks
- appreciate that "new" doesn't always mean "better" and that in certain situations, traditional channels of communication are preferable to new, high-tech ones

KEY TERMS

REAL WORLD

Differing Designs for the Future

Olds Young and Associates is one of the community's oldest architectural firms. One of the co-owners is Bud Olds, who founded the firm nearly three decades ago. The other owner is Betty Young, whose late father formed the original partnership with Olds.

In the five years since her father's death, Young has redirected the focus of the firm. Once known only as a local business, the firm has become nationally known for its designs of sports venues such as stadiums and arenas.

Because of increasing competition, your public relations agency has been asked to develop a public relations plan for Olds Young and Associates. As part of your initial research, you conducted separate interviews with the co-owners. It didn't take you long to discover a generation gap.

"We didn't use fancy public relations firms in the old days," said Olds. "If you wanted to generate new business, you went door to door and pressed the flesh. Who needs fancy Power-Point presentations when a handshake and a smile will do the job? Don't let Betty talk you into proposing something as silly as podcasts and blogs. Most people in this town have never even heard of digital whatevers."

"Bud Olds has been like a second father to me," said Young. "But we need to bring this firm into the 21st century. The days of Magic Markers and flip charts are gone forever. I want to see us on YouTube and Second Life. We have potential customers that we need to reach."

"I think this firm is getting too big for its britches," said Olds.

"I have some big plans for our firm's future," said Young.

You have a problem. You have asked for a joint meeting with Olds and Young. What are you going to tell them?

A WORLD OF POSSIBILITIES

Marc Andreessen, a Netscape founder and a Facebook board member, made a late-night visit to the San Francisco airport in February 2007 to talk with a stranger about the power of social media. The meeting had been arranged through a mutual acquaintance. Andreessen talked with the man about the vast possibilities of social networking and how it could help him overcome seemingly impossible odds to achieve his goal.

"What he was doing shouldn't have been possible, but we see a lot of that out here, and then something clicks," Andreessen said. "He was clearly super-smart and very entrepreneurial, a person who saw the world and the status quo as malleable."[1]

That impossible dream was becoming president of the United States. The stranger with curiosity about social media was Barack Obama.

The presidential election of 2008 was a watershed moment in U.S. history for a variety of reasons. Obama became the first black man elected to the nation's highest office. He also was the first person of the post–Baby Boom generation elected president. And more than any candidate before, Obama tapped into emerging social media to raise a record $747 million, with approximately one third of it in individual donations of $200 or less.[2] His campaign also created a 13-million member e-mail list as well as a second list of 3 million mobile and text subscribers—tools critical in communicating the candidate's unfiltered messages and in motivating supporters to go to the polls.[3]

Although most of the candidates in the crowded 2008 presidential primaries used some form of social media to their advantage, the Obama campaign proved to be their master. The numbers tell the story: Compared to the social media efforts of general election opponent John McCain, the Obama campaign had four times the number of YouTube viewers, five times the number of Facebook friends, and twice as many visitors to its website. This was no fluke; the Democrat nominee had 10 times as many online staff as his Republican opponent.[4]

"Thomas Jefferson used newspapers to win the presidency, F.D.R used radio to change the way he governed, [and] J.F.K. was the first president to understand television," said lawyer, money manager, and blogger Ranjit Mathoda. "Barack Obama understood that you could use the Web to lower the cost of building a political brand, create a sense of connection and engagement, and dispense with the command and control method of governing to allow people to self-organize to do the work."[5]

In so many ways that we are still trying to discover, the emergence of **digital** technology within most of our readers' lifetimes has brought dramatic changes to society. It is easy for today's college students to take computer-based communication for granted. However, when compared with traditional media, the **Internet** is a relative newcomer. The **World Wide Web**, which made the Internet more accessible to the masses, dates back to only 1990. In less than a generation, a digital revolution has affected almost every aspect of how we live, work, play—and, now, select our leaders. We truly are living in what Canadian philosopher Marshall McLuhan predicted in 1964 would be a **global village**, in which everyone can share simultaneous

President Barack Obama, shown with First Lady Michelle Obama on Inauguration Day, successfully used social media tactics to overcome better-known rivals to win the 2008 presidential election.

(Photo courtesy U.S. State Department)

experiences. However, even a visionary such as McLuhan might have been surprised by how much and how fast this digital revolution has transformed society.

Public relations professionals were among the first to ride this new media wave. Practitioners have always been among the first to adapt technological advances to their needs. Digital technology contributes to every step of the public relations process: research, planning, communication, and evaluation. Although the dizzying pace of change challenges us to keep pace, it also provides passage into a world of brave new possibilities.

Just ask Barack Obama.

It's All About You

Time magazine's decision to name *You* as its Person of the Year for 2006 was an acknowledgement of the power of **Web 2.0,** what the magazine described as "a tool for bringing together the small contributions of millions of people and making them matter."[6] The term *Web 2.0* was coined by a group of Silicon Valley consultants in 2004 to describe a new generation of Internet services that emphasize online collaboration and sharing. YouTube, the popular video-sharing service, and Wikipedia, the free—and not always accurate—online encyclopedia, are well-known examples of this phenomenon. Both are made possible through the voluntary efforts of thousands of contributors. Web 2.0 has unleashed a new force in mass communication: **social media.** *Time*'s editors said they decided to recognize the online individual "for seizing the global media, for founding and framing the new digital democracy, for working for nothing and beating the pros at their own game."[7]

To put this another way, the Digital Revolution has helped create new **social networks,** the often-informal structures through which individuals and/or organizations maintain relationships. Social networks can operate on many levels, such as families, civic organizations, trade associations, and neighborhoods. As a result of advances in communication technology, the number of these social networks is growing exponentially.

"There have been a lot of waves in technology and different types of media throughout history," said Jeffrey Robertson, assistant commissioner of U.S. Customs and Border Protection. "I think our challenge is to try to rise above the wave and take a look at 'What is the impact? How can I actually use this new media?'

"But the key for us as practitioners is how do you rise above, project what the impact may be, and then how do we use that to get our message out in a variety of ways?"[8]

Web 2.0 has made it possible for almost everyone to join the conversation. Granted, not everyone has something worthy to say. However, the debate is nothing if not lively. More important, these nontraditional online social networks have forced organizations to focus on new issues. Traditional media organizations, as well as the disciplines of public relations, advertising, and marketing, have had to reexamine how they reach targeted publics.

The reality of Web 2.0 comes down to this: It is all about you.

SOCIAL MEDIA APPS

Web 3.0

When it finally arrives, Web 3.0 is really going to be something special. What, exactly, it will be is unclear. It appears as if there are as many definitions for Web 3.0 as there are computer geeks. However, experts agree that it will transform the digital platform of social media and revolutionize the way we gather information from the Internet.

At the risk of looking foolish to some really, really smart people—including readers of this book—we offer this definition of Web 3.0, also known as the Semantic Web: the predicted third generation of the World Wide Web, one that will be more intelligent, intuitive, and capable of precisely gathering information based on content and meaning.

With Web 2.0, search engines, such as Google or Bing, gather information. But, as you may have experienced, a search term can result in a remarkable number of hits; for example, a Google search of *search engine* nets 52.9 million results. Your task becomes searching within those results to narrow the list and find the specific information you seek. For this reason, many organizations use search engine optimization (SEO) strategies designed to move their product or service to the top of search engine–generated lists.

The promise—or maybe it is just a hope—of Web 3.0 is that online information will include coding that allows computers to interpret content and meaning better. Instead of engaging in a lengthy online search, the Semantic Web will recognize relationships, link individual sources and different databases, and deliver more targeted and relevant information in just one mouse click. For public relations, this would bring more efficient research, better targeting, and improved media monitoring and measurement.

And that would be something special. ■

Risks and Rewards

Considering that the purpose of public relations is to build and maintain mutually beneficial relationships with publics critical to an organization's success, it is easy to see why practitioners have been at or near the cutting edge of the digital revolution. They are excited about the possibility of tapping into these online social networks and, in some cases, creating their own. Social networks also represent an opportunity to bypass traditional gatekeepers, such as those in the news media, to reach targeted publics directly.

However, the digital revolution can cut both ways. In a postmodern world, the impulse of many within these social networks is to redefine public policies and issues in a whole new narrative. They are not bound by traditional relationships and do not necessarily use traditional strategies and tactics. They also are adept at converting latent publics into active publics within a relatively short time frame. The challenge for the practitioner is to identify, monitor, and, if necessary, engage these social networks. The failure to do so could affect an organization negatively.

"Modern information technology is creating a new corporate communication landscape," said researcher Augustine Ihator. "Computer technology has altered the power structure and relationship between corporations and their publics, stakeholders and the media."

"There is an emerging power sharing," Ihator wrote in *Public Relations Quarterly*. "Publics now have ready access to the mass media to tell their story from their own perspective and complain vehemently if necessary."[9]

This brings us to the essential truth of social media: They are largely uncontrolled. Although organizations can frame their messages however they choose, they cannot command how others publicly react and respond to them. The idea of employees blogging about their jobs or customers tweeting candidly about a company's products or services terrifies many executives. And if organizations try to control social media—much like Nestlé unsuccessfully tried to in 2010 when it threatened to remove Facebook posts criticizing the company's environmental practices—they open themselves to a firestorm of criticism (see Case Study 16.1).

"The big corporate clients of all regulated industries have been reluctant to get involved in new media," said Bill Black, senior partner at Fleishman-Hillard. "They like the old way, where it's just a one-way path of communication." However, Black went on to say that in today's social environment, companies can't avoid new media or the loss of message control that comes with it.[10]

However, with social media, risks come with rewards. Organizations concerned about a loss of message control should also think of the credibility and trust gained by engaging in open communication with their key publics.

"Externally, one of the biggest problems [that business has now] is suffering from a lack of trust," said Harvey Greisman, a former executive with MasterCard International. "One of the ways you gain that trust is by engaging and by amplifying your communications. And social media really helps you engage."[11]

The decisions of when and how to use social media are among the most perplexing practitioners face. Jeffrey Robertson of U.S. Customs and Border Protection summed up the feelings of many when he said, "I enjoy my keyboard, but it is not my friend—and I don't trust that screen as much as I do hearing from someone who has the information."[12]

Media, Messages, and Values

For many, the selection of the medium has become an even more important decision than the content of the message to be delivered. However, even the best communications medium needs content. While it is true that the medium can alter the perception of a message, the reverse also holds true. An appropriate message delivered via an inappropriate medium is just as ineffective as an inappropriate message delivered via an appropriate medium. Message and medium must be equal considerations in communication. If not, true communication will not occur.

More to the point, the selection of both message and medium is closely tied to the values of the communicator, as well as to those of the targeted public. Those values are not linked to changes in technology. Instead, they are expressions of who we are and who we want to be. The first book ever produced in mass quantities was the Bible. Since the days of Gutenberg, millions of copies of the Bible have been produced using an increasing variety of media, including audiocassettes, videotapes, CD-ROMs, DVDs, and even as mobile telephone applications. Despite the many advances in communications technology, the values expressed in the Bible have not changed.

For an example of how values dictate the message and the medium, let's revisit the architectural firm of Olds Young and Associates mentioned in this chapter's "Real World" scenario. At the heart of the dispute between Olds and Young are conflicting values. Olds sees the firm as one with strictly local clientele. Young has a different vision: that of a firm competing on a global scale. Before any decisions can be made on *how* to communicate, the two partners must first reach a consensus on *what* to communicate and to *whom*. Only when those issues are decided is it appropriate to discuss messages and media.

Part of your job with Olds Young is to help the partners reach that consensus. Fortunately, you don't have to choose one option over the other. It is commonplace for different divisions within the same company to target different publics. If the architectural firm is willing to commit the necessary resources, *both* partners can have their way. Bud Olds can focus on local customers, using more traditional communication channels. At the same time, Betty Young can use more technologically advanced methods to reach out to clients more accustomed to communicating at that level. This is one generation gap that the sound application of public relations practices can close.

The point of this chapter is to put cyber-relations and the Digital Age in perspective. Advanced technology is a useful tool in the practice of public relations. However, it is only a tool. Ultimately, the expression of our values determines how we use all the tools available to us.

QUICK CHECK

1. What role, if any, did social media play in the 2008 U.S. presidential election?

2. What are the primary arguments for or against an organization's use of social media?

3. What role do values play in media selection in the Digital Age?

THE DIGITAL REVOLUTION

At the center of the explosion in communications technology is the *bit,* the basic element of transmission in digital communications. Nicholas Negroponte, cofounder of the MIT Media Laboratory, calls the bit "the smallest atomic element in the DNA of information."[13] Our increasing ability to transfer thoughts, images, and sounds into bits is changing the way we interact with our world.

Although it might be difficult to say where and when the first computer was created—there are many competing claims—most agree that the introduction of the Altair 8800 in a January 1975 *Popular Electronics* cover story was a major milestone. Invented by H. Edward Roberts, the Altair was the first inexpensive, general-purpose microcomputer, better known today as a personal computer or PC. It was a build-it-yourself computer designed for hobbyists. Roberts had hoped he could sell 200 of the gadgets to break even. He received 1,000 orders within the first month.[14] The computer's introduction also sparked the interest of Harvard freshman Bill Gates who, with partner Paul Allen, wrote software for the Altair and later set up a new business venture they called Microsoft—and, as they say, the rest is history. Just days before Roberts died in a Macon hospital in March 2010, Gates flew to Georgia to be at his bedside.[15]

Just how big is the Digital Revolution? According to *Social Times,* WebMedia-Brand's blog about social media, there were 1.73 billion Internet users worldwide as of September 2009. That compares with only 420 million people online at the start of the millennium. The largest block, 738 million, were in Asia, followed by 418 million in Europe, and 252 million in North America. An estimated 90 trillion e-mails, approximately 247 billion a day, were transmitted in 2009. Add to those impressive statistics these numbers: 234 million websites and 126 million blogs in 2009, 1 billion YouTube videos available at any time, 6 million Facebook page views per minute, and an average of 27.3 million tweets on Twitter each day. In early 2010, Ashton Kutcher had 4.63 million Twitter followers at @aplusk.[16] As new technologies develop, these staggering numbers will continue to grow.

Convergence and Hypermedia

Perhaps the most important consequence of the digital revolution is a **convergence of media.** As different media adopt digital technology in their production and distribution, barriers that have traditionally stood between them are tumbling down.

QUICKBREAK 11.1

The Internet by the Numbers

In December 1990, there was only one **website** in the world, located at CERN, the European Laboratory for Particle Physics, in Switzerland. By the end of 2009, that figure had grown to 234 million.[17] And with the advent of social media, there doesn't appear to be any end in sight for the Web's phenomenal growth. The Internet, which began as a rudimentary computer network linking military and academic researchers in the 1960s, has become a major force in society.

Based on the results of a December 2009 survey, the Pew Internet & American Life Project estimates that 74 percent of U.S. adults go online. Approximately six out of 10 U.S. adults use broadband connections at home, and 55 percent connect to the Web wirelessly. According Pew, there is no gender gap: Equal percentages of men and women use the Internet. A once wide race and ethnicity gap in Internet usage has narrowed: 76 percent of whites (non-Hispanic), 70 percent black (non-Hispanic), and 64 percent Hispanic go online. The study also suggests that the younger you are, the more income you have, and/or the higher level of education you attain, the more likely it is that you are online.[18]

According to the U.S Census Bureau, 36.1 million people living in its South region used the Internet in 2008. That was the highest regional concentration of Internet users in the nation, followed by the West (22.5 million), the Midwest (22.3 million) and the Northeast (19.1 million).[19] Alaska recorded the highest percentage of household Internet use of any state, 84.3 percent, compared with Mississippi, the lowest, at 59.7 percent.[20]

The public's dependence on the Internet as a source of news is growing. According to Pew, 72 percent of U.S. adult Internet users said they "ever" get news online in 2009. Thirty-eight percent said they got news online "yesterday." That is an increase from 2000, when those figures were 60 percent and 22 percent, respectively. More men get news online than women, 42 percent to 35 percent. People ages 30–49 years get news online more than any other age group. People with annual household incomes of more than $75,000 get online news more than any other income group.[21]

The Internet has really made its mark in business, where the level of **e-commerce** continues its steady rise. The Census Bureau estimates that e-commerce retail sales during 2009 were $134.9 billion, representing 3.7 percent of total U.S. retail sales. That might seem a small percentage, but it is nine times larger than it had been at the start of the decade. Almost 93 percent of all e-commerce is business to business, more than $3 trillion annually.[22] ■

Practically every medium we interact with now is digital, from flip-camera telephones, to satellite radio, to the Web. The television signal you receive in your home has been exclusively digital since 2009. The newspaper, seemingly an artifact of 18th-century technology, is currently produced—and may soon be delivered to your "electronic doorstep"—digitally.

TABLE 11.1

U.S. INTERNET USE BY GENDER, ETHNICITY, AND AGE (APRIL 2009)

	All (78%)	Gender		Ethnicity			Age		
		Male (78%)	Female (77%)	White (78%)	Black (66%)	Hispanic (84%)	18–29 (88%)	30–49 (87%)	50–64 (78%)
Read or send e-mail	90	88	93	92	82	90	94	91	89
Read the latest news	72	73	72	73	72	67	74	76	71
Read political information	60	64	57	61	58	54	53	68	61
Pass the time or for amusement	72	72	73	72	81	67	84	72	65
Buy product or service online	75	71	78	77	60	70	80	77	71
Gather job information	52	54	49	49	68	50	75	55	37
Look for religious or spiritual information	28	23	34	28	36	28	26	30	31
Participate in an online auction	27	32	21	28	15	19	24	35	23
Donate online to a charity	19	17	22	21	14	17	17	23	19
Use Twitter to communicate	11	13	9	9	18	14	20	11	5

Source: Pew Internet & American Life Project

A more dramatic development is the convergence of traditionally distinct media into one form. Integrated multimedia—called **hypermedia**—incorporate digital audio, visual, and text information. To see hypermedia in action, one need only log on to the website maintained by the Cable News Network, one of the Web's most popular sites. CNN.com combines text from magazines such as *Time* and *Sports Illustrated* with video and audio supplied by CNN. The site also provides links to other sites where more information on subjects of personal interest can be found.

The potential application of hypermedia goes beyond the Internet. Think of what the week before the start of each school year is like. You have to run to the bookstore to purchase the textbooks you need for the coming semester. Depending on how many classes you take, this errand can bring new meaning to the idea of "carrying a full load." In the future, however, it may not be necessary to leave home. You will be able to download the contents of all your texts into a single device, a digital book. These textbooks will be unlike any you have ever seen. You will be able to highlight a word and have its definition appear. Instead of footnotes, links will take you to vast quantities of background information. Video and audio will be inserted to complement the text. When you finish your assigned reading, you will be able to use the same electronic book to download the daily newspaper or one of the best-selling novels of the day.

However, students have been slow to embrace e-texts. Despite savings of nearly half the price of a printed book, the Government Accountability Office reports students "may run into technical difficulties" and "may not have the option at the end of the term to keep the textbook." Studies have also shown that words on a page are easier to read than those on a computer screen. The GAO noted that "according to publishers, electronic textbooks have not caught on with students, and sales of these products have been unsuccessful."[23]

Wireless Digital Communication

Another area in which technological advancements have had a tremendous impact on the practice of public relations is wireless technology. Our ability to communicate with others over great distances is no longer restricted by the length of a wire. The ability to communicate from anywhere using a variety of communication devices—telephones, computer modems, radios, video, facsimile (fax) machines, and satellites—has made us more mobile, responsive, and cost effective. Through the use of miniature transmitters and global positioning satellites, it is possible to locate the exact position of anyone and anything on the planet—particularly important in both commerce and travel. And what may have been the most important social, economic, and technological development of the 20th century, wireless communications technology, such as television, makes it possible for people in all corners of the world to share simultaneously in a common experience—in much the way the world watched in horror as terrorists attacked the World Trade Center and the Pentagon on September 11, 2001.

Look at what has happened in just the past few years. Because of the growth of the Internet, advancements in digital communications, and the availability of less expensive and more compact portable telephones, the demand for telephone service has exploded. Today's Smartphones are ubiquitous, palm-sized computers, which serve as mobile telephones, digital cameras, Web portals, music players, and global positioning system (GPS) devices.

Just as important, the growth in cheaper, more accessible wireless communication is making the world a smaller place. Globally, there are telephone lines for only one person out of every eight. Most of these lines are located in the

U.S. Census Bureau employees used GPS-equipped, hand-held computers to verify, add, and delete addresses during the 2010 census.

(Photo courtesy of U.S. Census, Public Information Office)

developed nations of the Western world. However, access to phones will change dramatically over the next quarter century as developing nations embrace wireless communications technology. Frances Cairncross, British economist, has written that this change will have significant geopolitical consequences. In her book, *The Death of Distance,* Cairncross argues that the expansion of wireless technology will remove one of the Western world's key competitive edges, the vast superiority of its communications system. The worldwide economic impact of this shift in competitive equilibrium, she believes, will rival that of the collapse of communism.[24]

Social Ramifications

Although digital technology opens up a world of possibilities for the 21st century, progress does not come without its price. Only now are we beginning to understand the social ramifications of this new digital world. New communications technology has raised numerous issues for public policy makers and individuals to address. Among these are questions about media mergers, personal privacy, job security, and intellectual property rights.

A NEW TOWN COMMONS   In the days before the Internet, television, and the telephone, people gathered in their community's main public square—the town commons—to hear the latest news. Arguably, new media have become the 21st-century town commons. More and more people are turning to digital media for breaking news. In some cases, they actually break the news. For example, the first Twitter reports of U.S. Airways Flight 1529's emergency landing in New York's Hudson River in January 2009 appeared within one minute of incident.[25] When pop music legend Michael Jackson unexpectedly died in June 2009, so many people flooded the Internet that several news sites crashed. CNN reported 20 million page views in the hour the story broke.[26]

REDEFINED COMMUNITIES   For those concerned that social media will destroy social relationships and a traditional sense of community, have no fear. "Instead of disappearing, people's communities are being transformed," conclude researchers for the Pew Internet & American Life Project. According to their analysis, "The traditional human orientation to neighborhood- and village-based groups is moving toward communities that are oriented around geographically dispersed social networks." However, the researchers also conclude, "People's networks continue to have substantial numbers of relatives and neighbors—the traditional bases of community—as well as friends and workmates."[27]

SOCIAL ISOLATION   A trio of sociologists published a controversial study in 2006, arguing that since 1985, Americans have become more socially isolated. Miller McPherson, Lynn Smith-Lovin, and Matthew Brashears also suggested that social media were advancing that trend.[28] However, the Pew Internet & American Life Project countered with a 2009 study that said social isolation has remained essentially unchanged over the past quarter century and that social media are more likely to increase demographic and psychographic diversity among individual social networks.[29] The debate likely will rage for some time.

MERGERS OF MEDIA COMPANIES   When General Electric and Comcast announced a $37 billion deal in 2009 to give the cable company control over NBC Universal, the move was the latest in a trend of big media mergers. These often are marriages of companies that produce content (such as news, television shows, and movies) with those capable of distributing that content over a variety of media platforms. Other notable media mergers include ABC and Disney, Time and Warner, and the Sirius and XM satellite radio services. Although a seemingly efficient arrangement, the concentration of numerous powerful channels of mass communications in the hands of a few corporations has caused some to worry about a loss of journalistic independence. One of the most vocal critics of the Comcast–NBC Universal merger was Sen. Al Franken (D-Minn.), a former cast member of NBC's *Saturday Night Live.* "Are we going to be seeing a situation where five companies are controlling the information we get?" Franken said. "I think that's a very dangerous situation."[30]

PRESERVATION OF PERSONAL PRIVACY   The digital revolution has made it easier for people to gather, store, and transmit personal information. This is a matter of convenience for individuals as well as for corporations. But there are risks. Even with sophisticated safeguards, digital information is not entirely secure. Privacy concerns extend to personal messages, whether sent via e-mail or wireless telephones. At a time when computer hackers are at least as knowledgeable as computer programmers, you never know who is accessing your private conversations. In the highly competitive economy of the 21st century, new technology opens the door to commercial espionage on an alarming scale.

JOB SECURITY   The good news is that improved technology can make people more productive in the workplace. The bad news is that increased ability to do more with less lowers the demand for highly skilled workers. New communication technology allows many industries to outsource corporate functions. We have seen this in public relations, where many corporate public relations offices have been downsized. Much of the slack has been picked up on a per-job basis by independent consultants who do not receive any of the traditional corporate benefits (e.g., health coverage, retirement plans, or stock options).

Then too, technological advances often disrupt successful companies, a phenomenon Clayton M. Christensen of the Harvard Business School has called "the innovator's dilemma" and about which he has written a book of the same name. The digital revolution has led to simpler, cheaper, and more user-friendly ways of doing things that can squeeze out the products of older companies. Although not a direct threat to public relations, these so-called disruptive technologies can threaten the organizations in which it is practiced.[31]

PROTECTION OF INTELLECTUAL PROPERTY The fact that digital copies are both identical to original works and easy to alter poses a huge problem in the Information Age. A person's intellectual property has value. When others ignore copyright law (see Chapter 15) and use someone's intellectual property without permission or compensation, it is tantamount to theft. Today's digital technology makes it easier to copy and distribute the results of someone else's labors. This is a particular problem in the music and film industries, where the performances of top artists and actors can be rapidly duplicated for illegal sale or downloaded illegally. And the problem is not limited to consumer goods. Specialized business software is also a prime target. In some instances, this piracy has national security implications.

QUICK CHECK

1. What is e-commerce, and how significant is its role in the U.S. economy?
2. What are the implications of the growth of wireless communication?
3. What are the social ramifications arising from the digital revolution?

THE BIRTH OF CYBER-RELATIONS

In many ways, the Internet and social media helped reduce the psychological distance that exists between an organization and the publics important to its success. Instead of being seen as a distant and obscure entity, the organization is now as close as the nearest Internet connection. It is as if the Internet has become the organization's new front door and its website the digital equivalent of the lobby, from which visitors are directed to various information sites within the organization.

Interactive websites allow visitors to communicate directly through e-mail links with key personnel within the organization. Through the integration of audio and video technology, visitors may be personally welcomed by the company CEO. For those looking for specific information, many websites are equipped with search engines that allow visitors to browse the entire site as well as company archives. Companies and organizations are connecting with key stakeholders through social media by developing large virtual communities of Facebook friends, YouTube channel subscribers, and Twitter followers. **RSS** feeds (Really Simple Syndication) can automatically send blogs, headlines, and other content to subscribers.

This has led to what we call **cyber-relations,** the use of public relations strategies and tactics to deal with publics via, and issues related to, the Internet.[32] Although cyber-relations does not exclude other forms of public relations, we use it to describe what has become a dynamic aspect of the practice of public relations with unquestionable social ramifications. With the rapid growth of the Internet over the past generation, practitioners have discovered that the Web is often both the cause of and the solution to the challenges they face.

Because the Internet is practically everywhere, it is an ideal medium for public relations practitioners. But the Web's omnipresence is also a challenge when it comes to targeting a specific audience. That's because different people use it in different ways. These differences were illustrated in *Generations Online in 2009,* a report issued by the Pew Internet & American Life Project. "Compared with teens and Generation Y (people born between 1977 and 1990), older generations use the Internet less for socializing and entertainment and more as a tool for information searches, e-mailing, and buying products," the report said. Online activities that teens and Generation Y dominate include watching videos, using instant messaging and social media sites, downloading music, and reading blogs. Older generations tend to search for health information, shop, bank, and seek spiritual information more than younger Internet users. According to Pew, some online activities previously dominated by either older or younger generations, such as using e-mail, researching products, and making travel reservations, are now being done more equally across almost all generations.[33] Research also suggests online gender differences: Men are more likely to turn to the Internet for financial or political information, whereas women are more likely to shop online or seek out religious or spiritual information.[34]

For an example of cyber-relations, you need look no further than one of the most basic tools on the public relations workbench, the news release. Not only has the method of distribution changed—e-mail versus so-called snail-mail—the structure is also changing to take advantage of digital technology. John Guiniven of Elon University wrote in *Public Relations Tactics* that reports of the death of the traditional news release "are greatly exaggerated." However, Guiniven also cautioned, "Social media releases are preferred by a growing number of journalists, particularly younger journalists in all media and practically all journalists in new media."[35] Social media releases can include imbedded hyperlinks that take the reader to supplemental information such as backgrounders, photographs, and video. "Including links to third-party sources does more than make life easier for reporters," writes Guiniven. "It adds credibility to your release and helps you control the debate over the issue that is the subject of the release."[36]

Another example of cyber-relations is **viral marketing,** the use of Internet-based platforms such as blogs, social-media sites, and e-mail to transmit messages along

QUICKBREAK 11.2

Making a Good First Impression

First impressions, it is said, are lasting. The first contact many people have with companies and organizations is on the Internet. Unfortunately, some of these websites do their creators more harm than good.

A problem with many well-intentioned websites is that their purpose is not well defined. A great advantage of the Internet is that it allows the delivery of multiple messages to multiple audiences. But who are these audiences, and what do you want to say to them? Unfortunately, many Web designers skip this crucial step. Internet researchers Candace White and Niranjan Raman have concluded that, in many cases, "website planning is done by trial and error, based on intuition, with little or no formal research."[37]

Websites can also assist in building and maintaining important relationships—especially in the area of media relations. However, an analysis of *Fortune* 500 company websites revealed that most were not being used to their full potential. Researcher Coy Callison said that journalists often complain that they can't find information they want and that "a few have even suggested that their coverage of companies with poor Web presence is skewed negative, if they cover these companies at all."[38]

This brings us to an important rule of Web design: Websites must be user-friendly. Just ask anyone who has spent time twiddling his or her thumbs waiting for a graphics-heavy page to download. Visitors should be able to find the information they want easily. Organizing the homepage by audience-specific categories is one way to achieve this. Another is to design pages that do not require the user to scroll down for additional information.

The website's hyperlinks should be carefully planned. "Developing your links strategy is one of the most crucial elements involved in Internet marketing," said Susan Sweeney, author of *101 Ways to Promote Your Web Site.* "Appropriately placed, links can be a real traffic builder."[39] Exchanging links with professional, business, and trade associations can help drive new visitors to your site.

Good writers always consider the medium. According to a study by Sun Microsystems, individuals take 50 percent longer to read from a computer screen than from a printed page.[40] Web writing consultant Sara Means Geigel noted, "You don't curl up with a website on your favorite chair or sofa or in bed to read it like a good book."[41]

Once the website is up and running, let people know about it. Place its address on all company communications. The site should also include easily accessible contact information. A good website that leaves a favorable first impression should be an integral part of an organization's branding. ∎

peer-to-peer channels. The concept is relatively simple: encouraging others to disseminate information through their own social networks in much the same way friends might share jokes, recipes, or the latest YouTube video. For example, following a 2003 outbreak of SARS, a potentially fatal flu-like virus, city and provincial officials

Federal Emergency Management Agency employees Ernie Martz (left) and Steve Crider record a podcast about flooding in Minnesota for distribution on the Internet. FEMA uses social media to deliver timely public information during disasters.

(Photo by Mike Moore, FEMA)

urged Toronto area residents to e-mail friends and relatives in the United States in an effort to stimulate the area's ailing tourism industry.[42]

Viral marketing can be a form of **word-of-mouth marketing** (WOMM), an effort to generate valuable third-party endorsements. "Nothing cuts through the weekly average of 35,000 marketing messages bombarding each of us like a friend or associate saying, 'You've just got to have dinner at my favorite restaurant' or 'I love my amazing product,'" said Ann Videan of vIDEAn Unlimited Marketing Connections. She said she frequently uses social media to create a community of "evangelists" for products and services."[43]

Virtual Public Relations

Another byproduct of the digital revolution is the emergence of **virtual public relations,** the networking of small, independent public relations consultants. Linked by telephones, fax machines, and the Internet, these informal practitioner networks successfully compete for business against traditional public relations agencies.

Here's how it works. A public relations consultant in Cincinnati has a client who needs to improve internal communications. This may require the services of a publications designer in Vancouver, a freelance writer in London, a Web developer

VALUES STATEMENT 11.1

INK Inc.

INK Inc., is a virtual public relations agency with its headquarters in Kansas City, Missouri—or wherever it chooses.

We Do the Job Others Can't

INK Inc. is a different kind of public relations firm. We don't bill by the hour, and we don't wax on for weeks about strategic positioning and research capabilities. We don't care about being the biggest firm with offices around the globe. We do care first and foremost about one thing above all else: achieving measurable results for clients.

Staffed exclusively by senior media professionals with actual newsroom experience, INK Inc. focuses on generating mainstream press coverage and placing stories in top-tier, national and international media. While we do offer a full range of services including broadcast production, writing, media training and special events, our specialty—and our bottom-line objective for every client—is publicity, or to put it bluntly, "getting ink."

—INK Inc., website ▨

in Sacramento, and an event planner in Charlotte. In many cases, these consulting arrangements are made on a project-by-project basis. However, in some virtual firms, such as INK Inc., of Kansas City, Missouri, these widely scattered practitioners are full-time employees of an agency, with its scattered operations linked by a secure intranet.

A reason for the growth of virtual public relations is its cost. "You can keep your overhead lower and pass that savings on to your clients," said Dick Grove of INK Inc. Virtual agencies offer client discounts of up to 40 percent over traditional firms by sharing the money they save on office space. When Internet security company nCipher Corp. Ltd. switched to a virtual agency, public relations manager Claire Collins said, "It was not important to us to see what kind of desks they had or what their lobby looked like to gauge the level of their work as PR professionals."[44]

Another reason virtual agencies are becoming more attractive is the freedom they give to practitioners. "I've never been very good in the corporate structure," said Grove. "People are not geographically dependent."[45]

 QUICK CHECK

1. What is cyber-relations?
2. What are the challenges of targeting specific publics on the Internet?
3. What is virtual public relations?

LIFE IN A DIGITAL WORLD

As anyone who has bought a new computer knows, technological change is so rapid that the computer is already outdated by the time you remove it from the box. During the digital revolution, change is the only constant. If public relations practitioners are to achieve success in this brave, new world, they must embrace and understand the changing environment. But this is about more than understanding technology. It is also about understanding the political, social, legal, and ethical ramifications of this change.

Courtesy of the U.S. State Department

Whenever we change the way we communicate with one another, that decision creates ripple effects that can change relationships. In a sense, we have to be more self-aware than ever before. How do these technological advances influence our messages? When we adopt new technology, we need to reevaluate whose needs are being served—ours, those of the targeted public, or both? How does the manner in which we communicate reflect our values? These are the questions we need to answer to live in a digital world. As always, the first step to finding answers is also the first step of the public relations process: research.

Individuals as Gatekeepers

In Chapter 5, we discussed the evolution of communication theory. As you might remember, theorists once believed that mass media could control the public opinion process. They thought editors at newspapers, magazines, and broadcast stations dictated what information people received and when they received it. However, the growth in communications technology changed all that. The magic bullet theory evolved into uses and gratifications theory—the belief that each person is his or her own information gatekeeper and picks and chooses from a wide variety of information sources.

What does this mean for public relations? For starters, **push technology**— a term that often means different things to different people—allows information to be automatically delivered or "pushed" directly to a user. By subscribing to various push services, individuals receive downloads of customized information. This can include news stories covering specific topics, sports scores, or the latest from the

QUICKBREAK 11.3

"I'm with Coco"

Although the brass at NBC sided with Jay Leno, the Twitterverse was decidedly "with Coco."

The concept of late-night television comedy took on new meaning in early 2010 when the peacock network unceremoniously ousted Conan O'Brien from his 11:35 p.m. Eastern time slot. Leno had handed the reins of *The Tonight Show* to O'Brien just seven months earlier. However, O'Brien trailed David Letterman's *The Late Show* in the ratings while those for Leno's nightly primetime show failed to meet expectations. Faced with the prospects of paying Leno an estimated $150 million to buy out his contract, NBC made what it thought was the most logical decision: Move Leno back to 11:35 p.m. and bump O'Brien and *The Tonight Show* to 12:05 a.m.[46]

The move may have made sense to the executives at "30 Rock" but was met with scorn in cyberspace. Immediately, dozens of pro-Conan protest groups appeared on Facebook. One of those upset by the late-night shake-up was Los Angeles artist Mike Mitchell. He posted a heroic sketch of the talk show host, one reminiscent of the Obama campaign's iconic "Hope" poster. Referring to one of O'Brien's nicknames, Mitchell added the words, "I'm with Coco."

"The idea started out as purely propaganda and somewhere down the line becoming an amalgam of propaganda and presidential campaign," Mitchell said. "I finished it at 1 a.m., posted it on Twitter, and I woke up the next day and it had already gone viral."[47]

Within days, the list of friends on the "I'm with Coco" Facebook page grew from a handful to more than 300,000. (By May 1, it had nearly 1 million friends.) On Twitter, people had a choice of joining either "Team Conan" or "Team Jay." According to Brian Roy, president of a social media monitoring company, it was "overwhelmingly Conan" on Twitter by a more than 50:1 ratio. *Advertising Age*'s Simon Dumenco wrote that O'Brien had become "an unlikely (Harvard-educated, multimillionaire) Everyman: the freckled face of American job insecurity."[48]

O'Brien had thrown down the gauntlet when he announced in a PR Newswire statement that he would not go along with the schedule change. In theory, NBC could have fired him for breach of contract. However, the network was losing the battle for public opinion. Hoping to avoid the negative publicity that accompanied Letterman's bitter exit from NBC in 1993, the network and O'Brien reached a reported $45 million settlement. Under the terms of the agreement, O'Brien agreed that he would not disparage either Leno or the network.[49]

Bill Carter, author of *The Late Shift*, a book that chronicled the Leno–Letterman controversy of 1993, wrote in the *New York Times* about the irony of the success of the "I'm with Coco" movement. "The online reactions highlighted the demographic gap between Mr. Leno's fans and the young tech-savvy fans of Mr. O'Brien," Carter wrote. "The plugged-in fans are not necessarily regular viewers; in fact, Mr. O'Brien fell short in NBC's attempt to gain younger viewers at 11:35 p.m."[50] ■

financial markets. If you represent a client that caters to people who travel extensively, a push service providing the latest in travel news and tips would be a cost-effective strategy for reaching this audience. What makes it most attractive is that it automatically delivers the information to an already receptive audience.

However, this also is an example of how communications innovations can mean both good news and bad news for public relations. Push technology can make it harder to get the attention of certain individuals. In the mass media, editors serve as information gatekeepers. But with push technology, individuals become their own editors. That can make reaching targeted publics more difficult. Opportunities for exposing your message may lessen, which, in turn, means making the best of the chances that remain.

Individuals as Publishers

Not only have individuals become information gatekeepers, they have also become self-publishers. Digital communications technology has made it possible for people to communicate more effectively and efficiently than ever before. In the past, if your campus organization wanted to typeset and print a meeting notice to post around campus, it was necessary to employ the services of a designer and the local photocopy shop. Today, those tasks can be accomplished by only one person using a laptop computer and a printer. In the past, if your organization wanted to contact a large number of people off campus, the job might require the use of direct mail, advertising, or telephone solicitations—expensive and time-consuming procedures. Today, e-mail and faxes can do the job cheaper and quicker, though they would reach smaller, more targeted publics. In the past, only media moguls had the resources necessary to reach a worldwide audience. Today, all you need is your own website.

Another popular form of Internet self-publishing is the **blog,** a regularly updated online diary or news forum that focuses on a particular area of interest. At first, most blogs were created by Web fanatics who had a story they wanted to tell. Blogs started catching on when reporters covering the Iraq war began posting their personal experiences. Employers have also begun to recognize their value as a communications tool. "Employer interest currently is the highest that I've ever seen it," said Google's Jason Shellen. "The interest is mainly in developing blogs as external communication tools with customers and clients, though some employers are beginning to consider ways they can use blogs internally."[51]

One reason practitioners find blogs attractive is that they target specific audiences. Some practitioners have begun pitching stories to bloggers with similar interests. However, before taking the plunge, practitioners should do their research, read through the blog, and determine whether its environment is right for their message.

A significant development in self-publication has been the introduction of wiki software that makes it easy for multiple people to author, edit, and remove online information. That's where Wikipedia, an online encyclopedia that contains articles from a community of contributors, gets its name. Although this collaborative authoring software has obvious advantages for internal communication, it has

TABLE 11.2

10 "Must Read" Public Relations Blogs

There are hundreds—perhaps thousands—of public relations blogs. This list represents a sampling of some of the most influential offerings. Although some focus on the latest industry news, others try to peer into the future. Although each has its own perspective, all share a passion for Digital Age public relations.

Blog	URL	What the bloggers say about themselves
PRoactive Report	www.proactivereport.com/	The blog is "about the shifts in the media landscape, social media strategy and online PR."
PR 2.0	www.briansolis.com/	"Brian Solis is globally recognized as one of the most prominent thought leaders and published authors in new media."
Richard Edelman – 6 A.M.	www.edelman.com/speak_up/blog/	"Richard Edelman is president and CEO of the world's largest independent public relations firm."
Strumpette – The Naked Journal of PR	strumpette.com/	"What you'll find here is an honest treatment of the PR business."
The Steve Rubel Stream	www.steverubel.com/	As Director of Insights for Edelman Digital, Rubel is "charged with helping clients identify emerging technologies and trends that can be applied in marketing communications programs."
The Buzz Bin	www.livingstonbuzz.com/	"It's not about being safe, it's about pushing the envelope, thinking and, hopefully, learning."
The Flack	theflack.blogspot.com/	"This weblog attempts to shine a brighter light on the subtle role public relations plays in politics, popular culture, journalism, business/finance, entertainment, technology, social media, consumer marketing and sports."

(continued)

TABLE 11.2 (*continued*)		
PRWeek Insider	www.prweekus.com/ prweek-insider/section/1255	"Over the years, *PRWeek* has established itself as a vital part of the PR and communications industries in the US, providing timely news, reviews, profiles, techniques, and timely research for in-house and agency professionals."
Strategic PR	prblog.typepad.com/	"Focused on strategy within integrated marketing communications."
The PRNews Blog	www.prnewsonline.com/prnewsblog/	"The latest news and strategies in PR and marketing."

been the use of **wikis** to create online social networks that has had the most profound effect.

Podcasts are another popular form of self-publication. They are audio and video files published online and downloaded by subscribers. (Video versions of podcasts are often referred to as *vodcasts*.) One of the most popular examples of a podcast service is iTunes, the Internet music and video provider. Podcasting sources range from individuals with something to say to giant corporations with something to sell (see Case Study 11.2). The value and technical quality of podcasts are as varied as the people who create them. Think of podcasts as online radio and television programs. The distribution of these programs is made possible through RSS (Really Simple Syndication), a computer programming language that simplifies downloading. In some instances, all the user has to do is connect an mp3 player to the computer—the software does the rest.

The dramatic growth in social media has resulted in a new phenomenon, the **citizen journalist.** Armed with cell phone cameras, wireless laptops, and wikis, ordinary people are changing the way news is covered. Though these citizens may not have been trained as journalists, the new technology allows them to bear witness to events that reporters often cannot.

This was made tragically apparent in April 2007 when a deranged gunman killed 32 students and professors on the Virginia Tech campus before turning the gun on himself. The most vivid images of that terrible day came from the cell phone camera of graduate student Jamal Albarghouti, who entered campus just as the shooting began. "His material is still the best of the day in terms of capturing on video what took place there," said Nancy Lane, CNN's vice president of domestic news.[52] The *San Francisco Chronicle* called the Virginia Tech shooting "the first major news story in which traditional media and new-media technologies became visibly interdependent."[53] When Virginia Tech students were not serving as the eyes and ears of an anxious world, they turned to social media such as Facebook and MySpace to console one another and let others know they were safe. Within 24 hours of the shootings, a Facebook group set up as a tribute to the victims had more than 130,000 members and 10,000 comments.[54]

As you can imagine, self-publication has a downside. The fact that everyone can become his or her own publisher doesn't necessarily mean that he or she should. It only takes a few minutes of Web surfing to realize that there are a lot of people on the Internet with nothing to say. And sometimes what they have to say is downright vicious. Numerous organizations, the subjects of grievances imagined or real, have been victims of what one author has called **cybersmears**—the use of the Internet to attack the integrity of an organization and/or its products and services.[55]

Cybersmear tactics include the creation of what are called **gripe sites.** One example is now-defunct "chasemanhattansucks.com," established by a disgruntled bank customer who said he had trouble removing an erroneous charge on his credit card account. What harm can one guy do? In its first two years of existence, that site recorded 300,000 hits.[56]

Perhaps an even bigger problem is that much of what is self-published, electronically or otherwise, does not go through the scrutiny that an editor applies to more traditional publications. Many self-published materials are inaccurate, incomplete, or biased, not to mention poorly written. Even Wikipedia acknowledges that information it receives from contributors may be inaccurate or open to substantially different interpretations.[57] Because of this, the need for constant monitoring of the Internet is growing. Organizations, especially publicly held companies, have a lot to lose from inaccurate information being flashed globally. The ease of self-publishing also brings into focus the need for rapid response plans to counter false or negative information on the Internet.

Internet pioneer Michael Dertouzos wrote before his death in 2001 that new communications technology will dramatically affect human behavior within organizations. With an increased ability to monitor all aspects of the organization, executives will be able to hold their employees more accountable for their actions. Dertouzos said this "will improve a firm's efficiency, even though its employees may be unhappy to have their individual work so open to inspection and critique."[58] Dertouzos also said the new technology will shift responsibility further down the corporate ladder, thus creating a greater need for employees to understand and embrace their organization's goals and values:

> For an organization to extract this increased decision power from its people, it will have to provide them with more knowledge about why some things are done and who does them, and why certain decisions are made and who makes them.[59]

With this growing reliance on employee communications, public relations will remain an important management responsibility in the 21st century.

QUICKBREAK 11.4

Flogging Walmart

The practice of using front organizations to hide the true source of communications goes back to the days of Edward L. Bernays. Unfortunately, a 21st-century version of this controversial and ethically questionable strategy has shed an unfavorable light on the world's largest retailer and one of the world's largest public relations agencies.

Walmart is unquestionably a financial success, with 803 discount stores, 2,747 Supercenters, 596 Sam's Clubs, and 158 Neighborhood Markets in 14 nations at the start of 2010.[60] During fiscal 2010, the company's net sales were a record $405 billion.[61] However, in its climb to the top, Walmart has made enemies. Complaints against the retail giant include low wages, the company's adverse effect on local retail stores, and the importation of cheap overseas products at the expense of U.S. manufacturing jobs. Legislators in Maryland passed a first-of-its-kind law in 2006 that would have forced Walmart to spend more on employee health care. Although the law was eventually struck down in two federal courts, the company knew it could be the target for further legislative assaults.[62]

Walmart launched a grassroots campaign to blunt its critics. Working with Edelman, a Chicago-based public relations agency, the company created Working Families for Walmart. Edelman Vice President Kevin Sheridan said WFWM would be "independent of the company" and "very transparent" in its dealings with the public and press.[63] When critics launched a bus tour publicizing their grievances against Walmart in 2006, WFWM launched its own bus tour. Using a recreation vehicle, "Laura" and "Jim" visited with Walmart shoppers from Nevada to Georgia. They kept company supporters abreast of their adventures with a blog.[64] Soon thereafter, a second blog, known as "Paid Critics," joined in the pro-Walmart chorus.

In one posting about the Maryland health-insurance controversy, blogger "Brian" wrote, "All across the country, newspaper editorial boards—no great friends of business—are ripping the legislation."[65]

To some, this kind of third-party endorsement seemed too good to be true. As things turned out, it was. Laura, Jim, and Brian were all Edelman employees. They had engaged in what critics call *flogging,* or false blogging. By failing to identify themselves as Edelman employees, they undermined the credibility of the company they were trying to help. The disclosure also hurt the reputation of Edelman, which was roundly criticized nationwide by public relations practitioners. CEO Richard Edelman apologized for what he said was an "error in failing to be transparent."[66]

"The shame is that if they'd been a little more up-front about the financial details of the [bus] trip, the integrity of the idea might have been protected," wrote Paul Parton of *Media Magazine.* "The thing I find staggering is that anyone really believed the ruse wouldn't eventually be uncovered."[67]

In its review of this and similar online deceptions, *Advertising Age*'s Noelle Weaver wrote, "The consumer is smarter than you think. Alternative marketing tactics must be genuine, authentic and in today's world, transparent."[68] ∎

QUICK CHECK

1. What are the benefits and risks of having individuals act as their own gate-keepers?

2. What are the benefits and risks of having individuals self-publish?

3. What are blogs? What do public relations practitioners see as their benefits?

Other Internet Issues

For all the possibilities created by the Internet, it is still not the answer to all the problems public relations practitioners face. Let's look briefly at a variety of Internet-related issues a practitioner should consider.

THE ONLINE GENERATION GAP   The next time someone says "everyone's on the Net," you should politely beg to differ. Although the number of senior citizens using the Internet is rising rapidly, the fact remains that most still are off-line. According to recent estimates, only 56 percent of persons ages 64–73 and 31 percent ages 73 and older are online. And although a higher percentage of persons 73 years and older use e-mail than teenagers, one researcher quipped, "Teens might point out that this is proof that e-mail is for old people."[69]

THE GLOBAL DIGITAL DIVIDE   More than half of people online globally speak either English or Chinese. English speakers are the largest group on the Internet, almost 496 million or 27.5 percent. Chinese is second 22.6 percent, followed by Spanish (7.8 percent), Japanese (5.3 percent) and Portuguese (4.3 percent). Despite a 400 percent growth in Internet access worldwide in the past decade, only one in four people on earth are online.[70] This uneven Internet access is known as the **digital divide,** and it has great social and economic ramifications for the future. In addition to access, cultural considerations exist. "[A] low context society, such as the United States, wants the essence of a message clearly and quickly," wrote researcher Augustine Ihator, "while [a] high context society, as in the Arab countries, appreciates the nuances and uses the physical context of the message to attribute meaning."[71]

INTERNET RESEARCH PROBLEMS   As a research tool, the Internet is, in many ways, a mile wide and an inch deep. For all the information readily available online, the total represents only a small fraction of what can be gathered through more traditional forms of research. For example, many libraries do not have the necessary resources to digitize everything in their archives; a lot of vital information exists in print and on the shelves, but not online. Also, more can be learned through a personal examination of historical artifacts than by looking at digitized pictures of them. In addition, although an overwhelming majority of investors turn to company websites to gather corporate information, a Burson-Marsteller study found that only one in five believes what he or she reads. Almost half of those polled said they considered newspapers and magazines to be the most credible source of information.[72]

UNWELCOME VISITORS Do you dread opening your e-mail in-box? Many do because of unsolicited **spam** e-mail, the cyberspace equivalent of junk mail. Spam has become so prevalent that it has created problems for legitimate Web users. For example, spam-filtering software can't always differentiate a mailing from an unwelcome marketer and one's own student organization. And who hasn't heard from a grieving relative of a former African ruler wanting to use your bank account number to move gold out of the country? Spamming doesn't build relationships—and can actually harm them. The Associated Press banned one public relations agency for sending too much "spam-like" e-mail.[73]

Another new headache is **spim,** the unwelcome commercial use of instant messaging. We must also guard against even more sinister visitors: **hackers,** who try to break into networked computer systems either to steal confidential information or just create mischief. And let's not forget the ever-dangerous **computer viruses** that can attach to a person's e-mail address book and spread to computers around the world, attacking data and causing incalculable personal and global economic damage.

PASSIVE COMMUNICATION It is important to remember that the Internet is a passive way for an organization to communicate. People have to go to a website; it does not automatically come to them. Although push technology allows organizations to send information via the Internet to subscribers, users must first sign up for the service. This is one of the reasons the Internet is best used as a component of a larger, integrated marketing communications plan (see Chapter 13).

CAREER IMPLICATIONS The rapid growth of the Internet has created a demand for college graduates capable of serving as Web masters. However, before you are tempted to skip all your other studies to focus on developing website programming skills, let us sound a cautionary note. One of the consequences of the advancement of technology is that, with the passage of time, it becomes more user-friendly. Because of advances in software, almost anyone can create his or her own website, thus pulling the rug out from under those who have only technical skills. Those who are more well rounded will be able to cope with this change and thrive. They are the folks who will be able to give websites substance. Therefore, the bottom line is that you should not give up on your studies quite yet.

 QUICK CHECK

1. When someone tells you that "everyone is on the Net," what can you say in response?
2. What is the global digital divide?
3. Why should you use other sources in addition to the Internet when conducting research?

WHY NEW ISN'T ALWAYS BETTER

The introduction of new communications technology does not automatically spell doom for the old. Let's go back to Gutenberg's invention of the movable-type printing press in 1455. Many at the time predicted that it would mean the end of handwritten text. However, it had just the opposite effect. As vast quantities of inexpensive reading materials became more accessible, literacy rates grew; and, in turn, so did the calligraphic arts. Similarly, audio books and downloadable digital books have not destroyed book sales. One book publishing trade association estimated U.S. book revenues at $40.3 billion in 2008; up more than 16 percent from 2005.[74]

The reason older technologies are able to survive the onslaught of newer technologies is that they are able to develop a niche in the New World Order. Despite their use of 18th-century technology, newspapers continue to publish in the 21st century. Why? Because they deliver something of value that consumers can't get elsewhere—in this case inexpensive and comprehensive coverage of local, regional, national, and global news. Similarly, although many people thought radio would fade into oblivion after commercial television was introduced to the United States in 1947, it didn't; instead, radio evolved from a national source of entertainment programming into a local source of music and information. And the beat goes on.

In a public relations context, the introduction of new communications technology has created new ways of reaching and being reached by targeted publics. It is hard to imagine what life for the public relations practitioner was like without fax machines, cell phones, e-mail, and satellite media tours. But even in this age of technological wonders, it is equally difficult to envision the practice of public relations without some of the old standbys such as brochures and good old-fashioned face-to-face communication. Dertouzos wrote, "The Information Marketplace must be supported with all the traditional methods for building human bonds, including face-to-face, real-life experiences, if it is to serve organizations as more than a high-tech postal system."[75] The real challenge for the future is to stay up to date on what is new without forgetting what has worked well in the past.

As with all communication, the choice of communications technology ultimately comes down to recognizing one's audience and purpose. Public relations practitioners must understand their audience and its values: What are its needs, what is its level of knowledge, and what are the best ways to reach it? Practitioners must also be clear about their values and purpose, especially because some media are better suited for certain purposes than for others. The choice of which technology to adopt rests more on whether the technology works than on whether it is new.

SUMMARY

The digital revolution has profoundly affected our personal and professional lives. It has resulted in the advent of online social media. It has also enabled a convergence of messages and images in multiple media and has created new social networks. The revolution has also forced traditional media to reinvent themselves and has had a profound effect on the practice of public relations. It has led to the creation of virtual public relations agencies that provide the same services as those of traditional agencies but at a fraction of the cost. For practitioners, the creation of new social networks brings both the benefits and risks that come with uncontrolled media. The challenge for the practitioner is to identify, monitor, and, if necessary, engage these networks.

Although the technology has brought many benefits, it also has raised a number of serious questions. Powerful channels of mass communication are being concentrated in the hands of relatively few corporations. In addition, issues of privacy, job security, and protection of intellectual property have come to the forefront. And although it is important to keep up with technological advances, it is also important to remember that when it comes to deciding strategies and tactics, new doesn't always mean better. Regardless of advances in technology, the decision about which message to deliver or which medium to use depends largely on the communicator's intended audience, purpose, and values.

DISCUSSION QUESTIONS

1. What are Web 2.0 and social media? How have they influenced the way people communicate?
2. In what ways has the introduction of digital communications technology influenced the practice of public relations?
3. What are some of the social ramifications of the digital revolution?
4. Name some considerations cyber-relations practitioners face when deciding whether to adopt new communications technology over more traditional channels.

MEMO FROM THE FIELD

CRAIG SETTLES
President; Successful.com
Oakland, California

As a broadband business strategist, marketing expert, author, and internationally renowned speaker, Craig Settles helps organizations use broadband technologies to improve government and stakeholder operating efficiency as well as local economic development. Settles is frequently called upon as a municipal broadband expert for journalists at CNN, the *Wall Street Journal, New York Times, Time,* and a host of business, technology, and local media outlets. He has spoken and chaired various conferences, including MuniWireless, the Wireless & Digital Cities Congress, and the North American Wireless Cities Summit. For more than 20 years, Settles has developed and executed innovative marketing campaigns for technology clients that include Microsoft, AT&T, and Symantec.

Social networks, particularly LinkedIn, Twitter, and Facebook, already play a key role in public relations for many professionals. That doesn't mean all the rules on effectively using these networks have been written. But there are some guideposts along these new stretches of the Information Highway you should note as you roll along.

Social networks enable two-way communication with the media and directly to the public you want to influence. They each have audiences that use the network for specific purposes and in distinct ways. Do some homework to learn these differences. Be clear in your strategy which audience you're trying to reach with what tactic. Communication is nearly instantaneous, far-reaching, and irreversible, so there's little room for errors.

LinkedIn, which is popular among managers, executives, and entrepreneurs, functions on the six-degrees-of-separation principle: no more than six layers of business/friend/family contacts separate you from anyone you want to meet. PR people use LinkedIn to build contacts with industry and/or market influencers. Some journalists use it, but I don't see as many there as on some of the other networks. Even fewer are the times I see it used to facilitate an introduction.

You can use some of the thousands of LinkedIn groups to reach hundreds of people at a time. There are often several for each industry or topic that your target audience finds interesting. You have to join the groups and become an active participant before you can reach out with effective results—or have your clients/senior executives join.

Many Twitter users are actually over 30, despite that service's attempt to come off as the domain of hip followers of sports and pop culture icons. It could be because Twitter enables older professionals to do the "old school" task they find most comforting: blast out lots of information (through heavy use of URL links) to audiences without having to engage in a lot of conversations. The 140-character limit discourages quite a few from replying to the person posting. However, a sizeable number of users do exchange thoughts, requests, and so on with each other, usually through direct messaging.

Twitter is great for keeping in touch with journalists, sometimes to reach out to them, but often to follow their writings so you can prepare more effective story pitches through other communication channels. It's great for getting breaking news ahead of the pack and monitoring developing trends. Clients and executives can use Twitter effectively by staking out an area of interest (need) and becoming a recognized expert in it through a regular stream of links to blogs, articles, columns, and so forth on this topic.

Facebook offers probably the broadest outreach. Almost all substantial media outlets have a Facebook presence even if their journalists don't engage there that much. Facebook can be a great catchall "outreach and update" tool for your business connections who don't use LinkedIn. Organizations can create pages that attract a lot of people who become your loyal fans and an audience to whom you can stream messages that support your PR campaign.

Despite its potential to boost your PR achievements, Facebook also can be the agent of your professional demise if you don't purge your college "Party Pics Greatest Hits" from this service. Social networks in PR can be, quite literally, your best friend and worst enemy, depending on how well you separate your social from your professional world. ■

CASE STUDY 11.1 It Can Happen to Anybody

Cyberspace can be unforgiving. Once you hit Enter or Send, you can't take it back. Once your e-mail, tweet, or instant message is gone, it's gone. And if you haven't chosen your words carefully or have been fast and loose with the facts, it doesn't take long for the whole world to know it. If you think mistakes can happen to anybody, that is exactly the point we want to make: Mistakes can and do happen to anybody.

Just ask Steve Rubel.

This is not to imply that Steve Rubel is *just* anybody. He is the senior vice president of Edelman Digital, the Internet and social media arm of one of the largest independent public relations agencies in the world. In fact, from 2004 to 2009, Rubel's *Micro Persuasion* blog was among the most influential on the Internet, with 50,000 readers daily. He also had 40,000 followers on Twitter and wrote a column for *Advertising Age.*

According to his Google profile, Rubel "studies emerging technologies, global media and online trends and shapes them into actionable insights and marketing communications strategies." It goes on to say, "Rubel's writings on emerging technologies and trends have been called must-read material by the *Wall Street Journal, Forbes, CNET, PC Magazine,* and *Forrester Research.*"[76]

Rubel's blog also was listed among *PC Magazine*'s "100 favorite blogs"—or at least it was until April 13, 2007, when a 15-word tweet drew the attention and ire of an important stakeholder. Responding to someone else's post about the irrelevancy of printed magazines, Rubel wrote, "PC Mag is another. I have a free sub but it goes in the trash."[77]

Because of who Steve Rubel is, a widely quoted expert on social media, the comment was bound to raise a few eyebrows. When one considers some of Edelman's clients—Microsoft, Palm, Mozilla, and Adobe—a backhanded swipe at the computer industry's leading publication with more than 11 million readers appeared to be a curious decision.

It certainly didn't sit well with Jim Louderback, editor-in-chief of *PC Magazine.* "When I saw the post, a torrent of thoughts flashed through my head," Louderback wrote in a guest column on the public relations blog *Strumpette.* "The first, of course, was to ring up the guys in the basement and cancel his free subscription.

"But then I started thinking about what this means for our relationship with Edelman. Did the rest of Edelman think like Steve? Were we no better than fishwrap to the entire company? Should I instruct the staff to avoid covering Edelman's clients? Ignore their requests for meetings, reviews, and news stories? Blacklist the 'Edelman.com' e-mail domain in our exchange servers?"[78]

Needless to say, Rubel got the message. And as any good public relations practitioner should do, he immediately apologized. "I have learned a valuable lesson," Rubel posted on his blog. "Post too fast without providing context and it can elicit an unintended response."[79] Rubel went on to say that although he didn't read the paper version of *PC Magazine,* he subscribed to the publication's RSS feeds and frequently cited the magazine in his own blog.

"My opinions and habits do not reflect the broader populace, our agency, or its clients," Rubel added. "While there is a subset of people who are reading blogs more than they do traditional media, magazines are in fact thriving. Therefore, the audiences that magazines like yours reach are important to our clients and agency."[80]

The good news for Rubel and Edelman is that the storm passed almost as quickly as it appeared. *PC Magazine* did not boycott the agency and kept *Micro Persuasion* on its "100 Favorite Blogs" list. Rubel ended his blog in June 2009 and focused his online publishing on one hub, *The Steve Rubel Stream.* At the bottom of its homepage is a disclaimer: "Note: Everything posted on this site is Steve's personal opinion. It does not represent the views of Edelman or its clients."[81] It serves as a cautionary reminder that when it comes to making gaffes in cyberspace, it can happen to anybody.

DISCUSSION QUESTIONS

1. Why do you believe the editor-in-chief of *PC Magazine* reacted so strongly to Steve Rubel's tweet?
2. What steps, if any, should social media users take to avoid incidents such as this?
3. Even with a disclaimer, is it possible for people to separate their expressed online personal opinions from those of their employer?
4. What degree of control, if any, should an employer have over employee use of social media? ∎

CASE STUDY 11.2 Corporate Podcasting

If you were Web surfing on February 10, 2005, and happened across the Oregon-based *Northwest Noise,* you might have thought the end of the world was near. The editor of the popular blog proclaimed, "Just now, as I look out my window and, yes, yes, there are pigs flying and a fat lady is singing,"[82]

What, you may ask, provoked such a reaction? That was the day General Motors entered the world of podcasting and, in turn, transformed what many saw as a vehicle for counterculture into a mainstream medium.

Podcasting, as both a term and practice, emerged in 2004. It is a marriage of the words *iPod,* Apple's revolutionary digital audio player, and *broadcasting.* Podcasts are audio files that sound like radio programs downloaded to computers or portable digital devices for on-demand listening. At the outset, podcasting was the domain of the eclectic, including what the *New York Times* described as "programs of weird monologists and couples capering, complaining and exposing their personal lives in ostentatiously appalling ways."[83] However, by April 2005, it was estimated that more than 6 million U.S. adults had downloaded podcasts— and that number was expected to grow rapidly.[84] The practice had become so prevalent that the editors of the *New Oxford American Dictionary* named *podcast* their Word of the Year for 2005.[85]

General Motors, for many a symbol of staid, conservative corporate values, entered the world of podcasting in connection with the 2005 Chicago Auto Show. In a five-minute presentation, GM North America President Gary Cowger introduced the 2006 Cadillac DTS and Buick Lucerne sedans. It was a no-frills production absent of music and sound effects.[86] Many in the podcast community were not impressed.

"Kinda looks like the time when ol' Dad put on the gangsta wear and hoodie, and tried to bust a rhyme," wrote software developer Dave Ritter. "You had to give him points for trying, but no matter how hard he tried to be hip, it wasn't going to fly."[87]

Despite the initial criticism of GM's first efforts in the new medium, the company logged approximately 10,000 downloads of the podcast within the first month of its release.[88] As the company increased both the quality and quantity of its podcast offerings, the number of downloads soared, an estimated 75,000 during August 2005.[89]

Although these figures look impressive, what do they *really* mean? As is often a challenge with many public relations tactics, the tangible impact of podcasting is difficult to measure. How can one equate downloads to sales figures, especially with high-end purchases such as automobiles? And as is true with any individual tactic that is part of an integrated marketing communications campaign, how does one measure its effectiveness in motivating the consumer when working in combination with other tactics?

"No one knows the impact of podcasts, or even how many hits constitute a success," said Travis Austin, director of creative services for the Washington-based Strat@comm agency. "Finding the right length and frequency to hold an audience in this format has not been established."[90]

Even with a lack of measurement, podcasts offer companies something they lack in traditional broadcast media. "Companies are completely losing control of their messages, and one way to get into the game is by blogging and podcasting," said GM Director of New Media Michael Wiley. "The companies that are early adopters stand tremendous opportunity to be winners in the long run."[91]

Other advantages to podcasts are that they are relatively inexpensive and their audience is self-selecting, meaning that people are already interested in the topic when they choose to download. "It is an interesting way to connect with niche audiences," Wiley said.[92]

Within a year of GM's first podcast, some of the biggest names in business and industry had jumped on the bandwagon. Disneyland celebrated its 50th anniversary with a series of podcasts recorded in the amusement park. The major broadcast networks began offering downloads of audio and video versions of their news and entertainment programming. IBM uses podcasts as an internal communications tool, one that reaches 7,000 employees weekly at an annual savings of $700,000 in conference-call costs.[93]

Some bloggers—including some on GM's *FastLane Blog*—said they feared the introduction of corporate marketing messages into what they saw as an alternative to commercial broadcasting. In other words, they were concerned that corporations will dominate the new medium. GM's Wiley's dismisses that argument, noting that the audience has ultimate control.

He said, "If you don't want to listen to it, don't."[94]

DISCUSSION QUESTIONS

1. What are the advantages and disadvantages of podcasting?
2. Does a traditional company such as General Motors take a risk in adopting cutting-edge communication tactics such as podcasting?
3. What differentiates a good podcast from a poor one?
4. Is podcasting a suitable tactic for both internal and external publics? ■

NOTES

1. David Carr, "How Obama Tapped into Social Networks' Power," *New York Times*, 10 November 2008, online, www.nytimes.com.
2. "Presidential Campaign Finance," Federal Elections Commission, online, www.fec.gov.
3. Monte Lutz, "The Social Pulpit: Barack Obama's Social Media Toolkit," Edelman, 2009, online, http://www.edelman.com.
4. Lutz.
5. Carr.
6. Lev Grossman, "Time Person of the Year—You," *Time*, 25 December 2006, 38–41.
7. Ibid.
8. "'There Is This Sense of Uncertainty': D.C. Roundtable Examines What's Ahead for the PR Profession," *Public Relations Strategist* (winter 2009): 12.
9. Augustine Ihator, "Corporate Communication: Challenges and Opportunities in a Digital World," *Public Relations Quarterly* 46, no. 4 (winter 2001): 15–18.
10. "There Is This Sense of Uncertainty," 9–10.
11. Amy Jacques, "What's Top of Mind Now for the Profession—and Where Are We Heading?"

Public Relations Strategist (spring 2009): 8. Brackets in original.
12. "There Is This Sense of Uncertainty," 9.
13. Nicholas Negroponte, *Being Digital* (New York: Knopf, 1995), 14.
14. Paul E. Ceruzzi, *A History of Modern Computing* (Cambridge, MA: MIT Press, 2003), 201–206.
15. Steve Lohr, "H. Edward Roberts, PC Pioneer, Dies at 68," *New York Times*, 2 April 2010, online, www.nytime.com.
16. "Twenty Impressive Internet Statistics," *Social Times*, WebMediaBrands, Inc, online, www.socialtimes.com/2010/02/20-impressive-internet-statistics/.
17. "Twenty Impressive Internet Statistics."
18. Lee Rainie, "Internet, Broadband, and Cell Phone Statistics," Pew Internet & American Life Project, 5 January 2010, online, www.pewinternet.org.
19. "Table 1120—Internet Access and Usage: 2008," U.S. Bureau of the Census, online, www.census.gov.
20. "Table 1119—Household Internet Usage by Type of Internet Connection and State: 2007," U.S. Bureau of the Census, online, wsww.census.gov.

21. "Table 1124—Online News Consumption by Selected Characteristics: 2000 to 2009," U.S. Bureau of the Census, online, www.census.gov.

22. "Quarterly Retail E-Commerce Sales, 4th Quarter 2009," U.S. Bureau of the Census, 16 February 2010, online, www.census.gov; and *E-Stats*, U.S. Bureau of the Census, 28 May 2009, online, www.census.gov/econ/estats/2007/2007reportfinal.pdf.

23. *College Textbooks—Enhanced Offerings Appear to Drive Recent Price Increases* (GAO-05-806), United States Government Accountability Office, July 2005.

24. Frances Cairncross, *The Death of Distance: How the Communications Revolution Will Change Our Lives* (Boston: Harvard Business School Press, 1997), 28.

25. Mathew Rose, "Miracle on the Hudson: The Lessons of Flight 1549," *Public Relations Strategist*, (spring 2009): 11.

26. Linnie Rawlinson and Nick Hunt, "Jackson Dies, Almost Takes Internet with Him," CNN, 26 June 2009, online, www.cnn.com.

27. Jeffrey Boase, John Horrigan, Barry Wellman, and Lee Rainie, "The Strength of Internet Ties," Pew Internet & American Life Project, 25 January 2006, online, www.pewinternet.org.

28. Miller McPherson, Lynn Smith-Lovin, and Matthew Brashears, "Social Isolation in America: Using Survey Evidence to Study Social Networks," *American Sociological Review*, 74, no. 4 (2009): 670–681.

29. Keith Hampton et al., "Social Isolation and New Technology," Pew Internet & American Life Project, November 2009, online, www.pewinternet.org.

30. Cecilia King, "Franken Presses Holder on Comcast–NBC Merger," *Washington Post*, 15 April 2010, online, www.washingtonpost. com. The Comcast–NBC Universal merger was under federal government review as this book went to press.

31. Paul T. Hill, review of *The Innovator's Dilemma, Education Week on the Web*, 14 June 2000, online, www.edweek.org/ew/ ewstory.cfm?slug= 40hill.h19.

32. David W. Guth and Charles Marsh, *Adventures in Public Relations: Case Studies and Critical Thinking* (Boston: Allyn & Bacon, 2005), 320.

33. Sydney Jones, *Generations Online in 2009*, Pew Internet & American Life Project, 28 January 2009, online, www.pewinternet.org.

34. "Internet Useage Over Time" database, Pew Internet & American Life Project, 15 July 2009, online, www.pewinternet.org.

35. John Guiniven, "Getting Social with Press Releases," *Public Relations Tactics*, November 2006, 6.

36. Ibid.

37. Candace White and Niranjan Raman, "The World Wide Web as a Public Relations Medium: The Use of Research, Planning, and Evaluation in Web Site Development," *Public Relations Review* 25, no. 4 (winter 1999): 405–419.

38. Coy Callison, "Media Relations and the Internet: How *Fortune* 500 Company Web Sites Assist Journalists in News Gathering," *Public Relations Review* 29 (2003): 29–41.

39. Joe Dysart, "Making the Most of Promotional Links," *Public Relations Tactics*, November 2002, 21.

40. Sara Means Geigel, "Web Writing That Wows," *Public Relations Tactics*, February 2003, 15.

41. Geigel.

42. Guth and Marsh, 312–316.

43. Ann N. Videan, "Consider Adding Word-of-Mouth Marketing Strategies to Your PR Mix," Independent Practitioners Alliance (blog), Public Relations Society of America, 15 September 2009, online, www.prsa.org.

44. Steve Jarvis, "Virtual Firms Win Respect for Performance, Savings Virtual Agencies Deliver Tangible Results," *Marketing News*, 8 July 2002, 4–5.

45. Dick Grove, telephone interview, 2 August 2004.

46. Bill Carter, "Conan O'Brien Opens Up about NBC Departure," *New York Times*, 30 April 2010, online, www.nytime.com.

47. Jon Chattman, "The Man Behind the 'I'm With Coco' Movement," *Huffington Post*, 5 February 2010, online, www.huffingtonpost.com.

48. Bill Carter.

49. Bill Carter.

50. Bill Carter.

51. Bill Leonard, "Blogs Begin to Make Mark on Corporate Communications," *HRMagazine* 48, no. 4 (September 2003): 30.

52. David Zurawik, "Eyewitness Testimonies and Footage Dominate News: Citizen Journalists, Online Communities Give Unique Perspective," *Baltimore Sun*, 17 April 2007, 8A.

53. Joe Garofoli, "Virginia Tech Massacre: New-Media Culture Challenges Limits of Journalism," *San Francisco Chronicle,* 20 April 2007, A1.

54. Mathew Ingram, "In a Crisis, a Wave of 'Citizen Journalism,'" *The Globe and Mail* (Canada), 18 April 2007, A15.

55. Nicole B. Cásarez, "Dealing with Cybersmear: How to Protect Your Organization from Online Defamation," *Public RelationsQuarterly* (summer 2002): 40–45.

56. Cásarez.

57. Wikipedia: About, online, http://en.wikipedia.org/wiki/Wikipedia:About.

58. Michael Dertouzos, *What Will Be: How the New World of Information Will Change Our Lives* (New York: HarperCollins, 1997), 210–211.

59. Dertouzos, 211–212.

60. SEC Form 10k, Wal-Mart Stores, Inc., 31 January 2010, http://investor.walmartstores.com.

61. Ibid.

62. Michael Barbaro, "Appeals Court Rules for Wal-Mart in Maryland Health Care Case," *New York Times,* 18 January 2007, C4.

63. Marilyn Geewax, "Spinning Wal-Mart—Retailer, Union Activists Wage High-Stakes PR Battle," *Atlanta Journal-Constitution,* 26 November 2006, 1C.

64. Geewax.

65. Michael Barbaro, "Wal-Mart Enlists Bloggers in P.R. Campaign," *New York Times,* 7 March 2006, online, www.nytimes.com.

66. Geewax.

67. Paul Parton, "The Consumer: Reining in the Flog," *Media Magazine,* December 2006, online, http://publications.mediapost.com.

68. Noelle Weaver, "What We Should Learn from Sony's Fake Blog Fiasco," *Advertising Age,* 18 December 2006, online, http://adage.com.

69. Sydney Jones.

70. "Top Ten Languages in the Internet," Internet World Stats, Miniwatts Marketing Group, online, www.internetworldstats.com/stats7.htm.

71. Ihator.

72. Howard Stock, "Web Site Users Don't Trust Corporate Content," *Investors Relations Business,* 27 October 2003, 1.

73. Susanne Fitzgerald, "Predictions for the New Millennium—Have They Come True?" *Public Relations Quarterly* 48, no. 4 (winter 2003): 28–30.

74. "*Book Industry Trends 2009 Indicates Publishers' Net Revenue Up 1.0% in 2008 to Reach $40.32 Billion,*" news release issued by Book Industry Study Group, 29 May 2009, online, www.bisg.org.

75. Dertouzos, 205.

76. Steve Rubel profile, Google, online, www.google.com/profiles/steverubel#about.

77. Jim Louderback, "*PC Magazine* Considers Edelman Boycott," *Strumpette,* 17 April 2007, online, http://strumpette.com.

78. Jim Louderback.

79. Steve Rubel, "Open Letter: A Lesson Learned Twittering," *Micro Persuasion,* 17 April 2007, online, http://www.micropersuasion.com/2007/04/open_letter_les.html.

80. Steve Rubel.

81. The Steve Rubel Lifestream, online, http://www.steverubel.com.

82. "GM Starts a Podcast," *Northwest Noise,* 10 February 2005, online, www.northwestnoise.com.

83. Virginia Heffernan, "The Podcast as a New Podium," *New York Times,* 22 July 2005, E1.

84. "Data Memo: Podcasting," Pew Internet & American Life Project, April 2005, online, www.pewinternet.org.

85. Nathan Bierma, "At Random—'Podcast' Is Word of the Year," Knight-Ridder/Tribune Business News wire, 28 December 2005, LexisNexis.

86. John Couretas, "Podcast Is New GM Marketing Tool," *Automotive News,* 14 March 2005, 25.

87. Jamie Smith Hopkins, "Corporations Podcast Their Marketing Nets," Knight-Ridder/Tribune Business News wire, 11 December 2005, LexisNexis.

88. Couretas.

89. Hopkins.

90. John Guiniven, "Podcast as a PR Tool: What Do You Need To Know?" *Public Relations Tactics,* September 2005, online reprint, www.prsa.org.

91. Hopkins.

92. Couretas.

93. Hopkins.

94. Couretas.

12

Crisis Communications

OBJECTIVES

After studying this chapter, you will be able to

- understand what crises are and how they develop
- recognize that crisis situations often create opportunities
- appreciate the importance of anticipating crises and planning for them before they happen
- explain the elements of an effective crisis communications plan

KEY TERMS

apologia, p. 384
cleanup phase, p. 370
credentialing, p. 381
crisis, p. 368
crisis communications planning, p. 377
crisis impact value (CIV), p. 378
crisis management team (CMT), p. 377
crisis manager, p. 379
crisis planning team (CPT), p. 376
crisis plotting grid, p. 378

REAL WORLD

The Rumor

You are the head of corporate communications for a company that produces one of the nation's most popular snack foods. The company prides itself on making products that are both delicious and nutritionally sound. In your advertising, you brag of using only natural ingredients with no artificial flavorings or other additives.

Recently, a rumor cropped up on the Internet asserting that a leak from a nearby nuclear power plant has made most of your company's snack foods radioactive. Officials at the nuclear power plant say there has been no such leak. Despite this reassurance, the company has noticed a small decline in sales. To make matters worse, a producer from a nationally syndicated tabloid television show has called and wants to know whether it is true that the company's snack food products glow in the dark.

What are you going to do?

THE STORM BEFORE THE STORM

It was the disaster everyone feared. The massive hurricane slammed the Louisiana coast with sustained winds of 120 miles per hour and up to 20 inches of rain. The storm surge topped levees in low-lying New Orleans, leaving portions of the city under 10–12 feet of water and thousands of people stranded on rooftops or trapped by floodwaters. Transportation in and out of the city was severely restricted by flooding or a shortage of fuel. Hospitals and other medical services were closed or cut off by the rising tide. Usually reliable communications networks failed.[1] New Orleans was dying, and there was little anybody could do about it.

Although this might sound like Hurricane Katrina, which ravaged much of the U.S. Gulf Coast in late August 2005, it is not. This is the scenario for Hurricane Pam, a fictitious storm simulation created by Baton Rouge–based Innovative Emergency Management, Inc., for a five-day training exercise for 270 representatives of local, state, and federal agencies. The purpose of the exercise was to learn what might happen if the much-feared "big one" made a direct hit on the Crescent City. More important, officials hoped to learn the steps they could take to minimize, if not eliminate, the threats posed by a Hurricane Pam–like storm.[2] The simulation occurred almost one year to the day *before* Katrina.

A FEMA Urban Search and Rescue task force member rescues a New Orleans resident from his flooded neighborhood. Despite this and countless other acts of heroism, emergency response officials were widely criticized for what many viewed as an inadequate response to Hurricane Katrina.

(Courtesy of Jocelyn Augustino, Federal Emergency Management Agency)

IEM consultants developed a 109-page report, "Southeast Louisiana Catastrophic Hurricane Functional Plan," within a few weeks of the exercise. In it, they described a scenario that eerily paralleled the human tragedy that played out in the streets of New Orleans less than a year later. In an ironically accurate prediction, state and federal officials concluded "the gravity of the situation calls for an extraordinary level of advance planning to improve government readiness to respond effectively to such an event." However, Katrina struck before the officials put the plan into action.

"We were still fairly early in the process," said IEM President Madhu Beriwal. "This was part of FEMA's initiative for doing catastrophic disaster planning. New Orleans was picked as the first place to be studied."[3]

Not Just Bad Luck

Hurricane Katrina was the worst natural disaster in U.S. history. It is easy to rationalize that people have no control over the forces of nature. It is also tempting to suggest that the onset of Katrina before officials had time to implement their newly minted emergency response plan was just a stroke of bad luck. But was it?

The dangers confronting New Orleans, much of which is situated precariously below sea level, had been well known for decades. Even in the days before the deadly storm made landfall, Dr. Max Mayfield, director of the National Hurricane Center, warned Federal Emergency Management Agency (FEMA) and Department of Homeland Security officials of the potential for a catastrophe. "It's not like this was a surprise," Mayfield said. "We had in the advisories that the levee could be topped."[4]

What happened next—as documented in Case Study 1.2—has been the subject of rancorous political debate, heated recriminations, and a slew of investigations. Local, state, and federal emergency management officials often took actions that were either too little or too late to make a difference. Although the death toll from Katrina was a fraction of that predicted by the Hurricane Pam scenario, it still exceeded 1,800 throughout the region. Although the media had a difficult time separating fact from fiction, the lasting image of the government's response was thousands of people stranded on rooftops or at the battered Louisiana Superdome pleading for help five days after the storm had passed. Regardless of whose version of the events one may choose to believe, there is an undeniable fact: a widespread belief that people charged with the responsibility of protecting their fellow citizens had failed in their duties when they were needed most.

The Katrina fiasco was not just an emergency management failure. It was a public relations failure. Central to the Gulf Coast tragedy was the failure to manage relationships among key stakeholders, including other public and private response agencies, the residents of the region, and the news media. "Communications is the glue that holds a crisis response together," said Kathy Baughman of HLB Communications in Chicago. "Without it, chaos quickly ensues, which, of course, was the case in the immediate aftermath of Katrina."[5]

"When action and communications are inconsistent, credibility goes out the door, and the public's trust disintegrates," said Dan Keeney of Texas-based DPK Public Relations. "You can't say that everything that can be done is being done while failing to deliver basic necessities to crowds of people."[6]

Part of the failure can be blamed on the reorganization of the federal government's emergency response apparatus following the terror attacks of September 11, 2001. Prior to that date, FEMA was a stand-alone agency with established relationships with other public and private agencies. That changed in 2002 with the creation of the Department of Homeland Security, an umbrella agency designed to coordinate the government's response to all public safety threats, especially terrorism. Several experts have said that this reshuffling of the federal bureaucracy disrupted long-existing relationships, many of which had not been adequately reestablished by the time of Katrina.

The reorganization also had another unintended consequence: a failure of values. Christopher Cooper, a *Wall Street Journal* reporter who has coauthored a book highly critical of the federal government's response, said that Homeland Security officials, who he said had a mind-set that "natural disasters are for pansies, and real men handle the terrorist stuff," undervalued FEMA's mission.[7] Michael Brown, the ex-FEMA director who many see as a central villain in the Katrina drama, has since told audiences that Homeland Security Secretary Michael Chertoff was "clueless" and that President Bush had turned "a deaf ear" to his concerns about FEMA's ability to handle major disasters.[8]

It is unfair to say that emergency management officials were totally unprepared for Hurricane Katrina. Nor would it be fair to suggest that they didn't do anything right. The truth is that they did a lot of things right: sheltering and feeding hundreds of thousands of evacuees, rescuing countless others, and mobilizing the largest relief effort in the nation's history. However, the storm exposed serious weaknesses. There was a failure of planning, evidenced by the slow response to the recommendations arising from the Hurricane Pam exercise. There was a failure to build and maintain relationships among the members of the emergency response community. Local, state, and federal officials should have spent less time pointing fingers of blame and more time talking to one another. There was also a failure of values. It didn't matter whether the threat came from Al Qaeda or Mother Nature, the priority for government officials was to protect their people. Unfortunately, on that count, they fell short.

The April 2010 explosion and sinking of the BP-licensed Deepwater Horizon drilling rig killed 11 people. Federal officials estimated that 4.9 million barrels of oil spilled into the Gulf of Mexico before the leak was plugged. The crisis was an environmental and economic disaster for the Gulf Coast. It was also a public relations nightmare for BP, which often came across in public statements as defensive and callous.

(Courtesy U.S. Department of Defense)

Crises Can Happen to Anyone

The unforgiving truth is that bad things do happen to good people. When we hear of misfortune happening to others, we may easily rationalize that "it couldn't happen here." However, recent history suggests otherwise:

- When Lehman Brothers, a global financial-services company, filed for bankruptcy in September 2008, it triggered the world's worst economic recession since the Great Depression of the 1930s.[9]
- On Valentine's Day 2008, a man armed with a shotgun stepped onstage in a Northern Illinois University lecture hall. Before fatally shooting himself, the man killed five people and wounded 16 others.[10]
- A Minneapolis highway bridge first buckled and then plunged into the Mississippi River without warning during evening rush hour in August 2007. Thirteen people died, and 145 were injured.[11]
- An April 2010 explosion on an oil well in the Gulf of Mexico resulted in 11 deaths and an environmental disaster. Despite British Petroleum's claims that its response was a "model of social responsibility," negative public opinion eventually forced CEO Tony Hayward's resignation.[12]
- As a result of a November 2009 one-car traffic accident and subsequent revelations of marital infidelity, Tiger Woods—one of the most intelligent, popular, and business-savvy athletes of his generation—saw his public approval ratings plummet to 15 percent.[13]

If anything, these and other incidents testify to this reality: Anything can happen. However unexpected, the sad truth is that most crises are not wholly unpredictable. Perhaps even sadder is the fact that many, if not most, are avoidable. By identifying and analyzing potential risks, we can eliminate many crises before they ever happen. With crisis planning, we can mitigate the damage when crises do occur.

 QUICK CHECK

1. Because people have no control over the forces of nature, is it fair to criticize public officials for the problems they had responding to a massive storm like Hurricane Katrina?
2. Was there a failure of values in governmental responses to Hurricane Katrina?
3. Are most crises unpredictable and therefore unavoidable?

THE ANATOMY OF A CRISIS

"If economics is the dismal science," disaster recovery consultant Kenneth Myers writes, "then contingency planning is the abysmal science. No one likes to look into the abyss."[14] But like it or not, crisis planning has become an imperative in the 21st century for big and small organizations alike. "Any small business owner who doesn't have a crisis management plan is derelict in his duties," says Martin Cooper of Cooper Communications in Encino, California.[15] As researchers Donald Chisholm and Martin Landau have pointedly noted, "When people believe that because nothing has gone wrong, nothing will go wrong, they court disaster. There is noise in every system and in every design. If this fact is ignored, nature soon reminds us of our folly."[16]

A series of surveys over the past two decades has unearthed a surprising pattern: Despite warning after warning, many organizations remain unprepared for crises and their consequences. In research conducted in the 1980s and 1990s, just over half of the organizations surveyed said they had written crisis plans. Only one third of them said they had practiced them.[17]

One could logically assume that the 2001 terror attacks would have been a wake-up call. However, that does not appear to be the case. In a survey of IABC members conducted years later, one in three of the respondents indicated that they had no crisis communications plan in place. Almost half of those who said they had been unprepared reported being forced to cobble a plan together quickly when a crisis struck.

QUICKBREAK 12.1

Textbook Examples: Exxon and Tylenol

Whenever people discuss the right way and the wrong way to conduct crisis communications, two names inevitably enter the conversation: Exxon and Tylenol.

Although both incidents date back to the 1980s, their lessons stand the test of time. In fact, much of the growth in the science and practice of crisis communications can be traced to the spectacular successes and failures of these two companies. They constitute what we call—somewhat apologetically—textbook examples of crisis communications.

No one wants to be remembered for being the poster child for how *not* to act during an emergency, but that is the woeful legacy of Lawrence G. Rawl. He was chairman and chief executive officer of the Exxon Corporation when one of its tankers, the *Exxon Valdez*, spilled 11 million gallons of crude oil into the pristine waters of Alaska's Prince William Sound. Oil contaminated shorelines nearly 600 miles from where the tanker ran aground just after midnight on March 24, 1989.

Rawl declined to go to the accident site. Critics said he should have gone to Alaska and personally taken charge of the cleanup. "From a public relations standpoint, it probably would have been better if I had gone up there," Rawl later told *Fortune*. "But I would have used up a lot of people's time."[18]

Rawl waited one week before making his first public comment, in which he blamed U.S. Coast Guard and Alaskan government officials for holding up the cleanup. He came across in television interviews as combative, ill at ease, and unprepared. Exxon newspaper advertisements apologized for the oil spill but did not take responsibility for it. When the company announced that it would pass along spill-related expenses to customers as a "cost of doing business," angry consumers returned more than 45,000 credit cards.[19]

(continued)

In an interview two months after the accident, Rawl said the spill and subsequent lawsuits would cost Exxon less than $1 billion.[20] In fact, a federal judge in Anchorage imposed $4.5 billion in punitive damages against Exxon in January 2004 on behalf of 32,000 fishermen and residents who had sued the company 15 years earlier. Exxon said it would appeal the decision.[21]

The actions of James E. Burke stand in sharp contrast to those of Rawl. Burke was CEO of Johnson & Johnson when one of its most successful products, Tylenol, was involved in deadly product tampering crises in 1982 and 1986. On both occasions, Tylenol capsules were laced with cyanide by unknown perpetrators and placed on store shelves. Seven people died in the two incidents.

Within two weeks of the first Tylenol tampering incident, the value of Johnson & Johnson stock dropped $657 million. It was also estimated that the company had received as much as $300 million worth of negative publicity.[22]

The Food and Drug Administration advised against a massive product recall out of fear that doing so might spawn "copycat" crimes. However, Johnson & Johnson officials said they had no choice but to demonstrate their concern for consumer safety by recalling their product: Their values statement placed customer safety above all else. To further calm an uneasy public, Tylenol capsules were placed in triple-sealed safety packaging after the first incident. After the second, Johnson & Johnson replaced the capsule with tamper-proof caplets.

Burke took another important step to maintain his company's credibility. Early Johnson & Johnson statements indicated that no cyanide was present in its manufacturing plants. However, that statement was wrong. Rather than risk discovery of this potentially damaging fact, the company immediately issued a news release correcting the error.

The textbook lessons of Exxon and Tylenol are clear. Companies that communicate quickly and compassionately with their stakeholders during crises have a far greater chance of saving their reputation—and their bottom line—than those that don't. People are more forgiving of those who admit their mistakes and move quickly to correct them than those who refuse to be held accountable and try to blame others. When the heat is on, success goes to those who keep cool and adhere to their values. ■

According to Robert J. Holland and Katrina Gill, the study's authors, "54 percent of the communicators who work in organizations without a crisis communications plan said it is because senior management there does not consider it a priority."[23]

What Is a Crisis?

The word *crisis*, just like the term *public relations*, is often misused by those who do not know it has a specific meaning. Everyone instinctively understands that flash floods, hurricanes, and earthquakes can usually be classified as crises. But what about a flat tire, missed homework, or being stood up on a date? Are these crises, too?

The difference between a **problem** and a **crisis** is a matter of scope. Problems are commonplace occurrences and fairly predictable. They usually can be addressed in a limited time frame, often without arousing public attention or without draining an organization's resources. On the other hand, crises tend to be less predictable. They require a considerable investment of time and resources to resolve and often bring unwanted public attention. And more than problems, crises can challenge an organization's core values.

Researchers Thierry C. Pauchant and Ian I. Mitroff have written that a crisis is "a disruption that physically affects a system as a whole and threatens its basic assumptions, its subjective sense of self, its existential core."[24] According to Pauchant and Mitroff, crises can threaten the legitimacy of an industry, reverse the strategic mission of an organization, and disturb the way people see the world and themselves.[25]

Steven Fink, a noted crisis consultant, has characterized crises as being prodromal situations (situations often marked by forewarning) that run the risk of

- escalating in intensity
- falling under close media or government scrutiny
- interfering with the normal operations of business
- jeopardizing the positive public image enjoyed by a company and its officers
- damaging a company's bottom line[26]

Laurence Barton refines the terminology even further, describing a crisis as a major event that "has potentially negative results. The event and its aftermath may significantly damage an organization and its employees, products, services, financial condition, and reputation."[27]

Crisis Dynamics

As you might imagine, crises come in many shapes and sizes. They can also influence public perceptions of organizations in vastly different ways. Some crises cast organizations in the role of *victim*. In other crises, organizations may be seen as the *villain*. And in a few cases, well-prepared organizations have emerged from crises in the role of *hero*.

Most people would rather be seen as a hero than as either a victim or a villain. At the same time, many people operate under a false assumption that crises and their consequences are unavoidable. However, public relations practitioners can do much to influence events before they happen and, in some instances, to avert crises altogether. That role of public relations is a focus of this chapter.

But before trying to change the course of events, we should understand the dynamics of a crisis. It is a mistake to believe that crises operate as randomly as next week's lottery. In fact, they follow predictable patterns. Although various researchers have adopted different terminology to describe these patterns, there is general agreement that crises tend to develop in four stages (Figure 12.1):

1. **Warning stage:** In reality, most crises don't "just happen." Usually, there are advance signs of trouble. At this stage, it may still be possible to avoid trouble, but the clock is ticking. This is a period in which we can be proactive and control

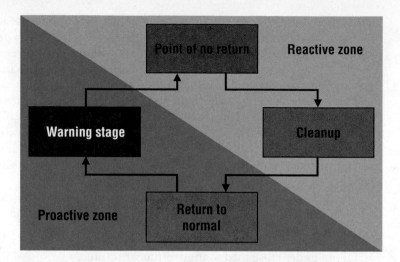

FIGURE 12.1
Crisis Dynamics

events *before* they happen. However, one of the greatest challenges in crisis communications is to recognize the potential for danger and then to act accordingly.

2. **Point of no return:** At this moment, the crisis is unavoidable, and we are forced to be reactive. Some damage will be done. How much remains to be seen and depends, to a large degree, on the organization's response. This is often the time when most of the stakeholders critical to the success of the organization first become aware of the crisis. And from this point on, they are watching very closely.

3. **Cleanup phase:** Even when the point of no return has been reached and the public spotlight shines upon the organization in crisis, an opportunity to minimize the damage remains. How long this period will last depends on how prepared the organization is to deal with the crisis. The cleanup phase is also a period of recovery and investigation, both internal and external. Fink says this is often the point at which the "carcass gets picked clean."

4. **Things return to normal:** If *normal* is defined as returning to the way things were before the crisis, then things probably will never be normal again. Following a crisis, operations may differ radically from before. New management may be in place. In addition to these changes, it is very likely that the organization learned valuable lessons. A vigorous evaluation of the organization's performance in dealing with the crisis can result in plans for coping with—or avoiding—the next crisis.

This brings us to an important point: The crisis dynamics model implies that this is a cyclical process, one in which we automatically move from one crisis to another. However, that doesn't have to be the case. Management has at least two opportunities to take steps to minimize or eliminate crises. One is identifying the warning signs of a looming crisis and taking forceful action before reaching the point of no return. The other comes after the crisis, when things return to normal. Management should then take the time to evaluate its performance and apply the lessons it learned. But if no such evaluation occurs, management runs the danger of making the same mistakes and creating a new crisis. After all, history has a tendency to repeat. Just ask NASA.

A Tale of Two Shuttle Disasters

Two dates are forever burned into NASA's collective consciousness: January 28, 1986, and February 1, 2003. On the first date, the space agency experienced its first fatal in-flight accident, when seven astronauts died in the explosion of the space shuttle *Challenger* shortly after liftoff. Seventeen years and four days later, another seven astronauts were lost when the space shuttle *Columbia* disintegrated during reentry following what had been a successful 17-day mission in Earth orbit.[28]

Although both tragedies came as a complete surprise to most people, a handful of NASA insiders knew that both shuttles had experienced problems that could lead to a catastrophe. Investigations of both accidents would attribute the failures, in part, to a NASA corporate culture known as "go fever": a strong desire to accomplish mission objectives on schedule without regard to NASA's long-standing value of putting safety first. In its report, the *Columbia* Accident Investigation Board said the disaster was "likely rooted to some degree in NASA's history and the human space flight program's culture."

However, from a public relations perspective, major differences separated the *Challenger* and *Columbia* accidents. Let's compare the two events and NASA's response to them during each of the four stages of crises.

WARNING STAGE

- *Challenger:* The explosion was caused by a failure of O-rings that sealed sections of the shuttle's solid-rocket boosters. The escaping propellant had the same effect on the shuttle's external fuel tank as a blowtorch on a gas tank. Engineers had identified the problem six months earlier and debated it as late as 12 hours before launch.
- *Columbia:* The shuttle's fate was sealed during liftoff when a chunk of insulating foam broke off the external fuel tank and struck the orbiter's left wing at almost 600 mph. It damaged some of the external tiles designed to protect the shuttle from the searing heat of reentry. NASA officials knew of the incident. After an internal debate, they decided that it did not pose a threat to the shuttle and its crew.

POINT OF NO RETURN

- *Challenger:* The shuttle exploded 71 seconds into the flight. The explosion was witnessed by millions on live television—including thousands of schoolchildren following the exploits of Christa McAuliffe, the first participant in NASA's Teacher in Space program.
- *Columbia:* The first signs of trouble appeared when temperature gauges on the left wing failed during reentry. Within a few minutes, all voice contacts

and data were lost. Simultaneously, people on the ground watched a blazing trail of debris following the shuttle's flight path. Television cameras captured the disintegration of the orbiter over Texas.

CLEANUP PHASE

- *Challenger:* Despite a crisis plan that required an announcement of an in-flight death or injury within 20 minutes, NASA was silent for five hours. When officials held their first postaccident news conference, they promised a thorough investigation. But even then, they gave no information on the fate of the crew. That was left to President Ronald Reagan, who addressed a grief-stricken nation more than five hours after the explosion.

- *Columbia:* Within 15 minutes of the loss of shuttle data, NASA declared a "Shuttle Contingency" and posted an announcement on the agency's website. Within 30 minutes, NASA spokesman Kyle Herring told NBC, "Obviously it is the break-up of something, and based on the timing it is more than likely that, yes, that is the shuttle."[29] Within four hours, President George W. Bush spoke to the nation, followed by NASA Administrator Sean O'Keefe. NASA then began a series of technical briefings on the accident.

NASA Administrator Sean O'Keefe (center) briefs reporters on the investigation into the loss of the space shuttle *Columbia* and its seven-person crew. The agency's handling of media relations during this crisis contrasted sharply with relations following the *Challenger* accident.

(NASA—Kennedy Space Center)

THINGS RETURN TO NORMAL

- *Challenger:* NASA's poor response to the crisis and subsequent loss of public confidence led to a White House decision to take the investigation out of the space agency's hands. An independent panel sharply criticized NASA management, resulting in the premature end of many promising careers.
- *Columbia:* NASA's quick response won it public praise. More importantly, it was allowed to conduct its own investigation of the accident. Although the investigating board criticized NASA for "cultural traits and organizational practices detrimental to safety," the agency avoided the traumatic restructuring it had faced 17 years earlier.

That NASA won public praise for its response to the *Columbia* tragedy brings us to what may be the most important lesson in crisis communications: Not all outcomes of crises have to be bad. In fact, when managed properly, crises can bring opportunity.

Crises Can Bring Opportunity

Gerald C. Meyers, a former automobile industry executive who has written and lectured extensively on the subject of crisis communications, says a "window of opportunity" opens during the warning and point-of-no-return stages of crises.[30]

QUICKBREAK 12.2

A Porcine Problem

It is ironic that efforts to avert one crisis can precipitate another. Just ask Chris Chinn.

Chinn is a fifth-generation hog farmer in northeast Missouri. He, along with other pork producers, lost a lot of money during 2009 as a result of falling demand and plunging prices. Chinn and his fellow pork producers laid a lot of blame on health communicators for what they say was an inaccurate labeling of a highly contagious and deadly disease. Government officials now refer to it as the H1N1 virus. But, in the early days of the pandemic, they called it swine flu.

"We can't get people who don't have a direct link to agriculture to realize the harm it is having," Chinn said. "They don't realize what impact that name has had."[31]

Whether it is called H1N1 or swine flu, one thing is certain: It is bad news. The 2009 outbreak first appeared in Mexico. The European Center for Disease Prevention and Control estimates that it claimed 14,286 lives worldwide—2,328 in the United States—in the first year since its detection.[32]

Once they identified the threat, public health communicators immediately launched strategies to minimize its spread. Typical were the efforts of the Centers for Disease

(continued)

Control, which used a variety of traditional and social media to encourage people to take preventive steps such as covering mouths while coughing and washing hands after visiting the rest room. The CDC used social media to knock down rumors and misinformation. Within the first six months of 2009, 90,000 at-risk persons were vaccinated. [33]

"The CDC's performance so far is likely to boost confidence in the government's ability to handle pandemics, and its use of social networks has been a big part of its strategy," wrote Chuck Raasch in *USA Today*.[34]

Unfortunately for pork producers, the successful publicity campaign had unintended side effects. People began to shy away from eating pork products out of an unfounded fear of contracting the disease, which can be transmitted only from human to human. The *Wall Street Journal* reported that the drop in demand, along with bans on U.S. exports, caused an estimated $270 million loss for the nation's pork industry in the second quarter of 2009.[35]

Under pressure from pork producers, the CDC stopped calling the affliction by its porcine moniker and began using its more clinical name, H1N1 influenza.

"In the public, we've been seeing a fair amount of misconception, that by calling it swine flu, there could be transmission from pork products," said CDC Acting Director Richard Besser. "And that's not helpful to pork producers."[36]

During these stages, key stakeholders tend to sit back and withhold their judgment while placing the organization in crisis under close scrutiny. How long the window of opportunity remains open depends on the organization's reputation.

Meyers says seven potential benefits can be reaped from a crisis:[37]

1. *Heroes are born.* Crises can make people the focus of public attention. Those who respond well to that scrutiny are often seen as heroes.
2. *Change is accelerated.* People and organizations resist change. When change is suggested, you often hear, "But we have always done it this way." Crises often finally compel organizations and individuals who have lagged behind various social and technological trends to change the way they do things.
3. *Latent problems are faced.* When things are going well, it is easy to ignore some problems. This fact is reflected by the "if it ain't broke, don't fix it" mentality. During crises, however, organizations often have no choice but to tackle these problems head-on.
4. *People can be changed.* This item has a double meaning. On the one hand, it means that the attitudes and behavior of people can be changed, as has been dramatically demonstrated by society's loss of patience with sexual harassment in the workplace. However, "changing people" can have a pragmatic meaning: Sometimes it is necessary to replace some people with others who have a fresh perspective and new ideas.
5. *New strategies evolve.* Important lessons can be learned from crises. We often discover a better way of doing things or perceive new paths to opportunity.
6. *Early warning systems develop.* Experience is a wonderful teacher. If we know what the warning signs are, we can recognize a crisis on its way. As a child, you

might have been told never to touch a pan on the stove without first checking to see whether the stove was hot. The same principle applies here.

7. *New competitive edges appear.* It has been said that nothing is more exhilarating than having someone shoot a gun at you and miss. Organizations and individuals often feel like this after surviving a crisis. The sense of teamwork and accomplishment that comes with a job well done often carries over to the next challenge. Because of the various changes that occur during the crisis cleanup, organizations are often better equipped to compete in the new environment.

QUICK CHECK

1. What is the difference between a problem and a crisis?
2. Do crises follow a predictable pattern?
3. Are the outcomes of crises always negative?

CRISIS COMMUNICATIONS PLANNING

Public relations, which by definition is a management function, plays a critical role during times of crisis. In an ideal setting, practitioners should be in a position to advise management before, during, and after each incident. Mayer Nudell and Norman Antokol, veterans of the U.S. Foreign Service, have written that communications specialists should be involved in every aspect of crisis communications.[38] Robert F. Littlejohn, who has experience in both academic and emergency management communities, favors the inclusion of a good communicator on a crisis management team, saying that strong communication skills are an essential quality of the team leader.[39]

Nobody likes to think about the consequences of disasters. However, the stark reality is that no one is immune to their effects. As the events of recent years have shown, crises can strike at any time and place. Public relations practitioners owe it to themselves, to their employers, and to all their stakeholder publics to confront these unpleasant issues head-on and map out a course of action for dealing with crises that is consistent with their organization's values. In the final analysis, planning for a hurricane while it is still out at sea is a lot easier than when you are in the eye of the storm.

Effective crisis communications, like the public relations process as a whole, involves four steps: *risk assessment, crisis communications planning, response,* and *recovery.* Let's look more closely at each of these phases in turn.

Step One: Risk Assessment

At the heart of proactive crisis communications is **risk assessment:** the identification of the various threats under which an organization operates. Some potential crises are common to most organizations. These include problems created by bad weather, fires, financial difficulties, and on-the-job accidents. Other crises are more closely related to the specific nature of the product or service a given organization provides. These can include dangers inherent in the product/service itself (e.g., accidents involving public transportation or contamination of a food product) and toxic by-products from manufacturing processes (e.g., radiation from a nuclear power plant). Compared with private companies, publicly owned companies operate in an environment in which their crises are often more visible. The same holds true for well-known as opposed to less-known organizations. Sometimes crises have to do less with *what* business you are in than with *where* you are doing business. For example, the location of an office within a floodplain or in a country with an unstable political environment entails risks not faced elsewhere.

But the goal of risk assessment is not just the identification of potential hazards. Once a threat is identified, steps should be taken to eliminate or lessen it. Unfortunately, some companies do not—a decision they later regret. The Toyota Motor Corp., once recognized as a maker of high-quality automobiles, took a severe hit to its reputation in 2010 because of its slow response to consumer complaints ranging from unexpected acceleration to steering problems. Federal safety officials linked 34 deaths to Toyota safety defects.[40] Although conceding no guilt, Toyota agreed to pay a record-high $16.4 million federal fine for its tardy response to the accelerator problems.[41]

Whereas other legal issues raised in the controversy might take years to resolve, there was almost immediate universal agreement on one point: Toyota's slow response to consumer complaints and subsequent recall of 8.5 million automobiles and trucks caused immeasurable damage to the company's image. "It's going to take a mighty powerful hose to wash off the mud that's soiled Toyota's reputation," wrote Carolyn Said of the *San Francisco Chronicle*.[42] Marketing and branding expert Peter Schaub said, "Right now, just saying the word 'Toyota' in conversation stirs up visions of runaway cars and poor quality. That kind of perception will not change overnight."[43]

Many organizations can avert crises by clearly articulating and actively implementing their core values. By doing so, they can make all aware of the legal and ethical limits under which they choose to operate. This is much easier to do during a period of relative calm than it is during the heat of a crisis. Decisions made during a crisis without consideration of organization values can have long-term ramifications that can eventually trigger new crises.

Once again, the Toyota case is instructive. When called before a congressional committee to explain their company's slow response to consumer safety complaints, Toyota officials were confronted with a "smoking gun"—an internal company memo in which executives boasted of saving $100 million by limiting the scope of its recall. When shown the document that seemingly put profits ahead of safety, Yoshimi Inaba, chief of Toyota Motor North America, acknowledged, "It is inconsistent with the guiding principles of Toyota."[44]

When undertaking a program of risk assessment, organizations can choose either to hire outside consultants or to perform an in-house evaluation. Some organizations, in fact, choose to do both. Often, outside consultants assume a training role after the planning is complete. These consultants can be expensive but worth every penny.

For those who decide to do in-house planning and training, the development of a broad-based **crisis planning team** (CPT) is a logical step. The makeup of these teams varies. According to a National Association of Manufacturers study, the chief legal counsel is the company official most often assigned to the CPT, followed by the director of public affairs, the director of security, and the chief operating officer.

It is not enough for the management to dictate a crisis response to the rank and file. The plan will be more successful if employees have some ownership of it. For this reason, employees at all levels of the organization should take part in the risk assessment process. This brings different and valuable perspectives to the process. If two heads are better than one, think how much better the risk assessment can be if many heads contribute to the final product.

 QUICK CHECK

1. What are the four steps of the crisis communications process? Do these remind you of any other process you have seen?
2. What is risk assessment?
3. What role do values play in crisis communications?

Step Two: Developing the Plan

Crisis communications planning means developing communications strategies for identified risks—making as many decisions and taking as many steps as you possibly can *before* a crisis occurs. The best decisions are usually made when you have time to think through their ramifications.

Because crises vary in their scope and nature, it is best to have a flexible crisis plan that is not event specific. The contents of such a plan include crisis definitions, a list of crisis managers, stakeholder communication strategies, planned coordination and information sites, and an employee training program.

CRISIS DEFINITIONS Different people conjure up different images when they hear the phrase *public relations*, and the same is true when the word *crisis* is mentioned. A good crisis plan eliminates the guesswork as to whether something is "an incident" or "a crisis." One pharmaceutical manufacturer has a "decision tree" on the first page of its crisis communications plan in which a series of questions helps gauge the nature and intensity of each situation. Developing a common language is also critical for interactions with those outside an organization. Electric utilities with nuclear generators are required to ensure that public agencies, as well as people residing within 10 miles of these facilities, are familiar with terminology that relates to various emergencies and the possible responses to those emergencies.

A LIST OF INDIVIDUALS WHO WILL MANAGE THE CRISIS RESPONSE When possible, crises should not be allowed to keep an organization from conducting its daily operations. A special **crisis management team** (CMT) should be assigned the responsibility for monitoring and responding to any crisis. These people should

QUICKBREAK 12.3

The Crisis Plotting Grid

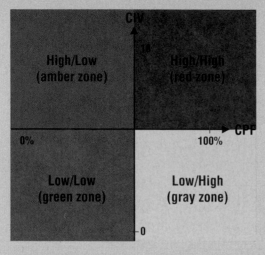

FIGURE 12.2
The Crisis Plotting Grid

Steven Fink is a public relations and management consultant who has firsthand knowledge of crises. During the Three Mile Island nuclear power plant crisis in 1979, Fink provided valuable advice to Governor Richard Thornburgh of Pennsylvania that, in the long run, helped prevent public panic. In his book *Crisis Management: Planning for the Inevitable*, Fink developed a useful tool for risk assessment: the **crisis plotting grid** (Figure 12.2). By placing every potential crisis on the grid, an organization can easily identify the areas where its crisis planning is most needed.

The vertical axis of the grid, which runs from 0 to 10, represents the **crisis impact value (CIV).** Fink says you should respond to the following five questions for each potential crisis on a scale of 0 to 10, with 0 being the lowest level of impact on your organization and 10 being the highest:

1. If the crisis runs the risk of escalating in intensity, how intense can it get and how quickly can it escalate?
2. To what extent will the crisis fall under the watchful eye of key stakeholders, including the media, regulators, shareholders, and so on?
3. To what extent will the crisis interfere with the organization's normal operations?
4. To what degree is the organization the culprit?
5. To what extent can the organization's bottom line be damaged?

Add up the total from the five questions (maximum 50 points) and divide by 5. The resulting figure is the CIV for that potential crisis.

The horizontal axis represents the **crisis probability factor (CPF).** Determine the CPF for the crisis in question by estimating the probability of the crisis on a scale of 0 percent (absolutely no likelihood the crisis will occur) to 100 percent (the crisis is an absolute certainty).

The CIV and CPF axes intersect at their midpoints (5 and 50 percent). Fink says the grid now becomes a barometer for crises facing an organization. Potential crises whose scores place them in the red zone are ones that present an organization with the greatest danger and require immediate attention. The next priority is to address crises that fall in the amber and gray zones. Potential crises located in the green zone shouldn't be ignored altogether but require less of your attention. ■

be identified by their job titles, not by name—who knows whether Frank Jones will be working here two years from now? Backup persons should also be identified. Ideally, this team should consist of the following members:

- *The CEO or a designated crisis manager.* Deciding whether the CEO should head the CMT depends on the nature of the crisis. Sometimes no one else will do. In other instances, however, someone who has the CEO's confidence can head the team. If the presence of the CEO inhibits frank discussion among the CMT members, it is better to appoint a **crisis manager,** someone who represents the interests of the CEO and to whom is delegated decision-making authority.

  What is not as clear is *when* the executive should publicly leap into the fray. A misjudgment can be very damaging. As noted in QuickBreak 12.1, Exxon Chairman Lawrence Rawl waited one week to comment on the *Exxon Valdez* oil spill in Alaska. He believed that public opinion issues should take a back seat to more important issues relating to the cleanup. "We thought the first task should be to assist our operating people to get the incident under control," Exxon President Lee Raymond told reporters. Based on public reaction, that was a mistake.

  "When a major crisis occurs, the CEO must step out immediately into the glare of TV lights and tell the public what is being done to fix the problem," said Andy Bowen of Atlanta-based Fletcher Martin Ewing Public Relations. "The CEO can't wait until all of the information is in."[45]

- *Legal counsel.* Lawyers often present business communicators with their most difficult challenges during crises. Gerald Meyers, a veteran of many skirmishes with attorneys while he was head of American Motors, believes that the best advice is often to "cage your lawyers." He wrote, "Smart executives are not intimidated by lawyers who do not have to run the business once the legal skirmishing is over."[46]

  This is not suggesting that legal counsel should be excluded from CMTs. Even their critics, including Meyers, say lawyers have an important role in crisis discussions and can provide valuable legal advice. But it is important to remember that the organization must answer to more than just a court of law. It also answers to the court of public opinion, where the judgment can be more devastating. That is why the legal and public relations counsels must have a good working relationship.

- *Public relations counsel.* Public relations is a management function. In this capacity, the practitioner advises how best to communicate with important stakeholders and, when necessary, represents these stakeholders' views to the CMT. The public relations counsel also advises the CMT on public opinion and potential reactions to the proposed crisis responses. The public relations practitioner is also responsible for serving as the organization's conscience, making certain the organization's actions square with its stated values.

- *Financial counsel.* Many crises have the potential for severely damaging the company's bottom line. Someone with hands-on knowledge of organization finances can be a valuable asset to the CMT.

- *Appropriate technical experts.* These people may vary from crisis to crisis. After identifying the various threats to the organization, the crisis communications plan should then identify experts who can assist in the resolution of each type of crisis.

■ *Support personnel.* The CMT may require any of a variety of support services, including people with secretarial skills, people with computer skills, and artist/illustrators.

STAKEHOLDER COMMUNICATION STRATEGIES   The plan should identify the various stakeholders who must be contacted and should provide appropriate telephone numbers, fax numbers, and e-mail addresses. Given adequate warning of a potential problem, some organizations prepare news releases and other stakeholder communications in advance.

The value of communicating with key stakeholders was demonstrated following an explosion at the Imperial Sugar Plant in Port Wentworth, Georgia. Fourteen workers died, and 32 were injured in the February 2008 blast. In addition to the need to respond to the crisis at hand, Imperial Sugar executives faced questions about the company's long-term survival. Lacking an internal communications department, they hired Edelman, which moved quickly to reassure key stakeholders: the families of victims, other employees, the local community, the media, and Wall Street investors. This decisive action allowed the company to resume production with full employment within nine months.[47] However, it should also be noted that the federal government hit Imperial Sugar with $8.77 million in fines for 108 safety violations in connection with the blast.[48]

Key stakeholders with whom organizations need to communicate during crises include the following:

■ *Employees.* This may be the most important group. Too often, employees are overlooked. Long after the reporters have left, these people remain. The plan needs to outline how employees will be notified of an emergency on short notice. It should also include plans for providing employees with updated information on a regular basis.

■ *The media.* It is critically important for an organization to speak with one voice during a crisis. The plan should designate an official spokesperson. A procedure should be established for the timely release of information through news releases or regularly scheduled briefings. The plan should also include provisions for monitoring media reports. The establishment of a media information center (MIC) is discussed below.

■ *Other key stakeholders.* The plan should designate the individual or individuals responsible for serving as liaisons with people who require "special" attention. These key stakeholders include members of the board of directors, major stockholders, financial analysts, regulators/public officials, unions, and community leaders.

■ *The curious public.* Some crises attract a lot of public attention. In those cases, it is a good idea to have a rumor control center where people can telephone and have their questions promptly answered. This is a very useful mechanism for tracking down the source of erroneous information and squelching false rumors before they spread.

Through the use of traditional and social media tactics, private organizations such as the Clinton–Bush Haiti Fund raised millions of dollars for earthquake relief in Haiti.

(Federal Emergency Management Agency)

WHERE THE RESPONSE IS COORDINATED The CMT meets in what is called the **emergency operations center (EOC)**. The EOC is the command post for the organization's crisis response; therefore, it should be in a secure location. That doesn't mean the meetings need to be held in Fort Knox. However, CMT members should be free to do their work without interruption and without the peering eyes of reporters, curious employees, and other rubberneckers. The meeting place should have adequate communications capabilities, including televisions and radios for monitoring the media (see Figure 12.3). It should also be close to the place where the media are briefed.

WHERE REPORTERS CAN GO TO GET INFORMATION The place set aside for meeting with reporters covering your crisis is the **media information center (MIC)**. The most important goal in its operation is to make the MIC the only place journalists can go for information during a crisis. When it comes to interagency and multiorganizational communication with the media, this is the place where all responding organizations ensure they are "singing off the same sheet of music." The MIC has to be close enough to the action to satisfy reporters but far enough away to prevent journalists from getting in the way. A procedure for verifying the identity of working reporters, known as **credentialing**, should be established.

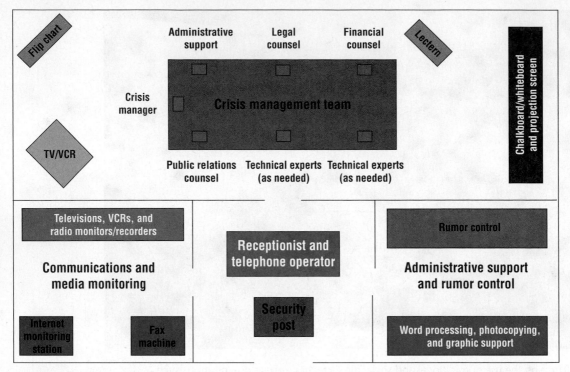

FIGURE 12.3
Emergency Operations Center Layout

Reporters and officials should have separate entrances into the building. Furnishings for the MIC should include a lectern or table capable of handling many microphones, adequate lighting and background for photography, tables and chairs for writing, access to telecommunications, and a place for distributing and posting news releases (Figure 12.4). The MIC should also be staffed at all times with a media center coordinator who can assist reporters in getting their questions answered.

THE ROLE OF THE INTERNET Organizations in crisis are increasingly turning to the Internet as a means of outreach. A website can serve several audiences, including news media, employees, and others affected by a crisis. American Airlines made extensive use of the Internet in the months following the 9/11 terror attacks. Facing possible bankruptcy, the world's largest airline used e-mail and a special website to communicate with its employees—including 20,000 who had been laid off because of the attacks—and investors. When a would-be terrorist attempted to ignite a bomb hidden in his shoe on a Paris-to-Miami flight, the airline used the Internet in an unusual way. The FBI had imposed a news blackout. However, it allowed American to tell its employees that the security breach was the fault of French officials—not a

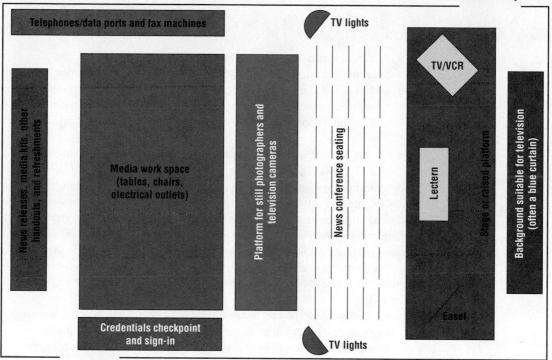

Restricted access entrance for officials only

Telephones/data ports and fax machines

TV lights

TV/VCR

News releases, media kits, other handouts, and refreshments

Media work space (tables, chairs, electrical outlets)

Platform for still photographers and television cameras

News conference seating

Lectern

Stage or raised platform

Background suitable for television (often a blue curtain)

Easel

Credentials checkpoint and sign-in

TV lights

Media entrance

FIGURE 12.4
Media Information Center Layout

result of the airline's actions. American posted the news on an employee website, knowing that the news media were monitoring it and would report what it said.[49]

EMPLOYEE TRAINING   Crisis communications training should occur as a normal part of employee orientation. Periodic reminders of each person's responsibilities also are in order, even if those responsibilities consist of nothing more than referring a matter to someone else. Mid- to upper-level managers should have more rigorous training, including tabletop exercises and role-playing scenarios. Part of this training should also focus on the language used and the information gathered when managers report a potential crisis. Inaccurate language and incomplete information can lead to misunderstandings that could cause an organization either to over- or underreact.

Every employee needs to know what to do when disaster strikes. Since Hurricane Andrew in 1992, one Miami law firm has issued a disaster-preparedness manual to all its employees. The manual includes emergency contacts, evacuation procedures, and instructions on what to do in the event of a variety of calamities.

QUICKBREAK 12.4

Hard to Say I'm Sorry

The year was 1982, a few years before many readers of this book were born. The rock group Chicago was topping music charts with "Hard to Say I'm Sorry." The song was part rock, part ballad, and all about the use of apology to mend fractured love. Although the music might seem outdated to today's college students, the sentiment of the song—the use of apology to salvage an important relationship—remains a strategic option for crisis communicators.

In fact, apology is just one of the strategies in **apologia,** which has been defined as "the speech of self-defense."[50] However, it should not be confused with *apology,* although it may include one.[51] Organizations engage in apologia as a way of presenting their side of the story in the face of negative events or to repair damaged reputations and limit losses.

Crisis communications experts don't agree on exactly how many apologia strategies exist. One of the dominant theories is known as **Image Restoration Discourse,** developed by communications professor William Benoit. He identified five apologia strategies: denial of wrongdoing, evasion of responsibility, reduction of the perceived offensiveness of the act, promise to take corrective action, and mortification, when one admits responsibility and seeks forgiveness.[52]

Benoit also notes that an apologia can involve more than one of these strategies and can progress from one strategy to another as events change. We saw that in the first Tylenol-tampering incident in 1982—the same year Chicago was singing its apologia tune. Although Johnson & Johnson was not responsible for the lacing of Tylenol capsules with cyanide, the tampering incident could have had a catastrophic effect on the company's financial stability (see QuickBreak 12.1).

CEO James E. Burke moved quickly to counter the damage, using two apologia strategies: by denying any wrongdoing and taking corrective action. Going against the government's advice, the company pulled 22 million bottles of Tylenol off store shelves. "We value that trust too much to let any individual tamper with it," Burke said in a television advertisement. "We want you to continue to trust Tylenol."[53] At another point in the crisis, Burke erred when he told reporters that there was no cyanide in company manufacturing plants. In fact, cyanide was used in the quality control process. After learning of his error, Burke employed the apologia strategy of mortification and admitted he had misspoken. In the end, these strategies helped save the Tylenol brand—and possibly the company.[54]

Apologia as a strategy has its risks. While a well-framed apologia can moderate stakeholders' anger, it can also strengthen negative associations between the company and the problem. Because of the diverse composition of an organization's stakeholders, not everyone requires an apology or an explanation.[55] "An admission of guilt could exacerbate legal difficulties stemming from the offensive act," said Benoit. "But I cannot recommend that an organization attempt to deny an accurate accusation."

He added, "Tylenol's response to the poisoning was exemplary."[56] ■

The firm has also set up an emergency telephone contact system so it can keep track of employees and their needs during crises.[57]

Everyone needs to know whom they should call at the first sign of a crisis. The most important person in a crisis is often the first person to recognize it as such. That person's actions (or inactions) go a long way toward dictating the nature and quality of an organization's response. Employees should feel comfortable reporting trouble if even the slightest thing seems amiss. If the culture of the organization discourages such feedback, the organization might end up missing early warning signs that, if acted on, could have averted trouble.

 QUICK CHECK

1. What are the advantages of designating a crisis management team? Who should be in charge of it?
2. Why must a good working relationship exist between an organization's legal counsel and its public relations counsel?
3. What is apologia?

 SOCIAL MEDIA APPS

Domino's Dilemma

Kristy and Michael said the video they posted on YouTube on Easter Sunday in April 2009 was meant as a joke. However, for the Domino's pizza chain, the prank suggesting that employees in its Conover, North Carolina, restaurant were handling food in unsanitary and disgusting ways quickly escalated into a Twitterstorm.

By the time *Ad Age* first reported the video the next morning, the prank video had received 21,000 YouTube views. Within seven hours, that figure had risen to 151,000.[58] Once alerted to the video, Domino's officials captured images of the video and circulated still pictures of the employees' faces on its internal network. By Monday evening, the company had identified both the restaurant and the employees. On Tuesday night, Domino's social media team noticed increasing chatter about the video on Twitter. By then, the number of views had reached 250,000. By noon Wednesday, the YouTube post hit one million views. For the first time, *Domino's* had surpassed *Paris Hilton* as a search term.[59]

After 48 hours, Domino's decided to fight fire with fire. It had YouTube remove the video and then posted its own response video featuring Patrick Doyle, president of Domino's USA. Domino's also opened a Twitter account to communicate with customers.[60] Although many observers in and out of the public relations industry praised Domino's for its eventual response, many also felt the restaurant chain was slow to react.

"On the one hand we're lauded for doing something unprecedented. And yet, we didn't do it fast enough," said Tim McIntyre, Domino's vice president, communications. "Nobody has been able to answer: How can you do something that's never been done before, but not fast enough?"[61] ■

Step Three: Response

Crisis **response** is the execution of crisis communications strategies. If all the necessary steps have been taken, this is where the organization is rewarded for its hard work. Critical decisions on whom to call and how to respond have already been made. In some cases, actions may have already been taken to avert or minimize the crisis.

At the risk of being repetitive, the response phase is when employee training provides its greatest dividends. Employees who have been trained in how to respond—even if the preferred response is to defer to someone else—are less likely to make critical errors that compound a crisis. That is why it is important for every employee to know what he or she should do.

However, just as with any public relations plan, a crisis communications plan must be flexible. Every crisis is unique. And although most crises are predictable, some are not. A crisis communications plan should guide, not dictate, the organization's response. It may be that because of some unanticipated factors, the organization's planned response will be inappropriate. The crisis in question could involve a group of stakeholders with whom the organization has little or no experience. And in some circumstances, such as the case of a catastrophic explosion, some of the response mechanisms anticipated in the plan may no longer be available.

Does this mean that a crisis communications plan is useless? Of course not. Think of a crisis communications plan in the same way a coach sees his or her game plan. Like a good game plan, a good crisis communications plan lays the foundation for success. All the training has been geared toward successful execution of the plan. However, both coaches and crisis managers can face circumstances that force them to change their plans. In sports, a key player may get hurt. In crisis management, some key decision makers might be unavailable. That can force some changes in the original plan, but the changes will be based on options and resources provided for in the plan. Even when one is forced to improvise, good planning can mean success.

Step Four: Recovery

When the immediate threat of a crisis ends, the natural instinct is to relax and return to a normal routine. However, it is important to resist that temptation. There is an important final step: **recovery**, in which the organization should evaluate the quality of its response and take appropriate actions on the basis of lessons learned. The questions asked at the end of one crisis can make the difference in averting or minimizing the next crisis. Some questions that need to be asked are

- Were our actions during and after the crisis consistent with our organization's values?
- What aspects of the crisis did our plan anticipate? How can we build on these successes?
- What aspects of the crisis did our plan fail to anticipate? What changes do we need to make?
- How well did our employees perform? Were they adequately trained?
- What are the lingering effects of the crisis? Are there follow-up actions we should take?

- How have our stakeholders' views of the organization changed since the onset of the crisis?
- What actions can either take advantage of new opportunities created by the crisis or repair damage created by it?

Not every crisis response is successful. Some organizations are better prepared for crises than others. Some events are more unexpected than others. However, there is little sympathy or tolerance for those who fail to learn the lessons of the past. That is why a period of honest evaluation is absolutely essential. Former Xerox CEO Anne Mulcahy said that crisis response is a lot like a farmer with a cow stuck in a ditch: The farmer has to get the cow out of the ditch, understand how the cow got into the ditch, and make changes so she never gets stuck again. Mulcahy said, "Do we really understand where we are, how we got there and how not to make the same mistakes in the future?"[62]

CRISIS PLANNING ETHICS

At a time when "big government" and "big business" are under increasing attack for being out of touch with the people, proactive crisis communications planning can be critical to an organization's continued success. Through this approach, many crises that confront organizations can be averted or, at least, minimized. However, many organizations' lack of planning for crises is a cause for great concern. Crises, as well as inappropriate responses to them, pose societal threats on a variety of levels. Tangible losses are associated with them, such as damage to property and financial setbacks. There are also intangible losses, as evidenced by the psychological damage to crisis victims and a loss of public confidence in organizations. Even more, who can determine a value and assess the cost when the outcome of a crisis is the loss of human lives?

VALUES STATEMENT 12.1

Department of Homeland Security

Created in 2002, the Department of Homeland Security mobilizes and organizes efforts to secure the United States from terrorist attacks. A major reason for the establishment of the department was to unify a vast national network of organizations and institutions involved in efforts to protect the nation. Its headquarters are in Washington, D.C.

Vision: Preserving our freedoms, protecting America . . . we secure our homeland.

Mission: We will lead the unified national effort to secure America. We will prevent and deter terrorist attacks and protect against and respond to threats and hazards to the nation. We will ensure safe and secure borders, welcome lawful immigrants and visitors, and promote the free-flow of commerce.

—DHS Vision and Mission Statements, DHS website ■

BE INFORMED
BIOLOGICAL THREAT

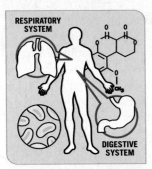

1. A biological attack is the release of germs or other biological substances. Many agents must be inhaled, enter through a cut in the skin or be eaten to make you sick. Some biological agents can cause contagious diseases, others do not.

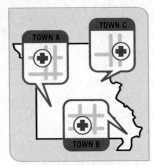

2. A biological attack may or may not be immediately obvious. While it is possible that you will see signs of a biological attack it is perhaps more likely that local health care workers will report a pattern of unusual illness.

3. You will probably learn of the danger through an emergency radio or TV broadcast.

4. If you become aware of an unusual or suspicious release of an unknown substance nearby, it doesn't hurt to protect yourself.

5. Get away from the substance as quickly as possible.

6. Cover your mouth and nose with layers of fabric that can filter the air but still allow breathing.

1

Poster

The Department of Homeland Security provided this example of citizen preparedness information on its special website, www.ready.gov.

(Courtesy of the Department of Homeland Security)

Is crisis communications planning an ethical imperative? In the minds of researchers Pauchant and Mitroff, the answer is a resounding yes. Although they have a certain degree of "empathy" for those caught in the vortex of a crisis, they also express "moral outrage" when crises and their subsequent fallouts are preventable.[63] Although PRSA's *Code of Ethics* does not specifically mention crisis communications planning, one of the professional values it identifies is honesty. "We adhere to the highest standards of accuracy and truth in advancing the interests of those we represent and in communicating with the public," the code states.[64] That wording prompts the question, "Can one claim to have acted in such a manner when one has failed to take reasonable precautions against predictable crises?"

It is not enough to develop technical contingencies to meet the logistical needs of an organization in crisis. Developing plans for communicating during times of stress is critical to the success, if not the very survival, of organizations. As one postmortem of Exxon's Alaskan oil spill noted,

> The *Exxon Valdez* spill clearly shows the penalty for perceived unreadiness in the face of an environmental disaster. But it also shows the importance of having insurance for when things go wrong. It would be unthinkable to go without liability insurance against claims for loss or negligence. Why then do some companies fail to take out strong public relations "insurance" for claims against image?[65]

Although ethical arguments might move some of the unconcerned and unprepared to action, tangible evidence of the consequences of such failures may prove more convincing.

SUMMARY

Crises don't just happen. Usually, warning signs indicate that trouble is on the way. Too often, however, people fail to recognize the signs. When this failure occurs, a considerable amount of an organization's time and resources must be spent dealing with a crisis.

Crises tend to develop in four stages: a warning stage, a point of no return, a cleanup, and a return to normalcy—although crises can alter what normalcy means for an affected organization.

Crises don't have to have exclusively negative outcomes. Good things can come out of a crisis—if an organization is prepared. But the sad truth is that most organizations are not. Many do not even have a written crisis communications plan. Among those that do, many have not properly trained their employees in its use.

Crisis communications planning is one of the most proactive things a public relations practitioner can do. However, it is not something he or she does alone. A good crisis plan is one that has been developed in collaboration with people throughout the organization *and* has the wholehearted support of top management. A good crisis plan also reflects an organization's values—and there is usually no more important time for communicating those values than during a crisis.

Good crisis communications planning begins with an honest assessment of the potential risks an organization may face. It follows with a plan that identifies the members of the crisis management team, key stakeholders, and the logistics necessary for a swift and appropriate response. The training of all employees is the key to a good response. Although the organization should be guided by its crisis communications plan, its response should not be dictated by it. As is the case with all plans, it should be flexible enough to address unanticipated circumstances. As the crisis ends and the organization moves into the recovery phase, it is important to evaluate what happened and why. This is the first step in preparing for—and possibly preventing—future crises.

DISCUSSION QUESTIONS

1. Can you name a crisis and identify how it proceeded through its four stages?
2. What lessons can be learned from the government's badly handled response to Hurricane Katrina?
3. What do you think are some excuses organizations might proffer for not having adequate crisis communications plans? How would you counter those arguments?
4. Identify some crises that officials at your college or university might face. Where would you place each on Steven Fink's crisis plotting grid?
5. What role do organizational values play in crisis planning?

MEMO FROM THE FIELD

MELANIE MAGARA

Assistant Vice President for Public Affairs; Northern Illinois University
DeKalb, Illinois

Melanie Magara is assistant vice president for public affairs at Northern Illinois University in De Kalb, Illinois. She, along with others in the NIU community were forced deal with the nightmare of a shooting rampage on campus in February 2008. Six people, including the gunman, died and 16 others were wounded. The details of the incident and its aftermath are chronicled in Case Study 12.2. For its efforts to keep the public informed and to help the campus community cope with the tragedy, the NIU Office of Public Affairs was awarded the Public Relations Society of America's "Best of the Silver Anvil" award in June 2009.

The term *crisis management* is something of an oxymoron, implying as it does that events bringing sudden shock, panic, and chaos can submit to project "management." Of course, it is imperative for us to have crisis plans in place and for those plans to be practiced on a regular basis. We know that first responders, counselors, communicators, and other support staff must know their roles. And clearly we must be ready to deal with the onslaught of media interest when tragedy strikes. Yet just as important as planning and practice is the acknowledgement that there is much for which we cannot prepare, and it is to those issues I direct this memo from the field.

First and foremost, each crisis is unique. We learned a great deal from Virginia Tech and others who have suffered tragedy, yet we encountered many situations at NIU for which we could not find a precedent. Instead, under the guidance of President John Peters, we proceeded in all our actions to be guided by compassion for the victims and their families and loving concern for all members of our university community. Throughout our ordeal, questions about media access, release of information, and the tenor of official statements were consistently put to that test.

Second only to compassion was our commitment to transparency, not only as an institutional value but also as a very practical response. We quickly learned that the news media—more than 300 reporters and photographers during the first 48 hours—were consistently ahead of us in terms of new information. They fanned out across campus and at the local hospital and found many witnesses and others willing to share what they had seen and what they were hearing. I recall sitting in crisis team meetings punctuated by updates from the conference room television that provided new details (some correct, some not) of which we had not yet officially been made aware. Whenever I am asked how we "controlled" the media during our crisis, I reflect on those early hours and days: "Control" is not the word I would use.

What we formed with the news media in those early hours—and indeed, throughout the duration of our crisis—was a partnership. As landline phones across campus rang off the hook and cell phone lines jammed, we realized as never before that the news media owned the platforms we needed to communicate to worried families across the Chicagoland area. We established media workrooms near the auditorium where we held our news conferences, and we supplied wireless Internet access so reporters could file their stories remotely. We kept those rooms stocked with food and beverages and arranged to have the building kept open 24/7. These were not enemy troops to be held at bay; they were partners in a sad but necessary task. The simple courtesies we extended to the news media were repaid many times over in fair coverage and advance notice when new story angles were about to emerge.

Finally, the aspect of crisis management for which we were least prepared was our own emotional responses. We knew it was important to project a sense of competence and to convey that we had things under control; that is standard operating procedure in crisis communications. Yet we learned as well the importance of speaking from the heart. Once the basic facts were known—and that happened fairly quickly—ours was a story of grief and remembrance. When the eyes of the world were on NIU, we felt a tremendous responsibility to show a caring community that loves and values all its members.

NIU leaders would be the first to advocate for planning and preparedness. There is no time during a crisis to consult a book or learn one's role for the first time. We also benefited tremendously from practice and emergency simulations. Yet each crisis produces new insight, and for me the sum of those revelations is simply this: There is much for which you cannot prepare. Many of our best decisions were made on the spot, guided by a shared commitment to compassion, transparency, partnership—and each other. In the words of our school fight song, "Forward, together forward." ■

CASE STUDY 12.1 False Hope

An explosion rocked a Sago, West Virginia, coal mine on the morning of January 2, 2006. Thirteen miners were trapped 260 feet belowground. Company, local, state, and federal authorities immediately began a frantic effort to rescue the men.[66] The mine's owner, International Coal Group (ICG), also activated its crisis communications plan. Company officials conducted regular news briefings, counseled the miners' families, and cooperated with state and federal regulators. The company received high marks for its initial crisis response.[67]

That changed just before midnight on Wednesday, January 3. Within a three-hour period, the families experienced the joy of being told that 12 of the 13 miners had survived—only later to suffer the shock and grief of learning that 12 of the 13 had died. Like the mining families who had just realized their worst fears, people around the world began asking the same question: How could this miscommunication have happened?[68]

A visibly shaken ICG President Ben Hatfield met with reporters on the day after the disaster and explained how poor communications conspired with good intentions. By the early evening hours of Wednesday, rescuers had already found the body of one of the miners near the site of the initial blast. The fate of the remaining 12 miners was unknown. Shortly before 11 p.m., rescue workers wearing full-face oxygen masks radioed the rescue command center that they had found the missing miners.[69]

In a muffled, barely audible voice over a crackling radio, a member of the rescue team announced that they had found the missing men. Six minutes later, an emergency medical technician radioed the rescue team and asked, "And what am I telling them?" The rescuer replied, "Twelve, and they're bringing them out." When the EMT said, "And they're all alive," the rescue worker replied, "Uh, as far as I know."[70]

According to Hatfield, this exchange was heard on an open speakerphone in the command center.

And as might be expected after 36 hours of nearly unbearable tension, the place erupted into a spontaneous celebration of joy and relief. Several people in the command center—exactly who is not known—could not wait to share the good news with the anxious families. In violation of the ICG's crisis response plan, they pulled out their cell phones and announced that the miners had been rescued.

The news spread like wildfire to the nearby Sago Baptist Church, where most of the trapped miners' families and friends had waited for news. According to media reports, a man burst through the front door of the church and screamed, "They've found them! All 12 are alive!" The church bell tolled as the crowd cheered, wept, prayed, and sang the hymn "How Great Thou Art." A friend of three of the trapped men proclaimed, "There still are miracles!"[71]

Back at the command center, a different picture emerged. The rescuers had initially thought the miners were unconscious but alive. However, 45 minutes later, the rescue team radioed that only one of the miners appeared to be alive. The company immediately dispatched more medical teams to the mine.

Hatfield was aware of the premature celebration back at the church and did not want to confuse matters by releasing unverified information. He decided to wait until he was certain of his facts. Three hours after the first erroneous report, Hatfield went to the church to tell the crestfallen families that only one of the 12 miners had survived.

Hatfield later said that he asked a state trooper to call the church and warn the families that the company had to sort out conflicting information. However, that was not done. If he had to do it all over again, Hatfield said that he, personally, would have gone to the church sooner and warned the people. "In the process of being cautious, we allowed the jubilation to go on longer than it should have," Hatfield said.[72]

Although ICG rightfully accepted blame for what turned out to be a cruel mistake, it shares the blame with others. The news media quickly accepted as fact unverified reports from unofficial sources. West Virginia Governor Joe Manchin, who first questioned the validity of the reports, admitted that he "got caught up in the euphoria" and helped spread the false rumor.[73]

The fact is that people heard what they desperately wanted to hear. No one wanted to compound the families' grief with a glimpse of false hope. But that's what happened when some well-intentioned people failed to follow the company's crisis communications plan.

DISCUSSION QUESTIONS

1. The case suggests that some of the families' heartache could have been avoided if "well-intentioned" people had followed the company's crisis communications plan. Where, specifically, did they fail to follow the plan?
2. How could ICG have improved its communications with the families?
3. Should ICG seek to share the blame with the news media for spreading the false rumor?
4. Knowing what you now know about the events at the Sago Mine, what would you have done differently had you been in charge of crisis communications? ■

CASE STUDY 12.2 "Gunman on Campus"

When the man dressed in black walked onto the stage during an ocean science lecture at Northern Illinois University, many of the students first wondered if it was some sort of prank. But when he leveled his shotgun at the center of the audience and opened fire, chaos ensued.

"All I could think about was, 'I could die at any moment,'" sophomore Geoff Alberti later said. "This could be the end."[74]

By the time former NIU student Steven Kazmierczak ended his rampage by killing himself, five students were dead and 16 others were injured. The horrible events of February 14, 2008, were sadly reminiscent of an even deadlier campus shooting less than a year earlier at Virginia Tech, where a troubled student killed 32 people and wounded 25 before committing suicide. However, the two schools were linked by more than just grief born of senseless tragedies. Within minutes of the shootings, Virginia Tech officials reached out to their NIU counterparts to help them cope with the worst day of their lives.

To their credit, NIU officials had already researched the April 2007 Virginia Tech shootings. And when terror visited their campus on that Valentine's Day, they had already learned valuable lessons from their colleagues in Blacksburg. NIU Assistant Vice President for Public Affairs Melanie Magara had heard a presentation given by Virginia Tech officials just a few months earlier. From that, she learned that the Internet had played a critical role in getting information to students, families, employees, and a concerned public.

"Our first priority was to get a warning out there," Magara said. "Our first message on the website was very simple: Gunman on campus. Remain in rooms and offices. Campus in lockdown."[75] NIU also issued emergency alerts via e-mail, voicemail, and the university's hotline.[76]

In the first hour after the shooting, NIU's website registered almost 4.4 million hits. By the end of the day, that figure had climbed to 14 million. However, the website handled the traffic, thanks to recently upgraded servers. That was not a lucky coincidence. In the months following the Virginia Tech tragedy, NIU officials twice had used their revised crisis response plans, once in response to local flooding and the other a result of a racially charged threat scrawled on a residence hall wall.

In evaluating their response to those crises, school officials realized they needed to beef up their computer server capacity.

As one might expect, media coverage of the NIU shootings was intense. More than 25 television satellite trucks descended on the campus to report the breaking news to the rest of the world. Magara said the university's crisis plan called for treating the media as partners—not as adversaries—because they had the communication channels needed to reach NIU's publics. She said transparency proved to be the university's best strategy for dealing with reporters.

"We told [students and staff] that the university neither encourages nor discourages you from doing an interview," said Magara. "If you [decide to speak to the media], then we simply advise you to stick with what you know and not speculate or share third-hand information."[77]

NIU Public Affairs also helped in coordinating the university's message, one of compassion for the victims and their families and of the commitment of the NIU community to stand together in the face of tragedy. This involved coordinating six news conferences; staffing a media center; and preparing talking points, speeches, and other public communications. The office also helped plan the memorial service attended by 12,000 people on February 24 and created a memorial website that allowed visitors to leave messages of condolence. The university also provided grief counseling for students, faculty, and staff within hours of the last shot being fired.[78]

As had been the case in the Virginia Tech shootings, students took it on their own to reach out to concerned family and friends via social media. This was especially important in the early stages of the crisis, when cell phone traffic spiked to more than 14 times its normal level. A 19-year-old student in the process of transferring to NIU created a "Pray for Northern Illinois University Students and Family" Facebook group within 90 minutes of the incident. Within five hours, almost 10,000 people had joined the group.

"Like with any tragedy, you feel like you need to say something," Jim Combs, the NIU Facebook group creator, said. "Since I'm going to be a part of the family, I felt like there needed to be a safe haven for the students."[79]

University President John G. Peters served as the public face of the university during the crisis. He also attended student funerals and spoke with those wounded during the rampage. He recalls one conversation, when a shooting victim asked him whether his professors might cut him some slack if he missed some assignments.

"It was at that moment," Peters said, "that I knew we were going to be OK."[80]

DISCUSSION QUESTIONS

1. Citing specific examples from this case study, describe the four phases of a crisis.
2. What role, if any, did evaluation play in Northern Illinois University's crisis response?
3. How did NIU use social media in response to this crisis?
4. What steps, if any, has your college or university taken in the wake of the Virginia Tech and Northern Illinois University tragedies? ∎

NOTES

1. Mark Schleifstein, "FEMA Knew Storm's Potential, Mayfield Says," *New Orleans Times-Picayune*, 4 September 2005, via NewsBank, online, http://infoweb.newsbank.com.
2. John McQuaid, "Before Katrina, There Was Pam," *New Orleans Times-Picayune*,

10 September 2005, via NewsBank, online, http://infoweb.newsbank.com.
3. McQuaid.
4. Schleifstein.
5. Ed Cafasso, "Going Back to Basics: Hurricane Katrina Illustrates the Importance of Aligning

Action and Communications," *Public Relations Tactics*, October 2005, 12.

6. Cafasso.

7. Eric Weslander, "Speaker: Government Compounded Disaster of Hurricane Katrina," *Lawrence Journal-World*, 15 March 2007, online, www.ljworld.com.

8. Steve Vockrodt, "Ex-FEMA Director: Nation Still Isn't Prepared for Major Disaster," *Lawrence Journal-World*, 5 April 2007, online, www.ljworld.com.

9. "Financial Meltdown: a Timeline," CBS News, online: www.cbsnews.com.

10. Kyra Auffermann, "It Still Chokes Me Up: Responding to a Deadly Campus Shooting at Northern Illinois University," *Public Relations Strategist* (summer 2009): 12–16.

11. Paul Levy, "Buckling and Swaying, Then 'Down, Down, Down,'" *Minneapolis Star-Tribune*, 2 August 2007, 1B.

12. Terry Macalister, "Tony Hayward's parting shot: 'I'm too busy to attend Senate hearing,' " *The Guardian*, 28 July 2010, online, www.guardian.co.uk.

13. NBC News/*Wall Street Journal* poll, as reported on *Polling Report*, online, http://www.pollingreport.com/sports.htm#Golf.

14. Kenneth N. Myers, *Total Contingency Planning for Disasters* (New York: Wiley, 1993), 2.

15. Jane Applegate, "Why Crisis Management Plans Are Essential," *Los Angeles Times*, 29 December 1989, D3.

16. Donald Chisholm and Martin Landau, "Set Aside That Optimism if We Want to Avoid Disaster," *Los Angeles Times*, 18 April 1989, sec. II, 7.

17. "Many Still Aren't Prepared," *Public Relations Journal*, September 1986, 16; David W. Guth, "Organizational Crisis Experience and Public Relations Roles," *Public Relations Review* 21, no. 2 (summer 1995): 123–136.

18. "In Ten Years You'll See Nothing," *Fortune*, 8 May 1989.

19. Allanna Sullivan and Amanda Bennett, "Critics Fault Chief Executive of Exxon on Handling of Recent Alaskan Oil Spill," *Wall Street Journal*, 31 March 1989.

20. Sullivan and Bennett.

21. Adam Liptak, "$4.5 Billion Award Set for Spill of *Exxon Valdez*," *New York Times*, 29 January 2004, online, www.nytimes.com.

22. "Tylenol Tries for a Comeback," *Newsweek*, 1 November 1982, 78.

23. Robert J. Holland and Katrina Gill, "Ready for Disaster?—A New Survey of IABC Members Reveals That Crisis Communications Are Not as Widespread as Expected," *Communication World*, March–April 2006, 20–24.

24. Thierry C. Pauchant and Ian I. Mitroff, *Transforming the Crisis-Prone Organization* (San Francisco: Jossey-Bass, 1992), 12.

25. Pauchant and Mitroff, 15–16.

26. Steven Fink, *Crisis Management: Planning for the Inevitable* (New York: AMACOM, 1986), 15–16.

27. Laurence Barton, *Crisis in Organizations: Managing and Communicating in the Heat of Chaos* (Cincinnati: South-Western Publishing, 1993), 2.

28. Except where otherwise noted, facts and figures about the *Challenger* and *Columbia* disasters come from the report of the *Columbia* Accident Investigating Board, issued August 2003.

29. NBC coverage, approximately 9:30 a.m. EST, 1 February 2003.

30. Gerald C. Meyers with John Holusha, *When It Hits the Fan: Managing the Nine Crises of Business* (Boston: Houghton Mifflin, 1986), 28.

31. Stephanie Desmon, "Hog Farmers Rue Swine Flu," *Baltimore Sun*, 21 August 2009, online, www.baltimoresun.com.

32. *ECDC Daily Update—2009 Influenza A (H1N1) Pandemic*, 18 January 2010, online, http://ecdc.europa.eu/en/healthtopics.

33. "*PRNews*: Nonprofit PR Awards," *PRNews*, 9 November 2009 (via ProQuest).

34. Chuck Raasch, "Pandemics in the Age of Twitter," *USA Today*, 7 May 2009, online, www.usatoday.com.

35. Curt Thacker, "Pork Producers Ache from Swine Flu," *Wall Street Journal*, 30 April 2009, online, www.wsj.com.

36. Press Briefing Transcripts, CDC Briefing on Public Health Investigation of Human Cases of Swine Influenza, 28 April 2009, online, www.cdc.gov.

37. Gerald C. Meyers.

38. Mayer Nudel and Norman Antokol, *The Handbook for Effective Emergency and Crisis*

Management (Lexington, Mass.: D.C. Heath, 1988), 36.

39. Robert F. Littlejohn, *Crisis Management: A Team Approach* (New York: American Management Association, 1983), 18–32.

40. Mark Glover, "Toyota Fumbling Recall Public Relations Crisis," *Chicago Tribune*, 27 February 2010, online, www.chicagotribune.com.

41. Ralph Vartabedian and Ken Bensinger, "Toyota Agrees to Pay Fine," *Los Angeles Times*, 19 April 2010, online, http://articles.latimes.com.

42. Carolyn Said, "Toyota Should Have Accelerated Response," *San Francisco Chronicle*, 10 February 2010, online, www.sfgate.com.

43. Glover.

44. Tom Raum and Ken Thomas, "Toyota Chief Blasted by Lawmakers Despite Apology," Associated Press, 24 February 2010, via Yahoo! News, online, www.yahoo.com.

45. Andy Bowen, "Crisis Procedures That Stand the Test of Time," *Public Relations Tactics*, August 2001, 16.

46. Gerald C. Meyers, 232–236.

47. "Crystallizing a Response to a Crisis," Silver-Anvil Award Campaign Profile 6BW-0911A05, Public Relations Society of America, online, www.prsa.org.

48. Julia Malone, "Sugar Maker Fined Millions," *Atlanta Journal-Constitution*, 26 July 2008, A1.

49. David W. Guth and Charles Marsh, *Adventures in Public Relations: Case Studies and Critical Thinking* (Boston: Allyn & Bacon, 2005), 307–311.

50. B. L. Ware and W. A. Linkugel, "They Spoke in Defense of Themselves: On the Generic Criticism of Apologia," *Quarterly Journal of Speech* 59 (1973): 273.

51. K. M. Hearit, "Apologies and Public Relations Crises at Chrysler, Toshiba, and Volvo," *Public Relations Review* 20(1994): 115.

52. William L. Benoit, "Image Repair Discourse and Crisis Communication," in *Responding to a Crisis: A Rhetorical Approach to Crisis Communication*, eds. Dan P. Millar and Robert L. Heath (Mahwah, N.J.: Lawrence Erlbaum, 2004), 263–280.

53. "Tylenol Tries for a Comeback," *Newsweek*, 1 November 1982, 78.

54. Bill Powell, "The Tylenol Rescue," *Newsweek*, 3 March 1986, 52–53.

55. Barbara Kellerman, "When Should a Leader Apologize—and When Not?" *Harvard Business Review* 84, no. 4 (April 2006): 72–81.

56. Benoit, 280.

57. Sharon Nelton, "Prepare for the Worst," *Nation's Business*, September 1993, 22.

58. Emily Bryson York, "Domino's Reacts Cautiously, Quietly to YouTube Gross-Out Video," *Advertising Age*, 14 April 2009, online, www.adage.com.

59. Amy Jacques, "Domino's Delivers During Crisis," *Public Relations Strategist*, (summer 2009): 6–10.

60. Greg Beaubien, "Domino's YouTube flap: "'A landmark event in crisis management,'" *Public Relations Tactics*, May 2009, 4.

61. Jacques.

62. "The Cow in the Ditch: How Anne Mulcahy Rescued Xerox," *Knowledge@Wharton*, 16 November 2005, online, http://knowledge.wharton.upenn.edu.

63. Pauchant and Mitroff, 5–6.

64. *Public Relations Society of America Member Code of Ethics*, online, www.prsa.org.

65. E. Bruce Harrison with Tom Prugh, "Assessing the Damage: Practitioner Perspectives on the Valdez," *Public Relations Journal*, October 1989, 42.

66. Vicki Smith, "12 Miners Found Dead after Rescue Effort," *Lawrence Journal-World*, 5 January 2006, 1.

67. Jim Jordan, "Mining Company Lost Control, Experts Say," Knight-Ridder Newspapers, 4 January 2006, online, www.charlotte.com.

68. Bob Dart, "Company Knew Report Was Wrong," *Kansas City Star*, 5 January 2006, 1.

69. Allen G. Breed, "Answers to Foul Up in Mine Disaster Sought," Associated Press, online, http://abcnews.go.com, 6 January 2006.

70. "Sago Mine Emergency Call Transcripts," ABC News, online, http://abcnews.go.com, 5 January 2006.

71. Breed.

72. Breed.

73. Breed.

74. Josh Noel, Mary Ann Fergus, and Megan Twohey, "An Instant of Uncertainty, Then Terror," *Chicago Tribune*, 17 February 2008, 1.

75. Chris Cobb, "With the Help of Virginia Tech, NIU Responds to Deadly Shooting," *Public Relations Tactics*, May 2008, 12–13.

76. "Putting Lessons Learned to Work: Managing Communications after a Campus Shooting," Silver Anvil Award campaign profile 6BW-0911B03, Public Relations Society of America, online, www.prsa.org.

77. Kyra Auffermann, "'It Still Chokes Me Up,' Responding to a Deadly Campus Shooting at Northern Illinois University," *Public Relations Strategist* (summer 2009): 12–16.

78. "Putting Lessons Learned to Work: Managing Communications after a Campus Shooting."

79. Kevin Pang, "Web Site Keeps Many Connected," *Chicago Tribune*, 15 February 2008, 19.

80. Jodi S. Cohen, E.A. Torriero, and Josh Noel, "Tough Road Ahead for NIU," *Chicago Tribune*, 24 February 2008, 1.

13

Public Relations and Marketing

OBJECTIVES

After studying this chapter, you will be able to
- describe recent changes in marketing
- define integrated marketing communications
- explain the differences among public relations, advertising, and marketing
- describe marketing public relations

- summarize the process of integrated marketing communications

KEY TERMS
advertising, p. 401
contacts, p. 414
customer relationship management (CRM), p. 402

REAL WORLD

Face the Music

What a dream job. You've just been appointed marketing director for a new website that features hard-to-find alternative rock mp3s and discounts on downloads. Most songs are from live performances.

Unfortunately, you've been hired only two months before the site goes online. Now your associates are asking you for a marketing plan that will attract thousands of loyal customers.

Some associates want advertising; others prefer public relations. But, fortunately, you soon determine that everyone is flexible and eager to be innovative in the marketing efforts.

You have an adequate marketing budget but not enough money to advertise on national television or in magazines such as *Alternative Press*.

What do you do?

PUBLIC RELATIONS AND MARKETING

Let's begin by addressing a question you may be asking right now: *Why am I reading about marketing in a public relations textbook?*

Good question. Here are some answers:

- Marketing focuses on consumers, as does consumer relations, or customer relations, which is part of public relations. Traditional consumer relations tactics, such as product-oriented news releases, can work hand in hand with marketing tactics such as direct mail and in-store displays.
- Other areas of public relations, such as government relations and employee relations, can affect the success of marketing programs—and vice versa. Some of the biggest headaches in public relations, in fact, come from mishandled marketing programs that damage important relationships. For example, the KFC restaurant chain ruffled feathers when it promoted its new grilled chicken menu with coupons for free meals. Thousands of customers downloaded the online coupons and flocked to KFC, only to cry foul when many locations ran out of chicken. The shortage sparked sit-ins and even lawsuits. KFC apologized and promised to honor the coupons when possible.[1]

■ Marketing in the 21st century is undergoing dramatic changes. Far from just persuading consumers to buy products *now,* new marketing strategies seek to build long-term, productive relationships with consumers. That should sound a lot like public relations to you. These new relationship-oriented marketing theories signal a profound shift from the mass-marketing programs of the past.

The Decline of Mass Marketing

Life seemed easier when professionals in public relations and advertising believed they could rely on the awesome power of the mass media. When Company X wanted to sell its new and improved gizmo to millions of eager customers, it simply bought ads on the right TV and radio shows and did the same with a few newspapers and magazines that delivered huge audiences. Company X often tried to place news releases in the same media. With the boom of network television in the mid-20th century, such a marketing plan really seemed to work . . . for a while.

However, we're now witnessing the weakening of the mass media. In a world with hundreds of cable and satellite channels, the traditional television networks (ABC, CBS, NBC, and Fox) can no longer automatically deliver a mass audience. In addition, thousands of specialized blogs, e-mail newsletters, websites, Twitter accounts, and other online media have helped plow over the few broad paths that once reached millions of consumers. No longer can public relations and advertising professionals reach a mass audience of consumers simply by placing news releases and ads in a few national print media and on the television networks your parents watched.

Modern marketing focuses on individual relationships. Successful long-term relationships, as you know from Chapter 7, involve control mutuality: a sharing of power. Today, buyers have unprecedented control of the purchasing process—and sellers have unprecedented control of consumer information. Advertising professor Robyn Blakeman links such control to technologies that are reshaping modern marketing:

> Technology has changed the way that corporations market their products and services. The customer now is in control of what he buys, when he buys, and where and how he buys. Computerized databases have given names and personalities to segments of the mass audience. . . . Because of this, thinking has gone from being sales oriented to being customer driven in a relatively short period of time.[2]

Bottom line? It's all about relationships with individual consumers.

The Growth of Consumer-Focused Marketing

In the past decade, marketers have decreased their reliance on mass communication. Instead, they are embracing what we will call consumer-focused marketing. Consumer-focused marketing uses a variety of media to build relationships with individual consumers. Since the 1990s, one of the most popular forms of consumer-focused marketing has been **integrated marketing communications (IMC)**. A recent study of marketing professionals in the United States, Korea, and Great Britain showed that "IMC is being taken seriously and implemented by agencies not only on both sides of the Atlantic Ocean, but also in the Far East."[3]

IMC differs from mass marketing in five respects:

1. IMC practitioners focus on individual consumers. Products are developed to fill consumers' specific needs, and sales messages are created to target specific consumers' self-interests. (Because IMC targets consumers, not all of public relations is part of IMC. Public relations, of course, targets other publics as well: employees, government officials, and stockholders, to name just a few.)
2. IMC practitioners use **databases** to target individual consumers rather than mass audiences. These databases contain a wealth of information on individual consumers' wants, needs, and preferences.
3. IMC practitioners send a well-focused message to each consumer through a variety of approaches: advertising, public relations, direct marketing, and all other forms of marketing communications, including packaging and pricing.
4. IMC practitioners use consumer-preferred media to send their marketing messages.
5. IMC practitioners favor interactive media, constantly seeking information from consumers. Thus, media such as interactive websites can be ideal for IMC.

Just as public relations has evolved over the decades, consumer-focused marketing is growing and changing. Although IMC is the best-known form of consumer-focused marketing, other forms exist, and they are helping shape the future of marketing. IMC was preceded by database marketing, which helped turn marketing away from mass audiences and toward individuals. Other approaches that can be grouped under the broad umbrella of consumer-focused marketing include relationship marketing, customer relationship management (CRM), and integrated brand communication (IBC). QuickBreak 13.1 discusses similarities and differences among these new consumer-focused marketing approaches.

Public Relations, Advertising, and Marketing

The three main pillars of IMC, as we said in Chapter 1, are public relations, advertising, and marketing. In addition, social media such as Facebook and Twitter have revolutionized how each of the three disciplines communicates with consumers. Although these three disciplines have much in common, much also differentiates them (Figure 13.1). Let's quickly review the definitions we established previously for each discipline:

Advertising is the use of controlled media (media in which one pays for the privilege of dictating message content, placement, and frequency) in an attempt to influence the actions of targeted publics.

Marketing is the process of researching, creating, refining, and promoting a product or service and distributing that product or service to targeted

QUICKBREAK 13.1

IMC and More

Databases and new methods of communication: In the 1990s, those two developments came together in integrated marketing communications (IMC), probably today's best-known consumer-focused marketing philosophy. But consumer-focused marketing includes other, closely related philosophies that you should know: database marketing, relationship marketing, customer relationship management (CRM), and integrated brand communication (IBC).

Database marketing. The new consumer-focused marketing philosophies began with database marketing. A computerized database can store vast amounts of information about individual consumers: what they buy, when they buy, how often they buy, how much they spend, how and how often your organization contacts them, and much more. "Database marketing," says management consultant Mindi McKenna, "involves the collection, storage, analysis, and use of information regarding customers and the past purchase behaviors to guide future marketing decisions."[4]

Relationship marketing. John Dalla Costa, president of the Centre for Ethical Orientation, says that the true value of modern organizations "involves a return on relationship. . . . The worth of companies depends more and more on the worth of [their] varied relationships."[5] Relationship marketing looks beyond profits to individual relationships with specific consumers, all in the belief that if the relationships are good, profits automatically follow.

Customer relationship management (CRM). The Conference Board, a U.S.-based business-research association, defines CRM as "the business processes an organization performs to identify, select, acquire, develop, retain, and better serve customers. These processes encompass an organization's . . . engagement with its customers and prospects over the lifetime of its relationship with them."[6] CRM combines the technology of database marketing with the philosophy of relationship marketing to develop lifelong relationships with individual customers. Applied to business-to-business relations, CRM becomes **partner relationship management.**

Integrated brand communication. According to marketing professors Don Schultz and Beth Barnes, integrated brand communication goes beyond IMC, which focuses on sales. It goes beyond CRM, which focuses on relationships between organizations and customers. Instead, IBC focuses on relationships between consumers and brands. Schultz and Barnes define brand as "the bond between the buyer and the seller."[7] In IBC, a brand is an individual consumer's perception of his or her relationship with a product or an organization. The goal of IBC is to discover each consumer's view of the brand and to align it with the organization's view. To do so, the organization must identify and integrate all forms of communication, sending one, clear message—just as in IMC.

These consumer-focused marketing strategies, including IMC, are closely related to one another. And with their increasing focus on building two-way, win–win relationships with important publics, they are closely related to public relations. ■

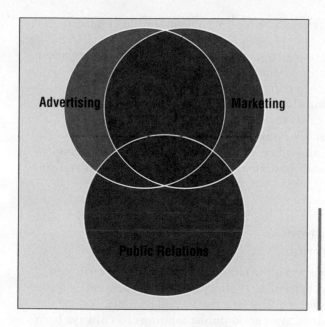

FIGURE 13.1

The Relationship among Advertising, Marketing, and Public Relations

Advertising, marketing, and public relations are three distinct professions with important areas of convergence. But not all advertising is marketing; nor is all public relations marketing.

consumers. Marketing promotion disciplines include sales promotions (such as coupons), personal selling, direct marketing—and, often, aspects of advertising and public relations.

Public relations is the values-driven management of relationships between an organization and the publics that can affect its success.

Advertising, marketing, and public relations follow the same process: research, planning, communication, evaluation. But unlike marketing, public relations focuses on many publics, not just on consumers. And unlike advertising, public relations doesn't control its messages by purchasing specific placements for them.

THE IMPACT OF CONSUMER-FOCUSED MARKETING ON PUBLIC RELATIONS

Consumer-focused marketing makes so much sense that some practitioners say, "We've been doing this for years. There's nothing new here." And, to some degree, they're right. Although certain aspects of IMC, for example, are relatively new, including the increasing use of social media such as blogs and YouTube videos, IMC is still based on a traditional commonsense approach familiar to most practitioners of good public relations: focusing on the values of a particular public and responding with a clear message.

But consumer-focused marketing *is* changing some aspects of public relations. The growing number of full-service agencies is evidence of this change. A generation ago, public relations constituted only a small portion of the activities of advertising agencies—almost an afterthought. But in recent years, ad agencies have widened their range of services to better serve clients and to counter a decline in advertising's share of marketing budgets. Some agencies are expanding through mergers. Others are forming strategic partnerships with public relations agencies or building public relations departments from scratch. Still others simply use freelancers to complement their range of services.

Consumer-focused marketing also is changing **marketing public relations,** the part of our profession that exists to promote organizations' products. More practitioners are learning—or at least learning about—disciplines such as **direct marketing,** product packaging, and other forms of advertising and marketing. They understand that IMC extends beyond any one discipline such as advertising or public relations.

The Impact of Public Relations on Consumer-Focused Marketing

But the influence flows both ways: Public relations has also had a profound influence on consumer-focused marketing. Public relations professionals have always believed in breaking down publics into their smallest units, just as consumer-focused marketing does. And good public relations has always been two-way; the best practitioners have always listened—not just talked—to their publics. Two-way symmetrical public relations by definition seeks to identify and honor the values and interests of important publics. Critics of traditional mass marketing charge—perhaps not altogether fairly—that consumer values and interests were left out of the traditional marketing process. Those critics say that companies designed products and sent marketing messages with very little analysis of what individual consumers really wanted. Whether or not that's true, it is undeniable that consumer-focused marketing has increased the power of the consumer in the marketing process.

Public relations practitioners communicate with publics through media those publics prefer; consumer-focused marketers do the same. Two-way symmetrical public relations involves the notion that sometimes an organization has to change to meet the needs of its publics, just as consumer-focused marketing involves realizing that a product might need to change. In fact, modern marketing's basic philosophy of respecting and listening to consumers may well be a contribution from the practice of successful public relations.

Differences between Public Relations and Consumer-Focused Marketing

A problem with some interpretations of consumer-focused marketing is the mistaken belief that all public relations is part of marketing communications. Knocking down that idea is easy. Marketing primarily focuses on a very important public: consumers. But that's only one public. Public relations must focus on developing healthy long-term relationships with employees, stockholders, news media, and any other public essential

VALUES STATEMENT 13.1

J.M. Smucker Company

The J.M. Smucker Company manufactures jams, jellies, preserves, ice cream toppings, and natural peanut butter. The company was founded in 1897 and is based in Orrville, Ohio.

Quality applies to our products, our manufacturing methods, our marketing efforts, our people, and our relationships with each other. We will only produce and sell products that enhance the quality of life and well-being. These will be the highest quality products offered in our respective markets because the Company's growth and business success have been built on quality. We will continuously look for ways to achieve daily improvements which will, over time, result in consistently superior products and performance.

At the J.M. Smucker Company, quality comes first. Sales growth and earnings will follow.

—Excerpt from "Our Basic Beliefs," J.M. Smucker website ■

to an organization's success. Certainly the two professions need to work together. But as Figure 13.1 indicates, public relations and marketing are distinct, complementary professions.

In *Excellence in Public Relations and Communication Management,* a landmark study on how award-winning public relations works, Professor Emeritus James Grunig of the University of Maryland declares, "The public relations function of excellent organizations exists separately from the marketing function, and excellent public relations departments are not subsumed into the marketing function."[8] Nearly 20 years ago, a panel of public relations and marketing experts concluded that the two professions were "separate and equal, but related functions."[9] Jack Bergen, senior vice president of corporate affairs and marketing for Siemens, a multinational corporation, says, "PR people understand the richness of audiences that have an interest in a company; advertisers just focus on customers."[10]

Public relations isn't advertising or marketing. But public relations and consumer-focused marketing certainly share important values. Both focus on the needs and interests of a public or publics. Both try to listen as much as they speak. And both act to strengthen an organization.

QUICK CHECK

1. How does consumer-focused marketing differ from mass marketing?
2. How and why does consumer-focused marketing use databases?
3. What are the differences among public relations, advertising, and marketing?

A CLOSER LOOK AT MARKETING

Before beginning this chapter, you probably had a basic understanding of marketing. After all, you encounter it every day. And earlier in this chapter, we defined marketing. But as you might suspect, we're about to tell you even more. Understanding how marketing works can make you a better public relations practitioner.

At its core, marketing means making the consumer want to buy your product. The so-called **marketing mix** consists of everything from product research and design to packaging, pricing, and product demonstrations. It even includes selecting the product's name. Years ago, marketing professors Jerome McCarthy and Philip Kotler defined the marketing mix with what they called the four P's of marketing:

1. *Product* (including name, design, and packaging)
2. *Price*
3. *Place* (where, exactly, can the customer buy it?)
4. *Promotion*

Public relations usually enters the marketing mix in the promotion category, and its importance is growing. The aforementioned study of IMC in the United States, Korea, and Great Britain found that public relations ranked first in "importance of [the] various disciplines" within IMC. The main components of IMC in order of importance, according to the study, were public relations, advertising, direct marketing, personal selling, sales promotion, and Internet-based functions.[11]

One of IMC's greatest contributions to marketing is the belief that every bit of the marketing mix sends a message to consumers. A product's name sends a message, as do design, packaging, price, purchase sites, and the promotions that publicize the product. For example, Redux Beverages definitely sent a message when it chose a name for its new energy drink: Cocaine. The name has faced legal challenges in the United States and Europe. However, by its own admission the company enjoys the product's "notorious" and "controversial" image: "With a name like Cocaine," said Redux Beverages founder Jamey Kirby, "half of the work was already done."[12] Like names, price and place also can send consumers a message. A lavishly packaged product that sells for an eye-poppingly high price at the most exclusive store in town has a different image in consumers' minds than a product sold for 25 cents at the town's grungiest gas station.

One problem with traditional marketing, some critics say, is that these various forms of communication may be sending different messages about the same product. And if consumers don't have a clear vision of the product, they won't buy it. For example, consumers may easily be confused by a product whose advertising suggests exclusivity and luxury—yet whose price suggests availability and cheapness.

"Most marketers send out a communications hodgepodge to the consumer, a mass message saying one thing, a price promo creating a different signal, a product label creating still another message, sales literature having an entirely different vocabulary, a sales force pitching nothing but 'price,' 'price,' 'price' to the retailer," say the authors of *Integrated Marketing Communications*, an excellent book on IMC. "Mixed-up, mass-directed, incompatible communication stems from the manufacturer's wishes rather than from customer needs."[13]

IMC tries to end that hodgepodge of messages by ensuring that every aspect of the marketing mix sends the same clear message to highly targeted consumers.

Marketing Public Relations

Before we take a closer look at how IMC in particular works, let's look at marketing public relations, which is the part of public relations that fits into marketing. Marketing public relations focuses on building relationships with consumers, with the intent, of course, of persuading them to buy a product.

Priceline.com, a leading provider of online travel services, uses marketing public relations, together with other IMC tactics, to gain competitive advantage in the multibillion-dollar travel industry. For example, knowing the power of celebrity, Priceline.com signed Emmy Award–winning actor William Shatner to star as "The Negotiator" in a long-running multimedia advertising campaign. But how did that translate into public relations? Just try to find an interview with or article about Shatner that doesn't mention Priceline.com. A recent *New York Post* profile of the actor mentioned Priceline.com in the second paragraph. The *San Francisco Chronicle* declared, "He's still a wise guy today, doing commercials for Priceline." ABC's *Good Morning America* described him as the "Priceline pitch man" even before

The Negotiator
William Shatner's popular commercials for Priceline.com have become a media-relations bonanza: Articles about the actor invariably mention his association with the provider of online travel services.

(Courtesy of Priceline.com)

mentioning his starring roles as Captain Kirk in *Star Trek* and Denny Crane in *Boston Legal*.[14]

How much did Priceline.com pay for those prominent media mentions? Zero. Zip. Nada. In fact, if interviewers won't mention Priceline.com, Shatner will. "And Priceline, don't forget Priceline," he told an interviewer on NBC's *Today* show. "I just finished a couple of Priceline commercials last week."[15] Said Priceline.com CEO Jeffery Boyd, "We've had a good run with William Shatner and The Negotiator ad campaign."[16]

Other tactics in marketing public relations include:

- product- or service-oriented news releases and media kits;
- video news releases (VNRs) featuring newsworthy products or services;
- news conferences to announce significant new products or services;
- blogs, interactive websites, messages in social networks such as Facebook, and other social media;
- satellite media tours (SMTs), in which a spokesperson for a newsworthy product or service gives individual interviews to local television stations via satellite;
- displays at trade shows, where industry analysts and interested consumers gather to examine new products and services;
- special events designed to attract media attention to a particular product;
- spokesperson appearances in the media (including Internet chat rooms) and at special events; and
- communication efforts that target employees, investors, government regulators, and other publics besides consumers that can influence the success of marketing campaigns.

Marketing public relations can work alone or, better, as part of a marketing campaign. Marketing public relations targets consumers, sometimes gaining independent endorsements by working through intervening publics such as the news media. Although all of an organization's relationships can have marketing implications—after all, everyone is a consumer—other areas of public relations work less directly with marketing, focusing instead on publics such as employees, government units, and investors.

A CLOSER LOOK AT IMC

Enough background. Let's jump into a deeper definition of integrated marketing communications. IMC, say the authors of *Integrated Marketing Communications*, is "planned, developed, executed, and evaluated with affecting one specific consumer behavior in mind, the process of making purchases now or in the future."[17]

Focusing on Individual Consumers

In IMC, individual consumers are the focus of thematically consistent messages sent through a variety of media. In fact, marketing professor Robert Lauterborn suggests that the traditional four P's of marketing have become the consumer-driven four C's:[18]

1. *Product* has become *consumer wants and needs:* These shape every aspect of the marketing process.
2. *Price* has become *consumer's cost:* For example, a price of $500 is a higher cost to a college student than it is to a movie star.
3. *Place* has become *convenience to buy.*
4. *Promotion* has become *communication:* This is two-way communication that actively seeks consumer input.

Sending thematically consistent messages through a variety of media might sound familiar. In Chapter 1, we discussed how an organization must identify its values and then ensure that all its actions, including its communications, are consistent with those values.

As we said earlier, IMC recognizes the ineffectiveness of trying to use only the old mass media to affect masses of people. Instead, IMC uses a variety of media to communicate with small groups and, ideally, individuals. For example, a combination of satellites, global positioning devices, and cell phones can allow marketers to send text messages to consumers as they near a favorite store. The messages can even offer discounts. "It drove me into the shop," said one recipient of such a message.[19]

IMC tactics can include rebate offers or other consumer-response promotions that gather information for databases. Databases are an indispensable element in IMC campaigns. As we've noted, computerized databases do more than record names, locations, phone numbers, and e-mail addresses; they can record when, where, and how a product was purchased. Databases also can record when and how consumers were contacted, when and how they responded, and what the organization and the consumer said. Every contact with a consumer becomes a chance to refine the database.

Sending One Clear Message

If the database lies at the heart of successful integrated marketing communications, so does the philosophy of sending one clear message—or, at least, thematically consistent messages—to consumers. Generally, marketing public relations helps send that one consistent message. However, with its expertise in supplying newsworthy stories to the news media, on some occasions marketing public relations may send a slightly different message than do the other tactics in an IMC campaign.

In the mid-1990s, a pioneering IMC campaign for First Alert carbon monoxide detectors helped show how public relations, by sending a slightly different message, could pave the way for following a related effort involving advertising, sales promotions, and more. Originally, the message for the entire campaign was simple: This product can save your life. But research revealed a problem: Wheatley Blair, Inc., the public relations agency assisting in the launch of First Alert's new detector, discovered through research that the U.S. public didn't understand how dangerous carbon monoxide gas is. Consumers, therefore, might not respond to a marketing message stressing safety—because they didn't know they were in danger.

Wheatley Blair and other members of the First Alert marketing team quickly retooled the campaign, crafting the following timetable and strategy. First, a public relations campaign targeting the news media would roll out. Mention of the First Alert carbon monoxide detector would be secondary; the campaign's primary goal would be to emphasize the threat of carbon monoxide poisoning. The detector itself then would be shipped to ensure availability. Finally, the advertising campaign would roll out in October, the beginning of the home heating season.

Radio and TV news stories were key to the public relations campaign. Wheatley Blair helped generate stories on CBS, NBC, and CNN network news.

Wheatley Blair's campaign included personal calls to science and home products editors, a comprehensive media kit, video news releases, and sponsorship of interviews with scientists and medical personnel.

Wheatley Blair's news-media strategy succeeded in raising public awareness of the dangers of carbon monoxide from 2 percent of consumers to 75 percent, and the entire First Alert IMC campaign was a success. Representatives of Walmart told the makers of First Alert that the new carbon monoxide detector was the most successful

QUICKBREAK 13.2

The Fall of Advertising?

Give a book a provocative title, and readers will come. For example, who wouldn't at least pick up a copy of author James Lee Burke's *In the Electric Mist with Confederate Dead*?

As noted in Chapter 1, the most provocative title in recent years for IMC practitioners may be Al and Laura Ries' *The Fall of Advertising and Rise of PR*. The father–daughter team of marketing consultants has made headlines with this claim: Public relations is more successful than advertising in introducing new brands.

"We're beginning to see research that supports the superiority of PR over advertising to launch a brand," the Rieses say. "A new study of 91 launches shows highly successful products are more likely to use PR-related activities."[20] According to the Rieses, public relations tops other IMC disciplines for building credibility and generating word-of-mouth publicity; advertising is most successful in maintaining awareness of established brands.

Recent IMC research shows that marketing agencies are increasing the amount of time they spend seeking alternatives to advertising.[21] In a 2006 study of traditional marketing communication functions, marketing executives believed public relations was the most effective discipline in five of eight key areas (product launches, generating word of mouth, building corporate reputation, managing a crisis, and changing perceptions); direct marketing was most effective in three (ongoing product promotion, targeting niche audiences, and increasing sales); and advertising was most effective in none.[22]

"Like Ries, I believe advertising has its place," says John Shattock of Shattock Communications and Research of New Zealand. "It should be a reminder of a perception that has already been established by more credible means. Public relations should come first, establishing perceptions and credibility."[23] ∎

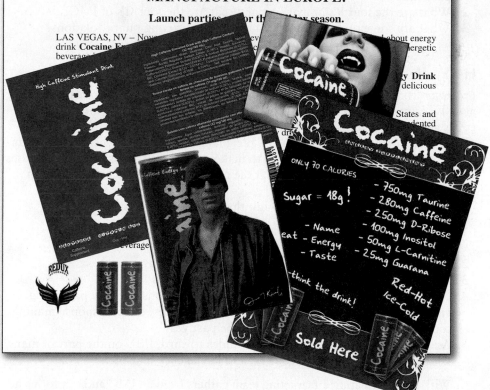

Media Kit Materials

To promote the debut of Cocaine energy drink in Europe, Redux Beverages created and distributed a media kit that included a news release, product shots, a poster of company founder Jamey Kirby, and other materials.

(Courtesy of Redux Beverages).

new product introduction, up to that time, in the history of Walmart's hardware/home products department. For its role in the First Alert campaign, Wheatley Blair won a Silver Anvil, the highest award bestowed by the Public Relations Society of America.[24]

In most IMC campaigns, public relations sends the same message that other elements of the marketing process send. But, as the First Alert example shows, marketing public relations is flexible. Using the tactics of public relations—or any other IMC profession—to help develop a market is called **premarket conditioning**.[25] By sending a slightly different preliminary message, public relations can help create receptivity for a subsequent IMC campaign.

 ## QUICK CHECK

1. What do public relations and IMC have in common? Is all of public relations part of IMC?

2. What are the four P's of marketing? What are the four C's of IMC?

3. What are some of the traditional tactics of marketing public relations?

HOW IMC WORKS

Professor Tom Duncan, author of a series of IMC textbooks, recommends starting an IMC campaign with an **IMC audit.** An IMC audit is similar in intent to the ethics audit (Chapter 6) and the communication audit (Chapter 7) we examined earlier in this book. As with all audits, the goal is to determine where an organization stands right now—and, perhaps, to make recommendations for future actions. Again and again, it's worth noting that the public relations process begins with good research.

Duncan recommends an IMC audit that consists of five steps:[26]

1. Analysis of the communications network used to develop marketing communications programs

2. Identification and prioritization of key stakeholder groups

3. Evaluation of the organization's customer databases

4. Content analysis of all messages (ads, public relations releases, packaging, video news releases, signage, sales promotion pieces, direct response mailings, social media, and so on) used within the past year

5. Assessment of knowledge of, and attitudes toward, IMC on the part of marketing managers, top management, and key agency managers

With the information a marketing team gathers from an IMC audit, it forms a good idea of the environment from which it intends to launch an IMC campaign. If that environment is favorable to an IMC campaign, great! Full speed ahead. But if the audit shows that an organization has no customer database and a hodgepodge of contradictory marketing messages, then it must make some technological and philosophical changes before it can launch a successful IMC campaign. Perhaps the organization must even reexamine its core values in light of the proposed IMC campaign.

IMC Tactics

To familiarize consumers with the new $50 bill, the U.S. Bureau of Engraving and Printing communicated through a variety of media, including an interactive website and, pictured here, news releases, school lesson plans, and cashier posters.

(Courtesy of the U.S. Bureau of Engraving and Printing)

Creating an IMC Campaign

With an IMC audit completed, we now know where we are. But how do we get to where we want to be? Using our knowledge of current resources and attitudes, how do we build a successful IMC campaign? The following seven strategies are among several recommended by Matthew P. Gonring, a consultant for the Gagen MacDonald strategic communications agency.[27]

1. *"Create shared performance measures. Develop systems to evaluate communications activities."* Recall Chapter 8 on planning: We need to have a goal and measurable objectives to prove to others the effectiveness of our program. Setting precise sales goals may be too ambitious, but we can certainly specify the number and nature of relationships we intend to create.

2. *"Use database development and issues management to understand your stakeholders."* Here's another expert telling us that a database is essential to a successful IMC campaign. A database details the individual consumer wants and needs that have been identified through interactive communication with consumers. Issues management, as we noted in Chapter 7, is a process of identifying and managing emerging issues that can affect your organization and the publics important to your organization.

3. *"Identify all contact points for the company and its products."* Some experts recommend an even broader look at contact points, or **contacts.** *"Contacts* will likely be a new term for many advertising and promotion people, particularly the way it is used in IMC," say the authors of *Integrated Marketing Communications.* "We define a contact as any information-bearing experience that a customer or a prospect has with the brand, product category, or the market that relates to the marketer's product or service."[28]

4. *"Create business and communication plans for each local market."* As your IMC program improves, you may want to strive for the goal of developing a plan for every individual customer within your database. Ideally, all those messages to slightly different publics must be consistent with one another.

5. *"Create compatible themes, tones, and quality across all communications media."* Remember: All elements of the marketing process need to send consistent messages about your product.

6. *"Hire only team players."* Jealousy and insecurity can destroy an IMC campaign. Public relations practitioners can't always insist on using public relations tactics, nor can advertisers always insist on using advertising. Members of the IMC team must agree to use the messages and the media consumers prefer.

7. *"Link IMC with management processes."* Robert Dilenschneider, the former head of Hill & Knowlton, one of the world's largest public relations agencies, offers solid advice: "Think in terms of what the manager wants to achieve, and tie everything you suggest to a financial or business result."[29]

If clearly identified consumer values, wants, and needs are shaping each step of your marketing process, from product design to follow-up after a purchase, the odds are good that you have a successful IMC campaign.

SOCIAL MEDIA APPS

Public Relations or Marketing? The "Tyranny of the *Or*"

Within large organizations such as corporations, who should manage social media activities? The public relations department—or the marketing department? That was one question in a recent survey of public relations and marketing professionals. The surprising answer? "In the future, 56% of respondents believe marketing will manage social media activities going forward; 18% say PR. . . ."[30]

Why surprising? A second survey of public relations and marketing professionals showed that, in such organizations, public relations tended to control the management of most online and social media activities, including blogging, podcasting, social networking, microblogging (including Twitter), and website content. Marketing tended to control the management only of e-mail marketing and search engine optimization.[31]

Asking which department should control social media activities, however, might be an example of the so-called "tyranny of the *or*." In other words, such a question might force us into an unproductive and unrealistic *either/or* choice. Additional survey research shows that, for their own purposes, *both* public relations professionals and marketing professionals use blogs and social networking; *both* groups also use search engine optimization.[32]

To counter the "tyranny of the *or*," James Collins and Jerry Porras, authors of *Built to Last: Successful Habits of Visionary Companies*, propose "the genius of the *and*."[33] As opposed to an *either/or* philosophy, a *both/and* approach to social media suggests that all communications departments within an organization should use social media when appropriate. Ongoing communication audits, as discussed in Chapter 7, could help ensure that all messages—social media or not, marketing-oriented or not—are coordinated, consistent, and effective. ■

Applying IMC

Let's return to this chapter's opening "Real World" scenario for a moment. What sorts of strategies and tactics might an IMC campaign for your music website include? After doing an IMC audit and learning that your organization will support an integrated marketing approach, you gain agreement on a consistent message to be sent to potential customers: "Hard-to-find music at hard-to-beat prices." A quick scientific survey of potential customers shows that this is an effective message. Your mission now is to deliver that message effectively and to bring buyers into your stores. Among the tactics you might consider are

- developing blogs, podcasts, and a few free downloads, all of which gather information for your database.
- placing ads in college newspapers, both print and online. The ads include your Web address and a discount coupon that requests names and phone numbers for free drawings. The coupons provide more information for your database.

- sponsoring alternative rock concerts and passing out flyers with coupons.
- offering company executives to local media as experts on little-known but high-quality bands. You particularly try to place the executives on call-in radio shows, where direct interaction with potential customers is possible.
- sending e-mail newsletters to customers who request them. You could simply spam everyone in your database, but you wisely decide not to.
- opening a Twitter account to announce new uploads.
- launching a direct e-mail and text-messaging campaign that lets customers know when one of their favorite bands has released a new recording. You know each customer's favorite bands because that information is in your database. And, of course, you send such messages only to customers who agree, in advance, that they want them. In those messages, you ask customers to let you know whether they're interested in other bands as well.

For each of these tactics, you also would establish some measures of evaluation. Evaluation of your tactics would help you determine which are most successful in helping your company achieve its marketing goals.

You can probably think of more and better ideas, but note what the tactics mentioned here have in common: They deliver approximately the same consumer-focused message, they tend to target individuals rather than mass audiences, they're not limited to traditional public relations and advertising tactics, they're interactive, and they seek information for an increasingly detailed database.

Hey, give yourself a raise.

QUICKBREAK 13.3

Mobile Marketing: The New Kid in Town

Among the many disciplines within integrated marketing communications, none has attracted as much recent buzz as mobile marketing. And oftentimes, that buzz is the ringing of a smartphone. In the words of the Mobile Marketing Association, **mobile marketing** is "the use of wireless media as an integrated content delivery and direct response vehicle within a cross-media or stand-alone marketing communications program."[34] In simpler terms, that generally means receiving marketing messages tailored for wireless telephones. Those messages, in turn, often are part of a larger IMC campaign that involves interactive messages through several media. In 2009, Forrester Research reported that 80 percent of U.S. households had at least one mobile phone.[35]

Here's just a sampler of how mobile marketing can work:

- downloadable wireless software apps that offer special services
- text message coupons
- microblog messages about product reviews, availability, or discounts
- GPS (global positioning systems) technology that issues coupons or other discounts when customers near their favorite stores or restaurants

In the best traditions of IMC, mobile marketing messages should focus on individual wants and needs: Either the individual has requested such communications, or a database helps ensure that company-initiated messages directly target an individual's known interests.

The new kid in town may also be the fastest-growing: *DMNews* reports that although mobile marketing expenditures were only 1.8 percent of all marketing expenditures in 2009, annual mobile marketing budgets grew by 26 percent—even though overall market budgets declined by 7 percent.[36]

Technological innovations never rule forever; 20 years ago, direct mail was the hottest thing around. But with an increasing allowance in a tough economy, mobile marketing—the new kid in town—shows staying power. ■

CHALLENGES TO CONSUMER-FOCUSED MARKETING

We hope you're excited about IMC, CRM, and the other approaches to consumer-focused marketing. However, we also hope that you're realistic. These relatively new approaches to marketing still face challenges that can limit their effectiveness.

We've already hinted at one: jealousy, or so-called turf battles, with every member of the marketing team promoting only his or her own area of expertise. IMC's new emphasis on social media may be increasing such concerns. Research shows that public relations units tend to supervise blogging, social-network involvement, and website development whereas marketing departments tend to supervise search engine optimization and e-mail marketing efforts (see Social Media Apps, p. 415).[37] To support new social media programs, organizations are shifting funds from advertising and direct marketing budgets much more than from public relations budgets.[38] Ironically, social media may be increasing antisocial tensions within IMC programs. Two tactics described earlier in this chapter—conducting an IMC audit and hiring only team players—can help reduce such tensions.

A second challenge to consumer-focused marketing involves measuring results. "I believe marketing is never going to be an exact science," says Philippe Schaillee, vice president of marketing, strategy, and research and development for Sara Lee North America.[39] "[There's] always a little bit of art and gut in it. PR is a difficult one to measure." A recent survey shows that, among the IMC disciplines, marketing managers find results easiest to measure in direct marketing, followed, in order, by online tactics in all disciplines; advertising; and, finally, public relations.[40]

A third challenge to consumer-focused marketing is privacy. For example, the United States and the European Union have significantly different standards regarding consumers' rights to privacy. And within the United States, concern for individual privacy increases as marketers seek more and more information on individuals. A survey of marketing professionals in the midwestern United States found that 74 percent favored government intervention to ensure additional privacy for consumers; only 7 percent strongly opposed government intervention. The authors of the study concluded, "The respondents . . . want legislation to protect privacy even though it might encroach upon their professional activities, partially to suppress their culpability and also because they desire such protections in their own lives."[41]

Finally, the very nature of consumer-focused marketing can be a challenge. Excessive focus on consumers' desires could pull a company away from its core values. An organization that lives only to satisfy the whims of consumers may well lack the deeply felt, enduring values that characterize successful organizations. Consumer-focused marketing will succeed best when it operates on a solid foundation of organizational values. "The integrity of the corporation that stands behind the brand is even more important than the marketing or promoting of the brand itself," says Frank Vogl, president of Vogl Communications in Washington, D.C. "So many people involved in the integrated marketing and communications of corporate brands have not paid adequate attention to the values that should be seen at the core of the brand itself."[42]

No one can deny that consumer-focused marketing faces serious challenges. However, as social media enter the new marketing mix, database-driven approaches to marketing offer significant opportunities for public relations practitioners.

QUICK CHECK

1. What is an IMC audit? What steps does it involve?
2. In marketing, what is a contact or contact point?
3. Why are team players essential to a successful IMC campaign?

SUMMARY

Consumer-focused marketing is not a passing fad. It's a growing reality for organizations that want their products to have clear, consistent, appealing images in the marketplace. It's also a growing expectation on the part of consumers, who seek more and more individual attention from organizations as new technologies make such communication possible. Unlike mass marketing, consumer-focused marketing begins not with a public but with an individual. Products are designed to accommodate, as much as possible, individual needs and desires. Sales messages focus on those same individual self-interests, which are discovered through two-way communication and are recorded in databases.

Integrated marketing communications unites a variety of communications disciplines to address individual self-interests: advertising, public relations, marketing promotions, packaging, pricing, direct marketing, and any other approach that can send an effective message to a potential customer. Despite the wide array of available tactics, the messages in an IMC campaign are integrated: Consumers should receive a consistent message about an organization's product or service. The message of an advertisement, for example, should be consistent with the message of the price and of a product-oriented news release.

Not all of public relations is part of consumer-focused marketing, of course. Marketing addresses one very important public: consumers. Public relations builds relationships with any public that can affect an organization's success, including employees, stockholders, and government regulators. But one of the most exciting areas in the future of public relations is its role in consumer-focused marketing. Today, marketing means building relationships with individual consumers, and that's good news for public relations.

DISCUSSION QUESTIONS

1. How are the philosophies of public relations and consumer-focused marketing similar? How are they different?
2. What is "integrated" about integrated marketing communications?
3. What are the benefits of using consumer-focused marketing instead of mass marketing?
4. Does IMC, as it is currently practiced, have any challenges or potential challenges?
5. How is an IMC audit similar to an ethics audit and a communication audit?

MEMO FROM THE FIELD

VIN CIPOLLA

President; Municipal Art Society of New York
New York, New York

Vin Cipolla is president of the Municipal Art Society of New York. Previously, he was president of the National Park Foundation, a private philanthropy dedicated to preserving, protecting, and improving U.S. national parks. He also led the integrated marketing agencies HNW, Inc., and Pamet River. He is a Phi Beta Kappa graduate of Clark University.

There's a very good reason why integrated marketing has become so popular lately. Basically, without it, we marketers are doomed. In fact, when a company doesn't present a consistent marketing message to the public, it not only wastes a lot of money, it also risks its own reputation.

But that's not all. These days it's not enough for marketing functions like advertising, PR, and direct mail to work together. Now, marketing needs to be integrated throughout the entire company—with departments like customer service, sales, distribution, and manufacturing all working together on corporate objectives. The goal today is to make certain that everyone in the company is conveying the same message. Not just the marketing department.

Not convinced? Think about it. Imagine watching a heartwarming television advertisement promoting a particular airline's commitment to friendly service. Now, the next time you fly, you certainly expect that airline's in-flight personnel to be extra friendly, right? You certainly expect that airline to have spent as much effort maintaining high customer service standards as it did creating that expensive television advertisement.

(continued)

The fact is, we expect more now as consumers than we did a few years ago. Interactive technology, websites, and sophisticated database marketing have all raised the standard of customer service by facilitating dynamic two-way communication between business and consumers. Today it's not enough simply to sell products; companies must also build relationships with customers if they want to compete.

For example, consumers like to feel remembered and appreciated. That's one reason some mail-order companies have started to track customer orders more effectively. Perhaps the next time you call, they may thank you for your repeat order and ask if you'd like the same size as before. It's that type of personal attention that is becoming the new norm.

That level of integration isn't easy to achieve. It requires a centralized database in which every customer contact position (e.g., billing, marketing, and service) is integrated so that valuable customer data is captured, analyzed, and maximized fully. That's a challenge. Maybe that centralized customer data isn't available yet. Or maybe it is, but the company doesn't know how to interpret it so the data provides valuable insight.

Another problem may be the company's own staff. Internal power struggles are responsible for the failure of many integrated marketing programs. Unfortunately, many employees aren't trained to work in cross-departmental partnerships. Finance managers speak a different language than marketing managers. Customer service has different priorities than sales. And rarely is there a company incentive for these disparate employees to work together in teams on company goals.

That's why the most successful companies have strong leadership at the top. Only the CEO or president has the authority to cross so many departmental borders. Without that senior-level support, a truly effective integrated marketing program will remain a distant dream.

So what does all this mean for you? It means your job just became a lot more difficult. Now you don't just need to work well with other marketing divisions. You also need to work well with customer service, billing, and distribution too.

The more you understand how the entire company functions, the better you'll perform your own job. The more you understand what these various managers consider important, the easier a time you'll have working with them on the corporate goals. And, finally, the more you understand how emerging technology is affecting marketing, the more successfully you'll play by today's new marketing rules.

As you take on the challenge, I wish you all the luck in the world. ■

CASE STUDY 13.1 Ford Has a Social Media Idea

A generation ago, Ford Motor Company touted its ingenuity with a catchy slogan: Ford has a better idea. So well-known was the motto that it became the punch line of a TV comedy skit: To his fiancée's request that they go for a walk, an actor portraying company founder Henry Ford smiled suggestively and said, "Ford has a better idea."

In the decades since, Ford, like many automobile companies, has traveled a bumpy road. But when *PRWeek* magazine announced the winner of its 2010 "Best Use of Social Media Award," one company clearly did have better ideas: Ford Motor Company.

In its successful efforts to improve young drivers' impression of the brand, Ford assembled an award-winning team of agencies, including Burson-Marsteller, Ogilvy PR, and Direct Impact, to create an integrated marketing campaign that relies heavily on social media.

"If you have a dedicated social media agency," said Scott Monty, Ford's manager of social media, "they need to be well integrated with the rest of your team because none of this stuff stands alone."[43]

The key tactic in Ford's new-age integrated marketing campaign might have been Fiesta Movement, a Web-based special event in which Ford selected 100 "agents"—basically media-savvy young adults—to drive Ford Fiestas for six months, compete with one another in various contests, and report on their experiences via blogs, Twitter, YouTube, Flickr, and other social media. Ford's Fiesta Movement, reported Slate.com magazine, showed that huge corporations could use social media effectively:

Fiesta Movement, most social media commentators agree, was a huge success. The 700 videos produced by the agents have generated 6.5 million views on YouTube, and there have been more than 3.4 million impressions of Fiesta Movement on Twitter. Even photos taken by the agents have been viewed more than 670,000 times.[44]

So successful was the program that Ford has created new versions of Fiesta Movement and has invited key opinion leaders and bloggers to drive other models and report on their experiences.[45]

"We're embracing a communications strategy [that's] shifted away from focusing primarily on financial and auto publications . . . and more toward consumer-facing [programs]," said Monty. "Social media is a big part of that."[46]

Additional social media tactics in the Ford campaign have included scheduling "Tweet-ups" with Ford executives, including CEO Alan Mulally;

posting company videos on YouTube; and corresponding with key bloggers through comments and Twitter. In 2009, Ford teamed up with BlogHer, a coalition of female bloggers, to sponsor test-drives and feedback sessions at a BlogHer convention.[47] In response, one member blogged to her readers:

I'm very excited about this. You know we are a Ford family. . . . So tell me, what do *you* want in a car? I will be participating in a roundtable with Ford staff and can ask questions or pass along comments. Follow the discussion on Twitter. . . .[48]

In praising Ford's social media programs, Jeff Davis of Sawmill Marketing Public Relations wrote, "That's the difference between stiff one-way traditional communications and social media. Sure, social media is riskier, but if executed properly it makes even the behemoth corporation feel more real and in touch with its customers."[49]

Social media blogger Jeff Bulas believes that the key to Ford's success involves intervening publics and independent endorsements. "People trust corporations less," he wrote, "so with the rise of social media, you need to allow other people [to] create trust for you through social media." Ford succeeded because it "reached out to those who are listening and let them do the talking and . . . connect with people like themselves."[50]

In its description of Ford's award-winning campaign, *PRWeek* wrote, "Ford research found that, prior to the campaign, an average of 29 percent of bloggers would have considered purchasing a Ford. Post-campaign, that number jumped to 89 percent."[51] When Vitrue, a social media marketing and measurement agency, posted its list of the "Top Social Brands of 2009," Ford ranked 24th, ahead of all other U.S. car manufacturers and, among all automakers, behind only Mercedes (17th) and BMW (20th). To compile its annual list, Vitrue searches popular social media sites for mentions of brand names. (Incidentally, the top social brand of 2009 was iPhone, with parent company Apple ranking eighth.)[52]

College students and other consumers needn't look far to find examples of large companies that have misused social media and damaged the relationships they sought to improve. However, with Fiesta Movement and its other social media tactics, Ford Motor Company clearly has a better idea.

DISCUSSION QUESTIONS

1. How are the concepts of intervening publics and independent endorsements relevant to Ford's social media marketing campaign?
2. Scott Monty, Ford's social media manager, said that "none of this stuff stands alone."

How might Ford integrate its social media tactics with other, more traditional relationship-building tactics?
3. Is Ford's IMC campaign a good example of two-way symmetrical relationship building? Why or why not?
4. In your experience, what large companies, besides Ford, have used social media to build successful relationships? What particular tactics succeeded?
5. In your experience, what large companies have tried but failed to use social media to build successful relationships? Why did they fail? ■

CASE STUDY 13.2 Ghost Story: A Questionable Tactic Haunts Medical Journals

Professor Adriane Fugh-Berman has encountered a ghost—twice. A professor of physiology and biophysics at Georgetown University School of Medicine, Fugh-Berman received an e-mail from a major international pharmaceutical company in 2004. The message offered her an article, already researched and written, that she could revise, if she wished, and submit to a medical journal under her own name. Journal articles can help professors gain promotion to higher ranks and higher salaries.

The professor looked at the article, which touted one of the company's drugs, but refused to submit it under her name. A short while later, however, she encountered the article again. This time, it carried another medical researcher's name: It had been submitted to a prestigious medical journal, and the journal's editors were consulting Fugh-Berman to see if the article merited publication. Rather than examine the article, she told the editors about the ghost.[53]

The ghost, of course, was a ghostwriter. Ghostwriting is a time-honored activity within public relations: Practitioners write speeches for executives, news releases without personal bylines, and a host of other documents for which others often receive the credit. Such ghostwriting is standard procedure. But some ghosts are scarier than others: Editors of

medical journals maintain that ghostwriting in the medical profession, especially when the ghostwriter is paid by a pharmaceutical company attempting to secretly promote its own products, is unethical and dangerous.

"Scientific research is not public relations," explains Robert Califf, vice chancellor of clinical research at Duke University. "If you're a firm hired by a company trying to sell a product, it's an entirely different thing than having an open mind for scientific inquiry. . . . What would happen to a PR firm that wrote a paper that said this product stinks?"[54]

Unfortunately, the ghost that appeared twice before Fugh-Berman may have lots of company. "I believe 50 percent of articles on drugs in the major medical journals are not written in a way that the average person would expect them to be," says David Healy, professor of psychological medicine at the University of Wales. "The evidence I have seen would suggest there are grounds to think a significant proportion of the articles in journals . . . may be written with help from medical writing agencies. They are no more than infomercials paid for by drug firms."[55]

Paraphrasing the charges of yet another angry medical professor who had seen a ghost, a *New York Times* reporter wrote, "Public relations firms hired by drug companies—furtive spin doctors—are ghostwriting articles in the journals to suit clients' interests."[56]

A survey published in the *Journal of the American Medical Association* found that ghosts had written at least 11 percent of articles in the top U.S. medical journals.[57] "It introduces another bias into the whole clinical drug trial picture," says Professor Thomas Bodenheimer of the University of California at San Francisco. "The American public and the physicians in the United States are not going to know, really, the true facts about the drugs."[58]

To combat ghostwriting, medical journals and medical researchers have enlisted their own writing skills: They are asking pharmaceutical companies and their ghostwriters to follow a written ethics code known as *Good Publications Practice: Guidelines for Pharmaceutical Companies*. In part, that document states:

- The Acknowledgments section of a paper should list those people who made a significant contribution to the study but do not qualify as authors. It should also be used to acknowledge the study's funding and the [pharmaceutical] company's involvement in the analysis of the data or preparation of the publication. . . .
- The named author(s)/contributors should approve the final version of the manuscript before it is submitted.

- The contribution of the medical writer should be acknowledged.[59]

By listening to their target audience—medical editors—and following the provisions of such ethics codes, public relations practitioners can help lay this ghost to rest.

DISCUSSION QUESTIONS

1. Is it ethical, in your opinion, for public relations practitioners to ghostwrite articles that tout a pharmaceutical company's product?
2. Is all ghostwriting in public relations unethical? Is it unethical for a public relations practitioner to write a speech for which another individual receives credit?
3. The vice chancellor of clinical research at Duke University suggests that a public relations agency that ghostwrote an honest article about a defective drug would lose its pharmaceutical client. What should public relations practitioners do when their research reveals that a pharmaceutical client's drug might have defects?
4. Would it be ethical for a public relations practitioner, in the employ of a pharmaceutical company, to openly assist a professor in writing a journal article about one of the company's products? ∎

NOTES

1. Russell Goldman, "KFC to Honor Oprah's Free Chicken Coupons," ABC News, 7 May 2009, online, http://abcnews.go.com; "Dumbest Moments in Business 2009 . . . Midyear Edition," CNNMoney.com, 1 July 2009, online, http://money.cnn.com/galleries/2009.
2. Robyn Blakeman, *The Bare Bones Introduction to Integrated Marketing Communication* (Lanham, Md.: Rowman & Littlefield Publishers, 2008), 14.
3. P. J. Kitchen, I. Kim, and D. E. Schultz, "Integrated Marketing Communications: Practice Leads Theory," *Journal of Advertising Research 48*, no. 4 (2008): 531–546.

4. "Will Database Marketing Work in Health Care?" *Marketing Health Services* (fall 2001): online, LexisNexis.
5. John Dalla Costa, *The Ethical Imperative* (Reading, Mass.: Addison-Wesley, 1998), 178.
6. "Customer Relationship Management Programs: New Hot Business Issue," news release issued by PR Newswire, 28 August 2001, online, LexisNexis.
7. Don E. Schultz and Beth E. Barnes, *Strategic Brand Communication Campaigns* (Lincolnwood, Ill.: NTC Business Books, 1999), 44.
8. William P. Ehling, Jon White, and James E. Grunig, "Public Relations and Marketing

Practices," in *Excellence in Public Relations and Communication Management,* ed. James E. Grunig (Hillsdale, N.J.: Lawrence Erlbaum, 1992), 390.

9. Glen M. Broom, Martha M. Lauzen, and Kerry Tucker, "Public Relations and Marketing: Dividing the Conceptual Domain and Operational Turf," *Public Relations Review* (fall 1991): 224.

10. "The Route to the Consumer," *PRWeek,* 17 May 2004, online, www.prweek.com.

11. Kitchen, Kim, and Schultz.

12. "The World Famous Cocaine Energy Drink Begins Manufacture in Europe," a news release issued by Redux Beverages, 5 November 2009, online, www.drinkcocaine.com.

13. Don E. Schultz, Stanley I. Tannenbaum, and Robert F. Lauterborn, *Integrated Marketing Communications* (Chicago: NTC Business Books, 1993), 22.

14. Michael Starr, "He's All Ears; Shatner Teeters on Edge of Personal Space," *New York Post,* 30 November 2009, online, NewsBank: America's Newspapers; Mick LaSalle, "They Boldly Go," *San Francisco Chronicle,* 8 May 2009, online, NewsBank: America's Newspapers; Robin Roberts, "William Shatner: Up Till Now," *Good Morning America,* 13 May 2008, online, LexisNexis Academic.

15. "Today," NBC News Transcripts, 8 December 2008, online, LexisNexis Academic.

16. Doug Tsuruoka, "William Shatner's Gone Where Relatively Few Have Gone Before," *Investor's Business Daily,* 11 March 2009, online, LexisNexis.

17. Schultz, Tannenbaum, and Lauterborn, 107.

18. Schultz, Tannenbaum, and Lauterborn, 12–13.

19. Patricia Odell, "Text Messaging Gets a Cautious Reception in the U.S.," *Promo,* May 2003, 25.

20. Al Ries and Laura Ries, "Part 1: The Fall of Advertising," Ries & Ries Focusing Consultants, online, www.ries.com.

21. "The Route to the Consumer."

22. "Marketing Management Survey 2006."

23. John Shattock, "The Fall of Advertising and the Rise of PR," Shattock Communications and Research, online, www.shattock.net.nz.

24. Bob Wheatley, telephone interview by author, 24 March 1994.

25. "The Route to the Consumer."

26. Tom Duncan, "Is Your Marketing Communications Integrated?" *Advertising Age,* 24 January 1994, online, LexisNexis.

27. Matthew P. Gonring, "Putting Integrated Marketing Communications to Work Today," *Public Relations Quarterly* 39, no. 3 (1994), online, LexisNexis.

28. Schultz, Tannenbaum, and Lauterborn, 51.

29. Cliff McGoon, "Secrets of Building Influence," *Communication World,* March 1995, 18.

30. "Social Media Survey 2009," *PRWeek* and MS&L Worldwide, October 2009, online, www.prweekus.com.

31. "Digital Readiness Report: Essential Online Public Relations and Marketing Skills," a report by iPressroom, Trendstream, Korn/Ferry International, and Public Relations Society of America, 2009, online, www.ipressroom.com.

32. "Digital Readiness Report: Essential Online Public Relations and Marketing Skills."

33. James C. Collins and Jerry I. Porras, *Built to Last: Successful Habits of Visionary Companies* (New York: HarperCollins, 1997).

34. "Glossary," Mobile Marketing Association, online, www.mmaglobal.com/glossary.pdf.

35. Charles S. Golvin, Jacqueline Anderson, and Reineke Reitsma, "The State of Consumers and Technology: Benchmark 2009," 2 September 2009, online, www.forrester.com.

36. Dianna Dilworth, "MMA Forum: Mobile Marketing Grows," *DMNews,* 3 June 2009, online, www.dmnews.com.

37. "Digital Readiness Report: Essential Online Public Relations and Marketing Skills."

38. "Social Media Survey 2009."

39. "Marketing Management Survey 2008," *PRWeek* and MS&L Worldwide, 23 June 2008, online, www.mslworldwide.com.

40. "Marketing Management Survey 2008."

41. Stuart L. Esrock and John P. Ferré, "A Dichotomy of Privacy: Personal and Professional Attitudes of Marketers," *Business and Society Review* (spring 1999): 113, 121, 123.

42. "Enviro Activists Use Ethics to Drive Powerful PR Strategies," *PRNews,* 12 March 2001, online, LexisNexis.

43. Brian Morrissey, "The New Social Gurus," *Adweek*, 18 January 2010, online, www.Adweek.com.

44. Matthew Yeomans, "Why Social Media Should Be about Far More than Marketing," Slate.com, 19 January 2010, online, www.thebigmoney.com.

45. See www.fiestamovement.com.

46. Nicole Zerillo, "CEO Involvement Buoys Ford's Social Media Drive," *PRWeek*, 15 April 2009, online, www.prweekus.com.

47. "Best Use of Social Media/Digital 2010," *PRWeek*, 11 March 2010, online, www.prweekus.com.

48. "Ford's What Women Want," Multi-Minding Mom, 12 July 2009, online, www.multimindingmom.com.

49. Jeff Davis, "Ford Understands Social Media," PR Buzzsaw, 8 December 2009, online, http://sawmillmarketing.com.

50. Jeff Bullas, "The 7 Secrets to Ford's Social Media Marketing Success," Jeffbullas's Blog, 18 February 2010, online, http://jeffbullas.com.

51. "Best Use of Social Media/Digital 2010."

52. "The Vitrue 100: Top Social Brands of 2009," Vitrue, 4 January 2010, online, http://vitrue.com.

53. Anna Wilde Mathews, "At Medical Journals, Writers Paid by Industry Play Big Role," *Wall Street Journal*, 13 December 2005, A1.

54. Mathews.

55. Antony Barnett, "Revealed: How Drug Firms 'Hoodwink' Medical Journals," *The Observer*, 9 December 2003, online, http://observer.guardian.co.uk.

56. Lawrence K. Altman, "The Doctor's World: Some Authors in Medical Journals May Be Paid by 'Spin Doctors,'" *New York Times*, 4 October 1994, online, LexisNexis.

57. Melody Petersen, "Madison Ave. Has Growing Role in Business of Drug Research," *New York Times*, 22 November 2002, online, LexisNexis.

58. Mathews.

59. Elizabeth Wagner, Elizabeth A. Ford, and Leni Grossman, "Good Publication Practice for Pharmaceutical Companies," *Current Medical Research and Opinions* 19, no. 3 (2003): 153.

14

Cross-Cultural Communication

Courtesy of USAID

OBJECTIVES

After studying this chapter, you will be able to

- describe broad areas that historically have distinguished one culture from another
- explain the differences between a culture and a public
- discuss traditional obstacles to successful cross-cultural communication

- describe a nine-step process organizations and individuals can use to achieve effective cross-cultural communication

KEY TERMS

communication, p. 436
communication model, p. 436
cross-cultural, p. 436
culture, p. 428

REAL WORLD

East Meets West

You are the new senior communications specialist for a multinational producer of breakfast cereals. Your company is based in the United States, and you are eager to begin traveling internationally. You've been to Mexico and Canada but have never been overseas. The director of corporate communications has just asked you to launch an internal social network—a kind of in-house Facebook—and a related magazine for employees in the three countries in which your company operates: the United States, Spain, and Japan.

You quickly learn the names of the company's senior communications officials in Spain and Japan and, with the director's permission, invite them to the United States to help plan the network and magazine. You know that a lot rides on the success of these meetings. You're new with the company, and you want to impress your employers. Your guests from Spain and Japan report to you, and you don't want

them to entertain doubts about their new boss. And you know that the director of corporate communications wants a great project that will impress the company's chief executive officer.

As the three-day meeting approaches, you're excited as you review the preparations. You've scheduled a comfortable meeting room, reserved tables in your city's best restaurants, and arranged entertainment for two evenings. You're startled, however, when a colleague asks about cultural differences.

Cultural differences? You will be dealing with individuals from highly developed economies who, in addition to their native languages, speak fluent English. Could there really be important cultural differences? And could those differences affect the success of your project?

That's a risk you must avoid, but what can you do? How do you cope with the challenges of cross-cultural communication?

CULTURES: REALITIES AND DEFINITIONS

The job seemed easy for the U.S.-based poultry company: It wanted to translate its English-language slogan—"It takes a tough man to make a tender chicken"—into Spanish. But the Spanish rendition may have startled Hispanic consumers: "It takes a sexually aroused man to make a chick affectionate."[1]

Affection was in short supply in 2010 when Japanese beverage giants Suntory Holdings and Kirin Holdings considered a merger to boost their international marketing efforts. In an article titled "Corporate Culture Clash Took Fizz Out of Merger," Japan's *Daily Yomiuri* newspaper reported that the companies' differing management styles "appear to have mixed about as well as oil and water." When months of negotiations finally collapsed, the newspaper concluded, "In the end, the two companies could not smooth over the differences in their respective corporate cultures."[2]

Promoters of a Seattle-area rave—a huge, uninhibited dance party—unintentionally offended Muslims when they lifted Arabic passages from the Koran, the holy book of Islam, to decorate a brochure. Devout Muslims honor the Koran so much that they wash their hands and mouths three times before touching and reading from the book.

"This is a disgrace to Islam," said a spokesman for a Seattle mosque. "The activities in raves are totally immoral."

The brochure's designer apologized and confessed that he found the passages in a school textbook. "We had no idea what any of it meant," he said. "It looked good on [the brochure]. It is a beautiful language. And we had a desert and a camel in there. It was a theme."[3]

The theme of these three anecdotes is cross-cultural communication. Each of these damaging mishaps occurred when different cultures intentionally or unintentionally met. In each case, important values were at issue. Those values grew, in part, out of **demographics** (nonattitudinal characteristics), **psychographics** (attitudinal characteristics), and **geodemographics** (characteristics based on where a person or group lives). But the values grew from more than these three "graphics." The values shaped and were shaped by unique cultures.

The term **culture,** in the sense of a group of people unified by shared characteristics, defies precise definition. "It seems obvious from the use of the word in our everyday language that it is impregnated with multiple meanings," says Anindita Niyogi Balslev of the Center for Cultural Research in the Netherlands.[4] In fact, as early as 1952, scholars had identified more than 150 definitions of *culture*.[5] The *Dictionary of Anthropology* defines a culture as "a social group that is smaller than a civilization but larger than an industry,"[6] with *industry* being an anthropological term for a small community. A culture, therefore, is usually larger than a public. In fact, a culture can consist of countless different publics, all of which are influenced by the traits of that culture. As if that weren't enough, the concept of culture can transcend a group of people: Culture is also the set "behavior patterns, arts, beliefs, institutions, and all other products of human work and thought" characteristic of that group.[7]

Why study cross-cultural communication? "Now, more than ever before in human history, more people are coming into contact with people from cultures other than their own," says Robert Gibson, author of *Intercultural Business Communication.* Gibson cites several reasons for the growth of cross-cultural contacts, including improved travel methods, the Internet, and increasingly diverse workforces.[8] To that list, we might add the increasing number of mergers and acquisitions in the business world, the growth of democratic governments around the world, and the consequent increase in international trade. Many of these forces help fuel **globalization,** the growing economic interdependence of the world's people.

Relationship-building errors such as those of the poultry company, Suntory and Kirin, and the Seattle rave occur because, in the words of Stephen Banks, author of *Multicultural Public Relations,* "scant attention is paid in research or practice to the predicaments of culturally diverse populations and the necessity for learning to communicate effectively across cultural differences."[9] A decade ago, a representative of the National Association of Corporate Directors recommended that, to negotiate successfully with diverse cultures throughout the world, each U.S. business should create an Office of Foreign Affairs to study trends, politics, moods, and opinions in regions where the business wishes to operate.[10] The authors of this book respectfully suggest that such an office should already exist: the organization's public relations department.

International Public Relations

Not all cross-cultural communication involves relationships between two nations. For example, the Suntory–Kirin situation involved the awkward meeting of two business styles. And the wealth of ethnic groups within the United States, Canada, and other nations can make cross-cultural communication an everyday occurrence. In the current global economy, however, when public relations practitioners study unfamiliar cultures, they often are studying consumers and business partners in other nations. "Cultural diversity and identity," says the author of *Multicultural Public Relations*, "tend strongly to conform to national borders."[11] For example, a recent survey of European tourists found that 25 percent of visitors to Italy went there hoping for a love affair with an Italian male. Only Italy's natural beauty scored higher; the lovers outscored museums and other attractions. Right or wrong, a large percentage of European tourists believe that romance, passion, and availability are cultural characteristics of Italian males.[12]

Musician Randy Newman has a satirical song that envisions the world becoming "just another American town"—a humorously offbeat premise for a song but a disastrous notion for international public relations. If the world were a town, it would be stunningly diverse—not at all a representation of a culture familiar to most students. A popular children's book, *If the World Were a Village*, shows that if Earth were a village of 100 people, demographic ratios in the first decade of the 21st century would make the village look like this:[13]

- 24 residents would have no electricity; most of the others would use it only at night to light their homes.
- 22 would speak Chinese; 9 would speak English; 7 would speak Spanish.
- 20 would earn less than a dollar a day.
- 17 would not be able to read or write.
- 10 would be younger than 5 years old; 39 would be younger than age 19; 1 would be older than age 79.
- 7 would own a computer.

Successful international public relations recognizes such diversity. Successful international public relations attempts to create harmonious, productive relationships through well-researched cross-cultural communication.

CULTURAL ATTRIBUTES

Without a research strategy, studying a different culture can seem impossible. Where do we start? What information should we gather? Fortunately, social scientists and business experts have created systems for categorizing important cultural

ТОРГОВЛЯ С АМЕРИКОЙ

СПРАВОЧНИК ПО ПРОГРАММАМ ПРАВИТЕЛЬСТВА США

Публикация BISNIS -
Службы деловой информации о странах Содружества независимых государств
Министерства торговли США

Business Guide

An indication of the increasing importance of cross-cultural communication is this U.S. Department of Commerce Russian-language publication, *Doing Business in America.*

(Courtesy of the U.S. Department of Commerce)

attributes. One of the best-known systems was created by marketing professional Marlene Rossman.[14] Rossman's system distinguishes among cultures by analyzing attitudes regarding eight characteristics. Let's examine each to see how it can differ from culture to culture.

Attitudes about Time

Different cultures have different attitudes about time. In some Latin American nations, a dinner party scheduled for 8 P.M. might not really begin until near midnight. In other cultures, arriving later than 8 P.M. would insult your hosts. In some cultures, a designated time is a flexible guideline; in others, it is a specific target. On a working vacation in Zurich, Switzerland, one of your authors was warned by Swiss colleagues to avoid the center of the city on a particular Thursday afternoon; college students would be holding a spontaneous demonstration at that time, he was told. A scheduled spontaneous demonstration: something to be expected from a nation famed for making clocks and other timepieces.

One survey of national attitudes toward time found that, of 31 nations studied, Switzerland ranked first in terms of a rapid, time-oriented pace of life. The United States ranked in the middle at number 16, and Mexico ranked last. In general, Japan and Western European countries had the fastest pace of life. Developing nations in Africa, Asia, the Middle East, and Latin America had the slowest, most flexible pace.[15]

In our East Meets West scenario, differing attitudes toward time could affect the success of your meetings. Japanese tend to be punctual about business meetings. If a meeting is scheduled for 9 A.M., businesspeople in Japan and the United States generally are ready to sit at the table and begin at that hour. In Spain, however, businesspeople are more casual about specified starting times. Says Miguel Angel Fraile, secretary general of Spain's Catalonian Commercial Confederation:

> It's true that Spain is behind the rest of Europe when it comes to punctuality at work meetings. . . . If I have a meeting in Brussels at 4 P.M., it starts at 4 P.M. Here in Spain we have what we see as 10 minutes of courtesy—so at a 4 P.M. meeting here you can be 10 minutes late. . . . We see this 10 minutes grace as being polite.[16]

And how about early-afternoon meetings? No problem for your Japanese guest, but will your Spanish guest expect a traditional siesta at that time? In Spain and several other nations in Europe and Latin America, businesses often close from lunch until late afternoon.

Attitudes about Formality

Should you address a new business associate from another nation by his or her first name? Should you hug? Bow? Shake hands? The answers depend, of course, on cultural preferences. As a rule, however, formality is safer than informality in new business relationships.

Syrians often embrace new acquaintances. Pakistanis shake hands, though rarely a man with a woman. Zambians shake hands with the left hand supporting the right. Norwegians rarely use first names until relationships are well established. Japanese almost never use first names in business settings.

A Quieter Quack

When AFLAC, a leading international insurance company, recently cast its famous duck in Japanese TV commercials, the company introduced a kinder, gentler quack. Japanese culture frowns on yelling, an AFLAC representative explained.

(Courtesy of American Family Life Assurance Company of Columbus—AFLAC)

What do cross-cultural experts say about the visitors you're expecting for your project planning meeting? A warm handshake and even an accompanying pat on the back would be acceptable as you greet your Spanish visitor. The Spanish make no distinction about shaking hands with men or women. With your Japanese guest, however, be prepared to bow, even though he or she may offer to shake hands. You can flatter your Japanese guest by bowing first. In Japan, the person who initiates a bow is acknowledging the high social status of the other person. If you exchange business cards with your Japanese visitor, bow slightly and extend yours with both hands. You should accept your visitor's card in the same manner and should look at it respectfully after receiving it.[17]

Attitudes about Individualism

People in the United States pride themselves on the rugged individualism that turned a diverse group of immigrants into a powerful nation of highly mobile individuals. It's comparatively rare in our society to live one's entire life in the town of one's birth surrounded by family. Other cultures, however, especially those of Asian and Hispanic origin, often place more emphasis on preserving extended families. Chinese names, for example, place the family name before the individual name.

Japanese businesspeople in particular see themselves as part of a team; in fact, a study of individual entrepreneurialism in 66 nations and self-governing territories ranked Japan second to last, ahead of only Puerto Rico.[18] In Japan, an individual may speak on behalf of an organization, but not until he or she has painstakingly built consensus on the issue under discussion. "Japan has a special phrase to describe such behind-the-scenes consensus-building, '*nemawashi*,' which translates as 'laying the groundwork,'" says Yuri Kageyama of the Associated Press. "Neglecting *nemawashi* is considered a foolish and sure way to walk into failure."[19]

VALUES STATEMENT 14.1

Special Olympics

Founded in 1968, Special Olympics is a nonprofit program of sports training and competition for individuals with intellectual disabilities.

Special Olympics Oath

Let me win. But if I cannot win, let me be brave in the attempt.

—Special Olympics website ∎

Because of the importance of *nemawashi* throughout their culture, the Japanese are reluctant to say no. In your project planning meeting, for example, it would be unusual for your Japanese guest to veto a particular proposal. Instead, he or she might meet the idea with thoughtful silence and a polite "If only. . . ."

Attitudes about Rank and Hierarchy

In cultural terms, rank and hierarchy extend beyond organizations: They exist within society itself. India, for example, still struggles to overthrow a traditional caste system of Brahmans—often Hindu priests—at the top and so-called untouchables at the bottom. Knowing the social status of a business associate and understanding the consequent signs of respect he or she expects can be essential to successful cross-cultural communications. For example, your Spanish guest would be honored to be seated at your right during meals—a sign of respect in Spain. And when you initiate a bowing sequence with your Japanese guest, you courteously suggest that he or she outranks you.[20]

Attitudes about Religion

Knowing the religious conventions and traditions of a culture can help prevent unintended errors that can hamper cross-cultural communication. For example, Muslims fast from dawn to sunset during the holy month of Ramadan. Inviting an Islamic business associate to a working lunch during that time could inadvertently suggest a lack of respect for his or her religious beliefs. The Jewish Sabbath extends from Friday evening to Saturday evening and, in Judaism, is a day of rest. Scheduling a Friday evening business dinner in Israel, where Judaism is the dominant religion, could be a serious cultural faux pas.

Cultural differences regarding religion became starkly apparent in 2005 when a Danish newspaper published editorial cartoons depicting the Islamic prophet Muhammad. Many Muslims feel that images of Muhammad are blasphemous, and riots broke out in Syria, Iran, Lebanon, and other nations. Meanwhile, believing the controversy threatened freedom of the press, newspapers throughout North America and Europe reprinted the cartoons. As different groups—religious and otherwise—clashed worldwide, the death toll exceeded 100.[21] An apology from the Danish newspaper failed to end the violence, and bloodshed continued for months.[22]

Attitudes about Taste and Diet

For many public relations practitioners, cuisine is the reward for mastering the subtleties of cross-cultural communication. Perhaps it's arroz con pollo (chicken with rice) in Costa Rica or couscous in Algeria or bratwurst in Germany or grits in the southern United States. The culinary diversity of the world's cultures is dazzling and gratifying but also rife with opportunities for serious blunders. Religion and other cultural influences often prohibit the consumption of certain foods. Hindus don't eat beef; cattle are exalted in that religion, which encompasses the belief that souls return to Earth again and again as different life forms. Strict Judaism forbids the consumption of pork products and shellfish, which are considered unclean.

QUICKBREAK 14.1

The Melting-Pot Myth

Much of this chapter focuses on cultures beyond the borders of the United States. Can we assume, then, that the United States is a uniform hot-dogs-and-apple-pie culture? Hardly.

In *America's Diversity,* a study of 200 years of U.S. Census data, the Population Research Bureau reported, "Residential separation of the races continues to be so pronounced that sociologists Douglas Massey and Nancy Denton have called it 'American Apartheid.' "[23] (Apartheid is the former South African policy of enforced separation of races.) A national survey of U.S. citizens indicates that *apartheid* may be too strong a word for some: 38 percent want a more uniform culture; 31 percent want cultural differences to remain; and 29 percent lack strong opinions on the matter.[24]

But can culture and race really be linked? Studies show that race can indeed be an indicator of a unique culture. A landmark survey of racial and ethnic groups within the United States at the end of the 20th century, for example, concluded that blacks, Asians, Hispanics, and non-Hispanic whites (a U.S. Census Bureau designation) spend their time in different ways. Asians spend more time each week on education than do blacks, Hispanics, or whites. Blacks devote more time to religion each week than do the other racial and ethnic groups. Hispanics spend more time caring for their children than do the other groups. Whites spend more time at work than Asians, blacks, or Hispanics.[25]

"The trend in every aspect of American life is toward greater cultural, ethnic, and linguistic diversity," says marketing expert Marlene Rossman. "Not only are minority groups increasing in size, they are also not assimilating the way many minority and ethnic (especially immigrant) groups did in the past. . . . Our cultural model is becoming the mosaic, not the melting pot."[26] ∎

Attitudes about Colors, Numbers, and Symbols

What's the unlucky number in mainstream U.S. culture? Thirteen, of course. How about in Japanese culture? It's four. One of your authors learned that the hard way when he titled an article for a multinational corporate magazine "Four from Japan." Every culture develops an unofficial language of colors, numbers, and symbols that often speaks louder than words. "It's worth knowing that the color white denotes death, to the Chinese," *New Zealand Management* magazine cautioned readers who do business in China. "So no gift should ever be wrapped in white paper. Similarly a bouquet of white lilies would be a definite no-no."[27]

Symbols can be just as fraught with meaning as colors and numbers. For example, most of us interpret the thumbs-up symbol used for case studies in this book as a sign of approval. In Australia and Nigeria, however, the symbol and the gesture mean anything but approval. In those societies, the upward thumb is an obscene sign of disrespect.[28]

Attitudes about Assimilation and Acculturation

How quickly can members of one culture adjust to the traditions of another? How accepting are people of new ideas and nontraditional thinking? Such flexibility can help characterize a culture. The more a culture resists outside influences, the more powerful its own traditions can become. The French Academy, for example, which is the legal watchdog of the French language as it's spoken in France, has officially banned English terms such as *hot dog* and *drugstore*. Russia has a similar anti-English campaign, instituting fines and even imprisonment for Russians who used English derivatives such as *biznismeni* for *businessmen*.[29] More tolerant is the attitude of former South African President Nelson Mandela, who drew cheers from young adults attending a rock concert in London by declaring, "I am now almost 100 years old, but I am so proud because my roots are in South Africa but my gaze reaches beyond the horizon to places like Britain where we are tied together by unbreakable bonds."[30]

Sometimes assimilation and acculturation occur so gradually that the process escapes our notice. More than one observer, for example, has noted that U.S. dominance of the technology and content of the Internet is subtly piping U.S. influences into offices and homes around the world. Says Andre Kaspi, a professor at the Sorbonne in Paris, "You have to know English if you want to use the Internet. . . . The main difference now in favor of American culture is the importance of technology—telephone, Internet, films. . . . American influence is growing. It's so easy to get access to U.S. culture; there are no barriers."[31]

No doubt true. But any public relations practitioner who assumes that the world has become one big U.S.-based culture runs the risk of studying a different phenomenon: the culture of the unemployment line.

To Rossman's list of eight characteristics, we might add one more: attitudes about business communication. For example, a recent report by Deloitte Consulting on "Technology Usage in the Global Workplace" came to this conclusion:

When in Rome, do as the Romans do. When in Brazil, better talk in person first: Brazilians are less likely to use their company intranets than their counterparts in other nations. Employees' preferred method of workplace communications varies somewhat by age, and a lot by nationality. Brazilians prefer in-person and e-mail communications for most workplace issues. In China, India, and the United Kingdom, the company intranet rules. Canadians and Americans are mixed in their communications preferences.[32]

 QUICK CHECK

1. What is the purpose of the analytical system created by Marlene Rossman?
2. Would it be fair to say that the United States is all one culture? Why or why not?
3. What is the difference between a culture and a public?

CROSS-CULTURAL COMMUNICATION: DEFINITIONS AND DANGERS

Clearly, this chapter uses the term *cross-cultural communication* to refer to exchanges of messages among the members of different cultures. But it's worth stopping to ask what, exactly, is meant by **cross-cultural.** Many sociologists and communication specialists use the term *intercultural* to denote exchanges of various kinds between cultures. Your authors, like many public relations practitioners, prefer the term *cross-cultural* because it prompts an image of crossing a border, of going into partially unknown territory. *Cross-cultural* urges caution and encourages you to stay constantly aware of the obstacles to successful communication between members of different cultures.

And what do we mean by **communication?** We mean more than words can say. In Chapter 13, for example, we noted that every aspect of a product sends a message to consumers. Besides the verbal messages of news releases and advertisements, a product's price, packaging, and distribution all send nonverbal messages to potential purchasers. Consumers in West African communities were horrified when one U.S. company tried to sell its popular brand of baby food in their stores. The labels featured a smiling baby—very popular in the United States, but intensely disturbing in a culture that relies on pictures to identify the contents of jars and cans.[33] Briefly, by *communication,* we mean any exchange of information—verbal and/or nonverbal—between the sender and the receiver of a message.

Encoding and Decoding

In Chapter 5 we examined a basic **communication model,** which is represented in Figure 14.1. More complex versions of this basic model include two elements that become particularly important in communication between cultures: encoding and decoding. **Encoding** involves the sender's selection of words, images, and other forms of communication that create the message. **Decoding** involves the receiver's attempt to produce meaning from the sender's message. This expanded communication model appears in Figure 14.2.

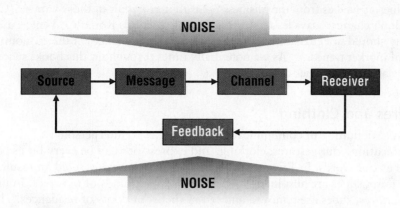

I FIGURE 14.1

In successful cross-cultural communication, senders must understand how a message will be decoded before they can effectively encode it. The perils of encoding errors are illustrated by yet another U.S. company's adventures abroad. When the Coca-Cola Company translated its name into Chinese, the phonetic version—KeKou Kela–instructed Chinese consumers to "Bite the wax tadpole."[34] It's hard to guess who was most surprised by that particular cross-cultural encoding–decoding glitch.

Even though an organization's message might need different encodings for different cultures, the message should ideally remain shaped by the values that unite the organization. A successful organization cannot embrace one set of values with the elderly in South Africa, a different set of values with women in China, a third set of values with Russian immigrants in Australia, and so on. Such duplicity would be more than dishonest; maintaining so many different personalities would be exhausting. In successful organizations, all messages emanate from a set of clearly understood

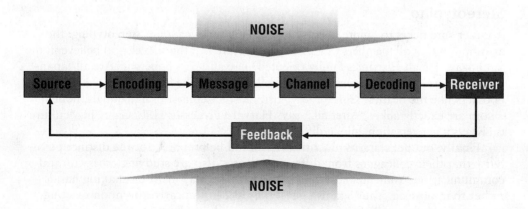

I FIGURE 14.2

core values as well as from the business goals that grow out of those values. "Core values don't change," says leadership consultant Jose Luis Romero. "Hence, a company should not change them in response to recent changes in the economy or to global market trends."[35] As we note many times throughout this book, successful public relations is a values-driven process.

Gestures and Clothing

Our broad definition of communication also applies to interpersonal communication. Our gestures, clothing, and expressions can be every bit as communicative as our words. In Taiwan, blinking at someone is considered an insult. In the Islamic faith, shoes are absolutely forbidden on the grounds of mosques. In many Asian cultures, shoes are removed and left at the front doors of residences. The A-OK expression made by forming a circle of the thumb and forefinger and raising the other three fingers is, like thumbs-up, a sign of approval in the United States. But in Japan it's a symbol for money. In Australia and some Latin American nations, it's an obscene gesture. During a 1950s visit to a Latin American country, Vice President Richard Nixon grandly made the A-OK gesture—and was stunned by an immediate chorus of boos.[36]

Because people from almost every culture use their hands when they speak, gestures—more so than clothing or expressions—can send unintended messages during cross-cultural communication. Speaking to a group of journalists in the Central Asian nation of Kyrgyzstan, one of your authors illustrated a point by bringing one fist down on top of the other two or three times. Halting in midsentence, his shocked interpreter leaned over and hissed in his ear that he was signaling, in the crudest possible way, that he wanted to make love to his audience. Fortunately, your author's stricken expression led his audience to forgive him with friendly laughter. That story has two morals: Cross-cultural mistakes can be very embarrassing—and people can be very forgiving if they sense your good will.

Stereotyping

Another sure ticket to failure in cross-cultural communication is **stereotyping**: the assumption that all members of a particular culture act, think, feel, and believe in the same way. Are all Hispanics family-oriented? Are all Swiss punctual? Are all Japanese polite? Are all U.S. citizens blunt? Do all teenagers like loud music? Do all baby boomers like the Beatles? Cultures *do* exist, but they consist of individuals, none of whom are exactly alike. "After all," says Harvard Professor H. L. Gates Jr., "culture is always a conversation among different voices."[37]

Finally, public relations practitioners should be prepared for the distinct possibility that their colleagues from different cultures *also* are studying cross-cultural communication. Your Japanese guest, for example, may insist on shaking hands rather than bowing. Your Spanish guest may ask for an early-afternoon meeting to show his or her willingness to adapt to your culture. So who prevails in such complicated situations? Often, it's easiest to follow the culture of the host, but the host still should seek opportunities to honor the cultures of his or her guests. An abundance of courtesy is a good beginning for cross-cultural communication.

Cross-cultural communication has become an unavoidable challenge for the public relations profession. One recent study shows that two thirds of international business mergers fail because "cultures and people are often incompatible, national differences emerging."[38] Says Elizabeth Howard, principal partner of an international consulting firm, "Today it is difficult, probably impossible, to find a business that has not been affected in one way or another by the new global economy."[39] Indeed, it's not unusual for farmers from the midwestern United States to find themselves part of trade delegations in Asia or Latin America, seeking new markets for U.S. agricultural products. And those farmers, like others engaged in cross-cultural business discussions, constantly confront the question posed by sociologist and anthropologist David Howes: "What happens when the culture of production and the culture of consumption are not the same?"[40]

These cultural gulfs must be bridged if the producers and the consumers are to achieve their goals. In the next section, we offer a nine-step process that can help organizations and individuals achieve successful cross-cultural communication.

 QUICK CHECK

1. What do *encoding* and *decoding* mean?
2. Should an organization's core values change as it communicates with different cultures?
3. What does *stereotyping* mean? How can it threaten successful cross-cultural communication?

ACHIEVING SUCCESSFUL CROSS-CULTURAL PUBLIC RELATIONS: A PROCESS

At this point in our chapter, two facts are clear: Cross-cultural communication can be difficult—and it is inevitable. Painstaking encoding and decoding of cross-cultural messages have become everyday challenges. Given that reality, how can public relations practitioners become effective cross-cultural communicators? We recommend a process consisting of nine stages: awareness, commitment, research, local partnership, diversity, testing, evaluation, advocacy, and continuing education. We begin with awareness. If public relations practitioners aren't sensitive to the presence or potential difficulties of a cross-cultural encounter, they have little hope of communicating effectively.

Stage One: Awareness

You can start enhancing your awareness of cross-cultural situations right now by studying a foreign language and enrolling in liberal arts courses that allow you to explore the traits and traditions of other cultures. If your college or university has an international students association, consider joining it. If it has a study abroad program, plan to spend a semester in another country. Higher education offers you rare opportunities to discover that the rest of the world doesn't think, act, dress, eat, and communicate as you do.

Achieving fluency in a foreign language can keep you from being the butt of an old joke that remains all too current. As the joke goes, someone who speaks three languages is trilingual; someone who speaks two languages is bilingual; someone who speaks one language is a U.S. citizen. English indeed has become the language of international commerce, but learning to speak the language of a foreign business acquaintance—even if you master only a few key phrases—can heighten your sensitivity to cross-cultural issues. More important, perhaps, learning a second language can improve the success of your cross-cultural communication by creating good will. On business in Paris, one of your authors was able to persuade a new acquaintance to work late by using his shaky knowledge of French, gained in college. When the Parisian apologized, in English, for missing a deadline, your author was able to

QUICKBREAK 14.2

Diversity in Public Relations

"To be more effective in our increasingly socially complex society," says Reed Byrum, former president of the Public Relations Society of America, "achieving diversity is more than just a matter of inclusiveness. The public relations profession needs to vigorously recruit minorities into the profession and into leadership positions."[41]

Since 2003, *PRWeek* magazine and public relations agency Hill & Knowlton have published the annual *PRWeek* Diversity Survey. The 2009 survey offered these findings:

- Sixty-one percent of practitioners are white; 17 percent are black; 15 percent are Hispanic; 4 percent are Asian/Pacific islander; 1 percent are Native American; and 2 percent are other.
- Before beginning a public relations career, only 46 percent of current minority-group practitioners knew someone who worked in public relations or a related profession; 54 percent of Caucasians knew someone.
- A lack of role models is the top barrier to the recruitment and retention of minority-group practitioners.
- Only 38 percent of minority practitioners believe that the profession of public relations is becoming more diverse; 48 percent of Caucasians believe the profession is becoming more diverse.[42]

"If we're supposed to be communicating with the public, surely we have to be reflective of the population and understand how to communicate with them," says MaryLee Sachs, chairman of Hill & Knowlton USA. "I cannot imagine why PR pros wouldn't see this as a critical aspect of doing business."[43] ■

respond *C'est la même chose pour tout le monde, n'est-ce pas?*—roughly, "It happens everywhere, doesn't it?" The Parisian was surprised that an American could speak even bad French. The conversation sputtered along in French until the amused Parisian switched back to English and agreed to stay late to finish the project.

Public relations organizations throughout the world now emphasize continuing education in multiculturalism and cross-cultural communication. The Institute for Public Relations, for example, has launched the Essential Knowledge Project, which includes a growing section on Global Public Relations. Public relations professionals, the institute concludes, are "likely to succeed in and to pursue further international assignments when acquiring adequate preparatory background or cultural competency."[44]

Another powerful way to increase awareness is to diversify the workplace, bringing multiculturalism and cross-cultural communication into the everyday business of the office. This strategy will be discussed in greater detail below.

Stage Two: Commitment

Reporters have a technique called "parachute journalism"—dropping into a locality the reporter doesn't know well to write a quick story about that same little-known locality. Journalists aren't proud of parachute journalism. Nor should public relations practitioners be proud of using a similar strategy in their profession: parachuting, so to speak, into a little-known culture to do some hit-and-run relationship building. Successful cross-cultural communication requires personal commitment, as well as commitment from an organization's highest levels, to doing the arduous background work that allows the effective encoding and decoding of messages to and from another culture.

Stage Three: Research

Commitment implies a willingness to do the research demanded by successful cross-cultural communication. Standard reference sources for this research include such magazines as *Communication World* and *National Geographic*; books such as Patricia Curtin and Kenn Gaither's *International Public Relations* and Krishnamurthy Sriramesh and Dejan Verčič's *The Global Public Relations Handbook*; and websites such as those of the Institute for Public Relations and the International Trade Administration, a division of the U.S. Department of Commerce. The ITA website includes information on business etiquette in almost every nation around the world. Hosting a meeting for colleagues from Botswana? Confirm your meeting 24 hours ahead of time, and don't be offended if your guests arrive late. Don't call them by their first names until they initiate that practice, and don't schedule the meeting for September 30: That's Botswana Day. Need more information? See ITA's Market Research Library at www.buyusainfo.net.

Believe it or not, the Central Intelligence Agency also makes available some of its highly detailed data on different nations around the world. Check out the CIA's *World Factbook* at www.cia.gov.

QUICKBREAK 14.3

Hofstede's Cultural Dimensions

Among the strategies for analyzing cultural diversity, the gold standard may well be **Hofstede's cultural dimensions.** In the 1970s, Dutch sociologist Geert Hofstede analyzed cultural information gathered by the multinational corporation IBM, which was trying to learn why particular employee relations strategies worked in some countries but failed in others. Hofstede's extensive research identified five "dimensions" that distinguish one culture from another:[45]

1. *Power distance* measures how tolerant a society is about unequally distributed power. Countries with a high acceptance of power distance include Mexico and France. Countries with a low acceptance include Austria and the United States.
2. *Individualism versus collectivism* contrasts loyalty to oneself with loyalty to a larger group. Countries in Asia and Latin America gravitate toward collectivism, whereas the United States, Canada, and most European nations gravitate toward individualism.
3. *Masculinity versus femininity* contrasts competitiveness with compassion and nurturing. Masculine nations include the United States, Germany, and Japan. Feminine nations include Sweden and Spain.
4. *Uncertainty avoidance* measures how well a society tolerates ambiguity. Nations that avoid uncertainty include Germany and Japan. Nations that tolerate ambiguity include Great Britain and the United States.
5. *Long-term orientation* measures a society's willingness to consider the traditions of the past and carry them into the future. China and other East Asian nations have a long-term orientation, whereas the United States has a short-term orientation.

Hofstede's national profiles, included in his 1991 book *Cultures and Organizations: Software of the Mind,* may be able to help you with the scenario that opens this chapter. For example, your Japanese associate comes from a masculine culture, whereas your Spanish colleague comes from a feminine culture. Several websites, including www.clearlycultural.com, also include Hofstede's national profiles. ■

A good reference librarian can steer you to other current sources. Such research might help you remember to take off your shoes when you enter the hotel room of your Japanese guest in our East Meets West scenario.

Stage Four: Local Partnership

No matter how much research you conduct, you'll never know as much about a foreign culture as does someone reared in it. When an organization begins a long-term cross-cultural relationship, it should consider bringing members of that culture into its communications team. "You must have representation on the ground in different parts of the world, but you should be extremely cautious about hiring a major global PR agency," says Robert Wakefield, former chairman of the International Section of the Public Relations Society of America. "Instead, tap into the worldwide network of small local agencies or talented native PR consultants who can guide you through the maze of PR issues in their own country."[46]

Stage Five: Diversity

Not all different cultures are beyond the borders of the United States. As QuickBreak 14.1 notes, the United States is hardly a melting pot; instead, it's a mosaic of different cultures. Diversity within an organization's public relations team can help ensure successful cross-cultural communication at home. Furthermore, it can increase an organization's awareness of cultural differences, which benefits communication both at home and abroad. Pitney Bowes, a multinational message-delivery company, believes that a diverse workforce boosts company profits.[47]

Stage Six: Testing

As every actor knows, it's better to bomb in rehearsal than on opening night. When possible, test your relationship-building tactics on trusted members of the culture you plan to address. For example, in this chapter's East Meets West

SOCIAL MEDIA APPS

Taking It to the Streets

Websites such as www.cia.gov and www.buyusainfo.net provide detailed overviews of different national economies and cultures. But what about the street-level view? What about individual opinions from citizens of the countries in question? Enter Global Voices (globalvoicesonline.org). In the words of the site's founders, "We wish to call attention to the most interesting conversations and perspectives emerging from citizens' media around the world by linking to text, photos, podcasts, video, and other forms of grassroots citizens' media."

Global Voices is searchable by Subject and Author, but for cross-cultural public relations, the most valuable search aspect might be Countries. A search of "Iran," for example, offers links to blogs about women's rights in Iran; a new political-protest ring tone; relations with Egypt; the dangers of blogging in Iran; and dozens of other topics.

The blogs on Global Voices specialize in linking to other blogs, videos, and similar social media that expand the particular topic.

In terms of research, blogs resemble focus groups and in-depth interviews: They cannot be considered representative of larger publics—but blogs often reveal issues and important personal viewpoints that formal research can overlook. Blogs can add the human element to the statistics of cross-cultural research.

To quote Global Voices' tagline: "The world is talking. Are you listening?" ■

scenario, you could show a detailed itinerary of your business and entertainment plans to natives of Japan and Spain. You just might learn, for example, that Spanish business dinners don't begin until late evening—often past 9 P.M.—and that Japanese business dinners can go on for hours and often end in nightclubs.[48]

Stage Seven: Evaluation

A constant goal in public relations is to learn from our successes as well as from our mistakes. As soon as possible, public relations professionals should evaluate the effectiveness of completed cross-cultural communication efforts, seeking ways to reinforce the good and revise the bad. In the East Meets West scenario, for example, did your Japanese guest wince when you offered her a gift as you met her at the airport? Your consequent research might show that although the Japanese enjoy receiving gifts, they often are embarrassed if they cannot reciprocate immediately.[49] The gift may have been a blunder, but it was a valuable misstep: It taught you to be sensitive to the intricacies of offering a gift to a member of another culture.

Stage Eight: Advocacy

Cross-cultural communication works best when an entire organization commits to it. Commitment requires a persistent focus, and a persistent focus requires an advocate. Perhaps that advocate can be you. Says international communication consultant Mary Jo Jacobi:

> No matter where a multinational company operates, it must remain conscious of the fact that it has audiences in many other parts of the world and that whatever its executives do and say locally could have far-reaching ramifications and business implications. As a result, we must seek to ensure that we communicate a consistent message worldwide, particularly on sensitive matters. Getting this clearly in the minds of colleagues is one of the most important roles that we, as professional communicators, must undertake.[50]

Stage Nine: Continuing Education

The Essential Knowledge Project, sponsored by the Institute for Public Relations, is an example of continuing education, as are exchanges of executives between local branches of multinational companies. Other forms of continuing education can be as simple as reading international publications, watching international television programming, attending lectures, or—gasp!—returning to a university for an occasional night course on a foreign language or an unfamiliar culture. Fortunately, learning doesn't stop at graduation. It's a big, exciting world out there, burgeoning with opportunities for anyone who can cross its boundaries with knowledge, diplomacy, and confidence.

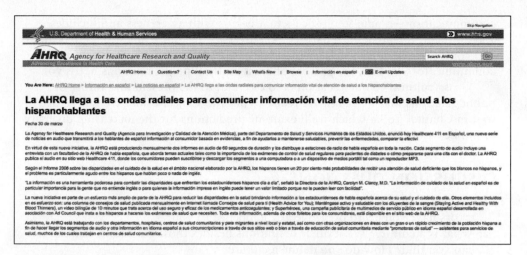

News Release

The growing importance of Hispanic publics in the United States has led progressive organizations such as the U.S. Department of Health and Human Services to issue news releases in Spanish. For an English-language version of this news release, see p. 282.

(Courtesy of U.S. Department of Health and Human Services)

QUICK CHECK

1. In the nine-step process for successful cross-cultural public relations, what does local partnership mean? Why is it necessary?

2. What sources could you consult for information on the cultures of other countries?

3. Specifically, how does cross-cultural communication mean more than international communication?

SUMMARY

As we noted in Chapter 11, a generation ago Canadian philosopher Marshall McLuhan argued that the world was becoming a "global village." In many ways, he was right. Modern technology can make communication between Kenya and China faster and easier than the task faced by a 19th-century Toronto resident who simply wanted to deliver a message across town. Yet the global village is hardly a community in the traditional sense. Every street has its own customs, biases, traditions, fears, religion, diet, and language. Every street, in other words, has its own culture.

If the global village is to thrive, those streets need to learn to communicate with one another. The conversations won't be easy. We need only to read a daily newspaper to see that the conversations often fail. We can increase the chances of success, however, by learning a process for effective cross-cultural communication—a nine-step process that begins with awareness and includes commitment, research, local partnership, diversity, testing, evaluation, advocacy, and continuing education. That process needs well-educated, talented, versatile communicators. In fact, the process of cross-cultural public relations needs you.

Cross-cultural communication is so essential to the present and future of public relations that we're not yet ready to put the subject aside. We will return to it in Chapter 16, in which we'll examine predictions for the increasing diversity of publics around the world.

DISCUSSION QUESTIONS

1. Besides the gaffes mentioned in this chapter, what cross-cultural communication errors have you heard of? Have any happened to you?
2. What is a culture? What other definitions besides those offered in this chapter can you find? How do *you* define a culture?
3. How might you respond to a colleague who makes the following statement: "You're wasting your time with that cross-cultural stuff. We're all humans, and we're a lot more alike than we are different"?
4. In the East Meets West scenario, would it be smarter to meet separately with your international visitors from Japan and Spain? Why or why not?
5. What cross-cultural educational opportunities exist at your college or university? Are you taking advantage of them?

MEMO FROM THE FIELD

BILL IMADA

Chairman and CEO; IW Group

Los Angeles, California

Bill Imada is the chairman and CEO of IW Group, a Los Angeles–based advertising and public relations agency specializing in the Asian American market. The agency represents a variety of major corporations and governmental agencies, including AT&T, Walmart, Merrill Lynch, Comcast, and McDonald's.

Values play a critical role in the way people think, react, relate, communicate, and make decisions. As a student of public relations, take a moment to think about the values that shape your own personality and the way you make decisions in life. As the authors of this book clearly note, there are a host of common values that people around the world share. When you walk into a room filled with nationals from Japan, Spain, or any other country in the world, consider all of the values you might share first. You will be pleasantly surprised by the number of values you have in common with your colleagues from another country or even another neighborhood or community. Your efforts to communicate will be made easier and more enjoyable when you find the values that bring you together. Afterward, take time to discover the things that make you different and unique. Celebrate what you have learned from one another, and share what you have learned with others.

As you move forward with your studies in public relations and communications, take a moment to think about some of the values you may take for granted. In this chapter, the authors talk about the concept of time. Many people from Western countries often talk about the lack of time we have to accomplish things. Americans, for instance, often say "time flies." On the contrary, many Latin American and Asian cultures may say "time walks." From a cultural point of view, which phrase is right? Both are right. How might this concept of time influence the way you interact and negotiate with your counterparts from Japan and Spain?

Now think of some other values that shape your views on life and ask yourself and your classmates to evaluate how these values might influence the way you think, react, relate, communicate, and make decisions. What thoughts come to mind when you think of these values: independence, family, sales, and equality?

Now ask people from other cultures to talk with you about their views on these values. I think you will find their answers enlightening and thought-provoking.

The authors also talk about the significance of gestures in other cultures. It is important to note that gestures are an important method of communicating in many cultures around the world. In Japan, public relations professionals often say that the Japanese can say "no" 40 different ways without even uttering the word. Facial expressions, hand movements, and body positions can signal a variety of different messages. As public relations practitioners, it is essential for you to learn how gestures can and will play a role in cross-cultural communication.

Lastly, think about what you have learned in the past about getting from one point in life to another. What did your teachers, professors, and parents tell you about getting from point A to point B? You and your classmates may say that the best way to get from point A to point B is a straight line. Why? Because it is considered the most efficient, cost-effective, and timely way to reach your desired destination. As you move forward in your public relations career, remember that there can be many different and unique ways to get from one point to another—and not necessarily by taking the direct approach. The most effective public relations practitioners will recognize early on that there are a myriad of different ways to reach where you'd like to go. Take time to explore each route. You'll be pleased that you did. ∎

CASE STUDY 14.1 Pro Bono: Bridging the Cultures of Rock and Politics

The world's news media call him "a political coalition builder" and a "hyper-agent."[51] The *New York Times* credits him with spearheading "a worldwide public relations campaign."[52] A reporter on the CBS program *60 Minutes* said, "He gets a lot of credit for lobbying [former] President Bush. They've met several times."[53]

Oh, and he also performs with a band. He's Bono, lead singer and songwriter of U2, the Irish rockers who rival Madonna for creative longevity.

Bono as a public relations practitioner? Maybe not quite, but to fight AIDS and poverty in developing nations, Bono has crafted a variety of relationship-building tactics to win resources from wealthy nations. He has hosted special events, held meetings with world leaders, and created photo opportunities by telephoning a U.S. president live from stage and by lending a pope his ever-present sunglasses. And he uses the language of his target publics: "When I'm speaking to corporate America," he says, "I always talk about countries being brands."[54]

For helping to raise billions of dollars for the world's poor, Bono and Microsoft's Bill and Melinda Gates were named *Time* magazine's 2005 Persons of the Year. So you'd think Bono's life, to quote a U2 song, might be "the sweetest thing." But you'd be ignoring the perils of cross-cultural communication.

In a scathing article titled "Saint Bono the Martyr," London's *Daily Mail* underscored the challenge of living on stage and in the corporate boardroom: "His obsession with changing the world has alienated both band-mates and fans. Could it now spell the end of the U2 singer's career?"[55]

Even less tolerant of Bono's cross-cultural odyssey was the *Ottawa (Canada) Sun:* "We resent spoiled brat rock stars . . . trying to dictate government policy decisions and telling us how to spend federal dollars."[56]

Less inflammatory critics still note the improbable clash of Bono's two worlds. CNN labeled Bono and former President George W. Bush the "odd couple."[57] The *New York Sun* calls Bono and a leading economist "an unlikely pair."[58] Melinda Gates herself said, "We'd certainly never had a rock star to the house before . . . but the whole reason we got together is because we have this joint cause."[59]

Bono himself tackles the cultural divide by confronting it head-on. In a meeting with U.S. government leaders, he said, "I'm the first to admit that there's something unnatural, unseemly, about rock stars mounting the pulpit and preaching at presidents. . . . Talk about a fish out of water. . . . Yes, it's odd having a rock star here—but maybe it's odder for me than for you."[60]

Bono is quick to admit that he sometimes stumbles in the alien cultures of world politics and corporate boardrooms. In one of his first meetings with President Bush, he says he pushed so relentlessly for more AIDS-relief money that Bush finally pounded the table to silence him. "He banged the table to ask me to let him reply," Bono recalls. "I was very impressed that he could get so passionate. And let's face it: Tolerating an Irish rock star is not a necessity of his office."[61]

An entire nation may have wanted to pound a collective fist when Bono—still seeking funds for the world's poor—declared, "Ireland is now the richest country in the European Union, second only to Luxembourg—and Luxembourg isn't really a country."[62]

To critics in Luxembourg and elsewhere, he concedes, "I'm sick of Bono—and I'm Bono."[63] He says he worries that his band-mates are "sick of the sight of me shaking hands with politicians."[64] Ironically, just as some scorn a rocker turned lobbyist, others decry the president's pal who still rocks: "He has courted ever greater risks to his street reputation," notes the *International Herald Tribune.*[65]

Why invite such culture clashes? One answer might be his success: "Bono charmed and bullied and morally blackmailed the leaders of the world's richest countries into forgiving $40 billion in debt owed by the poorest," *Time* declared in its story naming him one of its Persons of the Year.[66]

Bono himself believes that, if world poverty declines, he'll be remembered for his communications in just one culture: rock and roll. "Oddly enough," he says, "I think my work, the activism, will be forgotten. . . . I hope it will because I hope those problems will have gone away. But our music will be here in 50 years' and 100 years' time."[67]

DISCUSSION QUESTIONS

1. Do you agree with the *New York Times* that Bono's fundraising efforts can be called public relations? Why or why not?
2. Are the worlds of rock and roll and of politics and corporations really different cultures? Why or why not?

3. As Chapter 14 notes, stereotyping can interfere with successful cross-cultural communication. In what ways, if any, has stereotyping hurt Bono's fundraising efforts?

4. Before reading this case study, what were your impressions (if any) of Bono? Do his relationships with Bill and Melinda Gates and George W. Bush hurt his credibility as a rock star? ■

CASE STUDY 14.2 Walmart Works to "Export Our Culture"

You'd have to be crazy to question Walmart's success. Worldwide, the company owns more than 8,000 stores with more than 2 million employees. Approximately 4,000 of those stores and 680,000 of those employees are outside the United States. Sales in those overseas stores in fiscal year 2010 topped $100 billion.[68]

And yet . . .

When Walmart recently announced the promotion of Doug McMillon to president and CEO of Walmart's international division, the company's news release included a revealing quotation: "Doug is the right leader to continue to grow our international portfolio, export our culture, and leverage our global strengths in every market where we operate," said the executive whom McMillon succeeded.[69]

Laudatory quotations are typical in news releases, but, given Walmart's history, this quotation contained an interesting phrase: *export our culture.* For all Walmart's success, its attempts to export its culture without adequate consideration of the receiving cultures has led to repeated international setbacks.

In the 1990s, Walmart expanded into Canada, purchasing 122 stores from the Woolco retail chain. Always cost-conscious, Walmart gathered fliers printed for U.S. markets and distributed them throughout Quebec—French-speaking Quebec, where laws protect the prevalence of the French language. As potential customers bristled at the unintended insult, Walmart dropped another English bomb, this time on its own Quebecois employees. A letter from Walmart's Canadian headquarters that asked the employees to work longer hours was written in English.

"Vultures of savage capitalism," thundered the leader of Quebec's Confederation of National Trade Unions.[70] A columnist for *Le Journal de Montreal* shuddered at Walmart's very name, declaring, "Even uttering the word is disgusting, like chewing on an old Kleenex that was forgotten in the pocket of a winter coat."[71]

Other Canadians were more restrained in their assessment of Walmart's cross-cultural blunders. "They came so quickly to take advantage of the Woolco opportunity that they didn't have time to do their homework," said one retail analyst.[72]

Walmart sent letters of apology to its employees in Quebec and vowed to do better. "It never should have happened," said a Walmart representative.[73]

Months later, it happened again when the Mexican government announced a strict new law requiring Spanish-language labels for all imported products. As merchandise logjammed at the U.S. border, Mexican trade officials quickly instituted a 90-day grace period for compliance.

Six months earlier, Walmart had opened a 240,000-square-foot supercenter in Mexico City, selling mostly clothing with product tags in English. As the 90-day grace period came to an end, officials of the Mexican government gave the store another 30 days to comply with the labeling law. But after only six days, the officials returned and closed the store.

"It came out of the blue," said a Walmart representative.[74]

The store remained closed for less than 24 hours as the company rented a warehouse in Laredo, Texas, and in the summer heat hastily assembled a team to affix new labels to the products. "It wasn't fun," said one exhausted worker. Retail experts estimated that the Mexico City store lost $330,000 during the brief shutdown.[75]

The entire episode, said company officials, was "unfortunate"—doubly so, perhaps, because *unfortunate* was the same word Walmart had used months earlier to describe the cross-cultural confusion in Canada.[76]

"In the decade since Walmart Stores Inc. began its international exploits . . . its record abroad has been full of merchandising missteps and management upheaval," reported *Business Week* magazine. "[T]he Bentonville (Ark.) chain has learned some painful lessons about consumers, regulators, and suppliers around the world."[77]

Perhaps Walmart's greatest cross-cultural setback occurred in 2006, when the retail giant conceded failure and closed its German operations, its first stores in Europe. The *New York Times* reported that Walmart's American model simply didn't match German culture. The stores' outlying locations, for example, didn't match German demographics and psychographics: relatively low car-ownership rates and a preference for neighborhood shopping. German consumers preferred fresh butcher-shop meat to Walmart's packaged products and even interpreted Walmart employees' mandatory smiles as flirting.[78]

"It is a good, important lesson, a turning point," said a Walmart representative in addressing the company's rare failure. "Germany was a good example of [our] naïveté."[79]

Three years after that turning point, however, Walmart hired a new international leader to "export our culture."

DISCUSSION QUESTIONS

1. In the United States, Walmart has a very profitable business model. Why shouldn't it try to implement that approach in other nations?
2. What might Walmart do to prevent these cross-cultural misunderstandings?
3. Do you think the German experience will be a "turning point" for Walmart? Why or why not?
4. Can you describe other examples of cross-cultural clashes that have hurt particular organizations? ∎

NOTES

1. Marlene Rossman, *Multicultural Marketing* (New York: Amacom, 1994), 6.
2. "Corporate Culture Clash Took Fizz Out of Merger," Asia News Network, 10 February 2010, online, www.asianewsnet.net.
3. Mike Lindblom, "Muslims Protest Koran Use in Rave Ad," *Seattle Times,* 10 February 2001, online, LexisNexis.
4. Anindita Niyogi Balslev, ed., *Cross-Cultural Conversation* (Atlanta: Scholars Press, 1996), 10.
5. Stephen P. Banks, *Multicultural Public Relations,* 2nd ed. (Ames: Iowa State University Press, 2000), 9.
6. Charles Winick, *Dictionary of Anthropology* (Totowa, N.J.: Littlefield, Adams, 1972), 144.
7. *American Heritage Dictionary of the English Language,* 4th ed. (New York: Houghton Mifflin, 2000), online, www.bartleby.com.
8. Robert Gibson, *International Business Communication* (Oxford: Oxford University Press, 2000), 3.
9. Banks, ix.
10. John Budd Jr., "Opinion . . . Foreign Policy Acumen Needed by Global CEOs," *Public Relations Review* (summer 2001): 132.
11. Banks, 105.
12. "Italian Stallions," *Times* (of London), 1 May 2001, 17.
13. David J. Smith and Shelagh Armstrong, *If the World Were a Village* (Toronto: Kids Can Press, 2002).
14. Rossman.
15. Robert Levine, "The Pace of Life in 31 Countries," *American Demographics,* November 1997, 20.
16. Kathryn Westcott, "Bidding Adios to 'Mañana,'" BBC News, 1 March 2007, online, http://news.bbc.co.uk.
17. Much of the information in this section comes from two excellent books by Roger Axtell: *Do's and Taboos around the World* 3rd ed. (New York: Wiley, 1993) and *Gestures: The Do's and*

Taboos of Body Language around the World (New York: Wiley, 1991).

18. "Total Entrepreneurial Activity Ranked by Country: 2001-2008," International Entrepreneurship, online, www.internationalentrepreneurship.com.

19. Yuri Kageyama, "Reticent Toyota President Typical for Japan Inc.," Associated Press, 23 February 2010, online, www.associatedpress.com.

20. Axtell, *Gestures,* 150.

21. Lydia Polgreen, "Nigeria Counts 100 Deaths Over Danish Caricatures," *New York Times,* 24 February 2006, online, www.nytimes.com.

22. Colin Nickerson, "Danish Paper's Apology Fails to Calm Protests," *Boston Globe,* 1 February 2006, online, LexisNexis Academic.

23. Daphne Spain, "America's Diversity: On the Edge of Two Centuries," *Reports on America* 1, no. 2, (Washington, D.C.: Population Reference Bureau, 1999), 7.

24. Spain, 7.

25. John Robinson, Bart Landry, and Ronica Rooks, "Time and the Melting Pot," *American Demographics,* June 1998, 20.

26. Rossman, 6, 12.

27. Colin Taylor, "Great Gifts or Gifts That Grate?" *New Zealand Management,* August 2003, online, LexisNexis.

28. Axtell, *Gestures,* 50.

29. Alice Lagnado, "Putin to Purge Russian Tongue of Foreign Elements," *Times,* 1 May 2001, 16.

30. Adam Sherwin, "Mandela Steals Show in Trafalgar Square," *Times,* 30 April 2001, 8.

31. Mark Rice-Oxley, "The American World," *Seattle Times,* 18 January 2004, online, LexisNexis.

32. "Gen Y-ers, Baby Boomers & Technology: Worlds Apart?" Deloitte Consulting, 2008, online, www.deloitte.com.

33. David Howes, ed., *Cross-Cultural Consumption* (London: Routledge, 1996), 1.

34. Naseem Javed, "Naming for Global Power," *Communication World,* October/November 1997, 33.

35. Jose Luis Romero, "Values Based Leadership," Skills2Lead, 2010, online, www.skills2lead.com.

36. Information in this paragraph comes from Axtell's *Do's and Taboos* and *Gestures* (notes 18 and 19).

37. Henry Louis Gates Jr., "Whose Culture Is It, Anyway?" *Cast a Cold Eye* (New York: Four Walls Eight Windows, 1991), 263.

38. Budd, 126.

39. Elizabeth Howard, "Confranting Globalization Straight On," *Communication World,* June–July 1998, online, www.findarticles.com.

40. Howes, 2.

41. "Public Relations Society of America Finds Progress of Industry in Diversity Efforts 'Mixed' in Landmark Survey," news release issued by the Public Relations Society of America, 22 August 2003, online, www.prsa.org.

42. "*PRWeek* Diversity Survey 2009," *PRWeek* and Hill & Knowlton, December 2009, online, www.prweekus.com.

43. "Diversity Survey 2006," a report issued by *PRWeek* and Hill & Knowlton, 11 December 2006, online, www.prweekus.com.

44. Juan-Carlos Molleda, "Global Public Relations," Institute for Public Relations, 19 March 2009, online, www.instituteforpr.org.

45. The following description of Hofstede's cultural dimensions draws from Marieke de Mooij, *Global Marketing and Advertising: Understanding Cultural Paradoxes* (Thousand Oaks, Calif.: Sage Publications, 1998); and Geert Hofstede, *Cultures and Organizations: Software of the Mind* (New York: McGraw-Hill, 1991).

46. Cynthia Kemper, "Challenges Facing Public Relations Efforts Are Intensified Abroad," *Denver Post,* 1 March 1998, online, LexisNexis.

47. Pitney Bowes, online, www.pitneybowes.com.

48. Axtell, *Do's and Taboos,* 68, 89.

49. Axtell, *Do's and Taboos,* 90.

50. Mary Jo Jacobi, "Communications without Borders: Thinking Globally While Acting Locally" (speech delivered to the 1998 annual meeting of the International Public Relations Association, London, 17 July 1998).

51. Eric R. Danton, "The Many Faces of Bono," *Hartford* (Connecticut) *Courant,* 1 December 2005, online, LexisNexis; Alexandra Marks, "Celebrity Hyper-Agents Transform Philanthropy," *Christian Science Monitor,* 19 September 2005, online, LexisNexis.

52. Richard W. Stevenson and Alan Cowell, "Bush Arrives at Summit Session, Ready to Stand Alone," *New York Times,* online, LexisNexis.

53. Transcript, *60 Minutes*, CBS, 5 February 2006, online, LexisNexis.
54. Joel Selvin, "U2's Bono Makes Fiery Case," *San Francisco Chronicle*, 11 November 2005, online, LexisNexis.
55. Paul Scott, "Saint Bono the Martyr," *Daily Mail*, 24 December 2005, online, LexisNexis.
56. "Act Like Pro, Bono," *Ottawa Sun*, 7 July 2005, online, LexisNexis.
57. Transcript, "The Situation Room with Wolf Blitzer," CNN, 2 February 2006, online, LexisNexis.
58. John P. Avlon, "The Rock Star and the Economist," *New York Sun*, 7 October 2005, online, LexisNexis.
59. Jamie Wilson Washington, "Melinda, Bill and Bono Are Time's People of the Year," *The Guardian*, 19 December 2005, online, LexisNexis.
60. Bono, "Bono's Prayer for Africa," *The Record* (Kitchener-Waterloo, Ontario), 18 February 2006, online, LexisNexis.
61. George Rush and Joanna Molloy, "When Dubya Silenced Bono's Vox," *New York Daily News*, 26 January 2005, online, LexisNexis.
62. Richard Kay, "Bono's Little Bit of Bother," *Daily Mail*, 23 February 2006, online, LexisNexis.
63. "They Said What?" *The Journal* (Newcastle, England), 31 December 2005, online, LexisNexis.
64. "The Lobbyist Rock Star," CNN.com, 16 April 2004, online, LexisNexis.
65. Brian Lavery, "The Irish Love U2, Except When They Don't," *International Herald Tribune*, 28 June 2005, online, LexisNexis.
66. Desmond Butler, "Bill and Melinda Gates, Bono Named *Time*'s Persons of the Year for Work on Poverty," Associated Press, 18 December 2005, online, LexisNexis.
67. *60 Minutes*.
68. "International Data Sheet—February 2010," Walmart, 18 March 2010, online, www.walmartstores.com. "Total Company Data – February 2010," 18 March 2010, online, www.walmartstores.com.
69. "Doug McMillon Named President and CEO of Walmart International," Walmart, 7 January 2009, online, www.walmartstores.com.
70. Anne Swardson, "Top U.S. Retailer Heads North," *Washington Post*, 17 June 1994, online, LexisNexis.
71. Swardson.
72. Darren Schuettler, "Wal-Mart Predicts Dramatic Growth in Canada," *Reuter Business Report*, 2 May 1994, online, LexisNexis.
73. Schuettler.
74. *HFD: The Weekly Home Furnishings Newspaper*, 4 July 1994, online, LexisNexis.
75. Joanna Ramey and Jim Ostroff, "Wal-Mart Mexico City Unit Reopens after Shutdown," *Women's Wear Daily*, 24 June 1994, online, LexisNexis; John Freivalds, "Managing Languages in the 21st Century," *Communication World* (October/November 1997): 36.
76. *HFD*; Schuettler.
77. "How Well Does Walmart Travel?" *Business Week*, 3 September 2001, online, www.businessweek.com.
78. Mark Landler and Michael Barbaro, "Wal-Mart Finds That Its Formula Doesn't Fit Every Culture," *New York Times*, 2 August 2006, online, www.nytimes.com.
79. Landler and Barbaro.

Public Relations and the Law

OBJECTIVES

After studying this chapter, you will be able to
- understand the differences between and the regulation of political and commercial speech
- appreciate how privacy and copyright laws affect the practice of public relations
- identify the higher burden of proof public officials and public figures have in libel cases

- recognize the increasing role public relations has in the judicial system

KEY TERMS
actual malice, p. 473
administrative law judge, p. 461
annual report, p. 465
appropriation, p. 477
burden of proof, p. 472
cease and desist order, p. 461

REAL WORLD

Working in a Minefield

It has been a bad day at the Ferndale Corporation's investor relations office, and it almost got worse.

Your headache began when the corporate attorneys called and said that you would have to prepare a news release announcing the chief executive officer's sudden, unexpected resignation. Ferndale's revenues have fallen dramatically in recent months, and the board of directors wants to move in a new direction before the next annual meeting.

When you go to brief the staff on what is happening, you find a colleague illegally downloading music from the Internet. She tells you "downloading music doesn't hurt anybody." But you know differently.

As you sit down to write the news release about the CEO's departure, a number of questions come to mind. What should I say? What can I say? What must I say? Three questions similar in structure, but entirely different in their legal ramifications.

On top of everything, the timing for this could not be worse. The annual report is due at the printer this afternoon. Can you delay it?

It's times like these that everyone needs to talk to a friend. Your best friend from college is an investment analyst at a local stock brokerage firm. But before you start dialing, you suddenly hang up the telephone. You realize that you almost made the biggest mistake of your life, one that could have landed you in prison.

You think to yourself, "It's like working in a minefield."

THE STATUE OF RESPONSIBILITY

Freedom of expression is easily taken for granted—unless you don't have it.

In adopting the *Universal Declaration of Human Rights* in 1948, member states of the United Nations agreed that "Everyone has the right to freedom of opinion and expression."[1] Now, six decades later, nearly every nation has a free speech provision in its constitution. However, these are empty words in many places. Because of advances in communication technology, more people have access to more information than ever before. However, in its 2009 annual report on human rights, the U.S. State Department noted, "Yet, at the same time, it was a year in which governments spent more time, money, and attention finding regulatory and technical means to curtail freedom of expression on the Internet and the flow of critical information and to infringe on the personal privacy rights of those who used these rapidly evolving technologies."[2]

Fortunately, democratic nations are built on a free speech tradition. However, even in those countries, there are limits. Although the government enforces some of these restrictions, limitations on speech are often self-imposed. The First Amendment of the U.S. Constitution severely restricts the *government's* ability to regulate speech. However, those same rules often do not apply to *individuals*.

What is and is not considered acceptable speech is often affected by the ebb and flow of public opinion. For example, nearly half of those surveyed by the First Amendment Center in 2002 said they agreed with the statement that the First Amendment goes too far in the rights it guarantees. However, only 18 percent of respondents agreed when asked the same question four years later. In that same 2006 survey, 58 percent said that newspapers should be allowed to criticize the military, 63 percent said musicians should be allowed to sing songs with offensive lyrics, and 55 percent said people should be allowed to say things that might be offensive to religious groups. However, when asked if people should be allowed to say things in public that might be offensive to racial groups, 55 percent said they should not.[3]

Defining the limits of free speech is often messy. Many people were aghast when Fred Phelps, the pastor of a fundamentalist church in Topeka, Kansas, began picketing the funerals of U.S. soldiers killed in Iraq and Afghanistan. Phelps and his followers believe the soldiers' deaths are punishment for the nation's tolerance of homosexuality. The protesters often carry provocative signs, such as "God Hates the USA" and "Thank God for 9/11." When parishioners picketed the funeral of a

Maryland serviceman in 2006, the family sued Phelps and his church for emotional distress and invasion of privacy. A lower court awarded the soldier's family a $5 million judgment. But the 4th Circuit Court of Appeals overturned the decision, ruling that the signs contained "imaginative and hyberbolic rhetoric" protected by the First Amendment. The judges also ruled that the soldier's family had to pay for Phelps' appeal. By mid-2010, the matter was headed for the U.S. Supreme Court.[4]

Where does public relations fit into this debate? Do practitioners have a responsibility to engage in civil discourse—even when others do not? As noted in Chapter 3, free expression and First Amendment protections are foundations of public relations practice. We have also noted that practitioners have a boundary-spanning role between their organization and the many publics important to their organization's success. Their goal is to build and maintain strategic relationships.

Some forms of speech are regulated with well-defined boundaries. However, most speech is not. It is difficult for practitioners to identify the fine line between good and bad speech. To paraphrase the movie *Broadcast News,* "they keep moving that sucker."

Viktor E. Frankl, a holocaust survivor who went on to author *Man's Search for Meaning,* one of the most influential books of the 20th century, believed that freedom must be linked to personal responsibility. "Freedom is in danger of degenerating into arbitrariness unless it is lived responsibly," Frankl wrote. "That is why I recommend that the Statue of Liberty on the East Coast be supplemented by a Statue of Responsibility on the West Coast."[5]

Fundraising is under way to build Frankl's monument. Meanwhile, public relations practitioners are challenged every day to balance the benefits and responsibilities of free speech.

Public Relations, the Law, and You

In Chapter 6, we discussed ethical issues facing 21st-century public relations practice. We also noted the difference between conduct that is legal and ethical. There are times when an action may be legal but not ethical and vice versa. That is the nature of the complex and diverse society in which we live. However, there are many times when legal and ethical considerations *are* the same. Sometimes the world *is* black and white. That is why this chapter focuses on the legal environment in which public relations practitioners operate. And as anyone who has watched any television crime drama knows, ignorance of the law is not an excuse.

This fact should not be lost on public relations practitioners. They are often thrust into the limelight when their employer's actions face legal challenges. Practitioners also require an intimate knowledge of the laws governing what they may or must say or do in a variety of situations. For example, a certain degree of exaggeration is perfectly acceptable at times. However, at other times it is not. Depending on whom the practitioner is representing, some information can be considered public (for all to see) or very private.

The challenge for public relations practitioners is to understand the many laws and regulations that govern, or at least influence, their practice. Unfortunately, at least one study suggests that many practitioners do not have a good understanding of the laws and regulations governing the public relations profession. More than half the practitioners questioned in one survey indicated they had no familiarity with Securities and Exchange Commission regulations. In the same survey, more than 48 percent said they were not familiar with laws relating to professional malpractice, 45 percent were not familiar with laws governing financial public relations, and 40 percent were not familiar with laws pertaining to commercial speech. These responses led the author of the study to this conclusion:

> The finding that most practitioners are only somewhat or not at all familiar with important legal issues, combined with the finding that most of their work is either not reviewed or subject to limited review by legal counsel, suggests that many public relations practitioners may be placing both themselves and their clients at risk of legal liability.[6]

Attorney Morton J. Simon said that public relations practitioners "can and have cost companies millions of dollars. [Although] the incidence of legal implications [to the practice of public relations] may vary, their importance when they exist cannot be minimized."[7]

PUBLIC RELATIONS AND THE FIRST AMENDMENT

As noted in Chapter 3, the most important event in the development of public relations in the United States was the adoption of the **First Amendment** to the Constitution. The freedoms guaranteed by the First Amendment provide the framework for the nation's social, political, and commercial discourse:

> Congress shall make no law respecting an establishment of religion, or prohibiting the free exercise thereof; or abridging the freedom of speech, or of the press, or the right of the people peaceably to assemble, and to petition the Government for a redress of grievances.[8]

In the more than two centuries since its adoption, a great deal of thought and debate has surrounded what the First Amendment does and does not guarantee. There have been many instances in which free expression has come in conflict with other social interests. Does a person's First Amendment right to freedom of speech supersede someone else's Sixth Amendment right to a trial by "an impartial jury"? Does freedom of expression allow one to yell "fire" in a crowded theater? Clearly, the freedoms embodied in the First Amendment are not absolute. It has been left up to the courts, and, ultimately, the Supreme Court, to decide on the amendment's limits.

Political versus Commercial Speech

Although public relations enjoys certain protections under the First Amendment, these rights are not without some limitations. The practice of public relations often falls into a gray area between what the law characterizes as political speech and commercial speech. **Political speech** is defined as expression associated with the normal conduct of a democracy—such as news articles, public debates, and individuals' expressions of their opinions about the events of the day. In general, the U.S. Supreme Court has been reluctant to limit political speech. Justice William Brennan wrote in 1964 that there is a "profound national commitment to the principle that debate on public issues should be uninhibited, robust, and wide-open, and that it may well include vehement, caustic, and sometimes unpleasantly sharp attacks on government and public officials."[9]

Commercial speech, which is defined as expression "intended to generate marketplace transactions," is more restricted.[10] In fact, for much of the nation's history, commercial speech has been treated by courts as if it were unprotected by the First Amendment. However, toward the end of the 20th century, the tide began to change. In 1976, the Supreme Court ruled that a Virginia law prohibiting pharmacists from advertising prescription drug prices was unconstitutional and that some commercial speech enjoys First Amendment protection. "Generalizing, society also may have a strong interest in the free flow of commercial information," Justice Harry Blackmun wrote. "Even an individual advertisement, though entirely 'commercial,' may be of general public interest."[11] Two years later, in *First National Bank of Boston v. Bellotti*, the court also affirmed that corporations enjoy some political speech rights. The government's right to restrict commercial speech was further limited in *Central Hudson Gas & Electric Corp. v. Public Service Commission of New York* in 1980. In that decision, which still governs commercial speech today, the court ruled that government could restrict commercial speech only after demonstrating a substantial government interest and that the speech in question is misleading.[12]

"Today, the main danger to First Amendment rights in this context comes not so much from direct government regulations, but from private litigants seeking to ignore First Amendment rules by arguing that their opponents' statements are mere commercial speech," wrote attorney Bruce E. H. Johnson in an essay posted on the First Amendment Center's website. He added that several recent lawsuits have sought to narrow political speech protections available to commercial organizations.[13]

The most visible attempt at limiting corporate speech in recent years occurred when California antiglobalization activist Marc Kasky sued Nike over what he claimed were false and misleading statements in a public relations campaign. In response to concerns about labor practices at some of its overseas suppliers, Nike commissioned a study by former U.S. United Nations Ambassador Andrew Young. When Young found no evidence of widespread abuse of workers, Nike publicized his findings. Two lower courts sided with Nike and said the publicity campaign enjoyed First Amendment protection. However, the California Supreme Court ruled for Kasky, briefly igniting a controversy that threatened the practice of public relations. At first, the U.S. Supreme Court agreed to hear the case, but then abruptly kicked it back to the California courts. Eventually, the parties settled the matter out of court in 2003. However, most observers agree that *Kasky v. Nike* muddied the waters of corporate speech for years to come.[14]

Is public relations considered political speech, or is it considered commercial speech? The answer largely depends on the public being targeted, the purpose of the message, and the court's interpretation. Despite this somewhat murky answer, two things are very clear. First, there are limits to both political and commercial speech. And second, public relations practitioners need to know what those limits are.

 QUICK CHECK

1. Do public relations practitioners have a responsibility to engage in civil discourse—even when others do not?
2. What is the difference between the ways the U.S. Supreme Court has treated cases involving political speech and those involving commercial speech?
3. Is public relations considered political speech, or is it considered commercial speech?

QUICKBREAK 15.1

When Money Talks

Ever since Congress prohibited government officials from soliciting contributions from workers in Washington's Navy Yard in 1867, there has been public debate concerning campaign financing and free speech.[15] The central question is whether campaign contributions are a form of free expression protected by the First Amendment. More than 140 years later, the issue remains unresolved.

Just how big is money in politics? The Federal Election Commission (FEC) reports that candidates running for president in 2008 raised more than $1.6 billion for their campaign war chests. Add another $1.4 billion raised by candidates for the Senate and House of Representatives that year.[16] And that doesn't begin to address the money raised for state and local candidates or for ballot initiatives.

Some have argued that campaign contributions are a form of participation in the political process. Others have argued that unlimited campaign contributions allow those with deep pockets—notably corporations and labor unions—to wield an inordinate amount of influence on government policy.

In the wake of the Watergate scandal of the early 1970s, Congress created the FEC and gave it power to enforce limits on both contributions and spending. In an effort to level the playing field, it also created public financing of presidential elections through a check-off on federal tax returns. However, subsequent court challenges created loopholes through which large amounts of unregulated money could be pumped into campaigns.

The Bipartisan Campaign Reform Act of 2002—more commonly known as McCain-Feingold after its two chief sponsors—included several provisions designed to end the use of so-called soft money, money raised outside the limits and prohibitions of federal campaign finance law. It also placed restrictions on electioneering communications such as issue advertising and required candidates to appear in their ads saying they approved the ad's content.

A divided Supreme Court shocked the political world in 2010 when it overturned some of the provisions of McCain-Feingold. A five-justice majority ruled that corporations

(continued)

and labor unions may give money in support of or in opposition to candidates through independent (non-party or non-candidate) advertising. Within days of the court ruling, lawmakers introduced a flurry of legislation designed to reintroduce those restrictions. One proposal, the "Corporate Propaganda Sunshine Act," would require public companies to report what they spend to influence public opinion.[17]

"Whatever your opinion or affiliation, the decision could be a boon for public relations practitioners," said Public Relations Society of America Chief Operating Officer William M. Murray. "With limits gone, spending by corporations, unions, and special-interest groups is poised to explode.

"Standing to benefit are individuals and firms skilled in the art of election communications, government affairs, issues management and the like, who can apply these new sources of funding to the pursuit and delivery of political outcomes."[18] ∎

The Key: Know Your Own Business

It is not suggested here that every public relations practitioner should be ready to take the state bar exam. However, you don't have to be a lawyer to have a good working knowledge of the law. And that understanding should begin in the workplace. All public relations professionals need to know the laws and regulations that govern their organization.

Many of these laws and regulations relate to the handling of private information. For example, hospital public information officers need to know the rules pertaining to the confidentiality of patient records. Most of the information found in a patient's file is considered private. An improper release of that information could open the practitioner and the hospital to civil or criminal litigation.

The actions of practitioners can also be controlled by the legal status of the organizations they represent. Government practitioners must learn that all their records are open to public inspection, except records specifically exempted by law. The best-known federal law guaranteeing access to government information is the **Freedom of Information Act (FOIA)**. The FOIA applies to all federal agencies and departments except the president and his advisers, Congress and its subsidiary committees and agencies, and the federal judicial system.[19] Although there are specific exemptions to the FOIA, a vast majority of federal government records are available for anyone to inspect. Similar laws covering records held by state and local governments have been enacted nationwide. State and federal sunshine laws also require that meetings of government agencies at which official decisions are made must be open to the public. However, as is the case with open records laws, specific exemptions permit some government business to be conducted in private.

Practitioners employed by nongovernmental organizations enjoy a much greater degree of privacy than do their government counterparts. However, even they may be governed by state and federal requirements relating to disclosure (a concept that we discuss later in greater depth), taxation, and ethical conduct. For example, people hired for the purpose of influencing the actions of state and federal officials must register as lobbyists. Practitioners representing the interests of governments or organizations based outside the United States must also register as foreign agents. Both lobbyists and foreign agents must file periodic reports on their activities with designated agencies.

FEDERAL AGENCIES THAT REGULATE SPEECH

The federal government does not license public relations practitioners. Several federal agencies, however, do have a major impact on the practice of public relations. These agencies create and enforce regulations designed to protect the public's best interests. These rules often cover company or organization communications, especially in areas considered to involve commercial speech. Four of the most prominent of these agencies are the Federal Trade Commission, the Securities and Exchange Commission, the Federal Communications Commission, and the Food and Drug Administration.

The Federal Trade Commission

When public relations practitioners promote a particular product or service, their actions may fall under the watchful gaze of the **Federal Trade Commission (FTC).** The FTC was established in 1914 "to ensure that the nation's markets function competitively . . . are vigorous . . . and free of undue restrictions."[20] The commission is the source of most federal regulation of advertising. However, it also has jurisdiction over product-related publicity generated by public relations practitioners.

The Federal Trade Commission Act empowers the FTC to "prevent unfair methods of competition, and unfair or deceptive acts or practices in or affecting commerce."[21] This includes advertisements and publicity that may be considered false or misleading, including claims that are unsubstantiated, ambiguous, or exaggerated. The FTC is especially sensitive when the product or service being promoted might adversely affect personal health or when it requires a considerable investment of money before the consumer can determine its effectiveness.

If the FTC believes a violation of the law has occurred, it may obtain voluntary compliance through what is known as a **consent order.** However, if such an agreement cannot be reached, the commission can take a complaint before an **administrative law judge.** This person hears testimony and reviews evidence, much like the judge and jury in a civil or criminal case. An administrative law judge can issue a **cease and desist order.** This decision can be appealed to the full commission, then to the U.S. Court of Appeals, and ultimately to the U.S. Supreme Court. If the FTC's ruling is upheld, it can then seek **injunctions, consumer redress,** and **civil penalties** through the federal court system. In the case of ongoing consumer fraud, the FTC can go directly to federal court in an effort to protect consumers.[22]

An example of the FTC in action is the National Do Not Call Registry (www.donotcall.gov). Following a 2008 amendment to the law, consumers can block most telemarketers from calling their home telephone numbers permanently. However, the law does not block telemarketing calls made by charities, survey researchers, and political candidates. As of mid-2010, 189 million telephone numbers were registered.

SOCIAL MEDIA APPS

Mommy Bloggers Beware

On the surface, it seems like a sweet deal: Say something nice about my product and get something of value in return. If this were the 1950s and the medium was radio, we would be describing **payola,** unreported (and illegal) compensation for hidden endorsements. But this is the 21st century, and the issue now involves blogging.

The Federal Trade Commission amended its guidelines governing endorsements and testimonials in October 2009. This was in response to reports of so-called mommy bloggers, who *Public Relations Tactics* reported as receiving "perks like free washers and dryers and boondoggle trips to New York, Los Angeles, and Florida for writing enthusiastic posts, often featuring multiple exclamation points."[23] In announcing the amendments, the FTC news release said, "Bloggers who make an endorsement must disclose the material connections they share with the seller of the product or service." The news release went on to say, "The revised Guides also make it clear that celebrities have a duty to disclose their relationship with advertisers when making endorsements outside of the context of traditional ads, such as on talk shows and in social media."[24]

In response to the FTC's decision, Public Relations Society of America Chair and CEO Michael Cherenson told members, "From an ethics perspective, the new guidelines parallel key transparency principles in the PRSA Member Code of Ethics as well as Professional Standards Advisory PS-9 condemning 'pay for play' practices" (see p. 169). Cherenson noted that noncompliance could result in an FTC warning, a cease-and-desist order, or a fine.[25]

Does this mean that mommy bloggers will be fined? Not if they stop when asked, said the FTC's Richard Cleland. "We're focusing on the advertisers," he said, who could be penalized $16,000 per offense.[26] ∎

The largest fine levied by the FTC to date for violating DNC rules was $5.3 million to DirecTV and its telemarketers in December 2005.[27]

The Securities and Exchange Commission

In the wake of the 1929 stock market crash that triggered the Great Depression, Congress created the **Securities and Exchange Commission (SEC)** to "administer federal securities laws and issue rules and regulations to provide protection for investors and ensure that the securities markets are fair and honest."[28] Following the near collapse of the stock markets in September 2008—and allegations that the SEC had not adequately done its job—the agency today finds itself in a renewed effort to ensure transparency and fairness to the nation's securities markets.

The concept of **disclosure** is the foundation of SEC regulation. Under the Securities Act of 1933, publicly held companies—companies that issue financial securities, such as stocks and bonds, for public sale—have an obligation to disclose frankly, comprehensively, and immediately any information that is considered important to an investor's decision to buy, sell, or even hold the organization's securities.

Corporate disclosure, or a notable lack of it, was at the heart of several corporate scandals in the early 2000s. Companies such as Enron, WorldCom, and Adelphia focused intense public scrutiny on corporate disclosure. Before it issued **Regulation FD** (Fair Disclosure), companies often provided selective tidbits of information to favored analysts and money managers to curry favor among major investors. These companies may have been operating within the *letter* of existing disclosure law, but they were clearly outside of its *spirit*. However, Regulation FD, along with amendments to the SEC's disclosure rules, tightened disclosure loopholes. When the new rules were adopted, the SEC announcement said, "We believe that the practice of selective disclosure leads to a loss of investor confidence in the integrity of our capital markets."[29]

Congress further tightened disclosure rules in 2002 by passing the **Sarbanes-Oxley Act.** Under its provisions, CEOs and CFOs are held personally accountable

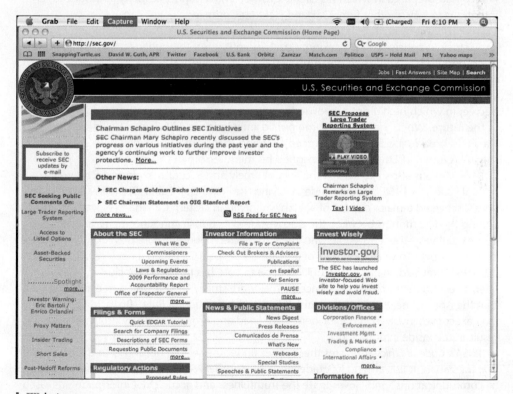

Website

The Securities and Exchange Commission operates a website that provides access to a variety of public records and updated information on federal regulations.

(Courtesy of the U.S. Securities and Exchange Commission)

QUICKBREAK 15.2

SEC Rule 10b-5

Any practitioner engaged in financial public relations must study SEC Rule 10b-5, which prohibits fraudulent or misleading corporate communications in matters that could affect investment decisions. Rule 10b-5 states that it is illegal "to make any untrue statements of a material fact or to omit to state a material fact necessary in order to make the statements made, in light of the circumstances under which they were made, not misleading." The rule also prohibits "any act, practice, or course of business which operates or would operate as a fraud or deceit upon any person, in connection with the purchase or sale of any security."[30]

One area in which this rule has a major impact on the practice of public relations is **insider trading**. That was the issue in 1985, when the SEC filed charges against Anthony M. Franco, the owner of a Detroit public relations firm and national president-elect of the Public Relations Society of America. The SEC complaint stemmed from a news release Franco had prepared in which his client, Crowley, Milner and Company, announced its intentions to buy another firm, Oakland Holding Company.

The SEC suit claimed that Franco purchased 3,000 shares of Oakland Holding Company stock in anticipation of making a sizable profit upon the public announcement of the proposed buyout. When the unusual transaction caught the attention of American Stock Exchange officials, Franco rescinded the trade. He claimed that his stockbroker had acted without his authorization. The SEC suit was resolved when Franco signed a consent decree, in which he did not acknowledge any wrongdoing but promised to obey the law in the future. When the affair became public knowledge in 1986, *after* he had assumed the PRSA presidency, Franco was forced to resign that post. Threatened with action by the PRSA Board of Ethics, he also resigned his membership in October 1986.[31]

Rule 10b-5 is also important in the area of timely and accurate disclosure. This was a central issue in a 1968 landmark case involving the Texas Gulf Sulfur Company. TGS geologists discovered a major deposit of valuable minerals in eastern Canada in November 1963. During the five months between the discovery and its public announcement, a handful of TGS executives—the few people who knew the secret—bought more than 20,000 shares of company stock. To squelch rumors of a major ore strike, TGS issued a news release on April 12, 1964, that said, in part, "The drilling done to date has not been conclusive."[32] Four days later, a second news release announced a major ore strike. An appeals court eventually ruled that the April 12 news release was misleading and a violation of Rule 10b-5. Many of the TGS executives involved in the incident were fined and ordered to repay profits made as a result of the inside information.

PRSA's *Code of Ethics* addresses these issues under the section dealing with the disclosure of information. It lists among its guidelines that members shall "be honest and accurate in all communications" and "investigate the truthfulness and accuracy of information released on behalf of those represented." The code cites as an example of improper conduct "Lying by omission: A practitioner for a corporation knowingly fails to release financial information, giving a misleading impression of the corporation's performance."[33] ■

for the truthfulness of corporate financial statements. Violators face up to 20 years in prison and a $5 million fine. The law limits the ability of company officers and their families to sell stock when employees are blocked from doing so. It created new laws against destroying, altering, or falsifying records in an attempt to impede investigations. It also required companies to publish a code of ethics annually.[34]

Although companies are required to file a large variety of reports with the SEC and other federal agencies, the most recognizable channels of disclosure are Form 10-K to the SEC and the annual report to shareholders. Publicly held corporations annually file a **Form 10-K** with the SEC. In it, a company is required to disclose specific information about its financial health and direction. This includes annual and multiyear reports on net sales, gross profit, income, total assets, and long-term financial obligations. The 10-K report also includes a management discussion and analysis of the company's financial condition.

Form 10-K usually provides the basis for the more familiar corporate **annual report,** which has to be in the hands of shareholders no fewer than 15 days before the corporate annual meeting. Typically, these annual reports are written and designed to make the investor feel good about his or her decision to own stock in the company. But serious investors and analysts look beyond the color pictures printed on glossy paper. They focus on Form 10-K, which is often inserted at the back of the annual report and printed on plain paper. All the small print may seem like gobbledygook, but it *is* necessary; and the information required in Form 10-K also has to be included in the annual report. Among the SEC requirements for an annual report are

- audited financial statements;
- supplementary financial information, such as net sales, gross profits, and per-share data based on income or loss;
- management discussion and analysis of the company's financial condition and any unusual events, transactions, or economic changes;
- a brief description of the company's business (products and/or services);
- the identities of company directors and executive officers; and
- a description of any significant litigation in which the company or its directors or officers are involved.

This is only a thumbnail sketch of SEC annual report reporting requirements.[35] It is a good idea to check with the SEC each year to keep up with changes in disclosure requirements.

Another SEC regulation that every practitioner needs to know is SEC Rule 10b-5, which prohibits, among other things, insider trading (see QuickBreak 15.2). Indirectly, that is what got Martha Stewart into trouble in 2004. A person violates insider trading rules if he or she buys or sells securities on the basis of insider information not available to other investors. Stewart was convicted of misleading federal investigators about selling shares of ImClone, a pharmaceutical company— just before the government announced an unfavorable ruling on one of the company's experimental drugs. An investigation alleged

United States Securities and Exchange Commission
Washington, D.C. 20549

FORM 10-K

☒ ANNUAL REPORT PURSUANT TO SECTION 13 OR 15(d) OF THE SECURITIES EXCHANGE ACT OF 1934
FOR THE FISCAL YEAR ENDED JUNE 30, 2009

OR

☐ TRANSITION REPORT PURSUANT TO SECTION 13 OR 15(d) OF THE SECURITIES EXCHANGE ACT OF 1934
FOR THE TRANSITION PERIOD FROM_____ TO_____

COMMISSION FILE NUMBER 0-14278

MICROSOFT CORPORATION

WASHINGTON	**91-1144442**
(STATE OF INCORPORATION)	(I.R.S. ID)

ONE MICROSOFT WAY, REDMOND, WASHINGTON 98052-6399

(425) 882-8080

www.microsoft.com/msft

Securities registered pursuant to Section 12(b) of the Act:

COMMON STOCK	**NASDAQ**

Securities registered pursuant to Section 12(g) of the Act:
NONE

Indicate by check mark if the registrant is a well-known seasoned issuer, as defined in Rule 405 of the Securities Act.   Yes ☒   No ☐

Indicate by check mark if the registrant is not required to file reports pursuant to Section 13 or Section 15(d) of the Exchange Act.   Yes ☐   No ☒

Indicate by check mark whether the registrant (1) has filed all reports required to be filed by Section 13 or 15(d) of the Securities Exchange Act of 1934 during the preceding 12 months (or for such shorter period that the registrant was required to file such reports), and (2) has been subject to such filing requirements for the past 90 days.   Yes ☒   No ☐

Indicate by check mark whether the registrant has submitted electronically and posted on its corporate Web site, if any, every Interactive Data File required to be submitted and posted to Rule 405 of Regulation S-T (§229.405 of this chapter) during the preceding 12 months (or for such shorter period that the registrant was required to submit and post such files).   Yes ☐   No ☐

Indicate by check mark if disclosure of delinquent filers pursuant to Item 405 of Regulation S-K (§229.405 of this chapter) is not contained herein, and will not be contained, to the best of registrant's knowledge, in definitive proxy or information statements incorporated by reference in Part III of this Form 10-K or any amendment to this Form 10-K. ☒

Indicate by check mark whether the registrant is a large accelerated filer, an accelerated filer, a non-accelerated filer, or a smaller reporting company. See the definitions of "large accelerated filer," "accelerated filer" and "smaller reporting company" in Rule 12b-2 of the Exchange Act.

Large accelerated filer ☒   Accelerated filer ☐   Non-accelerated filer ☐   Smaller reporting company ☐
(Do not check if a smaller reporting company)

Indicate by check mark whether the registrant is a shell company (as defined in Rule 12b-2 of the Exchange Act).   Yes ☐   No ☒

As of December 31, 2008, the aggregate market value of the registrant's common stock held by non-affiliates of the

Form 10-K

Publicly held corporations such as Microsoft are required to file a Form 10-K every year. Data from the form also have to be included in the company's annual report, which must reach shareholders within 15 days of the annual meeting.

(Courtesy of the U.S. Securities and Exchange Commission)

Annual Report

Publicly held businesses such as the Sonic restaurant chain are required by law to inform shareholders about the company's financial health and other issues that could affect the value of the shareholders' investments.

(Courtesy of Sonic, America's Drive-In)

that inside information might have come from ImClone founder Samuel D. Waksal, a close friend.[36]

Unfortunately, the SEC's biggest recent challenge has been restoring public trust in its ability to monitor the nation's securities markets. That trust was badly shaken in December 2008, when Bernard Madoff, one of Wall Street's most sought-after financial advisers, admitted to defrauding investors of more than $65 billion, the largest financial scandal in U.S. history. The SEC had been warned of Madoff's activities as early as 1999 but failed to act.[37] Madoff was sentenced to 150 years in prison, and the SEC was forced into full-scale damage control.

"As a result of economic turmoil, millions of Americans experienced significant losses in their retirement and family investments," SEC Chairman Mary L. Shapiro said. "That turmoil also had an impact on investor confidence.

"The SEC has moved swiftly to renew our commitment to protecting investors and restoring that confidence. Indeed, everything the agency has done has been with these goals in mind."[38]

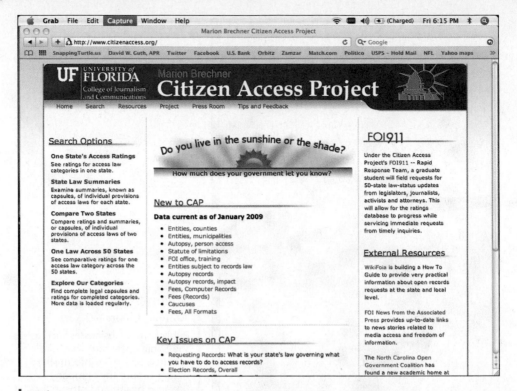

Website

In an effort to encourage more transparent government, the Marion Brechner Citizen Access Project has created a website where visitors can research and compare local, state, and federal open records and meetings laws.

(Courtesy of the Marion Brechner Citizen Access Project)

The Federal Communications Commission

Public relations practitioners who work for political candidates or whose clients may be subject to public criticism should be familiar with the federal agency that has regulated the nation's broadcast media since 1934, the **Federal Communications Commission (FCC)**. Originally created as the Federal Radio Commission in 1927, the FCC has the primary responsibility for ensuring the orderly use of the nation's airwaves in the public interest. Because a finite number of radio wave frequencies are available for public use, radio and television stations operate under licenses granted by the federal government. In contrast, print media face relatively little government oversight because of historic precedents and First Amendment protections. Since the Telecommunications Act of 1996, broadcast licenses are granted for a period of eight years and may be renewed after a review of the licensee's performance.

VALUES STATEMENT 15.1

Securities and Exchange Commission

Mission and Vision

The mission of the SEC is to protect investors; maintain fair, orderly, and efficient markets; and facilitate capital formation. The SEC's vision is to strengthen the integrity and soundness of U.S. securities markets for the benefit of investors and other market participants, and to conduct its work in a manner that is as sophisticated, flexible, and dynamic as the securities markets it regulates.

Putting Investors First: 2009 Performance and Accountability Report, www.sec.gov ■

It is not unusual for public relations practitioners and the people they represent to seek access to the public airwaves through the use of federal laws or FCC regulations. Best known is section 315 of the 1934 Communication Act, the **equal opportunity provision**. Legally qualified candidates for public office must be afforded equal access to the airwaves. If a candidate appears in a broadcast at no cost, for example, all other qualified candidates for the same office must be given the same opportunity. That is why *The Terminator* disappeared from California television broadcasts during Arnold Schwarzenegger's campaigns for governor in 2003 and 2006. Otherwise, every qualified candidate for governor would have been eligible to request equal time. However, the law does not apply to news coverage, such as news interviews or documentaries featuring qualified candidates.

Practitioners often seek access the public airwaves under the **personal attack rule,** through which stations are obliged to offer reasonable—not necessarily equal—opportunity to individuals who have been subjected to a broadcast character attack. In recent years, largely because of the perceived clout of talk radio, some in Congress have favored reinstating the **Fairness Doctrine,** a rule that had existed from 1949 to 1987. It required broadcast stations to provide balanced coverage on controversial issues. However, with the rapid expansion of media outlets during the 1980s, the FCC decided—and the courts agreed—that the Fairness Doctrine was outdated and unnecessary.

Public access to the airways has also been the central point of contention in an ongoing debate over media ownership. During the past decade, the FCC eased restrictions on the number of broadcast stations companies may own. Starting in 1975, the FCC banned cross-ownership of daily newspapers and broadcast stations within the same local market. However, because of the ever-changing media landscape, broadcast companies argued that they needed to expand their reach to compete in today's media-rich environment. The FCC ruled in December 2007 that broadcast companies may own as many stations as they want, just as long as their reach (primary coverage area) does not exceed 39 percent of all U.S. households.[39] Efforts to ease ownership rules have been opposed by a large coalition of opponents that cuts across the political spectrum. Those groups, including PRSA, have said this growing media concentration threatens to reduce the diversity of voices in the media.[40]

Another hot-button issue involving the FCC is a regulation making it unlawful to send an unsolicited advertisement to a facsimile (fax) machine without prior written permission from the recipient. Fines could range up to $500 for each violation.[41] The Junk Fax Prevention Act went into effect in 2005. It was opposed by a variety of business interests, especially professional associations such as PRSA that use fax messages to communicate with their members.[42] The FCC defines an unsolicited advertisement as "any material advertising the commercial availability or quality of any property, goods, or services which is transmitted to any person without that person's prior express invitation or permission, in writing or otherwise."[43]

The Food and Drug Administration

As public relations ventures deeper into the integrated marketing of products and services, practitioners are having to familiarize themselves with the regulations of yet another federal agency, the **Food and Drug Administration (FDA)**. The FDA was created to "protect, promote, and enhance the health of the American people." The agency has responsibility for ensuring that "foods are safe, wholesome, and sanitary; human and veterinary drugs, biological products, and medical devices are safe and effective; cosmetics are safe; and electronic products that emit radiation are safe."[44]

The area in which public relations practitioners are most likely to encounter this agency is in the promotion of products or services that are regulated by the FDA. The FDA enforces laws and regulations designed to ensure that regulated products are "honestly, accurately, and informatively represented."[45] FDA rules include restrictions on the labeling and promotion of prescription drugs. Both advertising and public relations professionals working in the health-care field must be aware of these limitations.

The FDA's Division of Drug Marketing, Advertising, and Communications (DDMAC) oversees prescription drug promotional labeling and advertising. Advertising includes commercial messages broadcast on television, radio, or the Internet, communicated over the telephone, or printed in magazines and newspapers. According to regulations, drug ads or promotions cannot be false or misleading and cannot omit material facts. Companies are required to submit their direct-to-consumer (DTC) ads to the FDA at the time they begin running. However, some companies seek prior approval.

"We look at a lot of DTC ads before they run," says Kathryn J. Aikin, of DDMAC. "Manufacturers typically want to be sure they're getting started on the right foot."[46]

News Conference

Health and Human Services Secretary Kathleen Sebelius (left) joined U.S. Justice Department officials in 2009 to announce a record $2.3 billion fraud settlement with American pharmaceutical giant Pfizer. The fine, the largest in U.S. history, was for the illegal promotion of certain drugs. It serves as a reminder of the strict regulatory environment food and drug manufacturers face.

(Lonnie Tague, U.S. Department of Justice)

 QUICK CHECK

1. Why is it important for public relations practitioners to understand the laws and regulations that govern their organizations?
2. Which federal agency serves as a watchdog against false and misleading advertising claims?
3. What does *disclosure* mean, and why are disclosure rules so vigorously enforced?

LIBEL

Another area in which public relations practitioners can be restricted in their use of free expression involves **libel,** which is loosely defined as "a false communication that wrongfully injures the reputation of others."[47] To put it another way, when you bad-mouth someone, you had better have your facts!

There are two major reasons public relations practitioners need to have a good understanding of libel law. First, they need to know that there are limits to free speech, especially when it involves another person's or company's reputation. They also need to understand that the courts have, under certain circumstances, given people great latitude in expressing their opinions on matters of public concern.

The Burden of Proof in Libel

Before 1964, people seeking damages under a claim that they had been libeled needed to prove five things: defamation, publication, identification, damage, and fault. These five things are known as the **burden of proof**.

DEFAMATION **Defamation** is any communication that unfairly injures a person's reputation and/or ability to maintain social contacts. Untruthful allegations that someone is a Nazi or has AIDS are examples of defamatory statements. It is also possible to defame a company, product, or service. In determining whether defamation has occurred, the court takes into account the context in which the statement was made, asking questions such as whether a reasonable person would understand the comment to be a parody or a joke. A truthful statement cannot be considered defamatory. Also, under the law, you cannot defame a dead person.

PUBLICATION **Publication** is the communication of a defamatory statement to a third party. Don't let the term *publication* fool you. This burden of proof is not restricted to print media; it is met regardless of the communication channel used. Another important concept closely related to this is the *republication rule*. If you repeat a defamatory statement made by someone else, *you* can be subject to a separate libel claim, even if you accurately quoted the original source. However, there are exceptions to the republication rule. For example, you may accurately repeat a defamatory statement contained in an official court document or during a meeting of an official governmental body such as Congress.

IDENTIFICATION **Identification** is the requirement that the person or organization alleging libel has to be identified in such a way that a reasonable person could infer that the defamatory statements applied to the plaintiff. This is easy to prove when names are used. However, this requirement can also be satisfied when no names are mentioned, if the defamatory statement provides information that can lead a reasonable person to believe it describes a particular individual or organization. It is even possible to defame members of a group. An allegation that someone at your college is a crook probably does not satisfy this burden. However, an allegation that someone in your family is a crook probably does.

DAMAGE There has to be evidence that the person or organization suffered injury or **damage** as a result of the defamation. This is not limited to financial injury, such as the loss of a job. Damage can also consist of loss of social esteem, such as losing all of your friends. Although this kind of damage may be intangible, juries have been known to give out some very high monetary awards as compensation for loss of social esteem.

FAULT   A plaintiff can demonstrate **fault** by proving that the defamatory statement is untrue. (Remember, a truthful statement is not defamatory.) Before 1964, the burden was on the defendant to show that the statement was true. Even if the statement was made as a result of unintentional error, the fact that an error was made was all that really mattered. However, it is on this burden of proof—fault, or falseness—that in 1964 the Supreme Court made what many have argued was one of its most significant rulings involving freedom of expression. In that ruling, the Court articulated the doctrine of *actual malice,* to which we now turn.

Actual Malice

In the case of *The New York Times v. Sullivan,* the Court set a higher burden of proof in libel cases involving public officials. It also shifted the burden of proving the falsity of a statement to the plaintiffs. In essence, the justices said public officials had to show not only that the statements made about them were not true but that the source of those statements knew—or should have known—they were not true. This higher burden of proof is known as **actual malice,** which the Court defined as knowing falsehood or reckless disregard for the truth.

Why did the Supreme Court make it harder for public officials to sue for libel? The case came out of the civil rights struggle of the 1960s. A civil rights group had run a full-page advertisement titled "Heed Their Rising Voices" in the *New York Times.* In the ad, the group accused Montgomery, Alabama officials of illegally suppressing lawful dissent. The basic thrust of the advertisement was accurate. However, some of the statements made in it were not, such as the number of times Martin Luther King Jr. had been arrested (four, not seven as stated in the advertisement). Because of the republication rule, Montgomery Police Commissioner L. B. Sullivan decided to sue the newspaper for libel. The purpose of this tactic was clearly understood by all: to make the nation's news media think twice before accepting the word of civil rights advocates. A jury awarded Sullivan $500,000 in damages, and the Alabama Supreme Court upheld the ruling. The U.S. Supreme Court, however, overturned the decision in a 5–4 vote.

In writing for the court, Justice William Brennan said this higher burden of proof was necessary to guarantee healthy public debate:

> A rule compelling the critic of official conduct to guarantee the truth of all his factual assertions—and to do so on pain of libel judgments virtually unlimited in amount—leads to . . . "self-censorship." Allowance of the defense of truth, with the burden of proving it on the defendant, does not mean that only false speech will be deterred. . . . Under such a rule, would-be critics of official conduct may be deterred from voicing their criticism, even though it is believed to be true and even though it is in fact true, because of doubt whether it can

be proved in court or fear of expense of having to do so. . . . The rule thus dampens the vigor and limits the variety of public debate. It is inconsistent with the First and Fourteenth Amendments.[48]

Subsequent court decisions have defined a **public official** as a person elected to public office (and potentially criticized in that role) or anyone who has significant public responsibility and is engaged in policy making. In another decision, *Gertz v. Robert Welch, Inc.*, the Supreme Court extended the actual malice burden to libel cases involving **public figures**—people who have widespread notoriety or have injected themselves into a public controversy in an attempt to influence its outcome. The Reverend Jesse Jackson may not be a public official, but when it comes to civil rights, he is considered a public figure.

This takes us back to something we stated earlier: People are often given great latitude in expressing their opinions on matters of public concern. As hard a pill as it may be to swallow, there is often little that public relations practitioners can do when they or their bosses are harshly criticized in the media. If a boss qualifies as either a public official or a public figure, then he or she is part of the public discourse and must meet a higher burden of proof, actual malice, to sue successfully for libel. Although a few public officials and public figures have won libel cases, most have not.

Other Forms of Libel

Although constitutional law applies to most libel cases, there are exceptions. Some cases grow out of common law, legal rules and principles that originate from judicial decisions, as opposed to those enacted by legislators or regulatory agencies.[49] **Common law libel** cases can create problems for practitioners because, by definition, they involve private communications that lack constitutional protection. In other words, actual malice, the higher burden of proof, is not available. The plaintiff needs only to demonstrate negligence to win punitive damages.[50] Even if the published information is accurate, plaintiffs can still claim damages under common law libel if that information is considered private and improperly made public.[51]

Then there are **food disparagement laws**—known informally as "veggie libel laws." Although these laws might sound somewhat frivolous, the reason for their creation is not. They are the outgrowth of aggressive news reporting that has had a negative effect—sometimes fair, sometimes unfair—on the marketplace. In the most famous of the veggie libel cases, talk show host Oprah Winfrey successfully defended herself against a suit brought by the cattle industry in 1996. Winfrey had suggested on her show that U.S. beef was not safe to eat. When beef prices fell as a result of what has been called "the Oprah effect," the Texas beef producers sued. However, they lost in the courts as well as in the court of public opinion.[52]

With the advent of blogs, podcasts, tweets, and e-mail blasts, the parameters of libel law are evolving. In the early days of the World Wide Web—about the time most of our readers were in kindergarten—many thought of the Internet as a sort of "wild, wild west" where anything goes. That feeling was fed by a lack of traditional gatekeepers and the ability of people to post comments anonymously. However, the courts have since reined in that notion. "The main issue to remember when dealing with the Internet is that people still have basic legal rights intact on the Net, and likewise, the Internet is not as completely anonymous as the typical person may presume," said Kelly O'Connell, editor of Internet Business Law Services. However, she also noted that laws pertaining to blogs are somewhat muddled. Although federal statues may legally protect a blog owner who has published defamatory material, a blogger posting on someone else's site can be held liable. However, even that can be difficult because of technical and legal hurdles involved in identifying authors of offending posts.[53]

PRIVACY

Libel is not the only area of the law to distinguish between truly private individuals and persons in the limelight. This distinction is also evident in privacy law. The legal debate over an individual's right to privacy is very complicated and, in many instances, unresolved. It often surprises people to discover that the U.S. Constitution does not specifically mention an individual's right to privacy. However, such a right has developed over the years through the passage of laws and through judicial decisions. As a general rule, private individuals have an easier time suing for invasion of privacy than do public figures.

The Four Torts of Privacy

Although the word *privacy* has one meaning in common everyday usage, it carries a different meaning when used in a legal context. *Black's Law Dictionary* has defined **privacy** as "the right to be left alone; the right of a person to be free from unwarranted publicity."[54] The law recognizes four torts, or wrongful acts, that constitute an invasion of privacy: intrusion, false light, publication of private facts, and appropriation.

INTRUSION Intrusion is defined as an improper and intentional invasion of a person's physical seclusion or private affairs. This area of privacy law hinges on whether a person has a reasonable expectation of privacy. Examples of intrusion involve trespassing on private property and illegally bugging telephone conversations. But if a television crew positioned on a public sidewalk photographed you inside your home through an open window, that would not, in a legal sense, be considered intrusion.

FALSE LIGHT You can be sued if you present someone in a **false light,** even if the communication in question isn't defamatory. For example, a picture of a man holding a mug of water in his hand is not, in and of itself, defamatory. But if the man is a member of a religion that prohibits its followers from drinking alcohol, and if the picture's caption implies that he is enjoying a beer, that could result in a claim of false

QUICKBREAK 15.3

The Pursuit of Privacy

The *right* to privacy and the *reality* of privacy are very different concepts in the Digital Age. In a world with a 24-hour news cycle and thousands of reporters needing to fill news holes, woe to anyone who unwittingly becomes a subject of media attention. It can be a suffocating experience.

This was the fate of the late Richard Jewell. He worked as a security guard in Centennial Park during the 1996 Summer Olympics in Atlanta. On a Friday night during the games, Jewell spotted a green backpack, suspected that it was a bomb, and helped hurry enough people from the scene that only one person was killed when it exploded. At first he was hailed as a hero. But when the media identified him as a suspect, he and his family suffered 88 days of unrelenting scrutiny.

"He would appear to be the victim of the beast that the media can turn into when there is blood in the water," *USA Today* reported years later. "The images of Jewell wading through the world press to get to an FBI interview never die."[55]

Jewell was eventually cleared of wrongdoing in the Centennial Park blast. Someone else was arrested. Several media organizations chose to settle libel suits brought by Jewell. Jewell died of natural causes in August 2007. He was 44 years old.[56]

The lines between legitimate news interest and prurient curiosity are often blurred. Consider the matter of Dale Earnhardt's autopsy photos.[57] When the racing legend tragically died from injuries received in the last lap of the 2001 Daytona 500, questions arose about NASCAR's official explanation for the driver's death, a seat belt failure. The *Orlando Sentinel* had reported that four drivers had recently died as a result of violent head whip, a preventable injury. In an effort to confirm its suspicions, the newspaper submitted a public records request for Earnhardt's autopsy photos. Although the *Sentinel* said it would not publish the photos, the family fought the request out of a fear that the photos would wind up on the Internet.

What followed was a flurry of legal and legislative activity. In court, the newspaper won a partial victory when it agreed to the selection of an independent medical doctor to examine the photographs under court supervision. The expert confirmed the newspaper's suspicion that violent head whip, not seat belt failure, was to blame. As a result, NASCAR reversed an earlier decision and required head and neck restraints for drivers.

However, in the court of public opinion, the Earnhardt family was a clear winner. Because of an outpouring of public outrage, state lawmakers passed the Florida Family Protection Act within 39 days of the crash. The bill severely restricts media access to autopsy photos. A Florida student newspaper challenged the constitutionality of the law all the way to the U.S. Supreme Court and lost.

And we haven't even begun to discuss hackers and eavesdropping technology that invade our privacy in ways we can't even imagine. The right and reality of privacy continues to evolve in the Digital Age. As with most other social conflicts, the issues will eventually boil down to a question of values. ■

light invasion of privacy. Categories of false light are distortion (the unintentional distortion of reality), fabrication (knowing falsehood perpetrated through alteration or embellishment of the facts), and fictionalization (publication of something, usually a book or movie, that is presented as fiction but closely mirrors real life).

PUBLICATION OF PRIVATE FACTS   **Publication of private facts** involves the public disclosure of true personal information that is embarrassing and potentially offensive. The courts have ruled, in essence, that we are entitled to keep some secrets about ourselves. However, to make a successful claim under this tort, a plaintiff must show that the information is neither newsworthy nor from a public record. If an ordinary person drinks too much in the privacy of his or her home and doesn't break any laws, it is likely that the courts will consider this private information. However, if this same person is an elected official and gets picked up for drunken driving, his or her drinking problem becomes a public matter.

APPROPRIATION   **Appropriation** is defined as the commercial use of someone's name, voice, likeness, or other defining characteristics without consent. For example, entertainer Bette Midler was once forced to tone down her stage act because she too closely mimicked the voice and mannerisms of legendary actress Mae West. "The Divine Miss M" herself later successfully used this aspect of privacy law to prevent a Midler sound-alike from appearing in an advertisement. The commercial use of a person's likeness without consent is often referred to either as *misappropriation* or as infringement of an individual's *right of publicity*. This right does not necessarily end with a person's death. In several states, California among them, the deceased's heirs retain the "right of publicity." However, the courts have said that in some circumstances a claim of misappropriation is not valid. For example, news content is not considered a commercial use. Nor is it considered a commercial use when a media outlet uses a likeness in promoting itself. Written consent is the best protection from a claim of misappropriation.

Privacy Issues in Public Relations

Privacy issues can arise in countless aspects of the practice of public relations. Practitioners routinely prepare news releases, publicity photos, videos, newsletters, annual reports, brochures, posters, and websites for public dissemination. An invasion of privacy suit can originate from any of these communications.

One area in which the practitioner has to be especially sensitive to privacy rights is employee relations. "It should not be assumed that a person's status as an employee waives his/her right to privacy," writes Frank Walsh, an expert in public relations law. "However, there are circumstances in which the employment relationship may provide an implied consent or waiver sufficient to invalidate an invasion of privacy suit."[58]

Privacy concerns also come into play when reporters make inquiries about employees. There are restrictions on the kinds of employee information that can be made public. The laws vary by location and profession. Typically, practitioners are limited to confirming a person's employment, job title, job description, date hired, and, in some cases, date terminated. A good guideline to follow: Check first with the personnel or human resources department about what is considered public or private employee information.

The growth of the Internet has raised many workplace questions. For example, the degree to which an employer may monitor an employee's e-mail can depend on whether a reasonable expectation of privacy exists. In some corporations, employees are told that their e-mail will be monitored. Other companies, in search of time-wasting and inappropriate behavior, regularly review printouts of the websites their employees visit while on the job.

COPYRIGHT

Although privacy protections are not specifically mentioned in the U.S. Constitution, **copyright** protections are. Copyrights protect original works from unauthorized use. Central to any discussion of copyright protections is the concept of **intellectual property,** which federal law defines as "original works of authorship that are fixed in a tangible form of expression." Copyrights cover seven forms of expression: literary works; musical works; dramatic works; pantomimes and choreographic works; pictorial, graphic, and sculptural works; motion pictures and other audiovisual works; and sound recordings.[59] Because the development of digital technology has made it nearly impossible to tell a copy from an original, the protection of intellectual property is a legal area of vital importance.

Copyright concerns about protecting one's own property and respecting the rights of others are a common issue for public relations practitioners. Copyright law confronts us all in many ways every day. Is it all right to take a funny editorial cartoon published in the morning newspaper and reprint it in the company newsletter? Can someone use one company's products to promote another's without permission? Is it legal to take an image off a website and use it in another medium? Are you allowed to photocopy this book?

Copyright Guidelines

As is true with other aspects of public relations law, the best place to get answers to these and other questions about copyrights are people who have expertise in this area—in this case, copyright lawyers and the U.S. Copyright Office. That said, some general rules of copyright are worth remembering:

- Copyright protection exists from the moment a work is created in a fixed, tangible form. In other words, the law presumes that a work becomes the intellectual property of the author at the moment of its creation.
- Copyrights do not protect works that have not been fixed in a tangible form of expression. Although it is possible to copyright an author's written description

of a particular location, that does not prohibit someone else from offering a different description of the same setting.

■ If a work is prepared by someone within the scope of his or her employment, it is considered **work for hire** and becomes the intellectual property of the employer. The work belongs to the employer if it was produced while the employee was "on the clock." Even after hours, the employer retains the rights if company resources (such as computers or copiers) were used.

■ It is possible for the copyright owner, such as a photographer or writer or artist, to grant limited use of the work while retaining copyright ownership.

■ Copyrights do not protect ideas, methods, systems, processes, concepts, principles, and discoveries. They do, however, protect the manner in which these are expressed.

■ Government documents and other publicly owned works may not be copyrighted.

The Digital Millennium Copyright Act

The ability to make exact copies of digital files without any measurable decline in quality is one of the great blessings of the Digital Age. However, in the view of copyright holders, it is also one of the great curses.

As noted in Chapter 11, digital technology has made it easier to copy and distribute the fruits of someone else's labors. This is of particular concern to the entertainment and computer software industries, which have seen their intellectual property rights eroded by the manufacturing and distribution of illegal copies.

These industries use special technology designed to foil piracy. For example, when a Hollywood movie studio distributes its latest movie on DVD, it encrypts the data on the disk to prevent unauthorized copying. That should be enough. However, in a world in which the frontiers of computer knowledge are breached every day, it is not. To use an analogy, locksmiths would face the same problem if every time they built a better lock, someone came along behind them and built an even better key.

In an effort to address this problem, the U.S. Congress passed the **Digital Millennium Copyright Act** (DMCA) in 1998. The DMCA established new rules for downloading, sharing, and viewing copyrighted material on the Internet. It made it a crime to circumvent antipiracy measures built into most commercial software, videos, and DVDs. It also outlawed code-cracking devices used to copy software illegally.

According to Scott Nathan, an attorney and consultant for iLinx International LLC, the penalties for violating the DMCA can be severe. "If the violation is willful for commercial gain, the first offense bears a fine of up to half a million dollars or five years imprisonment. Subsequent violations bear fines of up to one million dollars or ten years imprisonment." He added that civil actions might include an order to restrain the violation, damages for lost profits, damages for recovery of the infringer's profits, and fines up to $25,000. "Since each act of infringement can constitute a violation, the statutory fines can become quite substantial," Nathan said.[60]

QUICKBREAK 15.4

Online Music Piracy

Of all of the issues discussed in this chapter, the one that strikes closest to home for many readers is the battle over intellectual property. Of course, it is not often thought of in those terms. Many young people see it as the clash between the music industry and consumers over downloading music on the Internet. To some, this issue is nothing more than an attempt by the rich to get richer. But the music industry sees it as theft and estimates annual losses from piracy at $12.5 billion worldwide.[61]

In many instances, the law on intellectual property is clear. According to the U.S. Copyright Office, "Copyright is a form of protection provided by the laws of the United States (title 17, U.S. Code) to the authors of 'original works of authorship,' including literary, dramatic, musical, artistic, and certain other intellectual works. This protection is available to both published and unpublished works."[62]

Protection of intellectual property was included in the original draft of the U.S. Constitution. But that was before the Digital Age, the Internet, and the creation of technology that makes it easy to create and globally distribute perfect reproductions.

This is where the legal waters are muddy. At first, the music industry targeted file-sharing services such as Napster. The courts ruled that these services were guilty of abetting copyright infringement because they operated from a central server. However, when companies such as Grokster, KaZaA, and Morpheus moved to more decentralized peer-to-peer (P2P) technology, the music industry hit a snag. Citing the so-called 1983 Betamax case, the courts ruled that these P2P companies have no more control over the actions of consumers than manufacturers of home video recorders.[63]

That legal setback forced the music industry to take the controversial step of suing its own customers. The Recording Industry Association of America filed 261 copyright infringement lawsuits in September 2003.[64] RIAA claimed its lawsuits targeted people who illegally distributed, on average, more than 1,000 music files for millions of other P2P network users.

This tactic brought the music industry both scorn and embarrassment, especially when the media learned that one defendant was a 12-year-old New York honors student.[65] In recent years, RIAA backed away from suing individuals. Although the organization acknowledges that its litigation program had public relations "trade offs," it also says public awareness of the problem of illegal downloads has doubled. Although still a problem, RIAA says the rate of illegal downloads has leveled off since the start of the litigation campaign.[66] ∎

Fair Use

The courts have said it is all right to use copyrighted works without their owners' permission in some circumstances. These instances fall under the concept known as **fair use,** which the law has said is the use of copyrighted material "for purposes such as criticism, comments, news reporting, and teaching."[67] Again, fair use is a very complex area of the law. However, it is usually considered fair use if the copyrighted work is used for an educational as opposed to a commercial purpose.

The degree to which the copyrighted material is copied and the effect on its potential market value also affect whether a claim of fair use is valid. It is probably safe for professors to photocopy a paragraph from a book and distribute the copies to their classes. Copy shops have stopped reproducing book chapters for professors using course packets, however, because the courts have ruled that this practice harms the book's potential market value.

In a ruling that further defined fair use rights, the U.S. Supreme Court strengthened the rights of freelance writers in 2001. The court ruled by a 7–2 margin that major publishing companies may not reproduce the work of freelancers in electronic form without their consent. The effect of the ruling was to give the writers a voice in whether their work, originally published in one form, could be electronically published in an online database. As a practical matter, the Court's ruling largely affects only that material produced in the pre-Internet era—before freelance contracts specified whether the material could be used online.

Public relations practitioners often claim fair use when taking a quotation from a copyrighted publication for use in a news release, brochure, report, or speech. (For example, we have engaged in this practice in writing this book.) However, a claim of fair use cannot be made without appropriate attribution of the copyrighted material to its owner. As your writing and editing teachers will remind you, this is just one more reason it is necessary to use quotation marks and to cite sources of information properly.

Protecting Your Intellectual Property Rights

To assert a right of copyright protection, the work in question should bear a copyright notice that cites the year of the copyright and the name of its owner. An example: Copyright © 2011 Joan Q. Public. An even more complete way of securing copyright protection is to register a work within three months of its creation with the U.S. Copyright Office, Library of Congress, 101 Independence Ave. S. E., Washington, D.C. 20559-6000. There is a $35 nonrefundable fee for online basic registrations. Although registration is not required to claim ownership, it is required to bring an infringement of copyright lawsuit.

As a result of legislation proposed by the late Congressman Sonny Bono, a California Republican—the guy from Sonny and Cher for those who know pop music history—the owners of copyrighted works retain their rights longer than in the past. According to the U.S. Copyright Office website: "As a general rule, for works created after January 1, 1978, copyright protection lasts for the life of the author plus an additional 70 years. For an anonymous work, a pseudonymous work, or a work made for hire, the copyright endures for a term of 95 years from the year of its first publication or a term of 120 years from the year of its creation, whichever expires first."[68] The U.S. Supreme Court upheld the change in 2003. That decision relieved executives at the Walt Disney Corp., who were in danger of losing control over their most identifiable icon, Mickey Mouse.[69]

Similar to copyrights are trademarks and service marks. Both protect intellectual property rights. **Trademarks** (™) protect names, designs, slogans, and symbols that are associated with specific products. When you see the symbol ®, that indicates that the trademark is registered with the U.S. Office of Patents and Trademarks. For example, pick up a 12-ounce can of Coca-Cola®. Both the name Coca-Cola® and its derivative, Coke®, are registered trademarks. So is the design of the can and style of the lettering. When organizations want to protect names, designs, slogans, and designs associated with a particular service, they apply for a **service mark,** indicated by the symbol ᔆᴹ.

QUICK CHECK

1. What is the higher burden of proof that public officials and public figures must meet to make a claim of libel?

2. In terms of privacy law, what is appropriation?

3. What steps have been taken to protect intellectual property rights on the Internet?

LITIGATION PUBLIC RELATIONS

If you are an expert in movie or television trivia, you probably know about Dr. Richard Kimble. He was the lead character in the popular 1993 movie *The Fugitive* and the 1960s television series of the same name. What you may not know is that Kimble, a respected doctor on the run after his wrongful conviction for the death of his wife, is based on a real person. Dr. Sam Sheppard was convicted in 1954 of killing his pregnant wife. Twelve years later, the U.S. Supreme Court threw out Sheppard's conviction on the grounds that he had been denied a fair trial because of sensational media coverage before and during the trial.

The Sheppard case is often evoked when the conflict between a free press and a fair trial is debated. As a result of the Supreme Court's ruling, cameras and microphones were briefly barred from U.S. courtrooms. By the 1980s, they returned to most courtrooms—but not federal courts—under tight restrictions. This coincided with the growth in the number of media outlets, notably cable television and the Internet, and a series of highly publicized trials, particularly the 1995 double-murder trial of football legend O. J. Simpson. As lawyers for both sides played to the cameras, the battle for hearts and minds extended beyond the courthouse to the people on the streets. It is in this context that the controversial practice of **litigation public relations (LPR)** was born.

Litigation public relations is the use of mass communication techniques to influence events surrounding legal cases. Although it often focuses on lawyers' dealings with reporters, including preparation of news releases, coaching for interviews, and monitoring media, LPR can also involve the use of other public relations practices. These include focus groups and surveys as well as courtroom exhibit preparation.

Free Press versus Fair Trial

A clash of values is at the heart of the controversy surrounding LPR. The First Amendment guarantees freedom of speech and of the press. The Sixth Amendment guarantees fair and open trials. In this age of pervasive media, these two social interests often come into conflict.

While serving as chairman of the Criminal Justice Standards Committee of the American Bar Association (ABA), William Jeffress Jr. said, "A lot of us think defense attorneys and prosecutors shouldn't be playing to the press and becoming public relations agents for their clients."[70] One New York judge complained, "Lawyers now feel it is the essence of their function to try the case in the public media."[71]

Not surprisingly, some lawyers vigorously defend the use of public relations in connection with their practices. The late William M. Kunstler, who served as defense counsel in some of the most controversial trials of the past generation, believed that the use of pretrial publicity was necessary to balance scales of justice he thought were tipped unfairly toward the prosecution. "Whenever and wherever practicable, fire must be met with fire," Kunstler wrote.[72]

Because few states have laws that limit what prosecutors and defense attorneys can say before trial, it is generally left to state bar associations to regulate pretrial comment.[73] Most of these regulations mirror Rule 3.6 of the ABA's Model Rules of Professional Conduct. The rule states that "a lawyer shall not make an extrajudicial statement that a reasonable person would expect to be disseminated by means of public communication if the lawyer knows or reasonably should know that it will have a substantial likelihood of materially prejudicing an adjudicative proceeding."[74] However, this rule is rarely enforced.

The waters were muddied even further by the U.S. Supreme Court in June 1991, when the Court reversed sanctions against a Nevada attorney who had conducted a news conference to counter negative publicity about his client. In *Dominic P. Gentile v. State Bar of Nevada,* the Court said the rule, as interpreted by the Nevada state bar, was too vague. In his opinion for the majority, Justice Anthony M. Kennedy wrote, "In some circumstances press comment is necessary to protect the rights of the client and prevent abuse of the courts."[75]

"The stakes are inevitably high in litigation public relations situations," writes Dirk C. Gibson of the University of New Mexico. "At the least, your financial well-being may be affected by the outcome in a civil action, while in a criminal action a trial outcome may literally be a matter of life or death, or the deprivation of personal liberty and freedom."[76]

The Use of LPR Tactics

One survey of trial lawyers suggests that although most do not, as a rule, use mass communication techniques in their practices, a majority approve of their use. Nine out of 10 litigators surveyed said that in certain circumstances it is appropriate to speak to the media on behalf of a client. And by more than a 2:1 ratio, those who were surveyed and expressed an opinion said they thought the media had been fair in reporting cases in which they had personally been involved. Still, most lawyers appear to be uneasy about being under the media spotlight.[77]

When public relations practitioners are engaged in LPR, they usually work for the lawyer, not the client. LPR practitioners often aid in pretrial research by using public opinion polls and focus groups to determine the mood of the jury pool. Lawyers sometimes use this information to test specific approaches that may be employed in court. Practitioners often coach both lawyers and clients on how to deal with the

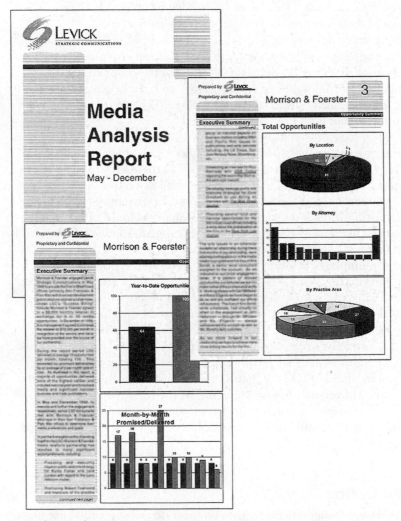

Media Analysis Report

A media analysis report can help litigation public relations practitioners show clients the effectiveness of media relations strategies and tactics.

(Courtesy of Levick Strategic Communications)

media, how to be interviewed, and how to be proactive in defending their reputation. A practitioner's roles also may include preparation of courtroom exhibits; service as a contact point for the media; and, in the most controversial aspect of LPR, assistance in efforts to influence the jury pool before a trial ever takes place.

Even when the practitioner works independently of a lawyer, it is often the lawyer who has the closest access to the client. The reason for this is simple: The lawyer, not the practitioner, has legal immunity. One very public example of this surfaced in 1998, when then presidential spokesman Mike McCurry told reporters that he had not asked President Clinton about his relationship with a White House intern. McCurry said he did not want to be subpoenaed by the special prosecutor investigating the allegations surrounding Clinton:

> On matters like this that are going to be under investigation, I think it could conceivably jeopardize the legal representation the president is entitled to, so I choose not to ask him directly about these things and rely on what counsel tells me. And then we work with the president to figure how we're going to respond to questions.[78]

For any practitioner, the reality of this lawyer–client **privilege** issue can be difficult to swallow, especially when it runs counter to the professional need to have direct access to management. It was especially frustrating for McCurry, who told reporters at one White House briefing, "I think you all know the constraints that I'm laboring under here, and I don't want to belabor the pain and anguish I feel."[79] However, as a general rule, courts have treated attorney work products—including case-specific public relations activity done under contract to an attorney—as privileged communication.

Is LPR in Society's Best Interests?

Is LPR a good thing for our society? No pun intended, but the jury is still out. On the one hand, people and companies should have every right to defend their reputations in the court of public opinion. However, many are bothered by attempts to use extrajudicial statements (statements made outside a court) to influence proceedings inside the court.

One place where this happens with increasing regularity is the Internet. According to a study released in 2004, a growing number of defendants are taking their side of the story to the Web.[80] In recent years, prominent figures facing legal troubles, such as Martha Stewart and the late Michael Jackson, turned to the Internet to tell their side of the story. A study of Stewart's and Jackson's personal litigation websites found similar content, including news releases, open letters, formal statements, downloadable court filings, responses to media coverage, and links for visitors to send messages of support. According to the authors of that study, "The analysis revealed that standard litigation public relations standards transfer well to the Internet and suggests that such websites are a promising means for disseminating and controlling a client's message."[81]

It all comes down to the difficult balancing act left us by the framers of the Constitution. A built-in conflict exists between the First and Sixth Amendments.

Judges, lawyers, and public relations practitioners must carefully navigate these uncharted waters. We must also remember that, as public relations practitioners, we have our own codes of ethics to uphold. The PRSA *Code of Ethics* says that practitioners must "serve the public interest by acting as responsible advocates for those we represent." The code also says that "a member shall preserve the integrity of the process of communication." Though not explicit statements on LPR, they do, nevertheless, provide meaningful guidance.

QUICK CHECK

1. What is litigation public relations?
2. Why must litigation public relations practitioners sometimes deal only with lawyers instead of with the lawyers' clients?
3. What are the arguments for and against the use of litigation public relations?

SUMMARY

At a time when many mourn a lack of civility in society, public relations practitioners face pressure to operate within both the letter and the spirit of the laws governing their profession. Practitioners must follow a wide array of rules and regulations that cover practically every aspect of their professional responsibilities. Unfortunately, many appear woefully ignorant of these laws.

First Amendment protection for the practice of public relations lies in the gray area between political and commercial speech. The underlying purpose of each communication determines the degree of constitutional protection it enjoys. In addition to constitutional issues, laws govern various aspects of specific businesses. Among the most notable of these are disclosure laws pertaining to publicly held companies. Practitioners also are often confronted by a need to understand libel, privacy, and copyright laws. In the case of libel and privacy laws, they also need to understand the different burdens of proof for public and private individuals. The growth of the Internet and digital technologies has triggered legal issues undreamt of a generation ago.

Public relations is having a growing—and not necessarily positive—effect on our civil and criminal justice systems. The practice of litigation public relations is expanding dramatically, thanks in part to the built-in conflict that exists between our constitutional freedom of expression and our constitutional right to a fair and open trial. Here, as in other areas of public relations, we should be guided by our values.

DISCUSSION QUESTIONS

1. Devise a response to this statement from a fellow public relations practitioner: "This is the United States. I have freedom of speech. I can say whatever I want on behalf of my clients."
2. How do federal agencies regulate commercial speech?

3. What is the burden of proof for libel? Are all persons treated the same under libel law?

4. How do privacy rights affect the practice of public relations?

5. What are some tasks undertaken by a practitioner of litigation public relations? Under what constraints do LPR practitioners operate?

MEMO FROM THE FIELD

JAMES F. HAGGERTY, ESQ
President; The PR Consulting Group, Inc.
New York, New York

James F. Haggerty, president and CEO of The PR Consulting Group, is an attorney with more than 20 years of experience in marketing, public relations, and public affairs. Among the nation's best-known experts in litigation communications, Haggerty has also earned a national reputation in professional services marketing, public affairs, and crisis management.

The intersection of public relations and law continues to widen, as interest in legal matters and legal media coverage grows. Unfortunately, the intersection is often littered with blind spots, potholes, and other hazards. For the PR practitioner with the right skills, however, it can be an avenue to a unique public relations career, combining media, law, regulation, government affairs, and public opinion in a way that is fast-paced, challenging, and, in the end, extremely satisfying.

Law now permeates most aspects of our lives, and media and news coverage are no exception. Watch CNN, MSNBC, or Fox News long enough and you begin to appreciate just how much legal news coverage is a part of our lives. A producer, for what until recently was known as Court TV, recently told me that the network became so successful that *all* news is now Court TV. She wasn't very far from the truth.

The ramifications for the public relations field are enormous. You don't have to be a lawyer to excel in this field, but nearly all PR practitioners at some time in their careers will now find themselves immersed in legal issues—or butting heads with the lawyers representing their client. Lawyers who still feel "no comment" is always the best response.

My company spends 70–80 percent of its time advising clients in the relatively new public relations specialty called litigation public relations. It combines the best elements of crisis communications, public affairs, and litigation strategy. In litigation public relations, it is not enough to deliver media coverage or other PR "results"—you've got to deliver coverage that helps to meet the client's litigations goals: whether it is discouraging legal action before it is filed, creating the proper atmosphere for a beneficial settlement, or controlling the effect on the client's reputation as a case moves to trial and beyond.

You need the ability to sift through 100-page legal filings for the sentence or two that catches the real "story" behind the case. You need the confidence to deal with lawyers and argue for a communications strategy that will enhance the litigation strategy. And you need to pick your media targets carefully: Giant media lists and mass-produced press kits are usually the exception rather than the rule.

But here's a fact most lawyers won't tell you: Sometimes what happens in the court of public opinion can be more important than what happens in the court of law.

An example: We recently worked with a client who spent eight years tangled in oppressive litigation with a large multinational corporation. Although the company's lawyers were doing an excellent job, the legal wrangling seemed endless. The other side's strategy was to bury the company in legal filings and discovery requests until virtually all of the defendant's resources were focused on fending off what was, at best, a very weak case. The litigation was sapping the lifeblood of a company that didn't have the resources to match the much larger multinational.

Then we got involved. Six months later, the case was withdrawn, with a simple joint statement that the parties would "agree to disagree."

How did this happen? In looking at the situation, we reasoned that the one thing that would stop the multinational plaintiff from continuing its frivolous litigation was a severe blow to the company's reputation. They needed to look not just wrong on the law but foolish for continuing what was obviously a mean-spirited, vindictive lawsuit designed to crush a smaller competitor. So we worked with thousands of pages of legal documents to assemble the kind of information that would convince an influential columnist to write an opinion piece exposing the true story of the case. Then we showed the column to an Associated Press reporter, who wrote a story on the column itself. The AP story was picked up in about a half-dozen cities nationwide. An editorial writer in one of the key trade publications covering the industry saw the AP story and wrote a very damaging editorial exposing the company's tactics. And so on.

It wasn't long before the multinational began to see that continuing the lawsuit was getting in the way of its own business goals. At that point, the plaintiff realized it was far easier to quit than to fight!

This is the value of litigation public relations. And while we usually can't have that kind of impact on every case, we can ensure that we create the kind of positive conditions that facilitate the best possible result for our clients: allowing them to get the litigation behind them and get back to the *real* work of their company or organization. ∎

CASE STUDY 15.1 Ethanol 2.0

You don't have to have an Ivy League business degree to know that in the complex world of global economics, good news is not always good, bad news is not always bad, and up is sometimes down. That is especially true for the Massachusetts-based Verenium Corporation and its attempt to bring the next generation of ethanol to your neighborhood gas station.

Since the days of the oil embargoes of the 1970s, many, especially farmers, have hailed ethanol as an answer to the United States' dependence on foreign oil sources. On paper, at least, it seems an elegant solution to a difficult problem: Instead of drilling for fuel, grow it. Of course, it is not that simple. The science of producing fuel from corn is complex, as are its economics. By the middle of the last decade, ethanol motor fuel consumption in the United States was less than 3 percent of the total gasoline pool.[82]

To make matters more difficult, ethanol has come under fire from environmental and consumer groups. Environmentalists claim the process of producing ethanol actually increases the amount of greenhouse gases released into the atmosphere. Consumer advocates also warn that the diversion of agricultural products into fuel production drives up food costs and increases world hunger.

A potential answer to this problem is cellulosic ethanol (CE), the next generation of ethanol, made from plant waste such as wood chips, corncobs, and unused parts of the sugar cane plant. Not only does CE have the potential for providing new revenue streams for farmers, it significantly reduces greenhouse gas emissions.[83]

By 2008, Verenium and other energy companies were hoping to make a big splash in this promising market. However, just as it appeared that CE's time had arrived, so had the Great Recession. Money needed for research and production facilities was tight. But there was an even bigger problem: Investors and the media didn't know the difference between ethanol and CE. Considering the warnings of environmental and consumer advocates, the financial community was having second thoughts about investing in ethanol. Even the U.S. government excluded Verenium from much-needed research grants.[84]

That's when Verenium sought out the services of Brandtectonics (BT), a division of Chandler Chicco Co., a global network of communication companies. The challenge was to differentiate CE from traditional ethanol in the eyes of financial reporters and investors while adhering to SEC restrictions against false, misleading, or hyperbolic statements. BT's first task was to analyze top-tier media outlets with influence among the energy, environmental, scientific, agricultural, and regulatory communities. From this, the agency created "a comprehensive media matrix with tailored strategies and newshooks for each reporter."[85] BT also conducted a competitive analysis and closely monitored Verenium's stock prices and analyst ratings.

From this research came a three-pronged effort: a steady news stream linked to events such as the passage of the federal farm bill, publicity surrounding the opening of the nation's first demonstration-scale CE plant in Louisiana, and promotion of partner investments and analyst upgrades. This was done to position Verenium as both an industry leader and a good investment. Tactics included media kits and advisories, op-ed commentaries, and letters to editors in support of ethanol legislation. One key tactic was an embargoed exclusive given the *Wall Street Journal* about British Petroleum's $90 million investment in Verenium. The agency also pitched Carlos Riva, the company's president and CEO, as an expert on whom journalists could rely for comment on energy-related issues.

In the end, Verenium secured four major capital infusions, including two Department of Energy grants. On the day the company announced its partnership with BP, its stock closed 64 percent higher than it opened, the biggest percentage gain on the NASDAQ that day. Key investors increased their holdings in Verenium by 27 million shares. Six investment firms increased, upgraded, or initiated coverage of the company. In terms of media relations, BT secured more than 65 unique placements in targeted media outlets.

In recognition of these efforts to rebrand the company and its cutting-edge product, Verenium and Brandtectonics received a Silver Anvil Award in Investor relations from the Public Relations Society of America in 2009.

DISCUSSION QUESTIONS

1. If, as the case study suggests, the public relations efforts focused on *rebranding* the company and its product, why did this campaign win an *investor relations* award?

2. What was done to target messages to specific publics?

3. What were the benefits and risks of giving the *Wall Street Journal* an exclusive on the company's $90 million partnership with British Petroleum?

4. If you had been advising Verenium, would you have placed a greater emphasis on using social media? Explain your reasons. ■

CASE STUDY 15.2 The Black List

After a decade of publishing an annual list of what it said were the best corporate citizens, the folks at *Corporate Responsibility* took a turn to the dark side in April 2010. Just a few weeks after publishing its "100 Best Corporate Citizens List," the magazine introduced its first-ever "Black List" of what it said were the 30 least transparent companies.

The Corporate Responsibility Officers Association publishes *CR*. Both lists, the good and the bad, rank Russell 1000 companies based on the availability of 349 data points. Specifically, the magazine looks at how much information companies disclose about their environmental, climate change, human rights, philanthropy, employee relations, financial performance, and governance policies.[86] The 30 companies that made the inaugural Black List had zero points of relevant data. They also had another thing in common: When *CR* contacted them to request data to gain a better picture of their corporate practices, none responded.[87]

"The notion of transparency as the first, best, primary value allows other players, players with a variety of values—be they journalistic, NGOs, competitors, collaborators—to weigh in according to their competing interests," said *CR* Editor-In-Chief Dirk Olin. "We decided to ask ourselves what the bottom of that list would look, never dreaming for a minute that we would uncover a full 30 corporations where no relevant data at all could be turned up."[88]

Among the corporations to achieve the dubious distinction of being on the first Black List were Abercrombie & Fitch, Bancorpsouth, Lorillard, Scripps Networks Interactive, and Weight Watchers International. This is in contrast to CR's 100 Best Corporate Citizens list, which in 2010 was headed by Hewlett-Packard, Intel, General Mills, and IBM.

"While being a '100 Best Corporate Citizens List' company is a major accomplishment requiring considerable commitment and cost, indulging in just enough transparency to get your company out of the cellar is not that hard, nor that expensive," *CR* publisher and president Jay Whitehead said. "It's less embarrassing than being on the 'Black List.'"[89]

Although the 30 companies on the inaugural Black List may have hit rock bottom in terms of overall transparency, many other companies are secretive in certain aspects of their corporate citizenship. The magazine noted that 60 percent of the companies studied have not disclosed any information relating to their greenhouse gas emissions, climate change policies, or broader environmental issues—something they are not required to do by law.[90]

The magazine suggested that increasing transparency in the future might do more than just help companies avoid public ridicule. It noted that companies on the "Best" list enjoyed a 2.3 percent return in shareholder value over a three-year period, compared with a 7.3 percent loss during the same time frame by blacklisted firms.

What does it take to get off the Black List? Not that much, said Whitehead. "All a 'Black List' company has to do is make a few CR-related data points about itself publicly available," he said. "Put your employees benefits policy online. Publish some human rights information. Get a formal climate change policy and put it online."[91]

There are some indications that some companies are taking steps to move out of the shadow of the

Black List. Whitehead cited Abercrombie & Fitch's "A&F Cares" campaign as a move in the right direction.

"I'm sure this is not the first they've heard this," Whitehead said. "This and many other voices raised against opacity and a lack of accountability have inspired them to respond in this way."[92]

A&F spokesman Eric Cerny said his company "does take our corporate responsibilities seriously" and that the A&F Cares website "now gives a consolidated voice discussing the company's efforts in all of those issues that we've been working on through the company's history." Cerny added that the company has established a committee "to focus on sustainability, philanthropy, human rights, and diversity and inclusion initiatives."[93]

"Companies on the 'Black List' represent the least transparent companies in the Russell 1000, which is a tough place to be in the era of corporate responsibility and its ever-intensifying drive for transparency," Whitehead said. "We expect companies on the 'Black List' will be unhappy with us."[94]

DISCUSSION QUESTIONS

1. Should companies such as those on the Black List be criticized for not publicizing information that the government does not require them to release?
2. Corporate transparency may be good public relations, but is it good business?
3. If your company were blacklisted, what steps might you suggest?
4. While *Corporate Responsibility*'s Black List may have increased the magazine's profile, does this kind of "finger-pointing" tactic carry with it potential risks? ■

NOTES

1. *Universal Declaration of Human Rights*, United Nations General Assembly resolution 217 A (III), 10 December 1948, online, www.un.org/Overview/rights.html.
2. *2009 Country Reports on Human Rights*, U.S. Department of State, 11 March 2010, online, www.state.gov.
3. *State of the First Amendment 2006*, First Amendment Center, 11 November 2006, online, www.firstamendmentcenter.org/sofa_reports/index.aspx.
4. "Westboro Church Protests Head to Supreme Court," Associated Press, 30 March 2010, as published by the *Huffington Post*, online, www.huffingtonpost.com.
5. Viktor Frankl, *Man's Search for Meaning* (New York: Pocket Books, 1984), 119–157.
6. Kathy R. Fitzpatrick, "Public Relations and the Law: A Survey of Practitioners," *Public Relations Review* (spring 1996): 1–8.
7. Morton J. Simon, *Public Relations Law* (New York: Meredith, 1969), 4.
8. *The Constitution of the United States and The Declaration of Independence* (Commission on the Bicentennial of the United States Constitution, 1992).
9. *The New York Times Co. v. Sullivan*, 376 US 255, 270 (1964).
10. *Virginia State Board of Pharmacy v. Virginia Citizens Consumer Council, Inc.*, 425 US 764, 765 (1976).
11. Ibid.
12. *Central Hudson Gas & Electric Corp. v. Public Service Commission of New York*, 447 US 557, 100 S. Ct. 2343 (1980).
13. Bruce E.H. Johnson, "Overview: Advertising & First Amendment," First Amendment Center, online, www.firstamendment.org.
14. Karla K. Gower, "*Kasky v. Nike, Inc.*: The End of Constitutionally Protected Corporate Speech?" Paper presented at the Association of Educators in Journalism and Mass Communications Annual Conference, Kansas City, Mo., August 2003.
15. "The Federal Election Campaign Laws: A Short History," Federal Elections Commission, online: www.fec.gov.
16. Federal Elections Commission, online, www.fec.gov.

17. Gordon T. Belt, "What's on the Horizon," First Amendment Center, online, firstamendmentcenter.org.

18. William M. Murray, "Is Supreme Court's Decision a Public Relations Boon?", *PRSAY* (blog), Public Relations Society of America, 22 January 2010, online, www.prsa.org.

19. David W. Guth and Paul Wenske, *Media Guide for Attorneys* (Topeka: Kansas Bar Association, 1995), 28.

20. Federal Trade Commission, online, www.ftc.gov.

21. FTC website.

22. FTC website.

23. Greg Beaubien, "FTC Rules Spotlight Mommy Bloggers, But Target Marketers," *Public Relations Tactics*, 14 December 2009, online, www.prsa.org.

24. "FTC Publishes Final Guides Governing Endorsements, Testimonials," news release, Federal Trade Commission, 6 October 2009.

25. Michael Cherenson, "PRSA Offers Clarity on the FT/C's Updated Guidelines to Regulate Bloggers," *Public Relations Tactics*, November 2009, 16.

26. Beaubien.

27. "Reporter Resources: The Do Not Call Registry," Federal Trade Commission website, http://www.ftc.gov/opa/reporter/dnc.shtm.

28. Securities and Exchange Commission, online, www.sec.gov.

29. Final Rule: Selective Disclosure and Insider Trading, 17 CFR Parts 240, 243, and 249; release Nos. 33-7881, 34-43154, IC-245999, File No. S7-31-99. RIN 3235 AH82, online, www.sec.gov.

30. John D. Zelezny, *Communications Law: Liberties, Restraints, and the Modern Media* (Belmont, Calif.: Wadsworth, 1997), 331; 17 C.F.R. §240.10b-5 (1992).

31. Dennis L. Wilcox, Phillip H. Ault, and Warren K. Agee, *Public Relations Strategies and Tactics,* 3rd ed. (New York: HarperCollins, 1992), 142–143.

32. *Securities and Exchange Commission v. Texas Gulf Sulfur,* 446 F. 2nd 1301 (2nd Cir 1966).

33. Public Relations Society of America, *Code of Ethics,* online, www.prsa.org.

34. "The Laws That Govern the Securities Industry," Securities and Exchange Commission, online, www.sec.gov/about/ laws.shtml.

35. Robert W. Taft, "Discretionary Disclosure," *Public Relations Journal,* April 1983, 34–35.

36. "A Chronology of ImClone and Martha Stewart," *Washington Post,* 8 July 2004, online, www.washingtonpost.com.

37. Binyamin Appelbaum and David S. Hilzenrath, "SEC Didn't Act on Madoff Tips," *Washington Post*, 16 December 2008, online, www.washingtonpost.com.

38. Mary L. Schapiro, "Message from the Chairman," *Putting Investors First: 2009 Performance and Accountability Report,* U.S. Securities and Exchange Commission, 2.

39. "FCC Consumer Facts: FCC's Review of Broadcast Ownership Rules," Federal Communications Commission, 23 June 2008, online, www.fcc.gov.

40. "Public Relations Society of America Strongly Supports the Overturning of FCC Ownership Rules by the U.S. Third Circuit Court of Appeals," news release issued by the PRSA, 25 June 2003, online, www.prsa.org.

41. "Unwanted Faxes: What You Can Do," Federal Communications Commission, online, www.fcc.gov.

42. "FCC Delays Amended Fax Advertisement Regulations," news release issued by the PRSA, 19 August 2003, online, www.prsa.org.

43. "Fax Advertising: What You Need to Know," Federal Communications Commission fact sheet, 28 March 2007.

44. Food and Drug Administration, online, www.fda.gov.

45. FDA website.

46. Carol Rados, "Truth in Advertising: Rx Drug Ads Come of Age," *FDA Consumer,* July–August 2004, online, www.fda.gov.

47. Zelezny, 519.

48. *The New York Times Co. v. Sullivan,* 376 US 254, 279 (1964).

49. This information on common law libels has been graciously supplied by Associate Professor Thomas W. Volek, William Allen White School of Journalism and Mass Communications, University of Kansas.

50. *Dun & Bradstreet v. Greenmoss Builders*, 472 US 749 (1985).

51. *Richard Garziano v. E.I. Du Pont de Nemours & Co., No. 86-4025*. U.S. Court of Appeals, Fifth Circuit. 818 F.2d 380 (1987).

52. "Texas Jury Has No Beef with Oprah," Associated Press story reported in the *Lawrence (Kansas) Journal World*, 27 February 1998, 3A.

53. Kelly O'Connell, "Internet Law—Understanding Internet Defamation," Internet Business Legal Services, posted 10 October 2007, online, www.ibls.com.

54. *Black's Law Dictionary*, 5th ed. (St. Paul: West, 1979), 1075.

55. Mike Lopresti, "Eight Years after Atlanta, Closure Difficult for Jewell," *USA Today*, 17 August 2004, 11D.

56. "Wrongly Suspected Richard Jewell," Court TV, online, www.crimelibrary.com.

57. David W. Guth and Charles Marsh, *Adventures in Public Relations: Case Studies and Critical Thinking* (Boston: Allyn & Bacon, 2005), 283–286.

58. Frank Walsh, *Public Relations & the Law* (New York: Foundation for Public Relations Education and Research, 1988), 15.

59. I. Fred Koenigsberg, *How to Handle Basic Copyright and Trademark Problems, 1991* (New York: Practising Law Institute, 1991), 31.

60. Scott Nathan, "Digital Millennium Copyright Act (DMCA): An Explanation," SearchEnterpriseLinux.com, posted 4 November 2004, online, http://searchenterpriselinux.techtarget.com.

61. Anti-Piracy Update, Recording Industry Association of America, n.d., online, www.riaa.com.

62. "For Students Doing Reports," Recording Industry Association of America website, online, www.riaa.com/faqphp.

63. Mark Thyer, "Understanding and Dealing with Common Peer-to-Peer (P2P) Application Security," *Information Systems Security*, Nov./Dec. 2003, 42–51.

64. "64 Individuals Agree to Settlements in Copyright Infringement Cases," news release issued by the Recording Industry Association of America, 29 September 2003, online, www.riaa.com.

65. "Downloading Girl Escapes Lawsuit," Associated Press, as reported on CBSNews.com, 9 September 2003, online, www.cbsnews.com.

66. "For Students Doing Reports."

67. Walsh, 61.

68. "Copyright Basics," U.S. copyright office, online, www.copyright.gov.

69. Gina Holand, "High Court Backs Longer Copyrights," *Kansas City Star*, 16 January 2003, C1.

70. B. Drummond Ayres, "Simpson Case Has California Debating Muzzles for Lawyers," *New York Times*, 21 August 1994, sec. 1, 40.

71. Hoffman.

72. William M. Kunstler, "The Lawyer: 'A Chill Wind Blows,'" *Media Studies Journal* (winter 1992): 79.

73. Ayres.

74. Rule 3.6 (subsection a), *American Bar Association Rules of Professional Conduct*, 1983.

75. *Dominic P. Gentile, Petitioner v. State Bar of Nevada, U.S. Supreme Court Reports*, 115 L Ed 2nd, 888–912.

76. Dirk C. Gibson, "The Paradoxical Nature of Litigation Public Relations," *Public Relations Quarterly* (spring 2003): 32–34.

77. David W. Guth, "The Acceptance and Use of Public Relations Practices among Kansas Litigators," *Public Relations Review* (winter 1996): 341–354.

78. White House press briefing, 23 January 1998, 1:35 P.M.

79. Karen Tumulty, "Caught in the Town's Most Thankless Job," *Time*, 9 March 1998, 68.

80. Bryan H. Reber, Karla K. Gower, and Jennifer A. Robinson, "The Internet and Litigation Public Relations," paper presented to the Public Relations Division, Association for Education in Journalism and Mass Communications, Toronto, Canada, August 2004.

81. Reber, Gower, and Robinson.

82. "Biofuels in the U.S. Transportation Sector," *Annual Energy Outlook 2007*, U.S. Department of Energy, February 2007.

83. *Verenium Corporation Form 10-K (Annual Report)*, filed with the U.S. Securities and Exchange Commission, 16 March 2010, 9.

84. "Not All Ethanol Is Created Equal," Silver Anvil Award Campaign Profile 6BW-0914A01, Public Relations Society of America, online, www.prsa.org.

85. "Not All Ethanol Is Created Equal."

86. "*Corporate Responsibility* Magazine to Announce First-Ever Black List—the Russell

1000's Least-Transparent Companies," news release, 9 April 2010, via Business Wire, online, www.businesswire.com.

87. Jeanine Poggi, "Least Transparent Stocks in America," *TheStreet.com Financial News Center*, 14 April 2010, online, www. thestreet.com.

88. Stephanie Clifford, "Magazine to Publish a Corporate 'Black List'," *New York Times*, 11 April 2010, online, nytimes.com.

89. "Bad Business—*CR*'s Black List," *Corporate Responsibility* website, 14 April 2010, online, www.thecro.com/content/bad-business-crs-black-list.

90. Jeremy Hance, "Black List Uncovers Least Transparent Companies," Mongabay.com, 14 April 2010, online, www.mongabay.com.

91. "Bad Business—*CR*'s Black List."

92. Tim Feran, "Abercrombie & Fitch Lands on Magazine's 'Black List.'" *Columbus Dispatch*, 14 April 2010, online, www.dispatch.com.

93. Feran.

94. "Bad Business—*CR*'s Black List."

16

Your Future in Public Relations

OBJECTIVES

After studying this chapter, you will be able to

- understand better the forces that are shaping the future of society
- recognize the trends that are changing the practice of public relations
- recognize the leadership role women and minority practitioners are playing and will play in public relations

- pinpoint steps you can take today to secure a successful future in public relations

KEY TERMS

baby boom generation, p. 503
breadwinners, p. 504
empowerment, p. 509
feminization, p. 504
globalization, p. 499

REAL WORLD
The Government Contract

The excitement of your agency's winning a big contract from a new client has begun to wear off. As the reality of this opportunity settles in, you realize you need to hire four more people to handle the increased workload.

Besides you, the agency you head has 10 people: three white females, two Hispanic females, three white males, one black female, and one black male. Your new client, a government agency, requires its contractors to have diverse workplaces that mirror the gender and racial makeup of society at large.

After advertising the positions in local and professional publications, you have determined that only four of the applicants meet your highly technical minimum education and experience requirements. However, all four finalists are white.

You are committed to cultural diversity in the workplace; you were particularly hoping to hire an Asian American practitioner. Both your client and various community groups are watching your hiring practices closely and insist on diversity. However, you have conducted what you considered an open and fair recruitment process. You also have four qualified applicants ready to go to work and a bunch of work piling up. What are you going to do?

WHAT'S NEXT?

Public Relations Tactics, a monthly publication of the Public Relations Society of America, celebrated its 10th anniversary in July 2004 by boldly predicting what the profession would look like in the year 2014. However, in a strategically wise move, the editors also reminded their readers of some past predictions that didn't pan out:

- "This 'telephone' has too many shortcomings to be seriously considered as a means of communication. The device is inherently of no value to us."— *Western Union internal memo, 1876*
- "This wireless music box has no imaginable commercial value. Who would pay for a message sent to nobody in particular?"—*NBC founder David Sarnoff's associates in response to his pushing for investment in radio in the 1920s*
- "Who the hell wants to hear actors talk?"—*H. M. Warner, cofounder and president of Warner Bros., 1927*

- "We don't like their sound, and guitar music is on the way out."—*Decca Recording Company rejecting the Beatles, 1962*
- "There is no reason anyone would want a computer in their home."—*Ken Olson, founder and chairman of Digital Equipment, 1977*[1]

Oops!

Obviously, there is peril in predicting the future. But everybody does it because we all have a stake in it. No one has a greater personal interest in your future than you. After all, isn't going to college about getting yourself ready for the challenges of the future? (OK, at least *one* of the reasons?)

How does one go about predicting the future, especially the future of a dynamic profession such as public relations? We'd hope that by this point of the semester, assuming that you haven't been reading this book backward, you would understand that the answer to any question about how anyone gets started doing anything has a one-word answer: *research*. Understanding the past and the present is the key to predicting the future. Social forces shaped public relations during its first century and will continue to do so in its second.

SOCIAL FORCES AND PUBLIC RELATIONS

Public relations, now and in the future, cannot operate in a vacuum. Just as its practitioners seek to exert influence on various aspects of society, social forces are at work that influence the profession. Understanding those forces is a key to unlocking the mysteries about the future of public relations.

The Global Spread of Democracy

One powerful social force is the global spread of democracy. Much of the history of the 20th century centered on the worldwide struggle against forces of tyranny and oppression. Most of that century's wars and great social movements grew out of a desire either to gain or to protect individual freedoms. With the end of the Cold War between democracy and communism, many nations embraced democratic institutions and ideas for the first time.

The changeover from an authoritarian to a democratic society is not easy. Democracy is more than just a set of rules. It is a way of life. Imagine what it would be like to live in a society in which the government watched over every aspect of your life. For as long as you can remember, someone was always telling you what you could do, think, or say. Now imagine what it would be like to have all those restrictions suddenly lifted. After the euphoria of liberation had dissipated, you would confront the cold reality of your new way of life. Before, someone else made your decisions for you. Now, you have to make your own choices and live with the consequences of those choices.

To ease this transition, many public and private agencies have engaged in aggressive programs of education and technical support in the newly emerging democracies. At the forefront of these efforts have been journalists, marketers, and

QUICKBREAK 16.1

A Global Snapshot

In 2009, the United States had the largest gross domestic product (GDP) of any nation in the world ($14.2 trillion), followed by China ($8.7 trillion), Japan ($4.1 trillion), and India ($3.5 trillion).[2] As is the case in the United States, the other three nations have vibrant public relations industries, each with unique characteristics.

Public relations is big business in China—and getting bigger each year. The China International Public Relations Association (CIPRA) reports that industry revenues topped 14 billion yuan ($2.05 billion) in 2008, a 30 percent increase over the previous year.[3] There is no licensing in China. However, the nation's practitioners must operate within restrictive laws established by China's communist government. CIPRA offers accreditation much like PRSA and IABC. The difference is that many agencies will hire only accredited practitioners.[4]

Because of the China's growing economic clout, accompanying demand for public relations consultants has created a shortage of practitioners. CIPRA, which has regulatory authority over the profession, has enacted rules restricting the poaching of talent from one agency to another.[5] Meanwhile, in an attempt to fill the void, an estimated 500,000 students are currently studying public relations.[6]

A rapid expansion of the economy has also heightened the need for public relations counsel in India.[7] According to the Global Alliance for Public Relations and Communication Management, more than 10,000 people work at more than 700 public relations firms in India. However, because of a lack of education and formal training, only 100 students enter the profession each year.[8]

According to the Public Relations Student International Coalition (PRSIC), Indian public relations suffers from a lack of self-regulation. "While public relations practitioners in India agree that ethical rules would help the profession's image, they do not agree that a code of ethics is truly necessary for practitioners themselves," a report said.[9] In fact, the Public Relations Society of India does not have a code of ethics.

Although Japan's public relations industry is far more evolved than either China's or India's, it faces similar issues. The Japanese public relations industry has a distinctly Western flavor. However, unlike Indian practice, which emerged from British colonial traditions, Japanese practitioners were heavily influenced by the American occupation following the Second World War.

The primary focus of Japanese public relations is media relations. "The nature of Japanese culture lends the practice of public relations a great deal of power," reports PRSIC. Apparently, in Japan, public relations is held in higher esteem than advertising, largely because of third-party endorsement.

However, the report goes on to say the most significant challenge facing Japanese practitioners is the nation's lax libel laws. "Without strict guidelines as to what press can and cannot say, media outlets can often twist messages and destroy company images," the PRSIC report said. "This necessitates the constant vigilance of practitioners."[10] ▪

public relations practitioners teaching the virtues of free expression. By the thousands, these professionals have crisscrossed the globe in an effort to instill democratic values and traditions in places where historically there have been none. The challenge is to do so in a culturally sensitive manner. The fact that something works well in the United States does not necessarily mean it will work somewhere else. The most successful efforts at spreading democracy have been those mindful of local traditions and values.

 QUICK CHECK

1. To what degree is the practice of public relations regulated in the four nations with the world's largest economies?
2. What are the challenges facing public relations practitioners in China, India, and Japan?
3. How has the end of the Cold War influenced the global growth of public relations?

Globalization

Another major social force influencing the future of public relations is **globalization.** The United Nations Development Program defines globalization as "the growing interdependence of the world's people through shrinking space, shrinking time, and disappearing borders."[11] With each passing day, the peoples of the earth are being drawn closer together by a vast array of forces. We live in a world where the economies of different nations are inexorably linked. Advances in communications technology have made it possible for us to know what is happening on the opposite side of the world instantaneously. Improvements in transportation have made it possible for you to travel in mere hours distances that took your grandparents weeks and months to cover.

Working in combination, these forces have given us a sense of **interconnectedness** and created a world of opportunities for public relations practitioners. Marshall McLuhan's global village (which we discussed in Chapters 11 and 14) has, in many ways, become a reality. Targeting certain audiences and effectively reaching them are, in many ways, easier than ever. But as we already have discussed in Chapter 11, these advances have also forced practitioners to face serious challenges and make some difficult choices. Thanks to the global reach of digital telecommunications, crises can now spread at the speed of light. And in a world in which the Internet makes it possible for anyone with a cause to become a self-publisher, it is becoming more difficult for organizations to identify potential threats.

Although some see globalization as an opportunity, others see it as a threat. Still others see it as both. Antiglobalization forces are concerned that the world's richest nations exploit the poorest in the name of economic development. They are concerned about the relocation of manufacturing jobs to poorer countries where laborers receive only a fraction of pay and have fewer human rights protections than their counterparts in industrialized nations. The exploitation of natural resources and the resulting damage to the environment are also a concern. In addition, technology and knowledge gaps are widening between rich and poor nations. Although it is difficult to gauge the strength of antiglobalization forces, they have made their voices heard. Massive protests in cities hosting international trade meetings have become commonplace in recent years.

The Changing Face of the United States

It is easy to think of globalization in simply economic terms. However, this increasing interconnectedness is changing society itself. This is especially true in the United States, where the nation's population is undergoing a dramatic demographic shift. According to census estimates, 64.7 percent of the U.S. population was "white alone, not Hispanic" on July 1, 2010. (The U.S. government treats Hispanic or Latino origin and race as discrete concepts.) By 2050, that figure is

The Spanish language version of the White House website is evidence of the growing political clout of the U.S. Hispanic/Latino community.

(The White House)

projected to drop to just 46.3 percent. Compare that with residents of Hispanic or Latino origin, who were estimated at 16.0 percent of the U.S. population in 2010 and are projected to increase to 30.2 percent in 2050. The percentage of "black alone, not Hispanic" residents will remain steady around 13 percent from 2010 to 2050.[12]

By the middle of the 21st century, the United States will be a much more diverse nation. "Minorities, now roughly one third of the U.S. population, are expected to become the majority in 2042, with the nation projected to be 54 percent minority in 2050," says one census report. "The working-age population is projected to become more than 50 percent minority in 2039 and 55 percent minority in 2050."[13]

In an ideal world, public relations should mirror the societies it serves. However, several studies have all come to the same conclusion: People of color are underrepresented in the profession. This issue confronts you as the head of the fictional agency in the "Real World" scenario of this chapter: You are being torn by competing values. On the one hand, you believe in the value of a multicultural workplace and know that the client and community expect it. On the other hand, you question the fairness to the four individuals who followed the rules you established and emerged as finalists. And not to be forgotten is the competing value of getting the job done.

This is a very real-life scenario; it has no easy answers. The choices are difficult:

- You could turn down the contract and avoid the hassles. But this could have a devastating effect on employee morale and could damage your agency's ability to compete for major contracts in the future.
- You could hire the four white males and defend the decision on the basis of sticking by the rules you established at the outset. However, you would do so at the risk of alienating the community and, possibly, losing the contract.
- You could reopen the search from scratch and expand the geographical area in which you advertise the positions. This might bring in more qualified candidates who are women or persons of color. But it might not, and you would run the risk of losing the candidates you have already identified.
- You could hire one or two of the finalists and expand the search for the remaining positions. This might ease the immediate situation; but, for reasons already mentioned, there is no guarantee that this course will lead to a long-term solution.

There is no one correct answer. It all comes down to which value you hold highest. The first option seems the least viable: You wouldn't have sought the contract if you didn't value entrepreneurship and the business it would bring to your agency. The second option indicates that the integrity of the process you established is your highest value. The third option places multiculturalism at the top of your list of values. Many would choose the fourth option because it has the appeal of addressing all three values: entrepreneurship, fairness, and multiculturalism. Of course, it is a compromise without any permanent guarantees. But it still has the advantage of leaving your options open.

The Growth in World Population

If you think dramatic social change is limited to the United States, consider this: By the time you finish reading this sentence, 21 babies will have been born into our global society. According to the U.S. Census Bureau, that's the rate of 4.2 births per second.[14] By most estimates, the world's population passed the 6 billion mark sometime during 1999. Experts predict it will pass 7 billion in 2012, 8 billion in 2026, and 9 billion in 2042.[15] It doesn't take a math major to understand that the world's population is growing at an astounding rate.

According to the Census Bureau, the U.S. population passed the 300 million mark in 2006. By the year 2050, that number is expected to climb to 439 million, a 42 percent increase. In comparison, the world population, estimated at 6.8 billion in 2010, is projected to reach 9.2 billion in 2050, a 35 percent increase.[16]

There is another way to look at this. See Table 16.1 for a list of the 10 most populated nations on Earth in 2010. Now compare those rankings with the projections for the year 2050 in Table 16.2 (p. 503). You may be thinking to yourself, "That's interesting. But what does it have to do with me?" In a word: Plenty.

With the world's population growing rapidly—especially in nations outside the industrialized West—the competition for Earth's limited resources is becoming more vigorous. In the best of all possible scenarios, this means increased economic trade and international cooperation—activities the practice of public relations can

TABLE 16.1

THE TEN MOST POPULATED NATIONS ON EARTH IN THE YEAR 2010

Rank	Country	Population
1	China	1,330,141,295
2	India	1,173,108,018
3	United States	310,232,863
4	Indonesia	242,968,342
5	Brazil	201,103,330
6	Pakistan	177,276,594
7	Bangladesh	158,065,841
8	Nigeria	152,217,341
9	Russia	139,390,205
10	Japan	127,804,433

Source: U.S. Census Bureau

TABLE 16.2

THE TEN MOST POPULATED NATIONS ON EARTH IN THE YEAR 2050

Rank	Country	Population
1	India	1,656,553,632
2	China	1,303,723,332
3	United States	439,010,253
4	Indonesia	313,020,847
5	Ethiopia	278,283,137
6	Pakistan	276,428,758
7	Nigeria	264,262,405
8	Brazil	260,692,493
9	Bangladesh	233,587,279
10	Congo (Kinshasa)	189,310,849

Source: U.S. Census Bureau

help foster. However, in the worst of all possible scenarios, the intense competition for Earth's dwindling resources could lead to wars, terrorism, and other forms of social unrest. The constructive application of public relations in its role as a catalyst for consensus is critical in helping human populations avoid these dire outcomes.

The growth in world population also foreshadows future environmental problems. The air we breathe, the water we drink, and the land on which we depend for our food are all threatened by an encroaching human population. One of the most immediate concerns is the loss of tropical rain forests, which are being clear-cut and burned to make way for people, animals, and crops. By destroying these rain forests, humanity is losing an irreplaceable source of numerous species of health-giving herbs and flowers, not to mention oxygen. Many of the people who clear-cut and burn the rain forests are not evil. They are just poor and looking for a way to improve their lives. Many companies, such as McDonald's, have developed partnerships that promote alternatives to the destruction of the environment. These and other public relations activities can serve as models for future environmental cooperation.

In addition to these global trends, major changes are taking place within the United States that will have a dramatic impact on future public relations practitioners in this country: the aging of the U.S. population. The **baby boom generation,** born between 1945 and 1964, will place a tremendous strain on the generations that have followed. Baby boomers began reaching retirement age in 2010. "In

2030, when all baby boomers will be 65 and older, nearly one in five U.S. residents is expected to be 65 and older," the Census Bureau reports. The report adds that the number of persons 85 and over will triple between 2010 and 2050 to 19 million.[17] From a political and social standpoint, this means that issues important to older citizens—such as Social Security, health care, and the stability of personal investments—will take on increasing importance.

However, the graying of America will have an even deeper impact on today's college students. The percentage of **breadwinners,** people between the ages of 18 and 65 who typically make up the nation's labor pool, is declining. The U.S. Census Bureau estimates that breadwinners constituted 60 percent of the U.S. population in 2010. By 2030, that estimate dips to 57 percent.[18] In other words, a smaller percentage of breadwinners will carry most of the tax burden for the rest of the nation. That trend, in turn, has a variety of implications for the future, including the likelihood that cost-effective public relations will become increasingly important.

 QUICK CHECK

1. Why is an increasing marketing focus being placed on the Hispanic community in the United States?
2. What are the implications of the higher population growth rate in non-Western nations?
3. What effect will the aging of the baby boom generation have on society?

Feminization of the Workplace

"The past several decades have been marked by notable changes in women's labor force activities," reported *Women in the Labor Force: A Databook*, a U.S. Labor Department publication updated in 2010. Nearly 60 percent of women 16 years of age and older were in the labor force in 2008, compared with 43 percent in 1970. "In 2008, women accounted for 51 percent of all persons employed in management, professional, and related occupations, somewhat more than their share of total employment (47 percent)." The report also notes that women's earnings relative to men's rose from just 62 percent in 1979 to 80 percent in 2008. The report links increasing salaries to the growing number of women attaining college degrees: 36 percent in 2008 compared with just 11 percent in 1970.[19]

It is easy for today's students to take for granted something that was relatively new just a generation earlier: the presence of women in the workplace. This movement—what some have called the **feminization** of the workplace—has dramatically changed our social and political landscapes. Women constitute more than 51 percent of the nation's population. They are an increasingly powerful political force. Despite these positive trends, there is still need for improvement

QUICKBREAK 16.2

The Hispanic and Latino Factor

There's a quiet revolution under way in the United States, one that moves to a decidedly Latin beat.

"The immense buying power of the nation's Hispanic consumers continues to energize the nation's consumer market," reports the Selig Center for Economic Growth. Its study on minority buying power estimated that the economic clout of the Hispanic–Latino community will reach $1.3 trillion in 2014, a nearly 300 percent increase since 2000. That is more than six times the increase in the buying power of all consumers during the same period. The report credited rising levels of population growth, entrepreneurial activity, and educational attainment for this community's upward mobility.[20]

The growing influence of the Hispanic and Latino community has caught the attention of the public relations industry. Practitioners are adjusting their approach to a rapidly diversifying marketplace. "It's not do-goodism," said Ofield Dukes, chairman of the Public Relations Society of America's National Diversity Initiative. "It's a matter of economics."[21]

Diversity is often easier said than done. Something as simple as assigning an adjective to describe this community is fraught with peril. Whereas many use *Hispanic* and *Latino* as if they are interchangeable, they are not. *Latino* refers to the Spanish- and Portuguese-speaking people of the western hemisphere. *Hispanic* is associated with Spain and the Iberian Peninsula.[22] The distinction is important to many.

"People from Latin America have immigrated to the U.S. because of hardships, dictatorships, drugs, poverty and the search for the American dream," said Venus Gines, founder of a Latino health awareness group. "Immigrants from Spain, a European, industrialized nation, usually don't come to this country hungry."[23]

Targeting this public is very complicated. It includes people from many countries and cultures. Mexican Americans constitute nearly three-quarters of the Hispanic and Latino population in the United States. Another 11 percent are of Puerto Rican heritage. Seven percent come from Central and South America. Five percent have ties to Cuba.[24]

There is also the language barrier. Not every word easily translates from English into Spanish. For example, Bayer Corporation executives trying to promote an antacid product were surprised to learn that Spanish has no word for heartburn. "We had to define what heartburn was," said one Bayer official.[25]

Then there is the challenge of adapting to cultural nuances. "When you're scheduled to be at a 2:30 meeting, it's OK to show up at 2:55," said account planner Sharon Brunot-Speziale, an Anglo American working at a Chicago Hispanic–Latino advertising agency. "I don't have that sense of urgency and Type A behavior that I've had in other positions."[26]

Many experts agree that success in communicating with a diverse audience starts with a diverse workforce. "Having a team of people with diverse backgrounds and perspectives is a business mandatory," said Kathy Bremer of Porter Novelli. "Effective communication begins with understanding the client's business and target audiences."[27] ■

QUICKBREAK 16.3

An Inconvenient Truth

When an organization attempts to focus public attention on its concern for the environment, this is called **green public relations.** However, skeptical environmental activists call it by another name, **greenwashing.** How an organization's actions are perceived often hinges on its credibility and motivations. These tactics can reflect an organization's values or an attempt to fend off public criticism and government regulation. Many times, they are a mixture of both.

Much environmental debate focuses on the issue of global warming. According to a 2010 Gallup Poll, 53 percent of Americans "agree that global warming is real [and] the effects of the problem have already begun."[28] However, it wasn't always this way. A survey conducted in 1981 indicated that only 14 percent of respondents had heard or read "a great deal" or "a fair amount" about the "greenhouse effect," a build-up of carbon dioxide in the atmosphere.[29]

The public relations battle over global warming is reminiscent of the profession's association with the controversy surrounding tobacco. During the early stages of the global warming debate, well-funded corporate practitioners—representing those who feared the economic impact of stiffer environmental regulations—appeared to have the upper hand. Much like the tobacco companies in the early days of public relations, corporations came together to form front organizations to refute the scientific research as nothing more than an unproven theory.

One of those organizations was the Information Council for the Environment, created in 1991. ICE was run by a Washington-based public relations agency and funded by several energy-related corporations, including the National Coal Association, the Western Fuels Association, and the Edison Electrical Institute. It launched a $500,000 campaign targeting "older, less-educated males from larger households who are not typically active information-seekers" and "younger, lower-income women."[30]

In later years, global warming skeptics and their practitioner allies helped block U.S. ratification of the Kyoto Protocol to the United Nations Framework Convention on Climate Change, an international treaty assigning mandatory limits for greenhouse gas emissions. Under intense political pressure, both the Clinton and Bush administrations declined to send the Kyoto Protocol to the Senate.

As reputable scientific evidence mounted and global warming activists became better organized, public opinion on global warming began to shift. (You can read about the evolution of public opinion in Chapter 5.) This, too, parallels the tobacco debate. *An Inconvenient Truth,* a documentary about global warming produced by former Vice President Al Gore, received widespread acclaim and won two Academy Awards. Gore also received the 2007 Nobel Peace Prize. A year earlier, the Ad Council released two television spots urging citizen action to reduce greenhouse gases. "In one, a man stands in the path of a speeding train, symbolizing the threat of global warming," reported *Newsweek.* "When he realizes the danger is decades away, he steps safely off the tracks—revealing a young girl standing behind him."

As *Newsweek* noted, "What's significant is that the issue now has the high-minded imprimatur of the Ad Council, which gave the world Smokey Bear."[31] ∎

In a visible display of the increasing power of women in government, Speaker of the House Nancy Pelosi, First Lady Michelle Obama, and Secretary of State Hillary Rodham Clinton joined the unveiling of the bust of abolitionist Sojourner Truth in the Capitol Visitors Center in April 2009.

(Courtesy of the Architect of the Capitol)

in significant areas such as workplace sexual harassment and **salary equity,** equal pay for equal work.

A 2007 report released by the American Association of University Women Educational Foundation showed that just one year out of college, women working full time earn 20 percent less than their male colleagues doing the same jobs. "These employees don't have a lot of experience and, for the most part, don't have care-giving obligations, so you'd expect there to be very little difference in the wages of men and women," said AAUW Director of Research Catherine Hill. "Unfortunately, we find that women already earn less—even when they have the same major and occupation as their male counterparts." The AAUW report, *Behind the Pay Gap*, also said that 10 years after graduation, women graduates get only 69 percent of the salary paid to their male counterparts.[32]

Findings in a 1986 study commissioned by the International Association of Business Communicators suggested that the field was becoming a **velvet ghetto**—an employment area in which women hold the numerous lower-paying technical positions and men predominate in the few high-paying managerial positions.[33] As one researcher noted:

> This "feminization" of the field has been heralded by some. Women, they argue, are uniquely suited for public relations because of their natural orientation toward "relationships" and their facility with verbal tasks. More often, though, women's entrance into public relations has been viewed with concern. People worry that so many women in the field will lower salaries and frustrate public relations' efforts to be taken seriously as a management function. These fears are bolstered by extensive research that shows women lag behind their male peers in salary and advancement. And this gender gap cannot be explained by age, level of education, or years of experience.[34]

Nearly two decades later, the IABC Research Foundation revisited its velvet ghetto study. Although some of the fears raised in the earlier report did not come to pass, researchers said there were still economic and social barriers for women in public relations to overcome:

- Although women continued to dominate the public relations industry, evidence suggested that the feminization of the field may have peaked in the 1990s and that the percentage of male practitioners was beginning to build slowly by approximately one half a percent per year.
- The velvet ghetto predicted that the feminization of public relations could lead to salary declines. That did not happen. But, as we have already shown, women continue to make less than their male counterparts.
- Access to senior management by women practitioners appears to have declined over the past two decades. In the velvet ghetto report, half of the respondents said they reported directly to the CEO. However, *IABC Profile 2002* placed that figure at only 35 percent.[35]

For those who think babies are the reason women's salaries lag behind those of men—think again. According to a 2007 study published in *Public Relations Journal*, there is statistically little difference in the salary growth rate between women who do and do not have their careers interrupted by childbirth. "In the messy world of survey research, no satisfactory rival theory has been posited to explain the differences between men and women practitioners," wrote the study's co-authors. "Gender discrimination remains the most compelling explanation."[36]

So how are women practitioners faring in terms of salary equity with their male counterparts at the start of the second decade of the 21st century? Sadly, they are not doing that much better than they were three decades ago. A 1979 survey of PRSA members found that, on average, women practitioners made only 58 percent of what men made. By 1991, that figure stood at 74 percent, what was then seen as a hopeful sign that the gap was narrowing. However, since that 1991 study, different studies using similar methodologies have shown that the gap has not significantly narrowed.[37] The most recent salary survey, conducted in 2010 by *PRWeek*

VALUES STATEMENT 16.1

League of Women Voters of the United States

The League of Women Voters encourages informed and active participation of citizens in government and influences public policy through education and advocacy.

The goal of the League of Women Voters of the United States is to empower citizens to shape better communities worldwide. We are a nonpartisan political organization.

We:

- act after study and member agreement to achieve solutions in the public interest on key community issues at all government levels.
- build citizen participation in the democratic process.
- engage communities in promoting positive solutions to public policy issues through education and advocacy.

We believe in:

- respect for individuals.
- the value of diversity.
- the empowerment of the grassroots, both within the League and its communities.
- the power of collective decision making for the common good.

We will:

- act with trust, integrity and professionalism.
- operate in an open and effective manner to meet the needs of those we serve, both members and the public.
- take the initiative in seeking diversity in membership.
- acknowledge our heritage as we seek our path to the future.

—"Vision, Beliefs and Intentions," LWV website ■

and Bloom, Gross, and Associates, said that women with five or more years of public relations experience made only 69 percent of the salaries of male practitioners with comparable experience. Among practitioners with less than five years experience, women made only 86 percent of their counterparts' salaries.[38]

Although many agree that gender discrimination exists, finding a solution has been elusive. Some argue that women should seek out more professional expertise—that improving their strategic and professional skills will allow them to compete at the same level as men. Others argue that women should push for **empowerment**—not only ensuring that they have the tools for success, but also demanding to be included in decision making.[39] Although sincere people may argue about which is the best path to take, none disagrees on the common goal: equity.

QUICKBREAK 16.4

Sexual Harassment

According to the U.S. Equal Employment Opportunity Commission (EEOC), sexual harassment is a form of sex discrimination that violates Title VII of the Civil Rights Act of 1964. The EEOC defines workplace **sexual harassment** as "unwelcome sexual advances, requests for sexual favors, and other verbal or physical conduct of a sexual nature . . . when submission to or rejection of this conduct explicitly or implicitly affects an individual's employment, unreasonably interferes with an individual's work performance or creates an intimidating, hostile or offensive work environment."[40]

According to the EEOC, 12,696 sexual harassment cases were filed with federal, state, and local agencies during fiscal year 2009. The good news: That's an almost 25 percent decline over the past decade. The agencies found "no reasonable cause" in 47.7 percent of the cases. Another 23.1 percent involved settlements or withdrawals with benefits. Nevertheless, sexual harassment is expensive. Victims were awarded $51.5 million in benefits in FY 2009—and that doesn't include any monetary awards obtained through litigation.[41]

Although there are legal remedies for dealing with blatant sexual harassment, many victims are reluctant to report it because of a fear of damaging their careers. Then there is a more covert form of harassment, dubbed by some as **lookism,** which is defined as a tendency to focus more on a woman's appearance than on her job performance. In one focus group, a female practitioner complained that she had to fight the perception of some of her older male colleagues that a woman traveling by herself or out alone after dark is "available."[42]

Sexual harassment in the workplace threatens more than just employees. Companies that do not take steps to enforce sexual harassment policies face increasing risk of stiff financial penalties. In an effort to force companies to take this problem more seriously, Congress amended the Civil Rights Act in 1991. The amendment made it possible for successful plaintiffs to collect not only lost wages but also up to $300,000 in punitive damages against offending companies.[43] The U.S. Supreme Court has also weighed in on this issue. The court said an employer is responsible for sexual harassment committed by a supervisor even if the employer was unaware of the supervisor's behavior. The court also ruled that workers can still file sexual harassment charges against supervisors even in the absence of adverse job consequences.[44]

It should be noted that sexual harassment is not just about men acting inappropriately toward women. According to the EEOC, men filed 16 percent of sexual harassment claims in FY 2009. The U.S. Supreme Court has also recognized that illegal harassment can occur between people of the same sex.[45]

Public relations practitioners will play a critical role in eliminating this offensive behavior from the work environment—both inside and outside their profession. As the EEOC has noted, employers "should clearly communicate that sexual harassment will not be tolerated."[46] That's one of the jobs of public relations.

The only way to rid the workplace of sexual harassment is to create a company culture that makes it taboo, said Naomi Earp, former chair of EEOC. She believes that antiharassment-policy education should be a part of every employee's regular training.[47]

"Management should talk about [the antiharassment policy] the way they talk about productivity and attendance," says Michael Fetzer of the EEOC's Cleveland office. "Otherwise, people won't think it's really that important to the company leadership."[48] ■

 ## QUICK CHECK

1. What is the meaning of the phrase *velvet ghetto*?
2. What are the differing views on how to level the playing field for men and women in public relations?
3. What is workplace sexual harassment?

Where Public Relations Is Headed

As modern public relations moves into its second century, the signs are generally positive. As it did during its first century, the profession of public relations has to adapt to a changing social environment. However, not everything will change. There will be a continuing need for the profession to address some of the same old questions, including those relating to its ethical standards and its social value. Let's survey briefly some of the key trends for the future of public relations.

GROWTH   According to the Bureau of Labor Statistics, "Keen competition will likely continue for entry-level public relations jobs, as the number of qualified applicants is expected to exceed the number of job openings." However, before you start rethinking your career choice, you should know that the bureau reports in its *Occupational Outlook Handbook, 2010–11* that "opportunities should be best for college graduates who combine a degree in journalism, public relations, advertising, or another communications-related field with a public relations internship or other related work experience. Additional job opportunities should result from the need to replace public relations specialists who retire or leave the occupation for other reasons."[49] Increasingly, this growth is being reflected in boardrooms, because more and more organizations recognize the profession's role in enhancing and maintaining relationships with key stakeholders.

THE STRUGGLE FOR CREDIBILITY   After 100 years, the modern profession still isn't sure what it wants to call itself. Because people who do not understand the profession have used *public relations* as a pejorative term since the time of Edward Bernays, many organizations have shied away from that phrase. Others have said the term is too broad or too narrow, depending on the context. By one accounting, "corporate communications" and "communications departments" outnumbered "public relations departments" at *Fortune* 500 companies by a 2–1 margin.[50] Concerns about the profession's credibility may be at the heart of this issue. The Public Relations Society of America Foundation created the National Credibility Index to track the way U.S. citizens perceive information sources. The good news: Many public relations tactics received a high index rating. The bad news: Public relations practitioners were rated near the bottom—below student activists, candidates for public office, and famous athletes.[51] Despite this apparent ambivalence, signs indicate that the profession is earning respect in surprising places. When Al and Laura Ries wrote *The Fall of Advertising and the Rise of PR* in 2002, they challenged the conventional wisdom that public relations plays second fiddle to advertising when it comes to launching or repositioning brands. They cite the Internet as proof of the power of public relations. "Amazon, eBay, Yahoo!, Priceline and even AOL benefited from enormous amounts of publicity," Al Ries said. "Sure, they may have done some advertising, but it was PR that built those brands."[52]

GREATER INTEGRATION Public relations activities are being more closely aligned with those of marketing and advertising. As we discussed in Chapter 13, the concept of integrated marketing communications (IMC) is the current rage. But as we also discussed, differences of opinion exist regarding just where public relations fits in the mix. Some see public relations as an element under a broad marketing umbrella. Others (your authors among them) see public relations practitioners as using a separate management discipline whose values often coincide with those of marketers. Regardless of one's point of view, one fact is undeniable: Today's clients are demanding more than just the persuasive messages of advertising and marketing. They also want the credibility that comes through third-party endorsement. For that, they need public relations. This is especially true when it comes to cause-related marketing, something for which public relations is well suited. According to New Jersey public relations executive John Rosica, "Cause-related marketing can increase brand equity, create a more positive image for corporations and establish a preferred brand name with customers and potential customers."[53]

GREATER ACCOUNTABILITY In the wake of the near meltdown of the world economy in 2008, it almost goes without saying: Public relations professionals and the organizations they represent are under greater scrutiny than ever before. Practitioners have always faced pressure to show tangible results as well as how they enhance revenue. Katie Paine of KDPaine & Partners, a public relations measurement and analysis firm, said, "I don't think that there's a program proposed any more that doesn't have a measurement element."[54] However, accountability now extends beyond an organization's bottom line. As recent scandals involving Enron, AIG, and Toyota have reminded us, the public expects organizations to value public interest as well as profitability. The role of public relations practitioners is well suited for monitoring the conduct of organizations. However, as Chrysler's decision to move its public relations function within its human relations department suggests (see Chapter 1, p. 5), access to top management might be the key to fulfilling such a role effectively. Accountability in public relations also requires that practitioners enthusiastically embrace equal opportunity without regard to gender, race, religion, national origin, or sexual orientation. That aspect of accountability will require aggressive recruitment of a more inclusive workforce, one that mirrors the diversity of society.

TARGETING   As a result of social and technological changes, we are living in a world of increasingly fragmented values and desires. Public opinion and public policies are being ruled by ever-shifting and constantly self-defining coalitions of interests. At the same time, the explosion in the number of communication channels has dispersed audiences. The challenge for public relations practitioners is clear: Reaching key publics in the future will require more targeted approaches. Designing those approaches, in turn, requires a greater precision in research methodologies and planning strategies.

RAPID RESPONSE   In the race to influence public opinion, time is an enemy. President Abraham Lincoln concerned himself with stories that appeared in the daily newspaper. President Franklin Roosevelt had to respond to stories on hourly radio newscasts. Today, the president is confronted with second-by-second developments in stories on 24/7 cable news channels, blogs, and Twitter. The window of opportunity for getting across one's point of view is narrowing. By implication, this means public relations practitioners must plan even further ahead. They must do a better job of anticipating events that could shape the public view of their organization. For that reason, issues management skills will in all likelihood become increasingly important.

A NONTRADITIONAL WORKPLACE   The amazing advances of the past decade in wireless communication and computing technology have redefined the traditional workplace. The federal government estimates that on an average day between 2003 and 2007, 12.2 percent of the U.S. labor force worked at home. The number was three times higher for self-employed individuals such as consultants.[55] *PRWeek* reports that telecommuting has become a popular solution for public relations agencies looking to keep employees who have undergone a change in lifestyle such as having a baby or moving to a rural area. "You have to accommodate talent," explained New York public relations executive Kimberley White. "That often means putting up with where that talent decides it wants to live."[56] However, telecommuting is not the only change in the workplace. As already noted, the labor pool is becoming more diverse in its gender and racial composition. By the time your children graduate from college, the workplace will look and feel very different.

VISION   The demands of a rapid-paced society tend to focus on the problems of the moment and to ignore the potential challenges of the future. The charge of short-term thinking is often leveled against business and industry in the United States.

Public relations practitioners share responsibility for this state of affairs. With public relations practitioners being held more accountable for a company's bottom line, many move from one planning cycle to another without having a real sense of direction. What organizations—and practitioners—need is a sense of vision. They need to have a sense of where they want to be 5, 10, and 20 years down the road. Here is where values, research, and strategic planning pay dividends. A longer-term outlook also requires practitioners to demonstrate that they have what is commonly referred to as "backbone": the courage to stand by their vision. Backbones do have flexibility, however; visions can change.

 QUICK CHECK

1. What trends are influencing the future of public relations?
2. In what ways will public relations practitioners be held more accountable in the future?
3. What is meant by the need for "vision"?

YOUR FUTURE IN PUBLIC RELATIONS

By now it should be obvious that modern public relations is a profession that continues to evolve as it moves into its second century. That is what makes it both challenging and exciting. Every day in public relations brings with it a new adventure. Are you ready for it? The short answer is no; at this stage of your academic and professional life, you probably are not quite ready. But the good news is that if you continue doing the right things, you will be.

Your decision to earn a college degree was the first big step in the right direction. Although exceptions to the rule exist, a college diploma is usually necessary if you are going to make the first cut in the employment process. As to what kind of degree you obtain, that is probably less important than what you studied in earning the degree. Not everyone in the profession has received a degree in public relations. And although the study of public relations is traditionally centered in either journalism or communications studies programs, degrees from other departments can also lead to successful public relations careers.

So what constitutes a good educational foundation for the practice of public relations? In a November 2006 report, the Commission on Public Relations Education said, "Public relations education should be interdisciplinary and broad, particularly in the liberal arts and sciences." In *The Professional Bond: Public Relations Education for the 21st Century*, the commission said, "A minor or a double major is recommended to broaden students' education and knowledge base."[57] The report also said that a strong public relations education is intertwined with business, language, social science, and other disciplines. Although the commission's recommendations echoed those of earlier years, the 2006 report also

QUICKBREAK 16.5

You Are the Future

You are the future of public relations.

As you make the transition from college life into a career in this dynamic profession, it is OK to pause for a moment and take a deep breath. After all, you are about to embark on a wonderful journey—but to where? No one knows for sure. But some pretty smart people have put some thought into what your future will hold. And they see a world of both opportunities and challenges.

"The PR industry has the chance to become the communications tool of choice in the next decade," said Richard Edelman, president and CEO of Edelman. "The opportunity for PR stems from the absence of trust in institutions and the splintering of audiences among various forms of media."[58]

Edelman based his prediction on the fragmentation of media, which he said has led to "information overload" and the creation of "individual webs of trust and triangulation among multiple sources of information." His reasoning: If organizations can establish credibility, they could become a part of these "webs of trust." That, he said, is the opportunity and challenge facing public relations.[59]

And how can future practitioners help establish this credibility? Mark Weiner, CEO of PRIME Research, said, "Match ethics with the delivery of meaningful business outcomes, and you'll earn credibility."[60]

According to a study of future trends conducted on behalf of the IABC Research Foundation, "An opportunity exists for communication professionals to change their roles. Communication officers are in the best position to provide information for leaders that flags new trends and anticipates potential changes on the horizon." This prediction was based on interviews with more than 30 senior practitioners and survey responses from more than 1,000 IABC members.[61]

However, with this shot of optimism comes a dose of reality. "Communication professionals need to increase their ability to measure results more concretely," the study said. "Proving the economic value of the communication function is becoming increasingly important." But that's the rub: Only 17 percent of the survey participants said they use before and after assessments to gauge communication performance.[62]

Gary Grates, of Edelman public relations, wrote in *Public Relations Quarterly* that practitioners must learn to sense and respond to changes in the environment: "In a way, we must become social scientists in our jobs, able to discern what people are looking at, listening to, and believing in."[63] Practitioners need to focus on problem solving, he said. "The wise firm will, in the long run, achieve greater profitability and stronger relationships by focusing on finding the solution instead of packaging the sell."[64]

The values and lifestyles of today's college graduates will also shape the future. According to Mike Marino, former head of human resources for Burson-Marsteller/New York, new practitioners are already beginning to question the traditional workweek and workplace. "In order to be able to effectively attract and retain this segment of the population," he said, "employers—including agencies—will need to adopt more flexible work arrangements."[65]

See, you are already molding the future of public relations. ∎

stressed the need for educators to focus on developing positive personal traits in tomorrow's practitioners:

> It continues to be crucial that graduates be responsible, flexible and professionally oriented self-managers. For communication to occur with and among diverse audiences, individuals must be able to respond and adapt to new and changing situations and to feel comfortable in having to make such adjustments without giving up personal identity. Students must have intellectual curiosity and be able to think conceptually. They must have positive attitudes and be able to take criticism. They must be organized self-starters who take initiative to solve problems. They must be both creative and pragmatic, and they must have integrity as team participants and leaders. Students should be able to demonstrate respect and empathy; even if practitioners do not belong to a group or agree with it, a practitioner must be able to show appreciation for those who are different and able to understand others' cultures and perspectives.[66]

The report also identified 22 essential skills that create a foundation for a successful public relations career. They included research methods and analysis, mastery of language in written and oral communication, problem solving, informative and persuasive writing, fluency in a foreign language, technological and visual literacy, and ethical decision making.[67]

Internships—supervised workplace experiences—also figure prominently in public relations career preparation, especially in light of corporate downsizing and the growth of virtual public relations. More than ever, internships give students the opportunity to get hands-on experience in a wide range of public relations activities. Think of internships as an extension of a college education—with one major difference: The "classroom" is the real world. If you are not certain what kind of public relations you want to practice—agency, government, nonprofit, or corporate—having several different internships during college can give you a taste of the different aspects of the field.

Internship experience can be crucial in getting that first job. "Internships are becoming vital to obtaining employment," reports the Bureau of Labor Statistics. "Employers seek applicants with demonstrated communication skills and training or experience in a field related to the firm's business—information technology, health, science, engineering, sales, or finance, for example."[68]

Membership in student public relations organizations also provides a good foundation for a public relations career. Some schools have **Public Relations Student Society of America (PRSSA)** chapters, which are affiliated with PRSA. IABC also sponsors student organizations. Other student groups operate independently. Whatever route one chooses, these student organizations can provide valuable job/internship information, networking opportunities, and professional experience that can be listed on a résumé. Some professional organizations give students who were active in their school's public relations organization a membership discount upon graduation. These student groups also offer opportunities for getting together with people who share common career interests. However, as with other student organizations, what you get out of any such group largely depends on what you put into it.

The Future of Values-Driven Public Relations

Some view the future with hope. Others fear the future. Either way, like it or not, the future is coming.

What kind of future lies ahead? At best, we can only make educated guesses. In QuickBreak 16.5, we choose to leave the prognostications to others. Perhaps our time is better spent on the present and on the things we can do today to prepare ourselves for tomorrow.

Each of us perceives the future in different ways. That's because we are unique individuals who view the world through different prisms. For that reason, the best preparation for the future is getting to know the one individual who will exert the most influence over the future as you will know it. In other words, the person you most need to get in touch with is yourself.

At the risk of being too philosophical, what is life but a series of choices? Some choices, such as what to have for lunch or what color socks to wear, are not particularly challenging. Other times, we are confronted with choices that can quite literally mean the difference between life and death. The funny thing about choices,

SOCIAL MEDIA APPS

The Changing Face of Facebook

The face of Facebook is changing.

The social networking service released a snapshot of its approximately 100 million members in December 2009. In a blog posting, Facebook said that 11 percent of its membership was black, with 9 percent Latino. That compares with only 7 percent black and 3 percent Latino in 2005, approximately one year after Facebook first surfaced.

"What we've seen over time is that Facebook has grown in the U.S. population; we've come to represent a cross-section, said Facebook's Cameron Marlow. "Diversity on the site is a good thing for the site and the users of the site."[69]

The Facebook study reflects a larger trend—the increasing diversity of Internet users, especially when it comes to Latinos. According to the Pew Internet & American Life Project, Web use among Latinos grew 10 percent, from 54 to 64 percent, between 2006 and 2008. In comparison, Internet usage grew only 4 percent among whites and 2 percent among blacks during the same period.

"The rapid increase in cell-only populations, particularly for Latinos and African Americans, coupled with the fact people in cell-only households tend to be slightly more likely to use other forms of technology than people who are reachable via landline telephone, suggests, if anything, the results here may underestimate increases in Internet use, especially for Latinos and African-Americans," said Susannah Fox, author of the Pew study.[70]

"You bring what you do in your daily life online, and social media is enabling that," said Manny Miravete, vice president of social media and strategy for MySpace and MySpace Latino. "It's the fabric of Hispanics online."[71] ■

however, is you can't always know the ultimate outcome of what might seem at the time to be the most trivial of decisions. Those are the decisions that steer us to unexpected paths in our lives. The best we can hope for is developing the habit of making good decisions.

That is why values are important. Values are the road map by which we, both as professionals and as individuals, chart a course into the future. Having values alone is not a guarantee of taking a smooth road. In fact, sticking to values can lead to a more treacherous road than traveling down the path of least resistance. But at least when we stick to our values we *know* we may be headed down a bumpy road. Often, the path of least resistance does not turn out to be as smooth as it looks.

After a century of modern public relations, it is somewhat disheartening to know that practitioners are still compelled to demonstrate their worth to employers, clients, coworkers—and even to themselves. In the words of a Public Relations Society of America report on the stature of the profession,

> Public relations has evolved from a fringe function to a basic element of society in a comparatively short period of time, despite a number of handicaps. One of the greatest of these is the field's failure to act according to its own precepts. It has allowed prejudices against it to persist, misconceptions to entrench themselves and weaknesses within the field to be perceived as endemic. Public relations, like most elements of society, is now confronted with critical questioning. Its practitioners are questioning its stature and role as pointedly as outsiders. Like other elements of society, it must respond to its challengers or lose even its present stature and role. That role must be clarified; its goals must be set; its practitioners must earn optimal stature; means to achieve the goals must be established.[72]

In its own way, this report, prepared by PRSA's College of Fellows, is a plea for the very same concept advocated throughout this book: *values-driven public relations*. It is a recognition—and a warning—that until practitioners fully embrace the relationship-building values on which this profession was supposedly built, our period of self-doubt will continue.

Granted, that's a heavy load to place on the shoulders of someone still in college. However, real change can occur if we remember that 21st-century public relations will be built one person at a time.

As you ponder the many choices that await you, here are some guidelines to help you steer down the uncertain paths of the future:

- *Be true to your values.* If you can't be true to yourself, then to whom can you be true? If something doesn't pass the "Can you look at yourself in the mirror?" test, don't do it.
- *Pay your dues.* No one is going to hand you the keys to the executive washroom—at least not yet. Hard work and personal commitment are your investments in the future. Your time will come.

- *Make your own luck.* A wise person once said that luck is where opportunity meets preparation. Circumstances may place you in the right place at the right time, but it will be your talent and professionalism that will keep you there.
- *Learn from your mistakes.* Mistakes are often more instructive than successes. If you are willing to look objectively at a situation and, when necessary, shoulder the blame, it is unlikely that you will make the same mistake again.
- *Celebrate victories.* Just as it is important to learn from mistakes, it is important to accept credit when credit is due. You want to encourage success, not ignore it. Life is too short not to enjoy the good times. Don't take them for granted.
- *Keep learning.* Your education is just beginning. The world is rapidly changing, and you need to keep up with it. Don't pass up opportunities to learn something new; you never know when this knowledge will come in handy. Knowledge is power.
- *Command new technology—and don't let it command you.* Technological advances offer new and exciting ways to reach out to targeted publics. However, having the ability to use a new technology doesn't mean we should. Values, audience, and purpose should govern our decisions on which channels we choose.
- *Pass it on!* It is very likely that you will owe some aspect of your career advancement to mentoring from a more experienced practitioner who took you under his or her wing. The best way you can honor that special person is to become a mentor yourself and show someone else the ropes.
- *Maintain perspective.* Former University of North Carolina basketball coach Dean Smith retired, at the time, with the most victories in the history of major college basketball. But he lost quite a few games as well. That's why he once told a reporter that he didn't treat every game as if it were a life-or-death situation. "If you do," Smith said, "you will be dead a lot."
- *Exercise your rights as a citizen—especially your First Amendment rights.* Freedom can't be taken for granted. It must always be defended and used responsibly. That's why it is important that you vote and speak out on important issues. That is also why you should resist anyone who tries to curb someone else's freedoms. How do you know that your freedoms won't be next on someone's hit list?

One practitioner at a time. That is how values-driven public relations will be established during the modern profession's second century.

SUMMARY

As modern public relations moves into the second decade of its second century, it has the potential to do both good and harm in society. Its good rests in the profession's ability to bring people together to reach consensus. However, some applications of public relations have been used to block consensus.

Major social forces are shaping the future. Among them are the global spread of democracy, the economic and cultural effects of globalization, the growth in world population, and the increasing feminization of the workplace. The growing presence of women has had and will continue to have a dramatic effect on the field of public relations. Although women in public relations continue to face the same challenges as women everywhere, there appears to be a consensus for addressing salary equity and sexual harassment issues in the industry.

The growth of public relations is expected to continue in the foreseeable future. Public relations will continue to work closely with other marketing disciplines—all of which will be held more accountable. Many of the old problems of the past, such as the search for respect, credibility, and ethics, will continue. Although the workplace in which public relations is practiced may change, the profession's need to adhere to enduring values remains constant.

DISCUSSION QUESTIONS

1. What social, political, or demographic trend will have the most significant impact on the practice of public relations in the 21st century? Please explain your reasoning.
2. How will world and national population trends affect public relations?
3. What steps do you think are necessary to make the profession of public relations more inclusive and representative of the population as a whole?
4. What steps are you taking to prepare for a career in public relations?
5. In a constantly changing world, what role will values play in the future of public relations?

MEMO FROM THE FIELD

REBECCA TIMMS
National President; PRSSA 2009–2010

Rebecca Timms served as 2009–2010 national president of the Public Relations Student Society of America while a senior at Rowan University in Glassboro, N.J. Before her election as PRSSA president, she served as PRSSA vice president of member services. Her Rowan University PRSSA chapter won the 2008 Teahan Chapter Award as the nation's outstanding PRSSA chapter. Before graduation, Timms completed four internships, including a position in the public affairs department of Campbell Soup Company. Her official PRSSA biography notes that "[i]n her free time, Timms relaxes with family and friends, travels, reads, listens to new music, seeks exotic foods and restaurants, cheers for her favorite ice hockey teams, explores Philadelphia, and continues her search for the perfect cup of cappuccino."

While progressing through your college years, looking to the wisdom and guidance of those who have come before you is a smart move. Your choice to pick up this textbook is one I hope will be particularly useful in your career.

In an age of social media explosion, graduates are expected to understand and use new communication channels to the benefit of companies and clients. Our industry is blazing its way through the social media space, and thousands of students, particularly those in public relations, have taken hold of it for personal and professional benefit.

As you move forward in college and into the workforce, take these lessons learned most recently through social media and apply them in your everyday public relations career.

1. **Be honest about yourself.** Although online media allow you to create an Internet-based extension of yourself, some mistrust of that portrayal must exist. Individuals have to be a bit biased about themselves, likely skewing their personality and abilities in a positive way. Use facts and other people to back yourself up. Be honest in your personal assessment.

   Also, be willing to combine personal and professional information on your sites. If these pages are going to be extensions of you, make them just as well-rounded and integrated as you are. Be sure to let that same mix play out in professional conversation as well. Your life experiences, few as they may seem, bring value to the table and a realness to your interaction with others.

2. **Be genuine in making connections.** Racking up friends and followers on social networking sites might seem beneficial, but know you are dealing with real people. Their impressions of your intentions, regardless of accuracy, can carry great weight in professional circles.

   That being said, take advantage of the ease social media allow in terms of networking. Research and contact professionals in your chosen field via social media and start a meaningful conversation. You never know where such connections can lead outside of the virtual world.

   As you meet professionals in real life, know that having a stack of others' business cards does not indicate your true network. Those with whom you intern, volunteer, or see at industry events are the people who will recommend you for other positions and propel you forward in your career.

3. **Speak from the heart.** Social media are about more than just networking; they allow users to express themselves on topics about which they care. No matter the subject, online or off, take time to talk about it. Professionals and personal friends alike can learn from what you have to say and gain insight on your thinking processes as they read more from you.

Just as speaking from the heart is important, so is following it. I firmly believe that this is key to success in public relations. Our profession consistently ranks high on lists of stressful jobs, and what alleviates that anxiety is a love for what you do. That's a feeling money and stock options cannot replace. ■

CASE STUDY 16.1 Social Media "Kat Fight"

The online video opens with an unshaven and somewhat disheveled office worker engaged in a monotonous task of shredding mountains of documents. As the worker looks at the clock, the question "Have a Break?" appears on the screen. In search of respite from his menial task, he unwraps a Nestlé Kit Kat candy bar.

Until this point, the video looks like a typical television commercial for the popular snack. But here's where things get weird: That's not chocolate the worker is eating—it is an orangutan's finger. The worker remains oblivious while blood drips everywhere. The screen turns red, and a message appears: "Give the orangutan a break. Stop Nestlé from buying palm oil from companies that destroy the rainforests." Only then do viewers learn that the source of the video is not the Swiss chocolatier but the environmental watchdog Greenpeace.[73]

At issue are the rainforests of Indonesia, home to vast expanses of palm trees and orangutan habitat. Palm oil is an important ingredient in many of the food products we use every day, including chocolate, margarine, and bread. It is also used in the production of cosmetics and biodiesel. Greenpeace accused Indonesia's largest palm oil producer, Sinar Mas, of logging, burning, or otherwise degrading an area twice the size of Germany. Although Nestlé said it didn't buy palm oil directly from Sinar Mas, it acknowledged that, through a vendor, its palm oil supplier might have.[74]

The issue has festered for years. One might say that Nestlé and Greenpeace haven't seen eye to eye on a number of issues. In fact, Nestlé is hardly a stranger to international controversy. The company has stood fast despite a 30-year boycott over its infant-care formula marketing practices in underdeveloped nations. This kind of corporate stubbornness, combined with Greenpeace's history of in-your-face tactics, was bound to create sparks.

It did, with Greenpeace's YouTube posting of its controversial Kit Kat parody on March 17, 2010. It coincided with the release of a Greenpeace report critical of Nestlé's environment practices. The cover of the report featured an altered version of the Kit Kat logo, with the brand name changed to "Killer." Greenpeace supporters began to flood Nestlé's Facebook page with highly critical wall posts. As if to drive home their point, Greenpeace protesters, dressed as orangutans, picketed outside of Nestlé's headquarters; one might call it a form of "gorilla warfare."[75]

Nestlé responded by filing a copyright infringement claim with YouTube, resulting in the video being removed from the site. A combative company employee told Facebook users that he would delete any posts featuring the altered "Killer" logo. Then, as if to pour palm oil on an open flame, the same Nestlé representative posted sarcastic comments into the increasingly hostile Facebook thread.[76]

What followed was nothing short of a twitterstorm. The online community didn't take kindly to what it saw as censorship. Greenpeace reposted the Kit Kat parody on another video-sharing website and used Twitter to spread the alarm about Nestlé's actions.[77] Before long, thousands of online protests were registered in the form of tweets. Nestlé's Facebook fan base, now comprised mostly of its critics, swelled to 95,000. As for the video, Greenpeace claimed it received 180,000 unique page views during the first 30 hours.

Within days, Nestlé severed all ties with Sinar Mas and promised to use only environmentally sustainable palm oil in its products by 2015. Greenpeace said that wasn't quick enough.

"Like all companies, we are learning about how to best use social media, particularly with such complex issues," Nestlé spokesperson Nina Backes said. "What we take out of this is that you have to engage."[78]

DISCUSSION QUESTIONS

1. What, if anything, should Nestlé have done differently to avoid the twitterstorm over its social media tactics?

2. What is your opinion of the tactics used by Greenpeace?

3. Citing examples from this case study, what are the benefits and risks of companies' using social media?

4. This case study suggests that, given the history of Nestlé and Greenpeace, a clash was inevitable. What, if anything, can be done to bring more civility to such relationships? ■

CASE STUDY 16.2 Guns and Greens

During the fall of 2004, a common complaint was heard throughout the Minnesota wetlands. "You can ask people from Baudette to Winona; Worthington to Ely," said Minneapolis *Star Tribune* columnist Dennis Anderson. "There were no ducks."[79]

A decline in the duck population in the "Land of 10,000 Lakes" brought more than 40 hunting, fishing, and environmental groups—a marriage of "guns and greens" as some called it—into an unusual coalition designed to pressure Minnesota's legislature to preserve the state's natural resources and outdoor heritage. What makes this unusual is that hunters and environmentalists are usually at cross purposes. However, with the U.S. Environmental Protection Agency rating 40 percent of the state's lakes and rivers as "impaired," the guns and the greens found a common cause. Minneapolis-based public relations agency Carmichael Lynch Spong helped them find their voice.[80]

It was Anderson, the *Star Tribune*'s outdoors columnist, who set events into motion. In a December 2004 column, he called for a rally at the state capitol to demand that legislators protect Minnesota's environment. Following the columnist's lead, the guns and greens came together to organize a "Rally for Ducks, Wetlands, and Clean Water." As a popular columnist at one of the Midwest's largest newspapers, Anderson had a ready-made pulpit from which to promote the cause. However, it wasn't long before organizers realized more expertise was needed. With only six weeks to marshal public opinion before the scheduled rally, CLS volunteered its services to the coalition on a pro bono basis.

The agency immediately embarked on primary and secondary research. This included a series of interviews with sportsmen and environmentalists who said they were frustrated by the manner in which state government funded and managed Minnesota's natural resources. Secondary research was used to identify key elected officials who wielded the greatest influence over environmental legislation—with special emphasis on locating those likely to support the coalition's cause. Perhaps most important, research helped to identify issues in which the groups—often at loggerheads with one another—could find common ground. From this research came the coalition's rallying cry and positioning statement: "One voice, many votes." Three goals also emerged: to raise public awareness of the issues facing Minnesota's ducks, wetlands, and waterways; to attract a large crowd to the rally; and to secure passage of coalition-supported legislation.

For the campaign to achieve success, CLS had to convince the guns and the greens that they, literally, had to follow their positioning statement and speak with one voice. To that end, David Zentner, a key rally organizer and prominent conservationist, was selected as the coalition's spokesman. Zentner was quoted in all news releases and offered to media outlets for interviews. Three other individuals were selected as alternate spokespersons. Zentner and the alternates received media coaching from CLS.

A variety of channels were used to attract people to the April 2, 2005, rally. Weekly news releases were distributed to more than 200 media outlets. Key elected officials received letters inviting them to the event. CLS created a special website, www.wetlandsrally.org, to inform both the news media and sympathetic citizens. The agency distributed more than 5,000 posters to outdoor retailers, bait shops, sporting clubs, and civic organizations throughout the state. Promotional efforts also included radio public service announcements and billboards donated by outdoor advertising companies. To defray costs, bumper stickers, sweatshirts, T-shirts, and baseball caps bearing the "one voice, many votes" tagline were sold on the Internet and at the rally. According to CLS, the campaign generated an estimated 14 million impressions—the number of times people were exposed to the coalition's message.[81]

On the day of the rally, approximately 5,000 people gathered at the steps of the state capitol in St. Paul. All the Twin Cities' network-affiliated television stations, as well as most of the state's major newspapers, covered the event. It even caught the attention of Sierra Club members, who named it as their favorite Earth Day story in an online poll.

The Rally for Ducks, Wetlands, and Clean Water also appeared to grab the attention of its most important target audience, Minnesota's politicians. "One of the most powerful forces in politics is a coalition with people from different viewpoints coming together," Minnesota Governor Tim Pawlenty told the gathering. "I think we are witnessing a historic birth of a powerful coalition for water, wetlands, and wildlife."[82]

Although the campaign achieved the first two goals, raising public awareness and attracting a large crowd to the rally, the outcomes for the third goal, changing public policy, were mixed. The 2006 legislature enacted a cornerstone of the coalition's legislative package, the Clean Water Legacy Act. It was designed to help restore the state's impaired lakes and rivers. However, lawmakers allocated only $15 million to enact the measure, well short of the $80 million supporters said was needed to do the job.[83] Another measure supported by the greens and the guns, a state sales tax dedicated to conservation and the arts, eventually passed both houses of legislature in May 2007. However, in what the bill's supporters must have felt was a cruel twist of fate, the clock literally struck midnight and the legislature adjourned for the year before the final version of the measure came to the floor for a vote.[84]

The guns and the greens didn't give up. The state legislature placed the renamed Clean Water, Land, and Legacy Amendment on the November 2008 ballot. The referendum passed with 56 percent of the vote. It created four new funds to allow Minnesota to invest in clean water, habitat, parks and trails, and youth arts access. Having won its big victory, the coalition held a victory party and then disbanded.

"We never intended this to be a permanent group," Zentner said.[85]

DISCUSSION QUESTIONS

1. Who are the "guns and the greens," and why is the coalition they built unusual?
2. Why do public relations agencies such as Carmichael Lynch Spong donate their services to organizations such as the Rally for Ducks, Wetlands, and Clean Water?
3. What steps were taken to ensure that the messages delivered by the guns and greens coalition were consistent?
4. What do you think are the reasons that, despite its success, the coalition disbanded? ∎

NOTES

1. Reid Goldsborough, "Unpredictions," *Public Relations Tactics*, July 2004, 25.
2. Country Comparison: GDP (Purchasing Power Parity), *World Factbook*, Central Intelligence Agency, online, http://www.cia.gov/library/publications/the-world-factbook.
3. China International Public Relations Association website, online, www.cipra.org.cn.
4. PR Landscape: China, Global Alliance for Public Relations and Communications Management, online, www.globalalliancepr.org.

5. China International Public Relations Association website.

6. David Zhou, "PR in China: 2008 Industry Overview," *Ampersand* (blog), Hill & Knowlton, 31 March 2008, online, http://blogarchive. hillandknowlton.com/blogs/ampersand/ articles/10492.aspx.

7. "Public Relations in India," Public Relations Society of India website, online, www.prsi.co .in/prindia.htm.

8. PR Landscape: India, Global Alliance for Public Relations and Communications Management, online, www.globalalliancepr.org.

9. Rachel Koontz, "Public Relations in India," Public Relations Student International Coalition, online, www.prssa.org/prsic.

10. Douglas P. Clements, "Public Relations in Japan," Public Relations Student International Coalition, online, www.prssa.org/prsic.

11. *Human Development Report 1999,* United Nations Development Program, online, www .undp.org/hdro.

12. "Table 5—Percent Distribution of the Projected Population by Net International Migration Series, Race, and Hispanic Origin for the United States, 2010 to 2050," U.S. Census Bureau, released 18, December 2009.

13. "An Older and More Diverse Nation by Midcentury," news release, U.S. Census Bureau, 14 August 2008.

14. "World Vital Events per Time Unit: 2010," U.S. Census Bureau, online, www.census.gov.

15. "Total Midyear Population for the World: 1950–2050," U.S. Census Bureau.

16. International Data Base, U.S. Census Bureau, updated 19 March 2010.

17. "An Older and More Diverse Nation by Midcentury."

18. U.S. Census Bureau

19. *Women in the Labor Force: A Databook*, U.S. Bureau of Labor Statistics, released September 2009, 1–2.

20. Jeffery M. Humphreys, "The Multicultural Economy 2009," Selig Center for Economic Growth, University of Georgia, *Georgia Business and Economic Conditions* 69, no. 3 (Third Quarter, 2009): 10.

21. Leon Stafford, "Missing Out on the Trend; Diversity Focus Can Open Doors," *Atlanta Journal-Constitution,* 27 October 2002, 1F, online, LexisNexis.

22. Yolanda Rodriguez, "Hispanic or Latino? It All Depends," *Atlanta Journal-Constitution,* 10 December 2003, 6F, online, LexisNexis.

23. Rodriguez.

24. Linda P. Morton, "Targeting Hispanic Americans," *Public Relations Quarterly* 47, no. 3 (fall 2003): 46–48.

25. Stafford.

26. Mindy Charski, "Crossing Cultures," *AdWeek*, 3 May 2004, online, LexisNexis.

27. Stafford.

28. Frank Newport, "Americans' Global Warming Concerns Continue to Drop," Gallup, 11 March 2010, online, www.gallup.com.

29. Opinion Research Corporation survey conducted March 26–31, 1981, reported by the Roper Center for Public Opinion Research.

30. Bob Burton and Sheldon Rampton, "The PR Plot to Overheat the Earth," *Earth Island Journal* 13, no. 2 (spring 1998): 29.

31. Jerry Adler, "The New Hot Zones; Books, Films, and a Slick Ad Campaign Make Global Warming the Topic du Jour," *Newsweek*, 3 April 2006, 42.

32. "Pay Gap Exists as Early as One Year out of College, Says New Research Report," news release issued by American Association of University Women, 23 April 2007, online, www.aauw.org.

33. L. L. Cline et al., *The Velvet Ghetto: The Impact of the Increasing Percentage of Women in Public Relations and Organizational Communications* (San Francisco: IABC Research Foundation, 1986).

34. Linda Hon, "Feminism and Public Relations," *The Public Relations Strategist* 1, no. 2 (summer 1995): 20.

35. Heidi P. Taff, "Times Have Changed? IABC Research Foundation's 'The Velvet Ghetto' Study Revisited," *Communication World*, February/March 2003, 10–11.

36. David Dozier, Bey-Ling Sha, and Masako Okura, "How Much Does My Baby Cost? An Analysis of Gender Differences in Income, Career Interruption, and Child Bearing," *Public Relations Journal*, 1, no. 1 (fall 2007), Public Relations Society of America, online, www.prsa.org.

37. Dozier, Sha, and Okura, 2–3.
38. *PRWeek*/Bloom, Gross and Associates 2010 Salary Survey, *PRWeek* (U.S. edition), March 2010, 30–36.
39. Linda Hon, "Toward a Feminist Theory of Public Relations," *Journal of Public Relations Research* 7, no. 1 (1995): 33–34.
40. "Facts about Sexual Harassment," U.S. Equal Employment Opportunity Commission, online, www.eeoc.gov/facts/fs-sex.html.
41. "Sexual Harassment Charges EEOC & FEPAs Combined: FY 1997–FY 2009," U.S. Equal Employment Opportunity Commission, 31 January 2007, online, www.eeco.gov/eeco/statistics/enforcement/sexual_harassment.cfm.
42. Hon.
43. Barry S. Roberts and Robert A. Mann, "Sexual Harassment in the Workplace: A Primer," *University of Akron Law Review*, online, www.uakron.edu/lawrev/robert1.html.
44. The applicable cases are *Faragher v. City of Boca Raton*, 118 S. Ct. 2275 (1998) and *Burlington Industries Inc. v. Ellerth*, 118 S. Ct. 2257 (1998).
45. The applicable case is *Oncale v. Sundowner Offshore Services, Inc.*, 118 S. Ct. 998 (1998).
46. "Facts about Sexual Harassment."
47. Candace Goforth, "Changing the Workplace Culture Can Help Stop Sexual Harassment," 5 November 2003, *Akron Beacon Journal*, online, LexisNexis.
48. Goforth.
49. *Occupational Outlook Handbook, 2010–11 Edition*, U.S. Department of Labor, Bureau of Labor Statistics, online, http://stats.bls.gov/oco/ocoso086.htm.
50. Cynthia Fritsch, researcher, "'Communications' Tops 'PR' by 2–1 Margin at Fortune 500," *O'Dwyer's PR Services Report*, February 1996, 1.
51. National Credibility Index, Public Relations Society of America, online, www.prsa.org.
52. Sean Callahan, "B to B Q&A: Proclaiming the 'Fall of Advertising'; Controversial New Book Argues That Public Relations Is the Best Way to Launch a Brand," *BtoB*, 14 October 2002, 3.
53. "Targeting, Relationship-Building Define Marketing Today," *PRNews*, 25 March 1996, online, LexisNexis.
54. "Measurement Driving More PR Programs," *PRNews*, 18 March 1996, online, LexisNexis.
55. "Work-at-home Patterns by Occupation," *Issues in Labor Statistics*, U.S. Department of Labor, Summary 09-02, March 2009.
56. Paul Cordasco, "Telecommuting Helps PR Firms Keep Their Top Talent at Home," *PRWeek—U.S. Edition*, 20 October 2003, 10.
57. *The Professional Bond: Public Relations Education for the 21st Century*, Commission on Public Relations Education, November 2006, 43.
58. Paul Holmes, "Embracing the Paradox of Change," *The Holmes Report*, 12 March 2001, online, www.holmesreport.com.
59. Holmes.
60. Mark Weiner, "The External Factors Shaping Public Relations in 2014," *Public Relations Tactics*, July 2004, 29.
61. Katherine Woodall, "What Will the Future Hold? Study Reveals Opportunities for Communicators," *Communication World*, February/March 2003, 18–21.
62. Woodall.
63. Gary F. Grates, "Through the Look Glass. Seeing the Future of Public Relations Relevance," *Public Relations Quarterly* (fall 2003): 15–19.
64. Grates.
65. Mike Marino, "Questions Abound for the PR Office of 2014," *Public Relations Tactics*, July 2004, 24.
66. *The Professional Bond*, 44.
67. *The Professional Bond*, 43–44.
68. *Occupational Outlook Handbook, 2006–07 Edition*.
69. Mike Swift, "Facebook Study Finds Network's Diversity Growing," *San Jose Mercury News*, 17 December 2009, 1A.
70. Susannah Fox, "Latinos Online, 2006–2008," Pew Internet & American Life Project, 22 December 2008, online, www.pewinternet.org.
71. Noreen O'Leary, "Why Social Media Is the 'Fabric' of Hispanics Online," *Brandweek*, 6 April 2009, online, www.brandweek.com.
72. "Excerpt from Report on Stature of PR: Factors Inhibiting Stature and Role of PR," *O'Dwyer's PR Services Report*, March 1992, 31.

73. "Ask Nestlé to Give Rainforests a Break," video, Greenpeace website, online, http://www.greenpeace.org/international/campaigns/climate-change/kitkat.

74. Paul Armstrong, "Greenpeace, Nestlé in Battle over Kit Kat Viral," CNN.com, 19 March 2010, online, www.cnn.com.

75. Emily Steel, "Nestlé Takes a Beating on Social-Media Sites," *Wall Street Journal*, 29 March 2010, online, www.wsj.com.

76. Greg Beaubien, "Nestlé Debacle Reveals 'Dark Side' of Facebook Fan Pages," *Public Relations Tactics*, posted 22 March 2010, online, www.prsa.org.

77. Paul Armstrong.

78. Emily Steel.

79. Lorna Benson, "Hunters and Environmentalists Rally for Ducks and Their Habitat," Minnesota Public Radio, 1 April 2005, online, http://news.minnesota.publicradio.org.

80. "Uniting Guns and Greens to Improve Minnesota's Environment," Silver Anvil Campaign Profile # 6BW-0603D07, Public Relations Society of America, online, http://prsa.org.

81. "Uniting Guns and Greens."

82. Dennis Anderson, "Progress Seems to Be on Horizon," *Star Tribune*, 8 April 2005, 5C.

83. Pat Doyle, "What Passed, What Failed in the Final Hours," *Star Tribune*, 22 May 2006, 3B.

84. Pat Doyle, "Time Runs Out for Outdoors-Arts Plan," *Star Tribune*, 22 May 2007, 8A.

85. Doug Smith, "Its Mission Accomplished, Duck Rally Group to Disband," *Star-Tribune*, 28 December 2008, 14C.

Member Code of Ethics 2000
Approved by the PRSA Assembly, October 2000

Preamble

Public Relations Society of America Member Code of Ethics 2000

Professional Values
Principles of Conduct
Commitment and Compliance

This Code applies to PRSA members. The Code is designed to be a useful guide for PRSA members as they carry out their ethical responsibilities. This document is designed to anticipate and accommodate, by precedent, ethical challenges that may arise. The scenarios outlined in the Code provision are actual examples of misconduct. More will be added as experience with the Code occurs.

The Public Relations Society of America (PRSA) is committed to ethical practices. The level of public trust PRSA members seek, as we serve the public good, means we have taken on a special obligation to operate ethically.

The value of member reputation depends upon the ethical conduct of everyone affiliated with the Public Relations Society of America. Each of us sets an example for each other—as well as other professionals—by our pursuit of excellence with powerful standards of performance, professionalism, and ethical conduct.

Emphasis on enforcement of the Code has been eliminated. But, the PRSA Board of Directors retains the right to bar from membership or expel from the Society any individual who has been or is sanctioned by a government agency or convicted in a court of law of an action that is in violation of this Code.

Ethical practice is the most important obligation of a PRSA member. We view the Member Code of Ethics as a model for other professions, organizations, and professionals.

PRSA MEMBER STATEMENT OF PROFESSIONAL VALUES

This statement presents the core values of PRSA members and, more broadly, of the public relations profession. These values provide the foundation for the Member Code of Ethics and set the industry standard for the professional practice of public relations. These values are the fundamental beliefs that guide our behaviors and decision-making process. We believe our professional values are vital to the integrity of the profession as a whole.

ADVOCACY
We serve the public interest by acting as responsible advocates for those we represent.

We provide a voice in the marketplace of ideas, facts, and viewpoints to aid informed public debate.

HONESTY
We adhere to the highest standards of accuracy and truth in advancing the interests of those we represent and in communicating with the public.

EXPERTISE
We acquire and responsibly use specialized knowledge and experience.

We advance the profession through continued professional development, research, and education.

We build mutual understanding, credibility, and relationships among a wide array of institutions and audiences.

INDEPENDENCE
We provide objective counsel to those we represent.

We are accountable for our actions.

LOYALTY
We are faithful to those we represent, while honoring our obligation to serve the public interest.

FAIRNESS
We deal fairly with clients, employers, competitors, peers, vendors, the media, and the general public.

We respect all opinions and support the right of free expression.

PRSA CODE PROVISIONS
Free Flow of Information
CORE PRINCIPLE
Protecting and advancing the free flow of accurate and truthful information is essential to serving the public interest and contributing to informed decision making in a democratic society.

INTENT
To maintain the integrity of relationships with the media, government officials, and the public.

To aid informed decision-making.

GUIDELINES

A member shall:

Preserve the integrity of the process of communication.

Be honest and accurate in all communications.

Act promptly to correct erroneous communications for which the practitioner is responsible.

Preserve the free flow of unprejudiced information when giving or receiving gifts by ensuring that gifts are nominal, legal, and infrequent.

EXAMPLES OF IMPROPER CONDUCT UNDER THIS PROVISION

A member representing a ski manufacturer gives a pair of expensive racing skis to a sports magazine columnist, to influence the columnist to write favorable articles about the product.

A member entertains a government official beyond legal limits and/or in violation of government reporting requirements.

Competition

CORE PRINCIPLE

Promoting healthy and fair competition among professionals preserves an ethical climate while fostering a robust business environment.

INTENT

To promote respect and fair competition among public relations professionals.

To serve the public interest by providing the widest choice of practitioner options.

GUIDELINES

A member shall:

Follow ethical hiring practices designed to respect free and open competition without deliberately undermining a competitor.

Preserve intellectual property rights in the marketplace.

EXAMPLES OF IMPROPER CONDUCT UNDER THIS PROVISION

A member employed by a "client organization" shares helpful information with a counseling firm that is competing with others for the organization's business.

A member spreads malicious and unfounded rumors about a competitor in order to alienate the competitor's clients and employees in a ploy to recruit people and business.

Disclosure of Information

CORE PRINCIPLE

Open communication fosters informed decision making in a democratic society.

INTENT

To build trust with the public by revealing all information needed for responsible decision making.

GUIDELINES

A member shall:

Be honest and accurate in all communications.

Act promptly to correct erroneous communications for which the member is responsible.

Investigate the truthfulness and accuracy of information released on behalf of those represented.

Reveal the sponsors for causes and interests represented.

Disclose financial interest (such as stock ownership) in a client's organization. Avoid deceptive practices.

EXAMPLES OF IMPROPER CONDUCT UNDER THIS PROVISION

Front groups: A member implements "grass roots" campaigns or letter-writing campaigns to legislators on behalf of undisclosed interest groups.

Lying by omission: A practitioner for a corporation knowingly fails to release financial information, giving a misleading impression of the corporation's performance.

A member discovers inaccurate information disseminated via a website or media kit and does not correct the information.

A member deceives the public by employing people to pose as volunteers to speak at public hearings and participate in "grass roots" campaigns.

Safeguarding Confidences

CORE PRINCIPLE

Client trust requires appropriate protection of confidential and private information.

INTENT

To protect the privacy rights of clients, organizations, and individuals by safeguarding confidential information.

GUIDELINES

A member shall:

Safeguard the confidences and privacy rights of present, former, and prospective clients and employees.

Protect privileged, confidential, or insider information gained from a client or organization.

Immediately advise an appropriate authority if a member discovers that confidential information is being divulged by an employee of a client company or organization.

EXAMPLES OF IMPROPER CONDUCT UNDER THIS PROVISION

A member changes jobs, takes confidential information, and uses that information in the new position to the detriment of the former employer.

A member intentionally leaks proprietary information to the detriment of some other party.

Conflicts of Interest

CORE PRINCIPLE

Avoiding real, potential, or perceived conflicts of interest builds the trust of clients, employers, and the publics.

INTENT

To earn trust and mutual respect with clients or employers.

To build trust with the public by avoiding or ending situations that put one's personal or professional interests in conflict with society's interests.

GUIDELINES

A member shall:

Act in the best interests of the client or employer, even subordinating the member's personal interests.

Avoid actions and circumstances that may appear to compromise good business judgment or create a conflict between personal and professional interests.

Disclose promptly any existing or potential conflict of interest to affected clients or organizations.

Encourage clients and customers to determine if a conflict exists after notifying all affected parties.

EXAMPLES OF IMPROPER CONDUCT UNDER THIS PROVISION

The member fails to disclose that he or she has a strong financial interest in a client's chief competitor.

The member represents a "competitor company" or a "conflicting interest" without informing a prospective client.

Enhancing the Profession

CORE PRINCIPLE

Public relations professionals work constantly to strengthen the public's trust in the profession.

INTENT

To build respect and credibility with the public for the profession of public relations.

To improve, adapt, and expand professional practices.

GUIDELINES

A member shall:

Acknowledge that there is an obligation to protect and enhance the profession.

Keep informed and educated about practices in the profession to ensure ethical conduct.

Actively pursue personal professional development.

Decline representation of clients or organizations that urge or require actions contrary to this Code.

Accurately define what public relations activities can accomplish.

Counsel subordinates in proper ethical decision making.

Require that subordinates adhere to the ethical requirements of the Code.

Report ethical violations, whether committed by PRSA members or not, to the appropriate authority.

EXAMPLES OF IMPROPER CONDUCT UNDER THIS PROVISION

A PRSA member declares publicly that a product the client sells is safe, without disclosing evidence to the contrary.

A member initially assigns some questionable client work to a non-member practitioner to avoid the ethical obligation of PRSA membership.

PRSA MEMBER CODE OF ETHICS PLEDGE

I pledge:

To conduct myself professionally, with truth, accuracy, fairness, and responsibility to the public; To improve my individual competence and advance the knowledge and proficiency of the profession through continuing research and education; And to adhere to the articles of the Member Code of Ethics 2000 for the practice of public relations as adopted by the governing Assembly of the Public Relations Society of America.

I understand and accept that there is a consequence for misconduct, up to and including membership revocation.

And, I understand that those who have been or are sanctioned by a government agency or convicted in a court of law of an action that is in violation of this Code may be barred from membership or expelled from the Society.

_____

Signature

_____

Date

GLOSSARY

Terms in the Glossary match those of the Key Terms section in each chapter and reflect the usage in the text. Thus, some entries in the Glossary are singular and others are plural.

account executive   A supervisory individual at a public relations agency who assists the account supervisor in the management of a client's account.

account supervisor   The individual at a public relations agency with the responsibility for managing a client's account and the people working on that account.

Accredited Business Communicator (ABC)   Designation given to accredited members of the International Association of Business Communicators.

Accredited in Public Relations (APR)   Designation given to accredited members of the Public Relations Society of America.

active public   A group whose members understand that they are united by a common interest, value, or values in a particular situation and are actively working to promote their interest or values.

active public opinion   Expressed behavioral inclination exhibited when people act—formally and informally—to influence the opinions and actions of others.

active voice   A grammatical term designating that, within a sentence, the subject does the action denoted by the verb (see *passive voice*). In most grammatical situations, writers prefer active voice to passive voice.

actualities   Recorded quotable quotes or sound bites supplied to radio stations on cassette tape or via a dial-in phone system or a website.

actual malice   The higher burden of proof that public officials and public figures must satisfy in libel cases: In addition to showing that a defamatory statement is false, a public figure must also show knowing falsehood or reckless disregard for the truth.

ad hoc plan   A plan created for a single, short-term purpose; from the Latin phrase meaning "for this purpose only."

administrative law judge   The presiding officer in hearings about alleged violations of government regulations. This person hears testimony and reviews evidence, much like the judge and jury in a civil or criminal case. If federal regulations are at issue, this judge's decision can ultimately be appealed in the federal court system.

advertising   The process of creating and sending a persuasive message through controlled media, which allows the sender, for a price, to dictate message, placement, and frequency.

advertising value equivalency (AVE)   A calculation of the value of publicity based on the advertising rates and the amount of media coverage received.

agenda building   The process through which journalists emphasize certain events, issues, or sources over others. The process is influenced by economic, cultural, and ideological variables; media ownership structure; media trends, and journalists' socioeconomic, political, and psychological orientations.

agenda-setting hypothesis   The idea that the mass media tell us not what to think, but what to think about. This hypothesis is the most widely accepted view of how mass media interact with society.

AIDA   An organizational scheme for persuasive messages that recommends this order: attention, interest, desire, and action.

annual meeting   A once-a-year informational conference that a publicly held company must, by law, hold for its stockholders.

annual report   A once-a-year informational statement that a publicly held company must, by law, send to its stockholders.

apologia   A speech of self-defense. People and organizations engage in it as a way to present their side of the story in the face of negative events or allegations as a means of repairing damaged images and/or reputations.

appropriation   A tort in libel law. In this context, it is the commercial use of someone's name, voice, likeness, or other defining characteristic without the person's consent.

association magazines   Magazines for members of associations, such as the American Library Association.

attitude   A behavioral inclination.

attributes   Characteristics or qualities that describe an object or individual, such as gender, age, weight, height, political affiliation, and religious affiliation.

attribution   The part of a sentence that identifies the speaker of a direct quotation. In the sentence *"Public relations is a values-driven profession," she said,* the words *she said* are the attribution.

aware public   A group whose members understand that they are united by a common interest, value, or values in a particular situation but who have not yet formed plans or acted on their interest or values.

aware public opinion Expressed behavioral inclination that occurs when people grow aware of an emerging interest.

axioms Self-evident or universally recognized truths.

baby boom generation People born between 1945 and 1964. The name comes from the record post–World War II surge in population. As the baby boomers reach retirement age early in the 21st century, they are expected to place a tremendous strain on services geared toward the elderly.

backgrounder A document that supplies information to supplement a news release. Written as publishable stories, backgrounders are often included in media kits.

belief A commitment to a particular idea or concept based on either personal experience or some credible external authority.

Bernays, Edward L. The man often acknowledged as the "father of public relations"—a notion he openly promoted. In his landmark 1923 book, *Crystallizing Public Opinion*, Bernays coined the phrase "public relations counsel" and first articulated the concept of two-way public relations. Bernays was a nephew of noted psychoanalyst Sigmund Freud.

bivariate analysis Analysis of research data that examines two variables.

blogs Regularly updated Internet journals or news forums that focus on a particular area of interest.

boundary spanning The function of representing a public's values to an organization and, conversely, representing the values of the organization to that public.

brainstorming A collaborative and speculative process in which options for possible courses of action are explored.

branding The process of building corporate and product identities and differentiating them from those of the competition.

breadwinners People between the ages of 18 and 65 who typically constitute the labor force. As the so-called baby boom generation reaches retirement age, the percentage of breadwinners relative to the total U.S. population will decline.

b-roll Unedited video footage that follows a video news release. Rather than use the VNR as provided, some television stations prefer using b-roll footage to create their own news stories.

B2B Abbreviation for business-to-business.

burden of proof The legal standard a plaintiff must meet to establish a defendant's guilt. For example, to prove a case of libel, the plaintiff must show defamation, identification, publication, damage, and fault or actual malice.

business-to-business communication The exchange of messages between two businesses, such as a manufacturer and a distributor.

business-to-business relations The maintenance of mutually beneficial relations between two businesses, such as a manufacturer and a distributor.

categorical imperative A concept created by Immanuel Kant; the idea that individuals ought to make ethical decisions by imagining what would happen if a given course of action were to become a universal maxim, a clear principle designed to apply to everyone.

causal analysis Aristotle's method of defining subjects by asking four questions: What is it? Who made it? What is it made of? What is its purpose?

cause marketing (cause branding) A concerted effort on the part of an organization to address a social need through special events and, perhaps, other marketing tactics.

CD-ROM The acronym for "compact disc—read-only memory," a medium for storage of digital data. It is a popular format for storage of music, computer software, and databases. CD-ROMs are increasingly popular among public relations practitioners for the distribution of multimedia and interactive communications.

cease and desist order An order issued by an FTC administrative law judge upon a ruling that a company or individual has violated federal laws governing marketplace transactions, including advertising.

census Survey of every member of a sampling frame.

channel The medium used to transmit a message.

citizen journalist Individuals not formally trained as journalists, but who through the use of digital technology assist in the traditional newsgathering and reporting process.

civil disobedience Peaceful, unlawful action designed to affect social discourse and/or change public policy.

civil penalties Penalties imposed under civil law for the violation of government regulations. These penalties usually involve the levy of a fine or placement of certain restrictions against the individual or organization found to be in violation.

cleanup phase The third stage of a crisis. During this stage, an organization deals with a crisis and its aftermath. How long this period lasts is influenced by the degree to which the organization is prepared to handle crises.

client research The gathering of information about the client, company, or organization on whose behalf a practitioner is working. Typically, this information includes the organization's size, products or services, history, staffing requirements, markets and customers, budget, legal environment, reputation, and mission.

closed-ended questions   Questions for which the response set is specifically defined; answers must be selected from a predetermined menu of options.

cluster sampling   A sampling technique used to compensate for an unrepresentative sampling frame. It involves breaking the population into homogeneous clusters and then selecting a sample from each cluster.

coalition building   Efforts to promote consensus among influential publics on important issues through tactics such as face-to-face meetings.

cognitive dissonance   The mental discomfort people can experience when they encounter information or opinions that oppose their opinions.

commercial speech   Expression intended to generate marketplace transactions. The U.S. Supreme Court has recognized a government interest in its regulation.

commitment   The extent to which each party in a relationship thinks that the relationship is worth the time, cost, and effort.

Committee for Public Information (CPI)   Committee created by President Woodrow Wilson to rally public opinion in support of U.S. efforts during World War I. Often referred to as the Creel Committee, it was headed by former journalist George Creel and served as a training ground for many early public relations practitioners.

common law libel   Libel defined by judicial rulings rather than by legislators or regulators; can occur in private communications such as internal business memoranda.

communal relationship   A relationship characterized by the provision of benefits to both members of the relationship out of concern and without expectation of anything in return.

communication   The exchange of information, verbal and nonverbal, between individuals. Also the third step in the four-step public relations process. Because the process is dynamic, however, communication can occur at any time.

communication audits   Research procedures used to determine whether an organization's public statements and publications are consistent with its values-driven mission and goals.

communication model   A diagram that depicts the elements of the process of communication.

communications grid   A tool used during communication audits to illustrate the distribution patterns of an organization's communications. The various media used are listed on one axis, stakeholders important to the organization on the other.

communications specialist   Job title given to some public relations practitioners, whose jobs usually entail the preparation of communications.

community relations   The maintenance of mutually beneficial contacts between an organization and key publics within communities important to its success.

compliance-gaining tactic   An action designed to influence the behavior of a person or public. Ideally, the action is consistent both with an organization's goals and values and with the person's or public's self-interests and values.

components of relationships   As defined by researchers Linda Childers Hon and James E. Grunig, the six key components that should be used in measuring the strength of a relationship: control mutuality, trust, satisfaction, commitment, exchange relationship, and communal relationship.

computer viruses   Software programming that attaches to a computer user's e-mail address book and is spread to computers around the world. Often the product of mischief, they have been known to erase or damage data on the computers they infect.

confidence levels   The statistical degree to which one can reasonably assume that a survey outcome is an accurate reflection of the entire population.

consent order   Ruling issued by the FTC when a company or individual voluntarily agrees to end a potentially unlawful practice without making an admission of guilt.

consumer redress   Compensation for consumers harmed by misleading or illegal marketplace practices. Under federal law, consumer redress can be sought by the Securities and Exchange Commission.

consumer relations   The maintenance of mutually beneficial communication between an organization and the people who use or are potential users of its products and/or services.

contacts   In marketing, all informative encounters, direct or indirect, that a customer or potential customer has with an organization's product or with the organization itself.

content communities   In social media, websites that seek particular kinds of input, such as videos or news stories, from individuals and organizations. Content communities also encourage comments on the content.

contingency plan   A plan created for use when a certain set of circumstances arises. Crisis communications plans are examples of contingency plans.

contingency questions Questions that are asked on the basis of questionnaire respondents' answers to earlier questions.

contingency theory of accommodation A theory of public relations that suggests its practice lies within a continuum from pure accommodation to pure advocacy, dependent on one or a combination of 87 variables.

controlled media Communication channels, such as newsletters, in which the sender of the message controls the message as well as its timing and frequency.

control mutuality The degree to which parties in a relationship agree on and willingly accept which party has the power to influence the actions of the other.

convenience sampling The administration of a survey based on the availability of subjects without regard to representativeness.

convergence of media A blending of media made possible by digitization. As different media adopt digital technology in their production and distribution processes, the differences among them become less apparent, and various media begin to incorporate one another's characteristics.

coorientation A process in which practitioners seek similarities and differences between their organization's opinions regarding a public and that public's opinion of the practitioners' organizations.

copyright A legal designation that protects original works from unauthorized use. The notation ©, meaning copyright, indicates ownership of intellectual property.

corporate social responsibility (CSR) An organizational philosophy that emphasizes an organization's obligation to be a good corporate citizen through programs that improve society.

creative thinking The systematic generation of unique and compelling ideas.

credentialing A process for establishing the identity of people working in an otherwise restricted area. Usually used in connection with reporters, credentialing involves issuing passes or badges that give access to an area such as a media information center.

crisis An event that if allowed to escalate can disrupt an organization's normal operations, jeopardize its reputation, and damage its bottom line.

crisis communications planning The second step in effective crisis communications. In this step, practitioners use the information gathered during risk assessment to develop strategies for communicating with key publics during crises; they also train employees in what they are supposed to do in a crisis.

crisis impact value (CIV) The vertical axis on Steven Fink's crisis plotting grid. Specific questions are used to measure the impact a given crisis would have on an organization's operations.

crisis management team (CMT) An internal task force established to manage an organization's response to a crisis while allowing other operations to continue.

crisis manager The person designated as the leader of a crisis management team. When this person is not the chief executive of an organization, he or she is usually someone appointed by the chief executive.

crisis planning team (CPT) A broad-based internal task force that develops an organization's crisis communications plan.

crisis plotting grid A risk assessment tool developed by crisis planning expert Steven Fink for prioritizing crisis communications planning needs.

crisis probability factor (CPF) The horizontal axis on Steven Fink's crisis plotting grid. It is an estimate of the probability that a given crisis will occur.

critical thinking The systematic, goal-oriented, comprehensive, objective analysis of a subject.

cross-cultural Occurring between members of different cultures.

Crystallizing Public Opinion Book authored by Edward L. Bernays in 1923, in which the term *public relations counsel* first appeared. In the book, Bernays also became the first to articulate the concept of two-way public relations.

cultural relativism The belief that no culture or set of cultural ethics is superior to another.

culture A collection of distinct publics bound together by shared characteristics such as language, nationality, attitudes, tastes, and religious beliefs.

customer relationship management (CRM) The use of individual consumer information, stored in a database, to identify, select, and retain customers.

Cutlip, Center, and Broom models A theory of public relations that categorizes the actions of practitioners into one of four models: expert prescriber, communication technician, communication facilitator, and problem-solving process facilitator.

cyber-relations The use of public relations strategies and tactics to deal with publics via, and issues related to, the Internet.

cybersmears Instances of using the Internet to unfairly attack the integrity of an organization and/or its products and services.

damage A burden of proof in libel. In that context, to prove damage is to demonstrate that the person or organization claiming libel suffered injury as a result of defamation.

database marketing The use of individual consumer information, stored in a database, to help plan marketing decisions.

databases Structured data storage and retrieval systems. In certain situations, such as with commercial online databases, these systems can be accessed by multiple computer users simultaneously.

decision makers Any persons or group of people who make decisions for publics.

"Declaration of Principles" Ivy Ledbetter Lee's 1906 articulation of an ethical foundation for the yet-to-be-named profession of public relations. In his declaration Lee committed his publicity agency to a standard of openness, truth, and accuracy—one that was not, unfortunately, always met.

decoding The process of deriving meaning from a message.

defamation A burden of proof in libel. In that context, defamation is any communication that unfairly injures a person's reputation and ability to maintain social contacts.

demographic information Data on nonattitudinal characteristics of a person or group, such as race, gender, age, and income.

dialectic A truth-seeking conversation.

dichotomous questions In a questionnaire, either/ or questions such as yes/no and true/false items.

diffusion theory A belief that the power of the mass media rests in their ability to provide information; individuals who act upon that information then influence the actions of others in their peer group or society.

digital Transmitted in a computer-readable format. Digital information is easy to use in a variety of media.

digital divide The term used to describe the uneven distribution of Internet access along geographical and socioeconomic lines.

Digital Millennium Copyright Act A federal law enacted in 1998 that established rules for downloading, sharing, or viewing copyrighted material on the Internet. It also makes it a crime to circumvent antipiracy and code-cracking measures.

direct marketing The delivery of individualized advertising to consumers one at a time as opposed to mass advertising.

disclosure The full and timely communication of any information relevant to investors' decisions to buy or sell stocks and bonds; a legal obligation of publicly held companies.

domestic publics Groups that are united by a common interest, value, or values in a particular situation and that exist primarily within an organization's home country.

downsizing Reduction in an organization's workforce. Because of economic globalization and technological advances during the last quarter of the 20th century, organizations were forced to do more with fewer employees to remain competitive.

due diligence A term originating in legal and financial circles that, in a public relations context, means the expectation that practitioners will conduct adequate research, analysis, and evaluation.

DVD (digital video—or versatile—disc) A computer disk that stores multimedia messages in a digital format.

e-commerce Financial activity conducted on the Internet.

e-mail A process by which a written message is sent electronically via computer to a receiver or receivers.

emergency operations center (EOC) The place where a crisis management team meets to develop its response to a crisis. It is in a secure location, one where the CMT can work free from interruptions.

employee relations The maintenance of mutually beneficial relations between an organization and its employees.

empowerment The process through which an individual or a public gains power and influence over personal and/or organizational actions.

encoding Selecting words, images, and other forms of communication to create a message.

equal opportunity provision The requirement that legally qualified candidates for public office be afforded equal access to broadcast media. This provision does not apply if a candidate's appearance is in the context of news coverage.

ethical imperialism The belief that a particular set of ethics has no flexibility and no room for improvement.

ethics Beliefs about right and wrong that guide the way we think and act.

ethics audit A process through which an organization evaluates its own ethical conduct and makes recommendations to improve it.

ethos An Aristotelian term denoting persuasive appeal based on a speaker's character and reputation.

evaluation The fourth step of the public relations process. However, because public relations involves a dynamic process, evaluation can occur at any time.

evaluation research Fact-gathering designed to help a practitioner determine whether a public relations plan met its goal(s) and objectives.

exchange relationship A relationship characterized by the giving of benefits to one party in the relationship in return for past benefits received or for the expectation of future benefits.

executive summary A description, usually one page in length, covering the essentials of a public relations proposal.

external publics Groups that are united by a common interest, value, or values in a particular situation and that are not part of a public relations practitioner's organization.

extranets Controlled-access extensions of organizations' intranets to selected external publics such as suppliers.

fact sheet A who–what–when–where–why–how breakdown of a news release. Unlike a news release, a fact sheet is not meant for publication; instead, it gives just the facts of the story contained in the news release. Fact sheets are often included in media kits.

Fairness Doctrine A Federal Communications Commission rule from 1949–1987 that required broadcast stations to provide fair and balanced coverage on controversial issues. Some in Congress favor reinstating the rule.

fair use A legal principle stating that portions of copyrighted works can be used without the owner's permission under certain conditions. Commonly, fair use includes noncommercial news reporting and certain educational purposes.

false light A tort in privacy law. A person can be sued for invasion of privacy if he or she presents someone in a false and offensive light, even if the communication in question isn't defamatory.

fault A burden of proof in libel cases involving private individuals. In that context, to prove fault (falseness) is to show that a defamatory statement is untrue.

Federal Communications Commission (FCC) A federal agency established to ensure the orderly use of the nation's broadcast airwaves in the public interest.

Federalist Papers Essays written to New York newspapers by John Hamilton, James Madison, and John Jay under the nom de plume "Publius" in support of ratification of the U.S. Constitution. The essays have been called "the finest public relations effort in history."

Federal Trade Commission (FTC) A federal agency established to ensure a competitive marketplace. The FTC is the source of most federal regulation governing advertising.

feedback The receiver's reaction to a message.

feedback research The examination of evidence—often unsolicited—of various publics' responses to an organization's actions. This evidence can take many forms, such as letters and telephone calls.

feminization The process through which the increasing influence of women is felt upon social, political, and economic issues.

figures of speech Sentence-level embellishments such as similes and metaphors.

First Amendment The constitutional guarantee of freedom of expression, freedom of the press, and freedom of religion. Its ratification in 1789 is considered the most significant event in the development of public relations in the United States.

focus groups An informal research method in which interviewers meet with groups of selected individuals to determine their opinions, predispositions, concerns, and attitudes.

Food and Drug Administration (FDA) A federal agency established to protect, promote, and enhance the health of the people of the United States. The FDA regulates the promotion of food, drug, and cosmetic products and services.

food disparagement laws Laws adopted in several states to protect products and services from defamatory statements that damage their market value; also known as veggie libel laws.

formal research Research that uses scientific methods to create an accurate representation of reality.

Form 10-K A comprehensive financial disclosure form that publicly held companies are required to file annually with the SEC.

Four-Minute Men A speakers' bureau used by the Committee for Public Information (Creel Committee) during World War I. Its members would make short presentations in support of the U.S. war effort during the four-minute intermissions between reels at movie theaters.

framing Communicating an idea in such a manner that an audience, either intentionally or unintentionally, is influenced by the way it is imparted.

Freedom of Information Act (FOIA) A federal law requiring all government documents, except those covered by specific exemptions, to be open for public inspection.

fully functioning society theory In public relations, the premise that organizations should help address important social needs, using two-way communication to build consensus, discover shared goals, and help societies reach their humane potentials.

gatekeepers Members of the news media, such as editors, who determine which stories a given medium will include.

geodemographics A marketing term for the examination of behavioral patterns based on where people live.

globalization The growing economic interdependence of the world's people as a result of technological advances and increasing world trade.

global village Concept first articulated by Canadian communications theorist Marshall McLuhan, suggesting that because of advances in telecommunications technology, we live in a world in which everyone can share simultaneous experiences.

goal The outcome a public relations plan is designed to achieve.

golden mean A concept created by Aristotle and Confucius. In Aristotelian ethics, the golden mean is the point of ideal ethical balance between deficiency and excess of a quality—for example, between deficient honesty and excessive honesty.

government relations The maintenance of mutually beneficial relations between an organization and the local, state, and federal government agencies important to its success.

grassroots lobbying Organized efforts by ordinary citizens to influence legislative and regulatory governmental processes.

green public relations Public relations activities geared toward demonstrating an organization's commitment to the environment. Increased environmental commitment is sometimes referred to as "going green."

greenwashing A term environmentalists use to describe disinformation disseminated by an organization in an effort to present an environmentally responsible image.

gripe sites Websites dedicated to airing complaints, either real or imagined, against individuals or organizations.

hackers Individuals who seek unauthorized access to websites and computer networks. Sometimes the motivation is personal amusement. However, a hacker's purpose may be to steal, alter, or damage data.

heuristic An informal, practical, trial-and-error problem-solving approach that often results in reaching a satisfactory, but not necessarily optimal, solution.

Hofstede's cultural dimensions Devised by Dutch sociologist Geert Hofstede, five variable elements that help distinguish one culture from another: power distance; individualism versus collectivism; masculinity versus femininity; uncertainty avoidance; and long-term orientation.

Hunt and Grunig models A theory of public relations that categorizes the actions of practitioners into one of four models: press agentry/publicity, public information, two-way asymmetrical, and two-way symmetrical.

hypermedia Integrated multimedia incorporating audio, visual, and text information in a single delivery system.

IDEA Aristotle's analysis of the message-generation process: idea-generation, arrangement, expression, and delivery.

identification A burden of proof in libel. To prove identification is to show that a reasonable person would infer that a defamatory statement applies to the plaintiff.

Image Restoration Discourse One of the dominant theories of apologia, developed by William Benoit. Benoit identifies five apologia strategies: denial, evasion of responsibility, reduction of offensiveness, corrective action, and mortification.

IMC audit An organization's examination and analysis of its own marketing communications: procedures, databases, personnel, messages, and so on.

independent endorsement Verification by a disinterested outside party, which can lend credibility to a message, as when the media decide to air or publish a news story based on an organization's news release.

independent public relations consultant An individual practitioner who is, in essence, a one-person public relations agency providing services for others on a per-job basis, contract, or retainer.

Industrial Revolution The period in the 19th and early 20th centuries during which the United States and other Western nations moved from an agricultural to a manufacturing economy.

informal research Research that describes some aspect of reality but does not necessarily create an accurate representation of the larger reality.

injunctions Court orders that prohibit the enjoined person from taking a specified action.

insider trading The purchase or sale of stocks or bonds on the basis of inside information that is not available to other investors. It is a violation of federal law and professional codes of ethics.

instant messaging An electronic process that allows two or more people to conduct a real-time, written conversation via computer.

institutional investors Large companies or organizations that purchase stocks and other securities on behalf of their members, usually in enormous quantities.

integrated brand communication The coordination of an organization's marketing communications to clarify and strengthen individual consumers' beliefs about a particular brand.

integrated marketing communications (IMC) The coordinated use of public relations, advertising, and marketing strategies and tactics to send well-defined, interactive messages to individual consumers.

intellectual property   Original works of authorship that are fixed in a tangible form of expression.

interconnectedness   The effect of a variety of forces that tend to draw the people of the world closer together. These forces include technological advances, world population growth, and multiculturalism.

internal publics   Groups that are united by a common interest, value, or values in a particular situation and that are part of a public relations practitioner's organization.

International Association of Business Communicators (IABC)   The world's second-largest public relations professional association, with approximately 15,000 members. It was founded in 1970 and is headquartered in San Francisco.

international publics   Groups that are united by a common interest, value, or values in a particular situation and that exist primarily beyond the boundaries of an organization's home country.

Internet   A global network, originally created for military and scientific research, that links computer networks to allow the sharing of information in a digital format.

internships   Temporary, supervised workplace experiences that employers offer students. Some interns work for academic credit. Others receive a nominal wage for their services. Internships are considered a valuable precursor to a public relations career.

intervening public   Any group that helps send a public relations message to another group. The news media are often considered to be an intervening public.

intranet   A controlled-access internal computer network available only to the employees of an organization.

intrusion   A tort in privacy law. In that context, intrusion is defined as an improper and intentional invasion of a person's physical seclusion or private affairs.

inverted pyramid   A symbol that represents the traditional organization of a news story. In a traditional news story, the most important information occurs within the first few sentences; as the story progresses, the information becomes less important.

investor relations   The maintenance of mutually beneficial relations between publicly owned companies and shareholders, potential shareholders, and those who influence investment decisions.

issues management   A form of problem–opportunity research in which an organization identifies and analyzes emerging trends and issues for the purpose of preparing a timely and appropriate response.

latent public   A group whose members do not yet realize that they share a common interest, value, or values in a particular situation.

latent public opinion   A behavioral inclination that exists when people have interest in a topic or issue but are unaware of the similar interests of others.

Lee, Ivy Ledbetter   Author of the "Declaration of Principles" in 1906. Lee became the first practitioner to articulate a vision of open, honest, and ethical communication for the profession—but became known by his critics as "Poison Ivy" for not living up to those standards.

libel   A false communication that wrongfully injures the reputation of another. To make a successful claim of libel, a plaintiff must meet the requirements of a five-point burden of proof.

litigation public relations (LPR)   The use of public relations research, strategies, and tactics to influence events surrounding legal cases.

lobby   In a public relations context, an organization that exists solely to influence governmental legislative and regulatory processes on behalf of a client. The word *lobby* may also be used as a verb to denote the act of lobbying.

logos   An Aristotelian term denoting persuasive appeal to the intellect.

lookism   A covert form of sexual harassment: attention that focuses more on a woman's appearance than on her job performance.

macroediting   A stage in the writing process in which the writer examines the "big picture" of a document, including format, organization, and completeness of information.

magic bullet theory   The belief that the mass media wield such great power that by delivering just the right message, the so-called magic bullet, the media can persuade people to do anything.

manipulation   In a public relations context, an attempt to influence a person's actions without regard to his or her self-interests.

marketing   The process of researching, creating, refining, and promoting a product or service and distributing that product or service to targeted consumers.

marketing mix   The four traditional aspects of marketing: product, price, place (distribution), and promotion.

marketing public relations   The use of the public relations process to promote an organization's goods or services.

Maslow's Hierarchy of Needs   Developed by psychologist Abraham Maslow, a multitiered list of ranked factors that determine a person's self-interests and motivations. Under Maslow's theory, people must meet their most basic needs before acting on less pressing needs.

media advisory   A fact sheet that is faxed or e-mailed to news media to alert them of a breaking news story or an event they may wish to cover.

media information center (MIC) A place where a large number of reporters can gather to collect information on a crisis. It should be close to, but separate from, the emergency operations center established for the crisis.

media kit A package of documents and other items offering extensive coverage of a news story to the news media. A media kit contains at least one news release as well as other materials such as backgrounders, fact sheets, photo opportunity sheets, and product samples.

media relations The maintenance of mutually beneficial relations between an organization and the journalists and other media people who report on its activities.

message The content of a communication that a sender attempts to deliver to a targeted receiver.

microblogs Brief, regularly updated Internet journal entries, often limited by character counts, such as Twitter tweets.

microediting A stage in the writing process in which the writer examines each sentence of a document for factual accuracy as well as correct grammar, spelling, punctuation, and style.

mission statement A concise written account of why an organization exists; an explanation of the purpose of an organization's many actions.

mobile marketing The delivery of marketing messages tailored for portable wireless devices, usually telephones.

modifiers Words or phrases that develop the meaning of another word, such as an adjective that modifies a noun or an adverb that modifies a verb.

monitoring In the context of issues management, the sustained scrutiny and evaluation of an issue that could affect an organization.

Monroe's Motivated Sequence Created in the mid-1920s by Purdue University Professor Alan H. Monroe, a five-step process (attention, need, satisfaction, visualization, and action) that organizes persuasive messages.

multivariate analysis Analysis of research data that examines three or more variables.

mutual fund managers Individuals responsible for purchasing stocks and other securities on behalf of a mutual fund's investors; the investors participate by purchasing shares in the fund.

news conference A structured meeting between an organization's representative(s) and the news media for the purpose of providing information for news stories.

news release A client-related news story that a public relations practitioner writes and distributes to the news media.

The New York Times v. Sullivan Landmark 1964 U.S. Supreme Court ruling that established a higher burden of proof in libel cases brought by public officials.

noise In the context of the communication model, distractions that envelop communication and often inhibit it. Noise can be both physical and intangible. It is sometimes referred to as static.

nonprobability sampling The process of selecting a research sample without regard to whether everyone in the public has an equal chance of being selected.

nontraditional publics Groups that are united by a common interest, value, or values in a particular situation but that are unfamiliar to an organization—but with which the organization now has a relationship.

normative In the social sciences, a term describing the ideal standard or model.

n-step theory A theory of mass communications suggesting that the mass media influence opinion leaders, who change from issue to issue, and that these opinion leaders, in turn, wield influence over the public.

objectives Specific milestones that measure progress toward achievement of a goal. Written objectives begin with an infinitive, are measurable, and state a specific deadline.

Office of War Information (OWI) An agency created by President Franklin Roosevelt to disseminate government information during World War II. Headed by former journalist Elmer Davis, it was a training ground for future public relations practitioners. It evolved after the war into the United States Information Agency.

open-ended questions Questionnaire items for which the number of possible answers is undefined and unrestricted.

opinion An expressed behavior inclination.

opinion leaders Individuals to whom members of a public turn for advice.

outcomes The actions of a targeted public generated as a result of a tactic or program.

outputs Measures of activity associated with implementation of a particular tactic or program.

partner relationship management The database-driven management of the relationships an organization has with its business partners, including vendors, distributors, and business customers.

passive voice A grammatical term designating that, within a sentence, the subject does not perform the action denoted by the verb (see *active voice*). Instead, the subject is affected by the action denoted by the verb, as in *She was hired*. In most grammatical situations, writers prefer active voice to passive voice.

pathos An Aristotelian term denoting persuasive appeal to the emotions.

payola Unreported and illegal compensation for hidden endorsements.

personal attack rule An FCC requirement that broadcast stations provide free air time to persons subjected to a character attack during a presentation on a public issue.

persuasion In a public relations context, an attempt to influence a person's actions through an appeal to his or her self-interest.

photo opportunity sheet A document that promotes the visual interest of an upcoming event. Photo opportunity sheets are sent to photojournalists and television stations. When appropriate, photo opportunity sheets are included in media kits.

pitch A persuasive message sent by a public relations practitioner to a journalist (via letter, e-mail, or telephone), often on an exclusive basis, describing a newsworthy human-interest story whose publication would generate helpful publicity for an organization.

planning The second step in the four-step public relations process. Because the process is dynamic, however, planning can actually occur at any time.

podcasts Downloadable audio essays or programs. Video versions are sometimes called *vodcasts,* though increasingly *podcast* now covers both audio and video.

point of no return The second stage of a crisis. Once this moment is reached, a crisis becomes unavoidable.

political action committees (PACs) Organizations representing particular special interests that collect money and contribute it to political candidates.

political speech Expression associated with the normal conduct of a democratic society. The U.S. Supreme Court historically has been reluctant to regulate it.

Potter Box A tool designed by Harvard Professor Ralph Potter for ethical decision making. Using the Potter Box involves defining an ethical issue and then identifying competing values, principles, and loyalties.

premarket conditioning Prior to a marketing campaign, the use of public relations tactics to build a sense of awareness, need, or desire within a targeted public.

press agentry/publicity model A form of public relations that focuses on getting favorable coverage from the media. In this model, accuracy and truth are not seen as essential.

press secretary The individual given the responsibility to speak for and handle media inquiries on behalf of a political or government official.

primary public Any group that is united by a common interest, value, or values in a particular situation and that can directly affect an organization's pursuit of its goals.

primary research Original research not derived from the results of any earlier researcher's efforts.

priming Conditioning the memories of people by framing complex issues in the simplest of terms, done in the belief that people will automatically draw on their memories to make judgments.

privacy A person's right to be left alone and be free from unwarranted publicity.

privilege Exemption of certain communications from court-ordered disclosure. For example, communication between a client and his or her attorney is considered privileged. However, communication between that same client and a public relations practitioner may not be privileged, and the practitioner could be required to testify.

PRM See *partner relationship management.*

probability sampling The process of selecting a research sample that is representative of the population or public from which it is selected.

problem A commonplace occurrence of limited scope. People often confuse problems with crises.

problem–opportunity research The gathering of information to answer two critical questions at the outset of any public relations effort: What is at issue, and what stake, if any, does our organization have in this issue?

Progressive Era Running from the early 1890s until the start of World War I, a period in which a series of political and social reforms, primarily in the United States, occurred in reaction to the growth of business and industry during the Industrial Revolution.

propaganda A systematic effort to disseminate information, some of which may be inaccurate or incomplete, in an attempt to influence public opinion. A propagandist advocates a particular idea or perspective to the exclusion of all others.

proposal A formal document that details specific, goal-oriented public relations tactics recommended for a client.

pseudoevent A special event, often of questionable news value, created for the purpose of attracting the attention of the news media.

psychographic information Data on attitudinal characteristics of a person or group, such as political philosophy and religious beliefs.

public In a public relations context, any group of people who share a common interest, value, or values in a particular situation.

public affairs officer The person responsible for maintaining mutually beneficial relations between a government agency or official and important publics. The term *public affairs* is also used by some nongovernment organizations as a synonym for government relations or community relations.

publication A burden of proof in libel. In that context, publication is the communication of a defamatory statement to a third party.

publication of private facts A tort in libel law. In that context, publication of private facts involves the public disclosure of personal information that is embarrassing and potentially offensive.

public figures For the purposes of libel law, individuals who have widespread notoriety or who inject themselves into a public controversy for the purpose of influencing its outcome.

public information model A form of public relations that focuses on the dissemination of objective and accurate information.

public information officer The individual given the responsibility to speak for and handle media inquiries on behalf of a government agency.

Publicity Bureau The first public relations agency, founded by George V. S. Michaelis and two partners in Boston in 1900.

public official For the purposes of libel law, any individual elected to public office and/or with substantial public decision-making or policy-making authority.

public opinion The average expressed behavioral inclination.

public relations The management of relationships between an organization and the publics that can affect its success. The term to describe the emerging profession was first used in 1923 by Edward L. Bernays in *Crystallizing Public Opinion.*

public relations agency A company that provides public relations services for other organizations on a per-job basis, by contract, or on retainer.

public relations managers Practitioners whose job responsibilities are more strategic than tactical in nature. These practitioners solve problems, advise others, make policy decisions, and take responsibility for the outcome of a public relations program.

Public Relations Society of America (PRSA) The world's largest public relations professional association, with approximately 21,000 members. Founded in 1947, it is headquartered in New York, and has 10,000 members.

Public Relations Student Society of America (PRSSA) An organization for public relations students. It is affiliated with the Public Relations Society of America.

public relations technicians Practitioners whose job responsibilities are more tactical than strategic in nature. Their primary role is to prepare communications that help execute the public relations policies of others.

public service announcements (PSAs) Broadcast announcements made on behalf of nonprofit organizations or social causes. Because of legal requirements to serve the public interest, the broadcast media do not charge for PSAs, as they do for commercial announcements. This term is also used to describe free advertising space granted by print media; however, the print media are under no legal requirement to provide the space.

push technology Computer software that permits users to customize information received automatically from the Internet.

rating scale questions Questionnaire items designed to measure the range, degree, or intensity of respondents' attitudes on the topic being studied.

receiver The person or persons for whom a message is intended.

recovery The fourth and final step in effective crisis communications. In this step, practitioners evaluate the quality of the organization's response to a crisis and take appropriate actions as a result of the lessons learned.

reflective paradigm (reflection) The belief that the most important role of public relations practice is to obtain and sustain the societal legitimization of organizations.

Regulation FD A regulation issued by the U.S. Securities and Exchange Commission in 2000 designed to tighten corporate disclosure requirements.

relationship management The use of public relations strategies and tactics to foster and enhance the shared interests and values of an organization and the publics important to its success.

relationship marketing Placing relationships with individual consumers above profits, in the belief that good relationships lead to increased profits.

representative sample Population sample selected by procedures that ensure that all members of the population or public being studied have an equal chance of being chosen for the sample. A representative sample must also be sufficiently large to allow researchers to draw conclusions about the population as a whole.

research The first step of the public relations process. However, because the public relations process is dynamic, research can occur at any time.

research strategy A plan that defines what the researcher wants to know and how he or she will gather that information.

resource dependency theory The premise that organizations form relationships with publics to acquire the resources they need to fulfill their values.

response The third step in effective crisis communications. In this step practitioners use their crisis communications plan.

return on investment (ROI) A business concept for getting more out of something than the original cost.

rhetoric The use of communication for the purpose of persuasion. In some of its applications, the practice of public relations is a rhetorical activity.

risk assessment The first step in effective crisis communications. In this step, practitioners identify potential hazards their organization may face.

RSS (Really Simple Syndication) Internet coding that permits automatic distribution of frequently updated content such as blogs or news stories.

salary equity Equal pay for equal work.

sample In a research context, the segment of a population or public being studied to enable researchers to draw conclusions about the public as a whole.

sampling frame The actual list from which a research sample, or some stage of the sample, is drawn.

Sarbanes-Oxley Act Legislation passed by Congress in 2002 that holds corporate officials personally accountable for the truthfulness of corporate financial statements.

satellite media tour (SMT) A series of interviews with reporters in different cities, conducted by means of satellite technology; the newsmaker stays in one location, eliminating expensive and time-consuming travel.

satisfaction When used in the context of Monroe's Motivated Sequence, the process of presenting an audience with a solution to a problem that has already been identified. When used in the context of measuring the strength of relationships, a reference to the degree to which the benefits of the relationship outweigh its costs. When used in the context of Mick Jagger, something of which he "can't get no."

scanning In the context of issues management, the process of identifying future issues that could affect an organization.

secondary publics Groups that are united by a common interest, value, or values in a particular situation and that have a relationship with a public relations practitioner's organization, but which have little power to affect that organization's pursuit of its goals.

secondary research Research using information generated by someone else, sometimes for purposes entirely different from your own; also known as *library research*.

Securities and Exchange Commission (SEC) A federal agency that administers federal securities laws to ensure that the nation's securities markets are fair and honest.

Seedbed Years A term coined by public relations historian Scott Cutlip that refers to the period during the late 19th and early 20th centuries in which the modern practice of public relations emerged.

service mark A legal designation indicated by the symbol^{SM} to protect names, designs, slogans, and symbols associated with a particular service.

sexual harassment Unwelcome sexual advances. Workplace sexual harassment is harassment that may affect an individual's employment, unreasonably interfere with an individual's work performance, or create an intimidating, hostile, or offensive work environment.

simple random sampling A basic and often impractical form of probability sampling that involves assigning a number to every person within the sampling frame, followed by random selection of numbers.

situation analysis In a written public relations proposal, a statement that accurately and objectively describes an opportunity or threat for which public relations actions are recommended.

social exchange theory The premise that relationships are built on the exchange of desired resources. Successful relationships are those in which the benefits of the relationship outweigh the costs.

social media Online technologies and practices that allow people to share information and opinions. They can take many forms, including text, images, audio, and video. Social media include blogs, wikis, online social networks, and more.

social media news releases News releases formatted for social media practitioners, particularly bloggers. Rather than standard news narratives, social media news releases feature snippets of information, such as facts and quotes, and links to other information.

social networks The often informal structures through which individuals and/or organizations maintain relationships. In social media, social networks link small, personal websites, often called "profiles," within a larger website.

soft money Money donated to national political parties for general expenses. Legislation passed in 2002 restricted such donations but allowed contributions to local political parties and national political conventions.

source The originator of a message.

spamming The mass distribution of an advertising-oriented e-mail message.

special event A planned happening that serves as a public relations tactic.

spim   The unwelcome commercial use of instant messaging.

spin   A popular term used to describe the framing of a message in what the source considers the most desirable context.

spin doctor   A popular term coined by *New York Times* editorial writer Jack Rosenthal in 1984 to describe the activities of political public relations practitioners.

stakeholder   A public that has an interest in an organization or in an issue potentially involving that organization.

stakeholder research   Research that focuses on identifying and describing specific publics important to the success of an organization.

standing plan   A plan that remains in effect over an extended period of time. Its tactics are routinely reenacted to sustain fulfillment of the plan's goal(s) and objectives.

statement of purpose   In a written public relations proposal, a declaration that the proposal presents a plan to address a given situation.

stereotyping   The assumption that all members of a particular group or culture are the same and act in the same manner.

strategic message planner   A document that advertising copywriters prepare to develop a research-based, persuasive message.

strategies   General descriptions of how practitioners propose to achieve a plan's objectives.

survey research   Formal research conducted through the use of carefully selected population samples and specifically worded questionnaires.

SWOT analysis   An assessment of the strengths, weaknesses, opportunities, and threats that an organization has or could confront.

systematic sampling   A probability sampling technique that uses a standardized selection process to create a sample that is both representative and easy to develop. At its most basic level, systematic sampling involves the selection of every Kth member of a sampling frame.

tactics   Specific recommended actions designed to help an organization achieve the objectives stated in a public relations plan.

text messaging   The process of sending a written message from one cell phone to another.

theoretical   A formal approach to decision making based on a system of rules or principles developed through scientific research.

things return to normal   The fourth and final stage of a crisis. During this stage, the immediate threat created by the crisis is over, but its lingering effects are still felt. Although things may have returned to "normal," normality now may be much different from what it was before the crisis.

third-party endorsement   Verification of a story's newsworthiness that the news media provide when they publish or broadcast the story. Appearance in an uncontrolled news medium lends credibility to a story, because the media are neither the sender nor the receiver but an independent third party.

trade magazines   Magazines for members of particular trades or professions, such as carpenters or lawyers.

trademarks   A legal designation indicated by the symbol ® that protects names, designs, slogans, and symbols associated with specific products.

traditional publics   Groups that are united by a common interest, value, or values in a particular situation and with which an organization has an ongoing, long-term relationship.

transition   A device that clarifies the introduction of a new topic within a document. One traditional transition device is a sentence that shows the relationship of the previous topic to the new topic. Such a sentence follows the previous topic and precedes the new topic.

transparency   A quality achieved when organizations and individuals conduct business openly and honestly without hidden agendas.

trust   The willingness of one party in a relationship to open itself to the other.

two-step theory   A theory of mass communication suggesting that the mass media influence society's opinion leaders, who, in turn, influence society.

two-way asymmetrical model   A form of public relations in which research is used in an effort to persuade important publics to adopt a particular point of view.

two-way symmetrical model   A form of public relations that focuses on two-way communication as a means of conflict resolution and for the promotion of mutual understanding between an organization and its important publics.

uncontrolled media   Communication channels, such as newspaper stories, in which a public relations practitioner cannot control the message, its timing, or its frequency.

units of analysis   What or whom a researcher is studying to create a summary description of all such units.

univariate analysis   Analysis of research data that examines just one variable.

Universal Accreditation Program   The availability of PRSA accreditation to members of eight additional public relations organizations; established in 1998.

uses and gratifications theory   The belief that people have the power to pick and choose the mass media channels that, in turn, influence their actions.

utilitarianism   A philosophy developed by Jeremy Bentham and John Stuart Mill that holds that all actions should be directed at producing the greatest good for the greatest number of people.

values   The fundamental beliefs and standards that drive behavior and decision making. They are also the filters through which we see the world and the world sees us.

values-driven public relations   The values-driven management of relationships between an organization and the publics that can affect its success.

values statement   A written declaration of the principles that an organization will strive to follow in all its actions.

variables   The logical grouping of qualities that describe a particular attribute. Variables must be exhaustive (incorporating all possible qualities) and mutually exclusive.

veil of ignorance   A term and concept created by philosopher John Rawls. The veil of ignorance strategy asks decision makers to examine a situation objectively from all points of view, especially from those of the affected publics.

velvet ghetto   Situation that exists when women predominate in lower-paying technical or middle-management jobs, with men dominating upper-level managerial positions.

video news releases (VNRs)   Videotaped news stories that an organization produces and distributes to the news media. VNRs often include b-roll footage.

viral marketing   Public relations or marketing information that is spread from person to person via e-mail.

virtual organizations   Temporary organizations formed by smaller units or individuals to complete a specific job.

virtual public relations   A term used to describe the work of many small public relations consultancies; as a result of advances in communications technology, these consultancies can have the look, feel, and service capabilities of much larger public relations agencies.

vox populi   Latin for "voice of the people." The phrase refers to the importance of public opinion.

warning stage   The first stage of a crisis. If warning signs are recognized and appropriate action is taken quickly, the negative effects of a crisis can be averted or minimized.

Web 2.0   A term coined by Silicon Valley consultants in 2004 to describe a new generation of Internet services that emphasize online collaboration and sharing.

webcast   Audiovisual telecasts, usually live, delivered through a website.

website   A series of computer files maintained by an organization or individual that can be accessed via the Internet. Websites are created to project an organization's image and to share information with various publics. They are also useful for marketing goods, services, or ideas and for generating feedback.

weighted media costs (WMC)   An alternative to AVE that employs a comparative index created over time.

wikis   Websites or multimedia documents that allow different individuals to contribute and edit content. Also, software packages that make it easy for multiple individuals to author, edit, and remove online content.

word-of-mouth marketing (WOMM)   The creation of strategies and tactics designed to stimulate public discussion of a brand, product, event, or issue.

work for hire   Anything prepared by someone within the scope of employment and, therefore, considered the property of the employer.

World Wide Web   A graphics-oriented computer network developed in 1991 that made the Internet more accessible and attractive and helped spur its rapid development.

writing process   An organized system for producing effective public relations documents. The writing process begins with the credibility of the writer and moves through nine separate steps: research, organization, writing, revision, macroediting, microediting, approval, distribution, and evaluation.

INDEX

TEXT CREDITS

p. 19: Courtesy of Hallmark Cards, Inc.

pp. 22–23: Courtesy of Gary McCormick.

p. 39: Reprinted with permission from the Public Relations Society of America (www.prsa.org).

pp. 47–48: Courtesy of John Echeveste.

pp. 78–79: Courtesy of Edward M. Block.

p. 104: Courtesy of PepsiCo, Inc.

pp. 119–121: Courtesy of David A. Narsavage.

pp. 149–150: Courtesy of APCO Worldwide (www.apcoworldwide.com).

pp. 152–154: Courtesy of Jane Hazel.

p. 176: Courtesy of Goodwill Industries of Orange County.

pp. 181–183: Courtesy of Mike Swenson.

p. 196: Courtesy of the Institute for Public Relations.

pp. 218–220: Courtesy of Dr. David B. Rockland.

p. 234: Courtesy of the Boeing Company.

pp. 247–248: Courtesy of Timothy S. Brown, APR, Ph.D.

p. 276: Courtesy of Johnson & Johnson.

pp. 286–287: Courtesy of Joshua Dysart.

p. 310: Courtesy of the Kellogg Company.

pp. 320–321: Courtesy of Regina Lynch-Hudson.

p. 343: Courtesy of INK Inc.

pp. 354–355: Courtesy of Craig Settles.

p. 387: Courtesy of the Department of Homeland Security.

pp. 390–391: Courtesy of Melanie Magara.

p. 405: Copyright © J.M. Smucker Company.

pp. 419–420: Courtesy of Vin Cipolla.

p. 433: Courtesy of Special Olympics, Inc. "Special Olympics" is a trademark and tradename owned by Special Olympics, Inc.

pp. 446–447: Courtesy of Bill Imada.

p. 469: Courtesy of the Securities and Exchange Commission (www.sec.gov).

pp. 487–488: Courtesy of James F. Haggerty, Esq., photo by Matt Flynn.

p. 509: Courtesy of the League of Women Voters of the United States.

pp. 520–521: Courtesy of Rebecca Timms.

pp. 528–533: Reprinted with permission from the Public Relations Society of America (www.prsa.org).